FOR REFERENCE

Do Not Take From This Room

EAST ASIA
AND THE
UNITED STATES

EAST ASIA
AND THE
UNITED STATES

An Encyclopedia of
Relations Since 1784

A–M

Edited by James I. Matray

G P

GREENWOOD PRESS
Westport, Connecticut • London

Library of Congress Cataloguing-in-Publication Data

East Asia and the United States: an encyclopedia of relations since 1784 / edited by James I. Matray.
    p. cm.
    Includes bibliographical references and index.
    ISBN 0–313–30557–9 (alk. paper : set).—ISBN 0–313–32446–8 (alk. paper : A-M).—ISBN 0–313–32447–6 (alk. paper : N-Z).
      1. East Asia—Relations—United States—Encyclopedias. 2. United States—Relations—East Asia—Encyclopedias. I. Matray, James Irving, 1948–
    DS518.8.E53 2002
    303.48'25073'03—dc21   2002019542

British Library Cataloguing in Publication Data is available.

Library of Congress Catalog Card Number: 2002019542
ISBN: 0–313–30557–9 (set)
     0–313–32446–8 (A-M)
     0–313–32447–6 (N-Z)

First published in 2002

Greenwood Press, 88 Post Road West, Westport, CT 06881
An imprint of Greenwood Publishing Group, Inc.
www.greenwood.com

Printed in the United States of America

The paper used in this book complies with the
Permanent Paper Standard issued by the National
Information Standards Organization (Z39.48–1984).

10 9 8 7 6 5 4 3 2 1

To the Memory of My Parents,
Theodore John Matray
and
Caroline Kathryn Werstler Matray

Contents

Maps follow page xxix.

Preface

In 1941, publisher Henry R. Luce told his readers in *Life* magazine that they were living in the "American Century," and subsequent events provided substantial support for the accuracy of his assessment. By 2000, the United States not only was the most economically and militarily powerful nation in human history, but its politics, society, and culture were worldwide sources of admiration, envy, and emulation. On 11 September 2001, however, the terrorist attack on the Pentagon in Washington D.C. and destruction of the World Trade Center in New York City demonstrated that a segment of the world's population considered U.S. dominance of the international system intolerably oppressive. Prior examples of hostility toward perceived American hegemony, although far less repugnant, provided further evidence that the U.S. record in foreign affairs has been mixed. American intervention made the difference in achieving victory over the Central Powers in World War I and the Axis in World War II. The United States also won the Cold War, resulting in the demise of the Soviet Union and the disappearance of Communist regimes across the globe. But U.S. policies in East Asia led to frustration in Korea and failure in Vietnam, as well as hostile relationships with revolutionary nationalist movements throughout the area. This helped explain why the only nations other than Cuba still under Communist rule after the Cold War ended were China, North Korea, Vietnam, and Laos. Despite a global focus early in the new century on waging a "war against terrorism," the future of these countries may well dictate the ultimate course of world affairs. In fact, some East Asia experts have predicted that the next 100 years will be "China's century."

American fascination with East Asia began at least as early as 1784 with the voyage of the *Empress of China* to Guangzhou in China. U.S. Secretaries of State John Quincy Adams, Daniel Webster, and William H. Seward all had visions of creating an American empire in the Pacific. In April 1870, Rear Admiral Robert W. Shufeldt, who later negotiated the first treaty between Korea and a Western power, spoke for them when he declared that "the Pacific Ocean is to be hereafter the field of our commercial triumphs. . . . [It] is and *must* be essentially *American*. Through it and by us, China and Japan must acquire a new civilization and adopt a new creed, for it is in this sense that 'Westward still, the Star of Empire takes its way.' " Students, scholars, and those with a casual interest in U.S.–East Asian relations will find this historical encyclopedia a useful guide for understanding the origins and impact of this American missionary quest to transform East Asia. Its primary emphasis is on diplomatic, economic, and political developments, with a secondary focus on military affairs and cultural interaction.

This encyclopedia contains descriptive essays covering all the significant people, controversies, treaties, agreements, and alliances affecting U.S.–East Asian relations over the past two centuries. In certain areas, entries appear in groups, such as battles, military operations, and treaties. There is an individual entry on almost every nation in East Asia, but in place of concise summaries, readers will need to consult entries about more narrowly defined issues, individuals, policies, and events related to Japan, China, Vietnam, and Korea. There also are an ample number of in-depth entries on specific topics that relate to Burma, Cambodia, Indonesia, Laos, Malaysia, Micronesia, the Philippines, Thailand, and Taiwan. References at the end of each entry provide guidance to sources for readers desiring more information. Entries appear in alphabetical order, with cross-references in the text of each, designated with an asterisk, assisting users interested in learning about related items. A chronology will help the student and layperson put the events in the entries into historical context. This book also contains a list of acronyms, a selection of maps, and a selected bibliography. Reprints of primary source documents on U.S.–East Asian relations from the 1850s through the 1960s are easily accessible in the Department of State's *Foreign Relations of the United States*. Organized by region, country, and event, individual series volumes are not listed in the bibliography to conserve space.

Completion of this valuable research tool would not have been possible without the participation of an outstanding group of contributors from nine different countries. Although most are established scholars in the field, many writers are graduate students just beginning their academic careers. Following each entry is the name of its author, and biographical summaries of all contributors appear in the section called "About the Editor and Contributors." This encyclopedia uses the current spelling of Korean names and places, and the pinyin rather than Wade-Giles spelling for Chinese, along with selective cross-references. I thank my colleague Kenneth J. Hammond for his help on the latter, as well as his insightful advice in ensuring analytical accuracy. As important, he prepared without complaint several entries at the end of the project that other contributors had abandoned.

Cynthia Harris of Greenwood Press deserves credit for providing outstanding advice and, for a second time, showing extraordinary patience. All authors should be so lucky to have an editor with her personal and professional skills. Most important, Juanita Stern devoted many hours to the encyclopedia, quietly and competently making seemingly endless editorial changes in the text. As always, my wife, Karin, provided unconditional affection and constant encouragement in my completion of this project, and my children, Benjamin and Amanda, were regular but welcome distractions. Finally, I dedicate this encyclopedia to the memory of my parents, who had unqualified faith in the power of education to improve the lives of their children. Both children of immigrants, they worked at difficult jobs to provide us with the opportunity to enjoy prosperous, productive, and happy lives. Thanks to them, my brother Paul and I are living their American dream.

Chronology

1856 Townsend Harris arrives in Japan as the first U.S. ambassador

Outbreak of the Second Opium War in China

Peter Parker recommends U.S. seizure of Taiwan

1857 Townsend Harris negotiates Convention of Shimoda with Japan

1858 The United States signs the Harris Treaty with Japan

Treaty of Tianjin signed between Western powers and China

1860 Beginning of the "Expel the Barbarian" Movement in Japan

1861 Japanese extremists assassinate Henry Heuksen, translator for U.S. Ambassador to Japan Townsend Harris

Convention of Beijing in 1860 forces China to establish the Zongli Yamen

Anson Burlingame named first U.S. minister in Beijing

1862 Frederick T. Ward forms the Evervictorious Army to fight the Taiping rebels

Russell and Company founds the Shanghai Steamship Navigation Company

Zongli Yamen creates a foreign languages academy named the Tongwen Guan

1866 Koreans attack U.S. ship *General Sherman*, killing all its crewmen

1867 United States purchases Alaska from Russia

Midway Island claimed as U.S. territory

Charles LeGrande stages punitive attack on Taiwan

1868 Meiji Restoration in Japan ends the Tokugawa shōgunate

United States signs the Burlingame-Seward Treaty with China

1869 Frederick F. Low appointed U.S. minister to China

1870 Young Men's Christian Association begins operations in China

1871 Low leads punitive expedition against Korea

Iwakura Mission leaves Japan on an inspection tour of Western nations

1872 U.S. Senate rejects a treaty negotiated with a Samoan chieftain

First Chinese students arrive for study in the United States

1873 Qing Dynasty agrees to end the requirement for Western diplomats to perform the kowtow during audiences with the emperor

Meiji government lifts the ban on practicing Christianity in Japan

1875 United States negotiates a reciprocity treaty with Hawaii

1876 Chefoo Convention signed between Britian and China

1877 First General Convention of Protestant Missionaries convenes

1878 United States signs a convention with Japan granting it conditional tariff autonomy

Commodore Robert W. Shufeldt begins around-the-world cruise

U.S. ratifies treaty with Samoa ceding the harbor at Pago Pago to the United States

1879 Japan and China clash over control of the Ryūkyū Islands

1880 United States signs Angell Treaty with China

1881 China's Zongli Yamen withdraws Chinese Educational Mission from the United States

1882 U.S. Congress passes the Chinese Exclusion Act

Chinese Consolidated Benevolent Association established

Shufeldt Treaty negotiated between the United States and Korea

1883 Lucius H. Foote arrives in Korea as the first U.S. ambassador

Kim Ok-kyun leads rebellion against the monarchy in Korea

1885 China recognizes France's colonial rule over French Indochina

Rock Springs Massacre of Chinese laborers in Wyoming

1887 U.S. missionaries involved in Pohnpei crisis

White planters stage uprising in Hawaii against the monarchy

Hawaiian King Kalakaua accepts new constitution, reducing his powers

United States renews treaty with Hawaii, adding a provision for an exclusive naval base at Pearl Harbor

1889 Young Men's Christian Association begins operations in Japan

Britain, Germany, and the United States agree to a tripartite condominium over the Samoan Islands

1890 General Conference of Protestant Missionaries convenes

Young Women's Christian Association begins operations in China

Publication of Alfred Thayer Mahan's *The Influence of Sea Power upon History, 1660–1783*

1891 United States and Britain sign an agreement to limit seal hunting

1893 Fur seal hunting arbitration decision issued

Hawaiian rebellion ousts Queen Lili'uokalani, ending the monarchy

James H. Blount begins investigation of Hawaiian Revolution

President Grover Cleveland withdraws Hawaiian annexation treaty from U.S. Senate consideration

1894 Signing of the American-Japanese Treaty

Renewal of Angell Treaty between United States and China

Outbreak of the Sino-Japanese War

Republic of Hawaii established

1895 Japan and China sign Treaty of Shimonoseki

Taiwan becomes part of the Japanese Empire

Triple Intervention forces Japan to return the Liaodong Peninsula to China

1896 Philippine Revolution begins against Spanish colonial rule

1897 Germany seizes Jiaozhou, Qingdao, and Yantai on Shandong Peninsula

Japanese warship arrives off the coast of Hawaii

U.S. Senate defeats a treaty to annex Hawaiian Islands

1898 Beginning of public references to the Ōkuma Doctrine

Formation of the American Asiatic Association

Outbreak of the Spanish-American War

Commodore George Dewey commands destruction of Spain's Pacific fleet at the Battle of Manila Bay

United States annexes Hawaii

Senator Albert J. Beveridge delivers "The March of the Flag" speech

Formation of the Anti-Imperialist League

1899 Treaty of Paris transfers the Philippines, Guam, and Puerto Rico from Spain to the United States

Outbreak of the Philippine-American War

Agreement signed between the United States and Germany to partition the Samoan Islands

U.S. Secretary of State John Hay issues first Open Door note

1900 Congress passes legislation establishing the Territory of Hawaii

Boxer Uprising begins in China

Multinational China Relief Expedition liberates foreign embassies in Beijing

Hay issues second Open Door note

1901 Balangiga Massacre occurs in the Philippines

Supreme Court issues rulings in Insular Cases

Chinese government accepts the Boxer Protocol

1902 Britain and Japan form the Anglo-Japanese Alliance

Philippine-American War ends

1903 Young Women's Christian Association begins operations in Japan

1904 Outbreak of the Russo-Japanese War

1905 Britain acknowledges Japanese control over Korea

George Kennan meets with President Theodore Roosevelt to promote an accord with Japan

Taft-Katsura Agreement signed

Formal enunciation of the Ōkuma Doctrine

Roosevelt mediates the Treaty of Portsmouth, ending the Russo-Japanese War

Establishment of Japanese-Korean Exclusion League in San Francisco

Homer B. Hulbert meets with Secretary of State Elihu Root in a failed effort to obtain U.S. support for ending Japanese rule in Korea

1906 Shanghai Drug Conference convenes

1907 Hulbert joins Korean leaders in delivering petitions to the Second Hague Peace Conference protesting Japanese colonial rule

Japan and Russia sign agreement recognizing each other's sphere of influence in Manchuria

U.S. Great White Fleet begins around-the-world cruise

1908 President Roosevelt finalizes Gentlemen's Agreement with Japan

United States remits Boxer Indemnity to China

Puyi becomes last emperor of China

Root-Takahira Agreement provides for the United States to respect Japan's control over Korea and Japan to respect U.S. control in the Philippines

1909 Japanese businessman Shibusawa Eiichi visits the United States

Knox Neutralization Scheme initiates Dollar Diplomacy in Manchuria

1910 Entente between Japan and Russia divides Manchuria into spheres of influence

Japanese annexation of Korea

1911 Chinese Revolution to establish a republic begins

First of three Hague Opium Conferences convenes

Signing of the American-Japanese Treaty

Renewal of Anglo-Japanese Alliance

Treaty to ban the hunting of pelagic seals signed

Beginning of Korean Conspiracy Case

1912 Sun Zhongshan becomes president of the Republic of China

Puyi abdicates as emperor, ending the Qing Dynasty

Yuan Shikai replaces Sun Zhongshan as president of the Chinese Republic

Six Power Consortium arranged

1913 United States recognizes Republic of China

California passes Land Law discriminating against Asian-Americans

Woodrow Wilson announces U.S. withdrawal from Six Power Consortium

1914 Outbreak of World War I

Japan declares war on Germany and seizes Qingdao on Shandong Peninsula and all German islands north of the equator

1915 Japan conveys its Twenty-One Demands to China

Secretary of State William Jennings Bryan announces nonrecognition of forcible changes in status quo in China that violate U.S. treaty rights

1916 Japan-American Relations Committee established

Beginning of the Warlord Era in China, lasting until 1928

1917 Negotiation of the Lansing-Ishii Agreement

Immigration Act extends the Chinese Exclusion Act to other Asians

1918 United States joins Japan in launching the Siberian intervention

1919 March First Movement in Korea protests Japanese colonial rule

Korean Provisional Government created in Shanghai

Outbreak of the May Fourth Movement in China

Peking Union Medical College opens with Rockefeller Foundation funding

Versailles Peace Treaty signed, establishing the League of Nations and the Mandate System, but rejecting inclusion of a racial equality clause in the League Covenant

Japanese retention of Shandong contributes to the decision of the U.S. Senate to reject ratification of the Versailles Peace Treaty

1920 Soviet Union creates the Far Eastern Republic, a puppet regime in Siberia

1921 Sun Zhongshan reestablishes the Republic of China at Guangzhou

Founding of the Chinese Communist Party in Shanghai

Washington Conference convenes

Four Power Pact signed to preserve the status quo in the Pacific

1922 Nine Power Pact affirms the Open Door Policy in China

Signing of the Five Power Pact to limit naval armaments

United States and Japan resolve the Yap controversy

Japan agrees to restore Chinese control over the Shandong Peninsula

Katayama Sen helps found Japan Communist Party

1923 United Front formed between the Guomindang and the Communist Party

Formal abrogation of the Anglo-Japanese Alliance

Abrogation of Lansing-Ishii Agreement announced

1924 First of four Geneva Conferences on the drug trade convenes

U.S. military leaders adopt War Plan ORANGE

Congress restricts immigration with a racial quota system with passage of the National Origins Act

California's legislature passes law barring Asian immigration

1925 Formation of the Institute of Pacific Relations

Creation of the Korean Communist Party

May Thirtieth Movement begins in China to protest unequal treaties

Socialist reformer and journalist Anna Louise Strong makes her first trip to China

1926 Jiang Jieshi, new Guomindang leader in China, begins the Northern Expedition to unify China and end Warlord Era

Hirohito becomes emperor of Japan

1927 Geneva Naval Conference convenes

Guomindang forces massacre Communist Party members at Shanghai, ending first United Front

1928 United States signs treaty with China restoring tariff autonomy

Signing of the Kellogg-Briand Peace Pact to outlaw war

Formation of the Taiwanese Communist Party

Socialist reformer and journalist Agnes Smedley first travels to China

Japanese military extremists assassinate Chinese warlord Zhang Zoulin

1929 Stock market crash in the United States ignites global depression

1930 London Naval Conference results in the adoption of new limits on naval armaments covering all classes of military vessels

Ho Chi Minh and others establish the Vietnamese Communist Party

1931 Japanese extremists assassinate Prime Minister Hamaguchi Yūkō

Mukden Incident initiates Manchurian Crisis

1932 U.S. Secretary of State Henry L. Stimson sends identical messages to Japan and China, refusing to recognize forcible changes in the status quo

Lytton Commission begins League of Nations investigation of the Manchurian Crisis

Kim Gu kills the head of the Japanese Residents Association and maims Japanese Ambassador Shigemitsu Mamoru in Shanghai

Japanese military and naval forces attack Shanghai

Japan's government accepts the creation of the puppet government in Manchukuo

Japanese Prime Minister Inukai Tsuyoshi assassinated in abortive military coup

1933 Japan withdraws from the League of Nations

1934 Japan enunciates the Amō Doctrine

Manchukuo's President Puyi made emperor

Tydings-McDuffie Act provides a timetable for the independence of the Philippines

Members of the Chinese Communist Party begin the Long March

1936 Young militant Japanese military officers assassinate government officials

London Naval Conference convenes

United States signs Silver Agreement with Republic of China

Japan and Germany join in forming the Anti-Comintern Pact

Xian Incident results in the Guomindang and the Chinese Communist Party forming a United Front to fight the Japanese

1937 Marco Polo Bridge Incident in China ignites World War II in Asia

General Claire L. Chennault begins to work for China's Jiang Jieshi

President Franklin D. Roosevelt delivers Quarantine Speech

Brussels Conference convenes

Release of the movie *The Good Earth*

Rape of Nanjing by Japanese military forces

Italy joins Ant-Comintern Pact

Japanese pilot sinks USS *Panay* on Yangze River in China

1938 Terms of the Lansing-Ishii Agreement made public

Publication of Edgar Snow's *Red Star Over China*

1939 Formation of the Hukbalahap in the Philippines

U.S. military leaders begin to develop War Plan RAINBOW

United States announces six-month notice of the termination of commercial treaties with Japan

U.S. Pacific Fleet transferred from San Diego to Pearl Harbor

Ida Pruitt begins work to create Chinese Industrial Cooperatives in China

Outbreak of World War II in Europe

Soviet Army defeats the Japanese at the Battle of Nomonhan

1940 China's government at Nanjing under Wang Jingwei signs treaty with Japan

American cryptologists first break Japanese code with *Magic*

French colonial officials sign the Hanoi Convention, allowing Japan to deploy military forces in northern French Indochina

United States embargoes scrap iron, steel, iron ore, copper, and brass to Japan

Tripartite Pact signed between Japan, Germany, and Italy

1941 U.S. Congress passes Lend Lease Act

Conversations between Secretary of State Cordell Hull and Japanese Ambassador Nomura Kichisaburō attempt to resolve U.S.-Japan differences

Ho Chi Minh organizes Vietminh to oust both the French and the Japanese

Japanese military forces occupy southern French Indochina

U.S. government freezes Japanese assets in the United States

United States rejects Japanese proposal for a meeting between President Roosevelt and Prime Minister Konoe Fumimaro

Japanese combat aircraft stage attack on Pearl Harbor

U.S. declares war on Japan

Japanese forces attack British Malaya, the Dutch East Indies, and the Philippines

1942 U.S. aid to China through "over the Hump" flights from India begin

Jimmy Doolittle leads air raid on Japan

Fall of Corregidor in the Philippines to Japanese forces

Bataan Death March

Battle of Coral Sea between U.S. and Japanese air and naval forces

Battle of Midway Island between U.S. and Japanese air and naval forces

United States signs Lend Lease agreement with the Republic of China

Song Meiling, wife of Jiang Jieshi, arrives in the United States to begin eight months of lobbying for U.S. support for the Republic of China

1943 Casablanca Conference issues unconditional surrender doctrine

Chindits launch invasion of Burma

U.S. Congress repeals Chinese Exclusion Acts

U.S. military begins island-hopping strategy against Japan in the Pacific war

Cairo Conference convenes, resulting in the issuance of the Cairo Declaration promising independence "in due course" to Korea and the return of land captured by Japan to China

1944 Merrill's Marauders begin military operations in Burma

Dixie Mission sent to Communist headquarters at Yan'an in China

U.S. Navy captures Tinian, Guam, and Saipan in the Pacific war

Japanese launch Ichigo Offensive against Guomindang forces in China

Battle of the Philippine Sea

Great Marianas Turkey Shoot

Battle of Leyte Gulf leads to U.S. recapture of the Philippines

President Roosevelt replaces Lieutenant General Joseph W. Stilwell with Lieutenant General Albert C. Wedemeyer as military adviser to Jiang Jieshi in China

1945 President Franklin D. Roosevelt, British Prime Minister Winston Churchill, and Soviet Premier Joseph Stalin meet at the Yalta Conference

Deer Mission arrives in French Indochina to assist the Vietminh in operations against the Japanese

Battle of Iwo Jima

Battle of Okinawa

Death of President Franklin D. Roosevelt

Operation OLYMPIC outlines plan for the occupation of Kyūshū

Massive Allied firebombing of Japanese cities

Germany surrenders, ending World War II in Europe

Potsdam Declaration issued

United States drops atomic bombs on Hiroshima and Nagasaki

United States and Soviet Union agree to divide Korea into military zones of occupation

President Harry S. Truman issues General Order Number 1

Formation of the Committee for a Democratic Far Eastern Policy

Ho Chi Minh proclaims the establishment of the Democratic Republic of Vietnam

Sukarno and Mohammed Hatta declare the independence of Indonesia

Japan formally surrenders, ending World War II in Asia

Chinese Civil War begins

U.S. occupation of Japan begins

U.S. occupation of southern Korea begins

Claire L. Chennault establishes Civil Air Transport in China

U.S. Ambassador Patrick J. Hurley escorts Mao Zedong to Chongqing for a meeting with Jiang Jieshi

France invites Bao Dai to establish the State of Vietnam

General George C. Marshall travels to China on a mission to end the fighting between the Communists and the Guomindang and secures a cease-fire

Moscow Agreement provides a plan to reunite Korea

1946 Outbreak of First Indochina War between France and Vietminh

Tōkyō War Crimes Trials begin

Chinese Civil War resumes

George F. Kennan outlines the containment policy in the "Long Telegram"

Joint Soviet-American Commission convenes in Seoul to implement Moscow Agreement to reunite Korea

Philippines gains independence from United States

Publication of Theodore H. White's *Thunder Out of China*

U.S. Congress passes the Fulbright Act

1947 Assassination of Aung San in Burma

Guomindang forces massacre Taiwanese in the February 28 Incident

President Harry S. Truman requests military and economic aid for Greece and Turkey in the Truman Doctrine speech to Congress

Creation of General Agreement on Tariffs and Trade

Promulgation of the new Japanese constitution

National Security Act establishes the Central Intelligence Agency, Joint Chiefs of Staff, Department of Defense, and National Security Council

U.S. administration begins over the Trust Territory of the Pacific Islands, which includes all the Marshalls, Marianas, and Carolines

General Wedemeyer conducts factfinding mission to China and southern Korea

Autumn Harvest Uprising occurs in southern Korea

Chinese Communist forces cross the Yellow River

United States refers the issue of Korea to the United Nations

Beginning of the "reverse course" in U.S. occupation policy in Japan

1948 Britain grants independence to Burma

Formation of the Federation of Malaya

Congress passes China Assistance Act

Establishment of Joint Commission on Rural Reconstruction in China

Open Payments Agreement signed

Beginning of the "Malay Emergency"

Establishment of the Republic of Korea ends the U.S. occupation of Korea

Establishment of the Democratic People's Republic of Korea

Soviet troops withdraw from North Korea

Execution of Tōjō Hideki, Hirōta Koki, and five other war criminals

1949 Japanese government establishes the Ministry of International Trade and Industry

Elysee Accords between France and Democratic Republic of Vietnam

Implementation of the Dodge Plan in Japan

Chinese Communist forces cross the Yangze River

U.S. forces withdraw from South Korea

Major military border clashes begin at the thirty-eighth parallel in Korea

State Department releases the China White Paper

Soviet Union explodes its first atomic device

Mao Zedong proclaims establishment of the People's Republic of China

China's government orders the imprisonment of U.S. diplomat Angus Ward

Retreating Guomindang forces begin military operations in Burma

Jiang Jieshi and his Guomindang government flee to Taiwan

Netherlands grants independence to Indonesia

Sun Liren conspires to stage a coup to oust Jiang Jieshi from power on Taiwan

1950 President Truman announces the end of U.S. involvement in China's civil war

Soviet Union begins boycott of the United Nations to protest the refusal to seat the People's Republic of China in place of the Republic of China

Secretary of State Dean G. Acheson delivers National Press Club speech

Senator Joseph R. McCarthy delivers speech in Wheeling, West Virginia, charging that 205 Communists worked in the State Department

Sino-Soviet Treaty of Friendship and Alliance signed

Tibet made an autonomous region in the People's Republic of China

Soviet Union and the People's Republic of China recognize the Democratic Republic of Vietnam

U.S. Congress approves the Korean Aid Act after almost two years of debate

United States recognizes Bao Dai's State of Vietnam

United States recognizes Norodom Sihanouk's government in Cambodia

Laotian Communist leader Souphanouvong founds Pathet Lao

President Truman names John Foster Dulles to negotiate a Japanese peace treaty

National Security Council Paper 68 proposes a huge increase in defense spending

U.S. State Department official John F. Melby leads mission to East Asia to Indochina, the Philippines, Malaya, Thailand, and Indonesia for recommendations on providing U.S. economic and military aid

Outbreak of the Korean War

UN Security Council passes two resolutions calling for international action for the defense of South Korea

Truman sends the U.S. Seventh Fleet into the Taiwan Strait

MacArthur named commander of the United Nations Command

UN forces halt North Korean offensive at the Pusan Perimeter

Philippine Defense Minister Ramon Magsaysay crushes Hukbalahap rebellion

Inch'ŏn Landing results in the liberation of South Korea

Adoption of the Colombo Plan

Chinese military intervention in the Korean War begins

At Wake Island, MacArthur predicts to Truman that China will not intervene in Korea

MacArthur launches Home by Christmas Offensive in the Korean War

Massive Chinese counterattack forces UN troops to evacuate North Korea

John S. Service dismissed from the State Department as security risk

1951 United Nations condemns China for aggression in Korean War

Counterattacks of UN forces restore battlelines in Korea at the thirty-eighth parallel

Sterling Payments Agreement signed

State Department dismisses O. Edmund Clubb as security risk

United States, Australia, and New Zealand sign ANZUS Treaty

United Nations approves moratorium resolution on discussing Chinese representation for the first time

Truman recalls General MacArthur

Lieutenant General Matthew B. Ridgway becomes commander in Korea and head of the U.S. occupation of Japan

Establishment of the Military Assistance Advisory Group, Taiwan

U.S. Congress holds hearings on recall of MacArthur

Military stalemate emerges in the Korean War

Opening of Korean War armistice negotiations at Kaesŏng

U.S.-Philippines Mutual Defense Pact signed

Signing of the Japanese Peace Treaty in San Francisco

U.S.-Japan Security Treaty signed

Korean War armistice negotiations resume at P'anmunjŏm

Japanese Prime Minister Yoshida Shigeru says in a letter to Dulles that Japan will recognize the Republic of China

1952 Chinese and North Koreans officially accuse United States of practicing germ warfare in Korean War

Establishment of the China Committee (CHINCOM) to restrict trade to the People's Republic of China

Japan regains its sovereignty and the U.S. occupation ends

Deadlock over prisoner of war repatriation begins at P'anmunjŏm

U.S. Army creates Special Forces unit known as the Green Berets

Sino-Japanese Peace Treaty signed

People's Republic of China expels missionaries

U.S. Congress passes McCarran Immigration Act

Committee for a Democratic Far Eastern Policy dissolved

1953 Burma Conference convenes

Zhou Enlai enunciates Five Principles of Peaceful Coexistence

U.S.-Japan Treaty of Friendship, Commerce, and Navigation signed

Korean Armistice Agreement signed

Navarre Plan implemented in French Indochina

1954 U.S.-Japan Mutual Defense Assistance Agreement signed

United States stages nuclear test at Bikini Atoll

Japanese ship *Lucky Dragon* showered with nuclear fallout

Opening of Geneva Conference on Korea and Indochina

Eisenhower refers to domino theory during press conference

Secretary of State Dulles fails to organize United Action for multinational military action in French Indochina

Fall of the French stronghold at Dien Bien Phu

Geneva Accords achieves cease-fire, ending the First Indochina War

United States helps with the creation of a special forces unit in Thailand

Formation of the Southeast Asia Treaty Organization

State Department terminates the employment of John Paton Davies

Start of the first Taiwan Strait Crisis

U.S.-China Mutual Defense Treaty signed as part of Operation ORACLE

United States ratifies Mutual Defense Treaty with the Republic of Korea

General J. Lawton Collins begins mission to South Vietnam

1955 Congress passes Formosa Resolution

American Friends of Vietnam formed

Bandung Conference of nonaligned nations convenes in Indonesia

Ngo Dinh Diem defeats Bao Dai in an election for president in South Vietnam

Establishment of the Republic of Vietnam

Michigan State University Group begins its training and advisory program in the Republic of Vietnam

Beginning in Geneva of ambassadorial talks between the United States and the People's Republic of China

Publication of Graham Greene's *The Quiet American*

1956 Souvanna Phouma leads coalition government in Laos

Kim Il Sung orders the execution of rival Pak Hŏn-yŏng in North Korea

South Vietnam's President Ngo Dinh Diem rejects nationwide elections

PRRI-Permesta rebellion begins in Indonesia

1957 Anti-American revolt occurs in Taibei, Taiwan

Britain grants independence to Malaysia

Last meeting of the Institute of Pacific Relations

United States agrees to revise U.S.-Japan Security Treaty of 1951

1958 Sukarno's military forces crush PRRI-Permesta Rebellion

Second Taiwan Strait Crisis occurs

Sino-American ambassadorial talks move from Geneva to Warsaw, Poland

U Nu tranfers authority in Burma to Ne Win

1959 Air America formed from Civil Air Transport

North Vietnamese leaders develop plan to expand and improve Ho Chi Minh Trail

Lee Kuan Yew becomes prime minister of Singapore

1960 Ouster of Syngman Rhee in South Korea

Jang Myŏn elected prime minister in the Republic of Korea

Anpo crisis in Japan protests renewal of U.S.-Japan Security Treaty

U.S.-Japan Mutual Cooperation and Security Treaty signed

Kong Le stages coup in Laos

Vice President Richard M. Nixon and Senator John F. Kennedy debate protection of Jinmen and Mazu in U.S. presidential campaign

Creation of the National Liberation Front in Vietnam

1961 Congress passes Fulbright-Hayes Act

Implementation of Strategic Hamlets Program in Vietnam

Opening of Geneva Conference on the Laotian Crisis

Pak Chŏng-hŭi stages coup and establishes military junta in South Korea

Establishment of the Peace Corps

Soviet leader Nikita Khrushchev tells President Kennedy in Vienna that his nation will support "wars of national liberation" against colonialism

Ikeda Hayato meets with Kennedy in Washington

President Kennedy meets with Chen Cheng of the Republic of China

Walt W. Rostow and Maxwell D. Taylor conduct mission to the Republic of Vietnam

Kennedy meets with Pak Chŏng-hŭi in Washington

1962 United States begins Operation RANCH HAND to defoliate South Vietnam

Ne Win stages coup and seizes power in Burma

Establishment of the Military Assistance Command, Vietnam (MACV)

Geneva Accords provide for the neutralization of Laos

United States begins secret air war in Laos against Communist forces

U.S. pressure persuades the Dutch to transfer West Irian to Indonesia

Indonesia begins clash with Malaysia

1963 Buddhist uprising against the Diem government

Battle of Ap Bac in Vietnam

Ferdinand Marcos elected president of the Philippines

Pak Chŏng-hŭi elected president of the Republic of Korea

Norodom Sihanouk of Cambodia ends U.S. military and economic aid programs

Ouster and assassination of Ngo Dinh Diem

Assassination of President John F. Kennedy

1964 President Lyndon B. Johnson approves OPLAN 34A

Nguyen Khanh seizes control of Saigon government

General William C. Westmoreland assumes command of MACV

DeSoto Patrols by U.S. military vessels begin off the coast of North Vietnam

Summer Olympic Games held in Tōkyō

North Vietnamese torpedo boats attack U.S. destroyer in Tonkin of Gulf

Congress passes Tonkin Gulf Resolution

1965 Nguyen Van Thieu and Nguyen Cao Ky take power in South Vietnam

Viet Cong attack U.S. Special Forces base at Pleiku in Vietnam

Operation ROLLING THUNDER begins systematic U.S. bombing of North Vietnam

First U.S. combat troops land at Danang in the Republic of Vietnam

Meeting between President Lyndon B. Johnson and Pak Chŏng-hŭi

Japan-Korea Treaty on Basic Relations signed

Singapore ends brief union with Malaysia and asserts independence

Norodom Sihanouk breaks relations between Cambodia and the United States

Suharto crushes Communist Party in Indonesia

Republic of China signs Status of Forces Agreement with United States

U.S. Congress passes Immigration Act, ending quota system

1966 Battle of the Ia Drang Valley

Johnson meets South Vietnam leaders Thieu and Ky in Hawaii

President Johnson confers with Pak Chŏng-hŭi in Seoul

Ouster of Sukarno in Indonesia

Republic of Korea signs Status of Forces Agreement with United States

Operation MARIGOLD attempts at peace in Vietnam initiated

Publication of J. William Fulbright's *Arrogance of Power*

1967 Operation CEDAR FALLS levels village of Ben Suc in Vietnam

Operation JUNCTION CITY staged in South Vietnam

Great Proletarian Cultural Revolution begins in China

Creation of Association of Southeast Asian Nations

Lyndon B. Johnson outlines San Antonio Formula for peace in Vietnam

Lin Biao's *Long Live the Victory of People's War* published

Thieu elected president and Ky vice president of the Republic of Vietnam

Implementation of the Phoenix Program begins in Vietnam

Japanese Prime Minister Satō Eisaku first outlines the Three Non-Nuclear Principles

1968 Winter Olympic Games held in Sapporo, Japan

North Korea seizes USS *Pueblo*, a U.S. surveillance ship

North Vietnam and Viet Cong launch Tet Offensive

Seige at Khe Sanh in South Vietnam

My Lai Massacre occurs in South Vietnam

Pak Chŏng-hŭi resists sending more South Korean troops to Vietnam in meeting with Johnson at Honolulu, Hawaii

Johnson announces partial halt in the bombing of North Vietnam

United States returns Bonin Islands to Japan

Start of Paris Peace Talks to end Second Indochina War

United States ends Operation ROLLING THUNDER

Committee of Concerned Asian Scholars splits from the Association for Asian Studies

1969 Death of Ho Chi Minh

Operation MENU begins secret bombing in Cambodia

Retina, later Team Spirit, military exercises begin in South Korea

Implementation of Vietnamization begins

President Richard M. Nixon announces Nixon Doctrine on Guam

Withdrawal of first U.S. combat troops from Vietnam

Provisional Revolutionary Government replaces National Liberation Front

Nixon-Sato Communiqué released, pledging U.S. return of Okinawa to Japan

1970 Henry A. Kissinger and Le Duc Tho begin secret talks to end Vietnam War

Formation of National League of Families of Americans Missing in Southeast Asia

Lon Nol stages coup and replaces Norodom Sihanouk in Cambodia

U.S. and South Vietnamese forces launch Cambodian incursion

Four students killed by Ohio National Guardsmen at Kent State University

1971 Lam Son 712 invasion by South Vietnamese forces into Laos

Ping-Pong Diplomacy begins rapprochement between the United States and the People's Republic of China

State Department official Marshall Green reportedly coins the term "Golden Triangle"

Korean Central Intelligence Agency fails in attempt to assassinate dissident Kim Dae-jung

Publication in the *New York Times* and other newspapers of the Pentagon Papers

Announcement that Nixon will travel to China early in 1972

Nixon Shocks damage U.S.-Japan relations

Prime Minister Tanaka Kakuei's concessions settle U.S.-Japan textile dispute

United States advocates UN representation for both Chinas

United Nations votes to expel Republic of China and seat People's Republic of China

1972   President Nixon visits China

Issuance of the Shanghai Communiqué

North Vietnam launches Easter Offensive in South Vietnam

Operation LINEBACKER 1 begins massive U.S. bombing of North Vietnam

Japan regains control over Okinawa

National Security Adviser Kissinger announces that "peace is at hand"

Operation LINEBACKER 2 stages "Christmas Bombings" of North Vietnam

1973   Paris Peace Accords end Vietnam War

Operation HOMECOMING brings U.S. prisoners of war back from Vietnam

United States and the People's Republic of China open liaison offices in each other's capital

Jiang Jingguo initiates "total diplomacy" to reestablish ties with nations that had broken relations with the Republic of China

Opening of the Tōkyō Round trade negotiations

Korean Central Intelligency Agency kidnaps dissident Kim Dae-jung in Tōkyō

1975   Vang Pao and his Hmong army flee into Thailand

Communist forces seize control of South Vietnam, Cambodia, and Laos

Establishment of the People's Republic of Kampuchea

Souphanouvong becomes president of the People's Republic of Laos

Indonesian troops invade East Timor

Death of Jiang Jieshi

President Gerald R. Ford orders raid to liberate the crew of U.S. ship *Mayaguez* in Cambodia

Lockheed Scandal

1976   Mao Zedong dies

Establishment of the Socialist Republic of Vietnam

Ax murders at the demilitarized zone in Korea

Koreagate Scandal

1977   President Jimmy Carter announces plans to withdraw U.S. troops from South Korea

U.S. Congress votes to deny any rehabilitation aid to Vietnam

Termination of the SEATO alliance

Fukuda Doctrine signals Japanese commitment to economic development of Southeast Asia

Mass exodus of boat people from Southeast Asia begins

Vietnam invades Cambodia

1978   Implementation of the Four Modernizations begins in China

Japan normalizes relations with the People's Republic of China

1979   United States formally recognizes the People's Republic of China

Congress passes the Taiwan Relations Act

United States announces that it will accept 15,000 boat people

Sino-Soviet Treaty of Friendship and Alliance expires

Assassination of Pak Chŏng-hŭi

Chŏn Du-hwan seizes power in South Korea

1980 People's Republic of China formally creates four Special Economic Zones

      Kwangju Incident occurs in South Korea

1981 Chŏn Du-hwan the first foreign leader to meet with Ronald Reagan

      Mohamad Mahathir becomes prime minister of Malaysia

      Prime Minister Suzuki Zenkō pledges to expand Japan's role in regional defense

1983 First meeting between Reagan and Prime Minister Nakasone Yasuhiro

      Soviet plane shoots down Korean Airlines Flight 007

      Former Japanese Prime Minister Tanaka Kakuei sentenced to four years in prison

1984 Guomindang operatives assassinate Henry Liu in the United States

      Brunei gains independence from Britain

1985 Compact of Free Association for Micronesia signed

1986 Ouster of Ferdinand Marcos in the Philippines

      Corazon Aquino assumes power in the Philippines

      Dangwai becomes the Democratic Progressive Party on Taiwan

1987 Protests in South Korea against military rule reach a crescendo

      Issuance of South Korea's Democracy Declaration

1988 South Korean President No Tae-u announces "Nordpolitik" policy

      Summer Olympic Games held in Seoul, Korea

      Li Dengwei elected president of the Republic of China on Taiwan

1989 Establishment of Asia-Pacific Economic Cooperation forum

      United States imposes trade sanctions against Myanmar

      Tiananman Square Massacre in China

      Chinese dissident Fang Lizhi takes refuge in U.S. embassy

      U.S. government support helps block coup against Aquino government in the Philippines

1990 First meeting between No Tae-u and Soviet leader Mikhail Gorbachev

      Burma's Khun Sa indicted for drug trafficking

      Mohamad Mahathir proposes creation of an East Asian Economic Caucus

1991 Japan deploys minesweepers in the Persian Gulf

      Tōkyō accepts a cost-sharing arrangement to fund U.S. military bases in Japan

      Gorbachev and No meet on Cheju Island in South Korea

      United States and Japan agree to the Structural Impediments Initiative

      CBS televises documentary of convict labor in China videotaped by Wu Hongda

      United Nations arranges elections in Cambodia

      Both Koreas admitted to the United Nations

      Beginning of North Korean Nuclear Controversy

1992 Kim Young-sam becomes first civilian president of South Korea since 1961

      U.S. naval forces leave Subic Naval Base in the Philippines

1993 Japan's Liberal Democratic Party loses power for the first time since 1955

      President Bill Clinton proposes creation of a "New Pacific Community"

1994 World Trade Organization replaces the General Agreement on Tariffs and Trade

      Agreed Framework temporarily ends the North Korean nuclear dispute

      Death of Kim Il Sung

1995 United States establishes formal relations with the Socialist Republic of Vietnam

Chinese dissident Wu Hongda expelled from the People's Republic of China

1996 People's Republic of China conducts military exercises in the Taiwan Strait and fires missiles at Taiwan

South China Sea Islands dispute focuses on Spratly Islands

1997 Beginning of the East Asian Financial Crisis

Thailand receives loan from the International Monetary Fund

Republic of Korea requests a loan from the International Monetary Fund

President Jiang Zemin visits the United States

Release of Chinese dissident Wei Jingsheng from prison

1998 President Clinton visits China

Japanese government implements economic stimulus package

Fall of the Suharto regime in Indonesia

2000 South Korean President Kim Daejung visits North Korea

President Clinton visits Socialist Republic of Vietnam

New Status of Forces Agreement provides greater jurisdiction to South Korea

2001 U.S. surveillance plane lands on Hainan Island after collision with a Chinese warplane

Acronyms

AAA	American Asiatic Association		CIDG	Civilian Irregular Defense Group
ABCFM	American Board of Commissioners for Foreign Missions		CMB	China Medical Board
			CMC	Central Military Commission
AFV	American Friends of Vietnam		CMSNC	China Merchant Steamship Navigation Company
AIT	American Institute in Taiwan			
AMG	American Military Government (in Korea)		COCOM	Coordinating Committee (on East-West Trade Policy)
ANZUS	Australian-New Zealand-United States (Security Treaty)		COI	Coordinator of Information
APEC	Asia-Pacific Economic Cooperation (forum)		COSVN	Central Office for South Vietnam
			CPSU	Communist Party of the Soviet Union
ARF	ASEAN Regional Forum			
ARVN	Army of the Republic of Vietnam		CPUSA	Communist Party of the United States of America
ASEAN	Association of Southeast Asian Nations		CPV	Chinese People's Volunteers
			DCI	Director of Central Intelligence
CAT	Civil Air Transport		DJP	Democratic Justice Party
CBI	China-Burma-India (Theater)		DLP	Democratic Liberal Party
CBS	Columbia Broadcasting System		DMZ	demilitarized zone
CCBA	Chinese Consolidated Benevolent Association		DOD	Department of Defense
CCP	Chinese Communist Party		DPP	Democratic Progressive Party
CDFEP	Committee for a Democratic Far Eastern Policy		DRP	Democratic Republican Party
			DPRK	Democratic People's Republic of Korea
CER	Chinese Eastern Railway			
CFC	Combined Forces Command		DRV	Democratic Republic of Vietnam
CHINCOM	China Committee		ECA	Economic Cooperation Administration
CIA	Central Intelligence Agency			
CIC	Chinese Industrial Cooperatives		EUSAK	Eighth U.S. Army in Korea
CIG	Central Intelligence Group		FBI	Federal Bureau of Investigation

FEC	Far Eastern Commission	MPR	Mongolian People's Republic
FEC	French Expeditionary Corps	MSA	Mutual Security Act
FER	Far Eastern Republic	MSU	Michigan State University
FSO	Foreign Service Officer	MSUG	Michigan State University Group
GATT	General Agreement on Tariffs and Trade	NATO	North Atlantic Treaty Organization
GDP	gross domestic product	NDC	National Defense Commission
GMD	Guomindang	NDP	New Democratic Party
GNP	gross national product	NGO	nongovernmental organization
IAEA	International Atomic Energy Agency	NKDP	New Korea Democratic Party
		NLF	National Liberation Front
ICP	Indochinese Communist Party	NPT	(Nuclear) Non-Proliferation Treaty
ICSC	International Commission for Supervision and Control		
		NNRC	Neutral Nations Repatriation Commission
IMF	International Monetary Fund		
IMTFE	International Military Tribunal for the Far East	NPA	New People's Party
		NSA	National Security Agency
IRC	International Rescue Committee	NSC	National Security Council
IPR	Institute of Pacific Relations	NSP	National Security Planning (Agency)
ITO	International Trade Organization		
IWA	International Wheat Agreement	NTB	non-tariff barriers
IWC	International Wheat Council	NVA	North Vietnamese Army
JCP	Japan Communist Party	OPA	Open Payments Agreement
JCRR	Joint Commission on Rural Reconstruction	OSS	Office of Strategic Services
		OWI	Office of War Information
JCS	Joint Chiefs of Staff	PAVN	People's Army of Vietnam
JSP	Japan Socialist Party	PEC	President's Export Council
KAL	Korean Air Lines	PI	Partai Indonesia
KCIA	Korean Central Intelligence Agency	PKI	Indonesian Communist Party
		PKO	Peace Keeping Operations
KMA	Korean Military Academy	PKP	Partido Komunista ng Pilipinas (Philippine Communist Party)
KPA	Korean People's Army		
KPG	Korean Provisional Government	PLA	People's Liberation Army
KPR	Korean People's Republic	POL	petroleum, oil, and lubricant
KWP	Korean Workers' Party	POW	prisoner of war
LDP	Liberal Democratic Party	PPS	Policy Planning Staff
MAAG	Military Assistance and Advisory Group	PRC	People's Republic of China
		PRG	Provisional Revolutionary Government
MACV	Military Assistance Command, Vietnam		
		PRRI	Pemerintah Revolusioner Republik Indonesia
MFN	most-favored-nation		
MIA	missing in action	PRK	People's Republic of Kampuchea
MITI	Ministry of International Trade and Industry	PRU	Provincial Reconnaissance Units
		PUMC	Peking Union Medical College

ROC	Republic of China	TCP	Taiwanese Communist Party
ROK	Republic of Korea	TEA	Trade Expansion Act
RSFSR	Russian Socialist Federated Soviet Republic	TRA	Taiwan Relations Act
RVN	Republic of Vietnam	TTPI	Trust Territory of the Pacific Islands
RVNAF	Republic of Vietnam Air Force	UCR	United China Relief
SCAP	Supreme Commander for the Allied Powers	UK	United Kingdom
SCNR	Supreme Council for National Reconstruction	UMNO	United Malays National Organization
SEATO	Southeast Asia Treaty Organization	UN	United Nations
		UNC	United Nations Command
SEANWFZ	Southeast Asia Nuclear Weapon-Free Zone	USAAF	U.S. Army Air Force
		USAFIK	U.S. Armed Forces in Korea
SEZ	Special Economic Zones	USAMGIK	U.S. Army Military Government in Korea
SFRC	Senate Foreign Relations Committee	USC	United Service to China
SISS	Senate Internal Security Subcommittee	USIS	United States Information Service
SKWP	South Korean Workers' Party	VIVA	Victory in Vietnam Association
SMR	South Manchurian Railway	VNA	Vietnamese National Army
SOFA	Status of Forces Agreement	VOC	Vereenigte Oost-Indische Compagnie
SOG	Special Operations Group	WTC	Wheat Trade Convention
SPA	Sterling Payments Agreement	WTO	World Trade Organization
SRV	Socialist Republic of Vietnam	YMCA	Young Men's Christian Association
SSNC	Shanghai Steamship Navigation Company	YWCA	Young Women's Christian Association
SVN	State of Vietnam		
TAC	Treaty of Amity and Cooperation (in Southeast Asia)	ZOPFAN	Zone of Peace, Freedom, and Neutrality

Modern Japan. From W.G. Beasley, *The Rise of Modern Japan* (Weidenfeld & Nicolson, 1955). Reprinted by permission of The Orion Publishing Group Ltd.

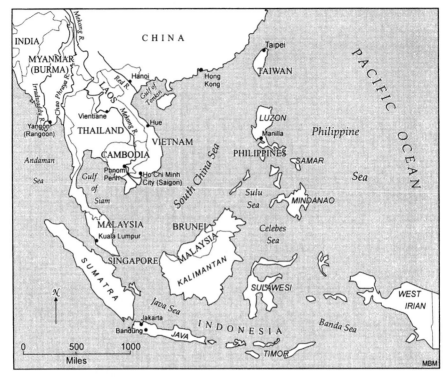

Above: Contemporary Southeast Asia. From *The Limits of Empire: The United States and Southeast Asia Since World War II* by Robert J. Mcmahon. © Columbia University Press, 1999. Reprinted with the permission of the publisher.

On opposite page: The Ryukyu Islands. From Gregory Smits, *Visions of Ryuku: Identity and Ideology in Early-Modern Thought and Politics* (Honolulu: University of Hawai'i Press, 1999). © 1999 University of Hawai'i Press. Reprinted with the permission of the publisher.

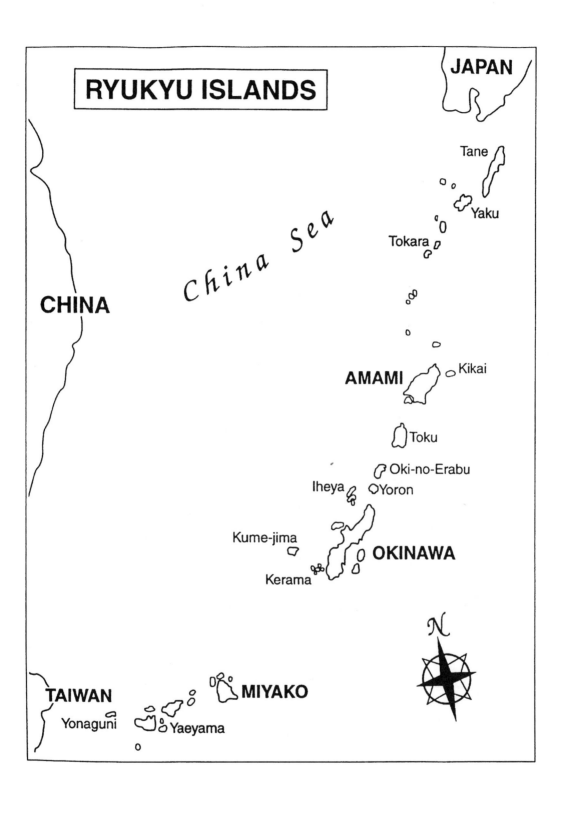

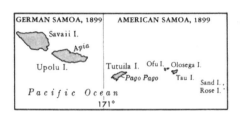

GERMAN SAMOA, 1899 | AMERICAN SAMOA, 1899

Savaii I.

Apia

Upolu I.

Tutuila I.   Ofu I.   Olosega I.

Pago Pago   Tau I.

Sand I.

Rose I.

Pacific Ocean

171°

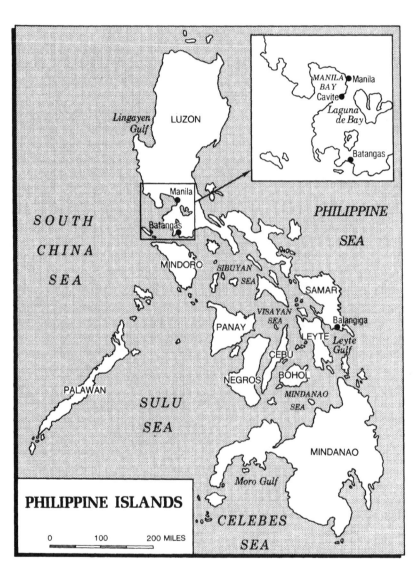

LUZON

Lingayen Gulf

MANILA BAY

Manila

Cavite

Laguna de Bay

Batangas

Manila

Batangas

SOUTH CHINA SEA

PHILIPPINE SEA

MINDORO

SIBUYAN SEA

SAMAR

VISAYAN SEA

Balangiga

PANAY

LEYTE

Leyte Gulf

CEBU

NEGROS

BOHOL

MINDANAO SEA

PALAWAN

SULU SEA

MINDANAO

Moro Gulf

PHILIPPINE ISLANDS

CELEBES SEA

0   100   200 MILES

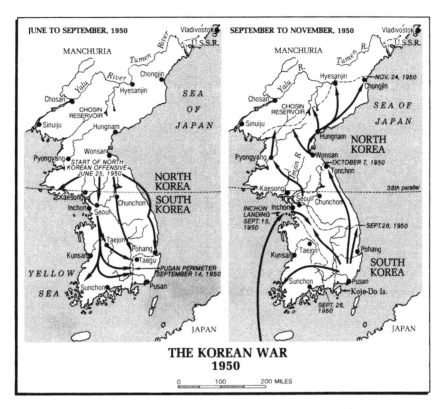

**THE KOREAN WAR
1950**

Opposite page, top: The Partition of Samoa, 1899. From *A History of American Foreign Policy*, 2nd ed., by Alexander DeConde (New York: Scribner's, 1971). Copyright © 1971 Charles Scribner's Sons. Reprinted with the permission of The Gale Group.

Opposite page, bottom: The Philippine Islands. Reprinted with the permission of The Free Press, a Division of Simon & Schuster, Inc., from *For the Common Defense: A Military History of the United States of America*, Revised & Expanded Edition by Allan R. Millet and Peter Maslowski. Copyright © 1984, 1994 by The Free Press.

Above: The Korean War, 1950. Reprinted with the permission of The Free Press, a Division of Simon & Schuster, Inc., from *For the Common Defense: A Military History of the United States of America*, Revised & Expanded Edition by Allan R. Millett and Peter Maslowski. Copyright © 1984, 1994 by The Free Press.

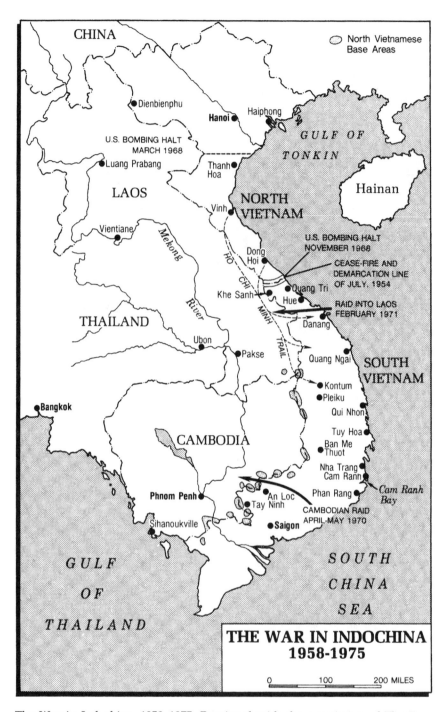

The War in Indochina, 1958–1975. Reprinted with the permission of The Free
Press, a Division of Simon & Schuster, Inc., from *For the Common Defense: A
Military History of the United States of America*, Revised & Expanded Edition by
Allan R. Millett and Peter Maslowski. Copyright © 1984, 1994 by The Free Press.

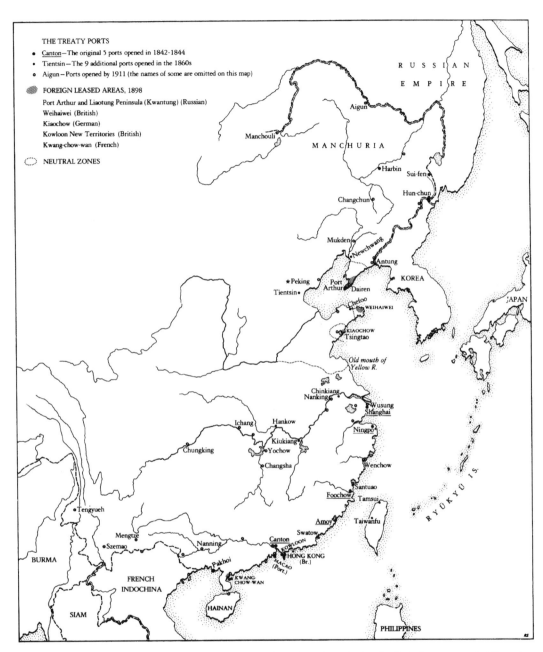

THE TREATY PORTS
● Canton—The original 5 ports opened in 1842-1844
• Tientsin—The 9 additional ports opened in the 1860s
○ Aigun—Ports opened by 1911 (the names of some are omitted on this map)

FOREIGN LEASED AREAS, 1898
Port Arthur and Liaotung Peninsula (Kwantung) (Russian)
Weihaiwei (British)
Kiaochow (German)
Kowloon New Territories (British)
Kwang-chow-wan (French)

NEUTRAL ZONES

Foreign Encroachment on China. From Fairbank, John K., Edwin O. Reischauer, and Albert M. Craig, *East Asia: Tradition and Transformation*, Revised Edition. Copyright © 1989 by Houghton Mifflin Company. Used with permission.

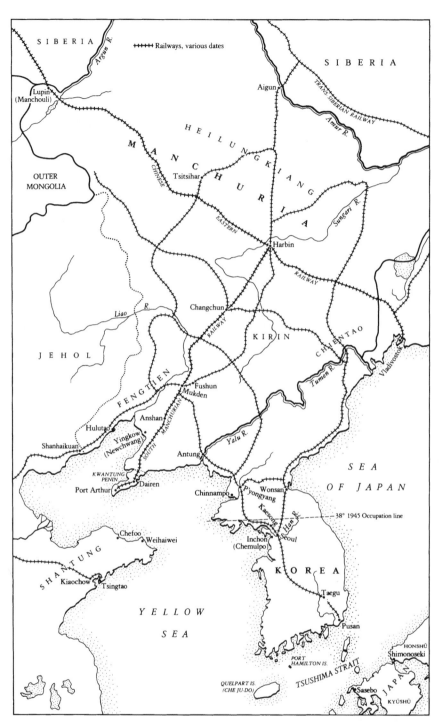

International Rivalry in Korea and Manchuria. From Fairbank, John K., Edwin O. Reischauer, and Albert M. Craig, *East Asia: Tradition and Transformation*, Revised Edition. Copyright © 1989 by Houghton Mifflin Company. Used with permission.

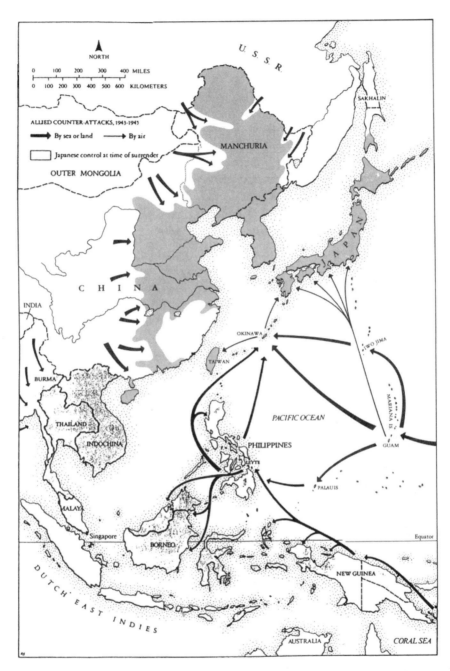

World War II in Greater East Asia. From Fairbank, John K., Edwin O. Reischauer, and Albert M. Craig, *East Asia: Tradition and Transformation*, Revised Edition. Copyright © 1989 by Houghton Mifflin Company. Used with permission.

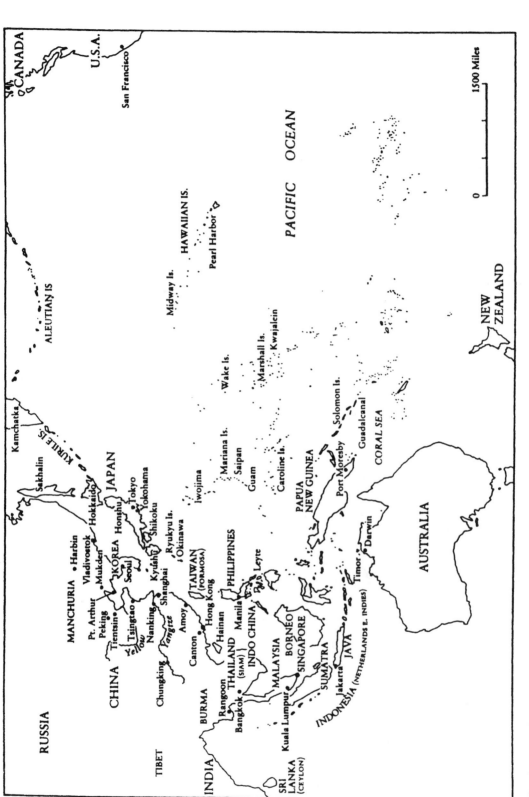

The Asia-Pacific Context. From Sydney Giffard, *Japan among the Powers, 1890–1990* (New Haven, CT: Yale University Press, 1997). Copyright © 1994 by Sydney Giffard. Reprinted with the permission of the publisher.

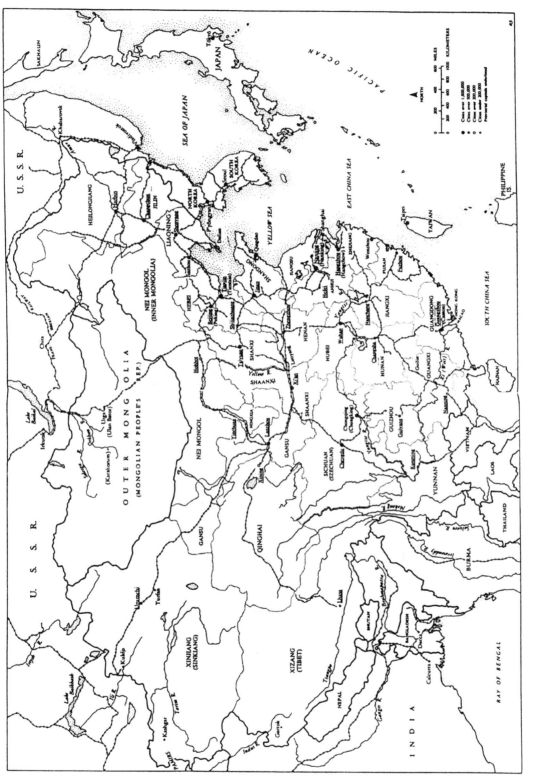

China: The People's Republic. From Fairbank, John K., Edwin O. Reischauer, and Albert M. Craig, *East Asia: Tradition and Transformation*, Revised Edition. Copyright © 1989 by Houghton Mifflin Company. Used with permission.

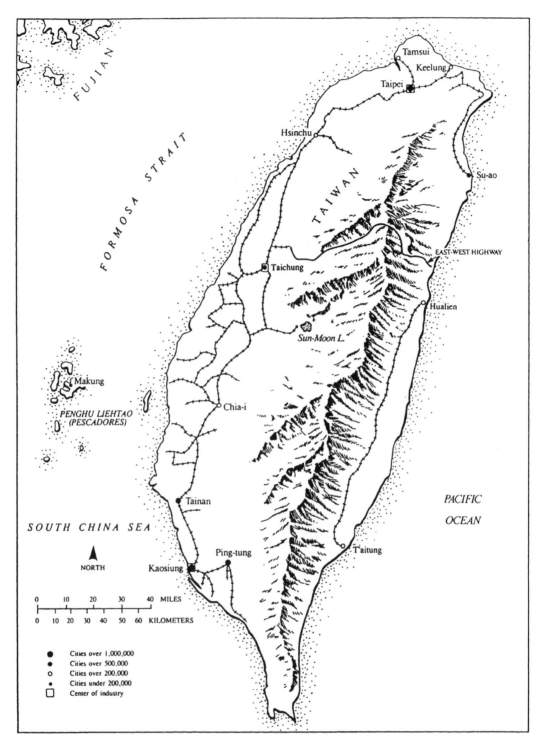

Taiwan. From Fairbank, John K., Edwin O. Reischauer, and Albert M. Craig, *East Asia: Tradition and Transformation*, Revised Edition. Copyright © 1989 by Houghton Mifflin Company. Used with permission.

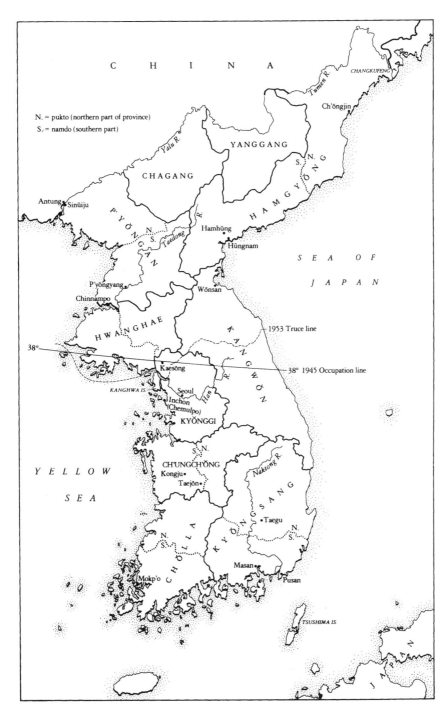

Korea in Recent Times. From Fairbank, John K., Edwin O. Reischauer, and Albert M. Craig, *East Asia: Tradition and Transformation*, Revised Edition. Copyright © 1989 by Houghton Mifflin Company. Used with permission.

Above: French Indo-China. From Fairbank, John K., Edwin O. Reischauer, and Albert M. Craig, *East Asia: Tradition and Transformation*, Revised Edition. Copyright © 1989 by Houghton Mifflin Company. Used with permission.

Opposite page, top: Singapore. From Fairbank, John K., Edwin O. Reischauer, and Albert M. Craig, *East Asia: Tradition and Transformation*, Revised Edition. Copyright © 1989 by Houghton Mifflin Company. Used with permission.

Opposite page, bottom: Hong Kong. From Fairbank, John K., Edwin O. Reischauer, and Albert M. Craig, *East Asia: Tradition and Transformation*, Revised Edition. Copyright © 1989 by Houghton Mifflin Company. Used with permission.

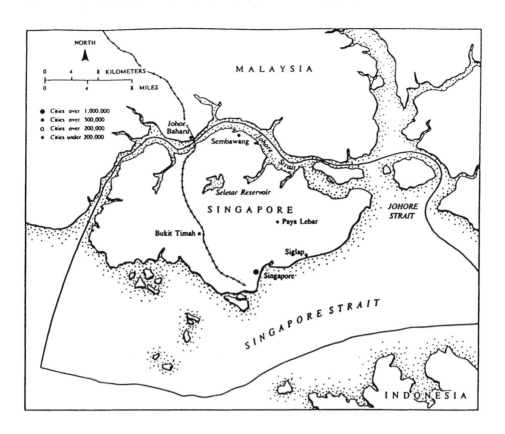

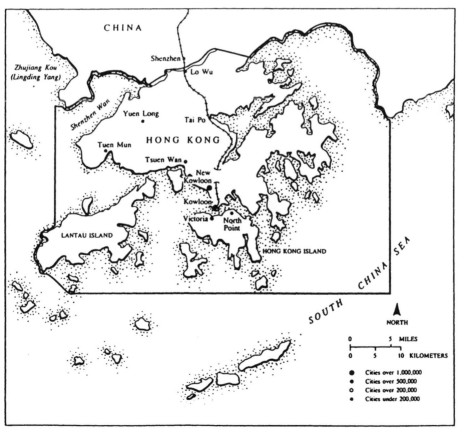

A

ABE NOBUYUKI (1875–1958)

Born in what currently is Kanazawa Prefecture, Abe Nobuyuki was a general in Japan's army and prime minister during World War II. He followed the Japanese Imperial Army's major career path, starting with graduation from the Army War College. Like many officers of his generation, Abe served in the Russo-Japanese War* and studied in Germany. After assuming the top command of forces in Taiwan in 1932, he worked his way up the army central bureaucracy and retired from active duty in 1936. Abe was virtually unknown in national politics when he received an imperial order to form a cabinet in August 1939 amid the shock and confusion in Tōkyō over the Nazi-Soviet Non-Aggression Pact. A product of compromise between recalcitrant middle-echelon army officials and civilian leaders hoping to rein in the army, the politically unambitious retired general was expected to restore unity of purpose in diplomatic and military affairs in the increasingly dysfunctional Japanese polity.

Inaugurated only a few days before the outbreak of war in Europe, the Abe cabinet failed to restructure Japan's misaligned foreign relations. Although Abe proclaimed neutrality in the European conflict, he failed to wean the major powers away from a position supporting Jiang Jieshi* of China. With the U.S.-Japan commercial treaty approaching expiration in January 1940, Foreign Minister Nomura Kichisaburō* and Ambassador Joseph C. Grew* opened a dialogue to ease the mounting tension in U.S.-Japanese relations. But Abe proved incapable of persuading the army to accommodate U.S. demands regarding China. He set up a binational committee to achieve reconciliation with the Soviets after the military clash at the Battle of Nomonhan*, but acquiesced in the army's sabotage of Ambassador Tōgō Shigenori's efforts to arrange a nonaggression pact with Moscow.

On the domestic front, Abe's inept handling of the army's attempt to rob the Foreign Ministry of jurisdiction over international economic matters discredited his cabinet. Amid the chronic shortage of goods, his cabinet's misguided fiscal policy exacerbated the price inflation caused in part by the war in Europe. As the House of Commons angled for a vote of no-confidence against the four-month-old cabinet, the army abandoned Abe, and the cabinet resigned en masse in January 1940. The highlight of Abe's postresignation life was an appointment in April 1940 as a special envoy to negotiate formal diplomatic relations with the collaborationist regime in Nanjing of Wang Jingwei*. Abe accepted Japan's defeat in World War II as governor-general of Korea, where he had encouraged the creation of the People's Republic to govern postwar Korea. In September 1945, Lieutenant General John R. Hodge* banned him from public offices during the U.S. Occupation of Korea*.

J. H. Boyle, *China and Japan at War 1937–1945: The Politics of Collaboration*. (Stanford, CA, 1972); Hayashi Shigeru and Tsuji Seimei (eds.), *Nippon naikaku shiroku* [The History of Japanese Cabinets], vol. 4 (Tōkyō, 1981); Matsushita Yoshio, *Araki Sadao to Abe Nobuyuki* [Araki Sadao and Abe Nobuyuki] (Tōkyō, 1935).

Shimizu Sayuri

ABRAMS, CREIGHTON (1914–1974)

General Creighton Abrams was reassigned from vice chief of staff of the U.S. Army to the post of deputy under General William C. Westmoreland* in command of all U.S. forces in Vietnam in April 1967. He coordinated the U.S. Army, U.S. Marine, and Vietnamese forces in the battle for Hue after the 1968 Tet Offensive*, then gradually took over command of the Military Assistance Command, Vietnam* (MACV) after the April 1968 announcement of Westmoreland's elevation to U.S. Army chief of staff, officially taking command in July 1968. He downplayed the "body count" and changed from Westmoreland's strategy of attrition to an emphasis on protecting the civilian population. Under President Richard M. Nixon*, Abrams was responsible for implementing Vietnamization* of the war and the Cambodian Incursion* in April 1970. He succeeded Westmoreland as chief of staff of the U.S. Army in June 1972, dying in office.

When Abrams went to Vietnam, he had the most combat experience of any general in the U.S. Army. A 1936 West Point graduate, he was the tank commander who led the forces that relieved the U.S. 101st Airborne at the Battle of the Bulge, ending the war as a thirty-year-old full colonel.

Abrams served as chief of staff of all three corps in Korea, then alternated Pentagon positions with command positions in Germany. As chief of staff, he was responsible for rebuilding the U.S. Army after Vietnam. When Abrams first went to Vietnam as a four-star deputy to his four-star West Point classmate, it was assumed that he would replace Westmoreland in a few months, rather than the fourteen that it eventually took. If he had assumed command a year earlier, Abrams's refusal to paint the rosy "light at the end of the tunnel" picture that Westmoreland presented to the press in 1967 and his emphasis on civilian control rather than search-and-destroy attrition tactics could well have softened the devastating impact of the Tet Offensive.

N. Sheehan, *A Bright Shining Lie: John Paul Vann and America in Vietnam* (New York, 1988); L. Sorley, *Thunderbolt: General Creighton Abrams and the Army of His Times* (New York, 1992); W. C. Westmoreland, *A Soldier Reports* (Garden City, NY, 1972).

Larry R. Beck

ACHESON, DEAN G. (1893–1971)

As undersecretary of state and secretary of state, Dean G. Acheson played a major role in formulating U.S. policy in East Asia after World War II, especially with respect to the Chinese Civil War*, the U.S. Occupation of Japan*, and the Korean War*. He was born in Connecticut, the son of an Episcopalian bishop, graduating from Yale University in 1915 and Harvard Law School in 1918. After serving briefly in the U.S. Navy during World War I, Acheson spent the greater part of the next two decades as an attorney for a Washington, D.C., law firm. In 1941, he became assistant secretary of state for economic affairs and was involved in the planning for postwar reconstruction and new international economic agencies. President Harry S. Truman* relied heavily on Acheson as undersecretary of state after 1945, because of his strained relations with

Secretary of State James F. Byrnes. They developed a close working relationship, built on mutual respect and common values. Acheson was instrumental in the formulation of the containment policy aimed at limiting the Soviet Union's influence in Europe until he resigned from the State Department in the summer of 1947 and resumed his legal practice.

Acheson was secretary of state from January 1949 until the end of the Truman presidency four years later. To Acheson, American priorities were in Europe, and he tended to view developments in Asia through a European perspective. This explains his lack of sympathy toward the nationalist revolutions that swept across much of South and Southeast Asia. Typical of Acheson's predisposition was his support of France in its prolonged warfare in French Indochina* against the Communist-led Vietminh*. In 1950, Acheson recognized the French-fostered State of Vietnam headed by Emperor Bao Dai* and began providing financial support for the French in the First Indochina War*. Acheson saw backing France in Asia as essential to assuring its acceptance of the rehabilitation of West Germany. But in 1949, the Chinese Civil War was the overriding American concern in Asia. With the Communist forces clearly in the ascendancy, conservative Republicans in Congress pressed the Truman administration to increase military assistance to the beleaguered Nationalists headed by Jiang Jieshi*. To Acheson, only direct U.S. military intervention could save the Guomindang*. In the summer of 1949, Acheson issued the China White Paper*, which argued that the impending Communist victory resulted from internal forces beyond the control of outside powers. When the victory of the latter became a reality in the fall of 1949, conservatives criticized Truman and Acheson for "selling out" Jiang and "losing China."

Attempting to clarify U.S. strategic interests in the aftermath of the Chinese Communist Party* victory, Acheson's National Press Club Speech* in January 1950 defined a "defensive perimeter" running from Japan, through the Ryūkyūs, and to the Philippines*. After the North Korean attack on South Korea on 25 June 1950, critics charged that Acheson had "invited" the invasion by not pledging U.S. defense beforehand. Throughout the Korean War, Acheson played the central role in formulating American policies, especially the decision to commit U.S. troops to a United Nations Command (UNC). Truman, who shared his conviction that aggression had to be resisted, invariably accepted Acheson's recommendations. Nevertheless, Acheson was reticent to challenge military leaders, especially General Douglas MacArthur*, who was given command of the UN forces. When the UNC took the initiative in the war in September 1950, Acheson supported the decision to cross the thirty-eighth parallel with the goal of Korean unification under UN auspices. Threats from China to intervene and the appearance of some Chinese units in Korea in late October and early November troubled him, but he took no initiative to reconsider military operations. In his memoir, Acheson blames himself for serving Truman poorly in this instance.

Open Chinese Intervention in the Korean War* came in late November, and the UNC forces retreated below the thirty-eighth parallel before managing to establish a stable front. This necessitated the Truman administration's return to the original objective of restoring Korea's division. Their policy seemingly in disarray, Truman and Acheson endured much criticism over MacArthur's Recall* in April 1951 and the stalemate on the battlefield that continued until Truman left office. Acheson was singled out by conservatives in Congress for what they considered the failures of policy in China and Korea. Meanwhile, Acheson pushed forward with the reconstruction of Japan and its incorporation into the Western economic system and the containment structure. After leaving office in 1953, Acheson resumed his legal practice and in the 1960s was called upon by Presidents John

F. Kennedy* and Lyndon B. Johnson*. Most significantly, he became the unofficial spokesman for the "Wise Men" whom Johnson consulted occasionally on Vietnam policy between 1965 and 1968. He began as a strident hawk, but in the aftermath of the Tet Offensive*, he and his fellow "Wise Men" advised Johnson that the time had come to negotiate an end to the unpopular Second Indochina War*.

D. Acheson, *Present at the Creation: My Years in the State Department* (New York, 1969); D. Brinkley, Dean Acheson: *The Cold War Years, 1953–1971* (New Haven, CT, 1992); J. Chace, *Acheson: The Secretary of State Who Created the American World* (New York, 1998); G. Smith, Dean Acheson (Cooper Square, NY, 1972).

Gary R. Hess

ACHESON'S NATIONAL PRESS CLUB SPEECH (12 January 1950)

In this speech, Secretary of State Dean G. Acheson* sought to refute Republican charges that the Truman administration had not done enough to prevent the Communist takeover in China during 1949. It was a defensive political gambit that Secretary of Defense Louis A. Johnson had forced him to write to silence administration critics. In addition, since the summer of 1949, Congress had been reluctant to approve the Korean Aid Act* and he wanted to build enough support for authorization. With American aid, Acheson claimed South Korea had "a very good chance" for successful resistance to Communist expansion. But he refused to pledge American military protection for the Republic of Korea* because it was outside the "defensive perimeter" of the United States. In the event of open aggression beyond Japan, the Ryūkyūs, and the Philippines*, "the initial reliance must be on the people attacked to resist it and then upon . . . the United Nations which so far has not proved a weak reed to lean on by any people who are determined to protect their independence." After the outbreak of the Korean War*, critics blamed Acheson for the North Korean invasion of South Korea, alleging that his National Press Club speech constituted a "green light" for the attack, since he implied that the United States would not act to prevent a Communist military conquest of South Korea. Soviet documents have since shown that the speech had no impact on Communist deliberations leading to North Korea's attack.

Prior emphasis on the effect on North Korea of this portion of the address has obscured its real significance as a definitive statement of American policy objectives and expectations in Asia. It merely restated policy decisions made late in 1949 and contained in National Security Council paper 48/2. For Acheson, the Soviet-inspired Communist military threat was not as immediate as the challenge of "subversion and penetration." Since Communism* thrived on social upheaval and economic dislocation, Asian nations could best withstand Communist political pressure by developing strong democratic institutions and stable economies. The United States could contribute to political and economic stability in Asia by providing economic aid, technical knowledge, and administrative advice. To substantiate his argument, Acheson pointed to China, explaining that Jiang Jieshi* had failed to satisfy popular needs and wants, causing the Chinese people to "brush him aside." By contrast, the South Koreans not only wanted American help, but would use it effectively. Acheson based his assessment on the key assumption that South Korea would not face open armed aggression. His National Press Club speech sought to persuade the American people that despite the fall of China, local strength and self-reliance would preserve stability in Korea and elsewhere in Asia beyond the "defensive perimeter." Ironically, North Korean leaders at first thought Acheson placed South Korea *inside* the perimeter.

D. Acheson, *Present at the Creation: My Years in the State Department* (New York, 1969); B. Cumings, *The Origins of the Korean War*, Vol. 2: *The Roaring of the Cataract, 1947–1950* (Princeton, NJ, 1990); J. I. Matray, "Dean Acheson's Press Club Speech Reexamined," *Journal of Conflict Studies* (Spring 2002); J. I. Matray, *The Reluctant Crusade: American Foreign Policy in Korea, 1941–1950* (Honolulu, HI, 1985); D. Rees, *Korea: The Limited War* (New York, 1964).

James I. Matray

AGUINALDO, EMILIO

See PHILIPPINE REVOLUTION OF 1896

AIR AMERICA

Air America was the wholly owned "proprietary" airline that the Central Intelligence Agency* (CIA) employed to support its clandestine operations in East Asia while undertaking legitimate business to maintain its cover. At its peak in the late 1960s, Air America employed more than 11,000 people, operated more than 175 aircraft, and fully lived up to its company motto "Anything Anywhere, Anytime: Professionally." Air America was a direct descendant of Civil Air Transport (CAT), a Chinese company organized after World War II, which bought surplus U.S. aircraft and facilities, and hired former pilots and technicians who had worked with General Claire L. Chennault* and his Flying Tigers. In 1950, the CIA acquired CAT as a temporary expedient with the intention of divesting its interests as soon as possible. The requirements of the Korean War*, logistical support for the French in the First Indochina War*, and continuing support of the Chinese Guomindang* operations in Burma* and China proved to the CIA the value of a covert airlift capability when an overt U.S. government connection was politically disadvantageous. During the later 1950s, CAT supported U.S. secret operations in the outer islands rebellion against Sukarno* in Indonesia* and provided logistical support to the resistance movement in Tibet*. Initially, the CIA provided a modest subsidy to CAT, but by the late 1950s, the company turned a profit. CAT was so successful and so prevalent in Asia's hot spots that it was generally known to be an arm of the CIA. Partly for this reason, CAT's name was changed in 1959 to Air America.

Air America did both overt and covert work in Vietnam in conjunction with the U.S. military buildup in the early 1960s, but Laos* was where Air America came into its own. The Geneva Accords of 1962* prohibited airlift of overt military assistance to any of the Lao factions, so Air America did the job of supporting the Lao non-Communists. With their signature Hawaiian shirts, heavy gold jewelry, and baseball or cowboy hats, Air America pilots earned a reputation for daring flying and hard living. They flew unarmed aircraft into remote airstrips in Laos, bringing supplies, ammunition, and weapons to support Hmong* or the regular Royal Lao Armed Forces. They airlifted regular and irregular Lao troops to and from the battlefields. The Pathet Lao* and North Vietnamese attacked Air America planes on sight, causing heavy losses of aircraft and personnel. Some Air America pilots actually flew combat missions in converted T-28 propeller-driven aircraft in the early days of the Secret U.S. Air War in Laos*. A few Air America pilots and officials became involved in Drug Trade*, smuggling either knowingly or by turning a blind eye, but the majority engaged in their dangerous occupation for motives other than money—love of flying, adventure, and/or anti-Communism. Air America's last big mission in East Asia was to evacuate Saigon when it fell to North Vietnamese forces in April 1975. Because Air America was no longer needed, the CIA sold its assets in 1976, returning a total of $20 million in proceeds. *See also* Guomindang Intervention in Burma; Second Indochina War.

W. M. Leary, *Perilous Missions: Civil Air Transport and CIA Covert Operations in Asia* (Tuscaloosa, AL, 1984); A. W. McCoy, *Politics of Heroin in Southeast Asia* (New York, 1972); J. Prados, *President's Secret Wars: Covert Operations Since World War II* (New York, 1986); C. Robbins, *Air America* (New York, 1979).

Edward C. Keefer

ALLEN, HORACE N. (1858–1932)

Horace Allen's chief fame was to serve from 1884 to 1905 in Seoul, Korea, for five years as a missionary doctor, seven years as secretary of the American legation there, and eight years as minister of the United States. He was a thin-skinned missionary, short-tempered, with a tendency to blurt out insults. Yet Allen's determination, his hard work ethic, and piety, together with his medical skills and blunt sincerity, won him esteem and support from the Korean monarch. He was a tall redhead who viewed the world through narrow steel-rimmed glasses and missionary eyes. His clipped mustache and goatee, with starched wing collar and black jacket, rounded out the archetypal late-nineteenth-century Presbyterian missionary appearance. Allen earned a bachelor's degree at Ohio Wesleyan in 1881 and also graduated from Miami Medical College in Cincinnati. He was assigned to China by the Presbyterian Board of Foreign Missions and went to Shanghai in September 1883, before being ordered to Korea in July 1884. He worked at first with General Lucius H. Foote*, who named him legation doctor, which freed him from the threat of persecution as a missionary. The camouflage fooled no one, and privately Allen dismissed Korean religion as a study of demons and spirits.

Allen observed two decades of intense Chinese-Japanese struggle to control Korea. He preferred an independent Korea, but operated close to the pro-Chinese group. He won influence at court with his doctoring skills, when in late 1884, he saved the life of Queen Min's nephew. Allen was made physician to the court and a champion of the third degree so that he could treat the royal family and the dowager queen mother. By this route he achieved the ear of King Kojong*, and during the next twenty years, became the most powerful foreign influence on the court. Thereafter, Allen always stuck to the path of royal favor. With court approval, he opened a hospital on 9 April 1885 with missionary doctors and nurses, and followed with a medical and scientific school within the hospital. When Allen left Seoul in 1905, there were eighty workers in the Presbyterian mission, and other denominations had double that number of Protestants. They reported 15,000 baptized Protestants, half of which were Presbyterians, and seven times as many adherents.

In the 1880s, Allen dueled politically with Yuan Shikai*, the Chinese resident general, who did not approve of Allen or his influence. In 1887, Kojong appointed Allen as foreign secretary of the Korean legation to the United States, where he served for two years. In August 1890, Allen was appointed U.S. secretary of legation in Seoul and used his influence to obtain concessions for American businessmen for franchises granted in Korea. His activities in Korea helped bring Korea's first railroad, its first waterworks, its first oil lighting and streetcar system, and its first modern mine. The biggest gold mine in Asia at Unsan became an American concession in July 1895 under the Korean Development Company for twenty-five years. But Allen's concession gathering was not a long-term success, as most eventually came under Japanese control. In 1895, Japanese military victory over China was the beginning of the end for Allen's influence, although he held on for an additional ten years. In September 1903, before the Russo-Japanese War*, Allen appealed to U.S. President Theodore Roosevelt* to make a stand against the Japanese takeover, but Roosevelt refused to intervene. When Japan effectively seized Korea and the United States withdrew its legation, Allen declared, "I fell with Korea." He returned to the United States and set up a medical practice in Toledo, Ohio, which flourished until his death.

F. H. Harrington, "An American View of Korean-American Relations, 1882–1905," in Y. Lee and W. Patterson (eds.), *One Hundred Years of Korean-American Relations, 1882–1982* (Tuscaloosa, AL, 1986); F. H. Harrington, *God, Mammon and the Japanese: Dr. Horace N. Allen and Korean-American Relations, 1884–1905* (Madison, WI, 1944); C. I. E. Kim and H. Kim, *Korea and the Politics of Imperialism, 1876–1910* (Berkeley, CA, 1967); W. Patterson, "Sugar-Coated Diplomacy: Horace Allen and Korean Immigration to Hawaii, 1902–1905," *Diplomatic History* (Summer, 1979); J. E. Wilz, "Did the United States Betray Korea in 1905?," *Pacific Historical Review* (August 1985).

Frederick C. Drake

ALLISON, JOHN M. (1905–1978)

John Moore Allison was influential as a State Department official and ambassador in the formulation of U.S. policy toward Korea, Japan, and Indonesia* after World War II. He joined the Foreign Service in 1932 and held various consular posts both in China and Japan before the Pearl Harbor Attack*, when Japan interned him and other U.S. diplomats. Shortly after repatriation in July 1942, Allison went to London to serve as second secretary and chief of the Far East Intelligence Section. He returned to the United States in September 1946 as adviser to the U.S. delegation at the United Nations and then became assistant chief of the Division of Japanese Affairs. Reorganization added Korea to Allison's responsibilities in 1947 as the new chief of the Division of Far Eastern Affairs. That year, the Truman administration adopted his plan to end the Soviet-American occupation of Korea, resulting in submission of the question to the United Nations, elections in South Korea alone, and creation of the Republic of Korea* in August 1948. By then, another restructuring made Allison the director of Northeast Asian Affairs. After a stint as consul general in Singapore*, he became special assistant to John Foster

Dulles* in May 1950 to help draft a peace treaty for Japan. Allison was in Tōkyō with Dulles when the Korean War* began, and the two men cabled Washington, urging use of U.S. troops to defend South Korea. Despite his later denials, Allison was influential in building support for the extension of military operations into North Korea, arguing that only unification would bring lasting peace.

In 1951, Allison, as counsel to the U.S. mission in Tōkyō, helped complete the Japanese Peace Treaty*. With Dulles, he negotiated security pacts with Australia, New Zealand, the Philippines, and Japan. Allison became acting assistant secretary for Far Eastern Affairs late in 1951 and then assistant secretary in February 1952. His next appointment was as ambassador to Japan, where from May 1953 to January 1957, he tried to persuade the reluctant Japanese to rearm and reduce a growing trade deficit. He completed delicate negotiations for the U.S.-Japan Mutual Defense Assistance Agreement* in March 1954, providing Tōkyō with $100 million in U.S. economic aid in return for its commitment of manpower, resources, and facilities to defend Japan and the Free World. Again displaying diplomatic talent, Allison resolved the *Lucky Dragon* Incident*, when twenty-three Japanese fishermen aboard the *Fukuryū Maru* were burned by radioactive ashes from U.S. thermonuclear tests in March 1954 near Bikini, resulting in payment of $2 million. In April 1955, he finished work on a new mutual defense pact providing for the United States to reduce by $50 million Japan's commitment of support for U.S. troops.

Allison chose in February 1957 to become ambassador to Indonesia rather than Pakistan, beginning "the most fascinating and frustrating period in my thirty years in the Foreign Service." To avert Communist takeover in that nation, he strongly urged in private cables that the United States press the Dutch to open negotiations for the transfer of West Irian to Indonesia, while providing President Sukarno* with both economic and military aid. But Washington ignored his advice, having decided that Sukarno was "beyond redemption." Allison believed his reassignment as ambassador to Czechoslovakia early in 1958 reflected the Eisenhower administration's conclusion that he had become soft on Communism* in East Asia. After a frustrating tenure in Prague, Allison retired in 1960. His autobiographical *Ambassador from the Prairie* is full of personal and professional anecdotes, but it also provides valuable insights about the making of U.S. policy in East Asia after World War II. *See also* PRRI-Permesta Rebellion.

Current Biography (1956); R. J. Donovan, *Tumultuous Years: The Presidency of Harry S. Truman, 1949–1953* (New York, 1983); J. I. Matray, *The Reluctant Crusade: American Foreign Policy in Korea, 1941–1950* (Honolulu, HI, 1985); W. W. Stueck, *The Road to Confrontation: American Policy Towards China and Korea, 1947–1950* (Chapel Hill, NC, 1981).

James I. Matray

AMERICAN ASIATIC ASSOCIATION

The American Asiatic Association was an organization of American business interests established to educate the public and lobby the U.S. government on East Asian policy issues. The association was formed in 1898 when the United States increasingly looked to foreign markets to absorb domestic industrial overproduction, and just as American exports to China began to surge. Although the group represented elements as diverse as Southern textile firms and New York trading companies, members found common ground on key issues, especially the overriding importance of maintaining U.S. access to Chinese markets and opposing partition of them. Through the work of two energetic early leaders, John Foord and Willard D. Straight*, the organization had a direct influence on policy during the early decades of the twentieth century. For instance, publicity campaigns on the importance of retaining

access to the China market helped generate the support leading to the W. W. Rockhill* memorandum and the implementation of the Open Door Policy*. But its influence on policy gradually waned after World War I.

American Asiatic Association, *Golden Anniversary Issue for the 50th Annual Meeting* (New York, 1948); *Journal of the American Asiatic Association* (New York, 1898–1917); J. Lorence, *Organized Business and the Myth of the China Market: The American Asiatic Association, 1898–1937* (Philadelphia, 1981).

Karl Gerth

AMERICAN BOARD OF COMMISSIONERS FOR FOREIGN MISSIONS

This first missionary society resulted from Congregationalists at Williams College in 1806 asking Congregationalist churches in Massachusetts to support missionary activities. The American Board of Commissioners for Foreign Missions (ABCFM) was active in the Pacific and elsewhere. The ABCFM was patterned after other Christian groups, such as the London, Baptist, and Netherlands Missionary Societies. Between 1820 and 1855, more than 150 Congregationalist ministers, farmers, printers, businesspeople, doctors, and teachers worked for it in Hawaii and Micronesia. In the latter area, the ABCFM in the 1850s established mission stations in Kosrae (Kusaie), Pohnpei, and Ebon, and in the 1870s in the Mortlock Islands and in Chuuk (Truk). By the 1880s, the board had established at least fifty churches in the Caroline and Marshall Islands. One of the most prominent and significant of the early missionaries was the Reverend Edward T. Doane, who had joined the ABCFM mission at Pohnpei in 1855, three years after it had been established. In 1857, he and his wife were posted to teach at Ebon in the Marshall Islands. They returned to the United States twice for medical reasons, and were released from service in 1878. The ABCFM ended in 1961, when the Congregational Christian Church and the Evangelical and

Reformed Church merged into the United Church of Christ, but continued to function as the United Church of Christ Board of World Ministries.

In 1887, Doane became a cause célèbre in American newspapers because of a diplomatic dispute involving American Protestant and Spanish Catholic rivalry and the mission's land rights. As a widower, he had returned to the Pohnpei station in 1885 and become the senior member. Pope Leo XIII had arbitrated the dispute between Germany and Spain over rights to the Caroline Islands by giving Spain sovereignty and Germany freedom of trade. Spain also had assured the United States that ABCFM mission efforts would be allowed to continue. In 1887, Posadillo, the newly appointed Spanish governor, arrived to establish a station on land at Kenan, Jamestown Harbor, now Kolonia, Pohnpei. Pohnpeian chiefs had deeded this area to the mission, but Doane had agreed to make a portion of it available to the Spanish. Shortly thereafter, Doane formally protested Spanish encroachment on other parts of the mission land and was arrested on 13 April 1887 for disrespectful behavior. He was deported on other charges, but on arrival in Manila, the governor-general of the Philippines* freed and repatriated him to Pohnpei. On his return in September, he and the Spanish ship captain were surprised to learn of the rebellion in July, which had resulted in the death of Posadillo and a number of soldiers. Conditions were temporarily stable, but Doane left Pohnpei for health reasons in 1889. ABCFM's claims for damages to property at Doane's station and the station at Oa, Pohnpei, that was destroyed in the 1890 naval bombardments of Pohnpeian rebels continued to be a subject of U.S. diplomatic negotiations with Spain in the 1890s.

R. D. Craig and F. P. King (eds.), *Historical Dictionary of Oceania* (Westport, CT, 1981); F. X. Hezel, *The First Taint of Civilization: A History of the Caroline and Marshall Islands in Pre-Colonial Days, 1521–1885* (Honolulu, HI, 1983); F. X. Hezel, and M. L. Berg (eds.), *Winds of Change: A Book of Readings on Micronesian History* (Saipan, 1979).

Dirk A. Ballendorf

AMERICAN FRIENDS OF VIETNAM

The American Friends of Vietnam (AFV) served as the formal organization of the Vietnam Lobby, a loose coalition of American citizens who advocated U.S. support for the Republic of Vietnam*. The association was formed in 1955 by Joseph Buttinger and Harold Oram. Buttinger was an Austrian socialist who became an admirer of Ngo Dinh Diem* after meeting Diem while supervising refugee relief projects on behalf of the International Rescue Committee (IRC) in Saigon. Oram was a fundraiser who worked closely with the IRC and became the Diem regime's public relations representative. Many of the AFV's first members were Buttinger's associates from the IRC, including the economist Leo Cherne and the patrician-diplomat Angier Biddle Duke. Other active AFV members were Wesley R. Fishel* and William Henderson, two academics who specialized in Asian politics, and Lieutenant General John W. O'Daniel, the former head of the U.S. military mission to Saigon. AFV correspondence also featured the names of such prominent figures as John F. Kennedy*, Mike Mansfield*, William O. Douglas, Henry R. Luce*, and Norman Thomas on its letterheads, a list that reflected the broadly based anti-Communist consensus of American political opinion during the Cold War.

Early accounts of the AFV's work claim that the non-governmental organization (NGO) pressured the Eisenhower administration to ignore the election provisions of the Geneva Accords of 1954*, and to back Diem's government, but the association actually had little influence over officials who already were committed deeply to the survival of an anti-Communist Vietnamese state. Moreover, many of its members already had worked closely with the

U.S. government since the early years of the Cold War. The AFV initially supported Diem as a democratic and modernizing leader, but by the early 1960s, some of its officers expressed doubts about his ability to stop a growing Communist insurgency. By 1963, the AFV's leadership had become bitterly divided over the issue of backing Diem, and his heavy-handed repression of Buddhist dissidents in that year persuaded most AFV members to make a break with the regime. A few members who still supported Diem quit the organization when its leaders endorsed the military coup that led to the overthrow of the Saigon government and Diem's Assassination* in November.

In the months after Diem's death, the AFV resumed its efforts to generate support for the Republic of Vietnam and backed the decision of President Lyndon B. Johnson* to use U.S. air strikes and ground troops to block a Communist victory in 1965, despite the resignation of some members, including Buttinger, who had become disillusioned with the Saigon government. The Johnson administration took notice of the AFV's support and worked with the group in sponsoring programs designed to counter the growing influence of the anti-war movement. The AFV's partnership with the administration suddenly ended in late 1965 when White House officials concluded that the group's financial and organizational difficulties, problems that had plagued the AFV since its inception, made it an ineffective ally. Thereafter, the NGO's work was sharply circumscribed by dwindling financial resources as the American public steadily lost confidence in the war effort. The AFV gradually phased out its activities in the early 1970s as U.S. troops withdrew from Vietnam. It staged a last-ditch attempt to amass American aid to South Vietnam during the Communist offensive of 1975, but this effort ended when Saigon fell on 30 April and the AFV's own demise quickly followed. *See also* Second Indochina War.

E. T. Chester, *Covert Network: Progressives, the International Rescue Committee, and the CIA* (Armonk, NY, 1995); J. T. Fisher, *Dr. America: The Lives of Thomas A. Dooley, 1927–1961* (Amherst, MA, 1997); J. G. Morgan, *The Vietnam Lobby: The American Friends of Vietnam, 1955–1975* (Chapel Hill, NC, 1997); R. Scheer, *How the United States Got Involved in Vietnam* (Santa Barbara, CA, 1965); R. Scheer and W. Hinckle, "The Viet-Nam Lobby," *Ramparts* (1965).

Joseph G. Morgan

AMERICAN-JAPANESE TREATY OF 1894

The U.S.-Japan Treaty of Commerce and Navigation was signed on 19 November 1894, to come into effect five years later, as was the case with the Anglo-Japanese Treaty concluded earlier in the same year. The benchmark Anglo-Japanese Treaty of Commerce and Navigation of 16 July 1894 abolished extraterritoriality and foreign settlements, and liberalized inland access, but did not address the issue of tariff autonomy and the right of perpetual lease. Foreign Minister Mutsu Munemitsu pushed through the Anglo-Japanese Treaty by shelving the issue of tariff autonomy and settling for rates set in consultation with Britain. Although the treaty was signed just before the de facto start of the Sino-Japanese War in Korea on 23 July, links between the formal declaration of war on 1 August and the Anglo-Japanese Treaty remain unproven.

Although the Anglo-Japanese Treaty created a precedent and template for U.S.-Japan negotiations, a number of points distinguished the American-Japanese Treaty. First, immigration, an issue not present in Anglo-Japanese negotiations, proved to be a sticking point. Mutual expansion in the Pacific, including the high-paced Japanese immigration to Hawaii, meant that Article 1 of the new treaty, dealing with the right of residence and travel, was subjected to intense debate in the U.S. Senate. Second, unlike Britain, the United States declined to set negotiated tariff rates, allowing Japan to set its own rates. Third, by the time the American-Japanese Treaty was signed, the Japanese Army had driven the Chinese forces out of northern Korea, meaning that in comparison to the Anglo-Japanese Treaty, the American-Japanese Treaty had fewer immediate military implications.

While the treaty was awaiting Senate ratification on 28 November, the *New York World* broke the story of the Japanese Army's massacre of civilians at Port Arthur. Mutsu quickly sent a statement refuting the incident to the *World*, defusing the mounting criticism. The U.S. government generally took a devotedly neutral position on the Sino-Japanese War, with only one instance of the U.S. ambassador in Tōkyō asking Japan not to violate Korea's sovereignty. In fact, both Japan, especially with the new treaty in hand, and China indicated that they would accept the United States as a mediator, as it had no direct interests on the Asian continent. Within the five years from the signing of the treaty to its taking effect, there was a publishing boom on booklets explaining the benefits of the new treaty. The consequences of the abolition of extraterritoriality and consular jurisdiction was put in clear and easily understood terms for the average citizen. The major issue left unaddressed, tariff autonomy, was not resolved until the signing of the American-Japanese Treaty of 1911*, when the 1894 treaty expired and new terms were negotiated. Right of perpetual lease was not abolished until 1937, when such rights were changed to land ownership rights. These issues notwithstanding, the 1894 treaty symbolized Japan's rising status within the international political arena, and constituted one of the legal accompaniments to Japan's military victory over China.

F. C. Jones, *Extraterritoriality in Japan and the Diplomatic Relations Resulting in Its Abolition* (New Haven, CT, 1931); J. W. Morley, *Japan's Foreign Policy, 1868–1941: A Research Guide* (New York, 1974).

Hyung Gu Lynn

AMERICAN-JAPANESE TREATY OF 1911

On 21 February 1911, the U.S.-Japan Treaty of Commerce and Navigation was signed, granting full tariff autonomy for Japan for the first time since the signing of the unequal treaties in the nineteenth century. In exchange, the United States obtained a promise from Japan to abide by the Gentlemen's Agreement* of 1908, and not let laborers leave the country for the United States. The revision of the unequal treaties by Japan in 1894 had not settled the issues of tariff autonomy and the right to perpetual leases on land. The 1894 treaty revisions ran out in 1911, and in preparation for the negotiations, the Japanese government enacted laws on the Rights of Foreigners to Own Land and on the Right to Fix Tariffs in April 1910. In July, Japan also sent out notices of abrogation to all the treaty countries concerned. With regard to tariffs, unlike Britain, the United States had declined to set agreed tariff rates in the American-Japanese Treaty of 1894*; thus the rates had been comparatively unprofitable for the United States in the intervening period. The United States had compensated for this with a 1907 law that allowed it to set unilaterally high tariff rates on goods from countries that had tariff rates disadvantageous to the United States. The 1907 law obstacle was overcome when Japan agreed to apply the most-favored-nation clause for tariffs. Japan conceded to the U.S. demand that the old terms remain valid for one year after notification of annulment. The new treaty also guaranteed the specific rights of the nationals of each country to reside, conduct business, and own and rent land.

Although there was increasing economic competition over the China market, immigration was still the second-most significant issue after tariff autonomy in the negotiations. Japanese Foreign Minister Komura Jutarō wanted to annul Article 2 of the 1894 revision regarding U.S. rights to limit immigration, whereas the U.S. government wanted to confirm the Gentlemen's Agreement. Komura wanted the principle of most-favored-nation treatment applied to those Japanese already in the United States, but ultimately conceded to the U.S. contention that such matters came under the jurisdiction of national law. This concession implied that the United States retained the right to regulate Japanese immigrants unilaterally. For Komura, this was an affordable price to pay for the new treaty, which realized the long-sought goal of restoring complete tariff autonomy to Japan. Indeed, the 1911 treaty laid the groundwork for further Japanese economic growth through trade, and capped a series of legally nonbinding agreements between the United States and Japan, such as the 1905 Taft-Katsura Agreement*, the Gentlemen's Agreement, and the 1908 Root-Takahira Agreement*. Signed in April, the 1911 treaty, along with the 1911 North Pacific Sealing Convention, marked some of the most significant efforts of Shibusawa Eiichi* at business diplomacy. Although the 1911 treaty was greeted with a mixture of sorrow and resignation by the Japanese community in the United States, it established the foundations for U.S.-Japan relations for subsequent decades until the treaty was unilaterally abrogated by the United States in 1940. *See also* Dollar Diplomacy.

A. Iriye, *Pacific Estrangement: Japanese and American Expansion, 1897–1911* (Cambridge, MA, 1972); J. W. Morley, *Japan's Foreign Policy, 1868–1941: A Research Guide* (New York, 1974).

Hyung Gu Lynn

AMŌ DOCTRINE

On 17 April 1934, Amō Eiji, the chief of the Intelligence Department of the Japanese Foreign Ministry, made a statement that, among historians, has been widely interpreted as Tōkyō's proclamation of an Asian Monroe Doctrine. But it also exposed a basic contradiction in Japan's China policy. At a routine press conference, Amō in-

formed his audience that Japan would oppose "any attempt on the part of China to avail herself of the influence of any other country in order to resist Japan." Because outstanding issues between China and Japan should be resolved bilaterally, Japan would oppose technical and financial assistance to China from other countries. The statement was understood in some diplomatic quarters as a warning to the United States, Great Britain, and the League of Nations, and it elicited strong reactions from some Chinese nationalists.

Close examinations of the documents surrounding the Amō statement have shown that it revealed, in distilled form, only the dilemma and dysfunction of Japanese foreign policy after the installation of Manchukuo* and the secession from the League of Nations. The military conflict between Japan and China, and a major power realignment was taking place in East Asia following U.S. recognition of the Soviet Union in November 1933. In this difficult situation, Foreign Minister Hirōta Koki* was able to craft only an incoherent diplomatic strategy. Although he posited a role for Japan as the maintainer of peace and order in East Asia, he wished to avoid an open clash with the United States and Britain. He portrayed the Japan-Manchukuo-China partnership as the cornerstone of regional order, but showed little regard for Chinese nationalism. The difficulty the other parties had in reconciling Japan's stated goals made any proclamation by Tōkyō regarding China susceptible to inflated interpretation.

After receiving negative reactions from some diplomatic quarters, the Hirōta government emphasized its noncombative intent in a particularly conciliatory gesture toward the United States. The official U.S. response was equally cautious. The State Department made no formal reaction to the Amō statement beyond an aide memoire to Japan on 29 April saying that the United States would adhere to the Nine Power Pact*. Many influential Chinese nationalists saw the Amō statement as a reflection of the status quo and understood that it contained nothing novel in Japan's attitudes toward China. The West's lukewarm reaction to the Japanese statement convinced them that gradualism was the only practical approach in fending off Japanese encroachment. The U.S. action in this diplomatic episode also showed that in the mid-1930s, a U.S.-Japanese clash in East Asia was not yet inevitable. *See also* Greater East Asia Co-Prosperity Sphere; Mukden Incident.

Inoue Toshikazu, *Kiki no nakano kyocho gaikō* [Diplomacy of Cooperation in Crisis] (Tōkyō, 1993); Nippon Kokusai Seiji Gakkai [Japan International Political Conference], *Taiheiyo senso eno michi* [The Road to the Pacific War] vol. 3 (Tōkyō, 1962); I. Nish, *Japanese Foreign Policy* (London, 1977); Y. Sun, *China and the Origins of the Pacific War, 1931–1941* (New York, 1993).

Shimizu Sayuri

ANGELL, JAMES B. (1829–1916)

Scion of an old Rhode Island family, James Burrill Angell made an important diplomatic mission to China in 1880, only to become something of a forgotten figure in U.S.–East Asian relations. From 1845 to 1849, he studied at Brown University and graduated as valedictorian, interested mainly in mathematics, modern languages, and English literature. He spent a year as assistant in the college library, and then worked as a civil engineer in Boston before studying for almost two years in Paris and Munich. In 1852, Brown University President Francis Wayland appointed Angell to a chair in modern languages. From 1859, he also served as temporary editor of the pro-Republican newspaper *Providence Journal*, then resigned his chair at Brown in the summer of 1860 to take over the editorship full time. Through the Civil War and Reconstruction crises, the *Journal* consistently supported Republican administrations, and Angell left it in August 1866 only to take the presidency of the University of Vermont. Becoming fund-raiser, public

speaker, and booster, he also taught rhetoric, history, German, and international law. In 1871, Angell was appointed to the presidency of the University of Michigan. He remained until 1909, dominating the university and leaving the legacy of a strong curriculum and a reputation of a leader who was popular with faculty and students.

Angell's importance in the field of U.S.–East Asian relations was confined to a diplomatic mission he undertook to China in 1880. By the terms of the Burlingame-Seward Treaty* of 1868, large numbers of Chinese gained entry into the United States. When President Rutherford B. Hayes vetoed congressional attempts to exclude the Chinese, Hayes was realistic enough to recognize that some modification of the Burlingame treaty was necessary, before Congress ran roughshod over the treaty rights. Angell was appointed minister to China in the spring of 1880, and was also to serve on a three-member commission to negotiate a new immigration treaty. Angell's fellow commissioners were William H. Trescott of South Carolina and John F. Swift of California, two politicians from states with vital interests in curtailing large numbers of Asian immigrants into the United States. Swift wanted total exclusion, but Trescott sided with Angell in seeking a modified treaty. The Angell Treaty* was signed 17 November 1880, in which the Chinese government agreed that the United States might "regulate, limit or suspend" but not "absolutely prohibit" the entry and residence of Chinese laborers into the United States.

Angell remained in Beijing as minister until October 1881, and left a reasonably flattering portrayal of Li Hongzhang,* with whom he negotiated. He also welcomed Robert W. Shufeldt*, who delivered drafts of two treaties for Angell when he presented his credentials as naval attaché to the legation. Angell arranged a reception for Shufeldt attended by "the whole foreign element," and urged the State Department to confer honors on some person to make a treaty with Korea. He may have meant himself, though he told Shufeldt he trusted that "the work will fall into your hands." Shufeldt used Angell as a sounding board when his frustrations with the slowness of the Chinese political bargaining process got the better of him. Angell thus served as an adviser to Shufeldt between July and October 1881. But the assassination of President James A. Garfield led Angell to suspend all formal diplomatic functions, and by October he turned the legation over to Chester Holcombe, the new chargé d'affaires. He left China, and returned to the United States to resume his academic duties at the University of Michigan in February 1882. President Grover Cleveland appointed Angell to the Anglo-American Northeastern Fisheries Commission in October 1887 and in November 1895, to the Canadian-American Deep Waterways Commission. Angell also was minister to Turkey from July 1897 to August 1898, and served with distinction during the Spanish-American War*.

J. B. Angell, *The Reminiscences of James Burrill Angell* (New York, 1912); S. A. Capie, "James B. Angell, Minister to China 1880–1881: His Mission and the Chinese Desire for Equal Treaty Rights," *Bulletin of the Institute of Modern History* (1982); F. C. Drake, *The Empire of the Seas: A Biography of Rear Admiral Robert Wilson Shufeldt, USN* (Honolulu, HI, 1984); E. M. Gale, "President James Burrill Angell's Diary as United States Treaty Commissioner and Minister to China, 1880–1881," *Michigan Alumnus Quarterly Review* (1942–1943).

Frederick C. Drake

ANGELL TREATY (17 November 1880)

The Angell Treaty was a modification of the Burlingame-Seward Treaty*, placing restrictions on Chinese immigration to the United States. Since 1854, after the discovery of gold in California, thousands of Chinese had been welcomed into the United States in the Coolie Trade* because of the desperate need for unskilled and inexpen-

sive labor. In July 1868, Anson Burlingame*, an American acting as China's envoy, concluded a treaty with U.S. Secretary of State William H. Seward*, stipulating that the people of both nations could immigrate freely to and reside in the other country. The treaty was obviously advantageous for the Chinese laborers. Thereafter, because of high demand for labor in building the Central Pacific Railroad, fresh batches of Chinese arrived in the United States. Nevertheless, with the end of the American Civil War, completion of the Central Pacific Railroad, and the decline of gold mining, the supply of immigrant labor became a surplus. American labor began to complain that the Chinese lowered the living standard by accepting low wages and were incapable of assimilation. Anti-Chinese hostility and violence, which traced back to the 1850s, began to develop and moved toward a climax. The center of the Exclusion Movement was in California.

In the 1876 presidential election, the California Committee of the Republican Party passed a resolution proposing the modification of the Burlingame-Seward Treaty. In 1880, President Rutherford B. Hayes accepted it and appointed James B. Angell*, the president of the University of Michigan, as the U.S. commissioner to negotiate with the Chinese. John F. Swift and William H. Trescott were appointed co-commissioners. Angell and his associates reached Beijing in early August 1880. The Chinese court appointed Baoyun and Li Hongzao as the representatives to negotiate with the American mission. On opening the talks on 13 October, Angell proposed the modification of the 1868 treaty. He said there were more than 100,000 Chinese laborers residing at American ports who harmed the security of the country, requiring restrictions on Chinese immigration. Angell wanted China to restrict immigration of certain classes of undesirables, not including laborers. Angell threatened that Washington would exclude Chinese laborers unilaterally if China did not cooperate then in putting together a satisfactory bilateral agreement. Nonetheless, the Chinese representatives thought that if the United States could impose restrictions on Chinese in spite of treaty commitments, then China could do the same to Americans. At last, the Chinese relented. Both sides agreed that only those classes of Chinese intent on "trade, travel, study or curiosity" would have the right to enter the United States.

On 17 November, a four-point treaty was signed in Beijing. As for the restrictions on labor immigration, the English version said that "the government of China agrees that the government of the United States may regulate, limit, or suspend such coming or residence, but not absolutely prohibit it. The limitation or suspension shall be reasonable and shall apply only to Chinese who may go to the United States as laborers, other classes not being included in the limitation." This modification of the old treaty was the crux. Between the two translations of English and Chinese, however, the word "suspend" did not appear in the Chinese version. Theoretically, the Angell Treaty just modified rather than overturned the Burlingame-Seward Treaty. Yet it was a watershed in the history of Sino-American relations, bringing to a close the era of free immigration. After that, the U.S. Bureau of Immigration could reject even Chinese of the expert class by making a laborer of anyone whom they could establish as having performed literally any kind of manual work.

M. R. Coolidge, *Chinese Immigration* (New York, (1969); W. F. Mayers, *Zhonghua diguo duiwai tiaoyue* [Treaties Between the Empire of Chinese and Foreign States] (Shanghai, 1906); Shen Iyao, *Haiwai paihua bainian shi* [A Century of Chinese Exclusion Abroad] (Beijing, 1980).

Xiang Liling

ANGLO-JAPANESE ALLIANCE

Negotiations begun in the fall of 1901, between the Conservative ministry of Lord Salisbury in Britain and the ministry of Count Katsura Tarō* in Japan, produced an alliance on 30 January 1902. The Triple Intervention* of France, Russia, and Germany to restrain the ambitions of Japan in China in 1895 and the diplomatic isolation Britain encountered during the Second Anglo-Boer War of 1899–1902 were part of the background that helped induce both Japan and Britain to seek out allies. The more immediate cause of the alliance was the coincidence of the two powers' interests in opposing Russian expansionism in Asia, as illustrated in the Russo-Japanese rivalry in Korea and the Russian occupation of Manchuria during the 1900–1901 Boxer Uprising* in China.

Count Hayashi Tadasu, the Japanese minister to England, was a strong supporter of the idea of an alliance with Britain and represented his nation in the negotiations with the British Foreign Secretary Lord Lansdowne. Britain had wanted to extend the scope of the alliance to cover Southeast Asia and the British Raj in India, but Japan succeeded in limiting the treaty's obligations to the "Extreme East." In a secret note exchanged between the powers, Japan had to accept the qualifying phrase "as far as may be possible" to the goal of each of them maintaining naval superiority over any third power's naval presence in that area. Japan, however, did extract from an initially reluctant Britain recognition of its right to take such measures as were deemed indispensable to safeguard its political, commercial, and industrial interests in Korea. The treaty was contracted for five years and committed the signatories to the Open Door Policy* in China and Korea; at the same time the two powers supported the right of each other to defend their interests in China. If one of them became involved in a war with another power in the "Extreme East," the other would be neutral. If, however, one of them found itself at war with more than one foe, the other would fight on its behalf. The Anglo-Japanese Alliance meant that when the Russo-Japanese War* began in 1904, Japan could have greater assurance that France

15

would not intervene on behalf of its Russian ally for fear of Britain coming to the aid of Japan.

In late August 1905, the Katsura ministry in Japan and the Conservative ministry of Lord Balfour in Britain agreed to expand provisions of the alliance. Although the commitment to the Open Door in China was reiterated, as well as the terms for the behavior of an ally when the other was at war, Britain now recognized the right of Japan to establish a protectorate over Korea. In exchange for this concession, Japan relented and agreed to extend the scope of the alliance to cover India. The alliance was renewed in July 1911 for ten years with slight changes. After the outbreak of World War I in August 1914, the Ōkuma Shigenobu* ministry invoked the alliance to enter into the war on the side of Britain against Germany, although technically the treaty of alliance did not obligate Japan's participation. The Japanese government was motivated more by self-interest, in that involvement in the war provided an opportunity to take over German holdings in China and the north Pacific. Although the alliance was renewed for another year in 1920, Britain had become increasingly dissatisfied with the growth of Japanese ambitions in China, which clashed with her own interests there. Furthermore, Britain wished to please the United States and the Dominions of Australia and New Zealand, who saw the alliance as a cloak for Japanese expansionism in Asia. As a result, the Anglo-Japanese alliance was replaced by the Four Power Pact* of December 1921, formally ending in August 1923 after the exchange of ratifications of this agreement.

C. Chang, *The Anglo-Japanese Alliance* (Baltimore, MD, 1931); W. Langer, *The Diplomacy of Imperialism: 1890–1902* (New York, 1972); I. Nish, *Alliance in Decline: A Study in Anglo-Japanese Relations, 1908–23* (London, 1972); I. Nish, *The Anglo-Japanese Alliance: The Diplomacy of Two Island Empires, 1894–1907* (London, 1966); A. M. Pooley (ed.), *Secret Memoirs of Count Tadasu Hayashi* (London, 1915).

Harold H. Tollefson

ANPO CRISIS

"Anpo Crisis" refers to the monthlong anarchy that gripped Japan in May and June 1960 in connection with the revision of the U.S.-Japan Security Treaty of 1951*. "Anpo" is shorthand for this agreement in Japanese. The disorder grew out of the longstanding differences among the Japanese people and political parties over foreign policy. One challenge the nation faced after the U.S. Occupation of Japan* was defining the terms of relations with the outside world. The security treaty was an unbalanced agreement, but no consensus existed on an alternative to being a virtual U.S. protectorate in the Cold War. Nationalists such as Hatoyama Ichirō* and Kishi Nobusuke* favored a more active role in the world as an ally of the United States. They called for a more equitable security treaty, revision of the no-war Japanese Constitution of 1947*, and additional rearmament. Their Socialist opponents, who favored a neutral role for Japan in the world, opposed constitutional revision and the alliance with the United States in any form. Socialists argued that the pact intensified East-West tension, and diminished Japan's security by identifying the nation as belonging to one of two armed camps. In between were the conservatives who followed the lead of former prime minister Yoshida Shigeru*. They supported the alliance with the United States, yet opposed constitutional revision, further rearmament, and the dispatch of Japanese forces overseas.

In 1957, Prime Minister Kishi won U.S. agreement to revise the security treaty. The U.S.-Japan Mutual Cooperation and Security Treaty*, signed on 19 January 1960, was a more equitable treaty, but it drew widespread criticism in Japan. The second of the Taiwan Straits Crises* in 1958 and the downing of an American U-2 aircraft over the Soviet Union in May 1960 aggravated popular Japanese mistrust of the United States. Numerous antitreaty organizations formed. Having recently prevented the Kishi government's various attempts to bolster the strength of the police and the bureaucracy at home, Socialists in the Diet were determined to stand firm. Unable to win a majority vote, they resorted to delaying tactics, including a sit-down strike. Kishi's aim was to secure Diet ratification of the treaty in advance of a trip to Japan by President Dwight D. Eisenhower*, scheduled for June. On 19 May, police guards removed the striking Socialists from the Diet building, and in the early morning of 20 May, the Liberal Democrats in the lower house approved the treaty in a snap vote.

Kishi's forceful tactics provoked a massive outpouring of popular support for antitreaty demonstrations the next month. On 10 June, hostile activists mobbed the car of Eisenhower's press secretary when he arrived at Haneda airport. Protest reached a climax on 15 June, when 5.8 million demonstrators gathered around the Diet building and one student was killed in the ensuing clash with riot police. Eisenhower postponed his visit indefinitely, and public pressure for Kishi's resignation grew. Kishi stepped down on 18 July, but the conservative Liberal Democratic Party* (LDP) remained in power and the revised treaty went into effect. Ikeda Hayato*, Kishi's successor, sought to avoid similar controversy by pursuing a low-profile foreign policy and concentrating on Japan's economic development instead. The LDP also reached out to accommodate Socialist concerns in policy making, rather than governing strictly as a majority party. Thus, Japan continued to straddle both the pacifist constitution and the Cold War alliance with the United States in the tradition established by Prime Minister Yoshida.

T. Kataoka, *The Price of a Constitution: The Origins of Japan's Postwar Politics* (Stanford, CA, 1991); M. Kosaka, *100 Million Japanese* (Tōkyō, 1972); E. S. Krause, *Japanese Radicals Revisited: Student Protest in Postwar Japan* (Berkeley, CA, 1974); G. R. Packard, *Protest in Tokyo: The Security Treaty Crisis of 1960* (Princeton, NJ, 1966).

Aaron Forsberg

ANTI-COMINTERN PACT
(25 November 1936)

On 25 November 1936, Nazi Germany and Japan concluded the Anti-Comintern Pact, which obligated its signatories to inform each other about the activities of the Communist International or Comintern and to consult with each other and coordinate their preventive policies against it. Although Japanese admiration for and imitation of German models in government, the army, and education went back to the Meiji Restoration period, other, more immediate factors help to account better for the pact. Both nations faced a common foe to their expansionist aims in the Soviet Union, who led the Comintern. Adolf Hitler, leader of Nazi Germany, sought to expand eastward in Europe in pursuit of living space for Germans, and Japan, coming increasingly under the control of the military, looked to dominate the Asian mainland. Because there was very little complementarity of commercial interests between Germany and Japan, the Anti-Comintern Pact represented the triumph of ideology over economics. The two powers viewed the pact as a logical step in the forging of a rightist authoritarian alternative to the Communists, as well as to the Western democracies.

Negotiations for a pact began in the spring of 1935, involving Joachim von Ribbentrop and General Ōshima Hiroshi, the Japanese military attaché in Berlin. The latter, a fervent admirer of Hitler, played an exceptionally important role in the negotiations for the Japanese side. A German draft emerged by the summer that served as the basis for working out the details of the proposed pact. The Hirōta Koki* ministry wanted to tone down the strongly worded preamble so as not to unduly offend the Soviet Union, with which it was trying to negotiate a new fisheries agreement. The existing language, however, was retained. Similarly, specific mention of the Soviet Union was kept in a secret additional protocol in spite of initial Japanese objections. This protocol provided that in the event of an unprovoked attack or threat of attack on one of the contracting parties by the Soviet Union, the other would take no measures to ease the situation for the Soviets. Furthermore, the parties would consult immediately on what actions to take to safeguard their common interests. The Germans originally envisaged a ten-year pact, but its term was reduced to five years at the behest of the Japanese. The Anti-Comintern Pact also invited other states to adhere to it. Fascist Italy, for instance, joined in November 1937.

The Anti-Comintern Pact paid dividends to Japan in that it helped to facilitate its aggression against China by reducing the threat of Soviet intervention. The pact actually had very little immediate positive effect of a concrete nature on German-Japanese relations, except for an agreement to exchange information concerning the Soviet Union. The chief difficulty was Japan's policy of aggression in China, with which Germany disagreed, because it ran counter to its own friendly relations with the Guomindang* (Nationalist) government and had the unintended effect of strengthening the position of the Chinese Communist Party*. In the end, Hitler decided to halt efforts at mediation in China to propitiate Japan, regarding it as a more valuable ally against the Soviet Union or Great Britain than China. In the first half of 1938, therefore, Germany recalled German military advisers from China, stopped arms deliveries to that nation, and recognized Japan's puppet Manchukuo* regime in Manchuria. Also, early in 1938, Germany began to sound out Japan on the formation of a military alliance. A second major crisis in German-Japanese relations resulted from the conclusion of the Nazi-Soviet Non-Aggression Pact in August 1939. Japan was discouraged by the news of the pact. It was not until September 1940 that Japan joined with Germany and Italy in a military alliance known as the Tripartite Pact*.

C. Boyd, "The Role of Hiroshi Oshima in the Preparation of the Anti-Comintern Pact," *Journal of Asian History* (1977); F. W. Iklé, *German-Japanese Relations, 1936–1940* (New York, 1956); Ohata Tokushiro, "The Anti-Comintern Pact, 1935–1939," in J. W. Morley (ed.), *Deterrent Diplomacy: Japan, Germany, and the U.S.S.R., 1935–1940* (New York, 1976); E. L. Presseisen, *Germany and Japan: A Study in Totalitarian Diplomacy, 1933–1941* (The Hague, 1958).

Harold H. Tollefson

ANTI-IMPERIALIST LEAGUE

This organization emerged in the aftermath of the Spanish-American War* to organize opposition against the annexation of the Philippines*. The Anti-Imperialist League was founded in Boston in November 1898 by reformers and intellectuals such as Edward Atkinson, Charles Eliot Norton, and Moorfield Storey. Most of its leaders were older men from established families, some of whom had been actively involved in the antislavery movement in their youth. Similar groups formed throughout the United States during the debate over ratification of the peace treaty with Spain and, in 1899, nominally consolidated into the American Anti-Imperialist League and claimed a membership of 700,000, but the Boston chapter remained the center of the movement against U.S. imperial expansion. The league drew support from old Mugwumps in the Republican Party, who had opposed government corruption during the 1870s, such as Carl Schurz and Charles Francis Adams. Other influential adherents included former President Grover Cleveland, labor leader Samuel Gompers, novelist Mark Twain, and industrialist Andrew Carnegie. But the organization was never truly united.

Members of the Anti-Imperialist League were distressed because they viewed acquisition of the Philippines as a reversal of the U.S. commitment not to annex Cuba in the Teller Amendment. They advanced a number of arguments against Philippine Annexation*, hoping to prevent this abandonment of American idealism. First, it was a violation of the U.S. Constitution to acquire territory not intended for statehood and with people ineligible for citizenship. One proposed congressional resolution said that "no power is given to the Federal Government to acquire territory to be held and governed permanently as colonies." Second, the Filipinos wanted independence, and annexation therefore contradicted the principle of national self-determination. Third, league members, sharing the racist assumptions of the time, argued that dark-skinned people, unschooled in democracy, were incapable of assimilation. More realistic were their arguments that acquisition of islands 6,000 miles across the Pacific constituted a dangerous overextension of U.S. commitments. The Philippines, they warned, offered few benefits and entailed major costs for protection, while inviting U.S. involvement in wars with powerful adversaries and without strategic advantages. Democrats led opposition to Senate ratification, but Republican Senator George F. Hoar* joined them in emphasizing the incompatibility between colonialism and American traditions.

President William McKinley* worked hard to counter the arguments of the Anti-Imperialist League, conducting a speaking tour in the fall of 1898 that stressed the humanitarian obligation of the United States to provide guidance for the Filipinos. Already, the expansionists had exploited successfully the flush of easy military victory over Spain to achieve Hawaiian Annexation* and the Samoa Partition*, in addition to the acquisition of Guam* and Puerto Rico. Whereas the U.S. military saw strategic value in acquiring the Philippines, Darwinists wanted to demonstrate the superiority of the American system and businessmen had visions of penetrating the China market. The anti-imperialists were unable to compete because of negativist arguments, limited funds, and an inferior propaganda machine. Perhaps worse, William Jennings Bryan*, the titular head of the Democratic Party, broke with the Anti-Imperialist League and endorsed ratification because he feared a continuation of the war. In February 1899, the Senate approved the treaty by just two votes, the same month that fighting began in the Philippine-American War*. In the 1900 election, the Anti-Imperialist League adopted a broader moral and educational strategy, initiating a propaganda campaign urging "government by the consent of the governed." Internal disagreements, elderly leadership, and shallow political organization meant that the Anti-Imperialist League, despite its prescience in warning about the dangers of imperialist expansion, was even less able to stop McKinley's reelection than the annexation of the Philippines.

R. L. Beisner, *Twelve Against Empire: The Anti-Imperialists, 1898–1900* (Chicago, 1968); F. H. Harrington, "The Anti-Imperialist Movement in the United States, 1898–1900," *Mississippi Valley Historical Review* (1935); C. Lasch, "The Anti-Imperialist, the Philippines, and the Inequality of Man," *Journal of Southern History* (August 1958); T. J. Osborne, *"Empire Can Wait": American Opposition to Hawaiian Annexation, 1893–1898* (Kent, OH, 1981); E. B. Tompkins, *Anti-Imperialism in the United States: The Great Debate, 1890–1920* (Philadelphia, 1970).

James I. Matray

ANZUS TREATY (1 September 1951)

The Australian–New Zealand–United States Security Treaty (ANZUS) has been the heart of the modern Australian-American security relationship. It was signed at San Francisco on 1 September 1951, ratified by the U.S. Senate on 15 April 1952, and entered into force two weeks later on 29 April. Conceived in close connection with the conclusion of a "soft" Japanese Peace Treaty*, and contrary to historical charges of subservience on the side of the junior partners, the ANZUS alliance was negotiated only after tough bargaining. The main source of contention was paradoxically the bipartisan determination of Australian leaders on both sides of the floor to establish a binding security relationship between their country and the United States and the equally firm and bipartisan resolve of American policy makers not to embark upon anything of the kind in the existing circumstances. Put simply, Canberra wanted strategic reassurance that the United States would come to Australia's aid in her next time of troubles, whereas Washington wanted cooperation and an opportunity to take advantage strategically of Australia's unique geographical position in the western Pacific. Neither got exactly what it wanted, Australia's future leaders reserving the right to see the alliance a little differently from the way the United States saw it.

According to Article 4, "each Party recognized that an armed attack in the Pacific area on any of the Parties would be dangerous to its own peace and safety and declared that it would act to meet the common danger in accordance with its constitutional processes." Since then barrels of ink were spilled on the actual meaning of those words. Most of them have highlighted the supposed differences between the presumably vague language of the ANZUS treaty and the Three Musketeers's language—one for all and all for one—of the North Atlantic Treaty Organization (NATO). The ensuing debate would have been news to President Harry S. Truman*. In the presidential news conference on 18 April 1951, a reporter asked Truman if the clause in question would mean that "an attack on one would be considered an attack on all." The president's reply was illuminating: "It would be similar to the guarantees that are in the Atlantic [NATO] Pact. They will be modeled on that treaty. That is what is to be conveyed there." In 1961, the National Security Council noted that ANZUS complemented, but did not duplicate, the later Southeast Asia Treaty Organization* (SEATO), giving the cornerstone of Australian foreign policy "a unique value by providing a means of military consultation on strategic prob-

lems in the Pacific outside the SEATO area as well as a forum for discussion of worldwide problems by the foreign ministers of the three governments." The ANZUS Treaty's value, coupled with the island continent's geographical position and affinity of attitude with the United States, was not lost on Washington.

C. Bell, *Australia's Alliance Options: Prospect and Retrospect in a World of Change* (Canberra, 1991); T. B. Millar, *Australia in Peace and War: External Relations, 1788–1997* (New York, 1978); J. M. Siracusa and Y. Cheong, *America's Australia: Australia's America* (Claremont, CA, 1997).

Joseph M. Siracusa

AP BAC, BATTLE OF

See BATTLE OF AP BAC

AQUINO, CORAZON (1933–   )

Corazon Cojuangco Aquino was the tenth president of the Philippines*, the first woman to hold that position. She led a disparate, multiclass social movement that mounted an electoral challenge to Ferdinand E. Marcos* after he called a "snap election" for February 1986 to show that his dictatorship remained popular and legitimate. With limited resources and organization, "Tita Cory" relied for support on popular hostility to the dictatorship and the public's image of her as the Filipina Joan of Arc and grieving widow of her slain oppositionist husband, Benigno Aquino Jr. Marcos "won" the elections through violence and manipulation of the vote count, but Aquino was clearly the "people's choice." Claiming victory, Aquino then called for a series of boycotts and strikes against Marcos and his cronies designed to wear down the regime. For the first few days, the strikes appeared successful. By the second week, however, they began to show signs of faltering. But whatever outcome the strikes would have had was superseded when rebels mounted an aborted military coup on 22 February 1986. Aquino, together with the Catholic Church hierarchy, called on the people to "protect" the retreating rebels. More than 1 million people massed outside the rebel camps and provided a "line of defense" against advancing Marcos troops. In the ensuing impasse, the rebels were able to erode military support for the dictatorship. On 25 February, an American military transport flew Marcos to Hawaii, and Aquino became president of the Philippines.

Aquino's ascension to power was enshrined as the triumph of a nonviolent "people power" revolution, a term that became part of the political vocabulary of the late twentieth century and an inspiration for social movements throughout Asia. It mattered little that the events of February 1986 were the result of failed plans and conspiracies by both sides. It also has been overlooked that the coalition Aquino led was fragile and fractious. Indeed, Aquino's presidency reflected the many contradictions inherent in the movement she led. Declaring that her central task was to restore political democracy, she immediately created a Constitutional Commission to replace the Marcos constitution. Despite opposition from her military allies, she freed political prisoners and entered into negotiations with the Communist Party of the Philippines and the secessionist Muslim group, the Moro National Liberation Front. She also created a government agency whose sole purpose was to recover the billions of dollars the Marcos family and their cronies purportedly stole from the national coffers. But these democratic features were counterbalanced by what one Filipino columnist described as a "return to political warlordism or tribal politics dominated by the family dynasties" and the reassertion of the power of the oligarchy in Philippine politics.

Disorganization and intense factional conflict within her cabinet on issues ranging from turf control to ideological differences in economic policy plagued Aquino's government. The military rebels who tried to oust Marcos also made their opposition to Aquino's policies clear, especially regarding her negotiations with the Communists. These opponents mounted, and Aquino survived, five coup attempts. The most serious, on 1 December 1989, was defeated only when the U.S. government openly showed its support for Aquino by authorizing two American fighters to "stray" over the skies of Manila. The coup attempts, however, helped push Aquino into a "rightward drift," abandoning not only her "leftist" allies but also many of the social programs she vowed to implement. She renewed counterinsurgency operations against the Communist movement, watered down a comprehensive land reform program (leaving her family's own estates untouched), and pushed for the extension of the military bases agreement with the United States, despite opposition from a nationalist senate. All this helped Aquino stabilize her government. In the last two years of the Aquino government, the Philippines was hit by massive earthquakes, typhoons, and a major volcanic eruption. The country also experienced a serious power shortage that the government was unable to resolve. Aquino ended her term in 1992, but remained extremely popular. *See also* Subic Naval Base Controversy.

C. Buss (ed.), *Cory Aquino and the People of the Philippines* (Stanford, CA, 1987); B. Dahm (ed.), *Economy and Politics in the Philippines Under Corazon Aquino* (Hamburg, 1991); R. Reid, *Corazon Aquino and the Brushfire Revolution* (Baton Rouge, LA, 1995); M. Thompson, *The Anti-Marcos Struggle: Personalistic Rule and Democratic Transition in the Philippines* (New Haven, CT, 1995).

Patricio N. Abinales

ARMACOST, MICHAEL H. (1937–)

Michael Armacost served as U.S. ambassador to the Philippines* (1982–1984) and to Japan (1989–1993), and as undersecretary of state for political affairs (1984–1989). After completing his doctoral degree at Columbia University in 1965, Armacost taught political science at Pomona College and then entered government service in 1969 as a White House fellow assigned to the Department of State. He served as a member of the State Department's Policy Planning Staff before moving to Tōkyō in 1972, where he worked as a special assistant to Ambassador Robert Ingersoll. He then returned to the Policy Planning Staff, and subsequently served on the National Security Council Staff, the International Security Affairs Division of the Defense Department, and the State Department's East Asia and Pacific Bureau. After becoming ambassador to the Philippines in 1982, he negotiated a military base agreement with the government of President Ferdinand E. Marcos*. Since public confidence in the Marcos regime was collapsing, Armacost was concerned about the gradual alienation of Philippine support for the United States, particularly if it seemed that the United States supported Marcos for access to the military bases in the country at the expense of Filipino hopes for greater democracy. He worked to distance U.S. policy from its close identification with Marcos while limiting the damage to the bilateral relationship.

When President George H. W. Bush* named Armacost ambassador to Japan in 1989, bilateral relations were unusually acrimonious. The growing U.S. trade deficit and a steep rise in Japanese investment in the United States alarmed many Americans. Although not a "Japan hand," Armacost, a trusted representative of the Bush administration, drew upon his rich experience in dealing with Asian affairs. He recognized the mutual benefits that flowed from interdependence. A high priority of his mission was a "sizable reduction" in the U.S. trade deficit with Japan, then more than $50 billion. Resisting domestic pressure for explicit Japanese market commitments, the Bush administration focused wisely on the structural sources of the imbalance instead. Armacost participated in the Structural Impediments Initia-

tive talks, which culminated in the spring of 1990. Policy coordination never became a top priority on either side, however, and the trade imbalance persisted. Economic fluctuations added to the complexity of the relationship. In the early 1990s, domestic recession curbed U.S. demand for imports, but the collapse of Japan's overinflated economy in 1990 also depressed Japanese demand for foreign goods.

The Bush administration also sought to adjust the U.S.-Japan alliance to the receding Soviet threat. The two nations continued their security cooperation in Asia, reflected in the 1991 cost-sharing agreement on the U.S. military presence in Japan. The virtual paralysis of Japanese decision making in the face of U.S. pressure for support of the Gulf War, however, tested the alliance. Armacost pressed hard for Japanese action, and Tōkyō responded with $13 billion in financial support and legislation that ultimately permitted Japan's participation in UN-sponsored peacekeeping activities. He also promoted broadening the bilateral relationship into a "global partnership" in support of initiatives such as an Asia/Pacific framework for economic cooperation, but in 1993 the promise of a wider partnership remained unfulfilled. Armacost's vigorous support of U.S. policies earned him the sobriquet *Gaiatsu-san* ("Mr. Foreign Pressure") in Japan. That expression reflected a broader pattern of frustration in bilateral relations, especially the huge structural differences in U.S.-Japan Postwar Trade Relations*. *See also* Subic Naval Base Controversy.

M. H. Armacost, *Friends or Rivals?: The Insider's Account of U.S.-Japan Relations* (New York, 1996); Y. Mikanagi, *Japan's Trade Policy: Action or Reaction?* (New York, 1996); C. V. Prestowitz, *Trading Places: How We Allowed Japan to Take the Lead* (New York, 1988); R. Sato, *The Chrysanthemum and the Eagle: The Future of U.S.-Japan Relations* (New York, 1995); L. T. Schoppa, *Bargaining with Japan: What American Pressure Can and Cannot Do* (New York, 1997).

Aaron Forsberg

ARMY OF THE REPUBLIC OF VIETNAM

The Army of the Republic of Vietnam (ARVN) had its roots in the Vietnamese National Army, which was created by the French in 1950. After the fall of Dien Bien Phu* and the creation of the Republic of Vietnam*, the Vietnamese National Army became the springboard for the ARVN. American sponsorship filled the vacuum left by the French departure, and American military "advisers" in Vietnam in the 1950s provided weapons and training in an attempt to model the ARVN after the U.S. Army. By the end of 1959, the ARVN totaled 234,000 troops, and remained at that size until 1964, when a major buildup began to fight off the National Liberation Front* (NLF). By the end of 1964, the ARVN had reached 500,000 troops, and it increased steadily until 1972, when it reached 1 million.

A number of highly skilled, first-rate military units, including the ARVN Airborne Division, the First Infantry Division, and the ARVN Marines, time and again distinguished themselves during the fighting. Overall, however, many ARVN units suffered from serious problems, including poor leadership, corruption, and low morale. Many officers, who were mostly Catholics commanding predominantly Buddhist troops, received command because of political connections rather than military skill. They operated their units based on personal financial enrichment, whereas soldiers were poorly paid and forced to buy their own food. Soldiers were drafted involuntarily, and many were reluctant to leave their home villages for indefinite periods. But the major force behind the ARVN's problems was the chronic political instability of the government. Fraudulent elections, corruption, constant infighting, and, especially in the mid-1960s, a series of impossibly confusing coups, undermined the credibility of the Saigon government and helped to incapacitate the military.

The last ten years of ARVN's existence were marked by an intensive American training program focused on junior officers and noncommissioned officers. These programs also provided helicopters to increase mobility and emphasized logistics and technical service units. This American effort, however, intensified divisions in the officer ranks between older, French-educated officers and junior officers trained in American tactics and procedures. Furthermore, the ARVN grew almost entirely dependent on American support. As the United States withdrew its troops and equipment during the early 1970s, ARVN units were faced with increasing inventories of unserviceable equipment. ARVN never had the consistent leadership and direction necessary for an effective combat force and could not overwhelm its highly motivated NLF and People's Army of Vietnam foes. Nevertheless, ARVN forces suffered 243,000 killed in action and more than 500,000 seriously wounded during the war. These statistics demonstrate considerable courage under fire, and belie the assumption that the ARVN was a uniformly poor fighting force.

G. C. Herring, *America's Longest War: The United States and Vietnam 1950–1975* (New York, 1996); S. Karnow, *Vietnam: A History* (New York, 1983); M. B. Young, *The Vietnam Wars, 1945–1990* (New York, 1991).

Robert K. Brigham

ASHIDA HITOSHI (1887–1959)

Ashida Hitoshi was a Japanese diplomat-turned-politician who served as foreign minister in the government of Katayama Tetsu* and then headed the same coalition as premier from March to October 1948. He was one of the architects of postwar Japanese defense policy. His postwar career also illustrates the unsuccessful effort of center-left politicians to challenge conservative rule. A graduate of the University of Tōkyō, Ashida entered the Foreign Ministry in 1910. Postings in Europe acquainted him with parliamentary democracy, and firsthand knowledge of the Russian Revolution affirmed both his liberal convictions and horror of Communism*. Ashida turned to popular politics in 1932, when he won a seat in the Diet. From 1933 to 1940, he also served as president of the English-language newspaper the *Japan Times*. His advocacy of internationalist diplomacy before and during World War II put him at odds with Japanese officialdom, but earned him the good graces of SCAP* during the U.S. Occupation of Japan*. He backed constitutional revision and took part in the Diet's review of the Japanese Constitution of 1947* as the chairman of the committee charged with the task. Unlike conservatives who acquiesced in the postwar reforms for opportunistic reasons, Ashida was both a nationalist and an advocate of egalitarian reform.

Although foreign minister only briefly (May 1947 to February 1948), Ashida enunciated the basic principles that guided Japan's postwar defense policy in a September 1947 document known as the Ashida memorandum. A statement of Japanese views on a peace settlement and posttreaty security arrangements, it essentially expressed Japanese willingness to be an American ally in the Cold War. Toward this end, the memorandum asked that the United States defend Japan's external security while Japan attended to its own internal security. Later, Prime Minister Yoshida Shigeru* was unable to persuade Ambassador John Foster Dulles* to agree on this formula in the unequal U.S.-Japan Security Treaty of 1951*. But the desire for greater "mutuality" in the relationship with the United States continued to guide Japanese defense policy.

As head of the Democratic Party in 1947, Ashida reached out to other center-left politicians to oppose Yoshida's conservative Liberal Party. The result was the Democratic Party's coalition with the Japan Socialist Party and the National Cooperative Party from May 1947 to October 1948. The inability of the Katayama and Ashida cabinets to govern effectively discredited the idea of coalition government. Although indictment in a bribery scandal cut short Ashida's tenure as premier, his advocacy of rearmament further divided the opposition and paved the way for conservative dominance in politics. His rearmament proposal of December 1950 transformed him into a leading advocate of rebuilding the nation's defenses, a proposition he insisted was consistent with the new constitution. Since rearmament was both widely unpopular and anathema to the political left, Ashida found himself increasingly drawn toward the conservative critics of Prime Minister Yoshida, such as Kishi Nobusuke*. In turning toward defenders of tradition in this manner, liberal advocates of rearmament such as Ashida self-destructed as an independent political force. In 1955, the Democrats merged with the rightist Liberals to form the Liberal Democratic Party*.

T. Kataoka (ed.), *Creating Single-Party Democracy* (Stanford, CA, 1992); E. Shindo (ed.), *Ashida Hitoshi nikki* [Ashida Hitoshi Diary] (Tōkyō, 1986); M. E. Weinstein, *Japan's Postwar Defense Policy, 1947–1968* (New York, 1971).

Aaron Forsberg

ASIA-PACIFIC ECONOMIC COOPERATION

The Asia-Pacific Economic Cooperation (APEC) forum sought intergovernmental cooperation to promote economic development in the Pacific. Although proposed in 1989 by Australian Prime Minister Bob Hawke, it enjoyed strong backing from the United States. APEC was conceived as a purely economic organization, out of frustration with the slow pace of the Uruguay Round of GATT (General Agreements on Tariffs and Trade*) talks and concern with the growing economic power of the European Union. Hawke invited only countries in the western Pacific, but Canada and the United States were interested and became founding members, along with Australia, Japan, the Republic of Korea*, New Zealand, Thailand*, Singapore*, Malaysia*, the Philippines*, Indonesia*, and Brunei*. In 1991, the People's Republic of China* (PRC), Hong Kong*, and Taiwan* joined, followed in 1993 by Chile, Mexico, and Papua New Guinea. These Pacific Rim nations were touted as the future high-growth region of the world. The leading U.S. role was seen variously as a component of single-power hegemony in the post–Cold War world, a consequence of the historic U.S. move west, and a sign of waning U.S. influence, because it had to work through multilateral institutions it could not dominate. The diversity among APEC countries led to dissension over both goals and structure. Washington generally promoted a more permanent and more political APEC than many other members wanted. Illustrative of this trend was when President Bill Clinton* convened the political leaders of APEC countries in 1993 to meet after the formal conference in Seattle to help create the "New Pacific Community."

Although the 1993 meeting resulted in few substantive measures, Indonesia's President Suharto* agreed to be host of a similar meeting in Bogor in 1994, creating a precedent for annual meetings of political leaders. The Bogor meeting resulted in the important declaration that APEC would form a "free and open trade" region, with deadlines set at 2010 for developed member countries, and 2020 for those with developing status. Clinton's failure to attend the 1995 Tōkyō APEC meeting, because of unrelated domestic political battles, signaled to some members of APEC that Washington was not reliable. Prime Minister Mohamad Mahathir* of Malaysia was pleased by that possibility, as the most vocal member of the group within APEC, composed primarily of ASEAN (Association of Southeast Asian Nations*) members, who wanted an Asian-controlled, or exclusively Asian, grouping. Mahathir had boycotted the 1993 meeting of political leaders, and continued throughout the 1990s to push his Asians-only alternative to

APEC, the East Asian Economic Caucus. Other member disputes have included reluctance by developing nations to lift protectionist measures supporting infant industries, Japanese insistence on continued protection for its agricultural sector, U.S. hesitance to move to cut tariffs, and predictable wrangling over status by the PRC and Taiwan (with Taiwan agreeing to join as an "economy" rather than as a state). The East Asian Financial Crisis* of the late 1990s placed even more strain on APEC, but with almost half the world's production and trade occurring in APEC countries, members also had incentive to make common cause.

M. Borthwick, *Pacific Century: The Emergence of Modern Pacific Asia* (Boulder, CO, 1998); D. C. Hellmann and K. B. Pyle (eds.), *From APEC to Xanadu: Creating a Viable Community in the Post–Cold War Pacific* (Armonk, NY, 1997); Symposium on the APEC Process, *Journal of Northeast Asian Studies* (Winter 1995).

Anne L. Foster

ASSOCIATION OF SOUTHEAST ASIAN NATIONS

As a regional organization, the Association of Southeast Asian Nations (ASEAN) was established on 8 August 1967 in Bangkok, Thailand*, with the signing of the Bangkok Declaration by the five original member countries: Indonesia*, Malaysia*, the Philippines*, Singapore*, and Thailand. The Bangkok Declaration united the ASEAN member countries in a joint effort to promote economic cooperation and the welfare of the people in the region. The ASEAN nations came together with three main objectives: to promote the economic, social, and cultural development of the region through cooperative programs; to safeguard the political and economic stability of the region against big-power rivalry; and to serve as a forum for the resolution of intraregional differences. Brunei* joined ASEAN on 8 January 1984. The Socialist Republic of Vietnam* became the seventh member of ASEAN on 28 July 1995. Laos* and Burma* (Myanmar) were admitted into ASEAN on 23 July 1997.

Political and security cooperation in the ASEAN began early in its formative years. Some of the most important accords adopted by ASEAN were the 1971 declaration designating Southeast Asia as a Zone of Peace, Freedom, and Neutrality (ZOPFAN), the Treaty of Amity and Cooperation in Southeast Asia (TAC), the Declaration of ASEAN Concord of 1976, and the Treaty of the Southeast Asia Nuclear Weapon-Free Zone (SEANWFZ) of 1995. The Declaration of ZOPFAN states ASEAN's peaceful intentions and commitment to building regional resilience free from any form or manner of interference by outside powers. The TAC represents a code of international conduct for peaceful relations among countries in the region in accordance with the charter of the United Nations. The UN General Assembly endorsed the TAC in 1992. The Declaration of ASEAN Concord, on the other hand, contains the principles and framework for ASEAN cooperation in the political, security, economic, and functional fields. The Treaty on SEANWFZ is ASEAN's contribution to the progress toward complete nuclear disarmament.

The ASEAN Regional Forum was established in 1994 as a multilateral consultative body aimed at promoting preventive diplomacy and confidence building among the states in the Asia-Pacific region. The forum consists of the nine ASEAN member countries, with Cambodia* as an observer, ten dialogue partners, and Papua New Guinea as a special observer. The South China Sea Disputes*, Indonesia's human rights abuses, and Myanmar's political unrest have tested the extent to which ASEAN would continue to function as a coherent entity. ASEAN has observed a policy of nonintervention based on its cardinal principle of noninterference in the domestic affairs of its members since its founding, making it difficult for it to deal with issues such as human rights or Indo-nesia's rule over the territory of East Timor. Thailand and the Philippines had proposed that ASEAN broaden its ability to become involved in cases in which internal policies affect other countries in the region, such as political unrest in Cambodia or Myanmar, which had caused a stream of refugees into Thailand. Their growing interdependence made it important for "enhanced interaction" among ASEAN nations on transnational issues. *See also* Asia-Pacific Economic Cooperation.

A. Broinowski (ed.), *ASEAN into the 1990s* (London, 1990); K. S. Sandhu, *The ASEAN Reader* (Singapore, 1992); G. Segal, *Rethinking the Pacific* (New York, 1990).

Han Kyu-sun

ASTOR, JOHN JACOB (1763–1848)

This powerful American merchant, through his near-monopoly of the American fur trade, was instrumental in establishing U.S. commerce with China in the early nineteenth century. Astor was born in Walldorf, near Heidelberg, Germany. At the age of sixteen, he left Germany to work in his brother's piano and flute factory in London. In 1783, he emigrated to New York to become agent for his brother's firm, Astor and Broadwood. Two years later, he traveled up the Hudson to enter the American fur trade. Within a decade, he had become one of the leading fur merchants in the United States. In 1796, through a London official of the East India Company, he received a charter to trade freely in any port monopolized by the company. That charter opened for him the China fur market, then the world's richest. He soon formed his own shipping company to carry his furs to Guangzhou, as well as St. Petersburg, London, and New York.

Astor used his friendship with American presidents to further his commercial ventures. President Thomas Jefferson permitted him to send a ship to China during the embargo after 1807, enabling him to reap a profit of $200,000. Through Jefferson, he secured the position of executive agent in the Northwest. As executive agent, Astor, in 1808, organized the American Fur Company to challenge the North West and Hudson's Bay companies that then dominated much of the northern fur trade. He added subsidiaries to operate in different regions of the country, especially around the Great Lakes. In 1811, he organized the Pacific Fur Company to gain control of the fur trade with the Orient. That year, he founded Astoria at the mouth of the Columbia River in the Oregon Territory, the first permanent American settlement on the Pacific coast. During the decades that followed, he bought out his rivals to create a virtual monopoly of the American fur trade. In 1834, Astor withdrew from the trade to deal in New York City real estate and other investments. He founded the Astor Library, later the New York Public Library. His Astor House was the forerunner of the later Astor Hotel and the Waldorf-Astoria in New York City. At the time of his death, Astor was the richest man in the United States, with an estimated fortune of $20 million.

H. M. Chittenden, *The American Fur Trade of the Far West* (New York, 1902); K. W. Porter, *John Jacob Astor* (Cambridge, MA, 1931).

Norman A. Graebner

ATOMIC ATTACKS

Eager to preempt possible German production of an atomic bomb, in late 1939, President Franklin D. Roosevelt* responded to a letter from Albert Einstein by ordering an American effort to develop such a weapon first. The program came under U.S. Army control, directed by General Leslie Groves, in mid-1942. A gun-type uranium-235 weapon, involving a supercritical mass that exploded instantaneously, was fashioned at the Los Alamos, New Mexico, laboratory headed by J. Robert Oppenheimer. There seemed to be no need to test this model, which was the one detonated at Hiroshima

(code name Little Boy) on 6 August 1945. A potentially even more devastating weapon, the product of a controlled chain reaction, was the plutonium implosion type of bomb, tested successfully north of Alamogordo, New Mexico, on 16 July 1945. Code-named Fat Man, this was the type of bomb dropped on Nagasaki on 9 August 1945. To conduct atomic bombing of Germany, the fifty-ninth Composite Group made up of modified B-29 aircraft was activated in December 1944 by Colonel Paul W. Tibbets. With the fall of Nazi Germany in May, the air group was transferred from Utah to Tinian Island in the Pacific. Only Tibbets knew the secret of the unit's mission; his men thought that some sort of "gimmick" was involved.

After the stationary test north of Alamogordo (Operation TRINITY), President Harry S. Truman* made the final decision about use of the bomb. On 26 July, the Allied leaders issued at the Potsdam Conference a dire declaration calling for Japan's unconditional surrender, though the atomic bomb was not specifically mentioned. Truman already had authorized the U.S. Army Air Force to dispatch Tibbets's group, on the president's order, to attack selected Japanese targets on or about 3 August, weather permitting. Additional bombs were to be employed as available. The target list included sizable urban industrial centers with psychological and experimental advantages: Hiroshima, Miigata, Kokura, and Nagasaki (replacing Kyōto, which Secretary of War Henry L. Stimson* had insisted on excluding). When word was received, incorrectly in fact, that Prime Minister Suzuki Kantarō* had rejected the Potsdam Declaration*, President Truman (on his way back from Europe) approved the dropping of the atomic bombs. Except in limited scientific circles, the senior decision makers gave little or no consideration to alternatives. Avoiding the bloody ground invasion of Japan was uppermost in their minds, although revisionist historians argue that other considerations were at play, such as anti-Soviet thinking and naked racism.

At 8:16 on 6 August 1945 the *Enola Gay*, piloted by Colonel Tibbets, dropped the first atomic bomb (Little Boy) on Hiroshima. Kokura and Nagasaki were saved from destruction, at least for the moment, by weather conditions, which allowed visual bombing of Hiroshima. With the energy equivalent of about 15,000 tons of TNT, the bomb destroyed 4.4 out of 7 square miles in the heart of the city, whipped up a merciless firestorm, and spawned the telltale mushroom cloud that soared within eight minutes to a height of 27,000 feet and was visible for 390 miles. The first U.S. estimate of casualties spoke of 60,000 to 80,000 people killed and as many or more injured. Hiroshima Police Bureau data as of late 1945 raised the total number to about 130,000, greater than half of the city's wartime population of 245,000. Continuing Japanese tabulations of the effects of atomic radiation reached a total of 108,000 deaths. It is believed in Japan that the grand total of casualties at Hiroshima exceeded 200,000.

In Tōkyō, the complexities of the traditional consensual process of decision making and the intransigence of the army prevented quick action to end the war. Therefore, U.S. Army and U.S. Navy aviation continued to attack Japan with conventional weapons, and the Soviet Union hastily decided to enter the Pacific war on 8 August, invading Manchuria, North Korea, and the Kurile Islands. Japan's military cruelly played down the effects of the atomic bombing. Consequently, the U.S. Army Air Force employed Fat Man, the plutonium bomb, on 9 August. The pilot of *Bock's Car* could not bomb Kokura visually, so he attacked Nagasaki instead. The airdrop took place at 11:02 A.M. Early American estimates placed the deaths in Nagasaki at 35,000 to 40,000. The energy equivalent of Fat Man was placed at 21,000 tons of TNT, causing a far larger scale of devastation, though the area razed was less

than at Hiroshima because of the off-target point of impact and the uneven terrain.

The nuclear weapons inflicted unprecedented mortality and casualty rates, especially at Nagasaki, that exceeded those caused by the devastating conventional raids against Tōkyō by 300–400 percent, even though the population densities at the two cities hit by the single atomic bombs were one-fourth to one-half those of the Japanese capital. Only one nuclear-armed B-29 Superfortress, flying unopposed above Japan, was employed against each of the stricken target cities. Doomed by the atomic bombs, in concert with the Soviet invasion on the Asian mainland, Emperor Hirohito* and the senior civil and military leaders finally accepted the terms of the Potsdam Declaration, five days after Nagasaki, and agreed to surrender. *See also* Thirty-Eighth Parallel Division.

A. D. Coox, *Japan: The Final Agony* (New York, 1970); W. F. Craven and J. L. Cate (eds.), *The Army Air Forces in World War II*, vol. 5 (Chicago, 1948); *Effects of Atomic Bombs on Hiroshima and Nagasaki* (Washington, DC, 1946); C. E. LeMay and M. Kantor, *Mission with LeMay: My Story* (New York, 1965); U.S. Strategic Bombing Survey, *The Strategic Air Operation of Very Heavy Bombardment in the War Against Japan* (Washington, DC, 1946).

Alvin D. Coox

AUNG SAN (1915–1947)

Aung San was the Burmese nationalist and military leader who brought his country to the brink of independence. He was assassinated in July 1947, only a few months before the formal handover by the British in January 1948. Aung San's own reluctance to allow Communists to play a prominent role in the government of Burma* improved his image for U.S. policy makers after World War II. Aung San had attended Rangoon University, where he had been a political activist as a student. He went to China seeking assistance in 1940. A series of mishaps led him to work with Japanese officials active in Xiamen, China. Colonel Suzuki Keiji invited Aung San and some of his associates to Japan for military training in 1941. They became known as the Thirty Comrades, from whom came many of the future political leaders of Burma, including Ne Win*. In Japan, the Thirty Comrades were formed into the nucleus of the Burma Independence Army, subsequently the Burma Defense Army, and then the Burma National Army, all under Aung San's command. This organization assisted the Japanese during the invasion of Burma in 1942, in exchange for the promise of future independence. Aung San soon became dissatisfied with the pseudo-independence offered by Japan. As early as mid-1943, he began to set up alternative political organizations. General Aung San cofounded the Anti-Fascist Organization (later renamed the Anti-Fascist People's Freedom League) in August 1944.

Aung San's military experience, loyal following among soldiers and civilians, and moderate anti-Japanese activities made him an acceptable representative of Burma's national aspirations to Admiral Louis Mountbatten, supreme commander for the Southeast Asia Allied Forces. U.S. officials at the end of World War II advocated quick action on self-government for Burma, arguing that Burma's pace should approximate India's, and that Burma and the Philippines* were the Southeast Asian colonies most ready for self-government. Although U.S. officials had no knowledge of Aung San before 1945, they quickly were impressed by his stated commitment to freedom of religion, his willingness to move more slowly than many Burmese on independence if necessary to accommodate British political requirements, and especially his ability to prevent the moderately popular Burmese Communists from gaining positions in the government. After agreements in January 1947, that stipulated the procedures for Burmese independence, the U.S. consul general in Rangoon met with Aung San to encourage his stance against Communism* and to promote U.S. investment in Burma. During June 1947, the two governments agreed to exchange diplomatic representatives. The details were still in negotiation when Aung San was assassinated with several members of his cabinet, by order of a political rival. Aung San's stature grew after his death. The two leaders of Burma to 1988, U Nu* and Ne Win, both claimed to be implementing his vision for the country. After 1988, Aung San's daughter, Aung San Suu Kyi, reclaimed that vision for Burma's as yet unsuccessful democracy movement. *See also* Ba Maw.

Aung San Suu Kyi, *Aung San* (Lawrence, MA, 1984); M. Maung, *Aung San of Burma* (The Hague, 1962); J. Silverstein (ed.), *The Political Legacy of Aung San* (Ithaca, NY, 1993).

Anne L. Foster

B

BA MAW (1893–1977)

Ba Maw was a Burmese nationalist leader and, from 1937 to 1939, first prime minister of Burma's government under British colonial rule. He received his education through the colonial regime in Burma* (now Myanmar) and as a foreign student in Britain and France. He attended Rangoon College, Calcutta University, Cambridge University, and the University of Bordeaux. He received a doctorate from the last of these in 1924, and was admitted to the bar in the United Kingdom the same year. Ba Maw then entered into law practice in Rangoon. He first achieved notoriety in 1931 when he was one of two Burmese attorneys defending Saya San, who had proclaimed himself king and set up a royal court in December 1930. His followers rebelled against British colonial rule, but were put down quickly by British and Indian troops. Ba Maw and his associates were unsuccessful in their efforts to defend Saya San, but in the process, Ba Maw emerged as a leading figure in nationalist circles.

Between 1931 and 1934, Ba Maw was outspoken as an opponent of British proposals to separate Burma from the rest of British India, fearing that Burma standing alone would have less power to negotiate with Britain about future independence issues. In 1934, however, he reversed his position. In the same year, he was named minister of education in the local government. Three years later, under a new constitution promulgated by the British, Ba Maw became the first prime minister, serving in this office until early 1939. As World War II broke out in Europe, he joined the Freedom Bloc, an alliance of nationalist Burmese opposed to assisting Britain in the war. In August 1940, he was jailed by the colonial authorities for these activities.

When Japan and the small Burma Independence Army led by Aung San* and other nationalists invaded Burma in 1942, Ba Maw was still in a British prison in the far north of the country. In 1943, he escaped and entered the Japanese zone, becoming *Adipadi*, or head of state, in the pro-Japanese government. When the war was coming to an end in 1945, he fled to Japan, where the Allies arrested and briefly imprisoned him early in the U.S. Occupation of Japan*. Upon his release, he returned to Burma, but was unsuccessful in regaining a significant role in postcolonial-era politics. He briefly joined with several other nationalist leaders in organizing the Democratic Nationalist Opposition to urge rejection of the London Agreement of 1947, but the mainstream of nationalist sentiment in Burma, now led by Aung San, was clearly in favor of accepting the British terms for independence, and Ba Maw's opposition group was marginalized. He retired soon after to private life.

J. F. Cady, *The United States and Burma* (Cambridge, MA, 1976); C. J. Christie, *A Modern History of Southeast Asia: Decolonization, Nationalism, and Separatism* (London, 1996); U. M. Maung, *Burmese Nationalist Movements 1940–1948* (Honolulu, HI, 1990).

Kenneth J. Hammond

THE BALANGIGA MASSACRE

The Balangiga Massacre of 28 September 1901, a successful guerrilla infiltration attack, was, for U.S. forces, the most costly single incident of the Philippine-American War* of 1899–1902. Company C of the Ninth U.S. Infantry arrived in the Philippines* in March 1899, was sent to Beijing during the Boxer Uprising* as part of the China Relief Expedition* of 1900, and returned to the Philippines in the summer of that year. In August 1901, it garrisoned the town of Balangiga on the southern coast of Samar, at that time one of the last islands in the archipelago still resisting U.S. authority under the leadership of a particularly skillful guerrilla commander, Vicente Lukban. Captain Thomas W. O'Connell, Company C's commander, was more concerned with improving the sanitary situation in Balangiga than with guarding against attack, since previously insurgents had not been active on the South Coast. Accordingly, O'Connell began to bring in young men from surrounding villages to discharge their tax obligations with sanitation and road maintenance work under the supervision of the town's mayor and chief of police, who, unknown to O'Connell, were insurgent officers under Lukban.

At 6:30 on the morning of 28 September, the men of Company C were eating breakfast with only three armed sentries securing their barracks and kitchen. At this moment a force of several hundred "bolomen" attacked the unarmed, sitting soldiers. All of the company's officers were killed immediately, but the senior surviving sergeant led a retreat twenty-five miles by sea to Basey, the nearest U.S. garrison. Of the 74 men present at Balangiga, 48 were killed or died of wounds. Of the 26 survivors, only 4 were unwounded. The next day, the U.S. commander at Basey reoccupied Balangiga, buried the U.S. dead, burned the town, and dispersed its residents.

In the immediate aftermath of the attack, General Adna R. Chaffee*, overall U.S. commander in the Philippines, assigned General Jacob H. Smith to command U.S. forces in Samar and the adjacent island of Leyte. Chaffee also provided Smith with the troops necessary both to reinforce coastal garrisons and form mobile columns to penetrate the interior of the island. To end resistance on Samar, Smith implemented a strategy of population concentration in coastal towns and the widespread destruction of homes, crops, and domestic animals outside U.S. garrisons. Although the written instructions Smith issued to his subordinates conformed to U.S. military occupation law, evidence exists that he also gave illegal verbal orders to shoot on sight all males able to bear arms. Smith also severed trade between Samar and Leyte to end the commerce in hemp that he believed was providing tax income to the guerrillas. Although extremely harsh, Smith's strategy succeeded. On 18 February 1902, Lukban was captured, and his last subordinate surrendered on 27 April. On 17 June 1902, a provincial civil government was established for the island of Samar. Several dozen more U.S. soldiers were killed during Filipino insurgent attacks, ambushes, and mismanaged patrols after Balangiga. After contemporary press reports on the pacification campaign led to Senate hearings, General Smith was court-martialed for "conduct to the prejudice of good order and military discipline," convicted, admonished, and retired from the U.S. Army.

W. T. Sexton, *Soldiers in the Sun: An Adventure in Imperialism* (Harrisburg, PA, 1939); J. R. M. Taylor, *The Philippine Insurrection Against the United States*, vol. 2 (Pasay City, Philippines, 1971); U.S. Army Adjutant-General's Office, *Correspondence Relating to the War with Spain, Including the Insurrection in the Philippine Islands and the China Relief Expedition*, vol. 2 (Washington, DC, 1902); U.S. War Department, *Annual Reports of the War Department for the Fiscal Year Ending June 30, 1902*, vol. 9 (Washington, DC, 1902).

John S. Reed

BANDUNG CONFERENCE

In April 1955, Asian and African leaders met at Bandung, Indonesia*, to discuss, without regard for regional bloc membership, a variety of issues, including colonialism, racism, international economic and social cooperation, human rights, and world peace. One year earlier, at the conclusion of the gathering of the heads of government of Burma*, Ceylon, Indonesia, India, and Pakistan at Colombo during April and May 1954, a joint statement had been issued, which proposed a wider international meeting of postcolonial states to deal with common problems. Under the sponsorship of the Colombo powers, representatives from twenty-nine Asian and African countries attended a conference at Bandung from 18 to 24 April 1955. Although there were notable exclusions from the conference, including Israel, the Republic of China*, and the two Koreas, the nations present did represent a quarter of the world's land area and two-thirds of its population. Being of pleasant climate, Bandung provided the ideal location for amity and discourse; the Indonesian government built hotels and imported 200 luxury cars especially for the occasion. Indonesian Prime Minister Ali Sastroamidjojo, who had provided the main impetus behind the organization of the conference, was elected its president and stewarded the gathering toward its end. All political ideologies were represented.

Through surprisingly free and frank exchange, the delegates reached agreement on several key issues based upon tentative compromises drawn up by three committees. National development was emphasized, with the promotion of intraregional trade, export diversification, and the undertaking of collective action to stabilize demand for primary commodities constituting the major economic recommendations. The establishment of cultural exchanges of information and artists to acquire knowledge of each other's countries received wide acclaim. The conference gave its full support to worldwide self-determination, with special reference to the Palestinian question. The delegates also declared that colonialism in all its manifestations was "an evil which should speedily be brought to an end." Turning to the problems of dependent peoples, the conferees emphasized the need to liberate French North Africa, states in Arabia under British protection, and West Irian, a territory claimed by Indonesia but still under Dutch rule. They further pledged to eradicate racism, including that expressed internally in each nation.

In international terms, the delegates sought to bridge the gulfs that divided the world along ideological lines and that in turn had separated them. One measure called for greater Afro-Asian representation in the United Nations and on its Security Council. Although the final communiqué did not recommend a seat for mainland China at the United Nations, the participation of delegates from the People's Republic of China* was significant unto itself. In terms of security, Bandung rejected passive resistance as impractical, and since military pacts were viewed as serving the interests of the great powers, a strong push occurred for extending the nonaligned areas of peace around the world to balance the major powers (although the establishment of an Afro-Asian bloc was roundly rejected). Also called for were the eventual destruction of all nuclear arsenals and universal disarmament as exemplified in the

Bandung Declaration of Peace. Bandung represented a new spirit of cooperation among non-Western states and became a key reference point in the development of the nonaligned movement in world affairs. *See also* Colombo Plan.

Angadipuram Appadorai, *Essays in Politics and International Relations* (Bombay, 1969); G. McT. Kahin, *The Asian-African Conference, Bandung, Indonesia, April 1955* (Ithaca, NY, 1956); R. Wright et al., *The Color Curtain: A Report on the Bandung Conference* (New York, 1956).

Kent G. Sieg

BAO DAI (1913–1997)

Bao Dai was the final emperor of the Nguyen Dynasty and the leader of the American-backed Associated States government of Vietnam in the early 1950s. Born as Prince Vinh Thuy, he was educated and spent most of his young adulthood in France. Although he became emperor on the death of his father in 1925, he was not permitted by the French to return to Vietnam until 1932, and his duties were severely constrained. When the Japanese overthrew the French colonial regime in March 1945, they invited Bao Dai to form a Vietnamese government with limited independence under Japanese protection. After Japan's surrender in World War II in August 1945, Bao Dai was pressured to abdicate by Ho Chi Minh*, leader of the Vietminh*, the Vietnamese independence movement, and offered a symbolic role in the new regime.

With the outbreak of the First Indochina War* in 1946, France sought to form an alternative government to that of Ho Chi Minh with Bao Dai as its head, resulting in the Elysee Accords of 1949 that established the Associated States of Vietnam. The new government remained under French control with no autonomy on military and diplomatic matters and did not attract widespread popular support. The United States was initially suspicious of France's agreement with Bao Dai, concerned about his ability to provide a credible challenge to the popular Ho government, and critical of French unwillingness to grant Bao Dai full independence. But with the recognition of the Democratic Republic of Vietnam* by the Soviets and Chinese in January 1950, the United States put its full support behind Bao Dai.

By 1954, levels of American assistance to Bao Dai's government and the French war effort were second only to U.S. aid to the Republic of Korea*. Nonetheless, this period was marked by bitter contestations between the French, Bao Dai, and the Americans over the political, economic, and social construction of the new Vietnamese state. With the defeat of the French and partition of Vietnam under the Geneva Accords of 1954*, the United States withdrew its support of Bao Dai in favor of Ngo Dinh Diem*, who ruled the Republic of Vietnam* until 1963. Bao Dai retreated from politics and lived in France until his death. *See also* French Colonialism; French Indochina.

Bao Dai, *Le dragon d'Annam* (Paris, 1980); P. Devillers, *Histoire du Viêt-Nam de 1940 à 1952* (Paris, 1952); L. C. Gardner, *Approaching Vietnam: From World War II Through Dienbienphu, 1941–1954* (New York, 1988); G. R. Hess, *The United States' Emergence as a Southeast Asian Power, 1940–1950* (New York, 1987).

Mark P. Bradley

BATAAN DEATH MARCH

The Bataan Death March was the journey to prisoner of war (POW) camps by captured Americans and Filipinos after their surrender on Bataan in the Philippines*, which hardened American attitudes to encompass the defeat of Japan. In December 1941, Lieutenant General Homma Masaharu's forces landed in the Philippines. The Japanese timetable indicated a quick campaign to defeat the Americans and win the Filipinos to the Greater East Asia Co-

Prosperity Sphere*. The Japanese offensive stalled, though the Americans and Filipinos suffered from malnutrition and disease. The last American stronghold on the Bataan Peninsula, Mariveles, surrendered on 9 April 1942. An argument has been made that many Japanese were surprised that so few Americans had held out for so long and had not fought to the death. They had planned to take 25,000 prisoners; instead they needed to deal with approximately 78,000 American and Filipino military and civilian personnel. These people were organized in a series of marches to walk toward the POW area at San Fernando, a distance of sixty miles, without food or water. Some Filipinos along the route tried to give food and water, which was sometimes permitted.

For most of the prisoners the experience was one of horror. Estimates of the number of POWs shot, bayoneted, or beaten to death, or who died of conditions of forced march in the tropics when already debilitated by malnutrition and disease, varies between 7,000 and 14,000 people, approximately one-third of them American. One eyewitness recounted that he observed one dead American or Filipino every couple of hundred yards. Because of bad publicity resulting from the march, General Homma was sent back to Japan in disgrace, although only the fact of surrender was broadcast in Japan. Rumors and reports reached Americans slowly; they were confirmed in the summer of 1943. The effect was to harden American determination to defeat Japan. General Homma was indicted as a war criminal following Japan's surrender. *See also* Corregidor; Tōkyō War Crimes Trials.

G. Daws, *Prisoners of the Japanese: POWs of World War II in the Pacific* (New York, 1994); W. A. Renzi and M. D. Roehrs, *Never Look Back: A History of World War II in the Pacific* (Armonk, NY, 1991); R. L. Spector, *Eagle Against the Sun: The American War with Japan* (New York, 1985).

Katherine K. Reist

BATTLE OF AP BAC (2 January 1963)

A small village south and west of Saigon, Ap Bac was the site of a battle between the Army of the Republic of Vietnam* (ARVN) and South Vietnamese guerrillas, known as Viet Cong*. The assault was supposed to demonstrate the fighting effectiveness of the ARVN troops who had been receiving American training and supplies since 1955. Instead, what it uncovered were the structural weaknesses and corruption of the government and the military leadership under Ngo Dinh Diem*. Watching the ARVN troops arrive by helicopter, Viet Cong troops decided to stand and fight, despite being heavily outnumbered. Viet Cong military leaders needed to demonstrate that they could handle the new technology—namely, helicopters and armored personnel carriers—introduced by the Americans with devastating effectiveness the previous year to bolster sagging morale. After they set down, the ARVN troops of the Seventh Division quickly were engaged by Viet Cong units and took heavy losses, which froze their commanders from proceeding with the operation. Viet Cong troops shot down five helicopters before noon and also destroyed M113 personnel carriers with far greater success than before.

American military adviser John Paul Vann observed the battle from the air and tried to relay instructions to the ARVN commanders without success. Certain South Vietnamese officers were reluctant to commit troops to battle if it meant taking casualties. Frequently beholden to Diem for their command, they understood that their political usefulness was predicated on unit strength. Thus, they proceeded into battle very slowly. The Viet Cong later escaped during the night. In desperation, U.S. military officials proclaimed victory because the Viet Cong had left. More than anything else, however, the battle demonstrated the vastly different nature of fighting in Vietnam. In addition, Ap Bac underscored the weaknesses of Diem's government, especially in terms of its reliance on maintaining control by playing one commander off against another, which undercut military cooperation on the battlefield.

A. F. Krepinevich Jr., *The Army and Vietnam* (Baltimore, MD, 1986); N. Sheehan, *A Bright Shining Lie: John Paul Vann and America in Vietnam* (New York, 1988).

T. Christopher Jespersen

BATTLE OF THE CORAL SEA (5–8 May 1942)

The Battle of the Coral Sea was the first setback suffered by the Japanese navy in the Pacific war and the first naval battle in which the adversaries' ships never came in sight of each other. Its genesis lay in Japanese determination to bolster their position in the southwest Pacific by the capture of Port Moresby, which also would provide a jumping-off point for a possible invasion of northern Australia. An attack planned for March was delayed when Allied naval strength in the area was reinforced, and the operation then was overshadowed by the planned operation against Midway Island. The Japanese invasion force set sail from Rabaul on 4 May, with a covering force comprising two large and one smaller aircraft carriers, commanded by Vice Admiral Inoue Shigeyoshi. Forewarned by signals intelligence, the Allies had scratched together a force to meet this threat. Rear Admiral F. J. Fletcher had available two aircraft carriers, three heavy cruisers, and a support group that included two Australian cruisers.

In their initial clashes, on 7 May, both sides launched attacks on targets that proved to be relatively insignificant. Not until early the next day did the main forces find each other and launch almost simultaneous strikes. In these exchanges, the Japanese carrier *Shokaku* was heavily damaged, and her consort, *Zuikaku*, suffered heavy losses to her air group. On the Allied side, the American carrier USS *Lexington* was mortally damaged, and USS *Yorktown* hit. Although the Japanese seemed to have the better of the engagement tactically, a somewhat defeatist Inoue, perhaps influenced by the substantial losses the Japanese had suffered in aircraft and trained naval aviators, called off the invasion attempt.

Insofar as the Japanese were denied their objective, the outcome was therefore a strategic reverse for them; Port Moresby's capture subsequently was sought in a difficult and ultimately unsuccessful overland campaign. The battle's wider impact was considerable. It resulted in the two Japanese carriers being absent from the crucial Battle of Midway* the following month, perhaps tipping the balance in American favor there. Moreover, it reinforced Japanese overconfidence and hence complacency, with important consequences for that later operation. The outcome was regarded as especially significant in Australia and New Zealand, where popular opinion believed, incorrectly, that an imminent invasion had been prevented by American action. It provided a firm basis for U.S. political relations with these two nations for a generation, and encouraged them to sign the ANZUS Treaty* in 1951. *See also* Battle of Midway.

P. S. Dull, *A Battle History of the Imperial Japanese Navy, 1941–1945* (Annapolis, MD, 1978); J. B. Lundstrom, *The First South Pacific Campaign, Pacific Fleet Strategy December 1941–June 1942* (Annapolis, MD, 1976); S. E. Morison, *History of United States Naval Operations in World War II*, vol. 4 (Boston, 1958).

Ian McGibbon

BATTLE OF THE IA DRANG VALLEY (14–17 November 1965)

This initial battle between the North Vietnamese Army (NVA) and the U.S. Army shaped both sides' approach in fighting the rest of the Second Indochina War*. A three-day battle at landing zone X-Ray in South Vietnam's Central Highlands, it was the first full-scale engagement between North Vietnamese regular forces and the U.S.

Army, specifically the First Cavalry Division (Airmobile), which was designed to use helicopters for mobility, firepower, and supply. The 450 men of the Air Cavalry First Battalion under Lieutenant Colonel Harold Moore landed at the staging area of three regiments numbering 1,750 and soon were reinforced by a third regiment. Using helicopter-transported artillery, more than 3,000 close air support sorties, and savage hand-to-hand fighting, Moore was able to withstand repeated NVA assaults on his perimeter with the loss of 79 killed and 121 wounded. One of the two battalions that relieved Moore, the second Battalion, Seventh Cavalry, was ambushed as it marched to landing zone Albany to be evacuated the next day. It suffered 154 killed and 121 wounded, an echo of the Little Big Horn for George Armstrong Custer's Seventh Cavalry. The monthlong Ia Drang Valley campaign cost the United States 305 killed, but the U.S. Army estimated that the NVA had lost 3,561 killed and more than 1,000 wounded of the 6,000 that they committed to battle in the area. This twelve-to-one kill ratio confirmed the strategy of attrition that General William C. Westmoreland* implemented for the next four years.

Both sides learned valuable lessons at Ia Drang. The NVA learned that the conventional roadblock ambushes it had set would be ineffective against the new helicopter assaults, but that troops en route to a landing zone could be effectively ambushed. The North Vietnamese learned not only the value of "clinging to the enemy's belt" to avoid the massive close air support available to that enemy, but that U.S. forces would not pursue them when they retreated across the border into Cambodia*. For the United States, the battle validated the air mobile concept, as well as demonstrating that the B-52s flying out of Guam* could support troops in combat. Both would become icons of the war. In a briefing to Secretary of Defense Robert S. McNamara*, Moore credited the new M-16 rifle with much of his success, leading

Westmoreland to push for more rapid production and distribution of the weapon. The number of casualties and Westmoreland's request for double the number of additional forces—raising the total requested to 400,000 by the end of 1966, and as many as 200,000 more the next year—were a "shattering blow" to McNamara. Thirty years later, he wrote that "they shook me and altered my attitude perceptibly." Westmoreland's request for more forces was based on the battle's revelation that the NVA could field and supply nearly four times as many forces in South Vietnam as previously estimated, despite heavy interdiction bombing of the Ho Chi Minh Trail*.

R. S. McNamara, *Argument Without End: In Search of Answers to the Vietnam Tragedy* (New York, 1999); R. S. McNamara, *In Retrospect: The Tragedy and Lessons of Vietnam* (New York, 1995); H. G. Moore and J. L. Galloway, *We Were Soldiers Once . . . and Young: Ia Drang, The Battle that Changed the War in Vietnam* (New York, 1992); N. Sheehan, *A Bright Shining Lie: John Paul Vann and America in Vietnam* (New York, 1988); W. C. Westmoreland, *A Soldier Reports* (Garden City, NY, 1972).

Larry R. Beck

BATTLE OF IWO JIMA (19 February– 26 March 1945)

Iwo Jima is one of the Bonin Islands*. During World War II, U.S. planners placed a high value on its seizure because the eight-square-mile island was almost exactly midway between Tōkyō and the B-29 bomber bases at Guam*, Saipan, and Tinian in the Marianas. Its radar gave a two-hour warning of bomber strikes, and its airfields were host to interceptors out of range of fighter escort. In January 1945, General Curtis E. LeMay* told the U.S. Navy that without Iwo Jima, he could not bomb Japan effectively. The island was defended by more than 22,000 Japanese dug into an elaborate network of trenches, tunnels, and caves. The invasion of Iwo Jima by the Third, Fourth, and Fifth U.S. Marine divisions was scheduled for five days beginning 19 February. After the heaviest advanced naval and air bombardment of the war, the initial landing was uneventful. Eight infantry battalions were ashore in thirty minutes. But then the defenders under General Kuribayashi Tadamichi emerged from their caves to pin the attackers to the black volcanic ash and sand of the beaches. Among the 30,000 marines landed the first day, 2,420 were casualties and 566 died. The well-entrenched Japanese held out for thirty-six days and inflicted 25,851 casualties, with 6,821 dead. Only 1,083 of the 22,000 Japanese survived the battle, none of them officers. General Kuribayshi would not approve "Banzai" charges, having his men sign a pledge to kill ten U.S. soldiers before they died. The defenders would commit suicide before surrender.

General Holland Smith said that "Iwo Jima was the most savage and most costly battle in the history of the Marine Corps." It was also their most decorated, with 22 of the 82 U.S. Marine Medals of Honor earned there. Of the 353 Medals of Honor awarded in all of World War II, 27 were for action at Iwo Jima, nearly half posthumously. Associated Press photographer Joe Rosenthal's photograph of the flag raising atop 550-foot Mount Suribachi immortalized the action at Iwo Jima, becoming the most celebrated picture of the war and the model for the U.S. Marine Memorial, even though it actually depicted the second (larger) flag to be raised and on the fourth day of a thirty-six day battle. Navy Seabees repaired the two airfields and constructed a third on the small island. The virtual collapse of Japan's air forces made Iwo Jima's use as a P-51 fighter escort base less necessary than originally believed, but in the next five months, B-29s made 2,251 emergency landings on the island. Several writers have noted the symmetry of the 24,751 crewmen on those planes with the number of U.S. Marine and U.S. Navy casualties during the battle. The fierce resistance of Iwo Jima's Japanese defenders alerted U.S. officials to the very high potential cost of the planned invasion of the home islands, to begin with Operation OLYMPIC*. This likely was a factor in the decision of President Harry S. Truman* to order the Atomic Attacks*. *See also* Battle of Okinawa.

J. Costello, *The Pacific War, 1941–1945* (New York, 1982); S. E. Morison, *The Two-Ocean War: A Short History of the United States Navy in the Second World War* (Boston, 1963); B. Ross, *Iwo Jima: Legacy of Valor* (New York, 1985); D. Wright, *The Battle of Iwo Jima: 1945* (London, 1999).

Larry R. Beck

BATTLE OF LEYTE GULF (23–26 October 1944)

The Battle of Leyte Gulf was the swan song of the Japanese Navy in the Pacific war. The largest naval encounter in history, it was precipitated by U.S. landings on the island of Leyte in the Philippines* on 20 October 1944, and encompassed a series of engagements fought in widely separated locations over a two-day period. In a desperate bid to restore the Japanese situation, which had been deteriorating steadily since the Battle of Midway*, the Japanese High Command had resolved to devote all of Japan's diminishing resources to seeking a decisive naval victory when the United States made its expected assault on the Philippines. For this "Victory Operation," the Japanese mustered virtually all of the warships still available to them, including the two superbattleships *Yamato* and *Musashi*. With their naval aviation arm a spent force—the remaining Japanese carriers possessed hardly any aircraft and few experienced pilots—Japan staked all upon the long-shot possibility of their powerful surface ships getting to grips with the American forces.

Three separate fleets under the overall command of Vice Admiral Ozawa Jisaburō were involved. Ozawa's Northern Force, coming from Japanese waters, would lure Admiral W. F. Halsey's powerful U.S.

Third Fleet away from the American landing zone at Leyte Gulf. This would open the way for a pincer attack by two striking forces, Central and Southern Forces, deploying from near Brunei* and Japan respectively, which would sweep aside the relatively weak U.S. Seventh Fleet and annihilate the American troop transports. When Ozawa's force made its presence felt on 24 October, Halsey responded as the Japanese hoped. In accordance with his instructions to give priority to engaging the enemy main fleet, he dispatched the whole of the Third Fleet northward to engage it. He assumed that the threat posed by the Central Force had been neutralized by successful air attacks, which he had launched at it in the Sibuyan Sea that same day.

Although Ozawa's four carriers all eventually were sunk—their lack of aircraft left them impotent—Halsey's absence from the landing areas left the gate open for the northern arm of the Japanese pincer. During the night, the southern arm met with disaster. Seeking to debouch from the Surigao Strait, the Southern Force was defeated severely by the Seventh Fleet. But when the Central Force emerged from the San Bernardino Strait the following morning, it surprised the American forces off Samar, and heavily damaged one of the Seventh Fleet's carrier escort groups with gunfire. Under incessant air attack, it then broke off the action, to the surprise and relief of the hard-pressed Americans, and retired through the strait. During the day, several kamikaze attacks by aircraft heralded a tactic the Japanese would use repeatedly in the last phase of the war. Although both the Central and Northern Forces managed to avoid total destruction, Japan had suffered a crushing defeat; its loss of the Philippines was now inevitable. The Japanese Navy was left incapable of playing any further strategic role in the Pacific war. Even if it had no chance of succeeding against the forces now arrayed against Japan and at best only could have delayed the American advance, this daring and characteristically complicated "Victory

Operation" had embarrassed the Americans briefly. *See also* Battle of the Philippine Sea.

T. J. Cutler, *The Battle of Leyte Gulf, 23–26 October 1944* (New York, 1994); P. S. Dull, *A Battle History of the Imperial Japanese Navy, 1941–1945* (Annapolis, MD, 1978); S. E. Morison, *History of United States Naval Operations in World War II*, vol. 12 (Boston, 1958).

Ian McGibbon

BATTLE OF MANILA BAY (1 May 1898)

A naval battle fought at the beginning of the Spanish-American War*, this contest resulted in the destruction of the Spanish fleet in East Asia. It paved the way for annexation of the Philippines* at the end of the war and made the United States an East Asian power. Just days earlier, the United States had declared war against Spain to free Cuba from Spanish rule. In these circumstances, it proved surprising that the first major battle of the war took place in Philippine waters thousands of miles from the Caribbean. But even before war commenced, Assistant Secretary of the Navy Theodore Roosevelt* cabled to Commodore George Dewey, commanding the American Asiatic Squadron based at Hong Kong*, ordering him to get his force ready to sail to the Philippines as soon as possible. Dewey did so, and when Roosevelt cabled the news of the declaration of war, Dewey was ready. He set out on 27 April for Manila Bay, where the Spanish fleet in the Philippines was based at Cavite. His squadron, consisting of his flagship, the protected cruiser *Olympia*, four other cruisers, two smaller gunboats, and a revenue cutter, practiced firing exercises on the way.

In Manila Bay, Rear Admiral Don Patricio Montojo, Spain's naval commander in the Philippines, was in an unenviable position. His fleet consisted of seven vessels, mostly small and obsolete. Only his flagship, *Reina Cristina*, was of much value, and it was only a little more than half the size of Dewey's *Olympia*. His ships took position in an anchored line in front of the Cavite navy yard, where he awaited the American attack. Dewey's squadron reached the entrance to Manila Bay in the night on 30 April. The fortress of Corregidor* and other island batteries covered the mouth of the bay, but the fleet got into the bay unscathed, even though some of the Spanish guns fired at Dewey's ships. After daylight on 1 May, the battle commenced. Dewey found Montojo's anchored ships, firing methodically, and turning about to bring its unengaged guns to bear as it passed the enemy ships again. The Americans completely outclassed the Spanish fleet in firepower and gunnery effectiveness. By noon the battle was over, with all the Spanish ships sunk or abandoned. Thanks to the safety offered by the nearby shore, the Spanish casualties were not heavy, with 381 killed or wounded. They made only about a dozen hits on the American ships, and the casualties on those ships were just seven wounded.

With Spanish naval power in the Philippines annihilated, Dewey turned to a blockade of Manila, for he was not strong enough to capture it without the aid of troops. At home in Washington, an expedition for this purpose was organized quickly and sent to the Philippines. On the way, a cruiser from the first convoy appeared at Guam* and secured the surrender of that island, whose governor was unaware that a war was in progress. As the troop convoys stopped at the Hawaiian Islands on their way across the Pacific, they gave added impetus to the movement to annex those islands, which took place in August. Upon arrival in early August, General Wesley Merritt, commanding the troops, and Dewey quickly made plans in concert with Filipino rebels to capture the fortifications guarding Manila. The troops, about 11,000 in number, landed on 13 August, and a day later the Spanish defenders capitulated. This was one day after the Spanish and American governments

signed a general cease-fire. The Battle of Manila Bay gave the United States grounds to force Spain to include Philippine Annexation* in the final treaty of peace. By taking the Philippines, the United States gained prestige as an Asian power, but also many headaches, not the least of which was growing tension with Japan. *See also* Hawaiian Annexation; Philippine-American War.

F. Freidel, *The Splendid Little War* (Boston, 1958); R. L. Spector, *Admiral of the New Empire: The Life and Career of George Dewey* (Baton Rouge, LA, 1974); D. F. Trask, *The War with Spain in 1898* (New York, 1981).

Ernest Andrade Jr.

BATTLE OF MIDWAY (4–6 June 1942)

The decisive encounter of the Pacific War, the Battle of Midway wrenched the strategic initiative from Japan's grasp, and henceforth it would lie with the United States. It also confirmed the lesson of the Battle of the Coral Sea*: the aircraft carrier was now the chief element of naval power. The battle was precipitated by Japanese determination to bring to battle the U.S. Fleet and complete the job begun with the Pearl Harbor Attack*. The driving force behind this decision was Admiral Yamamoto Isoroku*, the commander in chief of the Japanese Combined Fleet, who was convinced that Japan must concentrate upon decisively defeating the American naval forces ranged against it. The seizure of Midway Island in the Central Pacific, he argued, inevitably would force the Americans to respond in strength, leading to a showdown in which the Japanese would hold the advantage of surprise and material superiority.

Yamamoto's plan, which was endorsed in April, was complex and risky. A diversionary attack in the Aleutians would weaken Japanese strength at the vital point while introducing the danger of defeat in detail. More seriously, the Midway invasion was a potentially distracting element should a fleet action develop ahead of schedule. Nevertheless, the Japanese naval authorities were so confident of achieving surprise, and of ultimate success, that they gave insufficient attention to the potential dangers in their plan. Their careless approach was reinforced by the apparent power of the formidable armada that had been assembled for the Midway operation. The Combined Fleet consisted of eleven battleships, two light carriers, and ten heavy cruisers, as well as the four large carriers of the Carrier Striking Force under Vice Admiral Nagumo Chūichi. The fact that a third of Japan's strength in large carriers was unavailable, as a result of the Battle of the Coral Sea in early May, was not unduly troubling, since the U.S. Navy was expected to have the services of only two such vessels.

Far from being surprised or diverted, however, the Americans had sufficient warning through signals intelligence to prepare their response in the key area at Midway. Three large carriers—USS *Yorktown*, damaged at the Coral Sea, had undergone rapid temporary repairs to allow her to participate—and seven heavy cruisers were lying in wait when the approaching Japanese launched an air strike on the island early on 4 June. Although the Japanese had expected a clash of surface warships to settle the issue, the outcome of the battle effectively was decided when three of Nagumo's carriers were damaged fatally in quick succession by American dive-bombers later in the morning. Nagumo's remaining carrier, *Hiryū*, launched an attack that severely damaged *Yorktown* (later finished off by a Japanese submarine) before she, too, succumbed to American dive-bombers in the early evening. Yamamoto at first hoped that he might retrieve the situation using the rest of his fleet, but reconsidered and called off the invasion of Midway and retired to the west. Japan's only gains from the offensive were the insignificant islands of Attu and Kiska, in the Aleutians. With the destruction of the heart of the Carrier Striking Force, and its vet-

eran pilots, Japan had lost the key to the defense of its extensive gains of the previous six months. *See also* Doolittle Raid.

M. Fuchida and M. Okumiya, *Midway, The Battle that Doomed Japan: The Japanese Navy's Story* (Annapolis, MD, 1955); S. E. Morison, *History of United States Naval Operations in World War II*, vol. 4 (Boston, 1958); G. W. Prange with D. M. Goldstein and K. V. Dillon, *Miracle at Midway* (New York, 1982).

Ian McGibbon

BATTLE OF NOMONHAN (May– September 1939)

The Battle of Nomonhan caused the Japanese to temporarily abandon plans for war against the Soviet Union and instead shift their attention to Southeast Asia and the Pacific region, entailing hostilities in 1941 against the United States, Britain, and the Netherlands. Whereas Japanese and Western sources name the contingency war of 1939 after Nomonhan Burd Obo, a cairn in west Manchuria, the Russians use the name of Khalkhin Gol, the Halha River, which flows through the otherwise treeless steppes. Trouble began in the largely unmarked, remote region when Mongolian herders crossed the Halha. Responsible for defense of the vast flatland, the Japanese Twenty-third Infantry Division—a newly formed, green, ill-equipped, and relatively small force commanded by Russian specialist Lieutenant General Komatsubara Michitarō—sent elements from Hailar to sweep the zone east of the Halha stream. Finding the Mongolians gone, the Japanese withdrew. Thereupon the Mongolians reappeared, causing the Japanese to dispatch a much stronger punitive force to chastise the alleged interlopers once and for all. In the process, a Japanese reconnaissance regiment was annihilated. It was now apparent that the Soviet Russian garrison in the Mongolian People's Republic (MPR) was involved. Fierce dogfights raged overhead, to the detriment of the Russian flyers at this stage, and the Japanese even launched massive air strikes against air bases inside the MPR.

Meanwhile, Japanese higher headquarters in the Kwantung Army, egged on by hawkish staff officers Tsuji Masanobu and Hattori Tokushirō, hastily devised a plan to send the Twenty-third Division, reinforced by a regiment from the Seventh Division and involving most of the tanks in Manchuria (a paltry total of less than 100), across the Halha on 2 July to pincer Russian and Mongolian troops from both banks at the confluence with the Holsten. A debacle ensued for the Japanese. The infantry who traversed the feeble pontoon bridge constructed by the engineers immediately encountered swarms of unexpected enemy tanks and armored cars. About the best the Japanese could do was hurl gasoline bottles against the armor at close range. While Japan's foot soldiers' assault bogged down across the river, its tanks were destroyed on the right shore.

The overconfident Kwantung Army was compelled to cancel the offensive and pull back all forces after only forty-eight hours. The conclusion was reached that more artillery was needed if offensive action was to succeed. Reinforced accordingly, a new attack was launched south of the Holsten on 23 July. It, too, failed. Thereupon the Japanese made plans to settle in for the fast-approaching winter at Nomonhan and to resume offensive operations in spring 1940. The Russians allowed them no such time. General Georgi K. Zhukov, the Soviet combat commander since June, had received carte blanche from Premier Joseph Stalin and the High Command to mount a major counteroffensive designed to oust the Japanese from the Halha line by the end of August. After meticulous and powerful preparation, the Soviet attack jumped off on 20 August, the unsuspecting Japanese forces were shattered, and the Russian border claims were achieved entirely by the end of the month, though fighting continued at various sectors into September.

The Russians and the Japanese, on behalf of their respective client states of Outer Mongolia and Manchukuo*, had fought tenaciously on the ground and in the air between May and September 1939. On 16 September, diplomatic negotiations in Moscow, which had been dragging, achieved a cease-fire. By now, World War II had erupted in Europe, and the Japanese side was dazed by events. Their losses at Nomonhan had been severe—about 18,000 killed or wounded, from an engaged force exceeding 75,000. Japanese aerial superiority had been whittled away by the ceaseless combat. There was a wholesale shake-up of the Japanese Army staff, extending to the retirement of General Ueda Kenkichi, the Kwantung Army commander, and the temporary banishment of enfants terribles Tsuji and Hattori. Komatsubara, a broken man, died the next year. As for the Soviet side, recent data for Khalkhin Gol indicate between 7,974 and 8,931 killed or missing and 15,952 wounded or sick, for a total of 23,726 to 24,883 casualties, out of a total of 69,101 engaged.

A. D. Coox, *Nomonhan: Japan Against Russia, 1939*, 2 vols. (Stanford, CA, 1985); G. F. Krivosheev (ed.), *Soviet Casualties and Combat Losses in the Twentieth Century* (London, 1997); G. K. Zhukov, *Memoirs* (New York, 1971).

Alvin D. Coox

BATTLE OF OKINAWA (1 April–21 June 1945)

On 1 April 1945, the U.S. Tenth Army landed on the beaches of Okinawa in the Ryūkyūs, and for three months fought one of the bloodiest battles in the Pacific theater that ultimately claimed 100,000 military and civilian casualties, including the two opposing commanders. The command of Fleet Admiral Chester W. Nimitz targeted the island for invasion because of its proximity to the main Japanese islands. Once taken, Okinawa could provide air bases closer to Japan than those in use on Guam*. The island also would serve as a forward staging area for the ground troops assigned to the invasion of the main islands.

Realizing the importance of Okinawa, the Japanese defended the island tenaciously. The air battle prior to the actual invasion was a warning of the bloodshed to come. American air strikes did considerable damage to the urban areas on the island, and Japanese kamikaze pilots began to bloody the U.S. ships patrolling off the coast. Destroyers on picket duty took the brunt of the offensive as inexperienced pilots plunged on these small ships, thinking they were battleships. These kamikaze missions scored some considerable victories. The Japanese hit and damaged roughly a fourth of the U.S. fleet, sinking thirty-four ships, killing 5,000 sailors, and injuring another 5,000.

Initially, the ground invasion failed to match the intensity of the aerial battle, but this was intentional. The Thirty-second Army defending Okinawa lacked the strength to hold the entire island. Since the northern half of the island was mountainous and lacked military utility, the Japanese conceded the landing and the upper portion of the island to the enemy, and decided to fight a defensive action in the south. This decision essentially determined the outcome of the battle. The Americans would take the island if they could endure a protracted engagement with heavy casualties. American battle plans called for the Third Marine Amphibious Corps to take the northern portion of the island while the Twenty-fourth Army Corps conquered the south. When the marines in the first assault wave reached the beach, they were surprised to find no enemy opposition. The U.S. Marines marched north and accomplished their mission. The soldiers from the U.S. Army divisions had a more difficult time. The Japanese had built three fortified lines, using an interconnected series of tunnels, pillboxes, trenches, caves, and even Okinawan tombs on both the forward and reverse slopes of hills designed to channel attackers into prepared lanes of fire. This defensive system neutralized the advantage Americans had with artillery. The defenders also had more heavy weapons and artillery than any other Japanese force Americans had encountered. As a result, the attack on the southern portion of the island quickly became a slow and bloody process. According to American plans, the battle should have taken only a month, but it took more than four weeks to breech the first two lines.

As a result of the tenacious defense, Lieutenant General Simon B. Buckner Jr., the U.S. grand commander, decided to employ marines along the established front. In making this decision, he rejected a proposal from one of his division commanders to use a U.S. Army division and the Third Amphibious Corps to stage a second landing on the southern coast of Okinawa, which would have forced the Japanese to fight on two fronts, and presumably made their collapse more rapid. Reporters and columnists in June criticized Buckner for his conservative tactics, which they saw as the main reason for the heavy casualties. Buckner's more immediate concern was with the Japanese defenders. Heavy monsoons slowed the American march forward, turning roads into muddy traps that could stop trucks, tanks, and the movement of supplies. The storms allowed the Japanese to withdraw again and reform what would be their last line of organized resistance on a four-mile-long cliff wall. Buckner offered to enter into negotiations on terms for a surrender, but the Japanese refused. Nevertheless, coordinated Japanese resistance lasted until 15 June. Before the end of the month, General Joseph W. Stilwell* took command of the Tenth Army, and began preparing it and the island for its role in the invasion of Japan's main islands. Enemy stragglers, however, continued to pose a threat to U.S. occupation forces well into the spring.

R. E. Appleman, *Okinawa: The Last Battle* (Tōkyō, 1961); J. H. and W. Belote, *Typhoon of Steel: The Battle for Okinawa* (New York, 1970); B. M. Frank and H. I. Shaw, *Victory and Occupation* (Washington, DC, 1968); S. E. Morison, *History of United States Naval Operations in World War II*, vol. 14 (Boston, 1960).

Nicholas Evan Sarantakes

BATTLE OF THE PHILIPPINE SEA (19–20 June 1944)

The Battle of the Philippine Sea destroyed the remnants of Japanese carrier-based air power in World War II, ensured the American seizure of the B-29 bases in the Marianas, and set the stage for the American return to the Philippines*. In early 1944, the U.S. forces in the central Pacific were preparing to capture the Marianas Islands (Saipan, Guam*, and Tinian). The move was expected by the Japanese Navy, which had developed a plan to defeat the Americans. Japanese submarine and scouting forces were to alert their navy to the impending attack. Carrier forces under Vice Admiral Ozawa Jisaburō then would sortie to positions from which longer-range Japanese aircraft could attack while still remaining out of American reach. Although the nine Japanese carriers and 473 aircraft would be outnumbered by the Americans with 15 carriers and 956 aircraft, Ozawa was optimistic about the outcome because of the planned surprise. He also counted on the cooperation of aircraft from the First Air Fleet stationed in the Marianas. But in May 1944, faulty Japanese planning and a U.S. intelligence breakthrough caused the sinking of six Japanese submarines in fifteen days and the total disruption of a picket line protecting the Marianas. Before U.S. troops went ashore on Saipan on 15 June 1944, American carriers had damaged or destroyed half of the First Air Fleet, effectively removing it from the coming battle.

On the morning of 19 June, Ozawa's ships launched a multiple-wave attack against the U.S. carriers. In the midst of the morning launch, an American submarine sank one of the carriers, and a second one torpedoed Ozawa's flagship several hours later. The first wave was detected by the Americans from their ships more than 150 miles away. With sufficient warning and expert direction, massed U.S. fighters broke up the attacks, and the more experienced Americans completely dominated the resulting dogfights. The next three waves met similar fates, as the Japanese lost between 290 and 350 aircraft, and the Americans lost no fewer than 32 fighters—a battle so one-sided that it became known as the Great Marianas Turkey Shoot*. Vice Admiral Marc Mitschner, commander of Task Force Fifty-eight, did not learn the location of Ozawa's fleet until the next day, and then with only three hours of daylight remaining. Mitschner ordered an immediate attack. Most of the 215 aircraft reached the Japanese fleet and sank a third carrier and two oil tankers, destroyed eighty more Japanese aircraft, and damaged three of the remaining six Japanese carriers and a battleship. With fewer than forty operational aircraft left, Ozawa ordered the fleet to retire at full speed toward Okinawa. Later, Vice Admiral Raymond Spruance, Mitchner's superior, was subject to criticism for not allowing his subordinate to close aggressively with Ozawa's fleet on the night of 19–20 July. But Spruance thought the primary mission of his fleet was to protect the Marianas invasion force. The issue soon would reoccur at the Battle of Leyte Gulf*.

H. Gailey, *The War in the Pacific: From Pearl Harbor to Tokyo Bay* (Novato, CA, 1995); S. E. Morison, *The Two-Ocean War: A Short History of the United States Navy in the Second World War* (Boston, 1963); J. Prados, *Combined Fleet Decoded: Secret History of American Intelligence and the Japanese Navy in World War II* (New York, 1995); R. L. Spector, *Eagle Against the Sun: The American War with Japan* (New York, 1985).

Roger H. Hill

BERING SEA SEAL CONTROVERSY

This episode developed from an early conservation effort by the United States, that caused serious diplomatic difficulties with the governments of Great Britain, Canada, and Japan. The Bering Sea Seal Controversy had its roots in the fact that when the United States bought Alaska from Russia in 1867, it became the proprietor of the Pribilov Islands. The Pribilovs, along with other islands in the Bering Sea and the northern Kuriles under Russian and Japanese control, were the breeding grounds for thousands of northern fur seals, and they had been taken for their fur for many years. In the years after the transfer of the Pribilovs to American ownership, the U.S. government regulated the annual catch of seals on the islands, partly to preserve the herds and partly to safeguard the seal catch for American companies.

By the early 1880s, some conservationists were becoming concerned about the changing situation, for sealers, many of whom were Canadian, began taking the seals on the high seas, where the United States revenue cutters had no jurisdiction. Known as pelagic sealing, the practice of killing seals on the high seas was especially destructive to the seal population. First, it was impossible to distinguish female from male seals on the open ocean. Second, the use of firearms in the killing was wasteful, since up to half the seals shot sank and were lost. In 1885, the Grover Cleveland administration authorized U.S. revenue vessels to seize pelagic sealers on the grounds that even in international waters, the U.S. government had jurisdiction over the seals. As one wry comment at the time went, the seals were being considered somewhat like American citizens.

Since most of the seized sealing vessels were Canadian and operated mostly out of Vancouver, this practice brought immediate protests from the British government. Over the next several years, pelagic sealing and the American seizures became a diplomatic wrangle. The British claimed that the United States had no right to capture foreign ships in international waters and threatened to send naval vessels to protect the Canadian sealers. But after several years of arguing, the American and British governments reached an agreement in 1891 providing for international arbitration of the dispute. Representatives from France, Italy, and Sweden would meet in Paris in 1893 to decide the question. Until then, the British and Americans agreed to establish

patrols involving warships of both nations to police the Bering Sea to prevent pelagic sealing. The agreement was far from perfect. Enforcement, particularly by the British, was sporadic and only slightly effective. In the years between 1890 and 1893, the seal population declined rapidly.

The decision of the Paris Tribunal in August 1893 helped matters somewhat. It rejected the American case for protection of the seals on the high seas. A ban on sealing during certain months of the year was established, having some effect in arresting the decline of the seal population. But then problems with Japanese sealers, who began to take seals in increasing numbers in the Bering Sea after 1900, caused a resurgence of the problem. The Japanese took the same position as the British with regard to American attempts to capture sealers on the high seas. Another conference was convened at Washington, D.C., and in July 1911, a treaty was signed by representatives of the United States, Great Britain, Japan, and Russia. It provided that pelagic sealing would be banned permanently, and each country's sealers could share in the taking of seals on land under strict controls. In this way, the fur seals of the Bering Sea did not become just another addition to the list of extinct species.

J. Callahan, *American Foreign Policy in Canadian Relations* (New York, 1967); G. Williams, *The Bering Sea Fur Seal Dispute, 1885–1911* (Eugene, OR, 1984).

Ernest Andrade Jr.

BEVERIDGE, ALBERT J. (1862–1927)

Albert Beveridge, Republican senator from Indiana from 1899 to 1910, was imperialism's leading exponent in the United States at the turn of the twentieth century. Beveridge warned of the dangers of domestic overproduction and championed the need for foreign markets. A confirmed white supremacist, he regarded Anglo-Saxons as God's chosen people with the duty to export Christianity and capitalism. Philippine

Annexation*, in his mind, represented a logical extension of Manifest Destiny. "Shall the American people continue their march toward the commercial supremacy of the world? Shall free institutions broaden their blessed reign as the children of liberty wax in strength, until the empire of our principles is established over the hearts of all mankind?", Beveridge asked in 1898 in his most famous speech, "The March of the Flag." It was absolutely imperative, he declared, that Asia remain open to American trade.

Beveridge based his arguments for expansion on economic objectives and his belief in an American mission, as God's trustee of civilization in the world, to regenerate the world. The extension of U.S. naval and military power was central to both strains of his thought. Beveridge was reacting in part to anti-imperialists who objected to expansion on grounds that democracies should not practice colonialism, the United States should not absorb more peoples of color, and the U.S. Constitution could not extend across the Pacific. In a 1900 Senate speech, Beveridge stressed the need to retain the Philippines* because the "Pacific is our ocean," China "our natural customer," and the Philippines the gateway to the East. China was the most important market in the world and "peopled by a race which civilization demands shall be improved." Although the United States definitely should hold the Philippines, Beveridge argued, it was just as clear that the Filipinos were unready for democracy, being "not of a self-governing race. They are Orientals, Malays, instructed by Spaniards in the latter's worst estate." Beveridge thwarted anti-imperialists in the Senate, who sought to make U.S. atrocities in the Philippine-American War* an issue by manipulating hearings and emphasizing American courage over brutality.

In 1904, having traveled to China, Beveridge published *The Russian Advance*, detailing Russia's occupation of Manchuria in the wake of the Boxer Uprising*. In this influential book, echoing the arguments of Brooks Adams and Alfred Thayer Mahan*, Beveridge called for the U.S. government to assume a much larger role in Asian affairs and to exert a more powerful and direct military and commercial influence over the region: "diplomatic declarations and 'paper intentions' amount to little in the face of railroads actually built and building, and the concrete and tangible power that attends them." The senator was convinced (wrongly) that if war came in Asia, the Russians would defeat their Japanese rivals. As for U.S. policy, Beveridge promoted formal colonialism in the Philippines and informal empire in China. He advocated acquisition of a naval base on the Chinese coast and creation of a unified financial policy to minimize intra-American competition. As enthusiasm for imperialism waned, Beveridge shifted his focus to Progressivism at home, maintaining continuity, though, in many of his ideas about race and other issues.

A. J. Beveridge, *The Meaning of the Times and Other Speeches* (New York, 1968); A. J. Beveridge, *The Russian Advance* (New York, 1904); J. Braeman, *Albert J. Beveridge: American Nationalist* (Chicago, 1971); A. C. Carlson, "Albert J. Beveridge as Imperialist and Progressive," *Western Journal of Speech Communication* (Winter 1988); M. H. Hunt, *Frontier Defense and the Open Door: Manchuria in Chinese-American Relations, 1895–1911* (New Haven, CT, 1973).

Shannon Smith

BIDDLE, JAMES (1783–1848)

James Biddle, as U.S. commissioner to China, presided at the exchange of ratifications of the Chinese-American Treaty of Wangxia* at Guangzhou in late 1845. Born in Philadelphia, he entered the navy in 1800 and soon was captured in the war against Tripoli and held prisoner for nineteen months. During the War of 1812, he served as lieutenant on the *Wasp* when it captured the British *Frolic*. In early 1815, the government in Washington sent a small fleet under Commodore Stephen Decatur to Asian waters to protect American commerce and prey on British ships along the coasts of India and China. In Decatur's fleet, Biddle commanded the *Hornet*, which, in March 1815, captured the British *Penguin* while en route to the East Indies. Promoted to captain that year, Biddle received a gold medal from Congress in recognition of his services. In 1817, he presided at the American reoccupation of Astoria in the Oregon Territory, which had fallen to the British during the recent war. In subsequent years, Biddle protected U.S. shipping in South American waters when troubles facing the new Latin American republics rendered neutral rights precarious.

Following the U.S. Senate's approval of the Treaty of Wangxia with China, Biddle left New York in June 1845 with a small squadron to carry Alexander H. Everett, the new American commissioner, to China for the purpose of exchanging treaty ratifications with the Chinese government. Suffering ill health, Everett abandoned his mission at Rio de Janeiro and transferred to Biddle his instructions and assigned duties in China. On 31 December, Biddle exchanged ratifications with Chinese officials in elaborate ceremonies at Guangzhou. He then established the U.S. legation at the foreign settlement outside Guangzhou, presiding over it until April 1846, when he transferred the power of commissioner to Dr. Peter Parker*. On 7 July, he left for Japan, entering Tōkyō Bay to become the first U.S. naval officer to anchor a fleet in Japanese waters. The Japanese rejected his treaty of friendship. On 29 July, after ten days in Tōkyō Bay, he sailed to California for naval service on the Pacific coast during the Mexican War. *See also* Perry Mission to Japan.

C. O. Paullin, *American Voyages to the Orient, 1690–1865* (Annapolis, MD, 1971).

Norman A. Graebner

BINH XUYEN

Known for its involvement in organized crime activities, the Binh Xuyen played a notable role in South Vietnamese politics and the increasing American involvement in South Vietnam during the 1950s. Named for a village south of Saigon, the Binh Xuyen enjoyed influence during the decade immediately after World War II largely because of arms it had received from the Japanese during the end of their occupation of French Indochina*. After the war, the Binh Xuyen engaged in gambling, prostitution, and the Drug Trade* and came to possess an army numbering 25,000. In 1955, Ngo Dinh Diem*, the American-supported leader of the Republic of Vietnam*, targeted the group as a means of demonstrating to his supporters that he had gained control over South Vietnam. Diem's position was precarious in the twelve months after the Geneva Conference of 1954*, a year that saw the division of Vietnam at the seventeenth parallel, the French departure, and an increasing American presence in the southern half of the nation. Working closely with Edward G. Lansdale*, operative with the Central Intelligence Agency*, Diem struck in the spring of 1955. The South Vietnamese Army easily defeated Binh Xuyen forces, which Lansdale quickly used to proclaim Diem's control over the situation. Lansdale was seeking to undercut General J. Lawton Collins*, who was then pressing the Eisenhower administration to withdraw its support from Diem. Diem's defeat of the Binh Xuyen, however, persuaded President Dwight D. Eisenhower* not to remove U.S. endorsement of the Diem government. *See also* Cao Dai; Collins Mission; Second Indochina War.

D. L. Anderson, *Trapped by Success: The Eisenhower Administration and Vietnam, 1953–1961* (New York, 1991); G. C. Herring, *America's Longest War: The United States and Vietnam 1950–1975* (New York, 1996); M. B. Young, *The Vietnam Wars, 1945–1990* (New York, 1991).

T. Christopher Jespersen

BLOUNT, JAMES H. (1837–1903)

In 1893, new President Grover Cleveland sent James H. Blount to investigate allegations of U.S. involvement in the overthrow of the Hawaiian monarchy against the will of the native population. Born near Clinton, Georgia, he graduated from the University of Georgia in 1858. He was admitted to the bar the next year, but the outbreak of the Civil War interrupted his law career, and he rose from private to lieutenant colonial in the Confederate Army. Blount resumed his law practice in 1867 in Clinton, but five years later, moved to Macon. Although he opposed the Ku Klux Klan, he was, like fellow Southern Democrats, a supporter of states' rights and white home rule. In 1872, Blount was elected to the U.S. Congress. He held his seat until 1892, establishing a reputation for courage and ability as a parliamentarian. A fiscal conservative, Blount's state and party dictated his support for lowering tariffs, inflating the currency, and regulating railroads, but opposition to pensions for Union veterans, Chinese immigration, and merit hiring in the civil service. He also was an anti-imperialist who spoke against a large navy and building an isthmian canal. In 1892, Blount retired from Congress, hoping to position himself for election to the U.S. Senate.

President Benjamin Harrison strongly supported acquisition of Hawaii. As a result, he welcomed the actions of U.S. Ambassador John L. Stevens* in supporting the white elite who seized power under the leadership of Sanford B. Dole* early in 1893. But the Senate failed to ratify the treaty of annexation before Harrison's term expired, and the new Cleveland administration withdrew the document because Secretary of State Walter Q. Gresham believed Stevens's actions were inappropriate. Gresham also saw an opportunity to embarrass Harrison, the man who in 1888 had denied him the Republican Party's presidential nomination. At Gresham's urging, Cleveland named Blount as commissioner with "paramount" authority to investigate the circumstances surrounding the revolution in Hawaii, to make a judgment about

the advisability of ratifying the annexation treaty, and to determine whether the provisional government had gained power with the help of the U.S. Navy. He arrived in late March and quickly declared the U.S. protectorate at an end. On 1 April 1893, the U.S. flags were lowered from Hawaiian buildings and the U.S. Marines were sent back to the USS *Boston*.

After five months in Honolulu, Blount, without interviewing either Dole (who refused to meet with Blount) or other principal leaders of the revolution, and without questioning Stevens, mailed a report critical of the U.S. minister's actions. He wrote to Gresham that Stevens had conspired with the revolutionaries and had promised in advance of the rebellion the support of U.S. military forces to assist in the overthrow of Queen Lili'uokalani*. Gresham did not forward the report to the president, with his recommendations, until October. Blount's findings justified Cleveland's decision in December not to resubmit the treaty for Senate consideration. By then, Stevens and others had denounced Blount's report as inaccurate and biased. During 1894 Senate hearings, Blount defended his findings and recommendations while critics charged that his mission exceeded the president's authority because it lacked Senate approval. Blount then returned to Macon, where as one of the largest landowners in Georgia, he managed his plantations instead of practicing law or participating in public affairs.

T. S. McWilliams, "James H. Blount, the South, and Hawaiian Annexation," *Pacific Historical Review* (February 1988); T. J. Osborne, *"Empire Can Wait": American Opposition to Hawaiian Annexation, 1893–1898* (Kent, OH, 1981); M. Tate, *The United States and the Hawaiian Kingdom: A Political History* (New Haven, CT, 1965); U.S. Department of State, *Foreign Relations of the United States*, 1894, appendix 2 (Washington, DC, 1995); U.S. Senate, *The Hawaiian Islands: Report of the Committee on Foreign Relations*, Report 227, 2 vols., 53 Cong., 2nd Sess. (Washington, DC, 1894).

James I. Matray

BOAT PEOPLE

This is the term used to describe Vietnamese refugees fleeing Vietnam after the collapse of the U.S.-backed government of the Republic of Vietnam*. In April–May 1975, the United States assisted the evacuation of about 200,000 South Vietnamese with military and chartered aircraft. Other Vietnamese, mostly merchants and landowners, fearing for their lives as "exploiters of the people," under the Communist regime fled Vietnam abroad small boats and merchant ships to Hong Kong*, Singapore*, Malaysia*, and the Philippines*. These early boat people numbered about 50,000.

The mass exodus of boat people did not begin until June and July 1978, when the Vietnamese government implemented its policy of expulsion of ethnic Chinese from the Socialist Republic of Vietnam*. Persecution of the Chinese entrepreneurial class began in earnest with the crackdown on private enterprise by Hanoi in April 1978. First, the Vietnamese government began confiscating ethnic Chinese businesses and private property. Although ethnic Chinese constituted only 7 percent of the total population in Vietnam, they controlled nearly 80 percent of businesses. The economic success of the ethnic Chinese further exacerbated ethnic tensions between the two groups. Second, tensions between Vietnam and the People's Republic of China* (PRC) increased as the result of Vietnamese aggression into Cambodia*. In response to Vietnam's invasion of Cambodia and its alliance with the Soviet Union, the PRC invaded Vietnam in February–March 1979. This conflict further jeopardized the ethnic Chinese population in Vietnam. Between March and July, the largest number of ethnic Chinese fled Vietnam. The first wave of boat people from June 1978 to August 1979 consisted of at least 75 percent (217,788) ethnic Chinese. From August 1979 to June 1982, the pattern reversed, with roughly 75 percent (152,101) being ethnic Vietnamese and only 25 percent ethnic Chinese. A total

estimate of more than 600,000 refugees reached assorted destinations across the South China Sea.

The plight of these boat people captured the world's attention. In response to the crisis, Attorney General Griffin Bell announced in November 1978 that the United States would accept 15,000 boat people by the next spring. By then, the administration of President Jimmy Carter* was paroling 7,000 per month. In June, it announced that it would admit 14,000 monthly. New admissions thereafter pushed the total by early 1981 past the half-million mark. Further admissions during the administration of Ronald Reagan* brought the total number to approximately 700,000 by 1985. The international community responded to the crisis in June 1979 by holding a convention in Geneva to discuss what to do with the boat people turned away by first-asylum countries in Southeast Asia. The convention reached an agreement that stipulated that first-asylum nations would not turn away refugees and that second-asylum countries, the industrialized nations, would accept them for permanent settlement.

K. St. Cartmail, *Exodus Indochina* (Auckland, 1983); J. T. Fawcett and B. V. Carino (eds.), *Pacific Bridges: The New Immigration from Asia and the Pacific Islands* (New York, 1987); J. Hein, *From Vietnam, Laos, and Cambodia: A Refugee Experience in the United States* (New York, 1995); D. M. Reimers, *Still the Golden Door: The Third World Comes to America* (New York, 1985).

Roger Y. M. Chan

BONIN ISLANDS

The Bonin archipelago is a set of sparsely populated islands 300 miles from the bulk of Japan proper, which the United States administered as a territory from the end of World War II until 1968. In 1950, as part of an agreement between the U.S. military and the State Department that allowed progress to begin with Japan on a peace treaty, the United States government decided to retain exclusive control over both the Bonin and Ryūkyū Islands. Facing growing political sentiment concerning the fate of both sets of islands, Japanese Prime Minister Yoshida Shigeru* resisted surrendering formal claim to them in a peace treaty. John Foster Dulles*, the American representative charged with negotiating the treaty, was sympathetic and concerned, but the U.S. military's adamant opposition to any reconsideration made it impossible for him to act on this sentiment. During a briefing of the U.S. Senate Foreign Relations Committee, however, several senators informed Dulles that the language about the Bonin and Ryūkyū Islands reeked of imperialism. To satisfy both the U.S. military and the U.S. Senate, Dulles ultimately invented the legal concept of "residual sovereignty." According to this formula, the inhabitants of the islands would keep their Japanese citizenship and the territory eventually would revert to Japanese administration at some future date.

The Japanese government always claimed it wanted the return of both the Bonin and Ryūkyū Islands, but a variety of other issues dominated public attention in the 1950s. One of those was the negotiation of the U.S.-Japan Mutual Cooperation and Security Treaty* signed in 1960. Its ten-year limit eventually forced the Bonin Islands to the forefront of U.S.-Japanese relations because several political groups opposed to the alliance attempted to use the prolonged U.S. occupation of Japanese territory to turn nationalist sentiment against the United States. With this in mind, Japanese Foreign Minister Miki Takeo* on 15 July 1967, while discussing Okinawa with U.S. Ambassador U. Alexis Johnson*, recommended that Washington and Tōkyō focus on the Bonins, since there were too many issues blocking a settlement of the Okinawa Controversy*. Johnson privately agreed, and in a message sent back to Washington recommended that the United States return the islands. From that point, until the arrival of Japanese Prime Minister Satō Eisaku* in November, the U.S. government debated the fate of the islands. Secretary of State Dean Rusk* argued that Satō had been a staunch supporter of the U.S. effort in the Second Indochina War* and deserved help with his political problems. The Joint Chiefs of Staff, however, thought that returning the islands would increase pressure for the return of the Ryūkyūs. President Lyndon B. Johnson* was willing to return the islands, but was not about to give them up without getting something in return. Satō also wanted to get as much out of the meeting as he could, and give as little as possible in return.

Satō sent professor Wakaizumi Kei, an old friend of National Security Adviser Walt W. Rostow*, to Washington to conduct final negotiations. Wakaizumi proposed that the final communiqué say that the return of Okinawa would take place "within a few years." Although receptive, Johnson wanted to sample congressional opinion before he agreed. However, Senator Richard Russell of Georgia, chairman of the Armed Services Committee, believed it was unwise of the United States to commit to such an explicit statement. Johnson, unwilling to cross an old mentor, backed away from the proposed Japanese language. In his last meeting with Satō before the public release of the communiqué announcing the return of the Bonin chain, Johnson upped the cost of the islands. He told Satō he wanted Japan to increase its economic aid to Indonesia* and pay for an educational television system in the Republic of Vietnam*. Satō's reply was evasive. Johnson noticed the ambiguity of this response, and immediately announced their deal after their private meeting ended. Satō, later that day in a speech in which he referred to the importance of U.S.-Japanese relations, omitted a section expressing support for the American war effort, leaving it to his interpreter to read the section aloud in English. Few Americans noticed. He stalled on the other elements of his deal with Johnson, until events, such as the fall of Saigon, no longer made them relevant. The Bonin Islands were returned to Japanese administration in June 1968 through an executive order. *See also* Battle of Iwo Jima.

U. A. Johnson, *The Right Hand of Power* (Englewood Cliffs, NJ, 1984); N. E. Sarantakes, "Continuity Through Change: The Return of Okinawa and Iwo Jima, 1967–1972," *The Journal of American-East Asian Relations* (Spring 1994); N. E. Sarantakes, *Keystone: the American Occupation of Okinawa and U.S.-Japanese Relations* (College Station, TX, 2000).

Nicholas Evan Sarantakes

BORAH, WILLIAM E. (1865–1940)

William E. Borah, senator from Idaho and chairman of the Foreign Relations Committee, sought to protect China from great power despoilment and warned against the military power of Japan. Born in Illinois, he migrated to Idaho, where he practiced law and took part in a notable case involving the murder of a former governor. Elected to the U.S. Senate in 1907 and serving there until his death, Borah was supported indefatigably by the voters of his sparsely settled state, who were proud of his prominence nationally and internationally. The senator took interest in foreign relations during the fight over U.S. membership in the League of Nations in 1919 and 1920, in which he was one of the most intransigent of the irreconcilables whose swing vote ensured defeat of the Versailles Peace Treaty*. It was during the League fight that Borah began his advocacy of what he described as fair treatment for Communist Russia, which turned his attention to the increasing military power of Japan. He believed that if the U.S. government would support the new Communist government, it would be possible to deal with Japan. This would ensure better policy for a weak China, which needed American support.

Borah's positions on all issues, domestic and foreign, European as well as East Asian, were noted for their quixotic, unpredictable nature. On no single issue was this more apparent than his support and yet lack of support for the Washington Conference* of 1921 and 1922. It had been the Borah Resolution that had urged disarmament upon his own country and the other great powers. And yet when the senator observed Secretary of State Charles Evans Hughes* not merely championing limitation of naval arms in the Five Power Pact*, but offering a Four Power treaty that was to replace the no-longer-tolerable (to Americans) Anglo-Japanese Alliance*, he refused to vote for such an arrangement; he believed there should be no quid pro quo. The Four Power Pact* could not do an iota of good. As he wrote a friend, "it seems to me that the suggestion of settling the Far Eastern question in the same conference is to subordinate the question of disarmament to the settlement of the Far Eastern question, and that question will not be settled within your time or mine." Behind the quid pro quo he saw the "cloud" of the Treaty of Versailles, the recognition of military force instead of peace, the very reason he had voted against Versailles. To mollify Borah, among other critics (albeit in Borah's case to no avail), Hughes proposed the Nine Power Pact*, a mutual agreement to uphold the Open Door Policy*. Borah considered that treaty no proper guarantee of China.

Borah became chairman of the Foreign Relations Committee after the death of Henry Cabot Lodge* in 1924, lost the chairmanship with the beginning of the New Deal, when Democrat congresses replaced Republican, but was undeterred in stating his positions. When the Great Depression and the crisis over Japanese occupation of Manchuria following the Mukden Incident* coincided in the early 1930s, he desired recognition of Soviet Russia to assist in pacifying East Asia. He was against an arms embargo, on the grounds that it would benefit only Japan, a nation prepared for war, and discriminate against an unprepared China. In 1937, he favored the proposal of President Franklin D. Roosevelt* for a "quarantine" of aggressors of that same year, for it would be against Japan. But Borah felt only mild concern after the *Panay* Incident* when Japan sank U.S. Navy gunboat in the Yangze River. He began to think that the Japanese threat, increasingly talked about, was a decoy behind which the internationalists connived to carry out their European plans. When President Roosevelt failed to ask for renewal of the commercial treaty with Japan in the summer of 1939, he saw a blunder in policy. Renewal, he said, would not necessarily condone Japanese actions in China, and he was planning a campaign in favor of it, waged together with fellow isolationist friend Senator Arthur H. Vandenberg of Michigan, when he died.

J. M. Cooper, "William E. Borah, Political Thespian," *Pacific Northwest Quarterly* (1965); M. C. McKenna, *Borah* (Ann Arbor, MI, 1961); R. J. Maddox, *William E. Borah and American Foreign Policy* (Baton Rouge, LA, 1969).

Robert H. Ferrell

BOXER PROTOCOL

The Boxer Protocol marked the first time the United States participated in an international conference as an equal to the other world powers. It ended hostilities between China and several powers (including the United States) that began during the Boxer Uprising* in 1900. Its most contentious provisions established punishment for those Chinese who led the rebellion, and indemnities to be paid by China to foreign states, organizations, and people for losses suffered during the rebellion. Each of the foreign powers with interests in China participated in the treaty's negotiations. Each participating nation's minister to China served as its negotiator, and each nation had an equal vote, regardless of the depth of its involvement in China. The U.S. minister at Beijing, Edwin H. Conger*, was the lead American negotiator at the conference until replaced by W. W. Rockhill*, an Asian expert chosen by President William McKinley*. During the proceedings, Mc-

Kinley and Secretary of State John Hay* provided Conger and Rockhill with specific instructions in hopes of moderating the treaty's terms.

The outline for the protocol originated from a proposal circulated by the French minister prior to the conference. It outlined six points: (1) punishment of principal culprits responsible as designated by representatives of the powers at Beijing; (2) maintaining a prohibition on the importation of arms into China; (3) equitable indemnities for states, societies, and individuals; (4) establishment of a permanent legation guard at Beijing; (5) dismantling of the Chinese forts at Dagu; and (6) military occupation of two or three points on the roads from Tianjin to Dagu, ensuring that the roads would be open for the legations to reach the sea or for foreign reinforcements to reach Beijing. The protocol's final draft contained twelve articles. Hay disagreed with its arms embargo clause, believing it unrealistic and damaging to U.S. arms exporters. He also wanted to see his Open Door Policy* circular of 3 July 1900 incorporated into the final settlement. President McKinley opposed the punishment provision, which included the death penalty for guilty parties, so Conger petitioned for its removal. The other powers voted to keep both the arms embargo and the death penalty provision in the final draft.

The Chinese negotiators accepted the document's terms on 16 January 1901, but the government in Beijing ordered them to contest each of the protocol's articles in succeeding conferences. They attempted to clear Cixi*, the empress dowager, of all guilt for the rebellion by blaming her decision to support the Boxers on bad advisers. They successfully argued that she had to remain in power to ensure the allegiance of the Chinese people to the terms of the protocol. To satisfy the allies' demands for justice, the Chinese negotiators supported severe punishment for the pro-Boxer leaders who had misled the empress dowager. On 7 September 1901, the United States,

Germany, Austria-Hungary, Belgium, Spain, France, Great Britain, Italy, Japan, the Netherlands, Russia, and China signed the final treaty. It required the Chinese government to pay an indemnity of $333 million to the protocol's signatories. The U.S. share of the indemnity was $25 million, but in 1908 it remitted all but $7 million to cover private damages. The Chinese government used the remaining $18 million to establish a program that sent Chinese students to schools in the United States. U.S. negotiators only had limited success at moderating the treaty's terms. They succeeded in opposing the construction of an international fortress in Beijing, and negotiating for the removal of some Chinese from the executioner's list. They failed, however, in efforts to prevent China from being overburdened with an indemnity that it could not afford. *See also* Rong Hong.

J. S. Kelly, *The Forgotten Conference: The Negotiations at Peking, 1900–1901* (Geneva, 1963); C. C. Tan, *The Boxer Catastrophe* (New York, 1955); M. B. Young, *The Rhetoric of Empire: American China Policy, 1895–1901* (Cambridge, MA, 1968).

William E. Emerson

BOXER UPRISING

The Boxer Uprising was an antiforeign and anti-Christian movement in north China that reached its peak in 1900. The turmoil and violence associated with it triggered a foreign military response that, although it defeated the rebellion, jeopardized American hopes for the Open Door Policy*. Rooted in shamanism and inflamed by drought, the Boxer Uprising was an assault against foreign intrusion in China. Although the Boxers United in Righteousness originally clashed with Qing Dynasty soldiers and officials, the Empress Dowager Cixi* in 1899 formed an alliance with the Boxers, whose most widely used slogan became Support the Qing, Destroy the Foreign. Members of the Boxer movement employed a set of rituals intended to make

them invulnerable, including the belief in mass spirit possession. "Boxing" referred to a complex form of ritualistic martial arts, rather than fist fighting, and the movement's adherents also used more conventional weapons, including swords, fire, and guns. So armed, they attacked Chinese converts to Christianity and foreign missionaries, many of whom were isolated in the interior, other manifestations of the foreign presence, especially railroads, and American, European, and Japanese diplomatic and commercial personnel and their families.

In the summer of 1900, Boxers and Chinese soldiers killed the German minister to China and trapped the diplomatic legations, foreign businesspeople, and thousands of their Chinese servants in prolonged sieges in Tianjin and Beijing. Lurid tales of the torture and murder of missionaries and of the legation sieges attracted widespread attention abroad and prompted a substantial military response from the powers involved. Twenty thousand foreign troops were deployed, including 5,000 Americans who arrived via the new U.S. military base in the Philippines*. By August, they had relieved the sieges. President William McKinley* dispatched these troops without declaring war or consulting Congress, thus further expanding presidential power in the foreign policy arena. The Boxer Uprising threatened both the lives of Americans in China and the future of the Open Door in that country. Instability endangered trade. Even more troubling, though, was the prospect that the other powers involved, the Germans, British, Japanese, and especially the Russians, would seize upon the turmoil as a pretext to subdivide China. In July 1900, Secretary of State John Hay* issued the second of his famous Open Door notes, proclaiming U.S. respect for the "territorial and administrative integrity" of China.

As Hay and McKinley had feared, though, the Russians in particular continued to carve out a sphere of influence in northeast China. In response to the Boxers' assaults on the Manchurian extension of its valuable Trans-Siberian Railway, the Russian government sent thousands of troops to occupy Manchuria and then refused to withdraw, an act that contributed to the outbreak of the Russo-Japanese War* in 1904. In 1901, the powers extracted from China a $333 million indemnity in the Boxer Protocol* in payment for the destruction of property and for the loss of life. The United States had attempted unsuccessfully to have this penalty reduced, afraid that the financial burden only would place a weakened China further at the mercy of the imperialist powers. In 1907, President Theodore Roosevelt* promised to return a portion of the funds to China to be used to send students to U.S. schools and inculcate them, he hoped, with American values. *See also* Chinese Relief Expedition; Wu Tingfu.

P. A. Cohen, *History in Three Keys: The Boxers as Event, Experience, and Myth* (New York, 1997); J. W. Esherick, *The Origins of the Boxer Uprising* (Berkeley, CA, 1987); T. J. McCormick, *China Market: America's Quest for Informal Empire, 1891–1901* (Chicago, 1967).

Shannon Smith

BRITISH COLONIALISM

Colonialism can be generally divided into two types: British colonialism and French Colonialism*. A comparative analysis of British and French colonial practices shows several main differences between the two. Most prominent was Britain's indirect rule over her colonies, even though there was an exceptional case of Burma*, which was governed directly by the British government. The mode of indirect rule separated British colonialism from that of France and most other colonial powers, which exercised direct rule. Britain also allowed its colonies a measure of autonomy, buttressed by the establishment of rule of law. The experience of limited governance and participation in democratic representative institutions in British colonies explains the striking characteristic that the developing

countries after World War II with stable democracies were mostly former British colonies. India provided the representative example of this pattern. Britain's mode of indirect colonial rule also was conducive to creation of the British Commonwealth, composed of largely self-governing member states. Another characteristic of British colonialism was smooth decolonialization, which Britain pursued successfully despite the turbulence created by the Suez crisis during October and November 1956. French decolonization, by contrast, led to the costly First Indochina War* and the conflict in Algeria. The successful transition of the British Empire to the British Commonwealth represented a major achievement of British colonialism.

In Asia, Britain established herself as a major colonial power through the extensive conquest of India (1757–1857) and the acquisition of islands, trading posts, and strategic positions from Aden to Hong Kong*. New Zealand became officially British in 1840, after which systematic colonization there followed rapidly. In the wake of the Indian Mutiny (1857), the British crown assumed the East India Company's governmental authority in India. Britain's acquisition of Burma was completed in 1886. Elsewhere, British influence in East Asia expanded with the development of the Straits Settlements and the federated states of Malaya, and in the 1880s, Britain formed protectorates over Brunei* and Sarawak. Hong Kong Island became British in 1841, and an "informal empire" operated in China by way of British treaty ports and the great trading city of Shanghai.

After World War II, as nationalism developed rapidly in many of these areas, the decolonization process began. British decolonization proceeded along with the option of retaining an association with Great Britain and other former dependencies in the Commonwealth of Nations. India attained independence in 1947. Indian and Pakistani independence was followed by that of Ceylon (now Sri Lanka) and Burma (now Myanmar) in 1948. The last significant British colony, Hong Kong, was returned to Chinese sovereignty in 1997. By then, virtually nothing remained of the empire. But the Commonwealth remained a remarkably flexible and durable institution, with the role of Britain at the center declining by stages. World War II saw the emergence of the United States and the Soviet Union as interventionist superpowers. Britain tried to exert influence over Asia, though limited, through the Commonwealth. Britain, with its depleted resources, could no longer provide a worldwide defense shield. In 1967, the British withdrawal from Singapore* and other eastern bases out of financial necessity demonstrated that Britain no longer could pose as a global power. The withdrawal was regarded as a particular blow to Australia and New Zealand, which had long looked to Britain as a major contributor to their defense. To some extent, Australia replaced Britain in both Singapore and Malaysia*. By then, Britain contented itself with exerting influence over Asia, though limited, through the Commonwealth. *See also* Dutch Colonialism.

R. Emerson, *From Empire to Nation: The Rise of Self-assertion of Asian and African Peoples* (Cambridge, MA, 1960); D. K. Fieldhouse, *The Colonial Empires: A Comparative Survey from the Eighteenth Century* (London, 1966); J. S. Furnivall, *Colonial Policy and Practice: A Comparative Study of Burma and Netherlands India* (Cambridge, UK, 1948); W. D. McIntyre, *The Significance of the Commonwealth, 1965–90* (London, 1991).

Han Kyu-sun

BRUCE, DAVID K. E. (1898–1977)

David K. E. Bruce was among the most respected and professional of twentieth-century American diplomats, the only man ever to serve as U.S. ambassador to France, Germany, and Britain. Bruce's interest in what was then French Indochina* developed during his service in Paris as chief of the European Cooperation Administration

(1948–1949), U.S. ambassador to France (1949–1952), and American observer to the European Defense Community interim committee and U.S. representative to the nascent European Coal and Steel Community (1953–1955). In these years, Bruce, who did not share the anticolonialist leanings of many Americans, at first enthusiastically urged greater U.S. military and economic assistance for French efforts to subdue the Vietminh* and promote the Emperor Bao Dai*, to which he thought his own government too unsympathetic. He was relieved somewhat, however, by the final French defeat at Dien Bien Phu*, which he thought liquidated an important American ally's increasingly pointless and expensive commitment to an unwinnable war.

Dubious about the wisdom of American backing of the Republic of Vietnam*, Laos*, and Cambodia*, Bruce was unconvinced that U.S. military efforts were likely to succeed. In the 1960s, he nonetheless believed that, having pledged itself to help these states, the United States should keep faith, and he therefore loyally supported his nation's policies. The increasing public protests against the Second Indochina War* repelled him, particularly the violent demonstrations of which both the London embassy and his Georgetown home were targets. His growing private doubts as to the likelihood of an American victory and the war's political costs led him to hope for a negotiated settlement. Bruce supported various proposals that seemed likely to result in that, particularly an abortive attempt to end the war mounted in 1967 by British Prime Minister Harold Wilson, in collaboration with visiting Soviet Premier Aleksei Kosygin. He therefore welcomed the decision after the Tet Offensive* of the Johnson administration in 1968 to seek peace and American withdrawal, efforts in which he participated from 1970 to 1971. Bruce in fact headed the U.S. delegation at the largely nonsubstantive Paris Peace Talks*, which proceeded for several years. Here he often found himself irritated and frustrated by lengthy North Vietnamese propaganda barrages and came to regard his assignment as an empty charade.

Shortly afterward, Bruce, a friend of National Security Adviser Henry A. Kissinger*, was named by President Richard M. Nixon* as the first U.S. head of the new U.S. Liaison Office to the People's Republic of China* (1973–1974). In this essentially symbolic position, his seniority, ability, and charm were all important assets at a critical and delicate stage in the reopening of Sino-American relations. As early as 1955, Bruce had supported U.S. recognition of mainland China, deplored the efforts of Jiang Jieshi* to embroil the United States in war with Communist China, and hoped to be the first U.S. ambassador after the Chinese Civil War*. Because the convoluted power struggles of the Chinese Cultural Revolution* were still in progress, Bruce performed few substantive tasks and had no real responsibility for policy. Yet the very presence in Beijing of such a respected and experienced official indicated to the Chinese the significance the United States placed upon their new relationship.

D. Bruce, *Window to the Forbidden City: The Chinese Diaries of David Bruce*, P. Roberts (ed.) (Hong Kong, 2002); N. D. Lankford, *The Last American Aristocrat: The Biography of Ambassador David K. E. Bruce* (Boston, 1996); C. L. Sulzberger, *Postscript with a Chinese Accent: Memoirs and Diaries, 1972–1973* (New York, 1974).

Priscilla Roberts

BRUNEI

Brunei became the newest country of Southeast Asia when it achieved formal independence from Britain in 1984. It retained its monarchy, ruled by Sultan Hassanal Bolkiah. The United States was one of the first countries to establish diplomatic relations with Brunei, formally the Sultanate of Brunei or Brunei Darussalam. Brunei maintained thereafter a low international profile. Upon gaining independence, the sultan told the UN General Assembly of his nation's "wish to be left

alone and free from foreign intervention." Brunei would not be totally isolated, however. It joined the Association of Southeast Asian Nations* (ASEAN) almost immediately after gaining independence, and also became a member of the United Nations, the British Commonwealth, the Asia-Pacific Economic Cooperation* forum, and the Organization of the Islamic Conference. Brunei also supported, although not enthusiastically, the UN coalition against Iraq in the Gulf War. Many observers expected greater support for Kuwait, also a small, oil-rich sultanate. But Brunei official statements emphasized concern about the destruction of innocent lives and sacred sites. Brunei's world position has been maintained in large part because of its vast oil and natural gas reserves, which has put the sultan on *Fortune*'s list of the richest people in the world several times. The population, at least those native to Brunei, has benefited as well. The per capita income in the 1990s was approximately $19,000, and the government paid for much of the cost of education and health care. Japan, however, more than the United States, purchased this oil. Brunei has emphasized steadfastly regional relations, almost to the exclusion of extraregional ones.

Annual surveys, *Asia Yearbook* (Hong Kong); "Brunei in 1991," *Asian Survey* (February 1992); *Southeast Asian Affairs* (Singapore).

Anne L. Foster

BRUSSELS CONFERENCE

The Brussels Conference of November 1937 comprised a futile effort to resolve the burgeoning war between China and Japan. Japan's decision to convert the Marco Polo Bridge Incident* of July 1937 into a war with China had created a crisis mood throughout the West. A powerful isolationism limited the U.S. response to verbal appeals for peace. But on 6 October, the League of Nations invited members who were signatories of the Nine Power Pact* of 1922 to call an international conference to settle the Sino-Japanese dispute. President Franklin D. Roosevelt* suggested Brussels, but denied Belgium permission to send out invitations in his name. After the conference call, he selected Norman H. Davis*, the experienced American diplomat, to head the U.S. delegation. He instructed Davis to reject both joint action with the League or any European request for collective security. Instead, Roosevelt instructed Davis to join the delegates in posing questions that would embarrass the Japanese and thereby mobilize world opinion against them. But Japan refused to send a delegation to Brussels. Roosevelt's risk-free demands assured Davis's isolation at the conference. European delegations found the U.S. program of stopping Japan with an outraged world opinion untenable. Ordered to keep alive the principles of international law and morality, Davis sought to impose the American formula on the conference, but faced increased cynicism and resentment among the delegates. Three weeks after it opened, the conference adopted resolutions and disbanded. The Brussels Conference, determined, as was the United States, to avoid both compromise with Japan and war, merely pushed the Far Eastern crisis toward some unknown and inescapable future. *See also Panay* Incident; Quarantine Speech.

D. Borg, *The United States and the Far Eastern Crisis of 1933–1938* (Cambridge, MA, 1964); R. A. Dallek, *Franklin D. Roosevelt and American Foreign Policy, 1932–1945* (New York, 1979); H. Feis, *The Road to Pearl Harbor: The Coming of the War Between the United States and Japan* (Princeton, NJ, 1950).

Norman A. Graebner

BRYAN, WILLIAM JENNINGS (1860–1925)

William Jennings Bryan served as secretary of state to President Woodrow Wilson* from 1913 until 1915. He graduated from Illinois College in Jacksonville, Illinois, in 1881, and earned his law degree two years

later from Union College of Law in Chicago. Bryan ran unsuccessfully as the Democratic Party candidate for president in 1896, 1900, and 1908. He had no foreign relations experience before Wilson named him secretary of state as a reward for ensuring his party's presidential nomination in 1912. He played a key role in establishing a U.S. policy in East Asia leading to war with Japan. After the Chinese Revolution of 1911*, President Wilson and Secretary Bryan were among some of the first world leaders to officially recognize the new Chinese Republic in 1913. In so doing, they earned Beijing's goodwill, but also received Tōkyō's suspicion for recognizing a government that Japan considered its private preserve.

Japanese relations continued to prove troublesome for Bryan. In the spring of 1913, he found himself preventing war between the United States and Japan over a California law restricting Japanese citizens from owning land. Although California passed the bill in May, and Bryan did prevent a U.S.-Japanese war, sour relations with Japan continued under Bryan's watch until World War I created a new U.S.-Japanese crisis. In August 1914, Japan threatened to declare war on Germany and seize its Jiaozhou leasehold on the Shandong Peninsula of China. Beijing and Berlin begged Bryan to intervene and prevent war in East Asia. Tōkyō, still distrustful of the United States for the California Japanese land bill, awaited Bryan's decision as to whether the United States would attempt to block Japanese expansion into China and risk war or allow Japan to pursue a course of action that, to Tōkyō, did not threaten the United States in any way. Forced between aiding Beijing and Berlin, which the Triple Entente would interpret as Washington's endorsement of the Central Powers, and allowing Tōkyō to attack and capture Jiaozhou, Bryan chose the latter.

By allowing Japan's attack, Bryan saved the United States from war with Britain and Japan, but he tacitly encouraged Japanese expansion for the next three decades. Tōkyō interpreted Bryan's decision to mean that Washington would not interfere in Japanese expansion so long as that expansion did not threaten any vital U.S. interests in the Pacific. In 1915, Bryan further reinforced this assumption when he informed Tōkyō and Beijing that the United States would not recognize any limits on the Open Door Policy* after Japan imposed the Twenty-One Demands* on China. That year, Bryan resigned as secretary of state in protest over Wilson's failure to maintain a sufficiently neutral policy in World War I. But his legacy was a Japanese interpretation of U.S. policy in East Asia that guided Tōkyō's military and foreign policy until the Pearl Harbor Attack*. Shifting his attention away from foreign affairs after his resignation, Bryan successfully lobbied for Prohibition nationally and a ban in some states on teaching evolution in schools. He regained notoriety just before his death on the prosecution team in the famous Scopes Monkey Trial.

K. A. Clements, *William Jennings Bryan: Missionary Isolationist* (Knoxville, TN, 1982); L. W. Koenig, *Bryan: A Political Biography of William Jennings Bryan* (New York, 1971); A. S. Link, *Wilson: The Struggle for Neutrality, 1914–1915* (Princeton, NJ, 1960); U.S. Department of State, *Foreign Relations of the United States 1914, Supplement: The World War* (Washington, DC, 1928).

Shawn D. McAvoy

BRYANT AND STURGIS

This famed trading company loomed large in Boston's early penetration of the Pacific. New England merchants had brought the Oregon Territory into the China trade in the late eighteenth century. William Sturgis, a tough shipmaster, was active in the Pacific trade when he, with John Bryant of Boston, formed the firm of Bryant and Sturgis. This firm revived and dominated the Northwest fur trade after the War of 1812. Until 1830, this high road of Boston commerce, bartering fur obtained in Oregon for tea and silk in Guangzhou, offered both excitement and high profits. By the 1840s, the trade had disappeared, but through the decades, it had impressed much of the Pacific world on the minds of Yankee merchants and seamen. Meanwhile, Bryant and Sturgis dominated the burgeoning hide trade in California. That trade began in 1822 when William A. Gale, a company agent, arrived at Monterey. This aspect of Bryant and Sturgis's penetration of the Pacific became well renowned not only because California hides underwrote the Northeast's leather industry, but also because Richard Henry Dana, who sailed the California shores for Bryant and Sturgis between 1834 and 1836, dramatized the hide trade in his classic account *Two Years Before the Mast* in 1840.

R. H. Dana, *Two Years Before the Mast* (New York, 1899); S. E. Morison, *Maritime History of Massachusetts, 1783–1860* (Boston, 1979).

Norman A. Graebner

BUCK, PEARL S. (1892–1973)

Pulitzer and Nobel Prize–winning author Pearl Buck was born in China to missionary parents. Her significance for U.S. relations with East Asia came from the images she projected through her novels, as well as some nonfiction essays in popular magazines, of China and its people, extolling both at a time when Americans looked to East Asia in search of friends and kindred spirits. Of all her works, the most influential and popular was *The Good Earth*, published in 1931, the same year Japan began its conquest of China by occupying the northeastern province of Manchuria after the Mukden Incident*. Translated into thirty languages, awarded the Pulitzer Prize for fiction, and made into a Broadway play during 1933 and a multimillion-dollar motion picture in 1937, *The Good Earth* tells the tale of Chinese peasant Wang Lung and his family, including his wife, O-lan. This story of a common man and his attachment to his land and the travails he and his family endure struck a responsive chord with Americans during the Great Depression.

After the outbreak of World War II, Buck wrote essays for *Life* magazine and other publications, in which she defended the Guomindang* (Nationalist) government under the leadership of Jiang Jieshi*. She also began the East and West Association, a nonprofit organization designed to promote better understanding between the peoples of Asia and the United States. Buck's writings and activities, along with those of others such as Henry R. Luce*, were part of a wartime effort to see in the Chinese people kindred spirits, almost aspiring Americans, during that nation's brutal fight against Japan in the Pacific war. After World War II, this reinforced the hostility of the American people toward the Chinese Communist Party* during the Chinese Civil War* and then against the People's Republic of China*. Meanwhile, Buck created the Pearl S. Buck Foundation, which assisted Amerasian children, notably those born to U.S. servicemen who had returned to the United States.

P. S. Buck, *The Good Earth* (New York, 1931); P. J. Cohen, *Pearl Buck: A Cultural Biography* (New York, 1997); T. C. Jespersen, *American Images of China, 1931–1949* (Stanford, CA, 1996).

T. Christopher Jespersen

BUNDY, MCGEORGE (1919–1996)

As the principal foreign policy adviser for Presidents John F. Kennedy * and Lyndon B. Johnson* until 1966, McGeorge Bundy played a major role in the Cuban Missile Crisis in 1962 and the Dominican Intervention in 1965. Most important, however, was his central position in the evolving Vietnam debate, where he planned the U.S. escalation and bombing in the Second Indochina War*. Born in Boston, Bundy graduated from Yale in 1940 and was named a junior fellow in Harvard's Society of Fellows, a society of scholars so pure it did not acquire advanced degrees. During

World War II, he served in U.S. Army intelligence, and helped plan the invasions of Sicily and France. After his discharge, he collaborated with former secretary of war and secretary of state Henry L. Stimson* on his autobiography, *On Active Service in Peace and War*. He also served briefly as a consultant for the Economic Advisory Commission and worked as a foreign policy adviser to Republican presidential candidate Thomas E. Dewey, who ran unsuccessfully against President Harry S. Truman* in 1948. During 1949, he joined the government department at Harvard, where he became dean of the faculty in 1953. After working for Kennedy in the successful 1960 presidential election, Bundy became the new president's special assistant for national security affairs. The *New York Times* quoted an anonymous official as saying that Bundy was President Kennedy's "alter-ego . . . another Harry Hopkins—with hand grenades."

As a Cold Warrior with little knowledge of Vietnam outside the broad goals and presumptions of the Cold War, Bundy tended to view that nation solely through the lens of the war against Communism*. He believed that the Democratic Republic of Vietnam*, acting as the agent of the People's Republic of China*, sponsored the war in the Republic of Vietnam*. As a result, Bundy perceived Vietnam as a virtual test case for U.S. policy in the region. In late 1961, he reasoned for military intervention in Vietnam almost by default. By late January 1965, there was growing frustration with the quagmire in Vietnam, and Bundy headed a delegation to Saigon to investigate the necessity of initiating a bombing campaign against North Vietnam. Having witnessed the damage caused by a Viet Cong* mortar attack on a U.S. Special Forces base at Pleiku on 7 February, Bundy authored a pivotal policy memorandum saying "that the best available way of increasing our chance of success in Vietnam is the development and execution of a policy of sustained reprisal against North Vietnam—a policy in which air and naval action against the North is justified by and related to the whole Vietcong campaign against violence and terror in the south." This persuaded Johnson in response to the Pleiku Incident* to approve Operation ROLLING THUNDER*.

Bundy left the Johnson administration in acrimonious circumstances in December 1965. Secretary of Defense Robert S. McNamara* later speculated that "the true reason was his deep frustration with the war. I believe he was frustrated not only with the President's behavior but also with the decision-making process throughout the top echelons in both Washington and Saigon." Upon his return to private life, Bundy became president of the Ford Foundation. Early in 1968, after the Tet Offensive*, he played a leading role as one of the "Wise Men" in the discussions leading to recommendations Johnson accepted to deescalate the war. Nevertheless, Bundy himself remained convinced of his policy prescriptions with regard to the Vietnam War. "The war was polarizing to American opinion in ways that were certainly not foreseen by Lyndon Johnson and those like me who supported him in the basic decision he made in 1965," he wrote in 1988. "If Johnson could have carried the country with him, I believe he would have made the Vietnam War larger in the hope of making it shorter."

K. Bird, *The Color of Truth: McGeorge Bundy and William Bundy, Brothers in Arms* (New York, 1998); M. Bundy, *Danger and Survival: Choices About the Bomb in the First Fifty Years* (Melbourne, 1990); D. Halberstam, *The Best and the Brightest* (New York, 1972).

Peter Mauch

BUNKER, ELLSWORTH D. (1894–1984)

Ellsworth Bunker gained fame after President Lyndon B. Johnson* appointed him the ambassador to the Republic of Vietnam* (RVN) on 5 April 1967 after involvement in crises in Yemen, Panama, and the Dominican Republic. He became a diplomat only after a long career as a business executive in the sugar industry. During the 1950s, the unflappable and trusted troubleshooter was named to successive noncareer ambassadorial appointments to Argentina, Italy, India, and Nepal. In 1962, Bunker mediated the dispute between Indonesia* and the Netherlands over West New Guinea by successfully negotiating the transfer of that territory.

In Saigon, Bunker headed a massive mission and was in charge not only of the diplomatic corps, but also of military efforts and the Nation-Building Strategy*. Soon after arriving, the new ambassador oversaw the political evolution of South Vietnam from a military regime to an elected one. Bunker acted to prevent a split within the military, whose candidate would be most likely to win, and to ensure fair elections at the local and national levels. In the fall of 1967, he persuaded the RVN government to support an initiative to enter into direct negotiations with the National Liberation Front* (NLF) for the exchange of prisoners of war. The Tet Offensive* in January 1968 severely tested the ambassador. He portrayed it as a major disaster for Communist forces, guiding Saigon's recovery program and encouraging President Nguyen Van Thieu* to mobilize the populace. When the Paris Peace Talks* that had opened the following summer appeared to be on the verge of a breakthrough, Bunker was the point man in applying pressure on Thieu to enter into discussions with the Democratic Republic of Vietnam* (DRV) and the NLF. However, Bunker had not entirely attained Thieu's full assent, and after Johnson ordered a complete halt to the bombing on 1 November 1968, Thieu declared his opposition to participation in the negotiations.

Because of the great value of having such a senior statesman stewarding the war, President Richard M. Nixon* decided to retain Bunker in Saigon. During the Nixon years, Bunker pushed for an accelerated pacification effort and encouraged Thieu to expand his political base and to root out corruption. Eager to avoid an uncontested election in 1971 because of the serious impact it would have on South Vietnam's image, Bunker encouraged former chief of state Duong Van Minh* to run as an opposition candidate to Thieu. However, Minh eventually withdrew; neither could Bunker keep Nguyen Cao Ky* in the race. Thus, Thieu ran unopposed, forcing Bunker to face this public relations disaster. He also was a wholehearted advocate of Vietnamization*, despite the disappointing Army of the Republic of Vietnam* (ARVN) performances during the Cambodian Incursion* in 1970 and Laos* in 1971. When North Vietnamese regular forces invaded South Vietnam during the Easter Offensive* of 1972, Bunker curiously labeled it the enemy's last hurrah, although only extensive U.S. bombings kept ARVN troops from crumbling. Later that year, Bunker again became involved in the Paris Peace Talks and tried to persuade Thieu to acquiesce to the terms that Henry A. Kissinger*, Nixon's national security adviser, had negotiated with the DRV. After his return from Vietnam in May 1973, Bunker became an ambassador at large and, most significantly, co-negotiated the Panama Canal Treaty. The venerable diplomat retired from government service in 1978.

L. H. Burke, *Ambassador at Large: Diplomat Extraordinary* (The Hague, 1972); D. Pike (ed.), *The Bunker Papers: Reports to the President from Vietnam, 1967–1973* (Berkeley, CA, 1990); R. D. Schulzinger, *A Time for War: The United States and Vietnam, 1945–1975* (New York, 1997).

Kent G. Sieg

BURLINGAME, ANSON (1820–1870)

Anson Burlingame was the first U.S. minister to China, serving later as adviser and representative for the Qing Dynasty. He worked consistently to restrain Western exploitation of China and foster cordial Sino-American relations. Growing up and receiving his early education in the West,

Burlingame found his way to Harvard and graduated from its law department in 1846. Soon after setting up law practice in Boston, Burlingame entered public service with his election to the Massachusetts Senate in 1852. He was elected to the House of Representatives for three consecutive terms between 1855 and 1861. Having failed to win another reelection in 1860, Burlingame was appointed by President Abraham Lincoln as the American minister to Austria in 1861. When his appointment was rejected by the Austrian government, he was reappointed as the first minister to Beijing.

Unable to get to Beijing immediately because of cold weather, Burlingame had to spend the first six months in Macau to familiarize himself with the situation in China. Upon arrival in Beijing, Burlingame, with approval from Washington and support from British and French ministers there, carried out a policy of cooperation in China. He managed to coordinate all Western powers' dealings with the Chinese government, to persuade the other powers not to seek additional privileges beyond the existing treaties with China, to obtain their promise to support the Qing court's effort in suppressing the Taiping Rebellion*, and to remind other diplomats that they should learn more about the Chinese culture and be patient in dealing with Chinese officials, since the Chinese valued their own tradition. During his tenure, Burlingame successfully prevented the French from obtaining a new concession in Ningbo and stopped the effort to turn all of Shanghai into a "free city" under the jurisdiction of Western powers. While protecting U.S. interests in China, his efforts contributed to stable relations between China and Western powers in the 1860s.

Deeply impressed by his ability and fairness, the Chinese government, on learning of his intention to retire, appointed Burlingame as the Chinese envoy to Western powers in 1867. On his first Chinese mission to the West, Burlingame, accompanied by two Chinese envoys, was, in addition to training the Chinese in conducting

Western-style diplomacy, to inform the Western powers of Chinese difficulties and her sincere desire to be friendly and progressive so as to preempt any Western demand for more rights in China in 1868. Burlingame chose the United States as the first stop for his mission, receiving a warm welcome upon arrival at San Francisco in April. At public meetings as well as in Congress, Burlingame introduced the progress made by China and invited the Americans, in addition to a broader trade, to a more intimate examination of the structure of Chinese civilization. The climax of the mission was the treaty signed by Burlingame and Secretary of State William H. Seward* on 28 July 1868. Burlingame and his mission spent the next year and a half visiting Britain, France, Denmark, Sweden, Holland, Prussia, and Russia. He managed to moderate Britain's stern policy, but failed to achieve the same in France. He died of disease during his stay in Russia in February 1870. *See also* Burlingame-Seward Treaty; Yixin.

Li Dingyi, *Zhongmei zaoqi waijiao shi* [Early China-U.S. Diplomatic History] (Beijing, 1997); R. S. McMonigal, *Anson Burlingame: Chinese Minister to the Treaty Powers* (Washington, DC, 1946); F. W. Williams, *Anson Burlingame and the Chinese Mission to Foreign Powers* (New York, 1970).

Li Hongshan

BURLINGAME-SEWARD TREATY (28 July 1868)

This agreement made additions to the 1858 Treaty of Tianjin* between the United States and China. Anson Burlingame*, former U.S. minister to China, and U.S. Secretary of State William H. Seward* signed the treaty in Washington, D.C., on 28 July 1868. In 1867, the Chinese government had secured the services of Burlingame upon his retirement as U.S. minister to be its envoy to the Western treaty powers with the objective of reviving the floundering "cooperative policy" that called for restraint in making economic and political demands on China. Accompanied by two Chinese officials, Burlingame's mission was to visit the Western powers and inform them of not only China's difficulties, but its desire to be a friendly and progressive nation. The Chinese hoped that through personal persuasion and winning popular sympathy, he could preempt new Western demands for more rights in China. Burlingame chose the United States as his first stop, achieving there what he thought was a major success.

The Burlingame-Seward Treaty consisted of eight articles. It acknowledged Chinese territorial jurisdiction in China. While reaffirming U.S. privileges under the 1844 Treaty of Wangxia* and 1858 Treaty of Tianjin, it left decisions on future trade privileges to the discretion of the Chinese government. The United States disavowed any desire to intervene in China's internal affairs, and China granted immunity and unlimited privileges of travel, visit, residence, and immigration to U.S. citizens. It also provided the most-favored-nation status for each other in treatment of consuls and other rights. This last provision seemed to guarantee Chinese immigration to the United States. It provoked such opposition that it required negotiation of the Angell Treaty* in 1880, in which China agreed that the United States could suspend, but not prohibit, immigration. This led to passage of the Exclusion Acts*. But perhaps worse, Burlingame's speeches at the time wrongly implied that China could and did have sovereignty under a centralized government. His treaty also helped create the myth that the United States was China's main friend and adviser, leading to enunciation of the Open Door Policy* in 1899. In fact, U.S Minister Frederick F. Low* in Beijing knew that China saw the Americans as accepting concessions achieved at the point of a gun and thus "accomplices in the acts of hostility committed by" Britain and France.

D. L. Anderson, *Imperialism and Idealism: Ameri-*

can Diplomats in China, 1861–1898 (Bloomington, IN, 1985); T. Dennett, *Americans in Eastern Asia: A Critical Study of the Policy of the United States with Reference to China, Japan and Korea in the 19th Century* (New York, 1922); M. H. Hunt, *The Making of a Special Relationship: The United States and China to 1914* (New York, 1983); F. W. Williams, *Anson Burlingame and the Chinese Mission to Foreign Powers* (New York, 1970).

James I. Matray

BURMA

When Burma (Myanmar after 1989) gained its independence from Britain in January 1948, relations with the United States were cordial. But U.S. officials were wary about its new leader, U Nu*, and concerned about his anti-Communist credentials. Still, they saw that Burma occupied an important strategic place between India and China. It also produced valuable raw materials, namely rubber and oil. Burmese officials believed membership in international organizations, such as the United Nations, protected them as a weak nation near several strong ones. This consideration prompted Burma to vote for, and publicly defend, UN action in the Korean War* after 1950. This move was not entirely expected, since Burma had been the first Asian nation to recognize the People's Republic of China* (PRC) in 1949. Small amounts of U.S. assistance were sent to Burma from 1950 to 1953, when Prime Minister U Nu requested the cessation of aid because of the continued presence of Guomindang* (Nationalist) troops supported by Taiwan* on Burmese soil. Thereafter, U Nu moved more forcefully to an alternative strategy of neutralism, which he also found personally appealing. Burma played an early and leading role in preparation for and realization of the Bandung Conference*. Burma's neutralism meant it did not join such organizations as the Southeast Asia Treaty Organization* or the Association of Southeast Asian Nations* in the 1950s and 1960s. Burma's commitment to a neutralism that examined each issue

on its merits led as early as 1969 to its criticism of the Nonaligned Movement for creating its own bloc. Burma withdrew from the Nonaligned Movement in 1979.

During the 1950s, U Nu had been an active neutralist, but problems at home by the late 1950s drew his attention and that of General Ne Win*, his successor, inward in the 1960s and 1970s. Ne Win's "Burmese Way to Socialism," implemented soon after he took office in 1962, called for the elimination of as many foreign influences as possible to unify and develop from within. Concrete actions included the termination of the Fulbright Act*, Asia Foundation, and Ford Foundation programs, and the closing of the U.S. Information Agency office in Rangoon. Washington did not push too hard, however, and maintained normal relations. The low-key approach seemed effective. In 1966, General Ne Win visited Washington, and cultural exchanges resumed. Important also for the United States was Burma's muted criticism of American policy in the Second Indochina War*. Burma appreciated the 1967 provision of arms and equipment to Burmese armed forces during a time of tension with the PRC.

Relations after the 1960s were dominated by Burma's growing importance as a narcotics-producing country. Burmese politicians sometimes placed blame for the dramatic increase in poppy cultivation on the United States for having tolerated the opium-producing activities associated with the Guomindang Intervention in Burma*, and for providing a major market for the final product. Burma's own economic and ethnic troubles also were major factors explaining its involvement in the Drug Trade*, however. The United States supplied eighteen helicopters to Burma in 1974 for use in destroying opium crops; they were also useful for combating ethnic insurgents. In the 1970s and 1980s, various U.S. congressional delegations visited Burma to inspect antinarcotics programs, and to lend moral and financial support to what they often termed Burma's "sincere" efforts against drug production.

During the 1980s, trade, aid, and military relations between the two countries improved, but remained of minor importance to the United States. The democracy movement of 1988 brought Burma back to American attention and, for several years, the United States led attempts to isolate the military government. In response to congressional condemnation of Myanmar's human rights record, the administration of President George H. W. Bush* imposed an embargo on trade and aid in 1989. The military government worked to attract foreign investment, including some from major U.S. corporations. During the 1990s, some groups in the United States called for divestment from Myanmar. Official U.S. policy moved cautiously to reestablish some contacts in Myanmar while reminding military leaders that 1991 Nobel Peace Prize recipient Aung San Suu Kyi, daughter of the famous Burmese nationalist Aung San*, heads the political party that won the democratic elections of 1990. *See also* Baw Maw.

J. Badgley, "The Foreign Policy of Burma," in D. Wurfel and B. Burton (eds.), *The Political Economy of Foreign Policy in Southeast Asia* (New York, 1990); M. P. Callahan, "Myanmar in 1994," *Asian Survey* (February 1995); C. Liang, *Burma's Foreign Relations: Neutralism in Theory and Practice* (New York, 1990); D. I. Steinberg, *The Future of Burma: Crisis and Choice in Myanmar* (New York, 1990).

Anne L. Foster

BURMA CONFERENCE

The Burma Conference, formally known as the first Asian Socialist Conference, took place in Rangoon, Burma*, from 6 to 15 January 1953. The Socialist parties of Burma, India, and Indonesia* sponsored the gathering in an effort to bring together anticolonial forces that also wanted to forge a middle way between capitalism and Communism*. The U.S. official response to the conference was muted. Primarily, Washington seemed relieved that the conference delegates adopted one principle that declared that Communism "stands for the negation of all concepts of freedom, individual self-expression, and genuine mass responsibility." Of some concern, however, was the beginning of what even then was being called the Asian-African Group as a force in international relations. The attendees at the conference, which had more than 200 delegates, included official delegations sent by Burma, Indonesia, India, Israel, Japan, Lebanon, Malaya*, Pakistan, and Egypt, and observers sent by Algeria, Tunisia, Kenya, Uganda, and Nepal. Clement Attlee, former British prime minister, attended as representative of the Socialist International. Burma Conference delegates disagreed on much, but all united behind a strong call for national self-determination. Ernest A. Gross, the U.S. delegate to the UN General Assembly, tried to use some of the terms of the conference principles to promote U.S. objectives, stressing the affinity between U.S. foreign policies and the conference support for "freedom" and "individual self-expression." At the time, scholars noted a tendency toward neutralism among attendees. This sentiment proved to be among the most enduring of the Burma Conference. *See also* Bandung Conference; Colombo Plan.

R. H. Fifield, *Diplomacy of South East Asia, 1945–1958* (New York, 1958); A. Z. Rubinstein, "The State of Socialism in Asia: The Rangoon Conference," *Pacific Affairs* (June 1953); H. Tinker, *The Union of Burma: A Study of the First Years of Independence* (London, 1957).

Anne L. Foster

BURMA ROAD

The Burma Road was a route of supply to China during World War II, of particular importance to Americans in keeping the Republic of China* in active engagement against the Japanese before and during American participation in the Pacific war.

The road was originally a 350-mile pipeline to the government of Jiang Jieshi*, bringing in approximately 31 percent of outside goods to prewar China. Built by 200,000 Chinese laborers from Kunming (China) to Lashio (Burma*), the road became the principal outside means of supply to the Guomindang* (Nationalist) government after Japan captured much of China's coast during 1938 and closed the Haiphong (Vietnam) to Yunnan (China) railroad. The Japanese exerted heavy pressure on Britain to close the road, starving the Chinese government of outside support both actually and symbolically. The road was temporarily closed from July through October 1940, reopening when the Japanese invaded French Indochina*. Their invasion of Burma in December 1941 was in part to close the road. Efforts by the U.S. General Joseph W. Stilwell* and American, Chinese, and British troops to prevent the closure failed. Until Japan's control of north Burma could be broken, China received supplies only from "Over the Hump" Flights* from India. In January 1943, at the Casablanca Conference, the British promised increased aid to China and a new road from Assam Province to link with the northern part of the Burma Road. The Ledo Road was a 478-mile road and oil pipeline. As the Allies fought to push the Japanese from Burma, the road was constructed, beginning in October 1943. It was finished in January 1945. This road was notorious for its twenty-one hairpin curves, but it allowed the continuing supply of war materiel to China. *See also* Cairo Conference; Merrill's Marauders.

J. Costello, *The Pacific War, 1941–1945* (New York, 1982); E. P. Hoyt, *Japan's War: The Great Pacific Conflict* (New York, 1986); G. L. Weinberg, *A World at Arms: A Global History of World War II* (Cambridge, MA, 1994).

Katherine K. Reist

BUSH, GEORGE H. W. (1924–)

George Herbert Walker Bush served as president of the United States from 1989 to 1993, a critical period in world affairs that included the dissolution of the Soviet Union and the Tiananmen Square Massacre* in Beijing. He had prior experience with U.S.–East Asian relations as U.S. ambassador to the United Nations and head of the U.S. Liaison Office in the People's Republic of China* (PRC). After distinguished service as a navy fighter pilot in the Pacific during World War II, Bush attended Yale University and graduated with honors. Rather than enter his father's investment banking firm, he went to Texas and made a successful career in the oil business. He represented a Houston district in the U.S. House of Representatives from 1967 to 1971. President Richard M. Nixon* appointed him ambassador to the United Nations, where he served from 1971 to 1973. Ambassador Bush argued for a "dual representation" solution to the question of Chinese Representation in the United Nations* by allowing the Republic of China* (ROC) on Taiwan* to retain its membership. The United Nations rejected the appeal for a Two-China Policy* and expelled Taiwan, although it admitted the PRC in October 1971, but Nixon was pleased with Bush's work. The White House itself then was cultivating improved relations with Beijing, and Bush's defense of Taiwan helped offset criticism from conservative Republicans who had long championed the ROC. From 1973 to 1974, Bush was chairman of the Republican National Committee at Nixon's request and loyally supported the president through the Watergate investigations.

President Gerald R. Ford* rewarded Bush's loyalty to the Republican Party by giving him a choice of diplomatic assignments. Bush chose China. Although there were no formal U.S.-PRC diplomatic relations, each nation had created a liaison office in the other's capital in 1973. Replacing David K.E. Bruce* as head of the liaison office, Bush was de facto U.S. ambassador to the PRC. He learned a great deal about China and got to know its leaders during his year there, but was unable to accomplish much. Although Washington wanted to increase bilateral trade, and Bush had the business experience for such work, the PRC was not yet rushing into international capitalism. Also, Secretary of State Henry A. Kissinger* continued to dominate China policy from Washington and left no real independence for the ambassador. Ford brought Bush back to Washington in 1976 to head the Central Intelligence Agency* (CIA) as part of a leadership reorganization. In 1980, Bush sought the presidency, but Ronald Reagan* won the Republican Party's nomination and, after making the surprise choice of Bush as his running mate, the election. While serving as vice–president from 1981 to 1989, Bush made an official visit to China in 1985 to encourage more two–way trade, which then had reached an annual level of $7 billion from the 1972 figure of $100 million.

In February 1989, Bush made his first foreign trip after his election as president. A pragmatist on Asian issues, by then he thought of himself as somewhat of a China specialist. He traveled to Japan to attend the funeral of Emperor Hirohito*, and then proceeded to Beijing, his fifth time in China. He renewed his personal acquaintances with Deng Xiaoping*, Li Peng*, and other top Chinese leaders, believing that he had improved further the warming U.S.-China relationship. The one blemish on what Bush termed his "sentimental journey" to China came when Chinese security officers blocked Fang Lizhi*, the country's most prominent political dissident, from attending a gala dinner hosted by the president and to which Fang had an invitation. Already seriously at odds over free expression, in June 1989 the human rights issue exploded when the Chinese army killed hundreds of pro–democracy demonstrators gathered in Beijing's Tiananmen Square. Bush condemned the use of force, but opposed moves in Congress to impose a general boycott or to terminate China's most–favored–nation trading status. Privately, he dispatched top aides to Beijing to explain to the PRC's leaders that the United States could do much for China, but only if it stopped killing its people. Although sharply criticized for not being tougher, Bush held to his faith that engagement kept the way open for capitalist development that ultimately would lead to greater personal freedom in China and security for the United States.

H. Harding, *A Fragile Relationship: The United States and China Since 1972* (Washington, DC, 1992); H. S. Parmet, *George Bush: The Life of a Lone Star Yankee* (New York, 1997); R. S. Ross, "National Security, Human Rights, and Domestic Politics: The Bush Administration and China," in K. Oye, R. Lieber, and R. Rothchild (eds.), *Eagle in a New World: American Grand Strategy in the Post–Cold War Era* (New York, 1992).

David L. Anderson

C

CAIRO CONFERENCE

The Cairo Conference, code-named Sextant, was held during World War II, from 23 to 26 November and 3 to 7 December 1943. The conferees included British Prime Minister Winston Churchill, U.S. President Franklin D. Roosevelt*, and Chinese Generalissimo Jiang Jieshi*. It was the high point of collaboration among the three leaders. The major discussions at the conference focused on Southeast Asia and Jiang's wish to have the Western Allies launch amphibious attacks in the Bay of Bengal to coincide with a Chinese intervention in Burma*. Churchill was uninterested in these discussions. Despite Britain's cold attitudes, Roosevelt promised Jiang that the Allies soon would take amphibious actions against the Japanese. In the middle of the Cairo Conference, Roosevelt and Churchill met with Soviet leader Joseph Stalin at Teheran from 27 November to 2 December. Stalin did not come to Cairo, because he hesitated to meet with heads of states at war with Japan when the Soviet Union was not. The outcome of discussions at Teheran forced Roosevelt to retract his promise to Jiang.

The main results of the Cairo Conference included an agreement on military operations in China against the Japanese, a promise of postwar return of Manchuria, Taiwan*, and the Penghus to China, and a pledge of freedom and independence "in due course" for Korea. The Cairo Declaration of 1 December 1943 did not mention the future status of the Ryūkyūs, indicating that the Chinese view that the islands should revert to China was not shared by the Americans and the British. American officials in Washington who had studied the territorial question had concluded that the islands, if thoroughly demilitarized, could be retained by Japan. Nevertheless, the Chinese felt euphoric that at last China was accepted as a world power and assured an important role in the postwar international partnership. They also were gratified that Jiang was viewed as a major leader in the world. The Cairo Conference in effect formalized the framework of three-power collaboration. But the retraction of the Allied promise for amphibious warfare operations made the Chinese feel betrayed and belittled.

J. K. Fairbank, *The United States and China* (Cambridge, MA, 1948); T. Tsou, *America's Failure in China, 1941–1945*, 2 vols. (Chicago, 1963); B. W. Tuchman, *Stilwell and the American Experience in China, 1911–1945* (New York, 1971).

Song Yuwu

CAMBODIA

Cambodia occupies almost 70,000 square miles (about the size of Missouri) and is bordered by Vietnam to the east, Laos* to the north, and Thailand* to the west. By the end of the twentieth century, it had a population of approximately 10.5 million. The capital is Phnom Penh. A former colony in French Indochina*, Cambodia gained its independence under the Geneva Accords of 1954*. Until March 1970, it was ruled by Prince Norodom Sihanouk*. During U.S. escalation of the Second Indochina War* in the 1960s, Sihanouk tried to protect Cambodia from the conflict without overly antagonizing not only the Americans, but also the North Vietnamese, who were using Cambodian border territory along South Vietnam from which to launch attacks against the Republic of Vietnam*. He proclaimed Cambodia's neutrality and ended the U.S. military aid program in November 1963. And Sihanouk did not object publicly when the Democratic Republic of Vietnam* used Cambodian territory for transportation of troops and supplies, largely because there was nothing he could do to stop the North Vietnamese.

When the Republican Richard M. Nixon* became president in January 1969, having promised to end the war if elected, he began the Vietnamization* strategy to strengthen the Army of the Republic of Vietnam* so that it could assume the major burden of fighting the Viet Cong* guerrillas and North Vietnamese regular troops. More significant, however, Nixon decided to begin secret bombing of Cambodia. From 1969 until August 1973, Operation MENU* unleashed more tons of bombs on Cambodia than were dropped on Japan during all of World War II. The result was a radicalization of the peasantry in the areas hardest hit and a rise in support for the Khmer Rouge* under the leadership of Pol Pot*, Ieng Sary, and Khieu Samphan*. Meanwhile, dissatisfaction with Sihanouk led to the coup that brought Lon Nol* to power in March 1970. He received immediate backing from the United States and acquiesced to the American decision to launch the Cambodian Incursion* from South Vietnam on 30 April 1970. Nixon hoped to capture the elusive central headquarters for Communist operations in South Vietnam, disrupt supply lines, and capture enemy equipment. The mission failed in all three respects. Although the U.S. troops quickly withdrew from Cambodia, the bombing continued and was ended on 15 August 1973 only by congressional order.

With their military victory in April 1975, the Khmer Rouge renamed Cambodia the Democratic Republic of Kampuchea. They also initiated an ideologically driven program to realize Communist ideals. During its three-and-a-half years in power, the Khmer Rouge depopulated the cities, especially Phnom Penh, set up an interrogation center at a school that was turned into a prison named Tuol Sleng, where prisoners were known to enter but not leave, and designated certain crops for export, despite the massive starvation and suffering of the people. At first, the Khmer Rouge leaders avoided provocations toward the Socialist Republic of Vietnam*, but eventually radio Phnom Penh blared calls for each Cambodian to kill eight Vietnamese and in the process eliminate the entire population. Border attacks escalated in 1978 until the Vietnamese government decided to settle the situation with an invasion. The Khmer Rouge forces were no match for the better equipped and trained Vietnamese troops, who moved into Phnom Penh on 7 January 1979. Viewing the invasion as part of Vietnam's long-standing historical desire to dominate the region, Washington refused to recognize the coalition government Hanoi installed, which included former Khmer Rouge officers (who had fled to Vietnam) Heng Samrin* and Hun Sen*. Eventually, the latter came to dominate the coalition by the 1990s. Meanwhile, faced with the loss of economic support from the Soviet Union, Vietnam withdrew its troops in 1989. The United Nations decided in

1991 to sponsor elections, which were held in 1993 and saw 90 percent of the eligible population vote, despite Khmer Rouge threats of violence.

N. Chanda, *Brother Enemy: The War After the War* (New York, 1986); D. Chandler, *A History of Cambodia* (Boulder, CO, 2000); W. Shawcross, *Deliver Us from Evil: Peacekeepers, Warlords and the World of Endless Conflict* (New York, 2000); W. Shawcross, *Sideshow: Kissinger, Nixon and the Destruction of Cambodia* (New York, 1979).

T. Christopher Jespersen

CAMBODIAN INCURSION

The Cambodian Incursion was a major expansion of U.S. military operations during the Second Indochina War*. The decision of President Richard M. Nixon* to authorize the movement of U.S. and South Vietnamese forces against Communist positions in Cambodia* at the end of April 1970 had important military, political, and diplomatic consequences. Nixon, while gradually withdrawing U.S. forces as a part of Vietnamization* of the Vietnam War, also wanted to demonstrate his unpredictability to the North Vietnamese by employing U.S. power in ways that President Lyndon B. Johnson* had vetoed. The Cambodian operation was the most controversial of Nixon's military initiatives. In doing so, he granted the military leadership's longstanding request to send forces into Cambodia to attack Viet Cong* and North Vietnamese bases. It was also intended to strengthen the recently established Cambodian government headed by Lon Nol*.

In a nationally televised address, Nixon justified this expansion of the war as a military necessity: "I would rather be a one-term president than be a two-term president at the cost of seeing America . . . accept the first defeat in its . . . history." The incursion by some 20,000 American and South Vietnamese troops, supported by U.S. air power, disrupted the enemy's military operations, but the long-term strategic gains were marginal. Nixon's action initially won the support of most Americans, but it also touched off a wave of antiwar protest, especially on college and university campuses. Public outcry after National Guardsmen killed four students at Kent State University contributed to renewed congressional efforts to limit U.S. operations in Indochina. Diplomatically, the North Vietnamese and National Liberation Front* representatives broke off negotiations at the Paris Peace Talks*. In Cambodia, the incursion forced North Vietnamese and Viet Cong forces to operate from deeper inside Cambodian territory and to increase their support of the Khmer Rouge*, which contributed to a weakening of the Lon Nol government's hold on power. *See also* Operation MENU.

A. Isaacs, *Without Honor: Defeat in Vietnam and Cambodia* (Baltimore, MD, 1983); W. Shawcross, *Sideshow: Kissinger, Nixon and the Destruction of Cambodia* (New York, 1979).

Gary R. Hess

CAO DAI

The Cao Dai, a political-religious sect formally known as the Dai Dao Tam Ky Pho Do, played a major role in South Vietnamese politics during the First Indochina War*. Comprising between 1.5 and 2 million followers and an army of 10,000–20,000, the Cao Dai was a powerful force within the Republic of Vietnam*. Ngo Van Chieu, a young Vietnamese civil servant, founded the Cao Dai in 1919. Caodaism later became organized into a formal religion in 1926 under Vietnamese entrepreneur and colonial adviser Le Van Trung. Cao Dai means "high tower," a paraphrase for God who reigns over the universe. Caodaism was an eclectic blend of Buddhism, Catholicism, Taoism, Confucianism, and peasant beliefs in spirits and mediums. The Cao Dai played a significant role in serving as a hotbed for Vietnamese nationalism in French Indochina* before and during World War II. Moreover, it could compete with the Vietminh* politically, as both were grassroots movements that had the support of the Vietnamese people.

Caodaism began as a purely religious institution, but the strength of Vietnamese nationalism impelled the Cao Dai toward political objectives. The greatest concentration of Cao Dai adherents was in the area northwest of Saigon to the Cambodian border. The headquarters of its principal branch was in the border province of Tay Ninh, sixty miles northwest of Saigon. When the first temporal pope, Le Van Trung, died in 1935, Pham Cong Tac gained power and led the movement into nationalist channels. In 1938, the Cao Dai established its own private army to protect the property of members and gradually became a semiautonomous state in the Mekong Delta. As Caodaism spread rapidly among government officials, landowners, students, and peasants, the French colonial administration grew increasingly nervous, closing Cao Dai chapels, forbidding meetings, arresting leaders, and exiling Pham Cong Tac to Madagascar. In response, the Cao Dai cooperated with Japan during World War II to obtain protection from the French and joined the Vietminh in resisting the return of French troops to Cochin China. For a short time after French power collapsed in March 1945, the Cao Dai came close to gaining dominance over all other groups (including the Vietminh) operating in the south. After the Vietminh's attempts to liquidate them, after the end of World War II, most of the Cao Dai nominally cooperated with the French in return for arms, assistance, and autonomy in areas under Cao Dai control.

The Cao Dai was one of the few political groups outside the Vietminh that had any kind of popular base after World War II. Maintaining armies and imposing levies on local populations, it proclaimed allegiance only to Emperor Bao Dai*, who regularly appointed Cao Dai representatives to his cabinets. After the Geneva Conference of 1954*, Cao Dai leaders unsuccessfully resisted the attempt by Prime Minister Ngo Dinh Diem* to consolidate his authority over South Vietnam. In February 1955, the French ended their subsidies to the Cao Dai, causing the dissolution of the Cao Dai army. In March 1955, the Cao Dai and two other sects, the Hoa Hao and Binh Xuyen*, delivered an ultimatum to Diem, demanding that he broaden his government. Diem refused and the sects entered into open conflict with the Vietnamese National Army (VNA). American officials struggled to stop the fighting, fearing that the sects would bring down Diem's regime. However, Cao Dai leaders were forced under military pressure to yield their independence to Diem. Pham Cong Tac fled to Cambodia* in 1956, and the VNA seized control of Tay Ninh. Most Cao Dai leaders then were incorporated into the South Vietnamese bureaucracy and military. During the Second Indochina War*, the Cao Dai cooperated somewhat reluctantly with the Saigon regime against the National Liberation Front*. After reunification in 1975, the government of the Socialist Republic of Vietnam* restricted Cao Dai activities, but since the late 1980s, Caodaists have enjoyed more freedom and a reputed membership of between 4 and 5 million. *See also* Collins Mission.

J. Dalloz, *The War in Indo-China 1945–54* (Dublin, 1990); B. Fall, "The Political Religious Sects of Vietnam," *Pacific Affairs* (September 1955); E. Hammer, *The Struggle for Indochina, 1940–1955* (Stanford, CA, 1966); R. D. Schulzinger, *A Time for War: The United States and Vietnam, 1941–1975* (New York, 1997); D. Warner, *The Last Confucian: Vietnam, South-East Asia, and the West* (New York, 1964).

Kathryn C. Statler

CARTER, JIMMY (1924–)

As the first U.S. president after the Second Indochina War*, James Earl Carter sought to engineer major changes in both the tone and substance of American foreign relations, changes with profound implications for U.S.–East Asian relations. Above all, he strove to distance himself from what he considered the amoral policies of his immediate predecessors, Richard M. Nixon* and Gerald R. Ford*, by emphasizing the moral foundations of U.S. foreign policy. Carter also expressed his determination to abandon the single-minded American fixation with containment of the Soviet Union, and announced his intention to normalize relations with the People's Republic of China* (PRC). A former governor of Georgia who was not well known nationally, he owed his election in 1976 in no small measure to the anti-Vietnam, anti-Watergate revulsion that swept the American electorate. Echoing Woodrow Wilson* with his assertions that U.S. policy should be "rooted in our moral values" and "designed to serve mankind," Carter articulated a fresh, idealistic vision that highlighted the U.S. commitment to human rights while eschewing militaristic solutions to foreign affairs challenges. His early initiatives in East Asia flowed from those overarching precepts. For example, during the campaign, he promised that, if elected, he would remove U.S. troops from the Republic of Korea*; he even implied his intention to reconsider the U.S. security commitment to the regime of Pak Chŏng-hŭi* because of the South Korean president's "repugnant" repression of internal critics.

Upon becoming president, Carter reiterated his views regarding South Korea. In February, he created a commission to explore and make recommendations about the normalization of relations with Vietnam. Each of these initiatives quickly stalled, however. Carter's proposed withdrawal of U.S. troops stationed in Korea met strong resistance from South Korea, Japan, and even within his own inner circle. In a pattern frequently repeated throughout the Carter years, the president first postponed a final decision. Then, in July 1979, after frank talks in Seoul with President Pak, he reversed himself and decided that U.S. troops would remain in Korea.

The Vietnamese trial balloon fared no better. During direct talks in Paris with their American counterparts, Vietnamese diplomats sought to tie the issue of recognition to their insistence upon the provision of previously promised U.S. reconstruction assistance. That demand generated a sharp backlash at home. The House of Representatives voted 266–131 to forbid postwar aid, reparations, or payments of any kind to the Socialist Republic of Vietnam*. Domestic pressure groups, including the National League of Families of Americans Missing in Southeast Asia*, further tied Carter's hands by vigorously protesting any move to recognize Vietnam in the absence of a full accounting of Americans still missing in action in Vietnam.

Carter's human rights campaign foundered as well. Activists in Congress had appropriately singled out South Korea, the Philippines*, Indonesia*, and Thailand* as major violators of human rights. In each case, however, Carter refused either to apply sanctions or significantly reduce aid to those governments. The administration's interest in renewing U.S. base rights in the Philippines, to cite one telling example, easily trumped its commitment to forcing reforms upon the martial law regime of Ferdinand E. Marcos*. Carter similarly soft-pedaled his criticisms of Indonesia's bloody repression of freedom fighters in East Timor, after the Indonesian military's occupation of that former Portuguese colony late in 1975. His toothless human rights policy received another blow when Vietnam's invasion of Cambodia* in December 1978 once again brought security concerns to the forefront of U.S.–East Asian relations. Hanoi's aggression seemed to fit, according to many Carter administration insiders, a disturbing pattern of increasingly aggressive and adventuristic behavior by the Soviet Union and states closely allied with it. In an effort to contain Vietnam, the United States joined with the Association of Southeast Asian Nations* (ASEAN) to condemn the Vietnamese invasion and subsequent occupation of Cambodia. His normalization initiative regarding Vietnam was put in the deep freeze.

A sharp deterioration of Soviet-American relations during the second half of Carter's term directly affected U.S.-Chinese relations. Key administration strategists increasingly touted China's value as a counterweight to Soviet expansion, a view the president himself ultimately accepted. His decision to accord formal recognition to the PRC in January 1979 owed much to his interest in nurturing a strategic partnership with Beijing. That month, Vice Premier Deng Xiaoping*, the PRC's paramount leader, arrived in Washington for an official visit that underscored the importance attached to China as part of a re-invigorated U.S. effort to contain the Soviet Union. Significantly, Carter did not oppose China's decision to initiate a brief border conflict with Vietnam shortly after the Washington meetings. And after Vietnamese forces moved into Cambodia, the PRC joined with the ASEAN states and the United States in a common front against Vietnam, much to the president's satisfaction. Carter's China policy thus dramatized how his initial promotion of human rights and the concomitant emphasis on settling lingering disputes had given way by 1979 to a preoccupation with building military strength and strategic partnerships to contain the Soviet Union—and Vietnam. This shift even affected U.S. relations with Japan, relatively placid under Carter, as the United States began pressing the Japanese to assume greater responsibility for their own defense and pay more for it. By the end of the Carter presidency, containment of the Soviet Union once again dominated U.S.–East Asian policy.

Z. Brzezinski, *Power and Principle: Memoirs of the National Security Adviser, 1977–1981* (New York, 1983); J. Carter, *Keeping Faith: Memoirs of a President* (New York, 1982); R. J. McMahon, *Limits of Power: The United States and Southeast Asia Since World War II* (New York, 1999); G. Smith, *Morality, Reason, and Power: American Diplomacy in the Carter Years* (New York, 1986).

Robert J. McMahon

CASTLE, WILLIAM R. JR. (1878–1963)

Throughout his career in the State Department, and in particular from 1929 onward, the policy prescriptions of William R. Castle Jr. acted as a tempering influence on a U.S. policy toward Japan that was characterized by increasing friction. Born in Honolulu, Castle graduated from Harvard University in 1900. He held various administrative posts at Harvard until he became director of the Bureau of Communications of the American Red Cross during World War I. At the end of the war, he was appointed as a special assistant to the State Department, serving thereafter from 1921 to 1927 as chief of the department's Division of West European Affairs. In 1927, Castle was promoted to assistant secretary of state. Three years later, President Herbert Hoover*, his close friend, named him special ambassador to Japan. Upon returning to Washington, Castle became undersecretary of state. He returned to private life after the 1932 presidential elections.

Prior to 1929, East Asia had been of only peripheral interest to Castle, but after his posting to Japan, he devised a coherent formula for U.S. policy in the Pacific. He perceived Japan as the only hope for order in East Asia, arguing that the United States ought to anchor its policy to that nation to protect its economic and strategic interests in the region. By labeling himself a "friend of Japan," Castle placed himself in opposition to his direct superior Secretary of State Henry L. Stimson*. Stimson adopted a coercive stance toward Japan as chairman of the U.S. delegation to the London Naval Conference of 1930*, insisting that the Japanese accept the naval ratios agreed to at the Washington Conference* in 1921 and 1922. Eventually, Stimson was forced to negotiate, and later admitted that Castle's actions as ambassador to Japan helped secure Japanese agreement to the London Naval Treaty.

After the Mukden Incident* in September 1931, Undersecretary Castle reiterated his belief that Japan was a force for order in East Asia. He argued that Japan's control of Manchuria was to be preferred over that of China. Over the ensuing months, Castle worked hard to preclude Japanese resentment toward U.S. policy, successfully opposing Stimson's proposed economic sanctions. In January 1932, he exercised a vital influence over the Stimson Doctrine* of nonrecognition of conquests of aggression, restricting it to nonrecognition of "treaties affecting American rights which might be secured through military pressure of Japan on China."

In late 1931, after Ambassador to Japan Cameron Forbes's resignation, Castle worked to have Joseph C. Grew*, the ambassador to Turkey, appointed to Tōkyō. He took personal charge of preparing Grew for his new assignment, which included introducing him to Eugene H. Dooman, the State Department's premier Japan expert. As Castle's protégé, Grew lent to his Tōkyō post a distinctive diplomatic manner, which to some extent overcame the difficulties and strains that characterized U.S.-Japanese relations during the 1930s and early 1940s. Following the Pearl Harbor Attack*, and in the face of considerable opposition, Grew continued to represent the strain of policy that saw Japan as a force for order. On 28 June 1948, Castle and Grew were elected honorary co-chairmen of the American Council on Japan, which was the most important pressure group in the remaking of postwar Japan.

A. L. Castle, "Under Secretary of State W. R. Castle Jr., and the Manchurian Incident: A Case Study in Diplomatic Realism," *Mid-America* 78 (1996); L. E. Ellis, *Republican Foreign Policy, 1921–1933* (New Brunswick, NJ, 1968); R. H. Ferrell, *American Diplomacy in the Great Depression: Hoover-Stimson Foreign Policy, 1929–1933* (New Haven, CT, 1957).

Peter Mauch

CENTRAL INTELLIGENCE AGENCY

Since its creation in 1947, the Central Intelligence Agency (CIA) not only has gathered secret information about U.S. adversaries, but acted to destabilize and topple governments judged to be enemies of the United States, especially in East Asia. Its origins date from the operations of the Office of Strategic Services (OSS) in World War II, which had established a productive and successful record of intelligence gathering. Agents of the OSS worked with Ho Chi Minh* and the Vietminh* in southern China to monitor and disrupt Japanese military operations in French Indochina*. With respect to Korea, G. Preston Goodfellow, an OSS operative, established ties with Syngman Rhee* and other Korean exiles and provided assistance in plans for replacing Japanese rule in their homeland. But the main impetus for creating the CIA was the results of the investigation into Japan's surprise Pearl Harbor Attack*, which appalled President Harry S. Truman* as a massive intelligence failure. On 22 January 1946, he signed an executive order creating a Central Intelligence Group (CIG) modeled after the OSS to provide the U.S. government with high-quality analysis and coordination of information about foreign threats and advantageous policy initiatives. Despite opposition from the Federal Bureau of Investigation (FBI), Truman signed the National Security Act on 26 July 1947, replacing the CIG with the CIA. The legendary OSS spymaster William "Wild Bill" Donovan, the most vocal proponent of creating a permanent intelligence agency, was made the director of central intelligence (DCI).

Under Truman, the CIA had difficulty prevailing in bureaucratic struggles over turf and funding with the U.S. Army intelligence staff, the FBI, and the Atomic Energy Commission. Also, the State Department insisted that CIA personnel abroad operate under the U.S. ambassador. Walter Bedell Smith, who replaced Donovan in 1950, was a strong and talented DCI, but the CIA's power increased markedly when President Dwight D. Eisenhower* named Allan Dulles, brother of Secretary of State John

Foster Dulles*, as DCI in 1953. The CIA's budget was increased 80 percent, allowing for the hiring of 50 percent more agents and a major expansion of covert operations. As a result, the CIA was able to overthrow allegedly radical governments in Iran in 1953 and Guatemala in 1954. With the assistance of CIA Operative Edward G. Lansdale*, Defense Minister Ramón Magsaysay* was able to crush the Hukbalahap* rebellion in the Philippines*. After Lansdale secured U.S. support for his "miracle man" Ngo Dinh Diem* in South Vietnam, CIA agents infiltrated the Michigan State University Group under Wesley R. Fishel* that was training police and adminstrators in the Republic of Vietnam*. In Laos*, the CIA operated Air America* and provided support to rightist politicians such as Phoumi Nosavan*, while Donovan, now ambasssador in Thailand*, set up bases from which Thai paramilitary units fought Communist forces in neighboring countries. Although these covert operations in Asia experienced mixed success, the CIA's instigation of the PRRI-Permesta Rebellion* to topple Sukarno* in Indonesia* was a disaster and only strengthened this U.S. adversary. By then, not only revolutionary nationalists, but much of the general public in Asia saw the CIA as a sinister force.

President John F. Kennedy* lost confidence in the CIA after the embarrassing failure of the Bay of Pigs invasion to overthrow Fidel Castro in Cuba. Nevertheless, the agency not only implemented Operation Mongoose to kill Castro, but then was involved in the ouster of Diem. Although probably not behind Diem's Assassination*, the CIA was complicit in the murder later of Patrice Lumumba in Congo. As U.S. military action in the Second Indochina War* grew, covert operations there became less significant, but revived under President Richard M. Nixon* with the Phoenix Program*. The CIA was wrongly accused of a role in Sukarno's ouster in the Indonesia Crisis of 1965*, but its involvement in the coup bringing Lon Nol* to power in Cambodia* in 1970 remains a matter of debate. Revelations during 1975 about the assassination plots and the illegal Operation Chaos to spy on citizens protesting the Vietnam War led to the creation of the president's Intelligence Oversight Board and an Intelligence Committee in each house of Congress. In 1977, President Jimmy Carter* increased oversight of the CIA and reduced its budget, but then reversed this policy to show toughness after the Soviet invasion of Afghanistan. Under Ronald Reagan*, the CIA's power reached a new level under DCI William Casey, who authorized covert operations worldwide to undermine Communist regimes from Nicaragua to Afghanistan. After the Iran-Contra scandal brought new controls on the CIA, the collapse of the Soviet Union in 1991 came as a surprise to the agency. With the end of the Cold War, the CIA searched for new ways to show the value of intelligence gathering because there no longer was any need for secret manipulation of political and economic events in other nations. In 1996, new DCI John M. Deutch tried to consolidate the twelve intelligence agencies competing with the CIA, but dealt more with repairing damage to the agency's image resulting from the espionage of treasonous agent, Aldrich H. Ames in 1994. After George J. Tenet replaced him as DCI in July 1997, Deutch himself came under investigation in 2000 for mishandling classified documents.

W. Colby and P. Forbath, *Honorable Men: My Life in the CIA* (New York, 1978); R. Jeffreys-Jones, *The CIA and American Democracy* (New Haven, CT, 1898); R. J. McMahon, *The Limits of Empire: The United States and Southeast Asia Since World War II* (New York, 1999); J. Ranelagh, *The Agency: The Rise and Decline of the CIA from Wild Bill Donovan to William Casey* (New York, 1986).

James I. Matray

CHAEBŎL

Chaebŏl is a Korean word used to denote large family-run business conglomerates.

They were modeled after the Japanese prewar *Zaibatsu**, and the Chinese characters used for both terms are the same. In the era after World War II, Korean *chaebŏl* differed from their Japanese counterparts in two ways. First, they were not allowed to own shares in banks until 1981. Second, they generally did not guarantee lifetime employment. The relationship between the Korean state and the *chaebŏl* has gone through dramatic changes since the 1940s. In the developmental phase of Korea's industrialization, the state played a major role in providing the *chaebŏl* with loan capital and production targets. In the 1970s, Hyundai, Korea's largest conglomerate, grew at an annual average rate of 38 percent, almost five times the growth rate of the country's entire economy. By the late 1980s, the ten largest *chaebŏl* employed almost 12 percent of all manufacturing workers, dominating key sectors of the economy such as heavy industry and chemicals. By this time, the economic power of the *chaebŏl* gave Korean conglomerates greater relative autonomy from the state, and the government of the Republic of Korea* began to accept more of a regulatory role in South Korea's economy.

In the 1990s, Korean *chaebŏl* accelerated their investments in the United States. In 1994, Hyundai Electronic Industries bought Symbios Incorporated from American Telephone and Telegraph for $300 million. This deal inaugurated a wave of further Korean direct investment in the American marketplace. By the end of 1995, there were 109 nonbank branch plants of South Korean companies in the United States, employing some 23,000 people and selling almost $24 billion in goods. There were twenty-six Korean bank branch plants with seven subsidiaries by the end of 1996. The East Asian Financial Crisis* that began in late 1997 had a significant impact both on Korean investments in the United States and on American business relations with Korean *chaebŏl*. Many *chaebŏl* were blamed for South Korea's economic distress, and the government ordered them to restructure their businesses. In the United States, Korean bank branches lost their profitability and were forced to shut down. Samsung closed its American headquarters in New Jersey, and the SK Group began to lay off several hundred employees in New York. Symbios was sold to a California company at less than market price. There was speculation that the Lucky Goldstar Group might seek bankruptcy protection for its controlling interest in Zenith.

The economic crisis opened the door for increased foreign and U.S. investment in Korean *chaebŏl*. Daewoo encouraged General Motors to reinvest in its motor division. Ford announced an interest in purchasing Kia Motors, the only *chaebŏl* not managed as a family enterprise. Samsung also was engaged in discussions with General Electric and Hewlett-Packard to sell off assets to raise $13 billion and pay off debts. In the spring of 1998, the South Korean government of President Kim Dae-jung* passed legislation permitting 100 percent foreign ownership of Korean businesses. Although some U.S. businesses saw opportunities in the crisis, the surviving *chaebŏl* laid off up to 30 percent of their work orces, contributing to a social climate in South Korea that became much more unstable and insecure. The 1997 economic crisis caused the Kim administration to press somewhat reluctant *chaebŏl*s to implement a significant restructuring of their businesses.

E. M. Kim, *Big Business, Strong State: Collusion and Conflict in South Korean Development, 1960–1990* (Albany, NY, 1997); J. Lie, *Han Unbound: The Political Economy of South Korea* (Stanford, CA, 1998); *New York Times*, 1997.

Steven Hugh Lee

CHAFFEE, ADNA R. (1842–1914)

In 1900, Adna R. Chaffee was selected by President William McKinley* to lead the China Relief Expedition*, the contemporary term describing U.S. participation in the multinational force that relieved the siege of the European Legation Quarter in Beijing during the Boxer Uprising*. He stayed in Beijing for one year as commander of U.S. occupation forces, earning a positive evaluation from Qing civil servants with whom he cooperated to restore civil order, distribute food, and establish public health and sanitation programs. Born in Ohio, Chaffee fought with the Sixth U.S. Cavalry in the American Civil War, rising from private to first lieutenant. He served throughout the Indian War period in various cavalry regiments, rising to the rank of lieutenant colonel by 1897. During the rapid expansion of the U.S. Army during the Spanish-American War* and Philippine-American War*, Chaffee received several "volunteer" or temporary general officer commissions. During the Santiago campaign in Cuba, he commanded a brigade and later served as chief of staff to the first U.S. military governor of Cuba.

In 1901, Chaffee succeeded General Arthur MacArthur* as military governor of the Philippines*, where he presided over the final pacification campaigns in southern Luzon and on the Visayan island of Samar, both involving population concentration and widespread property destruction outside secure zones. Although several of his key subordinates were criticized severely or court-martialed for their roles in pacification of Samar, Chaffee does not appear to have issued any illegal orders leading to specific atrocities. In any event, he held senior leadership positions in all three of the nation's turn-of-the-century colonial occupations: Cuba, China, and the Philippines. He was promoted to lieutenant general in 1904, and served as chief of staff of the U.S. Army between 1904 and 1906. He retired from the service in 1906.

W. H. Carter, *The Life of Lieutenant General Chaffee* (Chicago, 1917); J. M. Gates, *Schoolbooks and Krags: The United States Army in the Philippines, 1898–1902* (Westport, CT, 1973); M. H. Hunt,

"The Forgotten Occupation: Peking, 1900–1901," *Pacific Historical Review* (November 1979); B. R. Linn, *The Philippine War, 1899–1902* (Lawrence, KS, 2000).

John S. Reed

CHANG HSUEH-LIANG

See ZHANG XUELIANG

CHANG MYŎN

See JANG MYŎN

CHANG TSO-LIN

See ZHANG ZUOLIN

CHEFOO CONVENTION

This agreement concluded between the Great Britain and Qing China in 1876 was one of the many unequal treaties between China and the foreign powers in the nineteenth century. It affected the position of the United States in China in that the privileges granted to the British were extended automatically to the Americans under the unilateral most-favored-nation treaty between China and United States. As a result of this, further Sino-American contact was made possible, including Chinese students being sent to study in American colleges on official scholarships. Under the leadership of Rong Hong*, the first group of about twenty teenagers arrived at the United States in 1877 and entered colleges in the East, mainly in Connecticut.

Beginning in 1870, Britain activated its scheme to expand access to the Chinese market, particularly the interior, southwest region. An exploration team was formed, with British Vice Consul Augustus Margary as the leader, for the purpose of opening a new trading route connecting the English base in Shanghai with British India. The Margary team traveled along the Yangze River and penetrated into its upper valley, where China was not open to the foreign trade. In 1875, the team reached the remote Yunnan Province in southwestern China and was raided by some non-Chinese ethnic aboriginals. Margary was killed in the battle. Britain responded by initiating negotiations with China for settlement, with military threat as a potential sanction. After a year of diplomatic wrangling, the Chefoo Convention was concluded. Under this agreement, the British acquired access to the southwestern Chinese provinces and a lower tariff on English imports. It also allowed the British to enter Tibet*, then a tributary state of China, either from India or from the Chinese adjoined provinces. As part of the settlement, China agreed to dispatch a high-ranking official as envoy to London to deliver a formal apology to Britain for the killing of Margary.

The United States then was preoccupied with Reconstruction after the Civil War and therefore did not play any part in the making of the Chefoo Convention. Under the Sino-American Treaty of Wangxia* in 1844, however, the United States enjoyed the most-favored-nation status and thus obtained all the above privileges that the English had secured. Also under the most-favored-nation treaty, China sent a separate official mission to the United States under Chen Lanbin, a third-ranked court official. Chen subsequently became the first Chinese permanent ambassador to Washington, whose tenure was between 1876 and 1878. Chen's was the first official mission by China's government to the United States since Anson Burlingame* led his mission in 1868. The Chefoo Convention therefore was significant for Sino-American relations in that it initiated a high-level official communication between the two governments, a goal that the United States had wanted since the *Empress of China** visited Guangzhou in 1784.

Gu Tinglong (ed.), *Zhongguo jindai shi cidian* [Dictionary of Modern Chinese History] (Shanghai, 1982); A. X. Jiang, *The United States and China* (Chicago, 1988).

Li Yi

CHEN GUANGFU (1881–1976)

Chen Guangfu was an important Chinese financial adviser during the years before World War II who negotiated a number of economic agreements with the United States improving and strengthening Sino-American relations. While attending the Louisiana Purchase Centennial Exposition in St. Louis in 1904, he decided to stay in the United States to pursue his studies in commerce and finance. On his graduation from the University of Pennsylvania with a doctorate in 1909, Chen returned to China and thereafter engaged in Chinese financial affairs. During his economic career, he always gave prominence to international trade, especially the economic connections with the United States. In 1935, China's government confronted a financial crisis and had to reform its currency system based on the silver standard. Chen was appointed chief representative to negotiate, in the capacity of a banker, a loan from the United States for China's new monetary system. In May 1936, Chen concluded the Silver Agreement with U.S. Secretary of the Treasury Henry Morgenthau Jr. Apart from helping to stabilize the Chinese foreign exchange, enable the new monetary system to be established, and thus to keep China from a financial crisis, the Silver Agreement promoted closer Sino-American economic relations and deepened American interests in China.

In 1938, the Japanese broadened the war begun in China the prior year with the Marco Polo Bridge Incident* and bombarded densely populated cities. In response, the United States began to emphasize the importance of assistance to China. President Franklin D. Roosevelt* was willing to help China, but was hindered by the Neutrality Laws of the 1930s. To find a way out of the difficulty, the Roosevelt administration secretly informed Chinese Treasury Minister Kung Xiangxi* of its hope for Chen to go to the United States to discuss the matter. On 9 September, Chen and his assistants left for the

United States in secret. With the support of Morgenthau, as well as Roosevelt, Chen secured the Tung Oil Credit of $25 million in December and then the Tin Credit of $20 million in April 1940. The two loans had such a positive effect on Chinese finances at a time when China was resisting Japan alone that, on hearing the news, Generalissimo Jiang Jieshi* sent a telegram to Chen praising his accomplishment. After returning home, to ensure repayment of the credits on time, Chen charged the Reconstruction Corporation to buy tung oil and hog bristles and transport the goods in every possible way. He also set up an office in the United States for receiving the goods and supervising repayment. His efforts resulted in payment on time, and his conscientious attitude earned him much prestige in the United States. When Lauchlin Currie, Roosevelt's personal representative, visited China in 1941, he praised Chen as an outstanding financier and urged Jiang to rely on him for advice. Jiang intended to name Chen as the treasury minister, but Chen refused the appointment.

Li Xin (ed.), *Zhonghua Minguo renwu zhuan* [Who's Who of the Republic of China], vol. 2 (Beijing, 1980); M. Schaller, *The U.S. Crusade in China, 1938–1945* (New York, 1979).

Cai Daiyun

CHENNAULT, ANNA CHEN (1925–   )

Anna Chen Chennault (née Chen Hsiengmei), the Chinese-born widow of General Claire L. Chennault* of the World War II Flying Tigers, has been an influential informal diplomat in U.S.–East Asian relations. Her activities built and cultivated trans-Pacific contacts and connections to political, economic, military, and social leaders. As the first female correspondent for the China Central News Agency, Anna Chen first met Chennault in 1944 when her beat was the U.S. Fourteenth Air Force. Following their marriage after the war, she made vital connections to Asian and American leaders while working as the public rela-

tions director for Civil Air Transport, his commercial airline in China that became the foundation of her later career. Anna Chennault was tied to her husband's unrelenting calls for American action against Communism* in Asia, and his identification with the China Lobby*. Upon his death in 1958, she was imbued with his standing, alliances, and causes, and with widow status launched her American career in business, politics, and informal diplomacy. The so-called 1968 October Surprise garnered her the most notoriety, but also created very mixed reviews of her actions. At the request of presidential candidate Richard M. Nixon*, who repeatedly promised an early end to the Second Indochina War*, Chennault urged her friends—President Nguyen Van Thieu* and other leaders of the Republic of Vietnam*—in their existing inclination not to participate in the Paris Peace Talks* that President Lyndon B. Johnson* announced just before the 1968 election. At the news of Thieu's refusal to join the peace talks, Nixon's poll standings rose again after a swing toward his opponent following the bombing halt announcement, and Nixon won.

Following these machinations, Chennault rose in visibility and power within the Republican Party, mostly as an ethnic minority group leader and a fund-raiser. She helped found the Asian-American Republican National Federation in the 1970s and later was co-chairperson of the National Republican Heritage Groups (Nationalities) Council. Her career boomed as vice president of international affairs for Flying Tiger Lines from 1968 to 1976 and as a consultant for corporations such as Northrop, Grummen, and Lockheed, as she acquired landing rights and jet sales for her clients. Her efforts deepened U.S. ties to non-Communist Asian nations, which advanced the prevailing U.S. diplomatic goals of building a contingent of pro-American capitalist nations with strong economies in East Asia, especially Japan, the Philippines*, and Taiwan*, to counterbalance Asian Communism. But Chennault was most visible in the public eye as the "Republican hostess" in Washington. American business, political, and military policy makers often met their Asian counterparts at her parties, making talk of mutual interests a common occurrence. In such a "salon atmosphere," networks of activity among leaders lubricated the wheels of diplomacy with its most essential elements of communication and influence. After Nixon's Visit to China* in 1972, Chennault altered her diplomatic standpoint from that of staunch anti-Communist refusing recognition of the People's Republic of China* (PRC) to one that thawed by the 1980s to allow for resuming communications, trade, and diplomacy with Asia's Communist nations.

Chennault's lifelong contributions to Asian journalism, as well as her stature as a Chinese author, made her well known among Chinese nationals and expatriates. She served as a model for many Chinese in particular to transcend the animosities engendered by the legacy of the Chinese Civil War*, thus playing an important role in changing public opinion about the opening to China. Chennault and Alaska's Republican Senator Ted Stevens traveled to Beijing in January 1981 to reassure the Chinese leadership that despite the confrontational tone of President Ronald Reagan* in the 1980 campaign, his administration planned to maintain a positive relationship. Her negotiation of American and Chinese business ventures, as well as her personal activities in Chinese-American organizations and her writing, conveyed the message of rapprochement to many Asia-watchers. Reagan recognized her value when he appointed Chennault to the President's Export Council (PEC). Soon elected as co-chairperson, she initiated, organized, and led the PEC's first trade mission in 1983, which went to Asia, where U.S. business executives explored trade opportunities. A second trip followed, which included the PRC, as well as Japan, Hong Kong*, and Singapore*. Both trips led to the expansion of U.S.–East Asian trade and

illustrated how much Chennault's and U.S. attitudes had changed since 1950.

A. Chennault, *The Education of Anna* (New York, 1980); C. M. Forslund, "Woman of Two Worlds: Anna Chennault and Informal Diplomacy in U.S.-Asian Relations, 1950–1990," Ph.D. dissertation, Washington University in St. Louis, 1997.

Catherine M. Forslund

CHENNAULT, CLAIRE L. (1890–1958)

Claire L. Chennault was a U.S. Army Air Force officer who retired because of a physical disability. In 1937, he went to China to work for Jiang Jieshi* as civilian adviser to the Chinese National Aeronautic Commission. Captain Chennault later commanded the American Volunteer Group, known as the Flying Tigers, prior to American entrance into the Pacific war. He was reinstated into the military and later promoted and given command of the Fourteenth U.S. Air Force in March 1943. Chennault enjoyed high standing with Guomindang* (Nationalist) leader Jiang and his wife, Song Meiling*, because he promised to defeat the Japanese through air power alone, without forcing the generalissimo to engage his troops. Jiang worried about fighting the Chinese Communist Party* after the war and did not want to commit his troops to battle, where they could suffer casualties. Working with Madame Jiang, her family, their connections, and influential columnist Joseph Alsop in Washington, he lobbied aggressively for more planes before and after the Pearl Harbor Attack* on 7 December 1941. He competed with General Joseph W. Stilwell* for supplies and the attention of President Franklin D. Roosevelt*. Chennault's strategy to bomb Japan drew early support because his were the only land bases from which U.S. planes could strike at the Japanese home islands.

With Allied victories in the Pacific during 1943 and 1944, U.S. military planners suddenly had other options for carrying the war to Japan's home islands. As a result, China's centrality within the strategic plan to subjugate Japan waned. But Chennault's influence over U.S. policy in Asia revived after the war. He stayed in China after 1945, where he created a civilian air cargo company called Civil Air Transport (CAT) that would become Air America*. In 1947, he married Chen Hsiengmei, the first female correspondent for the China Central News Agency, whom he had first met in 1944. Anna Chen Chennault* joined her husband as a strong proponent for Jiang Jieshi and the Republic of China*. Along with other political and military leaders who belonged to the China Lobby*, they pleaded for more economic and military assistance to the Nationalist government in the Chinese Civil War* against the Chinese Communists. The Chennaults had limited influence on the Truman administration's China policy, but the Republican administration of Dwight D. Eisenhower* was receptive to their insistence on the need to protect the Guomindang* regime on Taiwan*.

C. L. Chennault, *Way of a Fighter* (New York, 1949); M. Schaller, *The U.S. Crusade in China, 1938–1945* (New York, 1979); T. Tsou, *America's Failure in China, 1941–1950*, 2 vols. (Chicago, 1963); B. W. Tuchman, *Stilwell and the American Experience in China, 1931–1945* (New York, 1970).

T. Christopher Jespersen

CHIANG CHING-KUO

See JIANG JINGGUO

CHIANG KAI-SHEK

See JIANG JIESHI

CHIANG NAN INCIDENT

See JIANG NAN INCIDENT

CHINA

See PEOPLE'S REPUBLIC OF CHINA; REPUBLIC OF CHINA

CHINA ASSISTANCE ACT OF 1948

President Harry S. Truman* requested $570 million in economic assistance for China early in 1948, but Congress approved $368 million, appropriated just $275 million, and added $125 million in military aid. Truman signed the China Assistance Act on 3 April 1948. Under State Department supervision, the Economic Cooperation Administration (ECA) handled the economic assistance and the Joint Chiefs of Staff (JCS) administered the military aid, with the majority of both directed to the Republic of China* on Taiwan*. In early 1949, Secretary of State Dean G. Acheson* suspended aid briefly to force the appointment of Chen Cheng as a new governor. Because of Taiwan's strategic and economic importance to Japan, the JCS insisted on protecting it, but, short on military forces, asked Acheson to do the job through "diplomatic and economic steps." Analysts added that this might require creation of a new regime. Financed by the China Assistance Act, Acheson asked the ECA to forge a Taiwan rehabilitation program, including $17 million for industrial recovery. When talks with Chen bogged down, it was put on hold. Jiang Jieshi*, though he had resigned as president, then managed to block Acheson's efforts to replace Chen with U.S. favorite Sun Liren*.

Meanwhile, on advice from the Military Assistance and Advisory Group* (MAAG) in China, Truman approved a suspension of military aid. Of the $125 million, 50 percent had been delivered, 15 percent awaited shipment, and all but $15–$20 million had been allocated. On 7 February, Michigan Republican Senator Arthur H. Vandenberg warned Truman that he might be charged with pushing China "into disaster," and Truman quickly lifted the suspension. In a meeting with 31 Republican congressmen on 24 February, Acheson, paraphrasing from the MAAG report, spoke of "waiting for the dust to settle," which the Republicans then used to characterize his entire policy. Nevada Senator Pat McCarran fielded a bill to lend China $1.5 billion, but Acheson skillfully substituted an extension of the existing China Assistance Act to 15 February 1950. Later extensions produced much less infighting.

U.S. military aid exacerbated risks to U.S. prestige and lent legitimacy to Jiang, whom Acheson hoped to replace with Sun Liren. Hence, on 5 January 1950, Truman released a statement precluding any new military aid funds. By 10 March, nearly $124 million of the existing $125 million fund was allocated, but in April, Acheson increased economic aid disbursements by 90 percent to allow the Guomindang* to spend more of its own funds on defense. He needed only to forestall a Communist invasion until September, when winter would postpone it until spring. On 25 May, the State Department asked the JCS to expedite the final arms shipments of the China Assistance Act. Later, on 14 June, it asked the ECA to formulate plans for spending all of the economic fund's remaining $60–$70 million in just ninety days. Although actual disbursements never reached this rate, all the military funds and nearly all the economic funds from the 1948 China Assistance Act had been allocated by year's end. Defense of Taiwan from invasion ultimately was accomplished by the U.S. Seventh Fleet, when Truman ordered it into the Taiwan Strait at the onset of the Korean War*. With Taiwan thus protected, Acheson secured approval for National Security Council statement 37/10 on 3 August 1950, which provided for new economic and military aid appropriations to replace those of the fading 1948 China Assistance Act.

T. Graham, "Getting Right with China," Ph.D. dissertation, Northern Illinois University, 1993; R. L. McGlothlen, *Controlling the Waves: Dean Acheson and U.S. Foreign Policy in Asia* (New York, 1993).

Ronald L. McGlothlen

CHINA-BURMA-INDIA THEATER

The Americans, British, and Chinese formed a China-Burma-India (CBI) Theater in late December 1941 following the Pearl Harbor Attack*, with the Chinese Guomindang* (Nationalist) government under Generalissimo Jiang Jieshi* included as an ally at the insistence of the United States. Part of the Allied headquarters was allocated to the British in Delhi, India, and the other to the Chinese in Chongqing. Although secondary in World War II, the CBI Theater was characterized by a high degree of acrimony between the Allies, but the decisions and actions there during the fighting had a profound postwar impact. At first, the Allies were on the defensive after a string of Japanese military victories on the Asian mainland. Burma* was the last of the countries of Southeast Asia to fall to Japan by the spring of 1942. Stressing mobility, the lightly-equipped Japanese Fifteenth Army proved more adept at jungle fighting than the British forces and used the technique of establishing roadblocks effectively against their roadbound opponent, such as by felling trees in their path. Defeat resulted in a harrowing retreat by British forces, as well as in supporting Chinese troops under the command of General Joseph W. Stilwell*, U.S. chief of staff to Jiang. The loss of British Burma was a major strategic blow to the Allied cause, putting the Japanese in a position to threaten India and closing the Burma Road*, the overland supply route to China.

Great differences over strategy, sometimes magnified by personal rivalries, characterized inter-Allied relations in the CBI theater. Britain was dubious about American efforts to supply and train the Chinese army and, unlike the United States, was not eager to undertake an early reconquest of Burma, wishing to concentrate more on the European theater, the defense of India, and on an eventual landing in Sumatra and Malaya*. Jiang Jieshi, meanwhile, preferred to husband the American supplies the Chinese army was receiving through the treacherous "Over the Hump" Flights* for the expected end to the uneasy truce with the Chinese Communist Party* led by Mao Zedong* at the conclusion of the Pacific war, resisting Stilwell's pressure for the Chinese army to go on the offensive against the Japanese in China and Burma.

Disagreements also occurred within the armed services as to how to cope with the Japanese threat. Eccentric British Colonel Orde C. Wingate preached his theory of long-range penetration, in which soldiers were to operate well behind enemy lines to cut lines of communication and to wreak as much havoc as possible. Authorized with reluctance to proceed deep into Burma in February 1943, Wingate's troops became known as the Chindits, named for the sculpted lions guarding Burmese pagodas. After early successes, such as sabotaging the Mandalay-Myitkyina railway at numerous points, Wingate made a fateful error when he ordered the crossing of the Irrawadday River to go even deeper into Burma. Pursuing Japanese divisions forced yet another British retreat out of Burma during late March, this time with the Chindits suffering heavy casualties.

Based on the success of his Flying Tigers, General Claire L. Chennault* urged a larger role for air power against the Japanese. He claimed that if given most of the supplies coming over the Himalyas and a small air force, he could destroy Japanese air forces, disrupt enemy shipping lines in the China Sea, and move on to bomb the Japanese home islands, thereby bringing an end to the war. Persuaded that this plan would regain the strategic initiative for the Allies, President Franklin D. Roosevelt* ignored Stilwell's opposition and strongly supported it in May 1943 at the Trident Conference. The Fourteenth U.S. Air Force did go on to destroy many Japanese ships

and to carry out effective raids as far as Taiwan*, but it fell short of expectations.

Among the reasons for the delay in Allied efforts to reconquer Burma were the problems the British faced in India, where the Indian nationalist Mohandas Gandhi led the Quit India movement against the British and violence erupted in 1942 against small British outposts, railway lines, and Europeans. It took a major commitment of British force, including the wholesale arrest of Indian nationalist leaders, to restore order. There was also the fear of a Japanese invasion of India supported by the Indian National Army, formed under the auspices of the Japanese and composed of extreme Indian nationalists. Under U.S. pressure, however, and encouraged by improvements in the training of British and Indian forces, Britain was willing to agree to a limited offensive in northern Burma, whose goal was to build a Ledo Road to link up with the old Burma Road to reestablish a land route to China. By late 1943, Chinese soldiers had pushed into northern Burma, followed in early 1944 by British troops, as well as by Merrill's Marauders*, composed of about 3,000 American soldiers trained in irregular warfare. British superiority in numbers, tanks, artillery, and planes eventually prevailed despite a Japanese counterattack in March–April that initially forced the British to retreat back to Imphal. In September, British forces under General William Slim resumed the offensive, crossing the Irrawaddy in early 1945, seizing the important Japanese supply base at Meiktila in March, and occupying Rangoon in April.

Reconquest of Burma was the greatest Allied victory on the Asian mainland during World War II. It forced the Japanese to divert soldiers and supplies from the Pacific fighting, though at a high cost in Allied casualties and resources as well. But China remained to be liberated, where the Japanese had undertaken their biggest offensive of the war late in 1944 to eliminate Chennault's air bases. Their success against the Chinese army strained relations to the breaking point between Stilwell and Jiang, and the former was forced to resign. Lieutenant General Albert C. Wedemeyer*, his replacement, was able to bring about some improvement in the Chinese army, but the Japanese withdrawal from south China in 1945 was primarily motivated by the desire to protect the home islands. The American efforts through General Patrick J. Hurley* to bring about an anti-Japanese coalition government of the Nationalists and Mao's Communists failed, thus presaging the Chinese Civil War*. India and Burma soon gained their independence from Britain in the wave of decolonization that followed World War II. *See also* Ichigo Offensive.

C. Burdick and D. S. Detwiler (eds.), *War in Asia and the Pacific, 1937–1949*, vols. 6, 7, 8 (New York, 1980); S. W. Kirby, *The War Against Japan* (London, 1961); A. J. Levine, *The Pacific War: Japan Versus the Allies* (Westport, CT, 1995); C. Romanus and R. Sunderland, *United States Army in World War II*, Vol. 9: *The China-Burma-India Theater*, parts 1, 2, 3 (Washington, DC, 1956).

Harold H. Tollefson

CHINA HANDS

The China Hands were career diplomats such as John S. Service*, John Paton Davies*, George Atcheson, Raymond Ludden, and others from the State Department who were stationed in China during World War II. These diplomats had extensive experience and knowledge regarding China. Some of them were raised in American missionary families there. They were fluent in the Chinese language and familiar with Chinese history and culture. After World War II and the establishment of the People's Republic of China*, the China Hands were accused of disloyalty, of being sympathetic with Communists, and of contributing to the "loss of China." Although they were exonerated later, they suffered terribly from political persecution.

In World War II, the United States emerged as a major actor in Chinese affairs. As an ally, it embarked in late 1941 on a program of massive military and financial aid to the hard-pressed Guomindang* (Nationalist) government. The wartime policy of the United States was initially to help China become a strong ally and a stabilizing force in postwar East Asia. As the conflict between the Nationalists and the Chinese Communist Party* intensified, however, the United States sought unsuccessfully to reconcile the rival forces for a more effective anti-Japanese war effort. During the war, the China Hands became disillusioned with the Guomindang government, which they believed to be corrupt, inefficient, and undemocratic. Their observations about Jiang Jieshi* and his government led them to argue for a more realistic appraisal of China and a practical policy based on that assessment. Many of the reports sent by the China Hands provided descriptions of life in the Communist-controlled area that contrasted sharply with reports of life at Chongqing under the Guomindang.

The China Hands were convinced that the Communists would win the final victory in the Chinese Civil War*. Fearing that a Communist takeover would help the Soviet Union expand its influence in China, they urged the U.S. government to extend its aid to the Chinese Communists. They believed that to provide military aid to the Communists would shorten the war, because U.S. assistance would enable the Communist army to fight more effectively against the Japanese. They also reasoned that the strengthening of Mao Zedong* and his government would force Jiang to be more conciliatory regarding a coalition government in China. On 28 February 1945, the counselor of the U.S. embassy at Chongqing sent to the State Department a cable signed by all the embassy political officers, who recommended that "the President inform the Generalissimo in definite terms that military necessity requires that we supply and cooperate with Communists" because "through such policy . . . we could expect to hold the Communists to our side rather than throw them into the arms of Russia." U.S. Ambassador to China Patrick J. Hurley* stubbornly opposed this view. Supported by Presidents Franklin D. Roosevelt* and later Harry S. Truman*, Hurley's position prevailed. The China Hands in the embassy eventually were dismissed from their China assignments. Hurley's criticism and removal of the embassy staff helped trigger the purge of the China Hands that peaked in the witch-hunt started by Joseph R. McCarthy* in the early 1950s. *See also* O. Edmund Clubb; Dixie Mission; John F. Melby; Owen Lattimore; Theodore H. White.

J. Esherick, *Lost Chance in China: The World War II Dispatches of John S. Service* (New York, 1974); E. J. Kahn, *The China Hands: America's Foreign Service Officers and What Befell Them* (New York, 1975); B. W. Tuchman, *Stilwell and the American Experience in China, 1931–1945* (New York, 1971).

Song Yuwu

CHINA LOBBY

The term "China Lobby" usually refers to a loose and disparate collection of individuals and organizations dedicated to fostering sympathy and support for Jiang Jieshi* and his Guomindang* (Nationalist) government and to mobilizing opposition to the People's Republic of China* (PRC). First coined in a program memorandum on China policy publicized by the Communist Party of New York in January 1949, the expression "China Lobby" caught on in newspapers and magazines over the next few years at a time when relations with China were a vortex for controversy. Emotionally and politically charged, the catchphrase was construed differently by both critics and proponents of the Guomindang government. Critics oftentimes used it to suggest the existence of a shadowy network of Jiang's agents, family members, and fervent American admirers who cooperated to shift public opinion and the U.S. government in favor of the Nationalist cause. Nationalist partisans instead fixed the China Lobby label on those individuals they charged with trying to discredit or deny support to Jiang's government or to give succor to the Chinese Communist Party* (CCP).

Although organized activity in support of Jiang's regime dated back to the 1920s, the China Lobby gradually took shape as a loosely knit and diverse coalition during World War II and the early postwar years at a time when the Nationalists looked to the United States for assistance, first against the Japanese and then the CCP. By the late 1940s, it included members of Jiang's family and representatives and registered agents of the Nationalist government active in the United States, together with an array of prominent figures from the press, publishing, business, labor, the academic world, the churches, and the military. Among the Americans commonly identified with the lobby were Henry R. Luce*, the famed publisher of *Time* and *Life*; Roy Howard, owner of the Scripps-Howard newspaper chain; George Sokolsky, a nationally syndicated columnist; Frederick McKee, a Pittsburgh industrialist and philanthropist; and Alfred Kohlberg, a well-to-do textile importer. Kohlberg was known as "the China Lobby man" for his acrid and persistent denunciations of U.S. China policy. He wrote prolifically for right-wing publications, circulated open letters, press releases, and pamphlets to sizable audiences, bombarded the media and policy makers with propaganda, and fed information and advice to sympathizers in Congress, including Senator Joseph R. McCarthy*.

China lobbyists offered a simplistic explanation for the waning fortunes and ultimate defeat of the Nationalist government on the mainland, pointing the finger of guilt at incompetent, if not disloyal or treasonous, officials in the U.S. government. The China Hands*, various Foreign Service officers with China expertise, and top State Department officials responsible for China policy were accused of "selling out" Jiang and "losing China." Following the Chinese Civil War*, the China lobbyists agitated for resolute support for the Republic of China* (ROC) after it fled to Taiwan*. They also vehemently opposed U.S. recognition of the PRC or its admission to the United Nations. A so-called China bloc in the U.S. Congress consisting mainly of Republicans, most notably Congressman Walter H. Judd* of Minnesota and Senator William F. Knowland* of California, shared the basic outlook of the lobbyists and echoed many of their criticisms of U.S. China policy. Only a small minority in the legislative branch prior to the Korean War*, they sometimes exerted an influence beyond their numbers in intensifying partisan turmoil.

Chinese Intervention in the Korean War* gave the China Lobby a big boost, as it became a widely recognized and controversial entity. China lobbyists claimed that the Korean War could have been avoided had the Truman administration not given away China and neglected Asia. Through its impact on domestic opinion and politics, the lobby figured thereafter in the emergence in the U.S. government of a militant anti-PRC stance, a renewed association with Jiang Jishi's exiled regime on Taiwan, and a more assertive posture toward Asia as a whole. Under President Harry S. Truman*, some of the State Department's most capable officers were driven from the Foreign Service, producing a long-term chilling effect on dissent from a China policy now closer to the China Lobby's position. During the Eisenhower administration, both publicly declared U.S. China policy and the domestic consensus on China harmonized even more fully with views found within the pro-ROC, anti-PRC constituency. During the Kennedy and Johnson years, the dominant disposition toward China remained negative in policy-making circles and domestic opinion alike, but a trend toward a more accommodating posture slowly and fitfully gathered momentum. By 1968, the China Lobby had largely faded away.

S. D. Bachrack, *The Committee of One Million: "China Lobby" Politics, 1953–1971* (New York, 1976); J. C. Keeley, *The China Lobby Man: The Story of Alfred Kohlberg* (New Rochelle, NY, 1969); R. Y. Koen, *The China Lobby in American Politics* (New York, 1974); L. A. Kusnitz, *Public Opinion and Foreign Policy: America's China Policy, 1949–79* (Westport, CT, 1984); A. T. Steele, *The American People and China* (New York, 1966); N. B. Tucker, *Patterns in the Dust: Chinese-American Relations and the Recognition Controversy, 1949–50* (New York, 1983).

Robert D. Accinelli

CHINA RELIEF EXPEDITION

The China Relief Expedition of 1900 was the U.S. component of a multinational force that raised the siege of the Legation Quarter in Beijing during the anti-Western Boxer Uprising*. It was the third U.S. overseas military effort during the years 1898 to 1902, after the Santiago campaign in Cuba (1898) and the Philippine-American War* (1899–1902). On 30 May 1900, in view of the growing strength of the Boxer Movement and widespread reports of anti-European and anti-Christian violence in northern China, a small Japanese-European-U.S. force of sailors and naval infantry, including fifty-six U.S. Marines, were sent to Beijing from the port of Dagu. This group defended the Legation Quarter until it was relieved on 14 August. On 6 June, imperial Chinese forces cut the railway link south from Beijing and began to block allied access into northern China via the Beiho River at Tagu. On 9 June, an allied relief force departed Tagu for Beijing overland, but later fell back to Tianjin, eighty-four miles from Beijing.

On 20 June, the Boxer siege of the Legation Quarter began. Three days earlier, the allies had seized the Dagu forts blocking the Beiho River. Meanwhile, the general commanding U.S. forces in the Philippines* was ordered to send a regiment of infantry to Dagu. On 22 June, General Adna R. Chaffee* was selected to lead a U.S. expeditionary force that by late July comprised a force of 3,700, many of whom were shipped to China directly from the United States via the Japanese port of Nagasaki. President William McKinley* sent these troops to China to uphold U.S. national honor and prestige, defend Christian missionaries, lend credibility to the U.S. Open Door Policy* opposing further expansion of European concessions in China, and shore up the Qing Dynasty against further collapse. McKinley ordered Chaffee to preserve U.S. political influence in China at the lowest level of political involvement and military risk, relieve the Legation Quarter, protect existing U.S. economic interests, and restrain the conduct of his troops so as to earn the goodwill of the Chinese people.

On 13 July, the allies defeated an imperial army outside Tianjin. On 4 August, a combined Japanese-British-Russian-American-French force of 18,700, with a U.S. contribution of 2,100, left Tianjin for Beijing. After fighting two actions at Beicang and Yangcun, these troops entered Beijing, raised the siege of the Legation Quarter, and dispersed Boxer forces on 14–15 August. The next day, U.S. forces assumed their occupation district within Beijing. Contemporary Chinese sources describe U.S. troops as less abusive than the Germans and Russians. General Chaffee was generally successful in enlisting the collaboration of local Chinese elites in a joint effort to reestablish public order in the U.S. sector before the return of Qing civil servants. U.S. officials also briefly established public sanitation and health programs in Beijing, to include mass inoculations, similar to contemporary efforts in Cuba, Puerto Rico, and the Philippines. President McKinley was eager, however, to disengage from China. In August, General Chaffee was ordered to discontinue offensive patrolling outside Beijing and begin reducing U.S. forces in China. In May 1901, the last elements of the Relief Expedition departed China for pacification duties in the Philippines. Total U.S.

casualties during the operation were 32 killed in action and 177 wounded.

A. S. Daggett, *America in the China Relief Expedition* (New York, 1903); M. H. Hunt, "The Forgotten Occupation: Peking, 1900–1901," *Pacific Historical Review* (November 1979); U.S. Army Adjutant General's Office, *Correspondence Relating to the War with Spain, Including the Insurrection in the Philippine Islands and the China Relief Expedition*, vol. 1 (Washington, DC, 1902); U.S. War Department, *Annual Reports of the War Department for the Fiscal Year Ending June 30, 1900*, vol. 1, part 7 (Washington, DC, 1900); U.S. War Department, *Reports on Military Operations in South Africa and China* (Washington, DC, 1901).

John S. Reed

CHINA TARIFF AUTONOMY

China's struggle to recover tariff autonomy was one of the most contentious aspects of Sino-American foreign relations in the modern era. China ceded control over tariff rates in the Treaty of Nanjing* in 1842 and in subsequent "unequal treaties." As nation-states came to see tariff control as central to sovereignty, regaining control became a rallying point of Chinese nationalism and anti-imperialism in the first decades of the twentieth century. The Treaty Powers promised to restore autonomy in 1925, but delayed a final agreement. In 1928, the newly established Guomindang* (Nationalist) government made recovery a top priority. Foreign Minister Wang Zhengting announced the new government's intention to terminate unilaterally all treaties in 1928. In response, U.S. Minister John V. A. MacMurray*, acting on instructions from Secretary of State Frank B. Kellogg*, negotiated a new treaty, signed on 25 July and effective at the start of 1929. The treaty promised to set an important precedent and end the era of unequal treaties on tariff matters. It also provided an implicit recognition of the Nationalist government, but it was not a complete success. The United States stipulated that the most-favored-nation clause still applied; China still needed to renegotiate tariff autonomy with the other powers. The government promulgated new rates on 1 February 1929, but could not fully implement them until the Japanese consented in May 1930. *See also* May Thirtieth Movement.

S. E. Koo, *Tariff and the Development of the Cotton Industry in China, 1842–1937* (New York, 1982); W. Tung, *China and the Foreign Powers: The Impact of and Reaction to Unequal Treaties* (Dobbs Ferry, NY, 1970); S. Wright, *China's Struggle for Autonomy, 1843–1938* (Shanghai, 1938).

Karl Gerth

CHINA WHITE PAPER

The China White Paper was published by the Department of State in August 1949 to demonstrate to the American public that the collapse of the Guomindang* (Nationalist) government in China was caused by its own failings and not a lack of U.S. aid. Secretary of State Dean G. Acheson* in his letter of transmittal to President Harry S. Truman* dated 30 July 1949 summed up the department's case: "The unfortunate but inescapable fact is that the ominous result of the civil war in China was beyond the control of the government of the United States. Nothing that this country did or could have done within the reasonable limits of its capabilities could have changed that result; nothing that was left undone by this country has contributed to it." The massive volume included a 400-page narrative, drafted in the Office of Far Eastern Affairs by China expert John F. Melby* and revised by Ambassador at Large Philip C. Jessup, and more than 600 pages of documents on U.S. relations with China. Acheson's letter of transmittal also reflected his belief that China, even under the leadership of the Chinese Communist Party*, eventually would turn away from the Soviet Union. He predicted that China's "profound civilization" and "democratic individualism" ultimately would reassert themselves and that China would "throw off the foreign yoke." Moreover, he suggested, none too subtly, that the United States should try to support those in China who sought this outcome.

Truman and Acheson hoped the China White Paper would silence domestic criticism that the administration had given insufficient aid to the Chinese Nationalists and end agitation for further U.S. aid, so that the administration could continue to detach the United States from Jiang Jieshi* and the Republic of China* in anticipation of its final demise. The administration's effort was unsuccessful, because its critics neither were persuaded nor silenced. To their attacks on Truman's China policy, they now added charges that the White Paper was biased and that its timing would undermine the Nationalists while they still were fighting the Communists. The reaction of the Nationalists was muted, but in Beijing, Mao Zedong* seized on the White Paper to discredit the United States and those Chinese who sought to maintain ties between China and the United States. A series of bitter commentaries on the White Paper, most written by Mao himself, launched a campaign designed to expose "the imperialist nature" of U.S. policy on China and "the illusions about U.S. imperialism" harbored by some Chinese intellectuals. *See also* Acheson's National Press Club Speech; Chinese Civil War.

The China White Paper, with introduction by L. P. Van Slyke (Stanford, CA, 1967); *United States Relations with China with Special Reference to the Period 1944–1949* (Washington, DC, 1949); U.S. Department of State, *Foreign Relations of the United States, 1949*, Vol. 9: *China* (Washington, DC, 1976).

Harriet Dashiell Schwar

CHINCOM

The CHINCOM (China Committee) was a working group set up by allies of the United States to maintain strict export controls against Communist-controlled areas in Asia. The objective of the organization was to maintain higher trade embargoes against the People's Republic of China* (PRC) and other Asian Communist states than the European Soviet bloc. The CHIN-COM was established in September 1952. The founding members of the group were the United States, Britain, France, Canada, and Japan. Its main function was to deal with daily matters concerning export controls, whereas larger issues were dealt with by the Consultative Group, which consisted of senior officials who met quarterly in the U.S. embassy in Paris.

The CHINCOM was created as a result of differences between the United States on one side and Britain, France, and Canada on the other concerning an appropriate export control committee for Asia. The United States sought the establishment of a separate Far Eastern Group in Asia to maintain higher export controls toward the PRC and the Democratic People's Republic of Korea* than what the Coordinating Committee on East-West Trade Policy (CO-COM) maintained toward the European Soviet bloc. Moreover, Washington hoped that by establishing a Far Eastern Group, it would have greater influence over trade and export issues in East Asia, including trade flows between Japan and the PRC. Britain, France, and Canada opposed the U.S. proposal because none wished to see the United States gain greater influence over Asian trade. Moreover, the Far Eastern Group would have duplicated the work already undertaken by the COCOM, and it would have taken time and effort to form a separate bureaucracy. Therefore, U.S. officials agreed to the British proposal for creation of a separate Far Eastern Committee within the COCOM structure.

Despite the American compromise over the structure and the location of the Far Eastern Committee, U.S. officials were able to enforce stricter trade lists on exports to the Asian Communist countries than the European Soviet bloc. Furthermore, Japan was pressured to sign a bilateral agreement on 5 September 1952 that stipulated that Japan embargo 400 more goods against China than other CHINCOM members.

The signing of the agreement, therefore, precluded Japan from achieving one of its aims behind its entry into CHINCOM, which was to enjoy a relaxation in its trade relations with the PRC. U.S. pressure to restrict Japan's trade relations with mainland China inevitably led to political friction between Washington and Tōkyō. To ensure Japan's continued alignment with U.S. trade control policy, President Dwight D. Eisenhower* decided in 1954 to release Japan from the bilateral agreement on a gradual basis.

In 1954, differences between the CO-COM and the CHINCOM lists became more pronounced as export controls on the Soviet Union and Eastern Europe were relaxed. The CHINCOM members became increasingly dissatisfied with the high trade limits against the Asian Communist countries because the end of the Korean War* no longer justified a stringent trade embargo against the PRC. Moreover, the effectiveness of the embargo was questioned as goods embargoed against the PRC, but not the Soviet bloc, were reaching mainland China through Communist trade channels. Between 1955 and 1957, Britain and Japan increased pressure on the United States to relax the CHINCOM controls. Despite attempts to come to an agreement, the slow progress in talks eventually led to Britain's decision to abolish unilaterally the China differential on 27 May 1957. On 16 July 1957, Japan announced that as of 30 July it would follow the British initiative and adopt the COCOM levels to all trade with Communist China. In June 1958, the Consultative Group declared its decision to merge the two lists. Therefore, 1958 saw the end of the American attempt to maintain higher trade controls against the PRC, in part because of its inability to persuade the other CHINCOM members to maintain higher trade restrictions.

G. Adler-Karlsson, *Western Economic Warfare 1947–1967: A Case Study in Foreign Economic Policy* (Stockholm, 1968); M. Mastanduno, *Economic Containment: CoCom and the Politics of East-West*

Trade (Ithaca, NY, 1992); S. Qing, "The Eisenhower Administration and Changes in Western Embargo Policy Against China, 1954–1958," in W. Cohen and A. Iriye (eds.), *The Great Powers in East Asia, 1953–1960* (New York, 1990); U.S. Department of State, *Foreign Relations of the United States, 1955–1957*, Vol. 10: *Foreign Aid and Economic Defense Policy* (Washington, DC, 1989); Y. Yasuhara, "Japan, Communist China, and Export Controls in Asia, 1948–52," *Diplomatic History* (Winter 1986).

Yokoi Noriko

CHINESE CIVIL WAR (1946–1949)

The Chinese Communist and Guomindang* (Nationalist) armed forces began a full-scale war against each other for supremacy of the country shortly after Japan surrendered in World War II. The Chinese Communist Party* (CCP) won the fight on the mainland and founded the People's Republic of China* (PRC) in October 1949. The Nationalist government fled to Taiwan* in the same year. From 1937 to 1945, the CCP and the Guomindang (GMD) successfully established a wartime United Front* against Japan's invasion of China following the Marco Polo Bridge Incident*. After the Pearl Harbor Attack* in 1941, the United States supported the CCP-GMD coalition and provided military equipment and financial aid to China. As the head of the CCP, Mao Zedong* cooperated with Jiang Jieshi*, leader of the GMD, and mobilized guerrilla warfare behind Japanese lines, reducing rent and returning land to poor peasants. His successful strategy increased the number of CCP members from 40,000 in 1937 to 1.2 million in 1945, and his People's Liberation Army (PLA) increased to nearly 1 million, plus an additional 2 million militia at that time. In contrast, Jiang, having lost some of his best troops in frontal confrontations against Japanese offensive campaigns, withdrew his forces and removed the seat of his Republic of China* (ROC) from Nanjing west to Chongqing, a remote, isolated, mountainous city.

After the Pacific war suddenly ended in August 1945 after the U.S. Atomic Attacks* against Japan, Jiang found himself far away from the country's economic and population centers and facing an unprecedented challenge from Mao. In 1944, to avoid a collapse of the CCP-GMD coalition, U.S. Ambassador Patrick J. Hurley* visited Yan'an, Mao's wartime capital, and proposed a joint postwar government in China. In August 1945, Hurley personally escorted Mao from Yan'an to Chongqing for negotiations with Jiang. The negotiations failed and the two parties began their military conflicts in north China. After Hurley resigned in November, President Harry S. Truman* dispatched General George C. Marshall* as his envoy to China in December for further mediation. Though both parties agreed to a brief cease-fire mediated by Marshall in early 1946, Mao and Jiang rejected political compromise. Mao thought that the United States had intervened in the civil war on the Nationalist side by providing Jiang with military equipment and financial aid. Full-scale civil war broke out in the summer of 1946, signaling the failure of the Marshall Mission*.

The first phase of the civil war began in June 1946 when Jiang launched an all-out offensive campaign against Mao's "liberated regions" with a major attack in central China. With U.S. aid and support, the GMD had military superiority in both manpower and weaponry. But China's spiraling inflation, government corruption, and factional struggles within the ROC made elimination of the Communist forces impossible. Exploiting widespread complaints and the desire for peace after World War II, the CCP organized its second front against Jiang in major cities through student-led, popular antigovernment and antiwar movements to isolate the GMD politically. The second phase of the civil war, from June 1947 to August 1948, turned the GMD offensive into a CCP strategic offensive because of Jiang's military setbacks at the front and political frustrations at home.

By September, Deng Xiaoping* had led 120,000 PLA troops across the Yellow River, breaking through Jiang's lines and bringing his offensive to an end.

The civil war's third and final phase included three of the most important PLA campaigns in the civil war: the Liao-Shen campaign (northeast China), the Ping-Jin campaign (Beijing-Tianjin region), and the Huai-Hai campaign (east China), between September 1948 and September 1949. Jiang lost his main strength in the three campaigns and asked for cease-fire talks. Mao refused Jiang's request and ordered 1 million PLA troops to cross the Yangze River on 21 April 1949. Two days later, Nanjing, the ROC capital, fell and Jiang removed the seat of his government with 3 million GMD troops and government officials to Taibei, Taiwan. Then the PLA pressed on in its liberation drive into northwest, southwest, and central China. By September, the PLA occupied most of the country except for Tibet*, Taiwan, and other offshore islands. On 1 October 1949, Mao declared the birth of the PRC and the new republic's alliance with the Soviet Union. President Truman refused to recognize the new Communist China, a policy that remained in place until 1979, and continued his support and aid to Jiang's government on Taiwan. *See also* China Hands; China Lobby; China White Paper; Dixie Mission.

D. Borg and W. H. Heinrichs (eds.), *Uncertain Years: Chinese-American Relations, 1947–1950* (New York, 1980); J. K. Fairbank, *The United States and China* (Cambridge, MA, 1983); X. Liu, *A Partnership for Disorder: China, the United States, and Their Policies for the Postwar Disposition of the Japanese Empire, 1941–1945* (Cambridge, MA, 1996); S. Pepper, *Civil War in China: The Political Struggle, 1945–1949* (New York, 1999); T. Tsou, *America's Failure in China, 1945–1950*, 2 vols. (Chicago, 1963).

Li Xiaobing

CHINESE COMMUNIST PARTY

The Chinese Communist Party (CCP) grew out of the intellectual and political ferment in East Asia after 1900, as the critique of traditional political culture in China deepened and views toward Western liberal democracy darkened. The New Culture Movement promoted a broad rejection of Confucianism and a search for other models for China's national salvation and modernization. Although the ideals of representative democracy at first had been attractive to nationalist leaders, the decision by the Allies in the Versailles Peace Treaty* to allow Japan to retain German territorial concessions in China was seen by many Chinese as betrayal. The Russian Revolution provided inspiration for many radicals, who saw the Leninist Party as a way to realize China's liberation from imperialist domination. Agents from the newly founded Communist International went to China to assist in the establishment of a Communist Party there, providing both funding and organizational advice to Marxist study groups and labor organizations. In July 1921, the first CCP Congress was held with twelve participants in Shanghai and then, after fears of police raids arose, in Hangzhou. The party grew slowly until it formed a United Front* with the Guomindang* (GMD). The CCP at this time viewed a Socialist or Communist revolution as a future prospect, and so worked with the bourgeois nationalists in a joint effort to oppose imperialism in China.

After the death of Sun Zhongshan* in 1925, the GMD came to be dominated by military leader Jiang Jieshi*, who in April 1927 split with the CCP and precipitated a massacre of party leaders and activists in Shanghai. It took several years for the CCP to recover from this, and to reorient its political line in a way that would revive its prospects. Power struggles taking place in the Soviet Union also affected debates within the CCP, which made it more difficult for the Chinese leadership to respond to differing local conditions. Abortive efforts to spark mass uprisings in Changsha and Nanchang further decimated Communist military capacity. But by the early 1930s, a new strategy focused on the peasantry and building rural base areas began to emerge in Jiangxi Province and other remote areas across China. The shift is associated with Mao Zedong*, who although a founding member of the CCP in 1921, had remained a peripheral figure until he emerged as the key leader in the period of the Jiangxi Soviet from 1931 to 1934. During the retreat that became the Long March in October 1934, Mao's position as leader became stronger, and in January 1935, he was confirmed as chairman. Thereafter, the CCP's history was tied closely to the political life of Mao.

The Long March lasted a year, and at its end, the CCP established a new base in the remote area of northern Shaanxi Province, at Yan'an. This period was crucial in forging the so-called Yan'an Way, the political line that prevailed in the Anti-Japanese War from 1937 to 1945 of relying heavily on the concept of unity between the party, the Red Army, and the masses. Communist activists were to be like fish, with the people as the sea. A party culture of simplicity, honesty, and self-reliance developed, as well as Mao's view that intellectuals should serve the interests of the peasants and workers. The CCP's role in fighting the Japanese, especially after U.S. entry into the war in December 1941 following the Pearl Harbor Attack*, became increasingly important both in domestic politics and in the overall course of World War II. Although allied with Jiang's regime, American military intelligence sent the Dixie Mission* to explore possible cooperation with the Communists. After Japan's defeat in 1945 and perfunctory efforts at forging a postwar united front between the CCP and the GMD failed, the Chinese Civil War* resumed. The CCP enunciated a policy of New Democracy, calling for a new regime of national unity, and portraying Jiang and his followers as tools of American imperialism.

In October 1949, the CCP, after its military victory, oversaw the establishment of the People's Republic of China* (PRC). It now faced the daunting task of governing a vast territory and a huge population. The party at first adopted the Soviet model of modernization, but divisions soon arose among the leadership. Mao and his supporters wanted to continue the model of popular mobilization and egalitarianism developed at Yan'an, but Liu Shaoqi and others advocated reorienting the party to a more "pragmatic" approach, stressing technical expertise and playing down politics. During the later 1950s and early 1960s, conflict between these two basic orientations recurred around issues such as agricultural collectivization, the people's communes, the Great Leap Forward, and the Socialist Education Movement. The alliance with the Soviet Union fell apart in 1959, and along with crop failures and massive bureaucratic fraud, the economy collapsed and widespread hunger weakened the CCP regime. Mao had to retreat from daily leadership, and the pragmatists seemed to have triumphed until late 1965, when Mao launched the Chinese Cultural Revolution*. By 1969, new leaders were in place and the party resumed its monopoly of political power.

Mao's death in 1976 was a turning point, after which the pragmatists, now led by Deng Xiaoping*, rapidly purged the Gang of Four, leaders of the Maoist faction, and finally placed the PRC firmly on a path of modernization dominated by a party increasingly led by technocratic experts rather than Communist political activists. With the adoption in 1978 of the Four Modernizations*, the CCP sought to integrate China with the larger global system while retaining its role as the sole legitimate political force in the country. But plagued by corruption, and divided over the proper pace of reform, the party faced its greatest test in 1989 when students in Beijing led a large-scale protest, resulting in the Tiananmen Square Massacre*. Although this trauma further tarnished the CCP's image, the collapse of the Soviet Union in 1991 and the descent of Russia into poverty and criminality proved a counterpoint that has served to preserve the party's leading role. Under the leadership of Jiang Zemin*, the CCP has emphasized the need for stability above all, and managed to deliver adequate increases in living standards and a political and cultural environment much freer than any in modern Chinese history while still repressing anything directly challenging its own rule. The CCP cannot be seen as Communist in any meaningful sense, and in the summer of 2001 it moved to admit capitalist entrepreneurs to its ranks in the name of promoting economic development. *See also* Hu Yaobang; Hua Guofeng; Huang Hua; Lin Biao; Zhou Enlai.

L. Bianco, *Origins of the Chinese Revolution: 1915–1949* (Stanford, CA, 1971); C. A. Johnson, *Peasant Nationalism and Communist Power: The Emergence of Revolutionary China 1937–1945* (Stanford, CA, 1962); R. MacFarquhar (ed.), *The Politics of China: The Eras of Mao and Deng* (Cambridge, MA, 1997); H. E. Salisbury, *The Long March* (New York, 1985); F. Schurmann, *Ideology and Organization in Communist China* (Berkeley, CA, 1968).

Kenneth J. Hammond

CHINESE CONSOLIDATED BENEVOLENT ASSOCIATION

The Chinese Consolidated Benevolent Association (CCBA) is the umbrella organization of a variety of Chinese-American community associations in American Chinatowns. Founded in 1882, it was created as a Chinese response to growing anti-Chinese agitation in California and reflects an increasing sense of identity among Chinese in the United States as a community. The key components of the CCBA are the district associations, called *huiguan*, which originally were made up of people from contiguous villages who spoke similar dialects from the Pearl River delta and Siyi in China. The first two district associations in the United States, the Siyi Huiguan and the Sanyi Huiguan, were formed in 1851 in San Francisco. Almost as important as

these were the clan associations organized on the basis of common surnames. Because of the close identification of clans with locality in the Siyi area, some of the Siyi Huiguan were established with clan associations as the basic units. Chinese immigrants also organized trade guilds and secret societies, which eventually evolved into the system of the CCBA. All these organizations had their origins in Chinese society and offered their members mutual support in areas such as jobs and personal welfare. The associations, which were led by the merchant class, provided social order amongst the Chinese, as well as a buffer against the often racist mainstream American society.

In 1862, leaders of the existing six huiguan in California formed a loose federation called a *gongsuo* (Chinese Six Companies) to settle disputes among people of the different associations and to make decisions on matters affecting the general interest of the Chinese community. As the 1882 Chinese Exclusion Act went into effect, community leaders, pushed by Huang Zunxian, Chinese consul general in San Francisco, organized a formal umbrella association called the Zhonghua Huiguan (Chinese Consolidated Benevolent Association) to present a united front in the fight against the anti-Chinese movement. In subsequent years, additional CCBAs were established in other American cities. From the late nineteenth century to the first half of the twentieth century, the CCBAs functioned as local community leaders to protect Chinese rights and to promote each community's welfare. Both the Chinese and U.S. governments accepted their presidents as the unofficial mayors of Chinatowns. But since the repeal of the Chinese Exclusion Acts* in 1943 and the U.S. Immigration Act of 1965*, the CCBAs' command in the Chinese communities has declined primarily for two reasons: changes in the social, economic, and political background of the Chinese immigrant population became evident in the 1950s, and the U.S. government has made a variety of social services available to minorities since the 1960s. The immigrants of Chinese ancestry therefore have relied less on these traditional associations. In recent years, although the CCBA continues to be the major force in Chinatown, most residents see the CCBAs and the traditional associations as major obstacles to social reforms, because those in leadership are too old and too mercantile-oriented. *See also* Rock Springs Massacre.

S. Chan, *Asian Americans: An Interpretive History* (Boston, 1991); P. Kwong, *The New Chinatown* (New York, 1987); H. M. Lai, "Historical Development of the Chinese Consolidated Benevolent Association/Huiguan System," *Chinese America: History and Perspectives* (1987); S. H. Tsai, *The Chinese Experience in America* (Bloomington, IN, 1986).

Ena Chao

CHINESE CULTURAL REVOLUTION

Mao Zedong* unleashed this antibureaucratic struggle to try to salvage the Chinese Communist Party* (CCP) from revisionism, but his Great Proletarian Cultural Revolution degenerated into an internal party power struggle that devastated much of urban China from 1966 to 1976. It also delayed any progress toward U.S. diplomatic reconciliation with the People's Republic of China* (PRC). After the Great Leap Forward beginning in 1958 and the Lushan Plenum of 1959, Mao had withdrawn from his leading role in daily administration. From this position as elder statesman, however, he came to view the situation of the party and the revolution as gravely endangered. Mao developed a critique of the Soviet Union as a counterrevolutionary state in which its Communist Party exercised power as an alienated elite and viewed the people and the economy as its private property. He feared that the pragmatic economic policies advocated by such Chinese leaders as Liu Shaoqi, Chen Yun, or Deng Xiaoping* would lead China into similar difficulties. Moreover, Mao be-

lieved that he had lost the ability to reform the party from within because he saw himself as isolated from the central leadership. In the fall of 1965, he began an effort to force the party into one last attempt at self-criticism about its growing bureaucratization and alienation from the masses, but this move was thwarted by the central propaganda authorities and the Beijing municipal party leadership. Mao then turned to a strategy of mobilizing social forces outside the party to criticize and struggle against party leaders whom he saw as "taking the capitalist road."

In August 1966, Mao called on young people across China to "attack the headquarters," to "rebel against reactionaries," and to organize themselves to carry out a new stage of revolution, properly named the Great Proletarian Cultural Revolution. The Red Guards, groups of high school and university students now free to take part in politics while their academic institutions were closed, became the most visible symbols of the Cultural Revolution. Bureaucratic elements within the CCP consistently tried to divert the thrust of criticism from themselves onto intellectuals and others labeled as "rightists." Red Guard excesses against symbols of the "four olds" in thought and behavior spread an atmosphere of fear and chaos in the cities of China. Meanwhile, workers also were mobilizing in response to Mao's call, and criticizing the party leadership for its bureaucratic and authoritarian ways. In Shanghai, the workers' movement reached its peak early in 1967, when a crude form of popular government, labeled the Shanghai Commune, in emulation of the 1871 Paris Commune that Karl Marx had extolled as a model of proletarian self-rule, replaced the urban party leadership. But at this point, Mao backed away from his advocacy of popular initiative. The commune was disbanded and a Revolutionary Three-in-One committee created, combining leaders from the CCP, the People's Liberation Army, and the mass organizations.

With Mao's abandonment of efforts to

develop nonparty forms of popular self-government, the Cultural Revolution became essentially a struggle for control of the CCP machinery. Factional conflict continued in the late 1960s, some of it quite bitter and violent. Major party leaders such as Liu Shaoqi were not only driven from power, but died from maltreatment. At the same time many ordinary people became victims of personal vendettas or power grabs by officials and cadres as the CCP began to rebuild its central role in Chinese life. The Red Guards were demobilized, with many being sent for reeducation in the countryside. Then, in 1969, the Ninth Party Congress met to declare the victory of the Cultural Revolution, and to anoint Lin Biao* as Mao's heir apparent. Within two years, however, Lin fell from power as Mao shifted his geopolitical strategy away from seeing American imperialism as the main threat to China and took a strongly anti-Soviet stance, opening the way for U.S.-PRC Normalization of Relations*. Thereafter, leadership of the CCP remained polarized, with advocates of a more radical conception of China's revolution grouped under the so-called Gang of Four (Jiang Qing, Yao Wenyuan, Zhang Chunqiao, and Wang Hongwen) while mainstream party bureaucrats increasingly united around the reemerging leadership of Deng Xiaoping. By the time of Mao's death in September 1976, the radical elements within the CCP were weak and isolated, and were swept away in October of the same year with the arrest of the Gang of Four, on whom all the excesses of the Cultural Revolution subsequently were blamed.

H. Y. Lee, *The Politics of the Chinese Cultural Revolution* (Berkeley, CA, 1978); R. MacFarquhar, *The Origins of the Cultural Revolution*, 3 vols. (New York, 1974–1997); E. J. Perry and X. Li, *Proletarian Power: Shanghai in the Cultural Revolution* (Boulder, CO, 1997); M. Schoenhals (ed.), *China's Cultural Revolution, 1966–69: Not a Dinner Party* (Armonk, NY, 1996).

Kenneth J. Hammond

CHINESE INTERVENTION IN THE KOREAN WAR

In October 1950, the People's Republic of China* (PRC) entered the Korean War*, which thereafter became in essence a war between China and the United States, leading the two countries into the most mutually hostile period in their history. On 25 June 1950, the army of the Democratic People's Republic of Korea* (DPRK) attacked the Republic of Korea* (ROK). Two days later, President Harry S. Truman* authorized U.S. air and naval support for the ROK and ordered the Seventh Fleet into the Taiwan Strait to prevent the Chinese Communists from attacking the Republic of China* on Taiwan*. The next day, Zhou Enlai*, China's premier, denounced Truman's Neutralization of Taiwan* as "armed aggression against the territory of China." The United Nations adopted a resolution calling for using all possible means to aid the ROK on 7 July. That same day, at the suggestion of Mao Zedong*, party chairman and PRC president, the Central Military Commission of the Chinese Communist Party* (CCP) held the first meeting on national defense and decided to establish the Northeast China Border Defense Army, including four infantry armies totaling 260,000 troops, in case of an emergency situation along the Chinese-Korean border. On 4 August, when the invasion by North Korea was halted, Mao called a Politburo meeting to discuss possible involvement and preparation of Chinese forces for war. The next day, Mao ordered the Northeast China Border Defense Army "to get ready for fighting in early September" and later secured a promise from Soviet leader Joseph Stalin for Soviet air support.

On 15 September, the U.S. troops successfully staged the Inch'ŏn Landing* and in two weeks, crossed the thirty-eighth parallel. Kim Il Sung*, the DPRK's leader, asked the Soviet Union for help and told Stalin to ask China to send troops to Korea. Stalin telegraphed Mao on 1 October and suggested that China "should send at once at least 5 to 6 divisions to the 38th Parallel." Although Zhou had warned that China would intervene if U.S. forces invaded North Korea, Chinese leaders expressed divergent views when the Secretariat of the Central Committee met on 2 October. Mao then decided to hold an enlarged meeting of the Politburo, which on 5 October, agreed to his proposal and decided to send troops to aid Korea, even though Stalin had retracted his promise of air support. Three days later, Mao issued his order to establish the Chinese People's Volunteers (CPV) with Peng Dehuai* appointed commander in chief and political commissar. On 19 October, the first wave of the CPV, including four infantry armies and three artillery divisions, about 300,000 troops, crossed the Yalu River and entered Korea. On 25 October, the Chinese government announced that it was sending volunteers to Korea in the name of "Resisting U.S. Aggression, Aiding Korea and Defending the Homeland."

By late November 1950, China had dispatched to Korea thirty-three divisions and five regiments totaling 450,000 soldiers, including thirty infantry divisions, three artillery divisions, one anti-aircraft artillery regiment, and four engineering regiments. This quick deployment apparently was unexpected by U.S. generals. The CPV's superiority in manpower enabled the Chinese to overcome their inferiority in equipment and technology. It seemed rational to the Chinese leaders that a large force would be a decisive factor assuring victory. By the middle of April 1951, the Chinese forces in Korea had increased to 950,000 men. Their combat troops consisted of forty-two infantry divisions, eight artillery divisions, four anti-aircraft artillery divisions, and four tank regiments, totaling 770,000. Their supporting troops consisted of six supply services headquarters, four railroad engineering divisions, eleven engineering regiments, and one public security division, totaling 180,000. But despite Chinese expectations and efforts, the Korean War

reached a stalemate in June 1951. To achieve a favorable position in future negotiations, China sent more troops to Korea. By October, the number of CPV forces had reached 1,150,000, including 880,000 combat troops and 220,000 supporting forces. In addition, there were four divisions totaling 40,000 men undertaking airport construction in North Korea. By March 1953, the Chinese forces had reached a record high of 1,350,000 since intervening in the Korean War.

From 19 October 1950 to 27 July 1953, when the Korean Armistice Agreement* was concluded, China sent a total of 3 million troops to Korea. Confronted by U.S. air and naval superiority, the CPV forces suffered heavy casualties, including Mao's son, who was killed while acting as a Russian translator at the CPV headquarters in an air raid. According to Chinese military records, the Chinese casualties in the Korean War were 152,000 dead, 383,000 wounded, 450,000 hospitalized, 21,700 prisoners of war, and 4,000 missing in action. China had also spent in the war a total of $3.3 billion. In terms of war materials and supplies, the Chinese government transported into Korea a total of 5.6 million tons of goods and supplies during its intervention. Mao judged China's intervention a victory because the Communist regime in North Korea was saved, a perceived U.S. invasion of China was prevented, more Russian military and economic aid came to the PRC, and Beijing emerged as a world power. But it also caused the United Nations in February 1951 to condemn the PRC for aggression in Korea. *See also* Home By Christmas Offensive.

J. Chen, *China's Road to the Korean War: The Making of the Sino-American Confrontation* (New York, 1994); M. Hastings, *The Korean War* (New York, 1987); X. Li and H. Li (eds.), *China and the United States: A New Cold War History* (New York, 1998); A. S. Whiting, *China Crosses the Yalu: The Decision to Enter the Korean War* (New York, 1970); S. G. Zhang, *Mao's Military Roman-*

ticism: China and the Korean War, 1950–53
(Lawrence, KS, 1995).

Li Xiaobing

CHINESE REPRESENTATION IN THE UNITED NATIONS

The issue of Chinese representation in the United Nations was a constant irritant in U.S. relations with many of its allies and with the nonaligned countries in the 1950s and 1960s. U.S. administrations from Presidents Harry S. Truman* through Richard M. Nixon* expended an enormous amount of political capital to fend off proposals to oust the Republic of China* (ROC) from the United Nations and give China's seat to the People's Republic of China* (PRC). Chinese representation first became an issue with a 1950 Soviet resolution to admit Beijing. It was the defeat of that resolution in the UN Security Council that led to the Soviet boycott of the United Nations, which enabled UN Security Council action in Korea in June 1950. After the Chinese Intervention in the Korean War* and the UN condemnation of the PRC as an aggressor, U.S. representatives argued that this should bar PRC admission to the world body. Annual congressional resolutions threatening to end U.S. participation in the United Nations if the Guomindang* (Nationalist) government was ousted contributed to the determination of successive administrations to continue the battle.

In 1951, the Truman administration, with British support, won UN General Assembly approval of a U.S. resolution not to consider any changes in Chinese representation, which provided a way to avoid a public clash between London and Washington over this issue. A similar moratorium resolution was approved by the UN General Assembly every year through 1960, but U.S. representatives found it more difficult each year to muster a majority. By the time President John F. Kennedy* took office, it was evident that a new approach was necessary. The Kennedy ad-

ministration considered supporting PRC admission, provided that the Nationalists retained membership, on the assumption that Beijing would refuse to accept such an arrangement, but this idea ran aground because of adamant opposition from Jiang Jieshi*. Finally, the administration resolved the dilemma with a resolution to make any proposal to change representation of China an "important question" requiring a two-thirds majority. This resolution won UN General Assembly approval in 1961, but in 1965 the vote was very close, and the vote on a resolution to remove Taibei and seat Beijing was a tie.

In 1966, there was heavy pressure on Washington from Canada and other allies to support a special committee to study the question, on the assumption that it would recommend PRC membership. The administration of President Lyndon B. Johnson* reluctantly prepared to support this as a fallback position, but by the time the issue came to a vote in November 1966, the Chinese Cultural Revolution* was under way, and support for the PRC's admission had diminished. During the next few years, the UN General Assembly continued to support an "important question" resolution and defeat the annual Albanian proposals to admit the PRC and oust the ROC. Then, on 2 August 1971, Secretary of State William Rogers announced U.S. support for a policy of dual representation. The United States would support the PRC's admission to the UN General Assembly, but oppose any move aimed at expelling the Nationalists, and it would accept the decision of the UN Security Council as to China's seat in the council. President Nixon's announcement eighteen days earlier that he would visit China the next year already had fatally undercut this proposal. It was doomed from the start in any case because both antagonists had made their opposition to such an arrangement abundantly clear. On 25 October 1971, the UN General Assembly rejected 59–55 an "important question" resolution, with 15 abstentions. The Assembly then voted 76–35, with 17 abstentions, for an Albanian resolution to seat the PRC and expel the ROC. The United States voted against the resolution, but to no avail. *See also* Nixon's Visit to China; Two China Policy.

U.S. Department of State, *Foreign Relations of the United States, 1950*, Vol. 2: *The United Nations; The Western Hemisphere* (Washington, DC, 1976); U.S. Department of State, *Foreign Relations of the United States, 1951*, Vol. 2: *The United Nations; The Western Hemisphere* (Washington, DC, 1979); U.S. Department of State, *Foreign Relations of the United States, 1952–1954*, Vol. 3: *United Nations Affairs* (Washington, DC, 1988); U.S. Department of State, *Foreign Relations of the United States, 1954–1957*, Vol. 11: *United Nations and General International Matters* (Washington, DC, 1991); U.S. Department of State, *Foreign Relations of the United States, 1958–1960*, Vol. 2: *United Nations; General International Matters* (Washington, DC, 1996); U.S. Department of State, *Foreign Relations of the United States, 1961–1963*, Vol. 12: *Northeast Asia* (Washington, DC, 1996); U.S. Department of State, *Foreign Relations of the United States, 1964–1968*, Vol. 30: *China* (Washington, DC, 1998).

Harriet Dashiell Schwar

CHINESE REVOLUTION OF 1911

This was the pivotal event that led to the end of the Qing Dynasty, last of the imperial dynasties that ruled China for more than 2,000 years. The Chinese Revolution of 1911, Xinhai Geming in Chinese, opened the Republican period when army forces staged a mutiny in the city of Wuhan on 10 October. The dynasty had been in decline for many years, and since the death of Cixi*, the empress dowager, and her nephew the Guangxu emperor in 1908, the situation had become increasingly desperate. Efforts at institutional and political reform had accelerated, including a timetable for elections for a national assembly planned for 1916, but these were both too little and too late. Organizations such as the Revolutionary Alliance, led by Sun Zhongshan*, had formed to pursue the revolutionary overthrow of the imperial state.

Movements for provincial assemblies and calls for autonomy also had developed. For example, beginning in the spring of 1911, a crisis arose in the southwestern province of Sichuan, where local elites wanted to maintain control of railroad development and linked this to a desire for local political authority. A Railway Protection League was organized, which also functioned as a de facto provincial assembly, and defied the imperial government without openly repudiating it.

The mutiny at Wuhan in Hubei Province was an unplanned and uncoordinated response to local events, and the Revolutionary Alliance was not even involved in its initial stages. Instead, the mutiny was led by military men who belonged to the Literary Study Society (*wenxueshe*), a regional organization with broader contacts in the revolutionary movement in Wuhan. On 9 October, a bomb exploded in the offices of the Common Advancement Society, the leading local revolutionary group. When the group's leaders were arrested, revolutionary sympathizers in the military decided to act in their support. Four battalions mutinied on the evening of 10 October, and by the next day Wuhan was largely in military hands. The young officers who initiated the mutiny sought to legitimize their actions by bringing in more senior, respected figures. Tang Hualong was chairman of the Hubei Provincial Assembly, which had been created as part of the Qing reform program. He now accepted the job of running the civil administration of the province under the revolutionaries. He issued a call for other provinces to declare their independence from the Qing state, and by the end of October, Hubei had been followed by Hunan, Yunnan, Shanxi, and Shaanxi. Six more provinces declared independence in November.

As the collapse of the Qing Dynasty proceeded, leadership of the revolution was assumed by the Revolutionary Alliance. Sun Zhongshan, who had been in the United States on a fund-raising and speaking tour, returned to China at the end of December. The revolutionaries entered into negotiations with Yuan Shikai*, the commander of the Northern Army of the Qing, who acted on behalf of Puyi*, the boy emperor, and the regents of the Manchu ruling house. A settlement was reached under which Puyi abdicated the throne, and the Qing Dynasty came to an end, on 12 February 1912. Sun, who had been named president of the Republic of China* on 1 January, resigned that post in favor of Yuan Shikai. Yuan soon subverted the new republican government and ushered in the Warlord Era* in China, which lasted through the 1920s. The Revolution of 1911, known in Chinese by the calendrical term of the *xinhai* year in the sixty-year cycle of "stems and branches" and also as the Double Ten from its date in the Western calendar, is celebrated as the start of modern political developments in both the People's Republic of China* and on Taiwan*. *See also* Homer Lea.

J. W. Esherick, *Reform and Revolution in China: The 1911 Revolution in Hunan and Hubei* (Berkeley, CA, 1976); C. T. Hsueh, *The Chinese Revolution of 1911: New Perspectives* (Hong Kong, 1986); E. Shinkichi and H. Z. Schiffrin, *The 1911 Revolution in China: Interpretive Essays* (Tokyo, 1985).

Kenneth J. Hammond

CHŎN DU-HWAN (1931–)

Chŏn Du-hwan was president of the Republic of Korea* (ROK) from 1980 to 1988. He was born in South Kyŏngsang Province in a poor farming family. After graduating from the Taegu Technical High School in 1951, he entered the Korean Military Academy (KMA) as a member of its first regular four-year class. After graduating, he rose smoothly in the ranks as an airborne officer and studied at U.S. military schools in 1959 and 1960. After Major General Pak Chŏng-hŭi* led the coup on 16 May 1961 that brought him to power, Chŏn became one of his secretaries and then a section chief

at the Korean Central Intelligence Agency (KCIA). In 1964, he and other KMA graduates formed a secret club within the military called *Hanahoe* ("One Group"), which received fast promotions from Pak. After fighting in the Second Indochina War*, he was promoted in 1973 to brigadier general, the first star among his KMA classmates. Thereafter, Chŏn served in various posts, finally becoming commander of the Military Security Command in February 1979. Eight months later, he headed the investigation of Pak Chŏng-hŭi's Assassination*, providing him with the opportunity to seize power.

During the first months after Pak's death, General Chŏng Sŭng-hwa, ROK Army chief of staff and martial law commander, attempted to consign Chŏn Du-hwan to a local post. On 12 December 1979, Chŏn arrested Chŏng and assumed control of the government. "We have been through a coup in all but name," U.S. Ambassador William Gleysteen reported to Washington. By early 1980, Chŏn was promoted to lieutenant general and became acting director of the KCIA. Opposition leaders voiced strong protests, demanding the lifting of martial law, release of all political prisoners, abolition of antidemocratic laws, and restoration of full civil rights. "Seoul Spring" followed, with intellectuals, religious leaders, and students joining political dissidents in demonstrations against Chŏn. Then in May, martial law was extended to Cheju Island, putting all of South Korea under military rule. That month, the Kwangju Democratization Movement led to the Kwangju Incident*, when Chŏn sent special forces to suppress student demonstrations, resulting in the killing of hundreds of civilians. Kim Dae-jung*, a popular dissident and powerful opponent against Pak, was sentenced to death for allegedly instigating the "riots."

Consolidating power, Chŏn installed the Emergency Measures Committee for the Protection and Guard of the State, with himself as standing chairman. He then promoted himself to general and retired. The rubber-stamp National Council of Deputies for Unification elected Chŏn president in August 1980. Thereafter, he held a national referendum that approved a new constitution and formed the Democratic Justice Party. On 21 January 1981, the day after his inauguration as president, Ronald Reagan* announced Chŏn's impending visit to the United States. Three days later, Chŏn lifted martial law and also commuted Kim Dae-jung's death sentence to life in prison. His reception at the White House strengthened him politically, leading in February 1981 to his inauguration as president of the Fifth Republic. During his seven-year term, he used U.S. political and military support to retain power, but faced rising popular resistance against his regime, as well as widespread sarcastic gossip about himself and his wife. His answer was to create a police state. The National Security Planning (NSP) Agency, the successor to the KCIA, was held responsible for the mysterious deaths of many student protesters.

Chŏn tried to divert attention from his repressive rule with his proposals in 1981 and 1982 for a summit meeting with North Korea's Kim Il Sung*, but the Democratic People's Republic of Korea* responded by trying to assassinate him when he visited Rangoon, Burma*, in October 1983. In 1985, an agreement between the Koreas allowed families separated in the Korean War* to meet at both Seoul and P'yŏngyang for the first time and musical teams to exchange visits. Chŏn also stabilized inflation and boosted economic growth while preparing for No Tae-u*, a KMA classmate, to succeed him. But in 1987, opposition peaked, especially after revelations that police torture had resulted in the death of a student. This led to South Korea's Democracy Declaration* and a constitutional revision providing for a popular presidential election that year, which No won against divided opposition. As president, No bowed to pressure for an investigation of Chŏn and his family's corruption while in office, resulting in Chŏn and his wife being banished to a Buddhist temple. In 1995,

President Kim Young-sam*, No's successor, secured passage of a special law under which Chŏn and No were tried, convicted, and sentenced to life in prison for the 1979 military mutiny, treason in 1980, the Kwangju massacre, and corruption in office. During December 1997, Chŏn was freed under a special amnesty agreement between President Kim Young-sam and President-elect Kim Dae-jung*.

Ch'ŏn Kŭm-sŏng, *Hwangkangesŏ Pukakkaji: Inkan Chŏn Du-hwan* [From the Han River to the Pukak Mountain] (Seoul, 1981); D. Oberdorfer, *The Two Koreas: A Contemporary History* (Reading, PA, 1997).

Kim Hakjoon

CHUNG, HENRY (1890–1985)

Henry Chung (Chŏng Han-kyŭng) was a political associate of Syngman Rhee* who in August 1948 became representative of the new Republic of Korea* (ROK) to Japan. Born in northwest Korea, he went to the United States for study in 1904. But the Japanese Annexation of Korea* in 1910 caused him to participate in the Korean independence movement against Japan. He earned a bachelor's degree and a master's degree from the University of Nebraska in 1915 and 1917. Chung compiled *Korean Treaties*, including all the treaties Korea had concluded with foreign countries while independent, and wrote *The Oriental Policy of the United States*, both in 1919. In the latter book, he denounced Japanese policy toward Korea and other East Asian regions while criticizing U.S. policy in the Pacific because it had damaged American interests there and encouraged aggressive Japanese expansion.

There was significant opposition to Japanese Colonialism* in Korea among Koreans at home and abroad after 1910. When President Woodrow Wilson* delivered his address outlining the Fourteen Points in January 1918, asserting the importance of equality among nations, and an armistice ended World War I that November, Korean expectations for achieving self-determination in Korea rose. Thereafter, many Koreans expanded activities for independence. Chung agreed with Rhee, the leading Korean patriot in the United States, that the immediate independence of Korea was desirable, but it would not be easy to achieve because of a lack of American support. Chung and Rhee took a realistic interim step of sending two petitions to Wilson, the first on 25 November 1918. In the second petition on 25 February 1919, they urged establishment of a temporary mandate in Korea under the supervision of the League of Nations. But the State Department took steps to prohibit them from traveling to the Versailles Peace Conference. Worse, Chung was criticized harshly by many other Korean patriots outside the United States, because they thought his petition, issued before the start of the March First Movement*, weakened the campaign of all Koreans, who were demanding complete independence for Korea. His position in the Korean Independence Movement weakened, and Chung then became an aide to Rhee.

Chung was a member of the Korean Commission in Philadelphia beginning in 1919. He asserted that Japan at least should grant Korea self-government, if complete independence was impossible, in his article in the magazine *Asia* in May 1919. Chung then joined in submitting a petition to the Washington Conference* in 1921, but this call for Korean independence failed again. That year, he earned a doctoral degree from American University and published *The Case of Korea*. This book exposed the realities of harsh Japanese rule in Korea and the brutal suppression of the March First Movement. Chung continued to work thereafter for the independence of Korea in the United States as Rhee's aide, especially during the Pacific war. After Japan's surrender in August 1945, Chung returned to Korea after forty-one years, finding his country partitioned as a result of the Thirty-Eighth Parallel Division*. He supported the United States, urging it to

prevent the Soviet Union from extending Communism* to the south in his book *The Russians Came to Korea* in 1947. Rhee named Chung as South Korea's first representative to Japan in August 1948. Thereafter, he negotiated with Japan over the payment of reparations to Korea as compensation for Japanese colonial rule, but failed to achieve an agreement. After resigning in 1949, he went to the United States and spent the rest of his life in Colorado Springs.

Min Byŏng-yŏng, *Miju Imin 100 Nyŏng* [100 Years of Korean Immigration to the United States] (Seoul, 1986).

Nagata Akifumi

CIXI (1835–1908)

Cixi was the conservative, antiforeign empress dowager of the Manchu Qing Dynasty in China in the late nineteenth and early twentieth centuries. The daughter of a minor Manchu official of the Bordered Blue Banner, Yehonala, as she was originally named, entered the imperial palace as a concubine of the Xianfeng emperor in 1851. In 1856, she gave birth to a son, Zaiqun, who became the Tongzhi emperor in 1861. Along with Xianfeng's senior consort Ci'an, Cixi was designated empress dowager, a title she retained the rest of her life. She soon came to dominate Ci'an, and since the authorization of these two women was necessary for the issuance of any imperial documents, Cixi came to wield great power within the court. Then, when the Tongzhi emperor died in 1874, Cixi manipulated the succession to preserve her own power, with the new emperor being her nephew, ruling as the Guangxu emperor. In 1889, Cixi nominally withdrew from daily management of court affairs and retired to the Summer Palace in the western suburbs of the capital. This palace was constructed in part with funds originally designated for the development of a Chinese navy. This misappropriation became legendary, and continued to be part of the popular image of Cixi as a decadent ruler who squandered Chinese chances to modernize. From her vantage point in the Summer Palace, she kept close contact with officials, eunuchs, and palace women and monitored the emperor's activities. When in 1898 the Guangxu emperor embraced the reformist ideas of Tan Sitong, Kang Youwei, Liang Qichao, and others, Cixi at first tolerated his actions, but then turned against the reforms, executed leading reform officials and put the emperor under virtual house arrest.

In 1899 and 1900, Cixi became involved with the Boxer Uprising*, an antiforeign peasant rebellion in Shandong Province that soon spread to the capital region. After initially opposing the rule of the Manchus, the Boxers soon sought the support of conservative forces within the dynasty to drive the "foreign devils" out of China. Cixi endorsed the Boxer movement and encouraged the Boxers to come to Beijing. Once in the capital, Boxers besieged the Legation Quarter, where foreign diplomats resided. A military force led by Japanese and Russian troops, and including English, French, American, and other national contingents, marched to Beijing in August 1900 to lift the siege of the foreign missions. Cixi fled the capital in the face of the China Relief Expedition*, taking the hapless Guangxu emperor with her. After returning to Beijing in early 1902, she finally undertook a reform program. The classical Confucian examination system, which had served as the primary means of recruiting officials for government service since the tenth century, was abolished in 1905. Plans were developed to move toward establishing consultative assemblies, first on a provincial and later a national level. Other educational and administrative reforms were also contemplated. But Cixi did not live to see them implemented. She died on 15 November 1908, one day after the Guangxu emperor. Her last action was to select the boy Puyi* to be China's next, and last, emperor. The close proximity of the death of the Guangxu emperor and Cixi has led to much speculation that she may have had

him poisoned, but this has not been proven. *See also* Boxer Protocol.

P. S. Buck, *Imperial Woman* (New York, 1956); L. S. K. Kwong, *A Mosaic of the Hundred Days: Personalities, Politics, and Ideas of 1898* (Cambridge, MA, 1984); M. Warner, *The Dragon Empress: Life and Times of Tz'u-Hsi, 1835–1908* (London, 1972).

Kenneth J. Hammond

CLARK, MARK W. (1896–1984)

U.S. Army General Mark Wayne Clark served as commander of the United Nations Command (UNC) in the Korean War* from 23 June 1952 until after the secession of hostilities on 27 July 1953. Born in Madison Barracks, New York, the son of a career soldier, he graduated from West Point in 1917 and fought with the American Expeditionary Force in France the next year. During the interwar years, Clark held a variety of command and staff positions and was selected to attend U.S. Army Command and General Staff School and the U.S. Army War College. A lieutenant colonel in 1940, he was part of the U.S. Army general headquarters and had been promoted to temporary major general at the time the United States entered World War II. He was made chief of staff of ground forces in 1942, responsible for supervising the training of the multimillion-man wartime army. Reassigned to command the Second Corps, one of the first large U.S. units deployed to England, he quickly became deputy to General Dwight D. Eisenhower*, who was put in charge of Operation Torch, the plan to invade North Africa. Clandestinely landed in Algiers, Clark coordinated the advance surrender of the Vichy garrison with French leaders. After the successful landing and subsequent capture of all of North Africa and Sicily, Clark was made commander of the Fifth U.S. Army, which he led throughout the campaign in Italy from Salerno to the final German surrender in 1945. After the war, his troops occupied the U.S. sector of

Austria, where he was military governor until 1947. There, Clark was involved regularly in negotiations with the Soviet military over occupation matters and a prospective Austrian peace treaty.

After his return to the United States, Clark first commanded the U.S. Sixth Army, headquartered at the Presidio, California, and then the U.S. Army Field Forces Training Command, at Fort Monroe, Virginia. Although planning to retire in 1952, he agreed to replace General Mathew B. Ridgway*, who became U.S. commander in Europe. The uprising of North Korean and Chinese prisoners of war (POW) on Kŏje Island formally ended just the day before the change of command occurred; however, Clark's forces had to deal with the rebellions associated with the Korean War POW Controversy* through the remainder of 1952. Thereafter, Clark implemented the U.S. decision to continue the armistice negotiations to their successful conclusion and personally signed the Korean Armistice Agreement* on 27 July 1953. He played a key role in securing the cooperation of President Syngman Rhee* of the Republic of Korea* in implementing the agreement and in improving the training and equipping of the South Korean Army. Clark retired from active duty in 1953 and was president of The Citadel in Charleston, South Carolina, from 1954 to 1965. He published two books, *Calculated Risk* and *From the Danube to the Yalu*. In the latter, Clark expressed his discomfort with the compromise nature of the armistice, as well as his concern that Communism* had not been decisively defeated on the peninsula. He was later quoted as saying he believed that by his signature on the armistice agreement, he personally had become the victim of the American people's lack of will to win. *See also* P'anmunjŏm Truce Talks.

M. W. Clark, *Calculated Risk* (New York, 1950); M. W. Clark, *From the Danube to the Yalu* (New York, 1954); T. R. Fehrenbach, *This Kind of War: A Study in Unpreparedness* (New York, 1963).

Roger H. Hill

CLINTON, BILL (1946–)

William Jefferson Clinton was president of the United States from 1993 to 2001, achieving modest successes and avoiding potential disasters in guiding the transition of U.S. relations in East Asia into the new era emerging after the Cold War. Born in Hope, Arkansas, he was a Rhodes scholar while attending Georgetown University. To avoid serving in the Second Indochina War*, Clinton had promised to join the National Guard after graduation, but then reneged when he secured a high number in the 1969 draft lottery. After earning a law degree at Yale University, he entered politics and in 1976, became the youngest governor in U.S. history. Clinton won the Democratic nomination for president in 1992, running a campaign made famous by the pithy admonition "It's the economy, stupid!" Another reason for his deemphasis on foreign affairs was that this was the main area of strength for his opponent, incumbent President George H. W. Bush*. Nevertheless, Clinton criticized Bush for not being sufficiently critical of the People's Republic of China* (PRC) for its abuse of human rights, especially during the Tiananmen Square Massacre*. He won not because of world affairs issues, but because of the sagging U.S. economy and the third-party candidacy of Texas billionaire Ross Perot.

As president, Clinton immediately confronted the challenge of a nuclear threat from the Democratic People's Republic of Korea* (DPRK). In 1993, he came close to ordering air strikes to destroy the nuclear energy facility in North Korea. However, former President Jimmy Carter* mediated a settlement temporarily ending the North Korean Nuclear Controversy*. Under the Agreed Framework in 1994, the Republic of Korea* (ROK), Japan, and the United States agreed to fund construction of energy plants in the DPRK that did not produce weapons-grade nuclear waste. Despite criticism of Bush's China policy, Clinton did not alter course, pursuing Constructive Engagement* with the PRC, a policy focused on expanding trade and resolving contentious issues through cooperation. For example, Beijing joined Washington in 1993 in support of the United Nations when it supervised elections in Cambodia* that saw 90 percent of the eligible population vote. But congressional support for the Republic of China* contributed to rising tensions between Beijing and Taibei that reached a climax during 1996 when Clinton sent U.S. naval forces into the Taiwan* Strait after the PRC staged provocative military exercises in the area. Clinton ignored critics who favored a tougher stand toward China, welcoming President Jiang Zemin* for a state visit to the United States in October 1997 and traveling to China in spring 1998.

Less contentious were Clinton's steps in 1994 to end diplomatic and economic isolation of the Socialist Republic of Vietnam*, resulting in the establishment of full diplomatic relations in July 1995 and his own visit to Vietnam in 2000. Meanwhile, the East Asian Financial Crisis* beginning in 1997 had altered affairs along the Pacific Rim dramatically. While Thailand* teetered on the brink of financial collapse, a mass uprising in Indonesia* ended the dictatorial regime of Suharto*. Clinton supported loan packages from the International Monetary Fund (IMF) for both countries to achieve economic recovery. Japan's economic crisis provided him with the chance to press Tōkyō to boost domestic demand and lower tariffs, thereby reducing the U.S. trade deficit. South Korea had to secure an IMF loan, contributing to the election of former dissident Kim Dae-jung* as president. But the ROK also had to delay implementation, along with Japan, of the Agreed Framework, contributing to an impatient North Korea's launching of a missile over Japan in August 1998. Clinton strongly supported the policy of engagement with the DPRK that Kim used to reduce tensions, resulting in Secretary of State Madeleine Albright visiting P'yŏngyang in the fall of 2000. Clinton left office having

positioned the United States to pursue successfully its economic and strategic interests in East Asia early in the new century.

W. C. Berman, *From the Center to the Edge: The Politics and Policies of the Clinton Presidency* (New York, 2001); D. Maraniss, *First in His Class: The Biography of Bill Clinton* (New York, 1996); M. Walker, *The President We Deserve: Bill Clinton, His Rise, Falls, and Comebacks* (New York, 1996).

James I. Matray

CLUBB, O. EDMUND (1901–1989)

Oliver Edmund Clubb, one of the most prominent China Hands* charged with disloyalty during the McCarthy era, was a veteran of more than two decades in the Foreign Service when he was forced to resign in 1952. Born in Minnesota, he served in the U.S. Army during World War I, graduated from the University of Minnesota, and entered the Foreign Service in 1928. He spent most of his years as a diplomat in various posts in China. He was in Hanoi at the time of the Pearl Harbor Attack* and was interned by the Japanese for eight months, after which he returned to China. Consul general in Beijing from 1947 to 1950, he was there when Communist leader Mao Zedong* proclaimed the People's Republic of China* (PRC) in 1949 and closed the U.S. consulate general when all American diplomats were withdrawn from China in April 1950. On his return to Washington, he became director of the Department of State's Office of Chinese Affairs, the position he held when the department's Loyalty Security Board launched an investigation of him in December 1950.

The false allegations of Clubb's Communist sympathies that prompted the investigation derived in part from the extensive reporting on the Chinese Communist movement he had done as a young Foreign Service officer in China in the 1930s, at a time when little was known in the United States about the Chinese Communist Party* (CCP). Perhaps more important in stimulating the probe, however, was the chance encounter that Clubb had had in New York in 1932 with Whittaker Chambers, which Chambers mentioned during his testimony before the House Un-American Activities Committee. After several months during which Clubb endeavored to clear himself of suspicion without being permitted to face his accusers, the Loyalty Review Board charged in June 1951 that he was a security risk, and the State Department suspended him from active duty. In December, he was informed that the board had determined that although there was no reasonable doubt as to his loyalty, he was nonetheless a security risk and should be separated from the Foreign Service. Secretary of State Dean G. Acheson* reversed the ruling on appeal in February 1952, but Clubb was assigned to a position in the historical division with no policy-making responsibilities, and he promptly resigned. He subsequently had a distinguished career teaching at Columbia University and writing on Chinese history and Sino-Soviet relations.

O. E. Clubb, *The Witness and I* (New York, 1974); E. J. Kahn Jr., *The China Hands: America's Foreign Service Officers and What Befell Them* (New York, 1975); *New York Times*, 11 May 1989.

Harriet Dashiell Schwar

COLLINS, J. LAWTON (1896–1987)

General Joseph Lawton Collins played a significant role in U.S.–East Asian relations, beginning with his term as U.S. Army chief of staff during the Korean War* and continuing with his appointment as special representative in South Vietnam with full ambassadorial powers from November 1954 until May 1955. In Korea, Collins recognized the difficulties of conducting the Korean War in peacetime. In Vietnam, he was one of the few Americans who tried to work with the French to achieve a stable South Vietnamese state. Collins also provided a realistic assessment of the situation there, warning Washington that the

chances of Ngo Dinh Diem* creating a strong government were slim. As the United States became more committed to Diem's regime in the later 1950s and early 1960s, his words of warning came back to haunt American leaders.

Collins served under Dwight D. Eisenhower* in World War II and had been one of his most successful corps commanders, earning the nickname Lightning Joe for his aggressive tactics in the Pacific. During the Korean War, U.S. Army Chief of Staff Collins was executive agent for the Joint Chiefs of Staff (JCS). He was responsible for transmitting JCS instructions to the United Nations Command and for initiating appropriate recommendations for JCS studies or actions. Collins kept in touch, day and night, with the battlefront situation in Korea. In order to have firsthand evaluations of future requirements for men, materials, and money, Collins undertook regular trips to Japan and Korea for consultations with General Douglas MacArthur* and his successors, visiting commanders of the U.S. Eighth Army and South Korean Army in the field. These trips usually occurred during critical periods, notably when Collins consulted and raised concerns with MacArthur about plans for an amphibious Inch'ŏn Landing*. In late 1950, as U.S. allies became alarmed that premature action by MacArthur might provoke war with the People's Republic of China*, Collins was sent to gather firsthand information on MacArthur's estimates of his force capabilities and views about a possible cease-fire.

After the Korean War, Collins served as the U.S. representative to the Military Committee and Standing Group of the North Atlantic Treaty Organization. In November 1954, President Eisenhower appointed Collins as special representative in Saigon. The Eisenhower administration wanted an evaluation of conditions in the Republic of Vietnam* by a senior military officer to establish a concrete program of assistance as well as military, political, and economic reform. Having worked closely with Collins during World War II, Eisenhower believed he would provide a realistic assessment of the situation. In particular, Collins was to work on strengthening and reorganizing the South Vietnamese armed forces, concluding arrangements for their training and control. In addition, Collins was to assess the political viability of newly appointed Prime Minister Diem while trying to strengthen and stabilize his government. Collins left Vietnam in May 1955, convinced that the United States had erred in providing unqualified support to Diem's regime. *See also* Collins Mission.

D. L. Anderson, *Trapped by Success: The Eisenhower Administration and Vietnam, 1953–1961* (New York, 1991); J. L. Collins, *Lightning Joe: An Autobiography* (Baton Rouge, LA, 1979); J. L. Collins, *War in Peacetime: The History and Lessons of Korea* (Boston, 1969).

Kathryn C. Statler

COLLINS MISSION

The Collins Mission, which began on 3 November 1954 when President Dwight D. Eisenhower* appointed General J. Lawton Collins* as special representative in Saigon, was critical to future U.S. action in Vietnam. The Eisenhower administration wanted an evaluation of conditions in the Republic of Vietnam* after the First Indochina War* ended by a senior military officer to establish as quickly as possible a definite program of assistance and military, political, and economic reform. In particular, Collins's instructions were to reach agreement with General Paul Ely*, high commissioner in French Indochina*, on the strength and organization of the South Vietnamese armed forces and conclude arrangements for their training and control to be assumed by the United States. He was also to assess the abilities of newly appointed Prime Minister Ngo Dinh Diem*. Eisenhower sent Collins to Saigon on a temporary assignment expected to last sixty to ninety days, providing Collins with sweeping powers to direct and utilize all

the agencies and resources of the U.S. government in Vietnam.

Collins quickly developed a seven point program to strengthen South Vietnam. Working with General Ely, he succeeded in reorganizing and training the Vietnamese National Army, but had little luck in persuading Diem to broaden representation of his government. Nor did he have much success with the other points of his program, calling for resettlement of refugees and displaced people, land reform, creation of a national assembly, financial and economic assistance, and a program for training Vietnamese administrative personnel. Eventually, Collins became discouraged over Diem's chances for success in creating a viable South Vietnamese state and in rivaling the popularity of Ho Chi Minh*. In April 1955, he specifically recommended that the United States shift its support from Diem to other South Vietnamese leaders. At the end of April, after a series of meetings in Washington, Collins appeared to have convinced Eisenhower and Secretary of State John Foster Dulles* of the necessity of replacing Diem. In the meantime, Diem precipitated a confrontation with the Cao Dai*, Hoa Hao, and Binh Xuyen*, three principal politico-religious groups in South Vietnam that had formed a united front against him. Diem survived the crisis, and Washington decided to maintain his government.

Collins, the only American diplomat who consistently had tried to reduce Franco-American tensions in South Vietnam, left what became the Republic of Vietnam* on 14 May to return to duty with the North Atlantic Treaty Organization, warning that Washington was making a mistake in supporting Diem. In the years that followed, his assessments proved tragically correct, as Diem did not build popular support or broaden his government and instead relied increasingly on his family for political leadership. Collins was thinking of U.S. interests and the good of Vietnam when he recommended against keeping Diem in power. He also believed that unless there was firm and decisive agreement among the Americans, French, and Vietnamese, the United States should leave Vietnam. He feared that if the United States gave Diem unqualified support, he would become even more resistant to pressure. The Eisenhower administration's failure to listen to Collins meant that the United States became the guarantor not only of an independent South Vietnam but also of a particular South Vietnamese leader. *See also* Edward G. Lansdale; Nation-Building Strategy.

D. L. Anderson, "J. Lawton Collins, John Foster Dulles, and the Eisenhower Administration's 'Point of No Return' in Vietnam," *Diplomatic History* (Spring 1988); D. L. Anderson, *Trapped by Success: The Eisenhower Administration and Vietnam, 1953–1961* (New York, 1991); R. Buzzanco, *Informed Dissent: Three Generals and the Vietnam War* (Chevy Chase, MD, 1992); W. Duiker, *U.S. Containment Policy and the Conflict in Indochina* (Stanford, CA, 1994).

Kathryn C. Statler

COLOMBO PLAN

The Colombo Plan was hatched at a meeting in Ceylon (now Sri Lanka) of British Commonwealth foreign ministers in January 1950 and eventually developed into an organization of twenty-six nations. It initially was designed as a program of economic development for Asian nations to combat the spread of Communism* in the aftermath of the victory of the Chinese Communist Party* in the Chinese Civil War*. The possibilities of foreign aid in assisting nations in the period after World War II was stimulated by the U.S. Marshall Plan, which helped rebuild Western Europe. The plan's original members were Australia, Canada, Ceylon, Great Britain, India, New Zealand, and Pakistan. The first meeting in Sydney, Australia, in May 1950 created a Council for Technical Cooperation in South and Southeast Asia. The United States was at first hesitant to become a member because it was afraid of collaboration in British colonial policies

and being used as a money spigot. Nevertheless, it joined the Colombo Plan in 1951, along with Cambodia*, Laos*, and Vietnam. The United States began to see this as an opportunity not only to engage in closer cooperation with India and Pakistan, but "to contribute to the creation of economic strength in fields beyond the reach of bilateral U.S. programs," "draw Asian nations into a joint responsibility for stability in threatened areas," and "maximize the political advantages of economic aid for the U.S." The original members wanted this non-Commonwealth superpower for access to its huge financial resources.

The Colombo Plan is a series of "bilateral arrangements involving foreign aid and technical assistance for the economic and social development of Asia and the Pacific." Although it is a program of mutual assistance, the developing nations have been responsible for their own planning. Decisions are to be made by consensus after "mutual accommodation." Donor countries made up the Consultative Committee of the Colombo Plan. Recipient nations also have extended technical assistance to fellow developing countries. The plan has enjoyed some measure of success because it largely has been free of political pressures and aid with strings attached. But that was not always the case, as seen in late 1951 when the United States blocked Colombo aid to Ceylon after that nation allowed a Polish vessel to deliver a major shipment of Ceylonese rubber to the People's Republic of China* during the Korean War*. Most of the economic aid (as much as 85 percent) in the early years of the plan was provided by the United States. Technical assistance was provided in the fields of agriculture, education, and health.

As early as 1952, the United States sought membership in the organization for Japan as a means of reintegrating that defeated nation into regional affairs, although it sought Asian member sponsorship for their recent enemy. Initially, however, Japan's membership was opposed by Australia and India, among others. Washington also at that time favored membership for the Republic of Korea* and the Republic of China*, but recognized the unlikely possibility of that scenario. By 1960, it believed that by working through the Colombo Plan, it would be able to "make a special, sustained effort to help educate an expanding number of technically competent, pro-Western . . . leaders, both civilian and military." In the early years of the plan, the United States concentrated assistance in the fields of public health (especially malaria eradication), motor and air transportation, and food supply technical help. The principal Asian recipients of U.S. assistance during the 1980s were Indonesia*, the Philippines*, and Thailand*. U.S. aid toward Indonesia involved the promotion of agricultural efficiency and productivity. In the Philippines, Washington sought to open markets through small enterprise credit and privatization projects. In Thailand, U.S. designs focused on economic growth and environmental protection. In 1991, U.S. President George H. W. Bush* praised the Colombo Plan for "its ability to adapt itself to the changing needs of its member states" and specifically, for its role in curbing the Drug Trade*, a particular American concern. In fact, it was the United States that proposed the establishment of the Drug Advisory Program in 1973, which thereafter worked closely with the United Nations Commission on Narcotic Drugs. By the 1990s, Japan had replaced the United States as the largest distributor of aid within the plan.

The Colombo Plan for Co-Operative Economic and Social Development in Asia and the Pacific: 40th Anniversary Souvenir; The Colombo Plan Annual Report (1990/91); Records of the U.S. Department of State, Far East Files, Central Files (1955–1959), U.S. Department of State Conference Files, National Archives, College Park, MD.

Gregory J. Murphy

COMMITTEE FOR A DEMOCRATIC FAR EASTERN POLICY

Organized in August 1945, the Committee for a Democratic Far Eastern Policy (CDFEP) criticized U.S. Cold War Asian policy for its fierce anti-Communist orientation. It called on U.S. government officials to support colonial independence and social justice movements throughout Asia, while championing the right of free speech and democratic values in the United States. The brainchild of Frederick Vanderbilt Field, a member of the Communist Party of the United States of America (CPUSA), the CDFEP was first organized as the Committee for a Democratic China Policy to protest U.S. interference in the Chinese Civil War*. Bringing together progressive liberals, such as Brigadier General Evans Carlson and journalists Helen Foster Snow, Edgar Snow*, and Harrison Forman, with avowed leftists who included Israel Epstein, Maud Russell*, Agnes Smedley*, and Anna Louise Strong*, the CDFEP quickly expanded its concerns to U.S. policy throughout the entire Asian region. It was highly critical of U.S. government efforts to suppress all Asian Communist-led liberation movements, and to support any corrupt, ineffective, or colonialist forces that were not Communist. It waged a seven-year-long campaign to educate the American people about the negative consequences of their government's Asia policies in order to mobilize public opinion that would force policy makers to cooperate with "democratic" movements who combated the "authoritarian" regimes in power in Asia.

Most liberal members lent only the use of their names to be printed on the CDFEP publications, and gave their monetary donations to the committee's work. A core of leftists, who often associated with the CPUSA, compiled the CDFEP newsletter, the *Far East Spotlight*, press releases, and in-depth policy reports. These reports were sent to U.S. legislators, news agencies, and other political, social, and labor organizations. Active CDFEP members also organized public rallies and conferences in New York and San Francisco to bring public attention to their U.S. Asia policy critiques. As honorary chairman of the committee until his death in 1947, Brigadier General Evans Carlson was typical of most liberals who joined the CDFEP. Carlson had firsthand experience fighting in Asia during World War II. He witnessed the corruption and ineptitude of the U.S. wartime ally, the Chinese Guomindang* (Nationalist) Party. He was greatly impressed by the fighting zeal and commitment to social justice displayed by the Chinese Communist Party*, believing that it was more deserving of U.S. support than the Nationalist regime when the war with Japan ended. Moreover, as a great believer in the ideals of the American democratic tradition, he abhorred the U.S. decision to involve itself in the Chinese Civil War after 1945, rather than allowing the Chinese people to choose their own national leadership.

Much of the CDFEP's work was done by its paid executive director and small salaried staff. Harold Fletcher, a World War II U.S. Army veteran of the Pacific campaign, was executive director from 1945 to 1946. Maud Russell, a former YWCA foreign secretary in China, having joined the committee in 1945, replaced Fletcher and maintained the position until the CDFEP dissolved in 1952. During her tenure, the CDFEP came under attack from the political right wing. The connections of Russell and other active members to the CPUSA were investigated by government and non-government agencies. By 1947, because of its vigorous denunciation of the Truman Doctrine, the CDFEP was labeled a "Communist front" organization, and its liberal membership dropped off dramatically. Although the CDFEP was an active force in Henry Wallace's 1948 presidential campaign, the intense anti-Communist climate in the United States thwarted its effectiveness. The CDFEP lost all political credibility after 25 June 1950, when it condemned U.S. involvement in the Korean War* and support for South Korean leader Syngman Rhee*, questioned U.S. government claims

that Communist North Korea had initiated the war, and reported rumors that U.S. forces used chemical weapons during the Korean conflict. As support for the CDFEP dwindled to a few staunch leftists, it no longer could maintain the financial support needed to carry on its legal fight, begun in 1948, to challenge the U.S. government's designation of it as a "subversive" organization. The CDFEP dissolved in 1952.

K. S. Chern, *Dilemma in China: America's Policy Debate, 1945* (Hamden, CT, 1980); K. Garner, "Challenging the Consensus: Maud Muriel Russell's Life and Political Activism," Ph.D. dissertation, University of Texas at Austin, 1995; K. Kerpen, "Voices in a Silence: American Organizations That Worked for Diplomatic Recognition of the People's Republic of China by the United States, 1945–1979," Ph.D. dissertation, New York University, 1981.

Karen Garner

COMMUNISM

The term "Communism" is sometimes used synonymously with Marxism and Socialism, which can be a source of confusion. Josep Femia defines Marxism as theory and Communism as Marxism in practice. Communism has had such broad and varied usages that providing an exact definition is difficult. Andrew Haywood provides three usages of Communism. First, it refers to the utopian vision of a future society presented by Karl Marx. Second, it represents the ideas and policies of Communist parties. Third, it describes the type of government established by Communist parties. Some trace the origins of Communism to Plato's *Republic* or Thomas More's *Utopia*. Modern Communism, however, is identified with the writings of Marx in the latter half of the nineteenth century, and this is the usage of Communism applied here.

Marx used the term "Communism" to describe a political ideology advocating the abolition of private ownership of property, public ownership of the means of production, and distribution and consumption on the basis of common possession of goods and a communal way of life. In such a society, all forms of political domination and repression, in addition to the state itself, presumably would disappear. As time passed, Communism was modified and transformed by changing social, cultural, and historical factors. This caused several variants of Marx's original ideology. By 1977, for example, the Italian, French, and Spanish Communist parties had embraced Eurocommunism, which was based on the principle that "Communism had to conform to existing national traditions and culture." A central premise of Eurocommunism was the necessity to abandon the Leninist idea of revolution and adopt a strategy of a gradual and peaceful transition to Socialism.

Asian Communism established itself out of an anticolonial struggle rather than a class struggle. It placed more emphasis on the concept of colonial oppression than class exploitation. The mixture of national and Socialist principles in Asian Communism can be identified easily as one of its main characteristics. This occurred because Communism was imported as an ideological weapon against imperialism. No ideology has been free from the influence of nationalism in East Asia since these countries started to absorb foreign political ideas as a means to build independent nation-states as a solution to the threat of foreign aggression. This meant that a doctrine or ideology was viable in Asia only when it proved to be favorable to nationalism. Many Communist parties in East Asia effectively used this national aspiration of Asian people by claiming to be the leaders in a struggle for national liberation and opposing Western colonial domination and exploitation.

China's version of Communism represented well the characteristics of Asian Communism. The Chinese Communist Party* (CCP) adapted the theory of Communism to its particular needs and the Chi-

nese environment. Under the leadership of Mao Zedong*, the CCP eventually created its own version of Communism, known as Maoism. In the Democratic People's Republic of Korea*, elements of Marxist-Leninist theory have been combined eclectically with national ingredients into a novel mixture known as *Juch'e**. Although Communism remained strong in North Korea into the twenty-first century, capitalism by then had modified Asian Communism in the People's Republic of China*, the Socialist Republic of Vietnam*, Laos*, and Cambodia*.

J. V. Femia, *Contemporary Political Ideologies* (London, 1993); A. Heywood, *Political Ideologies* (London, 1992); L. Kolakowski, trans. by P. S. Falla, *Main Currents of Marxism* (New York, 1981); G. A. Lichtheim, *Short History of Socialism* (London, 1987).

Han Kyu-sun

COMPACT OF FREE ASSOCIATION FOR MICRONESIA

Passed by Congress in July 1985, the compact, President Ronald Reagan* said, "is the most complex legislation in U.S. history." It granted a new political status to specific island groups within the U.S.-administered United Nations Trust Territory of the Pacific Islands. The compact was the product of more than twenty years of negotiations involving a specially formed Office of Micronesian Status Negotiations within the U.S. Department of the Interior, and the U.S. House of Representatives Insular Affairs Subcommittee, with the supportive interest of the State and Defense Departments, and the National Security Council. The compact stressed the post–UN Trust Territory future of the Caroline Islands (Federated States of Micronesia), the Marshall Islands (the Republic of the Marshall Islands), and the Palaus (the Republic of Palau). The final agreement included hundreds of intricately negotiated articles, making it a larger diplomatic document than the Versailles Peace Treaty *. Particularly in its immigration and defense sections, the compact also affected the U.S. Territory of Guam* and the Commonwealth of the Northern Mariana Islands. Although politicians and academics differ on the origins and meaning of the term, most consider Micronesia the island groups of the western Pacific region.

Under public pressure from the Soviet Union to "decolonize the American Pacific," and given his own alleged interest in Third World "liberation," President John F. Kennedy* named Harvard University's Dr. Anthony Solomon in 1962 to investigate the political/economic troubles and ambitions of the Micronesian islands. After one year of work, he recommended some sort of "association" with the United States for these former World War II battlefields, although it did not necessarily have to be statehood, territorial/commonwealth status, or independence. The goal was to eliminate the colonial trappings of the UN Trust. The result, after twenty years of negotiations with many different cultures and islands, was "free association." This status permitted creation of new "nationlike" identities and governments, although the United States guaranteed their defense and the U.S. dollar remained the currency of choice. Immigration policies and international economic policy rights were negotiated carefully, and one new "freely associated" entity, Palau, refused to ratify the arrangement until guarantees of its nuclear safety were established.

Capitol Hill lobbying groups, including Greenpeace, complained that the compact was too convoluted to guarantee civil rights protection as well as the safe economic and environmental future of the islands. Other observers said the unique semi-independent status of the compact provided cultural respect and necessary U.S. connections at the same time. In addition to the different cultures and island-by-island political agendas, one reason for the long negotiation period was that the U.S. government saw Micronesia as a back-

water to major Cold War interests elsewhere in the Pacific. Yet some say otherwise, noting that the defense section of the compact, which upholds Cold War–championed U.S. security interests in the region, is the clearest article in the document. Although many argued into the 1990s that there cannot be a workable "free association" outside of traditional status agreements, such as independence or commonwealth, the compact negotiators, thousands of islanders, and several presidential administrations disagreed.

C. Heine, *Micronesia at the Crossroads: A Reappraisal of the Micronesian Political Dilemma* (New York, 1974); T. P. Maga, *John F. Kennedy and the New Pacific Community, 1961–1963* (New York, 1990); B. Rogers, *Destiny's Landfall: A History of Guam* (Honolulu, HI, 1995); J. Weisgall, "Micronesia and the Nuclear Pacific Since Hiroshima," *SAIS Review* (Summer-Fall 1985).

Timothy P. Maga

CONGER, EDWIN H. (1843–1907)

Edwin Hurd Conger served as minister to China during the Boxer Uprising* and as U.S. negotiator for the Boxer Protocol*. Conger entered the Foreign Service as minister to Brazil after careers as a rancher, farmer, banker, and U.S. representative from Iowa. He became minister to China in June 1898, during the early stages of internal unrest that led to the Boxer Rebellion. As reassurance against this agitation in China, Conger pressed the U.S. government to reinforce the legation guard in Beijing, permanently station a naval vessel at Tianjin, and acquire a naval base on the Gulf of Zhili. The U.S. Navy granted Conger's first two requests, but disregarded his third. Regardless, he continued to support calls for a naval base in China. His request for a reinforced legation guard in Beijing proved fortuitous when the Boxer unrest reached its zenith. By mid-June 1900, the Boxers (a nationalistic, antiforeign Chinese secret society) had killed hundreds of Christian missionaries and their Chinese converts before laying siege to the foreign legations in Beijing. Conger and the U.S. legation endured the siege barricaded in the British compound with the rest of the foreign legations. On 16 July 1900, as a Chinese gesture of reconciliation, Conger received a telegram from Secretary of State John Hay*. This was the first communication that the legations had received from the outside world since 15 June. Hay received Conger's response on 20 July 1900, thus reassuring the world that the Boxers had not massacred the legations as previously reported. The legations remained under siege until 14 August 1900, when the combined China Relief Expedition* freed them.

After the rebellion, Conger advocated maintaining a U.S. military presence in China. He lobbied for permanently stationing American troops in Beijing to maintain order. President William McKinley* disagreed, however, and ordered the withdrawal of all U.S. forces (except for the 150-man legation guard) by 31 May 1901. Hay, on 16 November 1900, proposed that Conger petition the Chinese for a naval base on the coast of Fujian in Samsah Bay. The Japanese (in whose sphere of interest Samsah Bay was located) quickly reminded the Americans that this request conflicted with Hay's Open Door Policy* as first stated in his circular of 3 July 1900, prompting Washington to withdraw its request. Thereafter, as minister to China, Conger was the primary U.S. negotiator at the Boxer Protocol talks until 25 May 1901, when W. W. Rockhill* replaced him. He remained minister to China until 1905, when he became minister to Mexico, a position he held for several months until he resigned because of the financial strain associated with his new post. Conger generally has received high marks from historians for his performance as minister to China during a turbulent period, despite his status as an amateur diplomat.

H. E. Mattox, *The Twilight of Amateur Diplomacy: The American Foreign Service and Its Senior Offi-*

cers in the 1890s (Kent, OH, 1989); U.S. Department of State, *Papers Relating to the Foreign Relations of the United States* (Washington, DC, 1901); M. B. Young, *The Rhetoric of Empire: American China Policy, 1895–1901* (Cambridge, MA, 1968).

William E. Emerson

CONSTRUCTIVE ENGAGEMENT

President Bill Clinton* adopted the policy of "engagement" or "constructive engagement" toward the People's Republic of China* (PRC) in the mid- and late 1990s. Clinton ran for election in 1992 on a platform that accused President George H. W. Bush*, his rival, of having "coddled" dictators, among whom China's leaders featured prominently. In particular, Clinton referred to Bush's reluctance to condemn China too harshly after the Tiananmen Square Massacre* of June 1989, his readiness to continue working with the Chinese as evidenced in the secret visit of National Security Adviser General Brent Scowcroft to China later in 1989, and his strong support for the renewal of most-favored-nation tariff treatment for China.

After his election victory, Clinton followed a policy toward China in practice almost indistinguishable from Bush's. In annual battles over most-favored-nation tariff treatment for the PRC, he argued that should the U.S. Congress rescind this, the Chinese economy and hence the pace of reform in China would slow, and conditions for ordinary Chinese would worsen rather than improve. Officials in the Clinton administration suggested that policies of "constructive engagement" would be more effective than those of containment toward China in promoting human rights and in winning its cooperation on such issues as nuclear nonproliferation, the cessation of arms sales to countries with which the United States was at odds, notably Iraq, Iran, and Pakistan, and adherence to international commercial standards. Critics suggested that in actuality, his stance resulted from pressure from U.S. businesses, who wished to minimize human rights and other contentious issues to win lucrative orders from mainland China and develop investments there. Relations between the United States and the PRC were strained severely in 1995 when Congress granted a visa to Li Denghui*, president of the Republic of China* (ROC) on Taiwan*, for a visit during which he made a well-publicized speech at Cornell University, his alma mater. This was followed by several months of rising tension between Taiwan and the mainland, culminating in the Taiwan Strait crisis of March 1996, during which the PRC conducted military exercises in that area designed to exert political pressure upon the ROC's first popular presidential elections. The United States sent two naval battle groups to the area, each headed by an aircraft carrier, and to the embarrassment of the PRC, President Li won a resounding victory.

Constructive engagement received repeated criticisms for being ineffective in winning concessions from the PRC on a number of matters, including the treatment of dissidents, observance of free market economic practices, adherence to internationally recognized commercial standards, noninterference with the former colony of Hong Kong*, which returned to Chinese rule in July 1997, and respect for Tibetan autonomy. Moreover, critics charged, China had embarked on a systematic campaign to enhance its military strength and influence in the Asia-Pacific region. Nevertheless, Clinton's adherence to the policy of engagement continued unchanged. Notwithstanding some congressional opposition, Clinton administration officials argued that such dialogue, combined equally with continuing U.S. diplomatic pressure on China on matters upon which the two disagreed and cooperation on other fronts, was the only realistic means by which the United States could moderate Chinese policy and discourage a course of unilateral disregard of generally accepted norms of international behavior in such ar-

eas as economic policies and China's treatment of Taiwan. This outlook led to numerous high-level exchanges of visits on both sides, culminating in October 1997 in a state visit by President Jiang Zemin* of China to the United States and a return visit by Clinton in spring 1998. It also resulted in continued U.S. naval port visits to Hong Kong, release of the noted Chinese dissident Wei Jingsheng*, and eventually in late 1999, the PRC making sufficient economic concessions to cause the United States to endorse its membership in the World Trade Organization. But it did not bring a peaceful and mutually satisfactory settlement of the relationship with Taiwan.

J. W. Garver, *Face Off: China, the United States, and Taiwan's Democratization* (Seattle, WA, 1997); D. M. Lampson, *Same Bed, Different Dreams: Managing U.S.-China Relations, 1989–2000* (Berkeley, CA, 2001); A. J. Nathan and R. S. Ross, *The Great Wall and the Empty Fortress: China's Search for Security* (New York, 1997); R. G. Sutter, *Shaping China's Future in World Affairs: The Role of the United States* (New York, 1996).

Priscilla Roberts

COOLIE TRADE

"Coolie," in Chinese *guli* (bitter labor), is the pejorative European term for Asian, particularly Indian and Chinese, laborers. "Coolie trade" refers to the virtual enslavement, through fraud, debt, and kidnapping, of hundreds of thousands of Chinese laborers during the period 1845 to 1875. Historians construe the coolie trade as a distinct facet of the larger migration of Chinese to Southeast Asia and the Americas from the fifteenth through the nineteenth centuries. Until the 1800s, most emigrants paid their own passages and were free on arrival. However, by the 1840s, circumstances were vastly different. There was a rising demand for labor around mines and plantations in the Americas and West Indies following the international abolition of the African slave trade (1814) and Anglo-

American agreement (1842) to police the west coast of Africa. Within China, emigration rose because of inflation, natural calamities, the impact of the opium trade, and internal unrest culminating in the Taiping Rebellion* (1851–1864). The Qing Dynasty's ban on emigration increased the vulnerability of those who sought to leave, opening the way for the combination of Western merchants and Chinese middlemen. The latter, often affiliated with secret societies and illegal activities, provided local knowledge and language skills; the former, primarily British, American, and Macau Portuguese, provided capital, ships, and the legal immunities given them by the unequal treaties that followed the First Opium War* and Second Opium War*.

By the late 1850s, conditions approximated the worst abuses of the African slave trade. Young Chinese males were coerced into "voluntary emigration," exchanging future service for paid passage. They were assembled in depots in southern Chinese ports, known as "barracoons," and passed from broker to broker, their debt increasing with each transaction. Domestic groups in England pushed for reform, and after 1850 the British government undertook halfhearted steps to curb the most egregious aspects of the traffic through the so-called Canton system, which called for inspecting ships and interviewing passengers. Qing officials initiated an active policy of protection of Chinese emigrants only in 1859, when it recognized the right of voluntary emigration and distinguished that right from the evils of the coolie trade. A series of incidents of notorious ill treatment and mutinies in the late 1860s and early 1870s finally brought international attention, and prompted British, American, and Qing officials to exert combined pressure on Portuguese-controlled Macau—by then the hub of the traffic—to abolish the trade, marking the beginning of the end of the practice. For Americans, the term "coolie" continued in common usage as a derogatory reference to Chinese laborers entering the United States.

M. Coolidge, *Chinese Immigration* (New York, 1909); J. Davids (ed.), *The United States and China*, Series 3, vol. 17 (Wilmington, DE, 1973); M. Farley, "The Chinese Coolie Trade, 1845–1875," *Journal of Asian and African Studies* (July–October 1968); S. Wang, *The Organization of Chinese Emigration, 1848–1888* (San Francisco, 1978); C. Yen, *Coolies and Mandarins: China's Protection of Overseas Chinese During the Late Ching Period, 1851–1911* (Singapore, 1985).

Eileen Scully

CORAL SEA, BATTLE OF

See BATTLE OF CORAL SEA

CORREGIDOR

An island fortress at the entrance of Manila Bay in the Philippines*, Corregidor was the last holdout of U.S. and Filipino forces against the Japanese after the Pearl Harbor Attack*. Japanese landings on Luzon had begun on 10 December 1941, when the Japanese fourteenth Army sent ashore the first of five distinct formations, which converged on Manila from north and south. On the same day, Guam* succumbed to a greatly superior Japanese force after a brief but spirited resistance by its tiny garrison of 365 U.S. Marines, 308 native militia, and a few naval officers and seamen. American air and sea forces scored a few successes against Japanese forces bound for Luzon, but they were too heavily outnumbered to make much of an impression. Without command of the air, General Douglas MacArthur*, overall U.S. commander in the Philippines, was obliged to fall back on the Bataan Peninsula near Manila Bay, but the U.S. Pacific Fleet was no longer in a position to come to his relief. Admiral Thomas Hart, commander of the U.S. Asiatic Fleet, left on 26 December for Java, bequeathing a miscellaneous force of gunboats, minesweepers, and other light naval craft to Rear Admiral Francis W. Rockwell, commandant of the Sixteenth Naval District. Meanwhile, Rockwell had moved from Cavite to Corregidor, establishing his headquarters in a tunnel. On 27 December, after his fourteen surviving heavy bombers had withdrawn to the relative safety of an airfield near Port Darwin, Australia, MacArthur declared Manila an open city and ordered his corps commanders to take up positions covering the Bataan Peninsula. On 2 January 1942, the Japanese captured Manila and Cavite.

Between January and April 1942, relentless Japanese pressure from superior forces with strong air support drove the defenders of Bataan slowly toward the southern extremities of the peninsula. Rockwell's miniature fleet was too weak to smother all attempts by the Japanese to land troops behind the American lines, and a bid to run supplies to Bataan from the southern Philippines was unsuccessful. On 11 March, after the submarine USS *Swordfish* had taken Philippine President Manuel L. Quezon* and other dignitaries to a place of safety, MacArthur handed over command to Major General Jonathan M. Wainwright and left, on orders from Washington, for Australia. Before departing, he promised the Filipinos that one day he would return. Redoubling their efforts, the Japanese succeeded in the course of the next few weeks in breaching Wainwright's front lines and sowing confusion in his defensive positions to the rear. On 8 April, he came to the conclusion that further attempts to hold Bataan without hope of relief and with dwindling reserves of food could serve no useful purpose. That night, he withdrew to Corregidor with the small part of his force that could be carried to the island before daylight, leaving the rest to lay down their arms. There, the U.S. Fourth Marine Regiment and the remnants of the U.S. Army stoutly continued to hold out until 6 May. On that day, General Wainwright surrendered the fortress and all surviving forces in the Philippines to the Japanese. *See also* Bataan Death March.

G. Daws, *Prisoners of the Japanese: POWs of World War II in the Pacific* (New York, 1994); *New York Times*, 5 January 1942; W. A. Renzi and M. D. Roehrs, *Never Look Back: A History of World War II in the Pacific* (Armonk, NY, 1991); R. L. Spector, *Eagle Against the Sun: The American War with Japan* (New York, 1985).

Dirk A. Ballendorf

CUSHING, CALEB (1800–1879)

Caleb Cushing's background made him a controversial choice as the first U.S. commissioner to China. Raised in Newburyport, Massachusetts, the son of a wealthy merchant and shipowner, he longed for foreign travel and accepted commercial expansion as a fundamental national interest. After graduating from Harvard College at age seventeen, Cushing pursued a career in law, literature, and politics. In addition to writing a pamphlet on international maritime law, he published numerous essays on a wide variety of subjects in such respected journals as the *North American Review* and the *United States Literary Gazette*. He also was a talented linguist proficient in several languages. On the long voyage from the United States to China in 1844, Cushing taught himself enough Manchu to be able to hold private talks with Chinese officials without the aid of an interpreter. As a politician, he gained a reputation as an independent-minded political maverick and an ardent advocate of commercial and territorial expansion. The willingness of this talented scholar-politician to place personal considerations and convictions above party interests helps to explain his appointment as the first U.S. commissioner to China.

Cushing entered national politics as a Whig during the 1830s, switched to the Democratic Party in the 1840s, and became a Republican in the 1860s. Beginning in 1835, Cushing served four consecutive terms in the U.S. House of Representatives. He became chairman of the Committee on Foreign Affairs in 1841. That same year, when the Whigs, under the leadership of Henry Clay, broke with President John Tyler and literally read him out of the party, Cushing sided with the president against his party leader. Tyler and Cushing became close friends, and on three separate occasions, the Whig-controlled U.S. Senate rejected Tyler's nomination of Cushing as secretary of the treasury. When Edward Everett declined the appointment as commissioner to China, Tyler named Cushing to the position during a congressional recess. By the time the Senate took up the nomination, Cushing was en route to China. In the 3 July 1843 entry of his celebrated diary, John Quincy Adams tartly observed that Cushing "had not made his court to Captain Tyler in vain." But Cushing justified his selection when he succeeded in negotiating the Treaty of Wangxia*, the first such agreement between China and the United States.

After his return from China, Cushing remained active in public affairs. An ardent expansionist, he supported the annexation of Texas, the claim to all of the Oregon Territory, and the war with Mexico, during which he served as a brigadier general. As President Franklin Pierce's attorney general, Cushing actively promoted the acquisition of Cuba. During the Civil War, however, he joined the Republican Party and endorsed the policies of President Abraham Lincoln. In 1873, President Ulysses S. Grant nominated Cushing as chief justice of the U.S. Supreme Court, but the nomination had to be withdrawn when it became clear that too many senators were unwilling to overlook Cushing's record of political opportunism. Cushing ended his career by serving as U.S. minister to Spain from 1873 to 1877. *See also* Peter Parker.

W. J. Donahue, "The Caleb Cushing Mission," *Modern Asian Studies* (1982); C. M. Fuess, *The Life of Caleb Cushing*, 2 vols. (New York, 1923); M. H. Hunt, *The Making of a Special Relationship: The United States and China to 1914* (New York, 1983); K. E. Shewmaker, "Forging the Great Chain: Daniel Webster and the Origins of American Foreign Policy Toward East Asia and the Pacific, 1841–1852," *Proceedings of the American Philosophical Society* (September 1985); R. E. Welch Jr., "Caleb Cushing's Chinese Mission and the Treaty of Wanghia: A Review," *Oregon Historical Quarterly* (1957).

Kenneth E. Shewmaker

D

DANGWAI

Dangwai was a group of Taiwanese intellectuals and politicians outside the Guomindang* (Nationalist) Party ranks who struggled to reform the political system established to serve the agendas of mainland Chinese immigrants to the island. The loosely organized Dangwai (literally, "outside the [Nationalist] party") evolved into the Democratic Progressive Party (DPP) in 1986, the largest opposition party in the Republic of China* (ROC). Dangwai presented a problem for the United States during the 1970s and early 1980s, as these political activists made a lie out of the ideal of "Free China" under Jiang Jieshi* and his successor Jiang Jingguo*. Americans found themselves torn between their ideals of democracy and the need to support the ROC as a Cold War ally. After switching recognition to the People's Republic of China* (PRC) in 1979, the United States found that the Taiwanese opposition became a major factor in Sino-American relations. In particular, the Dangwai/DPP stance questioned the idea that Taiwan* was no more than a province of China, and thus represented a constant source of conflict between Washington and Beijing. This party's electoral success forced the Guomindang to take a more ambiguous stand on reunification to maintain electoral support. These developments threatened the diplomatic understanding that was the basis for relations between United States and the PRC after issuance of the Shanghai Communiqué* of 1972.

Taiwanese, Han Chinese who immigrated to the island before 1945, made up about 75 percent of Taiwan's population after the arrival of supporters of the defeated Nationalist regime in 1949. But the Nationalist police state put mainlanders in a position of complete dominance over the island's political life, because the opposition was intimidated, new parties forbidden, and academic or media censorship widespread. Beginning in the 1970s, however, the declining international status of the ROC, the death of Jiang Jieshi, and the willingness of his son, Jiang Jingguo, to consider political reform, all served to increase the visibility and viability of the regime's critics, including the Dangwai. These political leaders also received support from American critics of the Nationalists in academia, the media, and Congress. A few key incidents helped crystallize opposition to the mainlander-dominated regime. For example, in the Gaoxiong Incident of December 1979, antigovernment protesters clashed with police, leading to the arrest of many

Taiwanese political activists. This event heightened calls for change in Taiwan and in the United States, and led to a slightly reformed election law in 1980.

In the context of internal reform and external pressure, Taiwanese politicians formed the Dangwai Public Policy Research Association in 1984. This grew into the Democratic Progressive Party (Minzhu jinbu dang) in September 1986. After the government lifted martial law in 1987, further reforms followed, including the relaxation of controls over the press, speech, assembly, and political opposition. The DPP competed in a series of elections to replace legislators and National Assembly members (most of whom had been elected on the mainland in the late 1940s). In late 1994, elections were held for the provincial governor and mayors of the two largest cities (Taibei and Gaoxiong) and, in March 1996, for the presidency of the ROC. The DPP steadily increased its influence on Taiwan because of better political acumen and fairer rules for political competition. The party also was bolstered by its ties with the growing middle class, gaining support by making quality of life issues an important part of its platform. By the 1990s, the DPP had developed a close relationship with many U.S. congressmen, an effective lobbying organization, and a network of student and immigrant organizations in the United States. Yet the party has been plagued by the same problems of corruption and cronyism as the Guomindang. In 2000, Dangwai activist-turned-DPP-politician Chen Shuibian won a closely fought race to become president of the ROC. *See also* Jiang Nan Incident; Taiwanese Communist Party; Two China Policy.

J. Copper, *Taiwan: Nation-State or Province* (Boulder, CO, 1996); D. F. Simon and M. Y. M. Kau (eds.), *Taiwan: Beyond the Economic Miracle* (Armonk, NY, 1992); H. Tien, *Taiwan's Electoral Politics and Democratic Transition: Riding the Third Wave* (Armonk, NY, 1996).

Steven E. Phillips

DAVIES, JOHN PATON (1908–)

John Paton Davies served as an adviser to General Joseph W. Stilwell* during World War II. His wartime recommendations that the United States cultivate friendly relations with the Chinese Communist Party* (CCP) led to charges that he harbored Communist sympathies, resulting in his dismissal from the State Department after Loyalty Review Board hearings during 1954. Although the U.S. government restored his security clearance in 1969, Davies never returned to government service. He was born to Baptist missionaries in remote Jiading, Sichuan Province. His family moved to the larger and more accessible city of Chengdu when he was young. In 1920, they traveled to the United States on missionary furlough. After returning to China, Davies attended the Shanghai American School and witnessed the start of the May Thirtieth Movement* in 1925 that sparked an intense anti-imperialist reaction among Chinese workers, students, and intellectuals. He returned to the United States soon afterward and attended the University of Wisconsin. In 1929, Davies went back again to China for his junior year of study at the Protestant-sponsored Yanjing University in Beijing before he completed his undergraduate degree at Columbia University.

Davies's experiences with travel and living abroad and his Chinese language skills had prepared him well for a career in the Foreign Service. After passing the civil service exams, he was assigned to a post at the U.S. consulate in Kunming, the capital of Yunnan Province, China. Within a few years, Davies was sent to the U.S. legation in Beijing for formal language study, where he met Clarence E. Gauss, legation counselor and later, ambassador to China. In 1935, Davies was appointed vice counsel to Shenyang, occupied by Japan since the Mukden Incident* in 1931, and remained there until Japan declared war on China after the Marco Polo Bridge Incident* in 1937. In 1938, he was transferred to Hankou, where he developed a respect for what he saw as the CCP's vigorous and sincere resistance to Japanese imperialism and a strong admiration for the CCP liaison, Zhou Enlai*. Assigned to Washington in 1940, Davies worked on the China desk of the Far Eastern Division until the United States declared war on Japan, when he was sent in 1942 to assist Joseph Stilwell, who had been appointed chief of staff to Jiang Jieshi*. Davies, Stilwell, Gauss, and Foreign Service officers John Carter Vincent* and John S. Service*, all posted to the U.S. embassy in Chongqing, grew increasingly frustrated with the Guomindang* (Nationalist) government's uncooperative attitude and the weaknesses of its army as a fighting force. Davies was impressed, however, by the CCP's significant popular support. He urged his superiors in the State Department to put pressure on Jiang to enact reforms within his government and army.

In January 1944, Davies recommended that Washington send an observer mission to the Chinese Communist headquarters in Yan'an, arguing that the CCP was the best-disciplined anti-Japanese fighting force in China. Cultivating better relations also would prevent the CCP from building an exclusive alliance with the Soviet Union when the war ended. Then, in September, Patrick J. Hurley* arrived in China to repair the strained relations between Stilwell and Jiang. Unable to reconcile them, he supported Jiang's request to remove Stilwell from his post in China. After Stilwell's recall in October, Davies secured reassignment to the U.S. embassy in Moscow. But before he left, Davies visited Yan'an in the fall of 1944. He recommended again that the United States develop friendly relations with what he described as the pragmatic and patriotic CCP leaders. However, Hurley, then U.S. ambassador to China, had determined that his mission in China was to unite the rival Guomindang and CCP forces in a coalition government. When Hurley resigned as ambassador in November 1945, he accused Davies and other China Hands* of having Communist sym-

pathies and sabotaging his efforts. His charges were investigated by the Senate Foreign Relations Committee. Although Davies was cleared of any wrongdoing at that time, and twice more in 1951, the U.S. government adopted new criteria in 1953 for loyalty and reevaluated Davies's case. Terminated in 1954, Davies moved to Lima, Peru, and went into business. See also Chinese Civil War; Dixie Mission.

J. P. Davies Jr., Dragon by the Tail: American, British, Japanese, and Russian Encounters with China and One Another (New York, 1972); R. Y. Koen, The China Lobby in American Politics (New York, 1974); P. A. Varg, The Closing of the Door: Sino-American Relations 1936–1946 (East Lansing, MI, 1973).

Karen Garner

DAVIS, NORMAN H. (1878–1944)

A leading Democrat and former businessman, Norman H. Davis entered public life first as assistant secretary of the treasury and then was assistant secretary of state in the administration of President Woodrow Wilson*, the man who would be his political idol for the remainder of his life. A firm supporter of the League of Nations, he rejected the opportunity of remaining in office under Wilson's Republican successor, yet continued his interests in international affairs, helping to organize the Council on Foreign Relations and the Woodrow Wilson Foundation, both of which he chaired for a period. For the rest of his life, Davis was one of those Americans most committed to the belief that the United States should play a substantial and active role in the world, preferably through those institutions Wilson had helped to establish. Throughout the 1920s and 1930s, he advocated American membership in the League of Nations and the World Court, serving on several League economic commissions and conferences in the 1920s. Davis's partisan loyalty to Wilson led him to attack treaties resulting from the Washington Conference* of 1921 and 1922 as a mere alliance of great powers, whose defects might well draw the United States into future wars.

For most of the 1930s, Davis took part in a series of disarmament negotiations spanning both the Hoover and Roosevelt administrations, becoming the leading U.S. representative and expert on the subject. Herbert Hoover* named him a member of the U.S. delegation to the Geneva Disarmament Conference in 1932, and Franklin D. Roosevelt* promoted him to its chairmanship, with the rank of ambassador. In this capacity, Davis attempted not only to implement arms limitation, but also to strengthen U.S. cooperation with the League of Nations. He persuaded Roosevelt to authorize him, should an agreement be concluded, to commit the United States to "consult" with other nations if any threat to peace arose, as well as possibly pledge that his country would not interfere with League sanctions against an aggressor. This remained a dead letter, since the conference never came near to reaching an agreement and lapsed in 1934. The London Naval Conference of 1935–1936*, at which Davis again led the U.S. delegation, was almost as fruitless. Japan withdrew from it, and Great Britain, France, and the United States, the other powers represented, reached only minor accords.

In 1937, Davis again headed a U.S. delegation, on this occasion to the Brussels Conference* to take action after Japan invaded China following the Marco Polo Bridge Incident*. He is believed to have drafted Roosevelt's Quarantine Speech* of October 1937, in which the president publicly called for a more forceful policy of international opposition to aggressor nations. From 1938 until his death, Davis was chairman of both the American Red Cross and the International Red Cross, supporting humanitarian efforts to alleviate the hardships of war in both Asia and Europe. He continued to advise the president on foreign policy and from 1941 took an increasing interest in postwar planning, which finally seemed likely to realize Davis's life-long hopes that the United States would be fully involved in international affairs.

R. A. Dallek, *Franklin D. Roosevelt and U.S. Foreign Policy, 1932–1945* (New York, 1979); T. C. Irvin, "Norman H. Davis and the Quest for Arms Control, 1931–1938," Ph.D. dissertation, Ohio State University, 1963; H. B. Whiteman Jr., "Norman H. Davis and the Search for International Peace and Security, 1917–1944," Ph.D. dissertation, Yale University, 1958.

Priscilla Roberts

DEER MISSION

This was one of a series of missions to French Indochina* during World War II by the U.S. Office of Strategic Services (OSS). On 16 July 1945, several members of the Deer Mission, under the command of Allison K. Thomas, parachuted into Vietnam near the Chinese border and were met by Ho Chi Minh*, Vo Nguyen Giap*, and some 200 members of the Vietminh*, the Communist-led organization seeking Vietnamese independence from French colonial rule. In the first weeks of August, the Americans provided the Vietminh with a modest number of weapons and supervised a series of training exercises. At the same time, Ho and Giap met with the leaders of the Deer Mission in hopes of winning American support for the Vietminh's wider aims. With the news of imminent Japanese surrender in mid-August, the OSS officers and the Vietminh forces made their way to the provincial capital of Thai Nguyen, where the Vietminh engaged the Japanese in a five-day street battle. The Deer Mission, along with other OSS missions to Vietnam in this period, have provoked significant historiographical debate. French historians have argued that the OSS was seeking to displace France and assert American control in Vietnam. Vietnamese historiography credits the actions of the Deer Mission with formation of a joint Vietnamese-American armed force aimed at fighting both the Japanese and the French. Available American evidence, however, suggests that the aims and activities of the OSS missions were considerably more modest, being confined to providing logistical support for the Japanese surrender and intelligence gathering on wartime conditions in Vietnam.

M. P. Bradley, *Imagining Vietnam and America: The Making of Postcolonial Vietnam, 1919–1950* (Chapel Hill, NC, 2000); A. L. A. Patti, *Why Vietnam? Prelude to America's Albatross* (Berkeley, CA, 1980).

Mark P. Bradley

DEMOCRATIC PEOPLE'S REPUBLIC OF KOREA

Formed in September 1948, the Democratic People's Republic of Korea (DPRK) occupies the mountainous northern half of the Korean peninsula. During World War II, the Soviet Union organized the Operating Group in Korea along with the Korean guerrilla leaders in its Eighty-eighth Division, naming Division Captain Kim Il Sung* as leader of the group. After the Thirty-Eighth Parallel Division* to accept Japan's surrender, Kim returned to the Soviet zone in the north on 19 August 1945. Taking leadership of the transitional pro-Soviet administration, Kim finally became the first premier of the DPRK in 1948 and the first chairman of the Korean Workers' Party (KWP) in 1949. At first, Kim Il Sung shared power with other Communist factions, including the indigenous Communists, Russian Koreans, and those who had completed the Long March with Chinese leader Mao Zedong*. North Korea enacted sweeping reforms, including land redistribution, nationalization of industry, public education, and women's rights. A determination to reunite Korea motivated Kim Il Sung's decision, with the support of the Soviet Union and the People's Republic of China* (PRC), to order the massive attack on South Korea on 25 June 1950. U.S. intervention not only prevented reunification, but almost resulted in the destruction of the DPRK. Three years of fighting

formed the basis for antagonistic relations with the United States. But Kim Il Sung skillfully exploited popular hatred and fear of American aggression to consolidate his political power, prevailing in a series of power struggles that climaxed with the execution in 1956 of rival Pak Hŏn-yŏng*. Thereafter, Kim ruled with an iron hand, promoting a personality cult centered on himself as the "Great Leader" of the Korean people.

In December 1955, Kim Il Sung initiated the ideology of *Juch'e** or self-reliance, possibly motivated by unsatisfactory support from the Soviet Union and unwelcome domination of the PRC during the Korean War*. *Juch'e* became the official ideology of North Korea only after the Sino-Soviet dispute became public knowledge when, in December 1962, a newspaper editorial in the *Nodong Shinmun* made it the approved code of conduct for the KWP. Then, in April 1965, Kim proclaimed "self-reliance in thought," "independence in politics," "autonomy in economy," and "self-defense in national defense," resulting in implementation of extreme policies aimed at isolation and autarky. In 1980, the DPRK proclaimed a new regime called Socialism of *Juch'e* and then renamed it Socialism of Our Type in the 1990s. This system was analogous to Stalinism, particularly in its reliance on the supremacy of the *suryŏng* or ultimate ruler. However, there were two important differences, as North Korea based the transformation of its society on Confucian culture, the "Socialist Great Family," and attached great importance to the military, the "Politics of Prior Military." Also, in 1986, Kim Jong Il*, Kim's son, explained that the North Korean society was a "sociopolitical living body" with the *suryŏng* as the cerebrum, the KWP the backbone, and the people the cells.

North Korea made strides toward industrialization during the 1950s, but its economy stagnated thereafter, contrasting sharply with the rising prosperity in South Korea. Nevertheless, the DPRK continued to claim legitimacy as the government of all Korea, refusing after 1948 to have any direct contact with the ROK. North Korea has maintained a huge military establishment while staging provocative incidents along the heavily fortified border between the two Koreas. It also has practiced terrorism, notably igniting a bomb in Rangoon, Burma*, in 1983 that killed several high-ranking ROK officials. Yet the end of the Cold War forced compromises on North Korea, such as accepting representation for both Koreas in the United Nations in 1991. After the Soviet Union fell in late 1991, the DPRK entered a period of serious socioeconomic crisis, as the end of foreign aid and several natural disasters produced shortages of food and consumer goods. Deterioration of industrial equipment and a paralyzed educational system brought productive activities to a virtual standstill. Widespread malnutrition and starvation destroyed the family, as parents abandoned children and relatives fled their villages. The state apparatus retained firm control, however, even after Kim Il Sung died in 1994. But despite measures to force citizens to return to their workplace, economic recovery has been difficult. Reports of popular dissatisfaction did not develop into organized resistance because North Korean authorities retained control of dissident elements with physical coercion and political repression.

During the 1990s, P'yŏngyang sought a relaxation of tensions with the United States in an effort to secure help in overcoming its economic difficulties. But in 1993, the North Korean Nuclear Controversy* renewed friction between North Korea and the United States. Negotiation of the Agreed Framework in October 1994 eased the crisis and led the DPRK to propose negotiations with the United States to achieve a peace agreement to replace the Korean Armistice Agreement*. It also was cooperative in satisfying U.S. demands to repatriate the remains of U.S. soldiers missing in action in the Korean War. But delays in implementing the Agreed Framework caused North Korea to stage missile tests

into Japanese airspace in August 1998. Another annoyance for Washington was the DPRK's sale of missiles to Arab states. But after Kim Jong Il, having succeeded his father, agreed to postpone missile tests, President Bill Clinton* in September 1999 lifted some economic sanctions against North Korea. Meanwhile, P'yŏngyang agreed to Four Party Talks between the two Koreas, the PRC, and the United States, resulting in the DPRK allowing American inspectors to visit suspected underground nuclear facilities in 1999 in return for 600,000 tons of American food aid. Thereafter, unofficial talks to normalize diplomatic relations resumed as the Clinton administration helped ROK President Kim Dae-jung* in implementing his "Sunshine Policy" of engagement with the DPRK to establish a stable peace on the peninsula. In June 2000, Kim Dae-jung made his historic trip to P'yŏngyang for talks with Kim Jong Il, and Secretary of State Madeleine Albright visited North Korea in October. But as the twenty-first century began, North Korea's future was a matter of speculation.

Chung'ang Ilbo Tŏkbŏylch'ŭijeban [Special Reporter Group of the *Chung'ang Ilbo*], *Chosŏn Minjujŭi Inmin' Gonghwagŏk* [The Democratic People's Republic of Korea], 2 vols. (Seoul, 1992, 1993); Yi Jŏng-sik, *Hyŭndae Bŭkhaneŭi Yihae, Sasang, Cheje, Jidoja* [Understanding Contemporary North Korea Ideology, Regime, and Leaders] (Seoul, 1995); D. Suh, *Kim Il Sung: The North Korean Leader* (New York, 1988); *Yonhap News, 2000 North Korea Year Book* (Seoul, 1999); *Yonhap News, 2001 North Korea Year Book* (Seoul, 2000).

Heo Man-ho

DEMOCRATIC PROGRESSIVE PARTY

See DANGWAI

DEMOCRATIC REPUBLIC OF VIETNAM

The Democratic Republic of Vietnam (DRV) was established in August 1945 by the Communist-led Vietminh* in the aftermath of Japan's surrender. Ho Chi Minh* declared the DRV's independence from France on 2 September, but his efforts to win diplomatic recognition for the DRV, including the sending of letters to President Harry S. Truman*, met with no success as French troops followed British and Chinese occupation forces into Vietnam. Ho agreed to negotiate with the French on the future of the DRV's status in 1946, but the talks broke down by the end of the year as fighting broke out between French and Vietminh troops. The DRV spent the next three years fighting against French efforts to destroy its forces and undermine its popular appeal by sponsoring the pro-French State of Vietnam headed by Bao Dai*. Its fortunes improved in late 1949, when Chinese Communist forces reached the Vietnamese border and provided the DRV with supplies and base camps for its troops. The People's Republic of China* and the Soviet Union extended diplomatic recognition to the DRV in January 1950, but the United States, which was hostile to its Communist leadership, committed itself firmly to the French and Bao Dai regime. The DRV received Soviet and Chinese military supplies that enabled its forces to launch a series of attacks against the French in the early 1950s. These offensives finally came to an end in May 1954, when the Vietminh decisively defeated the French garrison at Dien Bien Phu*, ending the First Indochina War*.

In the Geneva Accords of 1954*, elections for the reunification of Vietnam were scheduled for 1956 and the DRV gained control of Vietnam north of the seventeenth parallel. The DRV's leaders initially devoted most of their efforts to consolidating political control and creating a socialist economic system in North Vietnam, and they received Chinese and Soviet aid in doing so. They received only minimal Chinese and Soviet diplomatic support, however, in protesting the decision of Ngo Dinh Diem* to cancel talks for the 1956 elections. An opportunity to press the case for national reunification arose in the late

1950s as unrest against the Diem regime mounted. In party meetings held in 1959 and 1960, the DRV's leadership decided to send men and materiel to South Vietnam along the Ho Chi Minh Trail* to help Communist insurgents fighting against Diem. This support steadily increased in the early 1960s as the Kennedy and Johnson administrations raised the level of American support for the Republic of Vietnam* and the DRV's leaders eventually decided to send combat units to South Vietnam in the autumn of 1964. By 1965, the DRV was involved in a major Second Indochina War*, sending growing numbers of troops southward despite the heavy damage it suffered from American air strikes.

Both the United States and DRV made several attempts to begin negotiations to end the fighting, but neither side was willing to make the concessions needed to start peace talks until after the Tet Offensive* in 1968. The war, however, continued for several more years despite the Nixon administration's use of secret negotiations with the DRV to hasten a peace settlement. When the Paris Peace Accords* were signed in January 1973, the United States agreed to withdraw its military forces from Vietnam and the warring Vietnamese parties agreed to negotiate a settlement of the war in the south. These negotiations, however, never took place because of deep-seated mutual distrust. In the fall of 1974, the DRV's leaders planned a series of offensives to reunify Vietnam in 1975 and 1976. When the 1975 offensive led to a series of decisive victories over the South Vietnamese, the DRV's leaders decided to fight for a victory in 1975, and on April 30, the DRV's forces entered Saigon. Hanoi's leaders now named their united nation the Socialist Republic of Vietnam*. *See also* French Indochina; Le Ductho; Paris Peace Talks; Pham Van Dong; Vo Nguyen Giap; Xuan Thuy.

W. J. Duiker, *Ho Chi Minh: A Life* (New York, 2000); W. J. Duiker, *Vietnam: Nation in Revolution* (Boulder, CO, 1983); B. B. Fall, *The Two Viet-*

nams: *A Political and Military Analysis* (New York, 1967); G. Porter, *Vietnam: The Politics of Bureaucratic Socialism* (Ithaca, NY, 1993).

Joseph G. Morgan

DENBY, CHARLES (1830–1904)

Charles Denby, as minister to China from 1885 to 1898, sought to promote the interests of U.S. businesses and the work of American missionaries through a more assertive policy than the administrations in Washington were willing to support. He was born in Mount Joy, Virginia. After first attending Georgetown University, Denby graduated from Virginia Military Institute in 1850. During his youth, he lived briefly in Marseilles, France, where his father was a U.S. naval agent. After three years as an instructor of military tactics at Masonic University in Selma, Alabama, Denby moved to Evansville, Indiana, in 1853, where he worked as an editor for the *Daily Enquirer* while studying for the legal profession he would enter in 1855. He was elected to the state legislature as a Democrat in 1856 and, despite his Southern origins, fought for the Union in the Civil War as a colonel with the Indiana Volunteers. Wounded in 1862, he received a medical discharge three months later and returned to his legal practice.

Resuming his political involvements, Denby was a delegate to the 1876 and 1884 Democratic Conventions. His support of the successful presidential candidacy of Grover Cleveland and fellow Indiana Democrat Thomas Hendricks earned his reward of appointment as minister to China in May 1885. He remained in China for thirteen years, during which he became the dean of the diplomat corps in Beijing and gained the respect, if not the affection, of Chinese officials. In 1893, Denby remained in his post when Republican nominee Senator Henry W. Blair was declared unacceptable by the Chinese government because of his votes in favor of the Chinese Exclusion Acts*. As a lawyer in Indiana,

Denby had represented railroads, and in China he sought to assist American entrepreneurs in securing railroad concessions there during the 1880s. Meanwhile, Denby's central role in the promotion of various fraudulent efforts for telephone and banking concessions led to a warning from Secretary of State Thomas F. Bayard that the minister must remain "aloof" from U.S. business ventures. Denby had little respect for Chinese customs or culture, urging that antimissionary riots be punished by the demolition of whole towns.

During periods of strained relations with the Japanese, Denby managed the interests of the Japanese government in Beijing. Throughout the Sino-Japanese War (1894–1895), he served as an intermediary between the two warring nations while advising Chinese officials on correspondence related to peace negotiations eventuating in the Treaty of Shimonoseki*. He urged the Cleveland administration without success to assume an active role in mediating the conflict. Denby then was rebuked by Secretary of State Walter Q. Gresham, who instructed the minister to refrain from using his official status to press the case of particular American business interests. These instructions soon were modified by Gresham's successor, Richard Olney, allowing Denby to push unsuccessfully to secure the Beijing-Hankou Railroad concession for a U.S. syndicate, and another concession to build a North China–Manchurian railroad. As he completed his tenure in China, Denby expressed concern in 1898 about the German seizure of Jiaozhou and the Russian lease of Port Arthur on the Liaodong Peninsula. That same year, President William McKinley* named him a member of the commission investigating the conduct of the Spanish-American War*. Next, Denby served on the Philippine Commission that issued a report reflecting his personal views that the Philippines* should be held as a base to support U.S. national interests in East Asia. *See also* Open Door Policy.

D. L. Anderson, *Imperialism and Idealism: American Diplomats in China, 1861–1898* (Bloomington, IN, 1985); D. F. Healy, *U.S. Expansion: The Imperialist Urge in the 1890s* (Madison, WI, 1970); T. J. McCormick, "The Wilson-McCook Scheme of 1896–1897," *Pacific Historical Review* (February 1967); M. B. Young, *The Rhetoric of Empire: American China Policy, 1895–1901* (Cambridge, MA, 1968).

Michael J. Devine

DENG XIAOPING (1904–1997)

Deng Xiaoping was the most important Chinese Communist leader from 1978 to 1994. He opened China to the outside world and normalized diplomatic relations with the United States as the chairman of the Central Military Commission (CMC) of the Chinese Communist Party* (CCP), vice chairman of the CCP Central Committee, and deputy premier of the People's Republic of China* (PRC). While in France in 1923, Deng joined the Chinese Communist Young League in Europe, and in 1926 he studied Marxist-Leninist thought in Moscow. Returning to China, he organized armed revolts in Guangdong in 1929 and then served in various capacities in the Chinese Red Army in the 1930s and in World War II. After being appointed as secretary of the CCP Central China Bureau in 1945, Deng moved the CCP in the Chinese Civil War* from defense to strategic offense by leading his troops across the Yellow River in 1947 against the Guomindang* (Nationalist) army's attacks. His success in conducting the Huaihai campaign in 1948 and 1949, which eliminated more than half a million Nationalist troops and enabled Mao Zedong* to press on to victory, made him one of the CCP's top leaders.

After the founding of the PRC in 1949, Deng became deputy premier in 1954 and was general secretary of the Central Committee from 1954 to 1966. During the Chinese Cultural Revolution*, he was ousted from the PRC and CCP hierarchy in 1966. Deng and his wife were under house arrest in Beijing for two years before being sent to Jiangxi to work at a tractor-repair factory in a small town. Rehabilitated by Mao, Deng resumed his deputy premier post and was elected a member of the Central Committee in 1973. He led the Chinese delegation to New York to address the UN General Assembly in 1974 and then was appointed as first deputy premier. In 1975, Deng became vice chairman of the CMC and chief of the general staff of the People's Liberation Army (PLA) while being elected vice chairman of the Central Committee and a member of the Politburo Standing Committee. He was accused of criticizing Jiang Qing, Mao's wife, and dismissed again in April 1976 from all of his posts.

In 1977, Deng staged his third comeback as deputy premier after Mao's death. Firmly in control of Beijing and having removed the Maoists, he made a historic speech, "Emancipate the Mind," at the Third Plenary Session of the Eleventh Party Central Committee in 1978—a declaration calling for an opening to the outside world so as to bring the Four Modernizations* to China. This led to U.S.-PRC Normalization of Relations* in January 1979 to achieve economic growth and establish a market economy. That year, Deng became the first top PRC leader to visit the United States, holding talks with President Jimmy Carter* and signing protocols on trade, education, technology, and cultural exchanges. Later, he met Presidents Ronald Reagan* and George H. W. Bush* in Beijing during their state visits to China. Deng also began negotiations with the British government in 1982 for China to resume sovereignty over Hong Kong*, and with the Portugese government for Macau's return to China. He developed a theory of "one country, two systems" to apply to these territories, as well as to Taiwan*, for peaceful national reunification. After many years of negotiations, Hong Kong was returned to China in 1997, and Macau in 1999. Meanwhile, a rapid increase of cross-strait trade, visits, and exchanges occurred, and multilevel official negotiations began between Beijing and Taibei in the 1980s.

A pragmatist rather than an ideologue, Deng tried to keep China within the international system so as to seek maximum opportunities for its development by joining many international organizations and signing numerous treaties with foreign governments. Described in the West as a "mountain mover," he was one of a very few world leaders to be named *Time* magazine's Man of the Year twice (in 1978 and 1985). In 1987, he refused to become the chairman of the CCP, premier of the State Council, or president of the PRC, resigning from the Central Committee along with conservative senior party members to ensure continuity of his reform policies. Though officially retired, Deng remained at the center of power when the third generation of Chinese leaders faced many difficulties in the late 1980s and early 1990s. Lacking a plan to solve new economic and social problems and unwilling to carry the reform into politics, he and other Chinese leaders in the summer of 1989 were challenged by pro-democracy student demonstrations for nationwide political reforms and against corruption and power abuse. It was Deng who ordered PLA soldiers to open fire on protesting students in the Tiananmen Square Massacre* on 4 June in Beijing. In response, Western countries denounced the PRC, and the Bush administration joined international economic sanctions imposed on China by Western industrial countries. In 1992, Deng continued his reform with a new theory of "building socialism with Chinese characteristics." His health problems soon reduced his active political role, as Parkinson's disease and lung ailments eventually made him nearly blind and deaf. *See also* Constructive Engagement; Special Economic Zones.

X. Deng, *Selected Works of Deng Xiaoping, 1975–92* (Beijing, 1994); M. Goldman, *Political Reform in the Deng Xiaoping Era* (Cambridge, MA, 1994); L. Pye, *The Spirit of Chinese Politics* (Cambridge, MA, 1992); T. Tsou, *The Cultural Revolution and Post-Mao Reforms* (Chicago, 1986); B. Yang, *Deng: A Political Biography* (Armonk, NY, 1998).

Li Xiaobing

DENING, ESLER (1897–1977)

Sir Esler Maberly Dening arrived in Japan in 1951 to serve as the United Kingdom's head political representative and remained in Japan to become Britain's first postwar ambassador (1952–1957). In the lead-up to the signing of the Yoshida Letter*, he was seen as having attempted to influence Japan toward the recognition of the People's Republic of China* (PRC). He was thought to have acted in this manner to prevent Japan from becoming a threat to Britain's traditional trading areas in Southeast Asia. "Bill" Dening spent his early childhood in Japan, where his father had been a missionary. He began his public service when he joined the Australian forces in World War I. In 1920, he enlisted as a student interpreter in the Japan Consular Service, where he made use of his Japanese language skills. Dening spent the next two decades serving in the consular offices in Seoul, Dairen, Ōsaka, Kōbe, and Harbin. In 1941, he became the first secretary at the British embassy in Washington. Two years later, he became the political adviser to Louis Mountbatten in Singapore*. Although Dening did not get along well with Mountbatten, he made an impression on officials at the Foreign Office because of his careful reporting of events then taking place in Southeast Asia. His appointment as political adviser was followed by promotion to the position of assistant undersecretary of state. During the next four years at the Foreign Office, he was involved in formulating many of Britain's policies toward Asia, including the establishment of the Colombo Plan* and the "foot in the door" policy toward the PRC. Dening believed that Britain did not necessarily have to withdraw from Asia in the postwar period and thought that Britain could remain a predominant power in the region as long as it did not oppose the various independence movements there.

Between 1950 and 1951, Dening was appointed to head a special mission to Asia with the rank of ambassador to establish diplomatic contact with the PRC. But the outbreak of the Korean War* and China's entry prevented Dening from ever meeting with the Chinese Communist leaders. In 1951, Dening arrived in Tōkyō, where he took over as head of the United Kingdom (UK) liaison mission, but he soon became embroiled in discussions leading to the decision of Prime Minister Yoshida Shigeru* to recognize the Republic of China* rather than the PRC. The Americans believed he was trying to persuade Japan to normalize relations with the PRC to prevent the former from becoming a serious competitor in Britain's traditional trading areas in Southeast Asia. Ironically, U.S. officials misinterpreted Dening's actions. Dening in fact thought that an expansion of Japanese exports to Southeast Asia would lead to an improvement in the living standard of the people there and thus reduce the chances of Communist infiltration in the region. He also thought that Japan's economic viability would lead to the strengthening of the strategic defensive perimeter in Asia and therefore be of benefit to Southeast Asian defense as well. Thereafter, as the British ambassador in Tōkyō, Dening was sympathetic toward Japan, but he was unable to make a powerful impact on British decision making because of the growing anti-Japanese sentiment voiced by British industrialists. After his retirement in 1957, he served as the head of the UK delegation to the Antarctic Treaty Conference in 1959.

R. Buckley, "From San Francisco to Suez and Beyond: Anglo-Japanese Relations, 1952–60," in W. I. Cohen and A. Iriye (eds.), *The Great Powers in East Asia, 1953–1960* (New York, 1990); R. Buckley, "In Proper Perspective: Sir Esler Dening (1897–1977) and Anglo-Japanese Relations 1951–1957," in H. Cortazzi and G. Daniels (eds.), *Britain and Japan 1859–1991: Themes and Personalities* (London, 1991); P. Charrier, *Britain, India and the Genesis of the Colombo Plan, 1945–1951* (Cambridge, MA, 1995); T. Remme, *Britain and Regional Cooperation in South-East Asia, 1945–49* (New York, 1995); T. H. Tang, *Britain's Encounter with Revolutionary China, 1949–54* (London, 1992).

Yokoi Noriko

DESOTO PATROLS

Part of the Johnson administration's efforts to harass the armed forces of the Democratic Republic of Vietnam* (DRV) in the Second Indochina War*, the DeSoto Patrols were instituted during the spring of 1964 with the specific objective of finding shore-based North Vietnamese radar posts. U.S. destroyers ran along the coast of the DRV as part of Operation Plan 34 Alpha (OPLAN 34A*) to stimulate contact with radar installations, thus finding their positions for later targeting when the U.S. bombing campaign began. The U.S. destroyers USS *Maddox* and USS *C. Turner Joy* were part of the team that was participating in DeSoto Patrols when they reportedly were attacked by North Vietnamese torpedo boats in August 1964 in the Gulf of Tonkin Incidents*. President Lyndon B. Johnson* and Secretary of Defense Robert S. McNamara* took the case to Congress, which provided authorization for military action with the Gulf of Tonkin Resolution. The Johnson administration used this to justify its military escalation with Operation ROLLING THUNDER* in the spring of 1965. It later became clear that no attacks had occurred on the two destroyers. Moreover, the U.S. destroyers, as part of the DeSoto Patrols, were engaged in provocative acts against the DRV, a fact that Johnson did not communicate to Congress in 1964.

L. C. Gardner, *Pay Any Price: Lyndon Johnson and the Wars for Vietnam* (Chicago, 1995); F. Logevall, *Choosing War: The Lost Chance for Peace and the Escalation of the War in Vietnam* (Berkeley, CA, 1999); E. E. Moise, *Tonkin Gulf and the Escalation of the Vietnam War* (Chapel Hill, NC, 1996).

T. Christopher Jespersen

DIEM'S ASSASSINATION

Having served as the president of the Republic of Vietnam* since 1955, one year after the French defeat at Dien Bien Phu*, Ngo Dinh Diem* found his position becoming increasingly tenuous by early 1963. Widespread corruption and blatant favoritism, especially of landlords over peasants in legal, political, and economic matters, alienated much of the population and contributed to the rise of South Vietnamese resistance in the form of the Viet Cong*. Himself a Catholic, Diem hurt his public standing further when he launched a series of assaults on Buddhist monks in the spring because of his insistence that they were linked with the Viet Cong. Accordingly, by the summer of 1963, Diem's effectiveness was called into question by U.S. military personnel and members of the Kennedy administration. In addition, his brother Ngo Dinh Nhu* made public overtures to the Viet Cong, something anathema to the anti-Communist Americans. When certain South Vietnamese generals approached American officials about the possibility of a coup, worrying that such an action would be met with a termination of economic and military assistance, they were told that would not happen, and planning began in August.

After one aborted attempt, South Vietnamese troops moved on 30 October and surrounded the presidential palace. Diem tried stalling and called for units loyal to him to return to Saigon, a tactic that had saved him in 1960. In the meantime, after being rebuffed by Ambassador Henry Cabot Lodge Jr.*, Diem and his brother fled to the Chinese section of the city, Cholon, via an underground tunnel. They spoke with the coup leader, General Doung Van Minh*, and agreed to meet with the generals. On 2 November, Diem and his brother were executed in the back of an armored personnel carrier. Their deaths furthered the American involvement in Vietnam in two critical ways: first, since members of the Kennedy administration had known of the coup beforehand (though not of the plans to assassinate the Diem brothers), they bore some responsibility for the situation; second, the successors to Diem never were able to gain control of events in South Vietnam, leading to a growing American presence that culminated with the decisions in 1965 to begin bombing North Vietnam and to go with the major increase in the number of American troops.

L. C. Gardner, *Pay Any Price: Lyndon Johnson and the Wars for Vietnam* (Chicago, 1995); E. J. Hammer, *A Death in November: America in Vietnam, 1963* (New York, 1987); G. McT. Kahin, *Intervention: How America Became Involved in Vietnam* (New York, 1986); F. Logevall, *Choosing War: The Lost Chance for Peace and the Escalation of War in Vietnam* (Berkeley, CA, 1999).

T. Christopher Jespersen

DIEN BIEN PHU

The French defeat at the battle of Dien Bien Phu ended the First Indochina War* and brought a more direct U.S. involvement in the fate of former French Indochina*. In May 1953, the new commander of the French Expeditionary Corps, General Henri Navarre, developed a plan to seize the military initiative against the Vietminh*. As Navarre prepared for his offensive, General Vo Nguyen Giap*, the commander of the People's Army of Vietnam (PAVN), moved troops into northern Laos*, threatening French control there. In November 1953, Navarre responded by parachuting some of his best troops into the remote village of Dien Bien Phu. Located in the northwest corner of Vietnam, the village lay in a broad valley twelve miles long and six miles wide, surrounded by rugged terrain and hills as high as 1,000 feet. French troops (eventually numbering nearly 11,000) began to patrol the surrounding area and to construct a large fortress. By creating a "mooring point" deep in the interior, Navarre and his lieutenants hoped to close off enemy invasion routes into Laos, penetrate the Vietminh's rear areas, and lure enemy units into a major, set-piece battle. Giap accepted the challenge, dispatching 50,000 troops and 250 heavy weapons into the hills surrounding the valley and organizing a massive logistical effort to support his forces. On 13 March 1954, Vietminh artillery began an intensive bombardment of the French garrison on the valley floor.

French commanders had underestimated Giap's ability to move large forces and artillery through roadless terrain and to sustain them through a long battle. The fortress at Dien Bien Phu, consisting of an airfield and an interlocking series of fortified strong points, was poorly prepared for a determined enemy assault. French air transports had been unable to fly in sufficient materiel necessary for the construction of hardened bunkers, nor could they supply the garrison throughout a prolonged battle. As Giap pounded the fortress with his superior artillery, closed down its airfield, and encircled its strong points with trenches and tunnels, French generals realized that their days were numbered. Nevertheless, most French troops fought bravely, and even when the end was near, paratroopers volunteered to jump in to reinforce the garrison. On 7 May 1954, after fifty-five days of fighting, the occupants of the French command bunker surrendered, and the Vietminh flag, with its yellow star on a red background, was raised over the shattered fortress. Approximately 2,200 French soldiers died in the battle and 6,500 were taken prisoner, and Vietminh deaths numbered 8,000. France had suffered a stunning military and psychological defeat, one that brought the fall of the government of Prime Minister Joseph Laniel and his replacement by Pierre Mendes-France, who pledged to find a quick, negotiated settlement of the war. This he achieved at the Geneva Conference of 1954*. See also Paul Ely; Navarre Plan; United Action.

B. B. Fall, *Hell in a Very Small Place: The Siege of Dien Bien Phu* (Philadelphia, 1967); V. N. Giap, *Dien Bien Phu* (Hanoi, 1962); L. S. Kaplan, D. Artaud, and M. R. Rubin (eds.), *Dien Bien Phu and the Crisis in Franco-American Relations, 1954–1955* (Wilmington, DE, 1990); H. Navarre, *Agonie de l'Indochine, 1953–1954* (Paris, 1956); J. R. Nordell Jr., *The Undetected Enemy: French and American Miscalculations at Dien Bien Phu, 1953* (College Station, TX, 1995).

Charles E. Neu

DIXIE MISSION

The Dixie Mission was the first official U.S. delegation to visit the Chinese Communist Party* (CCP) base in Yan'an during World War II. Throughout the war, the Americans repeatedly were frustrated by the Chinese Guomindang* (Nationalist) leader Jiang Jieshi*, who, instead of fighting the Japanese vigorously as the Americans expected, opted to preserve his strength for a final showdown with the CCP, his political enemy. By 1944, when the land battles became more frequent in the Pacific, China's active participation became more vital. As Jiang's regime failed to meet U.S. expectations, the Roosevelt administration began to consider supporting the Chinese Communists as an alternative. John S. Service*, a U.S. diplomat, managed to contact Zhou Enlai*, the CCP's representative in China's wartime capital Chongqing, and accepted Zhou's invitation to visit the Communist base. To facilitate White House decision making, Service was ordered to arrange the visit of an official observation team to Yan'an. The team used the name Dixie to refer to the Communists, who, like the Confederacy fighting the Union in the American Civil War, were challenging the authority of the Republic of China* (ROC). The Dixie Mission consisted of twenty-four members, including technicians, inspectors, and analysts. They broke through various barriers laid by the Chongqing government, and arrived at Yan'an in July 1944. The purpose of their visit was to collect firsthand information concerning the Communists to provide guidance for President Franklin D.

Roosevelt* if he chose to alter wartime China policy.

In Yan'an, the Americans were given an extraordinary welcoming reception, including a celebration of the Fourth of July. The CCP viewed the coming of the Americans as a great opportunity, hoping to gain recognition and material aid. Communist leader Mao Zedong* tried to reassure the Dixie Mission that his men were nothing for the United States to worry about, and would respect and protect U.S. interests in China. Well-impressed by their Communist hosts, who appeared to be a more effective and uncorrupted force than the ROC, members of the Dixie Mission conveyed good words about Yan'an to Washington. Hoping to see the Communists become more active in the war against Japan, they began to show them how to use U.S. weapons. All signs suggested a promising future of cooperation. But Patrick J. Hurley*, the president's special envoy to China, did not share this opinion. Petitioned by the CCP, the Dixie Mission cabled Roosevelt directly from Yan'an, telling him that Mao and Zhou wanted to visit him in Washington. As both the defeat of Japan and the rising threat of Soviet expansion in Asia became apparent, conditions for a working relationship between the United States and the CCP became increasingly adverse. In the spring of 1945, as Washington's hostility toward the Chinese Communists grew, the Dixie Mission rapidly lost significance, and soon evacuated the Communist base. Service and other China Hands* were persecuted as targets of McCarthyism.

A. DeConde, *A History of American Foreign Policy* (New York, 1978); M. Schaller, *The United States and China in the Twentieth Century* (New York, 1980).

Li Yi

DODGE, JOSEPH M. (1880–1964)

Joseph Dodge traveled to Japan in 1949 to implement an economic stabilization pro-

gram that bears his name. He reached the heights of power in the financial community before entering government service during World War II. Dodge also was budget director (1953–1954) and chairman of the Council on Foreign Economic Policy (1954–1956) under President Dwight D. Eisenhower*. He began working as a bank messenger in his native Detroit and rose to become president of the Detroit Bank in 1933, a position he held for twenty years. He occupied various federal government posts during World War II and earned a reputation as one of the most capable troubleshooters on problems relating to the international economy. After serving as a consultant on monetary policy in occupied Germany and the Marshall Plan, Dodge agreed in 1948 to advise U.S. Army Undersecretary William H. Draper on Japanese economic problems. His appointment as financial advisor with ministerial rank comprised part of the Reverse Course* in U.S. policy toward occupied Japan.

By 1948, President Harry S. Truman* had adopted the containment policy in Europe to counter Soviet expansion. Administration officials such as Draper and George F. Kennan* were eager to promote Japanese recovery as part of a broader effort to fashion Japan into a strong anti-Communist ally. Economic conditions in Japan, however, were desperate. Inflation raged out of control. Production and foreign trade stood below prewar levels. The expansionary fiscal and monetary policies of the former Finance Minister Ishibashi Tanzan* exacerbated this price instability. The National Security Council approved a nine-point stabilization plan for Japan in December 1948. Dodge traveled to Japan in early 1949 to implement the program. As a fiscal conservative, Dodge opposed Keynesian theories and the government spending on social welfare and public works that they inspired.

The Dodge Plan sought to break Japanese dependence upon American aid and restore the competitiveness of Japan's exports abroad by means of a balanced government budget, tighter credit, and a single yen-dollar exchange rate. Working closely with Finance Minister Ikeda Hayato*, Dodge ordered severe reductions in government spending, more effective tax collection, and allocation of supplies to favor exports over domestic consumption. Dodge controlled the flow of money from funds raised through the transfer of the yen equivalent of the dollar value of raw materials provided under U.S. aid programs, thus enabling him to manage the money supply. By enforcing the single yen-dollar exchange rate of 360 yen to the dollar, he sought to integrate Japan's economy into the global capitalist system. Although the government of Prime Minister Yoshida Shigeru* agreed on the priority of economic rehabilitation, Japanese conservatives rightly feared that the severity of the Dodge Plan risked plunging Japan into a depression. U.S. Army officials and the State Department also worried about the social consequences of austerity. In the end, the outbreak of the Korean War* temporarily solved the problem. Overnight American military orders provided a market for Japanese output.

During Eisenhower's first year, Dodge served as budget director, rising to the familiar challenge of balancing the budget. He also stayed in touch with Japanese leaders such as Ikeda and continued to press them to hold the line on Japanese government spending. Although unpopular at the time, Dodge's exhortations had the salutary effect of encouraging Japanese fiscal and monetary discipline after the Korean War. Unlike the president, however, Dodge also favored the tightest possible embargo of the People's Republic of China* (PRC). As chairman of the newly created Council on Foreign Economic Policy, Dodge successfully defended the export controls of CHINCOM*, which called for allied nations to maintain tighter restriction on trade with the PRC than with the European Soviet bloc. One result was to place the United States and Japan at odds over Sino-Japanese trade. Dodge, a "granitelike,

no-nonsense official," disapproved of flamboyant behavior and avoided publicity. Americans are thus less familiar with his name than the Japanese. *See also* U.S. Occupation of Japan.

J. A. Garraty (ed.), *Dictionary of American Biography, 1961–1965* (New York, 1981); *New York Times*, 3 December 1964; H. B. Schonberger, *Aftermath of War: Americans and the Remaking of Japan, 1945–1952* (Kent, OH, 1989); Y. Sugita and M. Thorsten, *Beyond the Line: Joseph Dodge and the Geometry of Power in U.S.-Japan Relations, 1949–1952* (Okayama, Japan, 1999).

Aaron Forsberg

DOLE, SANFORD B. (1844–1926)

Sanford Ballard Dole was president of the Republic of Hawaii and first governor of the Territory of Hawaii. Born in Honolulu, the son of a prominent Congregationalist minister, he was educated in the missionary schools at Punahou and Koloa, and at Oahu College. Dole attended Williams College and then studied law in Boston, passing the Massachusetts bar in 1868. He returned to Honolulu that same year to begin a legal practice and pursue an interest in public affairs. Dole enjoyed a cordial relationship with Hawaii's native rulers and, at least in his early career, favored a constitutional monarchy as best suited to Hawaii's multiracial population. However, by the 1880s, he considered the "retrogressive tendencies" of the monarchy to be dangerous to public order. In 1884, Dole was elected to the Hawaiian legislature as a member of the Reform Party. In 1887, he participated in a revolution that forced King Kalakaua* to issue a new constitution, which Dole had a hand in drafting. This document reduced the power of the monarch and enhanced the control of the white planter class.

Neither Kalakaua nor Lili'uokalani*, his sister and successor, were satisfied with their lessened status. After her brother's death, Queen Lili'uokalani made it known that she intended to promulgate a new constitution, and Dole and the Committee for Safety acted to protect their interests, seizing power in the Hawaiian Revolution* of January 1893. Dole accepted the position as head of a provisional government and immediately sent a delegation to Washington to negotiate a treaty of annexation before the Harrison administration, defeated in the 1892 elections, left office. Although a treaty was drafted swiftly with the assistance of Secretary of State John W. Foster* and placed before the U.S. Senate for ratification, no action was taken prior to the inauguration of Grover Cleveland, who withdrew the treaty. Cleveland then appointed former Congressman James H. Blount* as a special commissioner with "paramount" authority to investigate matters related to the Hawaiian Revolution. Blount's report concluded that most of the Hawaiian people supported the deposed queen, rather than the provisional government, although he did not interview Dole and his associates. Accepting the Blount Report, Cleveland dispatched a new minister to Hawaii, Albert S. Willis, with instructions to pursue restoration of the monarchy.

Willis quietly urged the deposed queen to pursue a conciliatory and moderate policy if returned to power, but bent on revenge, Lili'uokalani declared her intention to have the leaders of the revolution beheaded. Meanwhile, Dole dealt tactfully with Willis and sensed correctly that the United States would not use force to restore a native monarchy in place of a self-declared republic headed by English-speaking whites. When asked by President Cleveland in December 1893 to restore the queen, Dole, acting as foreign minister for his provisional government, responded that the United States had no right to interfere in the internal affairs of Hawaii, but expressed the belief that at some point the island nation would be a part of the United States. On 4 July 1894, the provisional government replaced itself by declaring the creation of the Republic of Hawaii, with Dole as its president and the native population largely excluded from positions of power. Dole dealt successfully with a revolt in January 1895 by forces favoring Lili'uokalani's restoration. He also attended to diplomatic problems with Japan related to Hawaiian efforts to restrict Japanese immigration. Meanwhile, he pursued Hawaiian Annexation* to the United States, achieving this goal on 7 August 1898. Dole then served on a five-member commission that offered legislative recommendations to Congress for a territorial government for Hawaii and assisted in drafting the Organic Act of the Hawaiian Territory. President William McKinley* appointed Dole as governor of the new Territory of Hawaii, and he was formally inaugurated on 14 July 1900.

Dole's tenure as governor was marred by the legislature's lack of familiarity with the territorial system of government and the resentment many legislators held concerning the governor's role in the overthrow of the monarchy. Dole's aristocratic style exacerbated his problems with the legislature as well as his support of powerful plantation owners. Both houses of the legislature in 1900 sent a joint resolution to the president expressing a lack of confidence in the governor's leadership. Dole persisted in his duties despite his failures with the legislature until November 1903, when he resigned to accept appointment as a judge in the U.S. District Court for Hawaii. He retired from the court in 1915 and spent his remaining years writing memoirs and poetry while involving himself in civic and philanthropic organizations. He also remained an active advocate of Hawaiian statehood. Dole admired native Hawaiians and their culture, but in his legal and public careers he did much to disenfranchise them. He lived almost exclusively in the elite haole society and socialized publicly with neither natives nor Asians.

H. G. Allen, *Sanford Ballard Dole: Hawaii's Only President, 1844–1926* (Glendale, CA, 1988); E. M. Damm, *Sanford B. Dole and His Hawaii* (Palo Alto, CA, 1957); S. B. Dole, *Memoirs of the Ha-*

waiian Revolution (Honolulu, HI, 1936); H. M. Madden (ed.), "Letters of Sanford B. Dole and John W. Burgess," *Pacific Historical Review* (1936).

Michael J. Devine

DOLLAR DIPLOMACY

"Dollar Diplomacy" is the characterization for U.S. foreign policy during the Taft administration from 1909 to 1913. A global diplomacy, it also was the approach toward East Asia, where the major thrust of Dollar Diplomacy consisted of a series of efforts to prevent any imperialist nation, particularly Japan and Russia, from gaining a monopoly over the Chinese market so as to keep the commercial door open to the United States. It originated in the persistent attempts of E. H. Harriman* to purchase the South Manchuria Railway from Japan between 1905 and 1909. Though a failure, Harriman's effort sought to keep the door of East Asia open, a goal that the United States pursued for the next few decades. Upon coming to the presidency, William Howard Taft*, with Secretary of State Philander C. Knox*, quickly redirected U.S. diplomacy in East Asia and activated American financial involvement in that region. In October 1909, Knox told an American banking group of his plan to neutralize Manchuria's railroad. This Knox Neutralization Scheme* first worked on forming an international syndicate to lend money to China to purchase the Manchurian railroads, with the syndicate supervising them during the term of the loan. If this did not work, the syndicate would build a line to compete with Japan's South Manchuria Railway. The goal was to preserve the Open Door Policy* in Manchuria.

Knox's plan ran into resistance from both Japan and Russia, who responded by declaring that they would recognize each other's sphere of influence and take common action to deflect any challenge. But the Taft administration did not abandon its policy. In early 1911, China activated its prior reform scheme. The United States invited England, France, and Germany to participate in a four-power consortium to provide a loan for China for its ongoing currency reform, but the loan never was delivered. In May 1911, Washington managed to persuade the Chinese government to accept a loan of $30 million from the consortium to construct the Huguang Railway, linking Guangzhou in the south to Hankou in central China. Again, the U.S. attempt was frustrated. Revolutionaries accused the Qing government of "selling out" China, and the Chinese Revolution of 1911* that followed interrupted the processing of the loan. Early in 1912, however, chances for the execution of the Dollar Diplomacy became brighter. The newly founded Republic of China* needed money desperately, and Washington eagerly revived the four-power consortium. But Britain and France both wanted their allies, Japan and Russia, to participate as well, and the four-power consortium thus became a Six Power Consortium*. Japan and Russia agreed to join on the condition that their "special interests" in Manchuria be recognized. Fearing that the opportunity would be lost, the United States concurred. Thus, four years of Dollar Diplomacy ended with a closed door to Manchuria, with the United States outside.

P. H. Clyde, *International Rivalries in Manchuria, 1689–1922* (New York, 1966); W. I. Cohen, *America's Response to China: An Interpretive History of Sino-American Relations* (New York, 1980); M. H. Hunt, *The Making of a Special Relationship: The United States and China to 1914* (New York, 1983); C. Vevier, *The United States and China, 1906–1913: A Study of Finance and Diplomacy* (New Brunswick, NJ, 1955).

Li Yi

DOMINO THEORY

The domino theory said that if some key area of Southeast Asia fell to the Communists, a substantial number of other countries, most of them not even bordering on that key area, also would fall. In the early 1950s, the key area was said to be northern Vietnam, Vietnam as a whole, or French Indochina*. In the 1960s, it almost always was said to be the Republic of Vietnam*. Predictions about the number of countries that would fall, if the key area did so, varied widely. What might be called an average version of the theory held that if Vietnam fell to Communism*, the fall of Cambodia*, Laos*, Thailand*, Burma*, Malaya*, and Indonesia* would be inevitable, but there would be a chance of saving the Philippines*.

The theory was first developed by the French in the 1940s, though its later appearance in the United States is probably more a matter of independent invention than French influence. President Dwight D. Eisenhower* is the first known to have used the image of dominoes as a way of expressing the theory. In a presidential press conference of 7 April 1954, asked about the importance of Indochina, he replied:

Finally, you have broader considerations that might follow what you would call the "falling domino" principle. You have a row of dominoes set up, you knock over the first one, and what will happen to the last one is the certainty that it will go over very quickly....

When we come to the possible sequence of events, the loss of Indochina, of Burma, of Thailand, of the Peninsula, and Indonesia following, now you begin to talk about areas that not only multiply the disadvantages you would suffer through loss of materials, sources of materials, but now you are talking really about millions and millions and millions of people.

Minimalist versions said that only the fall of countries as far as Thailand would be inevitable, and that there would be a chance of saving Malaya and Indonesia. Maximalist versions reached as far as Japan and Western Europe.

Discussion of the domino theory subsided after 1954, but revived in the early 1960s. Vice President Lyndon B. Johnson*, on 23 May 1961, talked about a slightly modified version of the domino theory, using two key points, not just one:

Vietnam and Thailand are the immediate—and most important—trouble spots.... The basic decision on Southeast Asia is here. We must decide whether to help these countries to the best of our ability or throw in the towel ... and pull back our defenses to San Francisco.

Returning to the more usual pattern of specifying a single key spot, President John F. Kennedy* offered his definition of the domino theory on 2 September 1963:

These people who say that we ought to withdraw from Vietnam are wholly wrong, because if we withdrew from Vietnam, the Communists would control Vietnam. Pretty soon Thailand, Cambodia, Laos, Malaya would go, and all of Southeast Asia would be under the control of the Communists and under the domination of the Chinese.

Support for the domino theory faded among top U.S. officials in the late 1960s, but some influential people in other sectors of American society continued to endorse the theory into the 1970s.

Public Papers of the Presidents, 1954, 1963 (Washington, DC, 1960, 1963); N. Sheehan et al. (eds.), *The Pentagon Papers* (New York, 1971).

Edwin E. Moise

DONG XIANGUANG (1887–1971)

Dong Xianguang was a Chinese journalist who played a key role in bringing international publicity to Japan's efforts to impose the Twenty-One Demands* on China in 1915. He was from a Christian family in Zhejiang and educated in Shanghai. In 1909, he went to the United States to pursue his studies in Missouri. In 1912, when the Pulitzer School of Journalism opened at Columbia University, Dong immediately transferred to the school, studying journalism while working as a part-time newsman. In this period, he began to show solicitude for Sino-American relations and once distinguished himself for reporting the remarks President Theodore Roosevelt* made on the subject in an interview. In 1913, he returned to China and acted as the chief editor of *Peking Daily News*, an English journal.

In 1915, Japan pressed the Twenty-One Demands on China, which were so oppressive that even the submissive Chinese administration at that time could not accept them. Under great pressure of Japanese military strength, China's government had to resort to international protest as a means of countering the Japanese efforts to keep the fifth part of the Twenty-One Demands secret. Dong played an important role in China's strategy when he received a call from a secretary of the Foreign Ministry asking him to expose the contents of the fifth demand to the American press. Dong immediately called on his university teacher John B. Powell, who was then in Beijing. The next day, Dong and Powell went to the U.S. legation, where they met American envoy Paul S. Reinsch* and, after discussion, the three men reached full concurrence. According to the information Dong provided, Powell published an account of the event and then further reported it in detail at the invitation of the *Chicago Tribune*.

In the 1920s, Dong acted as associate editor of *Millard's Review of the Far East*. Gu Weijun*, Chinese envoy to the United States, asked him for help in preventing the United States from lending money to Japan. To carry out the mission, Dong stayed in the United States for ten months and served the *Peking Daily News* as correspondent in Washington. Dong was invited to be the general manager and chief editor of *China Press* in Shanghai and remained in this position for more than five years. At this time, Japan was planning aggression against Shanghai. Dong struggled with both limits on his access to the facts imposed by the administration and censure from his American colleagues for not publicizing the truth, resigning the position in 1935. In 1937, the Guomindang* (Nation-

alist) government placed Dong in charge of international propaganda affairs. He established an office to build world support for China's war effort against Japan, publishing a monthly in English and operating many branches abroad, including ones in New York, Washington, Chicago, and San Francisco. The New York branch was the largest, administering a news agency, publishing an English semimonthly, operating a broadcasting station, and often holding lectures on Chinese issues.

After the war ended, Dong was named head of the Bureau of Information in May 1947. Again, he resigned his position after being criticized by foreign journalists for the censorship he had enforced over their dispatches. In August 1949, Jiang Jieshi* authorized him to meet the admiral of the U.S. Seventh Fleet in Hong Kong*, asking for U.S. assurance of economic and military support for the Republic of China* (ROC) after its leaders had escaped to Taiwan*. During the next two years, Dong often made trips to the United States and Europe as Taiwan's messenger, eventually serving as the ROC's ambassador to the United States from 1956 to 1958.

Dong Xianguang zhuan [Autobiography of Dong Xianguang] (Taiwan, 1974); Zhu Xinquan and Yan Ruping (eds.), *Zhonghua minguo renwu zhuan* [Who's Who of the Republic of China], vol. 4 (Beijing, 1984).

Cai Daiyun

DOOLITTLE RAID

In the wake of the Pearl Harbor Attack*, the Japanese presumed that the United States would be unable to react coherently for a period of six months. However, the unscathed American carrier forces began a series of hit-and-run air attacks on the perimeter of the newly expanded Japanese Empire. Carrier-launched planes raided the Marshalls, Wake, Rabaul, and, on 4 March 1942, the Marcus Islands, a mere 1,000 miles from Tōkyō. Fear of an air attack on the home islands deeply affected Japanese strategic planning for the second phase of the Pacific war. The Japanese nightmare materialized before dawn on 18 April 1942, when Vice Admiral William F. Halsey's Task Force sixteen launched sixteen U.S. Army Air Force B-25 bombers under the command of Colonel James Doolittle from the carrier *Hornet*. This unprecedented feat resulted in the first air attack on Japan in its history. Tōkyō, Kōbe, Nagoya, Yokosuka, and Yokohama were bombed with little physical damage, because of the limited bomb loads permitted under the circumstances. After the raid, the bombers crash-landed in either China or Siberia, with seventy-one of eighty crew members surviving. Japanese occupation forces in China captured and executed Chinese civilians who had assisted their allies, as well as several of the flyers.

Although the Doolittle Raid was downplayed by the Japanese as the "Do Little Raid" and many historians have dismissed it as a mere morale booster rather than a significant military effort, the importance of the air strike has grown with historical perspective. Admiral Yamamoto Isoroku* (planner of the Pearl Harbor attack) became pale and depressed, shutting himself in his cabin for a full day after the raid. Even Premier Tōjō Hideki* was shaken when his plane was forced to dodge a U.S. bomber on his way to Tōkyō. The Doolittle Raid now is conceded to mark the end of the first phase of the Pacific war. Japanese strategic planning regarding the resilience of the United States had to be rethought completely. This war could not be continued on Japan's terms, as had the earlier Sino-Japanese War (1894–1895) and Russo-Japanese War* (1904–1905). Second, the Kuroshima Plan for a Japanese western offensive in the Indian Ocean with hopes of a final linkup with her Axis partners at Suez was doomed. Finally, Yamamoto's constant fear of carrier-based air attacks on Japan was confirmed and caused him to urge an early eastern offensive, finally supported by both the army and the navy, against Midway. Determined to force the

Decisive Battle of Imperial Navy doctrine, he reversed the plan from a defensive encounter to an offensive engagement. In his haste, Yamamoto approached the Battle of Midway* lacking two carriers, thus narrowing the odds to four for Japan and three for the United States.

J. Prados, *Combined Fleet Decoded: Secret History of American Intelligence and the Japanese Navy in World War II* (New York, 1995); G. L. Weinberg, *A World at Arms: A Global History of World War II* (New York, 1994); H. P. Willmott, *Empires in the Balance: Japanese and Allied Pacific Strategies to April 1942* (Annapolis, MD, 1982).

Errol M. Clauss

DRUG TRADE

The drug trade has been an issue in U.S.–East Asian relations since the early nineteenth century. American companies—chief among them Russell and Company*—were involved heavily in the opium trade with China, holding a virtual monopoly on the import of Turkish opium at the beginning of the 1800s, and becoming involved in the trade of Indian opium as well, starting in the 1830s. During the crisis of 1839–1840 precipitating the First Opium War*, American traders signed an agreement to halt opium imports, temporarily suspending their involvement in the trade. However, their decision to remain in Guangzhou and take over the task of transshipping for British companies that had withdrawn from the city proved vital in allowing the British to continue their China trade. By 1841, American companies had resumed their opium trade, but the U.S. government was coming under increasing pressure to ban the trade, both from missionaries who objected on moral grounds and commercial interests who thought it damaged their legitimate business with China. The 1844 Treaty of Wangxia* removed U.S. protection from Americans involved in the opium trade, but was revised in the 1858 Treaty of Tianjin*, after the British victory in the Second Opium War*, to legalize opium exports to China. Finally, the commercial treaty of 1880 banned the United States and China from export of opium to each other's ports.

The U.S. acquisition of the Philippines* led the United States toward a more international approach to the opium problem. Although the Philippine Commission originally favored the creation of an opium monopoly for the islands, the opposition led to the commission to appoint a committee to study the problem. The report of the Philippines Opium Committee in 1904 recommending progressive prohibition was distributed widely throughout the British Empire and was made the basis for a series of international conferences to deal with the problem: the Shanghai Conference of 1906, the three Hague Opium Conferences of 1911–1914, and the two Geneva Conferences of 1924–1925. Taken together, these conferences established the principle in international law that narcotics trade for other than "legitimate medical uses" constituted an illicit activity.

In 1930, the U.S. Congress established the Federal Bureau of Narcotics, headed by Harry Anslinger. Under Anslinger, the United States focused on Japan as the major source for opium trafficking in the 1930s. During the Tōkyō War Crimes Trials* after World War II, it was determined that Japan had pursued a deliberate policy to weaken resistance in Asia through its promotion of the opium trade. Subsequent to Japan's defeat, Anslinger accused the Chinese Communist Party* (CCP) of running the illicit opium traffic, although in fact the Communists carried out a mostly successful suppression policy after their victory in the Chinese Civil War*. By contrast, he dismissed evidence of Guomindang* (Nationalist) involvement in the trade. After their defeat in 1949, remnants of the Guomindang Army set up base in Burma* and greatly expanded opium production in the Golden Triangle*, eventually moving their operations to the Laos*-Thailand* border after the Burmese Army forced them out in 1961. Increasing American involvement in covert operations in the Golden Triangle provided the Guomindang, Hmong* guerrillas, and others involved in the opium trade with a means for transporting their opium to the global market via Air America*. U.S. involvement in the Second Indochina War* also created a new market for Golden Triangle heroin among U.S. soldiers, many of whom then became couriers taking heroin back to the U.S. market. See also Guomindang Intervention in Burma.

H. Chang, Commissioner Lin and the Opium War (Cambridge, MA, 1964); J. Jennings, The Opium Empire: Japanese Imperialism and Drug Trafficking in Asia, 1895–1945 (Westport, CT, 1997); A. W. McCoy, The Politics of Heroin: CIA Complicity in the Global Drug Trade (Chicago, 1991); A. Taylor, American Diplomacy and the Narcotics Traffic, 1900–1939 (Durham, NC, 1969); W. O. Walker, Opium and Foreign Policy: The Anglo-American Search for Order in Asia, 1912–1954 (Chapel Hill, NC, 1991).

Timothy L. Savage

DULLES, JOHN FOSTER (1888–1959)

As secretary of state from 1953 to 1959, John Foster Dulles played a central role in formulating and implementing policies that sought to check the spread of Communism* in East Asia—and, for that matter, everywhere else around the globe. His negotiation of mutual security pacts with the Republic of Korea*, the Republic of China*, and the multilateral Southeast Asia Treaty Organization* (SEATO) to deter Communist expansion were prime examples of how "pactomania" became synonymous with his tenure at the State Department. Born into a deeply religious and politically prominent family (both his grandfather John W. Foster* and uncle Robert Lansing* had been secretary of state), he earned a law degree at Princeton University. As senior partner for four decades in Sullivan and Cromwell, the renowed Wall Street law firm, Dulles handled a variety of clients from corporate, banking, and government circles, many actively involved in the world economy. Consequently, he gained intensive exposure to international economic questions during the years before and after World War I. As a U.S. representative at the Versailles Peace Conference in 1919, the young Dulles also honed his diplomatic skills. Other influences helped to shape his worldview, including his strong religious faith, his activism as a lay leader in the Federal Council of Churches, and his political partisanship as a lifelong Republican.

During World War II and the early postwar years, Dulles wrote extensively about current foreign policy issues, emerging as a leading foreign affairs expert within the Republican Party. President Harry S. Truman*, seeking bipartisan support, found it politically expedient to bring him into his administration as a foreign policy consultant in the spring of 1950. In that capacity, Dulles became chief negotiator for the Japanese Peace Treaty* that was approved in September 1951. With the election of Dwight D. Eisenhower* as president in 1952, he seemed the obvious choice as secretary of state. At the time, the former general confided to his diary that "there is probably no one in the world who has the technical competence of Foster Dulles in the diplomatic field." Dulles's main concern as secretary of state, naturally, was the Soviet Union and the People's Republic of China* (PRC), each of whom he saw as a dangerously aggressive state that threatened U.S. national interests. He was only slightly less concerned about the spread of revolutionary insurgencies in postcolonial Asia. Dulles was convinced that revolutionary nationalist regimes would prove as detrimental to U.S. interests as they would benefit the expansionist ambitions of Moscow and Beijing.

From the first, East Asian problems crowded the new chief diplomat's agenda. With the Korean War* still raging, Communist-led Vietminh* guerrillas effectively fighting U.S.-financed French forces in Indochina, and open hostility continuing to plague relations between the United States and the new Communist regime in China, Dulles worried that the U.S. position throughout the region stood in grave jeopardy. The Eisenhower administration, with Dulles playing a leading role, moved quickly to secure a Korean Armistice Agreement*. French Indochina* proved a far less tractable problem, especially after France's defeat at Dien Bien Phu* in May 1954. The Geneva Conference of 1954* was, for Dulles, a major Cold War blow to the West, prompting frenetic negotiations that led to creation of SEATO that fall. His manifold efforts throughout the rest of his tenure to persuade as many East Asian states as possible to "stand up and be counted" as Free World allies were especially vigorous in the Republic of Vietnam*, where the Eisenhower administration heavily supported the regime of Ngo Dinh Diem*. Eisenhower and Dulles also poured U.S. military and economic assistance into South Korea, Taiwan*, Thailand*, and the Philippines*, in the hopes that each could be molded into a reliable U.S. ally along the Japanese model. Government leaders who pursued the path of neutralism, from Sukarno* in Indonesia* to U Nu* in Burma* to Norodom Sihanouk* in Cambodia*, invariably aroused Dulles's ire. His support for a botched covert operation to oust Sukarno in 1957–1958 reflected his deep suspicion of nonaligned regimes. The Cold War, in his worldview, involved such basic issues of morality and order that it demanded commitment; neutrality, he once chided, was immoral.

Some historians recently have emphasized that Dulles was considerably more adept and nuanced in his diplomacy than the venerable stereotype of him as a rigid ideologue might allow. He evidently possessed a surer grasp of the fundamental tensions between Moscow and Beijing, for example, than his public rhetoric suggested and even took some actions designed to drive a wedge between the two Communist giants. Even so, virtually all of his East Asian policies derived from his overarching concern about the threat the PRC posed to peace and stability of the region. Indeed, his abiding fear of Chinese expansion and his determination to deter it constitute key unifying themes in his diverse diplomatic moves across the Southeast and Northeast Asian chessboards. Dulles was convinced that the PRC sought to expand its influence throughout East Asia and that only the United States had the power and will to check its aggressive proclivities. The Taiwan Strait Crises* that erupted between Washington and Beijing, first in 1954 and again in 1958, brought the two powers dangerously close to war. His brinkmanship in each case testified powerfully to his preoccupation with the Chinese threat, as did his responses to the other Asian challenges he faced. Dulles remained a consummate Cold Warrior until his death from cancer.

T. Hoopes, *The Devil and John Foster Dulles* (Boston, 1973); R. H. Immerman (ed.), *John Foster Dulles and the Diplomacy of the Cold War* (Princeton, NJ, 1990); R. H. Immerman, *John Foster Dulles: Piety, Pragmatism, and Power in U.S. Foreign Relations* (Wilmingon, DE, 1999); R. W. Pruessen, *John Foster Dulles: The Road to Power* (New York, 1982).

Robert J. McMahon

DUONG VAN MINH (1916–2001)

An influential South Vietnamese politician and general in the Army of the Republic of Vietnam* (ARVN), Duong Van Minh was born in the province of My Tho in the Mekong Delta and trained by the French at the Ecole des Chartres. Known as "Big Minh," he appeared on the public stage during the early years of the presidency of Ngo Dinh Diem*, and was considered a Diem loyalist. In early 1956, Minh was instrumental in subduing the Cao Dai* and Hoa Hao sects, whose insurrection threatened the stability of the Diem regime. Viewing Minh's popularity with the ARVN troops as a threat, Diem made him a "special adviser," a job without authority. Then, in

August 1963, Minh was a leader of the August 1963 plot to overthrow Diem. This scheme unraveled, however, when Minh and his co-conspirators failed to secure the backing of key army units and were unsure of American support. Determined not to make the same mistake twice, Minh initiated contact with Central Intelligence Agency* (CIA) operative Lucien Conein in October 1963. He requested a pledge of U.S. noninterference in the planned coup and asked for more military and economic aid after Diem's removal. By November, assured that the United States "would not thwart" a coup, Minh and his cohorts initiated a successful overthrow of the Diem regime. Minh played a key role, allegedly giving the order to assassinate the Ngo brothers, although he unconvincingly claimed that the two had committed suicide.

Minh became nominal chairman of the Military Revolutionary Council that replaced the Diem government, but seemed uninterested in ruling and preferred to play tennis and tend his orchids. American policy makers deemed Minh to be initially popular with South Vietnamese citizens because of his easygoing attitude and southern roots, but they worried that he lacked leadership ability. The junta was ousted in January 1964 by General Nguyen Khanh*, but Minh retained a position as titular head of state, largely because American officials feared that a feud between Minh and Khanh would divide the ARVN. A rivalry nevertheless ensued, and Khanh dismissed Minh in the summer of 1964. Anarchy erupted in Saigon as all the different factions of South Vietnamese society, including Buddhists, Catholics, students, and workers, protested. Khanh's regime disintegrated, replaced by a temporary government composed of a triumvirate of Khanh, Minh, and General Tran Thien Khiem, with Khanh appointed acting prime minister. Shortly thereafter, Khanh sent General Minh abroad on a "goodwill tour" and dispatched Khiem to Washington as the new Republic of Vietnam* (RVN) ambassador.

Upon Minh's return, he was confined to Pleiku with other generals by Khanh's allies.

After his incarceration, Minh returned to Saigon, where he became active in several pro-democracy groups, managing to maintain some respectability among the Saigon political elite. He also established some ties to the National Liberation Front* (NLF). During the Paris Peace Talks*, Minh functioned as a weapon in the negotiating strategy of the Democratic Republic of Vietnam* (DRV). The DRV demanded removal of RVN President Nguyen Van Thieu*, as a precondition for any peace accord, and suggested Minh as an acceptable alternative. Minh briefly challenged Thieu for the South Vietnamese presidency in the 1971 elections, but Thieu forced the removal of his opponents from the ballot. Four years later, as the Saigon regime disintegrated, some South Vietnamese officials and the French ambassador proposed replacing Thieu with Minh, who was supposedly less objectionable to Hanoi. Thieu abdicated on 21 April to Tran Van Huong, his vice president, who quickly resigned in favor of Minh. Minh was left with the unpleasant task of surrendering unconditionally to Colonel Bui Tin of the People's Army of Vietnam on 30 April 1975. In 1983, the government of the Socialist Republic of Vietnam* permitted Minh to move to France. See also Diem's Assassination; Second Indochina War.

G. C. Herring, *America's Longest War: The United States and Vietnam 1950–1975* (New York, 1996); S. Karnow, *Vietnam: A History* (New York, 1983); M. B. Young, *The Vietnam Wars, 1945–1990* (New York, 1991).

Robert K. Brigham

DUTCH COLONIALISM

Like the British in India, the earliest Dutch colonial presence in Asia was in the form of a trading company, the Dutch East India Company (in Dutch, Vereenigte Oost-Indische Compagnie, or VOC), which es-

tablished itself on Taiwan* in 1624 and Java in 1611, but shifted operations to Java exclusively after 1662. Gradually, the VOC was replaced by governmental authority, which spread slowly through what is now Indonesia*. The islands were not fully conquered until the early twentieth century; Indonesia gained full independence in 1949.

During the nineteenth century, Dutch-held Sumatra was an important trading point for Americans seeking pepper and, especially, tin. The Dutch presence was minimal still, and the fact of Dutch colonialism had little effect on trading relationships. After the United States acquired the Philippines* in 1898, some U.S. officials began to search for viable models for U.S. colonial rule. Dutch colonialism was by then turning toward the Ethical Policy, which asserted that achieving a civilizational goal for the colony could mesh with profitable business practices. This naturally had some appeal. Washington also strongly approved of Dutch public adherence to an "open door" trading policy for its colony. Both British Malaya* and the Netherlands Indies ran huge trade surpluses with the United States after World War I, caused by large U.S. purchases of tin, rubber, and other raw materials. The gap was smaller for the Indies, however, since Dutch laws were friendlier to both U.S. imports and U.S. investments. Dutch policy was designed to attract the support of Britain and the United States in defense of their vast colonial realm.

During the 1930s, the strategic importance of the oil-producing Netherlands Indies for both Britain and the United States increased. The British naval base at Singapore* was intended to provide mutual defense. Washington increased the status and quality of consular representatives in Batavia. President Franklin D. Roosevelt* was as maddeningly inconsistent in his judgments about Dutch colonialism as he was about the other European countries. Sometimes he criticized the Dutch in the same breath as the British and French for having held their colonies merely to exploit them economically. At other times, he praised the Dutch for comparatively enlightened policies. Perhaps because of his own Dutch ancestry, he seemed to believe the Dutch were more amenable to compromise. He therefore encouraged Queen Wilhelmenia, during World War II, to issue her famous statement promising Indonesia dominion status immediately upon the end of the war, and self-government soon thereafter. Roosevelt saw this policy as much closer to the U.S. policy in the Philippines than other European countries were willing to go.

In 1945, however, the situation was not so simply resolved. Not only did the Dutch want their colony back, but they believed Roosevelt had promised U.S. support for that endeavor. The Indonesians likewise thought that the Atlantic Charter applied to them, thus launching the Indonesian Revolution. Initially, U.S. policy supported Dutch claims, but a variety of factors, most important among them the staunch anti-Communism of Indonesian nationalists, gradually shifted the U.S. policy toward supporting Indonesian aspirations. The most important U.S. interests under Dutch colonialism, access to Indonesian exports and possibilities for investment, seemed secure under the new regime. *See also* British Colonialism; French Colonialism.

A. L. Foster, "Alienation and Cooperation: European, Southeast Asian, and American Perceptions of Anti-Colonial Rebellion, 1919–1937," Ph.D. dissertation, Cornell University, 1995; F. Gouda, "Visions of Empire: Changing American Perspectives on Dutch Colonial Rule in Indonesia between 1920 and 1942," *Bijdragen en Mededelingen betreffende de Geschiedenis der Nederlanden* (1994); G. D. Homan, "The United States and the Indonesia Question, December 1941–December 1946," *Tijdschrift voor Geschiedenis* (1980); R. J. McMahon, *Colonialism and Cold War: The United States and the Struggle for Indonesian Independence, 1945–1949* (Ithaca, NY, 1981).

Anne L. Foster

E

EAST ASIAN FINANCIAL CRISIS

Massive debt was the cause of the East Asian financial crisis of the late 1990s. As their economies boomed, Asian nations externally borrowed large amounts of then cheap capital, usually in the form of U.S. dollars, to splurge on costly projects of an often spurious nature. When the dollar started to rise against Asian currencies in mid-1995, exports from the region became more expensive. The resultant decreasing profit margin made repayment in dollars more difficult; deficits grew by at least 5 percent of gross domestic product (GDP). This development forced Asian nations to consider abandoning their overall 80 percent currency basket peg (a mechanism whereby a home currency is fixed to a basket of currencies comprising some of the major currencies such as the U.S. dollar and Japanese yen) to the dollar. But governments resisted when it was realized that the inevitable devaluation would cripple firms that had borrowed the huge dollar sums. Asian economies, however, then became increasingly vulnerable to speculation, and soon speculators sold local currencies and bought dollars in an effort to reap immense profits. As export growth halted, various Asian nations had no choice but to allow their currencies to devalue.

This crisis accelerated during July 1997 with a major slide in Southeast Asian currencies. Thailand* was the first Asian nation to abandon a fixed exchange rate with the dollar. The baht fell 20 percent almost immediately and continued to slide, forcing Thai officials to request a $17 billion package from the International Monetary Fund (IMF). By that fall, Indonesia* had asked for huge rescue packages from the IMF, having already responded by floating its currency (before its reserves were depleted) and by cutting fiscal spending. A reluctant President Suharto* seemed to backslide on reforms promised as a condition for IMF assistance (these posed a threat to business monopolies owned by family members and cronies). Inflation rose from 5 percent into the triple digits; the rupiah went from 2,500/dollar to 10,000/dollar. Growing unrest, generated not only by the economic downturn, but also frustration with three decades of autocratic rule, eventually led to Suharto's resignation in May 1998. Only Hong Kong*, because of its immense cash reserves, staved off the severe calamities that befell other Southeast Asian economies, but the value of its stock market also fell.

The crisis spread elsewhere, notably to Northeast Asia. The Republic of Korea* was hard hit because to fund economic expansion, the government had encouraged banks to make cheap loans to interlocking conglomerates, known as *Chaebŏl**. The return on these loans was below the cost of capital, and thus an inefficient allocation of resources, but the system was tolerated as a means of raising production, providing jobs, and eliminating competitors. As elsewhere, the troubled South Korean economy affected politics, contributing to the election of former dissident Kim Dae-jung* as president in the midst of massive layoffs and a request for a $57 billion bail-out from the IMF. By then, Japan's economy also had spun into a deflationary spiral. A ripple effect occurred, as not only the currencies of other nations fell, but their stock markets crashed, causing major Japanese financial institutions, notably Yamaichi Securities, to collapse. To avoid further recessional spread, the United States applied tremendous pressure on Japan, which it saw as the key to any regional recovery. As a result, on 9 April 1998, the Japanese government reversed generations of policy and, to correct the yen's weakness, implemented a $75 billion stimulus package designed to boost domestic demand and reduce trade surpluses. As the yen continued to slide against the dollar, a new Japanese government lamely attempted to address needed systemic reforms, including larger tax cuts and a massive budget expansion.

Since the Asia-Pacific Economic Cooperation* and other regional forums proved ineffectual, the IMF attempted to act as a global fireman and extinguish the financial fires in Asia. Its plans, based on a $100 billion bail-out, included provisions for restructuring the financial sectors, more stringent economic regulation, and opening domestic markets to outside goods as requirements for disbursement of resources. However, its fiscal proscriptions for South Korea and Thailand proved too tight and had to be relaxed, and IMF-recommended closure of sixteen of Indonesia's largest banks only further fueled a general unrest. Declining per capita income, rising unemployment, and increasing prices put a damper on the previously lauded Asian economic miracle. Washington's reaction appeared anemic in relation to the immensity of the crisis, the repercussions of which included a precipitous decline in the earnings of U.S. corporations in Asia, recurring downturns in world stock markets, and virtual economic collapse in Russia. Coupled with a Japanese government unable to retreat from the maintenance of a high level of exports and lowered inflation, U.S. policies inadvertently contributed to the yen's depreciation to a level that undermined the stability of other Asian currencies. Effects of the economic downturn lingered into the twenty-first century, made worse in 2001 by steadily rising energy costs.

"Asia on the Edge," *Foreign Affairs* (November/December 1998); F. Fukuyama, "Asian Values and the Asian Crisis," *Commentary* (February 1998); "The Essential Guide to the Crisis," *Asiaweek* (17 July 1998); S. Takashi, "The Currency Crisis and the End of Asia's Old Politico-Economic Setup," *Japan Echo* (August 1998); W. K. Tabb, "The East Asian Financial Crisis," *Monthly Review* (June 1998).

Kent S. Sieg

EASTER OFFENSIVE (30 March–16 September 1972)

In 1972, North Vietnamese leaders, believing South Vietnam to be vulnerable in light of the continued withdrawal of U.S. troops and as a means of breaking the stalemate that existed on the ground, staged the largest attack of the Second Indochina War*. The Easter Offensive revealed that Vietnamization* had not produced a modern and effective southern army that either could withstand a conventional assault from the north or launch a counteroffensive attack in response without U.S. direction. It began on 30 March when three North Vietnamese Army (NVA) divisions crossed the demilitarized zone and attacked the extreme northern provinces of the Republic of Vietnam*. In conjunction with this thrust, another wave of attacks soon occurred in the Central Highlands and Binh Long Province. The NVA forces contained large infantry, armor, and artillery units. A total of 120,000 NVA soldiers were committed to the action. As with the Tet Offensive* of January 1968, the South Vietnamese were caught off guard. Within weeks, the NVA had captured Quang Tri and part of Thua Thien Province, seized Loc Ninh, and laid sieges upon Kontum and An Loc. The Army of the Republic of Vietnam* (ARVN) made a stand at Hue and fortified the areas under seige by transferring units from one military region to another but quickly used up all its reserves.

President Richard M. Nixon*, still possessing the power and the will to defend South Vietnam, responded to the Easter Offensive firmly. He ordered a massive program of air strikes, including the utilization of more than half the Strategic Air Command's B-52 attacks, in a move known as Operation LINEBACKER that included a resumption of the bombing of North Vietnam, which had not occurred since 1968. In addition, Nixon closed the major port of North Vietnam, Haiphong, by laying mines. These measures took a heavy toll on the NVA, but neither the NVA's high losses nor even the bombing of four Soviet ships in Haiphong Harbor had an effect on Nixon's scheduled summit in the Soviet Union. By the summer, the Hanoi leadership ordered the withdrawal of its forces from An Loc and Kontum. On 16 September, after months of fighting and five days of clearing the city by hand-to-hand combat, the South Vietnamese finally recaptured and utterly destroyed Quang Tri City.

The North Vietnamese had miscalculated, suffering losses in men, materiel, and infrastructure that were staggering. General Vo Nguyen Giap*, the mastermind of what he termed the Nguyen Hue Offensive, thoroughly failed to coordinate armor and infantry units, ignored the fact that the enemy controlled the skies, and employed logistical lines, which proved woefully inadequate. The result of the failure of the Easter Offensive for the Democratic Republic of Vietnam* was that it was forced to accept the prospect of a negotiated settlement of the war—at least until U.S. support for South Vietnam had dissipated completely. Yet the poor performance of the South Vietnamese also foretold of more intrinsic difficulties to come. Some ARVN units had surrendered after only token resistance, but other units refused to coordinate with local commanders. When they did stand and fight, South Vietnamese losses were high. Military region commanders eschewed the front lines, and President Nguyen Van Thieu* made a number of tactical decisions himself from Saigon, often overruling his battlefield commanders. Only a ponderous NVA advance, coupled with the damage inflicted by the LINBACKER Bombings*, allowed the ARVN to hold their positions. In the aftermath, Thieu reorganized South Vietnam's army and cashiered several incompetent generals.

D. Andrade, *Trial by Fire: The 1972 Easter Offensive: America's Last Vietnam Battle* (New York, 1994); Ngo Quang Truong, *The Easter Offensive of 1972* (Washington, DC, 1980); G. H. Turley and J. Webb, *The Easter Offensive: Vietnam 1972* (Annapolis, MD, 1995).

Kent G. Sieg

EISENHOWER, DWIGHT D. (1890–1969)

Dwight David Eisenhower, as president of the United States from 1953 to 1961, brought an end to the Korean War*, confronted the People's Republic of China* (PRC) in crises, and led the United States into greater involvement in Southeast Asia. Raised in Abilene, Kansas, and graduated from the U.S. Military Academy in 1915, he held several posts during the interwar years, including a four-year stint in the Philippines* as assistant to General Douglas MacArthur*. After the outbreak of war in Europe in 1939, General George C. Marshall* appointed Eisenhower to prominent positions, culminating in his command of the D-Day invasion of occupied France. His role in the defeat of Nazi Germany made him into a celebrated war hero. After the war, he served as U.S. Army chief of staff, held the presidency of Columbia University, and became the first supreme commander of the North Atlantic Treaty Organization. Gaining the Republican presidential nomination in 1952, Eisenhower easily won the presidency and reelection in 1956.

Eisenhower was determined to achieve a breakthrough in the stalled P'anmunjŏm Truce Talks*, intimating, through secret channels, a willingness to use atomic weapons against the PRC if it did not cooperate in ending the war. Communist concessions helped to achieve the Korean Armistice Agreement* that was signed in July 1953, but the effect of his threat remains unclear. The willingness to engage in nuclear intimidation, however, was central to the Eisenhower administration's redefinition of the containment strategy, which was called the New Look. By giving greater emphasis to nuclear retaliation as a means of deterrence, reducing the size of conventional forces, enhancing reliance on regional allies, and engaging in covert operations against unfriendly governments, Eisenhower sought to reduce defense expenditures in the interest of fiscal responsibility and a stronger economy. Problems in East Asia, however, presented an especially difficult challenge to this New Look strategy. Twice during his presidency, Eisenhower dealt with the PRC's pressures on the tiny offshore islands the Republic of China* held between the mainland and Taiwan*. To some contemporaries, as well as historians, his handling of the Taiwan Strait Crises* demonstrated skillful diplomacy, which kept the ultimate decision in his hands. To others, it seemed unduly risky, given the negligible strategic value of the islands.

Besides the crises with the PRC, Eisenhower's most important challenges centered on Communist influence in emerging nations. Contrary to the antineutral rhetoric of Secretary of State John Foster Dulles*, he was also sensitive to the interests of nonaligned nations and worked for economic assistance and close relations with India in particular. But consistent with the priorities of the New Look, he supported economic and military aid programs to strengthen regional allies such as Thailand*, the Philippines*, and Pakistan. Eisenhower's effort at containment had the most lasting effect in French Indochina*, where he continued the Truman administration's policy of supporting France against the Vietminh* in the First Indochina War*. Yet in the spring 1954 crisis at Dien Bien Phu*, Eisenhower declined to provide direct military support. Distrustful of the French for their failure to grant genuine independence to the non-Communist Vietnamese and to follow U.S. military advice, he insisted that U.S. intervention required both British and congressional support, but both were lacking. So Eisenhower led the United States into essentially replacing the French in Vietnam. After the Geneva Accords of 1954*, the Eisenhower administration moved quickly to build an anti-Communist government from the remnants of the French regime in the southern half of the country. To deter further Communist advances in the region, the United States also led the establishment of the Southeast Asia Treaty Organization* in September 1954, which placed Laos*, Cambodia*, and the Republic of Vietnam* under its defense umbrella. Eisenhower made U.S. assistance to South Vietnam conditional upon reform that would rally the peasants behind the government of Ngo Dinh Diem*.

Meanwhile, in neighboring Laos, the Eisenhower administration became deeply involved, mainly through the activities of the Central Intelligence Agency*, in schemes to promote rightist political groups to counter the influence of the

Communist Pathet Lao*. But by the time Eisenhower was leaving office, these initiatives were unraveling. In Vietnam, the Viet Cong*, now supported by the Democratic Republic of Vietnam*, intensified its pressures on an increasingly precarious Diem regime. The situation in Laos seemed even worse, and Eisenhower in fact told President-elect John F. Kennedy* that it was the most critical problem facing the United States, one that might require military intervention. But the commitment to a weak South Vietnamese government was the most significant legacy of his Asian policy. In retirement, Eisenhower, who took pride in his presidency for having achieved eight years of peace, urged President Lyndon B. Johnson* to take decisive military action against North Vietnam as U.S. involvement escalated after 1964.

S. E. Ambrose, *Eisenhower: The President* (New York, 1984); G. Chang, *Friends and Enemies: The United States, China, and the Soviet Union* (Stanford, CA, 1990); W. I. Cohen and A. Iriye (eds.), *The Great Powers in East Asia, 1953–1960* (New York, 1990); R. A. Divine, *Eisenhower and the Cold War* (New York, 1981); R. Melanson and D. Mayers (eds.), *Reevaluating Eisenhower: American Foreign Policy in the 1950s* (Urbana, IL, 1987).

Gary R. Hess

ELY, PAUL (1897–1975)

French General Paul Henry Romauld Ely played a critical role in the transition from the *présence française* to the *présence américaine* in Vietnam during his tenure as high commissioner and commander in chief of the French Expeditionary Corps (FEC) in French Indochina* from 1954 to 1955. A highly respected military officer, he had a distinguished World War II record and continued to rise through France's command system after the war. Between 1950 and 1953, Ely was the French representative to the North Atlantic Treaty Organization, and then chairman of the French chiefs of staff. On 20 March 1954, Ely arrived in Washington to brief the U.S. de-

fense establishment on the military situation in Indochina. His mission was to explain the plight of the FEC at Dien Bien Phu* and to press for immediate additional aid in the form of supplies, bombers, and auxiliary U.S. personnel to raise the effectiveness of the French Air Force. He also was instructed to determine the U.S. response to a Chinese air strike against French forces. Finally, Ely was to inform the Eisenhower administration about the unwillingness of the French to carry on the First Indochina War*, urging instead a negotiated settlement of the war.

During Ely's visit to Washington, Admiral Arthur W. Radford*, chairman of the Joint Chiefs of Staff (JCS), outlined to Ely the possibility of an American air strike against Dien Bien Phu. Radford told Ely that France would have to make a formal request for assistance. Its hopes raised, the French government did ask for such aid, but President Dwight D. Eisenhower* then claimed that he would approve the air strike only with formal congressional approval and an internationalization of the war effort through United Action*. Bitterly disappointed over Eisenhower's refusal to consider unilateral military action, Ely then traveled to Saigon to provide an assessment of the military situation after the fall of Dien Bien Phu. The French government chose Ely to replace General Henri Navarre as military commander in chief in Indochina, as well as appointing him high commissioner. When he arrived in Saigon in early June, Ely accepted the necessity of complete French withdrawal from Vietnamese political life and the replacement of French political, economic, and military advisers by American ones. He established a cordial working relationship with General J. Lawton Collins*, the U.S. special representative in South Vietnam. Together, they tried to create a viable government in the Republic of Vietnam* that would be able to defeat Ho Chi Minh* and the Vietminh* in the proposed 1956 elections.

Ely differed with the Americans on prospects for success of Premier Ngo Dinh

Diem* in South Vietnam. From Diem's assumption of power in June 1954 until his consolidation of authority in May 1955, Ely remained hesitant to support him. The worst crisis occurred in the spring of 1955, when the Cao Dai*, Hoa Hao, and Binh Xuyen*, the three principal politico-religious sects in South Vietnam, united against Diem's government. Fearing Diem's loss of political control, the destruction of life and property, and the breakdown of all established authority, Ely moved to stop the fighting between the sects and government forces. After the crisis, Ely resigned in disgust over the American refusal to consider alternatives to Diem. His departure in June 1955 signaled the end of an active French presence in South Vietnam.

D. L. Anderson, *Trapped by Success: The Eisenhower Administration and Vietnam, 1953–1961* (New York, 1991); M. Billings-Yun, *Decision Against War: Eisenhower and Dien Bien Phu, 1954* (New York, 1988); W. Duiker, *U.S. Containment Policy and the Conflict in Indochina* (Stanford, CA, 1994); P. Ely, *Mémoires: L'Indochine dans la Tourmente* (Paris, 1964).

Kathryn C. Statler

EMPRESS OF CHINA

This ship, the first operated by American traders eager to participate in the lucrative tea trade with China, was built in Boston, then outfitted and launched from New York City on 22 February 1784. The financial consortium behind the venture included merchants from Boston, New York City, and Philadelphia. The ship carried a cargo of ginseng and silver, valued at £150,00. The export of ginseng to China from the United States had first been attempted in 1783 by the sloop *Harriet*, which had been intercepted near the Cape of Good Hope by British authorities, and its entire cargo purchased to block American entry into the China trade. The ship that became the *Empress of China* was purchased by the consortium primarily for its size, be-

ing one of the largest then produced by John Peck of Boston. The ship's cargo volume is uncertain, but it insured for 400 tons, and in addition the ship incorporated the speed and stability of the most formidable gunships then in use by the British.

The Americans, like the Europeans engaged in the China trade, had difficulty finding products in the China market. Europe, and Britain in particular, was burdened by a steep trade deficit, since the British market for tea imported from China was huge, and the market in China for anything British was small. The British had very modest success with finished cotton from India and rattan from Southeast Asia, but American ginseng was the first foreign product for which the Chinese market showed an appetite. Ginseng's medicinal properties made it a valuable commodity in China. People of Manchuria had for centuries grown wealthy on the Chinese demand for ginseng, but North America was another rich source of the root. The *Empress of China* consortium began its venture with the product, hoping eventually to develop a more profitable business by exporting furs from northwestern America to China.

The *Empress of China* traveled by way of the Cape Verde Islands, the Cape of Good Hope, and the Sunda Strait between Sumatra and Java, arriving at Guangzhou on 28 August 1784. At the time, the trade with Europe at Guangzhou was strictly regulated, and the *Empress of China*'s owners had not taken adequate steps to introduce their company or their ship to the officials there. Thanks to the intercession of French and British traders, as well as the flexibility of Chinese trade commissioners, the ship was admitted. The major European communities—British, Dutch, Danes, French, Swedes, and Austrians—maintained "factories" or closed residences in the city, and the American crew members of the *Empress of China* were installed in a small house in the British factory, where they pursued not only their commercial tasks, but also a series of visits with British and Europeans intended to establish the new republic as a serious but friendly participant in the China trade. The crew of the *Empress of China* spent the autumn in Guangzhou, when it was forbidden to leave because of the *Lady Hughes* Incident—involving the sentencing to death of a British gunner who had killed accidentally a Chinese boatman—on presumption that it was an English ship.

The Chinese authorities released the ship and in late December 1784 the return voyage was begun, with a cargo of teas, textiles (including silk), porcelain, gold ingots, and silver dollars. Arriving in New York City on 11 May 1785, its return immediately unleashed a bundle of business and legal disputes. The ginseng exported to China had brought less profit than the investors had hoped. A considerable sum of money had disappeared from the company's accounts, and for a time suspicion lay upon the ship's merchant-in-residence, Samuel Shaw. Shaw and another crew member had diverted a portion of the *Empress of China*'s intended return cargo to a second ship of their own. The original investors scrambled to sell off the *Empress of China*'s cargo before this second ship could arrive in New York; they also sold the ship. In February 1786, she set sail for China again. Thereafter, under several names, the *Empress of China* worked the trans-Atlantic trade until sinking off the coast of Ireland in February 1791. *See also* John Kendrick.

J. Goldstein, *Philadelphia and the China Trade* (University Park, PA, 1978); S. E. Morison, *The Maritime History of Massachusetts* (Boston, 1941); P. C. F. Smith, *The Empress of China* (Philadelphia, 1984).

Pamela K. Crossley

EVARTS, WILLIAM M. (1818–1901)

An underrated secretary of state under President Rutherford B. Hayes from 1877 to 1881, William Maxwell Evarts focused on Latin American and Asian markets while modifying U.S. tactics toward East Asia. Born to an elite Boston family, he be-

came a powerful New York City lawyer. During the Civil War, Evarts undertook missions to Europe for Secretary of State William H. Seward*. He learned about the importance of Asia from his law practice and especially from his close relationship with Seward. Both men realized, as Evarts declared in 1877, that the nation had reached a climactic point where its "vast resources . . . need an outlet." But he differed from his mentor on tactics. Whereas Seward believed Americans had to cooperate with the stronger Europeans, especially the British, to exploit Asia, Evarts followed a more unilateral policy. Thus, he signed a 1878 convention with Japan that displeased Europeans by granting the Japanese a large measure of tariff autonomy for the first time since the country had opened to the West in the 1850s. Evarts stipulated that the agreement would not take effect until other powers granted similar rights (thus he prevented any discrimination against U.S. goods), but he unilaterally had helped the Japanese break away from hated foreign controls. Evarts also signed the Angell Treaty* with China in 1880 that limited Chinese labor emigration to the United States, whereas Americans received new extraterritorial privileges and favorable duties for their goods.

In this context of their Asian policy, Evarts and Hayes paid special attention to that long-promised gateway to Asia, an isthmian canal. In 1878, when Ferdinand deLesseps began building a waterway across Colombia's Panamanian isthmus, Hayes sent warships to the region, warning that only the United States should control such a canal. Evarts tried to reinterpret the 1846 U.S.-Colombia treaty to mean that the United States must have "potential control" over such a passageway. He thus planned to override the 1850 treaty with the British that provided for cooperation in building any canal. Colombia coldly rejected Evart's claim, but deLesseps's project soon fell victim to Panama's swamps and diseases. But Evarts was more successful in his search for Asian markets when, at the business community's request, he ordered the issuance of monthly reports from U.S. consuls abroad. First appearing in October 1880, these reports provided vital, regular information to those who hoped to fulfill Evarts's expectations that "It is for us to enter into the harvest-field [of foreign markets] and reap it." He maintained his foreign policy interests as a U.S. senator from New York between 1885 and 1891, but his major contributions for U.S.–East Asian relations were his limited success in dealing with China and Japan, his prophecy that the United States, not European powers, would build the great canal, and the beginnings of the monthly consular reports.

C. L. Barrows, *William M. Evarts: Lawyer, Diplomat, Statesman* (Chapel Hill, NC, 1941); T. Dennett, *Americans in Eastern Asia: A Critical Study of the Policy of the United States with Reference to China, Japan and Korea in the 19th Century* (New York, 1922); B. Dyer, *The Public Career of William M. Evarts* (Berkeley, CA, 1933).

Walter LaFeber

EVATT, HERBERT V. (1894–1965)

Herbert Vere Evatt was Australia's minister for external affairs from 1941 to 1948, and worked to establish a postwar relationship approximating equality with the United States. He also played an important part in the establishment of the United Nations. After the Pearl Harbor Attack*, he was appalled to learn that the Americans originated the Atlantic First strategy, which assigned top priority to the defeat of Germany, rather than to Japan. This revelation engendered suspicions of American intentions in the Pacific that at times approximated paranoia. But Allied successes in the Pacific through 1943 gradually allayed Australian anxieties over the possibility of Japanese victory. Australian fears concentrated thereafter on signals that after the war, U.S. security might require the control of bases in the island groups of the British Commonwealth, as well as in the former Japanese mandates in the Pacific. Evatt acted to engineer with New Zealand a joint agreement affirming that there should be no change of sovereignty affecting any former colonial territories south of the equator without the sanction of Canberra and Wellington. Reactions in Washington were predictably unfavorable, as Secretary of State Cordell Hull* ridiculed the so-called ANZAC Pact as proposing "a Monroe Doctrine for the South Pacific," telling New Zealand Prime Minister Peter Fraser that it "seemed to be on all four, so far as the tone and method are concerned, with the Russian action toward Great Britain." Fraser agreed, thus strengthening Hull's disposition to cast Evatt as the villain of the piece.

After World War II, no more altruistic and unequivocally Western-aligned diplomat ever succeeded more than Evatt in making himself more detested by people he was most anxious to placate. State Department legal specialist Henry Reiff warned that Evatt's presence at the United Nations "bodes trouble" because his arguments were only a fascade to mask Australian ambitions in the region. Nelson T. Johnson*, U.S. representative in Canberra, reported that the Australian minister's "increasing megalomania" was more deserving of comment. It was not auspicious for a close and harmonious relationship. But these appraisals were also quite misleading. Evatt was anything but anti-American, either in his public policy or his private statements. He was perfectly sincere when he told Secretary of State James F. Byrnes that "leadership by your country is the basis of the Pacific settlement." The basic difficulty was that the Truman administration was not prepared to assume the kind of leadership role that Evatt had in mind. There were two main reasons for this. First, Evatt clearly believed that Australian-American relations should be conceived in terms of a partnership of equals, with full and effective consultations on all matters of common interest. The United States, however, was not prepared to recognize Australia as an equal partner. American policy makers were not ready to accept the right of Australia to be consulted on issues in which no real Australian interest could be discerned. Second, perhaps an even more serious concern was Evatt's other conviction that the United States should underwrite a formal military alliance in the Pacific, which the Americans considered to be both politically unacceptable and strategically counterproductive.

Australian-American confrontation on a string of postwar issues, therefore, was effectively guaranteed. First, Evatt was prepared to allow the U.S. Navy to establish a base on Manus Island in the Australian-mandated Admiralty Group, on condition that reciprocal facilities be made available to the Royal Australian Navy in U.S. ports. After the Americans abandoned the Manus project, he demanded that the United States include in its peace treaty with Thailand* a clause denying Bangkok the right to enter into any international commodity arrangements unless Australia had the opportunity to join. After both sides complained about unfriendly interference in Thai affairs, the peace settlement went through as planned. Undersecretary of State Dean G. Acheson* then advised President Harry S. Truman* that Evatt's concept of a "U.S.-Australia-New Zealand Joint defense scheme analogous to the U.S.-Canada joint defense scheme" should be opposed resolutely as "premature, inadvisable and likely to encourage the USSR to advocate similar over-all arrangements elsewhere not to the advantage of the United Nations or the U.S." But in July 1946, Acheson recommended that the two countries establish full ambassadorial relations as "the natural consequence of the increasingly close and cordial relations between Australia and the United States." Then, in 1947, Evatt complained when the United States chose not to consult Australia about authorization of a Japanese whaling expedition to the Antarctic. His unfailing skill at enraging his American colleagues

continued in 1948 and 1949, when Evatt, as president of the UN General Assembly, objected to U.S. efforts to create the Republic of Korea*. Nevertheless, his pressure for treatment of Australia as an equal paved the way for negotiation and signing of the ANZUS Treaty* in September 1951.

G. Barclay and J. Siracusa (eds.), *Australian-American Relations since 1945: A Documentary History* (Sydney, 1976); P. Crockett, *Evatt: A Life* (New York, 1993); H. V. Evatt, *Australia in World Affairs* (Sydney, 1946); T. R. Reese, *Australia, New Zealand, and the United States: A Survey of International Relations, 1941–1968* (Melbourne, 1969).

Joseph M. Siracusa

EXCLUSION ACTS

This series of late-nineteenth- and early-twentieth-century U.S. immigration treaties and regulations were directed against the Asian "yellow peril," particularly Chinese and Japanese. The U.S. Congress passed the first Chinese Exclusion Act in 1882, suspending Chinese immigration for ten years. It also called for identification certificates for Chinese laborers in the United States, deportation of those in United States illegally, and a ban on naturalization of Chinese as citizens. This was the same year Congress enacted a more general and equally restrictive Immigration Act establishing clear federal control over immigration and naturalization, and excluding idiots, lunatics, paupers, convicts, and prostitutes. The 1882 Exclusion Act marked the first occasion the United States blocked the immigration of a specific ethnic group, and was passed in response to pressure from the West Coast and from organized labor. Supporters of the legislation invoked Social Darwinist arguments about racial hierarchies and the fundamental immiscibility of Anglo-Saxon and Asian cultures. The limit of ten years on the immigration ban was intended to circumvent the 1868 Burlingame-Seward Treaty*, which had allowed unrestricted Chinese immigration to the United States, and the 1880 Angell Treaty*, allowing the United States to regulate, but not ban, Chinese immigration.

When coolie labor became a volatile issue in the 1884 presidential campaign, Congress broadened the definition of "laborer" and required Chinese residents in the United States who might visit China to obtain a return visa from American and Chinese officials in China. The U.S. Supreme Court upheld the right of the federal government to exclude aliens and regulate immigration in the 1889 landmark *China Exclusion Case (Chae Chan Ping v. United States)*. In an 1888 draft revision of the 1880 treaty, China accepted a twenty-year prohibition on immigration of Chinese laborers to the United States. But Congress refused ratification without a ban on the return of about 20,000 Chinese residents of the United States who had left to visit China. The 1880 treaty finally was renewed in 1894, when China—preoccupied with Japanese aggression at the time, and in need of international support—agreed to a ten-year suspension on immigration of Chinese laborers. In the interim, the 1892 Geary Act required all Chinese to register on threat of deportation. Although the Fourteenth Amendment ascribed citizenship to all those born on U.S. territory, American-born Chinese were excluded from this category in the 1890 case *United States v. Wong Kim Ark*. Courts continued to issue conflicting opinions as to whether Chinese could be naturalized U.S. citizens.

Sino-American conflict over immigration was a decisive factor in the largely unsuccessful 1905 anti-American boycott in China. The 1917 Exclusion Act established an Asiatic Barred Zone, embracing China, India, Burma*, Siam (Thailand*), Asian Russia, Arabia, French Indochina*, and the East Indies. The Philippines* already had been brought under exclusionary laws, and Japan was still bound by its Gentlemen's Agreement* of 1907–1908 for voluntary limits on Japanese immigration to the United States. The Japanese Exclusion Act of 1924 banned further Japanese immigra-

tion, and should be seen in the larger context of the 1924 National Origins Act*, which barred entry to immigrants who were not eligible for naturalization as U.S. citizens. This act also established a quota system, with group percentages to be drawn from the 1890 census. Restrictions on Asian immigration were not eradicated entirely until the combination of the 1952 Immigration and Nationality Act and the U.S. Immigration Act of 1965*. *See also* Coolie Trade; Wu Tingfang.

G. Neuman, *Strangers to the Constitution: Immigrants, Borders, and Fundamental Law* (Princeton, NJ, 1996); F. Ng (ed.), *The Asian American Encyclopedia*, vol. 3 (New York, 1995); R. Smith, *Civic Ideals* (New Haven, CT, 1997).

Eileen Scully

"EXPEL THE BARBARIAN" MOVEMENT

At the beginning of the seventeenth century, Japan cut itself off from the outside world to maintain a feudal social and political order. The arrival of Commodore Matthew C. Perry* and his ships, blackened by the smoke of the steam engines, off the coast of Japan in 1853 accelerated divisions within Tokugawa Japan, which led to the fall of the shōgunate. Recognizing the firmness of Perry's demands, Japan's leaders decided to buy time by granting the United States limited concessions and opening up to the outside world for the first time in 250 years (save for a tiny Dutch concession at Deshima Island). In quick succession, the imperial nations of Europe all made similar demands on Japan. By this time, the social order in Japan had decayed and all social classes were frustrated with the feudal system. Samurai were forced to borrow from and thus became impoverished to merchants, who were considered the lowest in the social hierarchy but were now powerful and desirous of outside contact for trade purposes. In addition, the peasants were taxed at incredibly high rates. Thus, the need for change within the Japanese order coalesced with the need to change the society to respond to foreign intrusion.

Thus, the shōgunate was forced to open Japan to foreign influences that undermined its own rule. For the first time, the shōgun had to turn to the emperor to decide how to deal with Perry. Like the emperor, the shōgun wanted to prevent, or at the very least stall for as long as possible, any opening, but powerful provincial lords such as Ii Naosuke* saw encroachment as an inevitability and wanted to try to channel it in Japan's favor. The arrival of Townsend Harris* in 1856, whose mission was to negotiate a commercial treaty, exacerbated the problems faced by the shōgun. Ii Naosuke persuaded both the shōgun and the emperor to accept the Harris Treaty*, since the alternative could be harsher treatment from the British and the French. However, the young, xenophobic samurai from the rebellious outer provinces never forgave him, and Ii was assassinated on 3 March 1860. With the death of this important figure, the shōgunate lost the last man who could have saved it.

The new thirteen-year-old shōgun was obliged to swear an oath to expel the barbarians from Japan within a decade. The rise of Jō-i, or barbarian-expelling movement, followed, with the slogan "Revere the emperor and expel the barbarian!" as its motto. A wave of murder against foreigners inside Japan ensued. But the foreign intrusion continued, and every step Japan's leaders took seemed to make things worse. For example, they tried to stem the activities of foreign merchants, who bought up Japanese gold coins and sold them overseas for great profits, debasing the currency. This action only triggered massive inflation inside Japan, generating more internal dissension. Then, on 25 June 1863, Chōshū samurai fired upon an American vessel, exposing the shōgunate's loss of control. Within a month, another U.S. ship was hit with the loss of five American sailors. Additional bombardments of foreign shipping and the closure of the Shimonoseki Strait soon followed. Secretary of State William H. Seward* advocated a forceful response and proposed an international naval expedition against Japan. Thus, the strait was opened by force in September 1864 and Japan's government was forced to pay a debilitating $3 million indemnity. Ironically, with British support, Chōshū quickly rebuilt its military might, and with the combined forces of other outside provinces, dispatched the shōgun's remaining troops in 1868, restored young Emperor Meiji to his rightful primacy of rule, and immediately began the most rapid modernization in history. *See also* Treaty of Kanagawa.

T. Huber, *The Revolutionary Origins of Modern Japan* (Stanford, CA, 1981); M. Nagai and M. Urritia (eds.), *Meiji Ishin: Restoration and Revolution* (Tokyo, 1985); E. O. Reischauer, *Japan: The Story of a Nation* (New York, 1981).

Kent G. Sieg

F

FAIRBANK, JOHN K. (1907–1991)

The foremost China scholar in the United States, John King Fairbank arrived in Shanghai aboard the German freighter *Aller* on a chilly February morning in 1932 to research nineteenth-century Chinese diplomatic relations with Western imperialistic powers for his dissertation. He left China four years later, devoting the rest of his life to promoting the study of modern China and better understanding between Chinese and Americans. Born in Huron, South Dakota, Fairbank enrolled at the University of Wisconsin at Madison in 1925 and transferred to Harvard University two years later. He left for Balliol College, Oxford, on a Rhodes scholarship in 1929, where, under the tutelage of Hose Ballou Morse, he became interested in China. Fairbank began his academic career at Harvard in the fall of 1936. As the only China specialist in a history department he described as "western-oriented and parochial," he endeavored to make the study of modern China not only an integral part of the curriculum, but also an area of serious research. By 1940, Fairbank had emerged as the central figure in a group of scholars known as "the church fathers of American China scholarship."

With the deepening crisis in East Asia, Fairbank recommended in June 1941 that the American people formulate an active foreign policy toward Japan and China. In August 1941, he began work in the Far Eastern section of the newly established office of the Coordinator of Information (COI) (renamed the Office of Strategic Services in June 1942) headed by Colonel William "Wild Bill" Donovan. His duties included the preparation of a study of the American Lend Lease* program in China and a China handbook for the U.S. Army. The COI sent Fairbank to Chongqing in April 1942 to collect information on Japan. After Japan's surrender in August 1945, he left for China to set up U.S. Information Service (USIS) regional offices to replace the Office of War Information (OWI). During his ten months in China thereafter, he observed firsthand the growing conflict between the Guomindang* (Nationalist) Party and the Chinese Communist Party* (CCP). Although he was convinced by neither the Marxist-Leninist doctrines nor the policies of the Chinese Communists, his own position was that the CCP possessed the keys to success. On the other hand, his view of the American policy of unequivocal support for the Nationalist government was less optimistic. "We seem to be fated to do the wrong things in Asia," he lamented in a letter to his mother prior to his departure from China, "and I wonder why." The CCP's victory in the Chinese Civil War* 1949 vindicated his observations.

Fairbank survived the McCarthy era by shying away from expressing publicly his views on the contemporary developments in either China or U.S. foreign policy. Instead, he devoted his efforts to research, writing, and expanding East Asian Studies programs in American institutions of higher learning. Fairbank believed that success in Sino-American relations depended on mutual cultural understanding. He saw the need to foster a new generation of Asian experts as cross-cultural emissaries to build a new relationship between the academic community and public interest. Fairbank returned to the public forum as American involvement in the Second Indochina War* intensified. He saw U.S. Vietnam policy as intimately tied to its China policy. He wrote to the Harvard *Crimson* in May 1965 that "we can expect no stability in Vietnam until we achieve some stability with China." In October 1969, he wrote in the *New York Times* that the United States should get out of the war, even if it required diplomatic and foreign policy sacrifices. When the decade of the 1970s brought a new Sino-American relationship, Fairbank praised President Richard M. Nixon* for his visit to Beijing in February 1972, calling the trip the "best thing in ten years" in U.S. policy toward East Asia. In the end, what he hoped for was that the American people would learn to identify cultural biases and recognize that China was different. As Fairbank noted, "Americans do not have to like China, merely to live with it."

P. M. Evans, *John King Fairbank and the American Understanding of Modern China* (New York, 1988); J. K. Fairbank, *Chinabound* (New York, 1982); J. K. Fairbank, *China Watch* (Cambridge, MA, 1987).

Roger Y. M. Chan

FANG LIZHI (1936–)

Beginning in the 1950s, scientist Fang Lizhi emerged as the leading human rights activist and dissident in the People's Republic of China* (PRC). He believed that China could assimilate into the modern community only after the characteristics of science, democracy, creativity, and independence became part of the spirit of the Chinese people. Fang entered Beijing University in 1952 to study theoretical and nuclear physics. Upon his graduation in 1956, he was assigned to work at the Chinese Academy of Sciences' Institute of Modern Physics. In 1957, Fang called for reform to China's educational system so that politics would not stifle scientific research. When he refused to recant his words, he was expelled from the Chinese Communist Party* (CCP) in 1958. What saved his career was the PRC's need for scientists in its early efforts to industrialize. The government assigned Fang to organize a new department of physics at the University of Science and Technology (Kexue Jishu Daxue or Keda) in Beijing. His outspokenness led him into trouble again at the beginning of the Chinese Cultural Revolution* in 1966. This time, he was imprisoned for one year and sent to the countryside in Anhui to work in mines and on railroads. During these years, Fang started to question the policies of Mao Zedong* and the feasibility of Communism*. After regaining his CCP membership, however, he received tenure and promotion to full professor in 1978 after the fall of the Gang of Four. In 1979, Fang began attending international scientific conferences under the PRC's open door policy. His travels not only made him one of a few Chinese scientists to receive international attention and acclaim, but also enabled him to reexamine the Chinese socialist system and the role of intellectuals within that system from a broader perspective.

Fang was dubbed by the foreign press as "China's Andrei Sakharov" after his dismissal from Keda in January 1987 for his support of student protests demanding immediate political reforms. Undeterred, he circulated a petition in early 1989 among Chinese intellectuals, advocating a general amnesty for political prisoners. When PRC authorities physically prevented him from attending a dinner that President George H. W. Bush* held during his visit to China in February, Fang appeared before a large number of Western journalists later that night to not only protest his exclusion, but also to raise the awareness of human rights abuses in China. With his image on television and newspapers around the world, he emerged immediately as China's first celebrity dissident. During the student protest at Tiananmen that spring, Fang and his wife, Li Shuxian, deliberately kept a low profile to avoid giving the CCP an excuse to crack down on the protest. After the Tiananmen Square Massacre* on 4 June, they sought refuge in the U.S. embassy in Beijing, causing the Chinese government to issue a warrant for his arrest. Fang received the Robert F. Kennedy Human Rights Award in 1989 for his activities. In his acceptance speech given in absentia on 15 November, he rejected the PRC's assertion that "China has its own standard of human rights." "The values that underlie human dignity are common to all peoples," he declared. "They are the universal standards of human rights that apply without regard to race, nationality, language, or creed." After staying in the U.S. embassy for a year, Fang and Li flew to England in June 1990 to take up temporary residence at the Institute of Astronomy at Cambridge University. In January 1991, they went to the United States, where Fang took a position at the Institute of Advanced Study at Princeton University before joining the University of Arizona as professor of physics and astrophysics. *See also* Wei Jingsheng; Wu Hongda.

C. Buckley, "Science as Politics and Politics as Science: Fang Lizhi and Chinese Intellectuals' Uncertain Road to Dissent," *The Australian Journal of Chinese Affairs* (January 1991); L. Fang, *Bringing Down the Great Wall: Writings on Science, Culture and Democracy in China* (New York, 1990); P. Link, *Evening Chats in Beijing: Probing China's Predicament* (New York, 1992); O. Schell "China's Andrei Sakharov," *The Atlantic Monthly* (May 1988).

Roger Y. M. Chan

FAR EASTERN REPUBLIC

This Russian puppet government was created in Siberia in 1920 in the midst of the political disorder resulting from World War I, the Bolshevik Revolution, the Russian Civil War, and the prolonged Japanese Siberian Intervention*. Its purpose was to present a "pink" face to the world and, it was hoped, counter the Japanese presence until Moscow was strong enough to assert its power in Russian East Asia. The U.S. government under both Presidents Woodrow Wilson* and Warren G. Harding supported the principle of the territorial integrity of Russia, despite abhorrence of the Lenin regime, and wished to counter Japan's forward position in Northeast Asia. Secretary of State Charles Evans Hughes* reluctantly permitted a warm and cordial relationship between the two "nations" while continuing to snub Moscow. Ignoring the embarrassing issue of recognition, Washington and the Far Eastern Republic (FER) exchanged diplomatic missions for an eighteen-month period in 1921 and 1922, which included the meeting of the Washington Conference*. Although neither Russia nor the FER was invited, the latter was physically present in the people of its envoys to the United States who made every effort to influence the powers in attendance.

During the course of 1922, momentous changes took place on the international scene that transformed the politics of Northeast Asia as well as the diplomacy of the United States. Soviet Russia began to emerge as a legitimate power in world affairs, attending the Rapallo and Genoa conferences, and Japan honored her pledge at the Washington Conference to withdraw her troops from Siberia. With Russia's territorial integrity secured, the FER officially thanked the United States for its support in a perilous time and casually announced its intent to rejoin the Russian Socialist Federative Soviet Republic (RSFSR) in November. In December 1922, the FER became a member of the newly proclaimed Union of Soviet Socialist Republics. *Izvestia*, newspaper and Soviet government mouthpiece, admitted publicly that the FER had been a sham devised to resist Japanese imperialism "against this distant frontier of Soviet Russia." "Smokescreen diplomacy" had been successful, however, in achieving the foreign policy objective of both Moscow and Washington for the stabilization of postwar Northeast Asia without resolving the recognition problem or precipitating conflict with Tōkyō. A decade later, formal U.S.-Soviet diplomatic relations would be established in the wake of another Japanese initiative in the region—the Mukden Incident* in Manchuria.

E. M. Clauss, " 'Pink in Appearance, but Red at Heart': The United States and the Far Eastern Republic, 1920–1922," *The Journal of American–East Asian Relations* (Fall 1992); L. Fischer, *Russia's Road from Peace to War: Soviet Foreign Relations, 1917–1941* (New York, 1969); H. K. Norton, *The Far Eastern Republic of Siberia* (London, 1923).

Errol M. Clauss

FEBRUARY 28 INCIDENT OF 1947

The February 28 Incident was a short-lived uprising by Taiwanese against the Guomindang* (Nationalist) government under Jiang Jieshi*. The incident represented a conflict between decolonization and reintegration on Taiwan*, when the legacy of Japanese rule and the drive for greater local autonomy clashed with the long-term centralizing efforts of the Nationalists. The bloody crackdown carried out by troops from the mainland cleared the way for unchallenged Nationalist domination of the island for the next forty years. The incident and its aftermath increased U.S. interest in the island's governance, and served as an example to many Americans of the fundamental defects of the Republic of China*.

At the end of World War II, the Nationalist Chinese government took control of Taiwan, ending fifty years of Japanese colonial rule. Taiwanese, Han Chinese who had immigrated to the island prior to 1945, soon found themselves living with the same corruption and incompetence that many provinces on the mainland then endured. Jiang's regime focused on the needs for postwar reconstruction and anti-Communism on the mainland, and paid little attention to the islanders' political aspirations or the material problems of reintegration. Taiwanese concerns over Guomindang misrule, linked to increasing criticism of specific policies during 1946, finally exploded in early 1947. The incident was sparked by the bungled arrest of a woman selling untaxed cigarettes in Taibei on 27 February. A police officer fired into an angry crowd and killed a bystander. The next day, Guomindang forces fired on protesting Taiwanese in what became known as the February 28 Incident. Jobless youths, workers, students, peddlers, and small-business men briefly wrested control of Taiwan from the provincial government. The island's elite initially moved to limit violence and to restore law and order, but then used the opportunity to press for reforms that soon threatened to weaken drastically Taiwan's ties with the central government.

After a week of increasing tensions, mainland reinforcements arrived and massacred Taiwanese—both those involved in the incident and others unfortunate enough to be on the streets. In March and April, the Nationalists embarked on the "exterminate traitors campaign" (*sujian*) and the "clearing the villages campaign" (*qingxiang*) to arrest and execute those who had opposed their rule. Although the exact numbers remain the subject of heated debate, Nationalist military or police killed probably about 10,000 Taiwanese over the next few months. The aftermath of the incident set the framework for the troubled relationship between the Taiwanese and the Guomindang government for the next forty years. Americans pointed to the events of early 1947 as further evidence of the incompetence and brutality of Jiang's regime. The Nationalist success at crushing the Taiwanese in 1947 helped create grievances that thereafter shaped opposition to the Guomindang—the Dangwai*, the Democratic Progressive Party, and independence activists.

G. Kerr, *Formosa Betrayed* (Boston, 1965); T. Lai, R. H. Myers, and W. Wei, *A Tragic Beginning: The Taiwan Uprising of February 28, 1947* (Stanford, CA, 1991); T. Liao, *Inside Formosa: Formosans vs. Chinese since 1945* (Tōkyō, 1960); M. Peng, *A Taste of Freedom: Memoirs of a Formosan Independence Leader* (New York, 1972); Yang Yizhou, *Er erba minbian: Taiwan yu Jiang Jieshi* [The February 28 Popular Uprising: Taiwan and Jiang Jieshi] (Taibei, 1991).

Steven E. Phillips

FENG YUXIANG (1882–1948)

During the chaotic Warlord Era* (1916–1928), Feng Yuxiang, known as the Christian General, controlled no territory, but played a critical role in the politics of the period. The second son of a minor army officer, he became a full-fledged soldier at age fourteen. In 1902, Feng joined the Beiyang Army of Yuan Shikai* and rose steadily in rank. His interest in Christianity began when he received medical care from missionary doctors. Impressed by the puritanical behavior of Christians, the intrinsic values of Christian teachings, and the missionaries' treatment of the poor and women, Feng joined a Bible class and was baptized in a Methodist church in 1914. During the Chinese Revolution of 1911*, he formed and commanded the Sixteenth Mixed Brigade. His training program, with a strong emphasis on physical and moral fitness through military training, competitive athletics, and moral indoctrination, made his unit one of the most formidable military forces of the time. Moreover, having gained the personal trust and loyalty of his officers and men, Feng was the only person who could order the brigade into action.

Feng joined the Guomindang* (Nationalists) in late 1926, and his army, which had expanded to thirty divisions, played an important part in the Northern Expedition and the reunification of China under Jiang Jieshi* and the Nationalist government. In 1928, he was named minister of war and vice chairman of the Executive Yuan in the Republic of China* (ROC) in Nanjing. Feng's relationship with President Jiang Jieshi became strained almost immediately over the issue of troop reduction, when he accused Jiang of trying to concentrate military power in his own hands. In May 1928, dismissed from all administrative and party offices, he declared his independence from the ROC. He completed his breach with Jiang in February 1930, when he joined with Shanxi warlord Yan Xishan* to form the Northern Coalition to oppose the ROC dictatorship. The Nationalist army's subsequent defeat of the Northern Coalition effectively ended Feng's military career. After 1930, cut off from the command of his troops, he exercised no real influence on national affairs.

After Japan's surrender in 1945, Feng left China to avoid the imminent Chinese Civil War*. In the spring of 1946, he headed a mission to the United States, ostensibly to study irrigation and conservation facilities. The real purpose of his trip, however, was politics. Setting up headquarters in New York City, Feng gave press conferences and wrote newspaper articles denouncing Jiang Jieshi and U.S. unequivocal support. Jiang's policies, he argued, were designed to perpetuate the conflict and the U.S. government instead should support moderate groups, such as the Democratic League and opponents of Jiang within the Guomindang, the so-called "Third Force" in China. On 9 November 1947, Feng and his associates in the United States organized the Overseas Chinese Association for Peace and Democracy in China to change U.S.

China policy, remaining in the United States until the summer of 1948. By this time, with the Communist Party* poised to take control of China, he saw no further need to convince the American public of Jiang's dictatorship. On 1 September, while on board a Russian ship returning to China by way of the Soviet Union, Feng died either of asphyxiation or a heart attack during a fire.

H. L. Boorman (ed.), *Biographical Dictionary of Republican China* (New York, 1968); D. G. Gillin, *Warlord: Yen Hsi-shan in Shansi Province, 1911–1949* (Princeton, NJ, 1967); J. E. Sheridan, *Chinese Warlord: The Career of Feng Yu-hsiang* (Stanford, CA, 1966).

Roger Y. M. Chan

FENOLLOSA, ERNEST F. (1853–1908)

Ernest Francisco Fenollosa, along with Lafcadio Hearn (1850–1904), was one of the most influential figures in establishing an awareness of East Asia, especially Japan, in the United States. He was the son of a Spanish-born musician, but grew up in Salem, Massachusetts. He attended Harvard University, graduating in 1878. Edward Sylvester Morse, the zoologist and collector of Japanese antiquities who had first interested the Boston Museum of Fine Arts in Japanese pottery, arranged for Fenollosa's appointment as professor of philosophy at the newly founded Tōkyō Imperial University. Over the next twenty years, he studied Japanese art and art history, and associated with collectors, artists, and scholars. In the process, Fenollosa amassed a large and important collection of Japanese paintings, sculpture, and objets d'art. In 1886, he sold his collection to the Boston Museum of Fine Arts, where, along with the collection of William Sturgis Bigelow, it formed the core of the museum's East Asian holdings. In 1890, Fenollosa returned to Boston and became curator of the museum's Japanese collection. He spent four years organizing, cataloging, and mounting displays of the finest pieces. In addition to his work bringing the collection to public view, Fenollosa wrote a two volume study titled, *Epochs of Chinese and Japanese Art: An Outline History of East Asiatic Design*, which was published in 1912.

While Fenollosa was bringing the artistic heritage of Japan and East Asia to the attention of Americans, Lafcadio Hearn, through his essays and travel writings published in American periodicals, was bringing images of daily life in Japan to readers in the United States. Hearn was born in 1850 in Greece, the son of a British army surgeon and a Greek woman. He was raised in Dublin, then moved to the United States in 1869. He became a reporter for the Cincinnati *Enquirer*, and traveled around the United States and the Caribbean. It was not until 1893 that he finally went to Japan, on commission from *Harper's Weekly*. Hearn first stayed in Tokyo, but soon moved to Matsue, on the southwest coast of Honshū, where he lived for the happiest years of his life in Japan. He later moved on to Kōbe, and finally back to Tōkyō, where he taught English at the Imperial University until his abrupt resignation in 1904. His emotional and mental state had deteriorated after his departure from Matsue, as had his physical health. Hearn's writings, in articles in periodicals, books, and anthologies, presented to readers in the United States an intimate and sympathetic image of Japan as it was transforming itself from a traditional, agrarian country into a modern, industrial nation. His early recognition of the potential power of Japanese militarism and sentiments for imperial expansion went largely unnoticed at the time, but seem remarkably prescient in retrospect.

V. W. Brooks, *Fenollosa and His Circle: With Other Essays in Biography* (New York, 1962); L. Chisolm, *Fenollosa: The Far East and American Culture* (New Haven, CT, 1963); L. Hearn, *Writings from Japan: An Anthology* (New York, 1994); J. Rosenfield, "Japanese Buddhist Art: Alive in the Modern Age," in M. R. Cunningham (ed.), *Buddhist Treasure from Nara* (New York, 1998).

Kenneth J. Hammond

FIRST INDOCHINA WAR (1946–1954)

The First Indochina War took place mostly in Vietnam, but fighting spread to some extent to Laos* and Cambodia*. The Japanese had occupied French Indochina* during World War II, and when the war ended, no French forces were in a position immediately to reimpose colonial control. Ho Chi Minh*, founder and leader of both the Indochinese Communist Party and the Vietminh*, proclaimed Vietnam's independence as the Democratic Republic of Vietnam* (DRV) on 2 September 1945. Within weeks, French forces began to return, and after fighting broke out in Saigon, soon had control over a large part of southern Vietnam. Efforts to negotiate some arrangement that would allow enough independence to satisfy the Vietnamese and enough French control to satisfy France proved unsuccessful, and war ensued. The French won the early battles easily because they not only had far superior weapons, but also far more competent troops and officers. The Vietminh were saved only because after World War II, it was politically impossible for the French government to send a large army to Vietnam. By 1949, the Vietminh were rebuilding their forces in the areas left to them and greatly improving their standard of training. In addition, France had difficulties destroying the Vietminh guerrillas because they had trouble finding them, either in the jungle or in the villages. Most peasants would not tell the French anything about Vietminh activities, but would tell the Vietminh all about what the French were doing. The Vietminh could stage many surprise attacks and ambushes, whereas the French often could not find the guerrillas to stage counterattacks.

Initially, the United States tried to avoid involvement. Washington opposed the Vietminh because it had Communist leadership, but refused to support the effort of its French ally to reimpose colonial rule. In 1949, France was working to create a Vietnamese government headed by Bao Dai*,

the former emperor. Many U.S. officials believed that as long as France tried to restore French Colonialism*, most Vietnamese people would oppose them, and any U.S. aid would be futile. But after Mao Zedong* triumphed in the Chinese Civil War*, Chinese Communist armies were at the border of Vietnam in January 1950 and the new People's Republic of China* was supplying weapons to the Vietminh. President Harry S. Truman* now applied the containment policy. On 7 February 1950, the United States granted formal diplomatic recognition to the State of Vietnam, without waiting for France to grant it anything approaching real independence. France still faced a very difficult dilemma. If it kept the State of Vietnam weak, it could not give it enough help against the Vietminh. But if France allowed its client to become strong, it probably would attempt to win independence. Despite American urgings, the French kept it weak. Nevertheless, by early June 1950, Truman, acting on France's request, had allocated $21 million in U.S. military aid to the French war effort. When the Soviet Union granted diplomatic recognition to the DRV, Secretary of State Dean G. Acheson* said this proved that Ho was "the mortal enemy of native independence in Indochina." So firmly did Americans reject the idea that the Vietminh might be a nationalist movement struggling for independence that when U.S. officials or newsmen referred to "the Vietnamese forces," they meant not Ho's troops, but the Vietnamese National Army fighting on the side of France.

Meanwhile, U.S. aid to the French in money, weapons, and equipment steadily grew. By 1954, the United States was paying for an estimated 78 percent of France's war effort. In 1953 and 1954, the U.S. Air Force sent hundreds of ground personnel, mostly aircraft mechanics, to work at French air bases in Vietnam. Pilots of Civil Air Transport, nominally a private company but actually under the control of the Central Intelligence Agency*, flew many of the planes delivering supplies and ammunition to units in the field. Ironically, the French did not want many U.S. advisers in Vietnam, for fear the Americans would help the State of Vietnam break itself free from French control. But when the Vietminh were about to overrun a major French force at Dien Bien Phu* early in 1954, France appealed for the United States to at least stage an air strike. Secretary of State John Foster Dulles* and Admiral Arthur W. Radford*, chairman of the Joint Chiefs of Staff, advocated military intervention, but the other four joint chiefs, including General Matthew B. Ridgway*, and congressional leaders opposed it. After European allies rejected United Action*, President Dwight D. Eisenhower* decided that he could do nothing. The French had hoped that the Vietminh would have to fight a conventional battle in the open, and Dien Bien Phu was that battle. When the French lost it, they lost faith in the war and sought to negotiate a settlement during the Geneva Conference of 1954*. The Geneva Accords of 1954* marked the end of France's war in Indochina and the beginning of U.S. involvement in the Second Indochina War*. See also Paul Ely; Navarre Plan.

B. B. Fall, *Street Without Joy: Indochina at War, 1946–54* (Harrisburg, PA, 1964); E. J. Hammer, *The Struggle for Indochina* (Stanford, CA, 1966); G. Lockhart, *Nation in Arms: The Origins of the People's Army of Vietnam* (Sidney, 1989); J. Prados, *The Sky Would Fall: Operation Vulture, the U.S. Bombing Mission in Indochina, 1954* (New York, 1983).

Edwin E. Moise

FIRST OPIUM WAR (1840–1844)

Britain precipitated this war to end Chinese restrictions on trade and open the rest of China to commercial penetration. Although it avoided direct involvement, the United States benefited from the concessions Britain extracted in the Treaty of Nanjing* that ended the war. U.S. merchants began their opium trade in China early in the nineteenth century, which expanded sharply to a large scale in the 1830s and made large profits. Among them, Russell and Company* was the principal. But in the opium prohibition in 1839, the Chinese government insisted that the merchants hand over opium stores, as well as provide written guarantees against smuggling in opium again. The British government was unwilling to accept this demand, stopping English merchants from complying and ordering them to leave Guangzhou, while threatening military force. By contrast, the Americans agreed to cooperate and resisted English pressure to leave together with them. They remained in Guangzhou and, after the opium had all been handed over to Chinese authorities, resumed trade. When the First Opium War broke out between China and Britain, the U.S. government instructed American citizens in China not to take any action hostile to either side.

American merchants and shipowners in Guangzhou, as well as in Boston, were worried about their merchant vessels being exposed to the pirates in Chinese waters because China's government at that time was preoccupied with the war and unable to provide protection. They requested that the U.S. government send a fleet, but without granting it the right to intervene militarily or diplomatically in the Sino-British war. The administration of U.S. President John Tyler approved the request, and during March 1842, Commodore Lawrence Kearney commanded two warships entering Guangzhou waters. This fleet did not intervene in the conflict as directed, but diplomatic negotiations did occur between Kearney and the Chinese administration. The Chinese fort had bombarded a small American barge of Olyphant and Company on 21 May 1841, resulting in one sailor being killed, some injured, and others captured. When Kearney's fleet reached Guangzhou waters, he negotiated with the governor-general and Guangxi Qigong, settling the outstanding dispute peacefully with Chinese payment of an indemnity.

After the Treaty of Nanjing was signed on 29 August 1842, Tyler, in response to the urging of American merchants, sent the Cushing Mission to China to negotiate for a share of the gains won by the British. Caleb Cushing* was a strong supporter of the China trade, maintaining an intense desire to equal or even outstrip the British in East Asia affairs, but in an amicable way. He criticized British measures as "outrageous" and "high-handed infraction of all law." After he arrived at Macau in 1844, Cushing negotiated the Treaty of Wangxia* on 4 July 1844. It gave the United States all the benefits Britain had obtained and promised by its most-favored-nation clause that if China in the future granted new favors to any nation, the United States must equally enjoy them. American merchants now could enter and leave freely five ports and carry on trade there. Thereafter, many American firms established offices in Shanghai and the American China trade expanded sharply.

Chouban yiwu shimo daoguang chao [Complete Record of the Management of Barbarian Affairs in the Qing Dynasty, Daoguang Period] (Beijing, 1930); K. S. Latourette, *Zhonghua diguo duiwai tiaoyue* [The History of Early Relations between the United States and China, 1784–1844] (Shanghai, 1906); W. F. Mayers, *Zhonghua diguo duiwai tiaoyue* [Treaties Between the Empire of China and Foreign States] (Shanghai, 1906); Zhao Erxun, *Qingshi gao* [Manuscript of Qing Dynasty History] (Beijing, 1977).

Xiang Liling

FISH, HAMILTON (1808–1893)

Hamilton Fish was secretary of state under President Ulysses S. Grant and the most able member of his cabinet from 1869 to 1877. Born in New York City and named after his father's friend Alexander Hamilton, he graduated from Columbia University in 1827. Three years later, Fish was admitted to the bar, specializing in his practice of real estate law. In 1842, he won a seat in the U.S. House of Representatives

as a Whig, thereafter supporting legislation to fund internal improvements and public education. Fish was lieutenant governor and governor of New York State from 1848 to 1850 and then a member of the U.S. Senate from 1851 to 1857. During the Civil War, he served on the Union Defense Committee and as a U.S. commissioner for the relief of prisoners of war. Grant asked him to be secretary of state, even though he had little experience in foreign affairs. An able administrator and judicious diplomat, he dominated Grant's cabinet and implemented a merit system for consular appointments.

Fish's tenure as head of the U.S. State Department was marked by attempts at U.S. acquisition of the Dominican Republic from 1869 to 1871, the settlement of the *Alabama* claims with Britain in accordance with the Treaty of Washington in 1871, and a crisis with Spain over the *Virginius* affair in Cuba. Like his predecessor William H. Seward*, he favored expansion of U.S. interests in the Pacific. For example, he was a proponent of negotiating a treaty to build a canal across the isthmus between North and South America. In 1871, Fish met with Japanese members of the Iwakura Mission* to discuss revision of the U.S.-Japan commercial treaty. That same year, he sent an agent to Samoa to determine whether Pago Pago was suitable for a coaling station. In response to his report that it was "the most perfectly landlocked harbor that exists in the Pacific," a U.S. naval officer went to Samoa and negotiated a treaty in 1872 with a local chieftain that provided the United States with an exclusive right to build a naval base, in return for protection from foreign encroachments. In May, the U.S. Senate refused to ratify the treaty, but Fish's successor, William M. Evarts*, gained approval of a similar accord in 1878 that led to annexation of some of these islands in the Samoa Partition* of 1898. In addition, Fish secured ratification in 1875 of the reciprocity treaty with Hawaii that Seward had negotiated in 1867. In 1887, this treaty was renewed, with a provision granting the United States the exclusive right to build a naval base at Pearl Harbor.

Three incidents that occurred during Fish's tenure as secretary of state signaled the growing American interest in China. In 1870, in response to the Tianjin Massacre of numerous French and other European residents, Fish authorized U.S. Minister to China Frederick F. Low* to join other Western diplomats in supporting French claims of reparations. He also induced Prussia to agree to a suspension of hostilities related to the Franco-Prussian War between each country's respective naval fleets in Chinese waters. In 1873, when the Tongzhi emperor came of age, the question arose whether Western diplomats would be allowed to present their credentials to China's monarch, rather than to the Qing regent as they had done previously. Fish instructed Low again to coordinate his actions with the other powers, but at the same time proceed with "tenderness" regarding Chinese opinion. Following the premature death of the Tongzhi emperor in 1875 and the ascension of the Guangxu emperor, Fish instructed U.S. ministers in Europe to inform European governments that the United States would act in unison with them in establishing an audience policy with the new emperor. His actions established the precedent of the United States joining with European powers to present a unified front in China. In 1877, Fish declined an offer to be chief justice of the U.S. Supreme Court and retired, devoting the rest of his life to philanthropy.

J. V. Fuller, "Hamilton Fish," in S. F. Bemis (ed.), *American Secretaries of State and Their Diplomacy* (New York, 1958); W. S. McFeely, *Grant: A Biography* (New York, 1981); A. Nevins, *Hamilton Fish: The Inner History of the Grant Administration* (New York, 1936).

Stephen E. McCullough

FISHEL, WESLEY R. (1919–1977)

Wesley R. Fishel holds a place of ignominy in most accounts of the origins of the Second Indochina War* because he was a central figure in the Michigan State University Group (MSUG) that managed a technical assistance program to the Republic of Vietnam* from 1955 to 1962. Born in Cleveland, he graduated from Northwestern University in 1941 and then during World War II was a U.S. Army language specialist in Asia. After earning a doctorate in international relations at the University of Chicago in 1948, Fishel worked for the University of California at Los Angeles teaching American servicemen in Japan. While there, he met Ngo Dinh Diem* and soon became his adviser, promoting him as the perfect anti-Communist leader for postwar Vietnam. Fishel joined the faculty of Michigan State University (MSU) in 1951, bringing Diem along as a consultant. When Diem became prime minister of South Vietnam in 1954, Secretary of State John Foster Dulles* asked MSU President John A. Hannah, who had been assistant secretary of defense in the Eisenhower administration, to send a survey team to devise a plan to strengthen the new regime. Hannah readily agreed because he saw fighting Communism* as part of his land grant institution's global service role and a way to raise money to increase faculty salaries and expand facilities.

Fishel, serving as Diem's consultant, negotiated the terms of the MSUG's contract, which focused on implementing a modern system of public and police administration, rather than land and economic reform. MSUG studied social problems and issued reports and recommendations to South Vietnamese and American policy makers. But differences in culture, language, and philosophy undermined its projects because most advisers, a minority from MSU, had no knowledge of Vietnam. A successful refugee resettlement plan failed to prevent favoritism toward Catholics, alienated Buddhists, and included relocation to the Central Highlands, which angered the Hmong*. MSUG built a modern civil servant training school, and a participant program sent Vietnamese to Malaya*, Japan, the Philippines*, and the United States for perfunctory education and training in modern administration and law enforcement methods. Attracting the most criticism was the program for material aid, training, and consultations with South Vietnam's law enforcement agencies, which Diem increasingly used to repress political opponents. But for Fishel, South Vietnam needed stability, not democracy. Diem's oppressive and authoritarian actions were unavoidable, he claimed, because of the necessity to combat the internal Communist threat. Corruption, Fishel argued, was a common malady of all Asian governments.

Allegations that Fishel was an operative for the Central Intelligence Agency* (CIA) remain unproven. In 1953, he held a top-secret security clearance while conducting a study for the U.S. Army in Korea on the effect of language and cultural differences on the United Nations military efforts in the Korean War*. But in Vietnam, Fishel was a freelance secret agent, and the State Department worked with him because he had influence with Diem. In 1956, he replaced the MSUG's first chief adviser, leaving Vietnam two years later, finally distressed and disillusioned with the growth of police-state repression. MSUG relations with Diem deteriorated thereafter, in part because it refused to train the civil guard as a paramilitary unit. In 1962, after former MSUG members wrote two articles criticizing political repression in South Vietnam and predicting that Diem would be overthrown within two years, Diem canceled the MSUG's contract. An article in *Ramparts* four years later charged that the MSUG was a CIA front. At its peak, perhaps five to eight of fifty MSUG advisers were in fact CIA agents. Fishel's knowledge of their presence and the U.S. military disaster that followed made him a pariah. During his last years at MSU, antiwar activists disrupted the classes of this former Teacher of the Year with chants of "murderer" and "butcher."

See also American Friends of Vietnam; Nation-Building Strategy.

D. L. Anderson, *Trapped by Success: The Eisenhower Administration and Vietnam, 1953–1961* (New York, 1991); J. Ernst, *Forging a Fateful Alliance: Michigan State University and the Vietnam War* (East Lansing, MI, 1998); F. FitzGerald, *Fire in the Lake: The Vietnamese and the Americans in Vietnam* (New York, 1972); R. Scigliano and G. H. Fox, *Technical Assistance to Vietnam: The Michigan State University Experience* (New York, 1965).

James I. Matray

FIVE POWER PACT (6 February 1922)

The Five Power Naval Treaty signed by Britain, Japan, France, and Italy was the major treaty of the Washington Conference* held from 11 November 1921 to 6 February 1922. Convened by the United States, which hoped to stop a threatening naval race between itself, Japan, and Britain in the Pacific, the conference began with a sensational opening proposal on naval arms limitation by Secretary of State Charles Evans Hughes*, who asked the participants to scrap seventy capital ships (battleships and battle cruisers) that were either already in existence, being built, or being planned. He also proposed a ten-year naval holiday on the building of capital ships and the creation of a total tonnage ratio of 5 (United States), 5 (Britain), 3 (Japan), 1.75 (France), and 1.75 (Italy) for the remaining capital ships, in hopes of creating a stable balance of power for those ten years. Delegates from the other four nations at first accepted the proposals in general, but then began to chip away at the foundations.

The U.S. proposal, kept secret and known to only about a dozen people, grew out of conversations between the four American delegates—Hughes, former Secretary of State Elihu Root*, Massachusetts Republican Senator Henry Cabot Lodge*, and Alabama Democratic Senator Oscar W. Underwood—and U.S. naval advisers, led by Assistant Secretary of the Navy Theodore Roosevelt Jr. The U.S. Navy, initially unwilling to accept deep cuts in the number of capital ships, found itself forced to acquiesce under severe pressures from Hughes and President Warren G. Harding, as the politicians, not the admirals, made the final decision to accept the "stop now" principle of limitation. Kept under control and muzzled both during the conference and the later Senate ratification debate (where the popular treaty had only one vote against it), the U.S. Navy did not come out in open opposition until the London Naval Conference of 1930*, where the naval holiday was extended for five years. The political skill of the Harding administration in keeping its naval advisers quiet and in line stands in stark contrast to the usual history of arms control negotiations. The Five Power Pact ended the capital ship race and temporarily established a better ratio of naval power for the United States against both Britain and Japan than the United States might have achieved if all three nations had completed their naval programs. As it happened, the United States did not even build up to the legal limits of the treaty during its fifteen-year existence.

The French prevented the adoption of the U.S. proposals that wanted to apply the 5–5–3–1.75–1.75 ratio not only to capital ships, but also to cruisers, destroyers, and submarines. The Japanese, not unexpectedly since the Americans, through the work of cryptographer Herbert O. Yardley and the American Black Chamber, were reading copies of Japanese cables between Tōkyō and Washington, wanted a higher ratio than the 60 percent allocated to them compared with the 100 percent figures of the United States and Britain. The desire of Tōkyō to come to a decision led to a compromise whereby the Japanese accepted the 60 percent ratio in return for a clause (Article 19) in the treaty that prohibited further construction of fortifications in the Pacific islands of the five nations. Nevertheless, the most aggressive wing of the

Japanese Navy remained dissatisfied, not only with the United States, but with its own leadership for accepting inequality. The end of the Anglo-Japanese Alliance*, formalized in the Four Power Pact* under U.S. pressure, added further to Japanese unhappiness, but Japan's government clearly recognized that the United States would not have accepted any naval limitation without the end of that alliance. Japanese pursuit of equality helped lead to the end of the Five Power Treaty in 1936. *See also* Geneva Naval Conference of 1927; London Naval Conference of 1935–1936.

T. H. Buckley, *The United States and the Washington Conference, 1921–1922* (Knoxville, TN, 1970); M. Krepon (ed.), *The Politics of Arms Control Treaty Ratification* (New York, 1991).

Thomas H. Buckley

FOOTE, LUCIUS H. (1826–1913)

Lucius Harwood Foote's father held Congregational pastoral ministries in New York, Ohio, Illinois, and Wisconsin. Born at Winfield, New York, he attended Knox College and Case Western Reserve, but did not graduate from either. In 1853, he traveled overland to California, and began to study law. Admitted to the bar in 1856, Foote served a four-year term as a municipal judge in Sacramento and was collector at the port there during the Civil War. A thorough Republican, Foote was adjutant-general of California from 1872 to 1876 and also a delegate to the Republican National Convention, before President Rutherford B. Hayes named him as consul to Valparaiso, Chile, in March 1879. When the American minister died, Foote assumed control of the embassy until July 1882. In August, he returned to the United States on leave. After the Shufeldt Treaty* with Korea in May 1882, Foote was appointed by President Chester Arthur as the first U.S. envoy extraordinary and minister plenipotentiary to that nation. His task was to treat Korea as a sovereign and independent nation, but not to interfere with its relations with

China "unless action be taken prejudicial to the rights of the United States." Accompanied by his wife and private secretary, Foote arrived in Japan in April, and in Korea on 13 May 1883.

Foote confronted a difficult situation, as China and Japan used all diplomatic and political pressures to resolve the question of the control of Korea in their own favor. King Kojong* was alleged to have danced with joy at his arrival, and granted him an audience a day later. Kojong consulted Foote repeatedly and, perhaps unwisely, saw him as spokesman of a United States that was not prepared to make the degree of commitment to Korean independence he desired. Not unexpectedly, the Chinese and Japanese watched him carefully, especially when Foote encouraged the Koreans to extend commercial trading privileges to American merchants and firms. Foote himself dabbled in Korean trade, and made considerable profit. He also urged Korea's king to send a mission to the United States, which went from August 1883 to May 1884. He desired to see a foreign settlement in the open ports, similar to the ones at Shimonoseki, Japan, or Shanghai, China. The Korean government was willing to establish one at In'chŏn, which began rapid growth as a port and center for American milling, timber and rice cleaning, and military equipment. Foote also welcomed the Protestant missionary Dr. Horace N. Allen* as a legation doctor, though Allen's original purpose had been to spread missionary influence, which was forbidden in Korea.

During December 1884, pro-Japanese "progressives" sought to overthrow the rule of the pro-Chinese Min family conservatives, and more than 300 people lost their lives. Foote sought to protect foreigners and progressives at court against the backlash of the conservative elements, and received the thanks of the Japanese government for his "brave and humane conduct." Brought in by Yuan Shikai*, the Chinese resident in Korea, Chinese troops had entered Kojong's palace and ejected a detachment of 200 Japanese "legation guards" in a dispute over who should defend and protect the king. The Chinese government extended thanks to Foote for his efforts, but probably did not know that he had telegraphed U.S. naval forces then at Nagasaki, which brought the USS *Trenton* steaming into Chemul'po's harbor on 17 September. Meanwhile, the U.S. Congress passed a new diplomatic and consular act in July 1884 that reduced the rank of Foote's office in Korea with no change in salary. Foote declined the new post, explaining that "to these people, proud that the United States should have sent to them a Minister of the first rank, it is impossible to explain the reasons for the change without leaving the most unfortunate impressions." After the State Department suggested he depart on leave, to avoid an explanation, Foote and his wife returned to the United States in January 1885, stopping in Tōkyō en route, where they received an audience with the emperor. Back in the United States, he was elected treasurer of the California Academy of Sciences and secretary to the board of trustees, positions he held until his death. Regrettably, Foote's papers and correspondence were destroyed in the San Francisco fire of 1906.

H. Conroy, *The Japanese Seizure of Korea, 1868–1910: A Study of Realism and Idealism in International Relations* (Philadelphia, 1960); O. Kim, "Early Korean-American Relations," *Journal of Social Science and Humanities* (1976); Y. Lee, *Diplomatic Relations Between the United States and Korea, 1866–1887* (New York, 1970); G. M. McCune and J. A. Harrison (eds.), *Korean-American Relations: Documents Pertaining to the Far Eastern Diplomacy of the United States*, Vol. 1: *The Initial Period, 1883–1886* (Berkeley, CA, 1951).

Frederick C. Drake

FORD, GERALD R. (1913–)

Gerald R. Ford was president for the United States from August 1974 to January 1977, presiding over the transition of U.S. policy in East Asia after the Communist triumph in the Second Indochina War*. He spent four years in the U.S. Navy during World War II on active service in the Pacific, during which he reached the rank of lieutenant commander. Ford later ascribed to this experience his conversion from prewar isolationism to confirmed internationalism, pledging himself to help keep the United States sufficiently strong militarily to deter future enemies. As a rising young Republican congressman from Michigan, he embraced Cold War policies of staunchly anti-Communist opposition to the Soviet Union and its allies, backing the Truman administration's Marshall Plan, North Atlantic Treaty Organization, and Foreign Economic Assistance Act of 1950, as well as intervention in the Korean War*. As a member of the House Appropriations Subcommittee for Military Expenditures he became an expert in crafting defense budgets. In 1952, he visited both French Indochina* and the Republic of Korea*, where he began a lasting friendship with General William C. Westmoreland*.

During the 1950s, Ford was a loyal soldier in Congress for President Dwight D. Eisenhower*, who found his help in obtaining the foreign aid budgets he requested invaluable. As a member of the Appropriations Committee's subcommittee for the Central Intelligence Agency*, he became a dedicated advocate of secret intelligence operations. In 1960, Ford's "American Strategy and Defense" report approved the Eisenhower administration's policy of moving toward detente with the Soviet Union, but said heavy defense budgets remained essential to U.S. national security. As House minority leader in the 1960s, Ford, who believed in a bipartisan foreign policy, endorsed his country's attempts to support the Republic of Vietnam*. Even so, he questioned the wisdom of the increasing American commitment of ground troops, suggesting that a naval blockade combined with sea and air bombardment might be more effective and that land forces should be contributed by U.S. allies. Although Ford continued to defend

U.S. conduct in the war, he endorsed in 1967 the concept soon known as Vietnamization*. He made it clear that this did not imply the sudden and precipitate withdrawal of U.S. forces, but a carefully orchestrated reduction over time. A visit to China in 1972 convinced Ford, who was initially suspicious of reopening relations with the People's Republic of China* under President Richard M. Nixon*, that rapprochement was justified, since China's leaders were strongly anti-Soviet.

Ford's surprise nomination to the vice presidency in 1973 was followed in 1974 by his succession to the presidency after Nixon's forced resignation. An admirer of Henry A. Kissinger*, Ford retained his services as secretary of state and attempted to continue Nixon's foreign policies unchanged. The depressing experience of watching helplessly in 1975 while the Democratic Republic of Vietnam* annexed the south, as Americans made frantic and humiliating attempts to escape, was one painful legacy he inherited from his predecessor. Striving to stress the positive aspects, Ford publicly announced the war was "finished as far as America is concerned," though privately he feared a resurgence of isolationism domestically and the development of contempt for the United States internationally. In May 1975, he therefore reacted forcefully when Cambodia* seized an American freighter in the *Mayaguez* Incident*. Ford continued the Nixon-Kissinger policy of playing Beijing against Moscow and thereby impelling both antagonists to reach an understanding favorable to the United States. He turned down a proposed Soviet alliance against the PRC in 1974, but signed Soviet-American agreements on arms control and human rights. Never an original thinker, Ford represented the prevailing conventional position on foreign affairs throughout his career.

J. Cannon, *Time and Chance: Gerald Ford's Appointment with History* (New York, 1994); G. R. Ford, *A Time to Heal: The Autobiography of Gerald*

R. Ford (New York, 1979); J. R. Greene, *The Presidency of Gerald R. Ford* (Lawrence, KS, 1995); E. L. and F. H. Schapsmeier, *Gerald R. Ford's Date with Destiny: A Political Biography* (New York, 1989).

Priscilla Roberts

FORMOSA

See REPUBLIC OF CHINA; TAIWAN

FORMOSA RESOLUTION (29 January 1955)

The Formosa Resolution, adopted by Congress on 29 January 1955 during the first of the Taiwan Strait Crises*, authorized the president to use U.S. armed forces to secure and protect Taiwan* and the Penghus (Formosa and the Pescadores) against armed attack, including the securing and protection of "such related positions and territories of that area now in friendly hands" as he judged required or appropriate to assure their defense. The language was designed to provide authority for U.S. action to defend offshore islands that the Guomindang* (Nationalist) government occupied without mentioning them explicitly. The resolution also declared that possession by friendly governments of the western Pacific island chain was essential to U.S. vital interests and that Taiwan was a part of that island chain.

President Dwight D. Eisenhower* requested the resolution in January 1955, when Communist forces of the People's Republic of China* (PRC) threatened to seize the Nationalist-held Dachen islands, 200 miles north of Taiwan. Eisenhower and Secretary of State John Foster Dulles* wanted congressional authorization for U.S. naval support for Nationalist evacuation of the Dachens and U.S. action to defend the Nationalist-held islands of Jinmen and Mazu, as well as congressional action to underscore the U.S. commitment to defend the Republic of China* (ROC) on Tai-wan, especially because the U.S.-China Mutual Defense Treaty of 1954* signed in December had not yet been ratified. Eisenhower's original draft message to Congress declared his intention to join in defending Jinmen and Mazu until the area had been stabilized by a UN resolution, but he dropped that statement when the British objected that it would destroy the possibility of UN action. The message that he sent to Congress said that he did not suggest expanding U.S. defense obligations beyond the territory covered under the Mutual Defense Treaty.

Some Democratic leaders questioned the necessity of any congressional action, arguing that the president had the authority he needed as commander in chief of U.S. armed forces. Some also doubted the wisdom of U.S. involvement in the defense of the offshore islands, but the resolution passed by huge majorities of 410–3 in the House and 85–3 in the Senate. A substitute resolution that Senator Estes Kefauver of Tennessee proposed, which would have authorized only the defense of Taiwan and the Penghus, was defeated on the Senate floor. The "related positions and territories" clause of the resolution never was invoked, although Dulles used it to argue for the protection of Jinmen and Mazu during the Taiwan Strait Crisis of 1958. Perhaps the greatest significance of the resolution was the precedent that it set for congressional advance authorization of the use of U.S. forces, notably the resolution Congress passed after the Gulf of Tonkin Incidents*. *See also* Operation Oracle.

R. Accinelli, *Crisis and Commitment: United States Policy Toward Taiwan, 1950–1955* (Chapel Hill, NC, 1996); G. Chang, *Friends and Enemies: The United States, China, and the Soviet Union, 1948–1972* (Stanford, CA, 1990); R. Foot, "The Search for a Modus Vivendi: Anglo-American Relations and China Policy in the Eisenhower Era," in W. I. Cohen and A. Iriye (eds.), *The Great Powers in East Asia, 1953–1960* (New York, 1990).

Harriet Dashiell Schwar

FOSTER, JOHN W. (1836–1917)

John Watson Foster was the most prominent career diplomat in the period between the Civil War and World War II. Tenacious, pragmatic, and legalistic in his approach to diplomacy, he was noted for a tough negotiating style. Foster was active in the promotion of American missionary efforts and the advancement of American business interests in China. Born in Pike County, Indiana, he graduated from Indiana University in 1855. After attending Harvard University for a year, Foster returned to Indiana to establish a law practice in Evansville and soon became active in Republican Party politics. During the Civil War, he attained the rank of brevet brigadier general in the Indiana Volunteer Infantry. After the war, Foster published the Evansville *Daily Journal* (1865–1973), worked as city postmaster (1869–1973), and advanced Republican Party causes. Party loyalty then earned him an appointment as minister to Mexico in 1873. During his seven years in Mexico, he established a close personal relationship with Porfirio Díaz, the nation's dictator. Foster was appointed minister to Russia in 1880, but resigned after deciding that both the Russian monarchy and its government were backward and corrupt. He then served as minister to Spain from 1883 to 1885.

In the 1880s, Foster opened a law practice in Washington, D.C., with an international clientele that included the governments of Mexico, Chile, Russia, Spain, and China. His work for the Qing Dynasty included directing opposition to the Chinese Exclusion Acts* and seeking an indemnity for the families of Chinese killed at the Rock Springs Massacre* in 1885. Foster then served as a special plenipotentiary to Spain to negotiate reciprocity arguments for Cuba and Puerto Rico, and reciprocity agreements for the West Indies with Brazil, Germany, and Great Britain. As a special agent, he represented the United States in 1892 before an international tribunal in the arbitration of an international dispute to regulate the fur seal trade. Foster became secretary of state after the abrupt resignation of James G. Blaine, serving from June 1892 to February 1893. During his brief tenure, he negotiated a settlement of the USS *Baltimore* Affair with Chile and led an unsuccessful attempt for Hawaiian Annexation*. Despite his initial frustration, Foster helped draft in 1898 the joint congressional resolution that finally made Hawaii a U.S. territory.

In 1895, Foster served as an adviser to Chinese Viceroy Li Hongzhang*, whom Foster knew personally from a visit to China a year earlier. While there, he possibly was involved with a conspiracy involving American railroad tycoon James H. Wilson, U.S. Minister to China Charles Denby*, and William Pethick, Li's American private secretary, to overthrow the antiforeign Qing Dynasty and place Li or his son on the throne. After the plot disintegrated, Foster remained on good terms with Li and the Chinese government. His continuing services as a legal adviser included acting as host for Li during the aged viceroy's visit to the United States in 1896 and serving as counsel, along with his young grandson John Foster Dulles*, to the Chinese delegation at the Second Hague Conference in 1907. Meanwhile, Foster was the "handyman" of the State Department. He accepted appointments as special ambassador to Britain and Russia in 1897 to seek a conference to regulate the hunting of fur seals in the Bering Sea Seal Controversy*, and as a representative before an international tribunal in London in 1898 to arbitrate Canadian-American disputes. President Theodore Roosevelt* appointed him agent for the American case presented before the Alaskan Boundary Tribunal in 1903. An advocate of U.S. expansion in the Pacific and wider acceptance of international law and arbitration, Foster urged creation of a professional diplomatic corps, expanded American trade through the use of reciprocity agreements, and worldwide advancement of Christian missionary work.

W. R. Castle Jr., "John W. Foster, Secretary of State, June 29, 1892, to February 23, 1893," in S. F. Bemis (ed.), *American Secretaries of State and Their Diplomacy* (New York, 1928); M. J. Devine, *John W. Foster: Politics and Diplomacy in the Imperial Era, 1873–1917* (Athens, OH, 1981); J. W. Foster, *Diplomatic Memoirs* (Boston, 1909).

Michael J. Devine

FOULK, GEORGE C. (1856–1893)

George Clayton Foulk was a critical actor in East Asian politics in the 1880s, and became the source of a legend. A gifted student, he graduated third in his class at the U.S. Naval Academy in 1876. Shortly thereafter, Foulk was assigned to the Pacific squadron of the U.S. Navy, and for a time was stationed at Nagasaki, where he learned Japanese. In 1882, he joined an exploration expedition in Siberia, and except for a brief return to the United States in 1883, Foulk remained in East Asia for the rest of his life. By 1884, he was naval attaché to the legation of U.S. ambassador Lucius H. Foote* at Seoul. Foulk's assignment to Seoul may have been occasioned by a request from the Korean government, whose representatives met the young officer during a visit to the United States in 1883. By the time of his arrival in Seoul in 1884, Foulk could converse in Korean, and he quickly became a promoter of Japanese-supported "progressives" in Korea, who advocated an end to the traditional subordination of Korea to China.

In November, progressive Koreans attempted a coup, and violent traditionalist reaction temporarily drove Japanese diplomats from Korea. Foulk was among the U.S. military officers who intervened to save Japanese representatives from the mob, and who escorted the Japanese diplomats back to their residences after their return to Seoul. He knew and encouraged the young nationalist Kim Ok-kyun, and despised the pro-Chinese intermediary P. G. von Möllendorf, who arranged for the Korean court to become deeply indebted to Russia. It is probable that Foulk not only

was a sympathizer with the progressives, but that he and Japanese agents actively encouraged the progressives in their political actions of 1884. If so, he acted with the approval of Foote and of the U.S. government, not surprising in view of the fact that during the crisis of 1884, Foulk supported the legation staff with his own money. He remained at his embassy post until 1887, when he accepted a commercial job with the American Trading Company at Yokohama. From 1890 to his unexplained death, he was professor of mathematics at Doshisha College.

In his memoir, *At the Court of Korea*, William Franklin Sands recounts the legend of Foulk as known in the U.S. Navy. Allegedly, in the days when he was stationed at Nagasaki, a Japanese couple who spoke English ran a teahouse that was frequented by American sailors and officers. The couple had a daughter, who was rarely seen by any but the most courtly of the officers. Foulk soon began to keep company with her, and beat out all competition by conversing regularly with her in Japanese. According to local rumor, the young woman was the last survivor of a noble family that had been all but obliterated in the violence culminating in Japan's Meiji Restoration of 1868. Her ostensible parents were old family retainers raising her in protective obscurity. Foulk married her, took her with him to Korea, and later returned with her to live in Japan. The story, given a tragic twist, inspired Puccini's plot in *Madame Butterfly*.

T. Dennett, *Americans in Eastern Asia: A Critical Study of the Policy of the United States with Reference to China, Japan and Korea in the 19th Century* (New York, 1922); W. F. Sands, *At the Court of Korea* (London, 1987); Y. Lee, *Diplomatic Relations Between the United States and Korea, 1866–1887* (New York, 1970).

Pamela K. Crossley

FOUR MODERNIZATIONS

Adoption in 1978 of this new pragmatic reform policy in the People's Republic of

China* (PRC) altered Sino-American relations dramatically. Zhou Enlai* first mentioned the economic strategy of "four modernizations" in 1965, calling again in 1975 for China to modernize its agriculture, industry, national defense, and science and technology by the beginning of the twenty-first century. However, it was not until the third Plenum of the Eleventh Central Committee of the Chinese Communist Party* (CCP) in late December 1978 that Deng Xiaoping* and the reformist faction sanctioned the decisive shift from emphasis on politics to economic development. The reforms called for dismantling the communes, ending the overconcentration of authority in economic management, permitting the establishment of private enterprises and joint ventures, opening China's market to foreign capital and competition, and importing advanced science and technology for economic modernization and improvement of national defense. To achieve these ambitious objectives, China intended not only to gain access to advanced technologies, but also to maintain good relations with the United States and other Western nations.

Historically, the United States had adopted a restrictive trade policy toward socialist countries, such as with CHINCOM* in East Asia. But Sino-American trade surged after President Jimmy Carter* announced in the fall of 1978 plans to normalize diplomatic relations with the PRC, coinciding with Beijing's adoption of its Four Modernizations policy that same year. This had important economic and political implications for both nations. Normal economic relations not only enhanced U.S. business opportunities in China, but also provided Washington with political and diplomatic leverage over Beijing as a result of the annual debate in the U.S. Congress over renewal of most-favored-nation (MFN) status for the PRC. Similarly, as long as economic development remained the highest priority for the PRC, the continual need for new technology and capital

investment to fuel economic growth forced Beijing to adopt a more moderate position in its foreign and domestic policies.

Strategically, commitment to the Four Modernizations gave China a stake in joining the United States in maintaining peace and stability in Asia, notably on the Korean peninsula. However, this relationship was constrained by the rise of Chinese nationalism and the thorny issue of Taiwan*. The Taiwan Relations Act*, signed into law by President Carter on 10 April 1979 after U.S.-PRC Normalization of Relations*, guaranteed Taiwan's security and continuation of sales of defensive weapons to the Republic of China*. Chinese nationalism dictated that the Chinese leadership pursue an independent foreign policy, resulting in Beijing criticizing U.S. policies on Taiwan and portraying the United States as a hegemonic power. Connecting these two issues, Beijing's view of Taiwan as a renegade province and refusal to renounce the use of force as a means for reunification contradicted U.S. China policy. Nevertheless, the PRC's adoption of the Four Modernizations strategy had a significant positive effect on Sino-American relations after 1978. As long as Beijing's primary objective was to pursue national power and wealth through economic development, its nationalistic passion was subject to rational constraints.

J. Howell, *China Opens Its Doors* (Boulder, CO, 1993); Q. S. Tan, *The Making of U.S.-China Policy: From Normalization to Post–Cold War Era* (Boulder, CO, 1992); G. White, *Riding the Tiger: The Politics of Economic Reform in Post-Mao China* (Stanford, CA, 1993).

Roger Y. M. Chan

FOUR POWER PACT (13 December 1921)

The Four Power Pact, signed by the United States, Great Britain, France, and Japan at the Washington Conference* on 13 December 1921, was the effort of the major Pacific powers to restore order and stability in

Asia after World War I by creating a consultative arrangement among themselves to preserve the status quo. The pact was a product of diplomatic compromise. The United States, who felt threatened by the growing power of Japan in the Pacific, firmly opposed the continuation in any form of the Anglo-Japanese Alliance*, which was first concluded in 1902 and last renewed in 1911 for a term of ten years. The United States regarded the alliance as an instrument of old imperialism that allowed Japan to establish its spheres of influence in Asia. The British government, despite mixed feelings about its increasingly ambitious ally in Asia, still saw some merits in keeping the alliance and preferred to retain some form of security arrangement in the Pacific. Japanese leaders were reluctant to surrender the alliance, but sensed little enthusiasm from the British about its renewal. Moreover, realizing that it was vital to avoid any war with the United States, Tōkyō did not want to fight to retain the alliance if it would antagonize the Americans.

At the beginning of the Washington Conference, the British representative, Arthur J. Balfour, drafted a tripartite agreement among the United States, Great Britain, and Japan to replace the Anglo-Japanese Alliance. However, the leading Japanese negotiator, Shidehara Kijūrō*, changed the proposed tripartite agreement into a consultative pact because he was afraid the British proposal was too close to a military alliance for the United States to be able to accept. Even that modification was not yet acceptable to Secretary of State Charles Evans Hughes* and he proposed to invite France into the arrangement to make it more acceptable to the American public, as well as the U.S. Senate.

The outcome was an ambiguous and general consultative agreement. The pact merely bound the four signatories "to respect their rights in relation to their insular dominions in the region of the Pacific Ocean" and to hold "a joint conference" in case a "controversy" arose among them.

The four also agreed that if their rights were "threatened by the aggressive action of any other power," they would "communicate with one another fully and frankly in order to arrive at an understanding as to the most efficient measures to be taken, jointly or separately, to meet the exigencies of the particular situation." There was no suggestion of any military commitment in the treaty. However, because it essentially terminated the Anglo-Japanese Alliance, the Four Power Pact alleviated the tension between the United States and Japan. By its creation of a mechanism to solve potential security problems in the Pacific, the treaty also facilitated the conclusion at Washington of the Five Power Pact* for naval arms limitation and the Nine Power Pact* affirming the Open Door Policy* in China.

R. V. Dingman, *Power in the Pacific: The Origins of Naval Arms Limitation, 1914–1922* (Chicago, 1976); A. Iriye, *After Imperialism: The Search for a New Order in the Far East, 1921–1931* (Cambridge, MA, 1965); I. Nish, *Alliance in Decline: A Study in Anglo-Japanese Relations, 1908–23* (London, 1972).

Kawamura Noriko

FREE THAI MOVEMENT

The Free Thai movement was the U.S.-trained and-supported anti-Japanese resistance movement in Thailand* during World War II. At the outbreak of hostilities between Japan and the United States after the Pearl Harbor Attack* in December 1941, Japanese troops moved into Thailand from French Indochina*. The Thai government, led by Prime Minister Field Marshal Phibulsongkram, allied itself with Japan, and in early 1942, declared war on the United States. Seni Pramoj, the Thai ambassador in Washington, met with Secretary of State Cordell Hull*, but did not deliver the declaration of war. Instead, Seni cooperated with the U.S. Office of Strategic Services to organize the training and deployment of about fifty Thai guerrilla fighters who, under the name Seri Thai, later were infiltrated into the country and played a largely symbolic role in anti-Japanese activities. Whereas Seni led the movement in exile, the leading role within Thailand was played by Pridi Banomyong, a French-educated leftist intellectual who became Thailand's first elected postwar prime minister.

J. B. Haseman, *The Thai Resistance Movement During World War II* (DeKalb, IL, 1978); E. B. Reynolds, *Thailand and Japan's Southern Advance, 1940–1945* (New York, 1994); D. K. Wyatt, *Thailand: A Short History* (New Haven, CT, 1984).

Kenneth J. Hammond

FRELINGHUYSEN, FREDERICK T. (1817–1885)

Frederick Theodore Frelinghuysen was U.S. secretary of state from December 1881 to March 1885, displaying dignified stewardship, courtesy, and sound judgment. His guidance and soft approach in seeking equality of commercial opportunity and in safeguarding and enlarging U.S. trading opportunities in the future were supportive in the signing of a treaty opening Korea in 1882. After graduation from Rutgers University in 1836, Frelinghuysen trained in law in his uncle's law firm in Newark, New Jersey. He was admitted to the bar in 1839, serving clients such as the Central Railroad of New Jersey and the Morris Canal and Banking Company. He entered public life as city attorney of Newark in 1849 and then was elected to the city council. From 1861 to 1866, he served as attorney general of New Jersey, and worked for impeachment of President Andrew Johnson. In July 1870, President Ulysses S. Grant named him for the position of ambassador to Britain, which he declined on the grounds that he preferred an American education for his children. In 1871, he joined the U.S. Senate for New Jersey, and became a leading figure in the Stalwarts. After he served on the electoral commis-

sion that selected Rutherford B. Hayes as president late in 1876, Frelinghuysen left the Senate and returned to his law practice.

In 1881, Frelinghuysen agreed to President Chester A. Arthur's request that he replace James G. Blaine as secretary of state. He reversed some of his predecessor's Latin American policies, especially in offering mediation of a border dispute between Chile and Peru, but maintained Blaine's Asian policies. Like Blaine, Frelinghuysen encouraged commercial advancement there on the basis of reciprocity, as well as in Latin America and Africa. He supported moves to gain a naval base at Pearl Harbor, Hawaii, and cautiously, but consistently, backed the efforts of Robert W. Shufeldt* to open Korea to American trading interests from 1881 to 1882. On 7 January 1882, he telegraphed Chester Holcombe, the U.S. chargé at Tianjin, interpreted to mean that Frelinghuysen and the Arthur administration supported the negotiations for a treaty, previously sanctioned by Blaine, and that Shufeldt was to be the U.S. commissioner. Frelinghuysen held Shufeldt on a much looser rein than Blaine did, and told him in the State Department's instruction to him of 14 November 1881, that the length of time required for communication in so isolated a nation as Korea left the commodore to his own discretion in carrying it out. He outlined his ideas of what might constitute a good basis for an initial treaty, with a shipwreck convention as first necessity. With regard to a commercial treaty, Frelinghuysen indicated that a "moderate degree of friendly and mutually profitable intercourse [at] first will bring about its natural and necessary enlargement in time cannot reasonably be doubted." He therefore instructed Shufeldt to seek a most-favored-nation clause as a provision in the treaty.

Frelinghuysen allowed Shufeldt a discretionary time to negotiate the treaty by May 1882. Although he neglected to provide advice when his envoy asked whether he should recognize China's claim to suzerainty over Korea, he did not withdraw his support when Shufeldt criticized the Chinese government and character in a long and bitter letter to California Senator Aaron Sargent. Shufeldt, for his part, made certain to keep the secretary informed, detailing long and careful observations on the state of negotiations, and especially the policies and tactics of Li Hongzhang*. Frelinghuysen was adamant about what the Shufeldt Treaty* had accomplished: "In view of all the circumstances, I cannot but regard the administrative independence of Korea as an established fact, abundantly recognized by the events of the past few years, and not created by or recognized by the conclusion of our treaty.... We regarded Korea as *de facto* independent, and ... our acceptance of the friendly aid found in China was in no sense a recognition of China's suzerain power." When he sent the treaty to the Senate Foreign Relations Committee, he declared that it "did not create Corean independence any more than like engagement concluded or now in process of negotiation between Corea and the western powers." Frelinghuysen's policy thus implicitly supported the pro-independence group in Korea and its supporters in Japan, an approach that Lucius H. Foote* would maintain as the first U.S. ambassador to Korea.

P. M. Brown, "Frederick Theodore Frelinghuysen, Secretary of State, December 19, 1881, to March 3, 1885," in S. F. Bemis (ed.), *American Secretaries of State and Their Diplomacy* (New York, 1958); F. C. Drake, *The Empire of the Seas: A Biography of Rear Admiral Robert Wilson Shufeldt, USN* (Honolulu, HI, 1984); G. A. McCune and J. A. Harrison (eds.), *Korean-American Relations: Documents Pertaining to the Far Eastern Diplomacy of the United States*, Vol. 1: *The Initial Period 1883–1886* (Berkeley, CA, 1951); J. W. Rollins, "Frederick Theodore Frelinghuysen, 1817–1885: The Politics and Diplomacy of Stewardship," Ph.D. dissertation, University of Wisconsin, 1974; H. Sunoo, "A Study of the U.S.-Korean Treaty of 1882," *Korea Review* (1949).

Frederick C. Drake

FRENCH COLONIALISM

French colonialism in Indochina resulted in expanding Vietnamese nationalism that eventually vanquished the French in 1954 and the Americans in 1975. French colonization in East Asia focused on Vietnam (Cochin China, Annam, and Tonkin), gaining momentum in the middle of the nineteenth century. French interest in East Asia had existed since the 1600s, developing out of Catholic missionary activity. France's conquest of French Indochina* (Cambodia*, Laos*, and Vietnam) was carried out with hesitancy during times of political and economic stability and interrupted in times of internal revolution and external war. French colonization in East Asia never represented a specific and organized plan, but resulted from international rivalry and a strong pro-colonial party in France. Perhaps the most important factor in French colonialism was French national pride—of culture, reputation, prestige, and influence. French colonizers embraced the idea of a *mission civilisatrice* (civilizing mission), in which France would civilize those peoples whose way of life seemed, from a Parisian perspective, primitive and barbaric. The specific colonial policy to carry out this civilizing mission was a *politique d'assimilation* (policy of assimilation), which professed to convert and eventually absorb colonial peoples into the French nation.

Until the middle of the 1800s, French attempts at colonization were intermittent and ineffective. To increase their influence in Southeast Asia, France began a serious military campaign to colonize Indochina. Only after 1880, spurred on by a drive for national prestige and rivalry with other powers, did France completely occupy Indochina. By the 1890s, Indochina was the richest and most populous of the French colonies—the jewel of the empire. French colonizers saw Indochina as the first step to an Asian empire that France hoped also would encompass Siam (Thailand*), Yunnan, and southern China. But France lacked the military resources to colonize these areas and was forced to look on Indochina as the limit of French East Asian expansion, rather than as the foundation of a still larger empire. French rule of the colony was harsh, as the colonial overlords sought to exploit economically the resources of Indochina, in particular rice, rubber, and coal. For the Vietnamese, who had enjoyed a relatively comfortable standard of living prior to colonial rule, their lives became worse. Most Vietnamese became impoverished and landless, and literacy actually plummeted from near universality to less than 20 percent of the populace. In addition, heavy taxation and poor administration served to break up the traditional institutions of Vietnamese society. France maintained its rule over the colony through force of arms, and harsh retributions followed each localized uprising.

French colonial development in Indochina reached its height between 1919 and 1929, but Vietnamese nationalist activity fomented underneath the surface. Resistance against French colonization always had existed. Hardly had the French conquered Tonkin when the nationalist Can Vuong movement emerged. After the turn of the century, resistance centered around Phan Boi Chau*, who turned to Japan for support in his efforts to create a Vietnamese republic. During World War I, France promised political, social, and economic reforms, but Vietnamese hopes quickly were dashed. Insurrectionary movements began to sweep the countryside in 1925, reaching their peak in 1930. That year, an uprising led by the Vietnam Quoc Dan Dang Party erupted at the Yen Bey garrison in Tonkin. Vietnamese nationalist Ho Chi Minh* also was active at this time, founding the Indochinese Communist Party in 1929, which advocated overthrowing the French imperialists and creating an independent country. Although Ho would become the principal figure associated with Indochina's wars of liberation, historically he stands at the end of a long line of leaders and movements that stretch back to the first years of French colonization in the region.

Strong resistance against colonial rule continued during World War II. In May 1941, Ho established the Vietminh* or League for Vietnamese Independence. During the war, the Japanese occupied the territory and in March 1945, when the collapse of the Japanese empire appeared imminent, they removed the French altogether from power and installed a puppet state ruled by Annamite Emperor Bao Dai*. Toward the end of the war, France attempted to reestablish its power, although U.S. President Franklin D. Roosevelt* opposed the French return and Ho Chi Minh in 1945 declared a provisional government of the Democratic Republic of Vietnam*. Harry S. Truman*, Roosevelt's successor, refused to support Ho, providing military and financial aid to the French instead. The First Indochina War* between France and Vietminh started in 1946. Ironically, Indochina, which had been the jewel of the French empire, became the catalyst that hastened the empire's total dissolution. Vietnamese nationalism emboldened other nationalist movements under French rule in Africa, and by 1962, little remained of the French Empire. *See also* Dien Bien Phu; Paul Ely; Navarre Plan; Phan Chu Trinh.

C. Andrew and A. S. Kanya-Forstner, *The Climax of French Imperial Expansion, 1914–1924* (Stanford, CA, 1981); R. Betts, *Tricouleur: The French Overseas Empire* (New York, 1978); J. Cady, *The Roots of French Imperialism in Eastern Asia* (New York, 1967); J. Dreifort, *Myopic Grandeur: The Ambivalence of French Foreign Policy Toward the Far East, 1919–1945*, (Kent, OH, 1991); M. Shipway, *The Road to War: France and Vietnam, 1944–1947* (Providence, RI, 1996).

Kathryn C. Statler

FRENCH INDOCHINA

This French colony in Southeast Asia was destined to figure prominently in U.S. policy during the late twentieth century. Using as a pretext antimissionary measures by successive emperors of Vietnam, Napoleon III began the conquest of Indochina in 1858. After initially establishing a toehold at Tourane and then at Saigon, the French gradually expanded outward. Within five years, they had taken the three southern provinces of the Vietnamese empire. By late 1867, all of southern Vietnam had been organized into a colony France termed Cochin China. After a series of abortive efforts at further conquest, Hanoi finally fell to the French in 1882, and Tonkin was converted into a protectorate. Emperor Tu Duc resisted the superior French military might, but his death in July 1883 paved the way for the ultimate loss of Vietnamese independence. Within a month, an emasculated imperial court signed a treaty making Annam a protectorate of the French Empire, although active native resistance to French rule continued almost to the end of the century. After a brief period of armed conflict, China, to whom the Hue court retained a tributary status, recognized French rule in Indochina in 1885. In similar fashion to what had occurred in Vietnam, the French compelled the kings of Cambodia* in 1863 and Laos* in 1893 to acquiesce to protectorate status, thereby completing the organization of the territories constituting French Indochina.

American interest in the area remained minor at first, as evidenced by the abrupt dismissal of a petition for the independence of Indochinese people submitted to the U.S. delegation at the Paris Conference in 1919 by Ho Chi Minh*. However, the coming of World War II elevated French Indochina's significance. Japanese military occupation of northern Indochina, a move designed to prevent resupply of forces then fighting the Japanese in China, followed Nazi Germany's conquest of France in 1940. In response, President Franklin D. Roosevelt* prohibited scrap metal shipments to Japan. In the summer of 1941, the Japanese began to occupy the rest of Indochina and Roosevelt terminated oil shipments to Japan, a move believed to have contributed to the Japanese decision to strike into Southeast Asia and launch the Pearl Harbor Attack* in Hawaii. During the Pacific war, the Deer Mission*, composed of American agents of the Office of Strategic Services, worked with Vietminh* nationalists fighting against the Vichy French administrators of Indochina and their Japanese overlords. Recognizing the long-standing suffering of the Vietnamese people, Roosevelt initially opposed the return of French Colonialism* in Indochina after the war, but already had wavered on this issue before his death.

At war's end, the Vietminh had displaced a puppet regime established by the Japanese and set up the Democratic Republic of Vietnam* (DRV). However, British Empire troops facilitated the return of French forces in the south, and the French return to the northern part of Vietnam was negotiated with the Chinese occupation force in March 1946. The First Indochina War* ensued between the French, bent on reconquest of their lost colonial glory, and the Vietminh, who was just as determined to maintain independence. With the advent of the Cold War, the United States began to underwrite the French war effort, reaching 80 percent of its costs in the effort to vanquish the Vietminh. However, the Truman administration also pressed France to move Indochina toward independence and in February 1950, recognized the State of Vietnam and the kingdoms of Cambodia and Laos. These states had been established in the mechanism known as the Associated States of Indochina of the French Union, a measure undertaken by France to grant limited autonomy, but to retain actual control. With the Geneva Accords of 1954*, the war ended and the Associated States became independent of France. Within two years, all French forces had left Vietnam, and stewardship of the struggle against the Communists had become an American affair. *See also* Dien Bien Phu; Republic of Vietnam; Second Indochina War.

J. Buttinger, Vietnam: *A Dragon Embattled* (New York, 1967); W. Duiker, *Vietnam: Nation in Revolution* (Boulder, CO, 1995); P. M. Dunn, *The*

First Vietnam War (New York, 1985); A. L. A. Patti, *Why Viet Nam?: Prelude to America's Albatross* (Berkeley, CA, 1980).

Kent G. Sieg

FUKUDA TAKEO (1905–1995)

Fukuda Takeo became prime minister of Japan in 1976. He played the leading role for almost five years in the recovery of the Japanese economy after the oil crisis of 1973 as finance minister and then as prime minister in his own administration. Fukuda was born in a farm town in Gunma Prefecture. After graduating from Tōkyō University, he entered the Ministry of Finance in 1929. Fukuda rapidly climbed the bureaucratic ladder during the years coinciding with the Great Depression, World War II, and the U.S. Occupation of Japan*. In 1947, he became director of the Budget Bureau, one of the most influential posts in the Finance Ministry, when he became involved in a bribery scandal. Even though he was cleared, Fukuda resigned in 1950 and became a successful Diet candidate for the lower house in the 1952 elections. His moderately nationalistic and independent orientation made him somewhat critical of unqualified pro-Americanism, resulting in him becoming a protégé of Kishi Nobusuke*. When Kishi became prime minister in 1957, Fukuda began a rapid rise in Liberal Democratic Party* (LDP) politics, serving as chairman of the policy bureau and then secretary general. After remaining an opposition leader in the LDP under Prime Minister Ikeda Hayato*, Fukuda came into the political spotlight again in the Satō administration, first becoming the finance minister and then the party's secretary general.

Although regarded as heir apparent to Satō Eisaku*, Fukuda was defeated in the 1972 LDP presidential election by Tanaka Kakuei*, who had built a strong following within the party because of his energetic style and wealth of campaign funds. In the face of a serious recession caused by the first oil crisis, Fukuda agreed to become the finance minister again in 1973. He was highly successful in controlling inflation and producing economic recovery, but the premiership was again snatched from him in 1974, this time by Miki Takeo*, after Tanaka's resignation in a money scandal. After Miki was forced to resign under pressure from Fukuda and other LDP leaders, Fukuda finally became prime minister in December 1976. In international affairs, he searched for *jishu-gaikō* (independent diplomacy) within the larger framework of Japan-U.S. security cooperation. The typical example of this was his Fukuda Doctrine of August 1977, in which he proclaimed Japan's determination not to become a military power again and to seek cooperation with Southeast Asians as equal partners for peace and economic development, including the Socialist Republic of Vietnam*. Fukuda also successfully concluded the Sino-Japanese Peace Treaty in August 1978. However, he was unable to end friction over the growing trade surplus with the United States and others. Fukuda also inherited a political reform agenda, which resulted in the introduction of an open primary election for the LDP president. Ironically, the first primary was carried out in November 1978, and Fukuda was defeated by Ōhira Masayoshi* with Tanaka's backing.

Fukuda Takeo, *Kaiko kyujūnen* [Remembering His 90 Years] (Tokyo, 1995); H. Kenji, *The Japanese Prime Minister and Public Policy* (Pittsburgh, PA, 1993); J. I. Matray, *Japan's Emergence as a Global Power* (Westport, CT, 2000); Watanabe Akio (ed.), *Sengo Nihon no saishō tachi* [Postwar Japanese Prime Ministers] (Tōkyō, 1995).

Kamimura Naoki

FUKUZAWA YUKICHI (1835–1901)

Fukuzawa Yukichi was the most articulate advocate in Japan of wholesale Westernization during the Meiji period. Born into a low-ranking samurai family in the Nakatsu clan in Kyūshū, he developed a deep resentment against the rigid feudal hierarchy imposed by the Tokugawa shōgunate. In 1854, the year after the arrival of Commodore Matthew C. Perry*, Fukuzawa went to Nagasaki and then to Ōsaka to study Dutch and English. Four years later, he was sent by his domain to Edo to open his own school for Dutch studies, where he introduced the teaching of English. His school was renamed Keiō University in 1871 and became one of the most prestigious private universities in Japan. Fukuzawa also worked for the Translation Office of the shōgunate.

In 1860, Fukuzawa went to the United States as the personal steward of the captain who headed the shōgunate's first official mission to the United States for the purpose of ratifying the Harris Treaty* signed in 1858. His autobiography indicates that he was more fascinated by American social practices and institutions than scientific and technological achievements. He visited the United States again in 1867. Based on his first trip to the United States and the subsequent trip to Europe in 1862, Fukuzawa published *Seiyō Jijō* (Conditions in the West) in 1866, which became a phenomenal best-seller and one of the most influential books published in modern Japan. Through the book, the Japanese people were exposed for the first time to the knowledge of Western social institutions and customs. *Seiyō Jijō* also introduced the two important American documents that symbolized Western enlightenment—the Declaration of Independence and the U.S. Constitution.

Although Fukuzawa did not directly participate in the Meiji Restoration of 1868, which ended the Tokugawa shōgunate and restored imperial rule in Japan, and refused to join the new Meiji government, he was the intellectual driving force that pushed Japan's new leaders to adopt modernization and Westernization policies. He vigorously attacked the Japanese feudal system and traditional values based on Confucianism, and preached the fundamental transformation of Japan through the adoption of Western values and institutions as well as Western science. Fukuzawa especially emphasized such qualities of individualism as independence and self-help as the essence of modern civilization. His other best-selling book, published in 1872, was *Gakumon no susume* (An Encouragement of Learning), which began with his most famous words: "Heaven did not create men above men, nor set men below men." However, Fukuzawa later became less radical. By the late 1870s, his admiration of the United States had been replaced by his celebration of the British parliamentary system and constitutional monarchy, which he believed would serve as a better model for Japan. In the 1880s, he became critical of the freedom and people's rights movement. He also supported the government's expansionist policy on the Asian continent. *See also* "Expel the Barbarian" Movement; Ii Naosuki; Iwakura Mission.

C. Blacker, *The Japanese Enlightenment* (Cambridge, MA, 1964); Y. Fukuzawa, *The Autobiography of Yukichi Fukuzawa*, trans. E. Kiyooka (New York, 1966); K. B. Pyle, *The New Generation in Meiji Japan* (Stanford, CA, 1969).

Kawamura Noriko

FULBRIGHT ACT (1 August 1946)

The Fulbright Program has provided U.S. citizens with fellowships and grants for graduate study, postdoctoral research, teaching experience in both elementary and secondary schools, and lecturing at institutions of higher learning in countries abroad. Foreign grantees usually come to the United States for education and training at the graduate level. J. William Fulbright*, the new senator from Arkansas, introduced in September 1944 the Amendment to the Surplus Property Act of 1944. Congress passed it with little resistance, and President Harry S. Truman* signed it into law on 1 August 1946. The act said that foreign currencies and credits derived from the sale of surplus U.S. properties left in foreign countries at the end of World

War II could be used to provide for the exchange of students, scholars, and professionals between the United States and other nations participating in an educational exchange program with the United States. The act's purpose was to avoid possible problems resulting from the sale of U.S. surplus properties to promote study and research by U.S. scholars abroad and foreign scholars in the United States, as well as to enhance mutual understanding between the people of the United States and other countries.

Fulbright based the introduction of the bill on the precedent the United States had set in its handling of the surplus of the indemnity it received from China under the Boxer Protocol*. When Washington returned the excessive part of the indemnity to China's government first in 1908 and then in 1924, it asked the Chinese government to place the money in a trust fund for the education of Chinese students in the United States. Believing that the exchange of students had been one of the most successful of U.S. international policies, Fulbright recommended that a similar program be administered among several nations. Fittingly, China was the first country to sign the Fulbright exchange agreement with the United States in November 1947. Derk Bodde, a well-known Sinologist at the University of Pennsylvania, was the first American Fulbright grantee and went to China in 1948 to work on a translation of Chinese philosophy. The first group of foreign Fulbright grantees came to the United States from Burma*, which signed an agreement with the United States in December 1947.

The Fulbright-Hayes Act of 1961 consolidated all previous laws under which the U.S. exchange program operated, becoming thereafter the basic charter for all U.S. government–sponsored educational and cultural exchanges. The Fulbright Program was supervised by the Board Foreign Scholarships, comprising twelve members drawn from academic, cultural, and public life. An amendment to the Fulbright-Hayes Act in 1990 changed the formal name of the board to the J. William Fulbright Foreign Scholarship Board. The Bureau of Educational and Cultural Affairs of the State Department administered the Fulbright Program until 1978, when the U.S. Information Agency took over the responsibility. By the fiftieth anniversary of the Fulbright Act, approximately 215,000 students and scholars, 80,000 from the United States and 135,000 from 140 nations, had participated in the program. Many foreign governments have contributed to this educational exchange with the United States.

W. Johnson and F. J. Colligan, *The Fulbright Program: A History* (Chicago, 1965); L. R. Powell, *J. William Fulbright and His Time* (Memphis, TN, 1996); R. B. Woods, *Fulbright: A Biography* (New York, 1995).

Li Hongshan

FULBRIGHT, J. WILLIAM (1905–1995)

Representing Arkansas in Congress from 1944 to 1974, James William Fulbright as both an intellectual and an internationalist had a great moderating influence over U.S. foreign relations. Born in Sumner, Missouri, he graduated from the University of Arkansas in 1925 and then attended Oxford University as a Rhodes scholar. After graduating from George Washington University Law School in 1934, Fulbright taught law there and at Arkansas, ascending to the presidency of the latter university in 1939. He ran successfully for Congress in 1942 and soon established himself as an outspoken advocate of enlightened internationalism after proposing a resolution that declared U.S. support for creation of and participation in an international peacekeeping organization. Two years later, he began a thirty-year career in the U.S. Senate. In 1959, Fulbright became chairman of the powerful Senate Foreign Relations Committee (SFRC), a role that vaulted him into the public spotlight as a critic of U.S. foreign policy in the 1960s.

A Cold War realist rather than an ideologue, Fulbright agreed that Communism* should be contained, but argued that American resources were limited and that therefore the nation's interests had to be specific. A staunch Europeanist, he thought the United States could live with the communization of all Asia, but could not tolerate Soviet domination of Western Europe. Thus, after Chinese Intervention in the Korean War*, Fulbright had no qualms about suggesting the withdrawal of American combat forces. Ever the pragmatist, he opposed the suggestion that the United States intervene in the Laotian Crisis of 1961* because the terrain and political conditions there were not proper for sending American troops. Yet he supported possible American intervention in South Vietnam because he viewed it as strategically important to the defense and security of the United States. Historians have made much of his role in guiding the passage of the Tonkin Gulf Resolution in August 1964, particularly given his later opposition to the war. Although he initially supported U.S. policy in Vietnam, Fulbright had his doubts about the commitment to Southeast Asia, which he had expressed to President Lyndon B. Johnson* in private. He endorsed the resolution more from fear of the potential election of Senator Barry Goldwater than out of the conviction that the resolution—and the burgeoning U.S. commitment in Vietnam—was necessary.

Fulbright became the most prominent and effective congressional critic of the Second Indochina War* as the conflict became Americanized and U.S. efforts to defeat Ho Chi Minh* and the Viet Cong* bogged down. His dissent was especially irritating to Johnson because Fulbright was a pragmatic Cold War liberal who could not be dismissed as an extremist. Fearing that Johnson's escalation of the war could jeopardize chances for improved relations with the Soviet Union and might provoke a war with the People's Republic of China*, Fulbright proposed a negotiated end to the war in 1965 based on a Titoist solution that would make Vietnam a counterweight to China. He feared that continued military involvement would lead to a "bloody and interminable conflict" that would poison American political life. When this proposal failed, Fulbright took to the offensive. Beginning in 1966, he held a series of hearings in the SFRC to debate the merits of the Johnson administration's policies in Vietnam and the validity of the entire U.S. commitment. These hearings gave opponents of the war and critics of the administration a high-level forum for expressing their views. His 1966 book, *The Arrogance of Power*, helped legitimize domestic opposition to the war. Fulbright's intellectual dissent directly challenged the administration's assertion that South Vietnam was of vital geopolitical interest to the United States.

Although Fulbright had no great love of Richard M. Nixon*, he was cheered by Nixon's election in 1968 because he viewed it as a repudiation of Johnson's policies in Southeast Asia. When his hope faded that Nixon would fulfill his campaign promise to end the war honorably, he argued that Vietnamization* was merely an attempt to avoid serious negotiations with the Democratic Republic of Vietnam*. Fulbright also vocally denounced Nixon's Cambodian Incursion*, deployment of combat troops in Thailand* and Laos*, and massive bombings throughout the region. He also worked for passage of the Cooper-Church amendment, repeal of the Tonkin Gulf Resolution, and approval of the War Powers Act to restore what he had come to consider a proper constitutional balance of power on the use of the military. Ironically, the end of U.S. involvement in Vietnam also brought the end of Fulbright's political career. Despite having the nation's best interests at heart and having fought for a termination of the fighting, he became a symbol of the divisiveness and rancor in American society over Vietnam. He lost the Arkansas Democratic primary for the Senate in 1974 and quickly faded into obscurity. It was not until the election of his protégé Bill Clinton* that his public image was rehabilitated. In 1993, Clinton awarded Fulbright the Medal of Freedom, the highest civilian honor the United States can bestow on an individual. *See also* Fulbright Act.

W. C. Berman, *William Fulbright and the Vietnam War: The Dissent of a Political Realist* (Kent, OH, 1988); J. W. Fulbright, *The Arrogance of Power* (New York, 1966); L. R. Powell, *J. William Fulbright and America's Lost Crusade: Fulbright's Opposition to the Vietnam War* (Little Rock, AR, 1984); R. B. Woods, *Fulbright: A Biography* (New York, 1995).

Andrew L. Johns

G

GENERAL AGREEMENT ON TARIFFS AND TRADE

The General Agreement on Tariffs and Trade (GATT) was a multilateral agreement negotiated in 1947. It became one of the cornerstones of the economic order after World War II. The principle behind the GATT was to prevent the recurrence of protectionism and the high tariffs of the 1930s, which was thought to have been one of the major causes of World War II. Originally signed by twenty-three states, GATT was a series of bilateral agreements and was to operate under the umbrella of the International Trade Organization (ITO), which was to become the third pillar of the Bretton Woods System (the other two pillars being the International Monetary Fund and the International Bank for Reconstruction and Development). With the failure of the U.S. Congress to ratify the ITO charter, the ITO never came into being. Instead, the GATT took over its functions. Thus, members became contracting parties to it and decisions were made either by two-thirds majority vote or by consensus.

The two cornerstones of the GATT were equality of treatment between nations and the application of the most-favored-nation clause in trade relations between the members. The GATT succeeded in reducing global tariff levels through eight "Rounds" of intensive negotiations: Geneva (1947), Annecy (1949), Torquay (1950), Geneva (1956), Dillon (1961), Kennedy (1962–1967), the Tōkyō Round* (1973–1979), and Uruguay (1986–1994). Early in its history, the GATT faced problems over the extension of the most-favored-nation clause, as in the case involving Japan's membership. Britain and the Commonwealth led the opposition because they were afraid that once most-favored-nation rights were extended to Japanese goods, serious Anglo-Japanese trade competition would follow in textiles and in other manufactured goods. Although Japan became a GATT member in 1955, fourteen countries invoked Article 35, the nonapplication clause, which was unprecedented in GATT history. In later years, the GATT shifted its attention to tackling nontariff barriers and protectionism in the agricultural sector. By the early 1990s, it was clear that the GATT could no longer function effectively, as participants in the treaty had increased to more than 100 countries. Therefore, the GATT was replaced by the World Trade Organization in 1994. *See also* International Wheat Agreement.

T. Akaneya, *Nihon no GATT kanyu mondai: Regimu riron no bunseki shikaku ni yoru jirei kenkyu*

[The Problem of Japanese Accession to the GATT: A Case Study in Regime Theory] (Tōkyō, 1992); R. Gardner, *Sterling-Dollar Diplomacy in Current Perspective: The Origins and the Prospects of our International Economic Order* (New York, 1980); J. H. Jackson, *Restructuring the GATT System* (London, 1990); J. Kasto, *The Function and Future of the World Trade Organization: International Trade Law Between GATT and WTO* (Surrey, UK, 1996).

Yokoi Noriko

GENERAL CONFERENCE OF PROTESTANT MISSIONARIES

The General Conference of the Protestant Missionaries of China, held in Shanghai from 7 to 20 May 1890, was one of the largest gatherings ever of Western missionaries engaged in proselytizing in China. A total of 445 delegates attended—233 men and 212 women. Most were American or British, although a few Canadian, Swedish, and German missionaries also participated. The conference was a follow-up to the conference of 1877, at which it was decided to hold another conference in ten years, although the Shanghai Missionary Association later chose to delay the second conference.

The General Conference provided an opportunity for interregional and cross-denominational discussions of the most important aspects of missionary work. Although delegates sought to forge consensus, the conference revealed some significant divisions. A major topic of discussion was the question of providing standardized translations of the Bible. Committees were created to translate the Bible into Mandarin, Cantonese, and vernacular dialects. Another committee recommended providing introductions and notes to help the Chinese better understand the scriptures, but several delegates strongly objected to the concept.

Women's roles in missionary activities also received a great deal of attention, not surprisingly given that nearly half the delegates were women. The earliest women missionaries were predominantly the wives of male missionaries, but by the time of the conference, an increasing number of single women were joining the missionary force. "An Appeal from the Ladies of the Conference" was issued, calling for more Western women to devote themselves to this undertaking. The conference delegates agreed that women were better suited than men for certain aspects of missionary work, particularly the education of children, medical services, and the evangelization of Chinese women.

The conference devoted significant opprobrium to the Drug Trade*, reflecting the consensus against opium that had emerged among missionaries in China by this time. The conference also revealed the tensions that existed between the missionaries and the rest of the foreign community in China. One of the missionaries, Arthur Moule, went as far to declare that Western businessmen should consider it "obligatory not optional to come out actively on the missionary side in the great fight." Most missionaries agreed, however, that the advance of Western influence in China, whether imperial or commercial, helped pave the way for the Christianization of the heathen masses.

Delegates to the conference voiced a wide disparity of opinions on the degree to which native customs should be tolerated among Christian converts. Although most agreed that Christians need not be required to abandon such cultural trappings as their native dress, the degree to which native customs were "idolatrous" generated much controversy. In particular, the delegates condemned the Reverend W. A. P. Martin's speech calling for toleration of ancestor worship, to the extent that the conference adopted a resolution announcing its dissent from Martin's views.

P. Barr, *To China with Love: The Lives and Times of Protestant Missionaries in China, 1860–1900* (London, 1972); J. K. Fairbank (ed.), *The Missionary Enterprise in China and America* (Cambridge, MA, 1974); J. Hunter, *The Gospel of Gentility: American Women Missionaries in Turn-of-the-*

Century China (New Haven, CT, 1984); K. L. Lodwick, *Crusaders Against Opium: Protestant Missionaries in China, 1874–1917* (Lexington, KY, 1996); *Records of the General Conference of the Protestant Missionaries of China, Held at Shanghai, May 7–20, 1890* (Shanghai, 1890).

Timothy L. Savage

GENERAL ORDER NUMBER 1

Drafted by the War Department and promulgated by President Harry S. Truman* on 14 August 1945, this unilateral declaration attempted to halt the momentum of Asian revolutionary movements during the crisis of Japan's surrender at the end of World War II. Having capitulated under the twin hammer blows of the Atomic Attacks* and the Soviet declaration of war, many Japanese troops in East and Southeast Asia had no legitimate Allied forces to whom to surrender. Fearful of the rise of Communist-led guerilla movements in this political vacuum, Washington laid down guidelines for Japanese surrenders, in due course, to "appropriate" authorities rather than the local resistance forces. The Americans sent General Order Number 1 to Soviet Premier Joseph Stalin and Britain for their information, rather than approval. General Douglas MacArthur*, as Supreme Commander for the Allied Powers (SCAP*), was to direct Emperor Hirohito* to issue the order outlining the precise forces to whom the Japanese were to surrender in the various theaters of operation. Most crucial for later developments included the surrender of Japanese forces in China to Guomindang* (Nationalist), not Communist, authorities. Korea was split into a Soviet and U.S. zone of surrender in the Thirty-Eighth Parallel Division*, whereas French Indochina* was divided between a Nationalist Chinese zone in the north and a British zone in the south. Japan and her mandates were to surrender to U.S. forces. *See also* U.S. Occupation of Japan.

H. Feis, *Japan Subdued* (Princeton, NJ, 1961); G. Kolko, *The Politics of War: The World and United States Foreign Policy, 1943–1945* (New York, 1968).

Errol M. Clauss

GENERAL SHERMAN INCIDENT

On 9 August 1866, the *General Sherman*, an eighty-ton trading schooner armed with two twelve-pounders in broadside, owned by American W. B. Preston, was chartered by the Tianjin-based British shipping house of Meadows and Company for a trading voyage to the west coast of Korea. Besides Preston, she carried George Hogarth, a British supercargo, Robert Jermain Thompson, a Scottish missionary, two Americans as master and mate, and among the crew, two Malays and five Chinese. She cleared the northeast boundary of Korean and Russian possessions, and after touching at Chefoo, entered the Taedong River. Whether she was on a pirate venture to rifle the graves of the dead Korean kings, alleged to be buried in gold caskets at P'yŏngyang, or to engage in legitimate trade never has been clarified. In the Taedong, she was carried by unusually high tides over rapids and anchored near an island, where she became stranded. For several days, she was supplied by local villagers, but after taking and holding hostage a local official, the crew was attacked with fire rafts and all on board were killed. To the outside world, she had simply vanished.

Concerned about her fate, Rear Admiral Henry H. Bell, commanding the U.S. Far Eastern squadron, ordered Captain Robert W. Shufeldt* and his USS *Wachusett* to investigate the disappearance of the *General Sherman*. He complied shortly after the Taewŏn'gun, the regent of Korea during the minority of King Kojong*, had ordered the expulsion of French Roman Catholic missionaries in the country, which resulted first in the deaths of three bishops, seventeen priests, and many native converts, and second, in an unofficial French military expedition being organized. Six ships and 600 troops under Admiral Pierre Gustav Roze, commander in chief of the French forces, burned the town on Kanghwa Island in the summer of 1866. Admiral Roze, returning from his attack on Kanghwa, brought the first news of the *General Sherman*'s disappearance, and the murder of her crew, to Chefoo, having gained his information from a French priest escaping from Korea. It is possible that Roze wished to implicate the U.S. Asiatic squadron, following the precipitate withdrawal of his own. The news passed from E. T. Sanford, U.S. consul at Chefoo, to Anson Burlingame*, U.S. minister in Beijing, who raised the matter with Prince Gong (Yixin*), head of the Zongli Yamen*, only to be told that China was not responsible for the activities of Koreans.

Burlingame then notified Bell, who already had heard of the schooner's loss from Meadows and Company, to move quickly in case the French returned with a large fleet to open the country. Bell urged Shufeldt to investigate the loss, while requesting support for an enlarged squadron and 2,000 troops to awe the Chinese and Japanese and "disclose to the world who are the masters of the Pacific." Bell sent Shufeldt to Chefoo in December 1866 and authorized him to investigate and demand the delivery of any survivors. Shufeldt conducted a series of interviews with French naval captains, the Chinese pilot, and French priest Father Rydell. Shufeldt had five possible rivers to explore and learned from Rydell it was the Taedong, about 120 miles northwest of Seoul. His research in January 1867 led him to believe that a local mob had murdered the crew, who feared they were pirates (the Chinese pilot's version), rather than from any command of the Taewŏn'gun (Rydell's version). He took his vessel to P'yŏngyang, wrote a letter to the king of Korea, and communicated with local authorities, who repeatedly suggested he return and leave Korea. Unable to communicate with anyone who could help him, Shufeldt left, fearing that his vessel might be trapped in winter gales.

After Shufeldt's return, he recommended using force to punish Korean authorities, and the possible seizure of the island of Port Hamilton. He claimed many years later that this first visit led him to consider the possibility of making a treaty with Korea. But he also recommended to Admiral Bell that the squadron could assail the Korean government in the south. In 1867, Captain John C. Febiger went to Korea and received a copy of the king's answer to Shufeldt's letter (the original was sent overland to Beijing), which gave an account satisfactory to both Febiger and Shufeldt of how the *General Sherman* was destroyed by the work of the local angered people, not the government. The *General Sherman* affair was the precursor and leading cause of an expedition to Korea that placed U.S.-Korean relations on a war footing. When Shufeldt visited Korea again at the end of his world cruise on the USS *Ticonderoga* in 1880, Korean officials informed him that they considered themselves in a state of war. The chains of the *General Sherman* were hung for a long time in the Great East Gate of P'yŏngyang as a warning to marauding foreigners. *See also* Lucius H. Foote; Charles LeGendre; Frederick F. Low.

H. G. Appenzeller, "The Opening of Korea: Admiral Shufeldt's Account of It," *Korean Repository* (1892); S. Choi, "A Study of Early Korean-American Diplomatic Relations," *Political Science Report* (1960); F. C. Drake, *The Empire of the Seas: A Biography of Rear Admiral Robert Wilson Shufeldt, USN* (Honolulu, HI, 1984); J. S. Gale, "The Fate of the *General Sherman*: From an Eye Witness Account," *Korea Review* (1895); E. M. Tate, "Admiral Bell and the New Asiatic Squadron," *American Neptune* (1972).

Frederick C. Drake

GENEVA ACCORDS OF 1954

The Geneva Accords of 1954 ended the First Indochina War*. After Communist forces under Vo Nguyen Giap* defeated the French at Dien Bien Phu*, an international convention met in Geneva, Switzerland, to determine the political future of French Indochina*. The Geneva Conference of 1954* originally had been convened in hopes of converting the Korean Armistice Agreement* into a permanent peace settlement, but those efforts failed. Meeting from May to July, delegates from the United States, the Soviet Union, the People's Republic of China* (PRC), Britain, France, India, the State of Vietnam, the Democratic Republic of Vietnam* (DRV), Laos*, and Cambodia* eventually drafted several complicated political arrangements. A proposal advanced by the United States and the State of Vietnam called for the disarmament of the DRV and the unification of the country under the State of Vietnam, but this was ignored by serious negotiators, since the DRV had achieved a military victory. U.S. Secretary of State John Foster Dulles* knew this proposal would not be accepted, but saw little hope for the emergence of an agreement that Washington could approve. Dulles left Geneva, and the U.S. delegation was headed at various times by Undersecretary of State Walter Bedell Smith or U.S. Ambassador to Czechoslovakia U. Alexis Johnson*, who were instructed not to participate in the talks, but to sit and listen.

The Geneva Accords left the Laotian and Cambodian governments associated with the French Union as the head of each country, with the exception of a region in northeast Laos under the control of the Communist Pathet Lao*. Vietnam was divided along a demilitarized zone at the seventeenth parallel. A cease-fire was imposed throughout Vietnam, and arrangements were made for peaceful withdrawal of French forces from the DRV and the People's Army of Vietnam from the south. During the period of troop withdrawal, civilians could move freely from one zone to another. Many northerners, mostly Catholics, chose to move south; few southerners went north. The placement of new foreign troops was prohibited throughout Vietnam. Finally, the Geneva Accords provided for free elections in North and South

Vietnam in 1956 to reunify the nation. An International Control Commission, which included representatives from Poland, India, and Canada, was established to oversee troop withdrawal and the elections.

During the negotiations in Geneva, both the PRC and the Soviet Union put pressure on the DRV to conclude a settlement and provide the French a face-saving defeat. The Korean War* had just ended, and these nations were eager to avoid a new military confrontation. As a result, the DRV leaders reluctantly agreed to surrender large amounts of territory and population then under their control in exchange for the promise of later reunification. South Vietnamese delegates did not sign the Geneva Accords, but expressed public support for them. Ngo Dinh Diem*, the new premier of the State of Vietnam, did not approve of the agreements, but had little ability to block them or even influence their content. He endorsed the concept of reunification, but rejected the process the accords established to achieve this outcome. The Eisenhower administration refused to sign the agreements, but pledged to uphold them, to avoid use of military force in the region, and to support the principle of self-determination throughout Indochina. Nevertheless, as a nonsignatory power, the United States could appear supportive of the accords without having to adhere to their provisions. Washington decided to forge a separate path, creating the Southeast Asia Treaty Organization,* and throwing its efforts behind a Nation-Building Strategy* in the Republic of Vietnam*. When it appeared that Ho Chi Minh* had majority support in North as well as South Vietnam, and undoubtedly would win the 1956 elections for reunification, the United States supported Diem's refusal to hold those elections.

G. C. Herring, *America's Longest War: The United States and Vietnam 1950–1975* (New York, 1996); S. Karnow, *Vietnam: A History* (New York, 1983); M. B. Young, *The Vietnam Wars, 1945–1990* (New York, 1991).

Robert K. Brigham

GENEVA ACCORDS OF 1962

Although outgoing President Dwight D. Eisenhower* advised President-elect John F. Kennedy* to draw the containment line against Communism* in Laos*, during the first months of his administration Kennedy came to the conclusion that Laos was not the place to fight in Southeast Asia. Instead, Kennedy sought to neutralize Laos, using the same venue and mechanism as had been used at the Geneva Conference of 1954* on French Indochina*. On 24 April 1961, the co-chairmen of the 1954 meeting in Geneva, the Soviet Union and Britain, called upon the twelve countries whose representatives attended that conference—Laos, Cambodia*, the Republic of Vietnam*, the Democratic Republic of Vietnam* (DRV), Thailand*, Burma*, France, the People's Republic of China* (PRC), and the United States, plus the International Commission for Supervision and Control (ICSC) members Canada, Poland, and India—to join them at Geneva to resolve the fate of Laos after a cease-fire came into effect. This call occasioned frenetic last-minute fighting for tactical advantage in Laos between the Communist Pathet Lao* with DRV support and their neutralist allies against the Phoumi Nosavan* government with U.S. backing. On 16 May, the Geneva Conference began with high officials in attendance, but absolutely nothing happened. The reason for the inactivity was the inability of the factions in Laos to agree on a coalition government in separate talks.

Fighting flared again in Laos and continued throughout the entire span of the conference. In Zurich during June, the three princes leading the Lao factions, Souphanouvong*, Souvanna Phouma,* and Bon Oum (front man for Phoumi) agreed in principle to a second coalition government for Laos, but over the next year they could not work out the details. Chief U.S. negotiator W. Averell Harriman* became exasperated with Phoumi's obstructionism and eventually persuaded Washington to suspend support for his faction to force him to join Souvanna Phouma's neutralist coalition. As for the Pathet Lao and North Vietnam, Harriman relied on assurances from Soviet delegate Georgi Puskin that Moscow could control them. After much wrangling, the three Lao factions agreed to a coalition government. At Geneva, the participants hammered out a series of accords constituting a declaration on Laotian neutrality and a protocol of nineteen articles to ensure that neutrality. The accords were signed on 23 July 1962. Essentially, the declaration committed Laos to neutrality, prohibited it from accepting anything more than essential military aid channeled through the coalition government to unified armed forces, barred Laos from joining military alliances, and called for withdrawal of all foreign troops. The fourteen nations agreed not to interfere in Lao affairs and to respect Lao neutrality. The protocol spelled out in detail how this was to be achieved and relied heavily for supervision on the ICSC.

Few expected the Geneva Accords on Laos to succeed fully, but its virtual total failure was a surprise, at least to Washington. The North Vietnamese withdrew only minuscule numbers of their troops in Laos and maintained control of the Ho Chi Minh Trail*. The Pathet Lao joined the coalition government, but had no intention of giving up their strongholds in the north. Phoumi and the rightists agreed to join the coalition only because of U.S. pressure and remained uncommitted to its success. The United States initially withdrew virtually all of its military and covert support of Laos, but it established extensive contingency plans in case the agreement did not hold. Within less than a year, the Kennedy administration realized that the Geneva Conference had failed and reestablished clandestine support of anti-Communist forces in Laos. All that Geneva created was a tacit understanding between Washington and Hanoi to accept a de facto partition of Laos and maintain it as a secret and secondary theater of the Second Indochina

War* fought along the de facto line that separated the lowlands from the highlands. Having failed to neutralize Laos through international agreement, the United States used air strikes and covert ground incursions from South Vietnam to impede infiltration into South Vietnam in combination with secret air power and covert support of the Hmong* to contest the North Vietnamese and Pathet Lao in north Laos. *See also* Air America; Laotian Crisis of 1961; Secret U.S. Air War in Laos.

A. J. Dommen, *Conflict in Laos: The Politics of Neutralization* (New York, 1971); N. B. Hannah, *The Key to Failure: Laos and the Vietnam War* (Lanham, MD, 1987); C. A. Stevenson, *American Policy Toward Laos Since 1954* (Boston, 1972).

Edward C. Keefer

GENEVA CONFERENCE OF 1954

This international conference to discuss questions regarding the future of Korea and French Indochina* began on 26 April 1954. Discussions on Korea were attended by all members of the United Nations that sent troops to fight in the Korean War*—except for South Africa, which chose not to participate—plus the Republic of Korea* (ROK), the Democratic People's Republic of Korea* (DPRK), the People's Republic of China* (PRC), and the Soviet Union. It was the last major occasion the postwar international community exerted influence on the Korean question. It was also a last chance for the British Commonwealth to participate in deliberations on postwar Korea, with Britain acting as a major power during the meeting. The conference opened a new phase in world power competition. It was the initial opportunity for China's new Communist regime to establish itself as a major actor in international politics. Throughout the conference, the United States made every effort to maintain its hostile position against the PRC, making light of Beijing's position or refusing to recognize its status. Such American attempts,

however, proved futile because it was clear to all the conference participants that the PRC would be a major player in addressing the issues.

One characteristic of this conference was that from the beginning, none of the participating countries expected the meeting to achieve solutions to the major questions separating the Western powers and the Communist bloc. For all who attended, the hidden but real purpose was propaganda exchanges and probing action to confirm the other side's position and intention. The leading nations of both sides, the United States and the Soviet Union, tried to test the solidarity of its counterpart's camp, with Washington focusing on the extent of the partnership between the Soviets and China. Nevertheless, the conference also presented the possibility for a relaxation of bipolar Cold War tension. Britain sought to assume her traditional role of balancer in world politics, having an impact when discussions turned to Indochina.

The Geneva Conference was called in accordance with the Korean Armistice Agreement* of July 1953. That accord provided that three months after the agreement became effective, a political conference would convene to achieve withdrawal of all foreign troops and the "peaceful settlement of the Korean question." The political conference was held at P'anmunjŏm in October 1953, but it broke down in December. It then was decided at the Allied foreign ministers meeting in Berlin in February 1954 that a conference would meet in Geneva to seek a peaceful settlement of the Korean issue. In Switzerland, the ROK representatives submitted a fourteen-point proposal on 22 May that included three major provisions. First, the authority of the United Nations over the Korean problem would be acknowledged. Second, free elections would be held under supervision of the United Nations for the purpose of creating a united, independent, and democratic Korea. Third, UN forces would remain in Korea until this UN mission had been accomplished. But the Communist side rejected this approach. In its counterproposal, the Soviets advanced five points, with withdrawal of all foreign troops from the Korean peninsula taking precedence over all other issues. Since neither side would compromise, negotiations on Korea's future deadlocked.

On 15 June, the sixteen nations that had fought on the UN side in the Korean War issued a declaration saying that the United Nations was fully empowered to take collective action to repel aggression, to restore peace and security, and to provide its good offices to achieve a peaceful settlement in Korea. Also, genuinely free elections should be held under UN supervision for the purpose of establishing an all-Korean national assembly in which representation should be in direct proportion to the indigenous population in the north and the south. That day, discussions at Geneva on Korea closed with the country still divided and with opposing forces still facing each other across the demilitarized zone. During subsequent years, this "Geneva formula" for the reunification of Korea was reaffirmed annually by the UN General Assembly. Meanwhile, there was progress toward a settlement on Indochina, largely because France wanted to withdraw after its defeat at the hands of the Vietminh* at Dien Bien Phu* in April. The Soviets and Chinese persuaded Ho Chi Minh* to accept the Geneva Accords of 1954* that Britain played a central role in negotiating. The United States, however, refused to actively participate in this part of the Geneva Conference.

G. C. Herring, *America's Longest War: The United States and Vietnam 1950–1975* (New York, 1996); S. Karnow, *Vietnam: A History* (New York, 1983); J. Na, *Unended War: 1950–1954* (Seoul, 1994); I. Neary and J. Cotton (eds.), *The Korean War in History* (Atlantic Highlands, NJ, 1989); U.S. Department of State, *The Korean Problem at the Geneva Conference, April 26–June 15, 1954* (Washington, DC, October 1954).

Han Kyu-sun

GENEVA NAVAL CONFERENCE OF 1927

This meeting was a failed effort by the governments of Britain, the United States, and Japan to resolve differences over limitation of warships left unregulated by the Five Power Pact* of 1922. For five years, all the major naval powers constructed warships in the unrestricted classes of cruisers, destroyers, and submarines. The focus was particularly upon cruisers, since they were the most powerful type of warship left unrestricted. Under the Five Power Pact, a clause provided that no new warship with a displacement larger than 10,000 tons could be built during the fifteen-year life of the treaty. This limitation fixed the maximum size of cruisers, and it was no surprise that practically all the cruisers built during the period before 1927, and even beyond, were about that size. Since these vessels were larger than other existing cruisers from the World War I period, there was created what amounted to a new kind of warship—the 10,000 "treaty" cruiser. This type of cruiser was the main focus of naval building worldwide after 1922.

Alone among the major naval powers, the United States did not engage in the construction of treaty or heavy cruisers. Not until 1925 did Congress provide funds for building any of these expensive warships. The U.S. government, faced with the necessity of building several of these cruisers to match the other powers, especially Japan, sought instead to try to secure an agreement that would establish limitations upon future construction of unrestricted warships. In the spring of 1927, President Calvin Coolidge issued invitations to the five main naval powers to meet at Geneva for this purpose. France and Italy declined to attend. Convened on 28 June, the conference soon fell into wrangling over the proportion of heavy to light cruisers to be allowed to the navies of Britain, the United States, and Japan, as well as their total numbers. The British, with their extensive sea lanes, naval bases, and need to protect commerce, preferred to have more light cruisers and limit the heavies. The Americans, with their long lines of communications across the Pacific Ocean and a scanty network of bases, preferred the longer-range and heavier-gunned heavy cruiser. The highest priority for the Japanese at the conference was to get a higher total tonnage ratio for cruisers than they had received for battleships in the Five Power Pact.

The conference collapsed over the cruiser question, which could not be resolved. Although the major argument had been between the British and American delegations, the United States was more concerned about Japan than Britain. The failure of the Americans to build either heavy cruisers or destroyers in the period before 1927, and only a few submarines, was in marked contrast to Japan's building programs, which threatened to surpass the U.S. Navy in these categories in the near future. American naval leaders thus refused to accept the Japanese demand for a larger tonnage ratio for cruisers. That and the American unwillingness to agree to a smaller number of heavy cruisers than the British possessed were the main reasons for the collapse of the conference. The failure of the Geneva Naval Conference had two main results. First, the United States initiated in 1929 a major warship construction program, which included fifteen heavy cruisers. Second, the major powers realized that continued unrestricted building of warships would be expensive and ultimately threatening to the security of all of them. *See also* London Naval Conference of 1930.

L. E. Ellis, *Frank B. Kellogg and American Foreign Relations, 1925–1929* (New Brunswick, NJ, 1961); R. G. Kaufman, *Arms Control During the Pre-Nuclear Era: The United States and Naval Limitation Between the Two World Wars* (New York, 1990); U.S. Department of State, *Records of the Geneva Conference for the Limitation of Naval Armament* (Washington, DC, 1927).

Ernest Andrade Jr.

GENTLEMEN'S AGREEMENT (18 February 1908)

This agreement was the first attempt to curb Japanese immigration to the United States. It was also the first in a series of U.S. immigration policies that repeatedly offended the Japanese people and government in the first half of the twentieth century. The United States and Japan signed the American-Japanese Treaty of 1894* to replace the 1858 Harris Treaty* as a gesture of establishing the two nations on a more equal footing. The treaty included a provision allowing for the free travel and immigration of their respective citizens, but with each government retaining the right to limit the immigration of laborers. However, with the anti-Asian movement already in full swing since the passage of the first of the Chinese Exclusion Acts* in 1882, anti-Japanese sentiment was gathering strength on the West Coast prior to the treaty. In May 1892, Dennis Kearney, leader of California's anti-Chinese movement, harangued a crowd in San Francisco about the Japanese "menace" and predicted the rise of Japanese immigration to an annual level of 120,000 by the turn of the century. Nevertheless, with the increasing need for labor in the West, recruitment of Japanese laborers both from Hawaii and Japan remain unabated. Anti-Japanese sentiments intensified with the formation of the Japanese and Korean Exclusion League in May 1905 in San Francisco. The crisis came to a head in October 1906 when San Francisco's school board ordered the segregation of Japanese children in public schools.

The Japanese government's official response was swift and strong. Japanese Ambassador Viscount Aoki Keikichi met with Secretary of State Elihu Root* to protest the San Francisco School Board order as a violation of the 1894 treaty. To defuse this potential international incident, President Theodore Roosevelt* successfully placated three separate interest groups: Californians, Congress, and the Japanese government. First, he persuaded the San Francisco

School Board to revoke the segregation order. Second, he issued an executive agreement, which required no congressional approval, to prevent the entry of foreign workers into the United States. Finally, more than a year and a half of negotiations and six notes exchanged between Root and Foreign Minister Tadashi Hayashi culminated in the Gentlemen's Agreement in February 1908. Its key provisions stipulated that the Japanese government withhold passports from Japanese laborers who wanted to emigrate to the United States and end Japanese immigration to the United States through Hawaii, Mexico, and Canada.

The Gentlemen's Agreement temporarily averted a diplomatic crisis between the United States and Japan. In the long run, however, it further exacerbated tensions between the two Pacific powers. With the Japanese government limiting passports, Japanese immigrants in the United States made the momentous decision to settle permanently on American soil. Thousands of Japanese men either brought their families over or used the "picture bride" practice to get married. The doubling of the Japanese-American population on the West Coast in less than twenty years after the Gentlemen's Agreement further inflamed the nativists' anti-Asian passion. Congress passed the National Origins Act* in 1924, the most restrictive immigration legislation in American history. This act effectively excluded all Asian immigration to the United States.

R. Daniels, *The Politics of Prejudice: The Anti-Japanese Movement in California, and the Struggle for Japanese Exclusion* (Berkeley, CA, 1968); Y. Ichioka, *The Issei: The World of the First Generation Japanese Immigrants, 1885–1924* (New York, 1988); B. O. Hing, *Making and Remaking Asian America Through Immigration Policy, 1850–1990* (Stanford, CA, 1993).

Roger Y. M. Chan

GERM WARFARE

During the Korean War*, the Democratic People's Republic of Korea* (DPRK), the People's Republic of China* (PRC), and the Soviet Union made allegations that the United States used germ or bacteriological weapons in North Korea and northeast China against the Korean People's Army (KPA) and the Chinese People's Volunteers (CPV). In 1951 and 1952, the CPV headquarters warned the Chinese field generals that U.S. airplanes had dropped infected insects, such as fleas, mosquitos, flies, crickets, spiders, and sand flies over CPV positions in North Korea. Tests by CPV medical officers identified more than ten types of insect-borne germs and viruses that might cause such diseases as plague, anthrax, cholera, typhoid, dysentery, meningitis, and encephalitis. In May 1951, Pak Hŏn-yŏng*, the DPRK foreign minister, first issued a protest statement condemning the "criminal conduct of using germ weapons by the American invaders." In February 1952, he sent a formal statement to the UN Security Council. According to the DPRK's charges, bacteriological warfare affected about seven provinces including forty-four counties. Chinese commanders asked their troops in Korea to apply "emergency measures" to extinguish the insects immediately, adopt preventive methods, and work on improving the morale of the troops.

On 8 March 1952, Zhou Enlai*, the PRC premier and foreign minister, accused American military aircraft of dropping bacteriological bombs in Fushun, Xinmin, Dandong in northeast China, and Qingdao in east China on sixty-eight occasions between 29 February and 5 March. The China Central Commission for Epidemic Prevention, created in March and with Zhou as chairman, within one month organized 129 provincial and local prevention teams with 20,000 members. Meanwhile, 5,800,000 vaccine kits were shipped from China to Korea to meet frontline needs. The Red Cross of China, various social groups, and experts and scholars joined to organize the American Germ Warfare Crime Investigation Team. Some exhibitions of objects and pictures showing Chinese soldiers infected by the bacteriological weapons were held in Beijing and Shenyang, and the Chinese News Agency successively issued public statements made by twenty-five captured U.S. pilots admitting using germ weapons. The PRC and DPRK invited the International Association of Democratic Lawyers that spring and the International Scientific Commission that summer to investigate. Both commissions supported North Korean and Chinese allegations in their reports.

These charges, however, were controversial. Both U.S. government and UN officials denied in early March 1952 any employment of biological or bacteriological agents to further the goals of military operations in North Korea and China. Dean G. Acheson*, U.S. secretary of state, and General Matthew B. Ridgway*, commander of UN forces in Korea, denied the claims of using biological agents against the Chinese and North Korean troops and civilians, though the United States did not ratify until 1975 the Geneva Convention of 1925, which outlawed the first use of chemical and biological weapons in war. The Soviet Union kept reiterating that the United States never had ratified the protocol, and repeatedly called on Washington to do so during 1952 and 1953. However, the Soviets, like the PRC and DPRK, provided neither solid information nor material evidence to support their allegations. Since the Korean War ended in 1953, historians and military experts in the West have not found sufficient evidence in U.S. military archives, UN official documents, or any English sources to prove the allegations of germ warfare. In 1998, some classified Soviet documents became available that said the charges were "contrived and fraudulent." This was the first evidence from the Communist side refuting the long-standing allegations that UN or U.S. forces used biological weapons in the Korean War. See also Korean Armistice Agreement; Korean War POW Controversy; P'anmunjŏm Truce Talks.

S. Endicott and E. Hagerman, The U.S. and Biological Warfare: Secrets from the Early Cold War and Korea (Bloomington, IN, 1997); J. Halliday and B. Cumings, Korea: The Unknown War (New York, 1988); M. Leitenberg, "New Russian Evidence on the Korean War Biological Warfare Allegations: Background and Analysis," Cold War International History Project Bulletin (Winter 1998); W. W. Stueck, The Korean War: An International History (Princeton, NJ, 1995); K. Weathersby, "Deceiving the Deceivers: Moscow, Beijing, Pyongyang, and the Allegations of Bacteriological Weapons Use in Korea," Cold War International History Project Bulletin (Winter 1998).

Li Xiaobing

GOLDEN TRIANGLE

The term "Golden Triangle" refers to the opium-producing region of Southeast Asia, comprising parts of Burma*, Laos*, and Thailand*. The term was apparently coined by U.S. Assistant Secretary of State Marshall Green* in 1971. The centrality of the Golden Triangle to the global heroin trade, U.S. involvement in covert activities in the region during the Cold War, and its relation to the problem of heroin use among the U.S. military during the Second Indochina War* have combined to make the Golden Triangle an important focus for U.S. international narcotics policy. Although the cultivation of poppies in the Golden Triangle dates back for several centuries, the British colonization of Burma starting with the first Anglo-Burmese War of 1824–1826 greatly expanded the Drug Trade* in this region. Later British attempts at opium suppression had only limited success, particularly in the Shan states that were not under direct British control.

Remnants of the Guomindang* (Nationalist) army arriving in Burma after their defeat in the Chinese Civil War* in 1949 quickly became involved in the opium trade as a source of revenue. U.S. General Claire L. Chennault*, former head of the Flying Tigers, persuaded the Central Intelligence Agency* (CIA) to set up an air supply operation for Guomindang forces, originally called Civil Air Transport and later Air America*. The CIA used these aircraft for its covert operations in Southeast Asia, using these nominally civilian airlines for transportation and supply not only for the Guomindang, but also for Hmong* guerrillas fighting against the Communist Pathet Lao*. Most scholars agree that at least some opium was carried on these U.S. aircraft for export to the global market, although they continue to dispute both the amount of such traffic and to what degree U.S. officials were aware of it.

Increasing U.S. involvement in Southeast Asia had a profound effect on the economics of the drug trade in the Golden Triangle. First, U.S.-backed governments in the Republic of Vietnam* were unable or unwilling to stop the flow of drugs into South Vietnam, thus providing a seaport for opium produced in the landlocked region of the Golden Triangle to reach the global market. Second, high casualties among U.S.-supported guerrillas and the resulting continued demand for fresh young recruits left poppies—traditionally cultivated by women—as the only economically viable crop in the region. Finally, the increase in heroin use among U.S. military personnel in Vietnam starting in 1970 created a new market for Golden Triangle opium, which continued and expanded when addicted soldiers returned to the United States.

In the 1970s and 1980s, Chinese-Shan warlord Khun Sa* began consolidating his control over the Golden Triangle opium trade. Rebels in the Shan states started to fight for independence from Burma in 1959, trading opium for weapons in Thailand. This rebellion provided an opportunity for Khun Sa to rise gradually to dominate the opium trade, overcoming a series of setbacks to defeat his enemies and gain a near monopoly on Golden Triangle opium by the late 1980s. Joint U.S.-Burmese efforts at poppy eradication in the late 1970s proved only temporarily effective. In February 1990, the United States indicted Khun Sa for drug trafficking. In

January 1996, Khun Sa surrendered to the Myanmar government. He was placed under house arrest in Rangoon, and the Myanmar junta refused his extradition. See also Guomindang Intervention in Burma.

A. W. McCoy, *The Politics of Heroin: CIA Complicity in the Global Drug Trade* (Chicago, 1991); R. Renard, *The Burmese Connection: Illegal Drugs and the Making of the Golden* (Boulder, CO, 1996); W. O. Walker, *Opium and Foreign Policy: The Anglo-American Search for Order in Asia, 1912–1954* (Chapel Hill, NC, 1991); J. Westermeyer, *Poppies, Pipes, and People: Opium and Its Use in Laos* (Berkeley, CA, 1982);

Timothy L. Savage

GONG, PRINCE

See YIXIN

GORBACHEV-NO SUMMITS

These meetings symbolized South Korea's rising power and prominence in East Asian affairs as the Cold War was ending, while placing diplomatic pressure for accommodation on an increasingly isolated North Korea. Since its establishment on 15 August 1945, the Republic of Korea* (ROK) had had no relations with the Soviet Union. South Korea followed a staunch anti-Soviet, anti-Communist policy, and the Soviet Union recognized the Democratic People's Republic of Korea* (DPRK) in the north, denouncing South Korea as "an American puppet state." In the early 1970s, following Soviet-American detente, South Korea began formal efforts to improve relations with the Soviet Union, but Moscow responded coldly. In 1985, Mikhail Gorbachev adopted a conciliatory policy toward the ROK after assuming Soviet leadership. In response, South Korean President No Tae-u*, in his inaugural speech in February 1988, pledged to pursue a "Nordpolitik" (Northern policy). He repeated his intentions in his speech at the UN General Assembly later that year. Gorbachev, in September at Krasnoyarsk, suggested the possibility of economic cooperation between the two countries. The Soviet Union then participated in the Seoul Summer Olympics of 1988, with political and economic contacts increasing considerably thereafter.

In April 1990, No learned that Gorbachev would be visiting the United States for talks with President George H. W. Bush* in June. In response to No's request to meet with him in the United States, Gorbachev replied that he would send former Soviet Ambassador to the United States Anatoli Dobrynin to Seoul to meet with No. On 22 May, Dobrynin told No that Gorbachev, on his return to Moscow, would meet him in San Francisco on 4 June. But he advised the South Koreans not to attempt to confirm Gorbachev's verbal message through any other channel, warning that this might torpedo the proposed summit. For a conference site, Moscow suggested the Soviet Consulate General in San Francisco on grounds of security, but No strongly opposed this idea because in 1896, King Kojong* had taken refuge for a year in the Russian legation in Seoul in an act of national shame. Then former U.S. Secretary of State George Shultz helped persuade former President Ronald Reagan* to vacate the presidential suite at the Hotel Fairmont in San Francisco so that No could use it for his meeting with Gorbachev, and the Soviets agreed to this arrangement.

On 4 June 1990, the first Gorbachev-No summit confirmed the improvement of relations between the ROK and the Soviet Union. Discussions focused on the rapidly changing global situation and its relationship to bilateral relations between the two countries. The two leaders agreed that this new trend to openness and reconciliation had to include Northeast Asia with the objective of fostering cooperation among all concerned nations toward establishing peace and stability in the region. With respect to the Korean peninsula, Gorbachev and No agreed on the need to reduce tensions and preserve peace. The meeting led to the establishment of diplomatic relations between the ROK and the Soviet Union on 30 September 1990 at UN headquarters. This historic event restored ties severed in 1904 between the Korean kingdom and imperial Russia.

In December 1990, No visited the Soviet Union, the first time in history that a South Korean president had done so. While in Moscow, No and Gorbachev issued a joint proclamation of basic principles, which included the declaration that "through consultation between the two nations and concerned parties in the Asia-Pacific region, peaceful and constructive cooperation should be encouraged." As an act of diplomatic reciprocation, Gorbachev visited South Korea's southernmost island of Cheju in April 1991 on his return to Moscow from Tōkyō. This was the first visit to either Korea by a Soviet head of state or Communist Party secretary general. At his meeting with No, Gorbachev privately committed the Soviet Union to support South Korea's entry into the United Nations, even if North Korea continued to reject the joint entry of the two Koreas, a step that the DPRK had claimed would perpetuate national division. Also, Gorbachev publicly urged North Korea to open its nuclear facilities to international inspection and pledged to stop supplying its nuclear power plants with fuel until it took this step. No's Nordpolitik then achieved its greatest success in October 1991 when the two Koreas were admitted to the United Nations in accordance with ROK policy objectives. *See also* North Korean Nuclear Controversy.

H. Kim, "The Process Leading to the Establishment of Diplomatic Relations between South Korea and the Soviet Union," *Asian Survey* (July 1997).

Kim Hakjoon

GREAT CIRCLE ROUTE

The Great Circle Route from the Pacific coast of North America to East Asia became the high road of commerce that tied the great harbors of San Diego, San Francisco, and even Puget Sound to the markets of the Orient. What mattered in the early nineteenth century was not the reality of those markets, but their promising commercial future for those who could exploit the Great Circle sea lanes of the north Pacific. The United States, in the 1844 Treaty of Wangxia*, gained access to China's major ports and freedom from the arbitrary and capricious exactions imposed by Chinese merchants in the old Guangzhou trade. The Great Circle Route from San Francisco to China brought American ships off the Japanese coast. To bring Japan into the sphere of American commerce and gain an added measure of security on the long trans-Pacific voyage, the United States rapidly perceived the importance of opening Japan to American seamen. It was a small step from the acquisition of Puget Sound and San Francisco Bay to the expedition of Commodore Matthew C. Perry* to Tōkyō Bay in 1853. Fortunately for the Perry Mission*, the Japanese were prepared to compromise their historic isolation. Upon his return to Tōkyō Bay in February 1854, Perry's negotiations with the Japanese produced the famed Treaty of Kanagawa* on 31 March 1854 that offered good treatment for shipwrecked sailors and opened the two ports of Shimoda and Hakodate. Although the treaty's provisions were meager, they moderated Japan's traditional fear and hatred of foreigners, and gave U.S. shippers traveling the Great Circle Route new markets and some respite from danger. *See also* Bryant and Sturgis; John Kendrick; Russell and Company.

N. A. Graebner, *Empire on the Pacific: A Study in American Continental Expansion* (New York, 1955); N. Inazo, *The Intercourse Between the U.S. and Japan: A Historical Sketch* (Baltimore, 1891); A. Walworth, *Black Ships off Japan: The Story of Commodore Perry's Expedition* (Hamden, CT, 1966).

Norman A. Graebner

GREAT CRESCENT

This term was featured in early U.S. Cold War policy papers and referred to a geographical area stretching from the Kurile Islands to the north of Japan, extending in a sweeping arc westward as far as Iran and Afghanistan. Common in Department of State reports, the phrase is often cited in Cold War historiography as shorthand for an ambitious, but ultimately unrealized, U.S. postwar strategy of regional economic integration centered on Japan and seeking to shore up the countries of Southeast Asia against Communist encroachment. Conceptually, the strategy could be likened to a Marshall Plan for East Asia and envisaged the provision of U.S. economic aid to Japan to facilitate the purchase of raw materials from Southeast Asia, allowing the nations of the region to earn dollar receipts and buy Japan's expanding manufactured exports.

Early U.S. regional integration policy developed incrementally through a series of internal policy discussions and initiatives in the Truman administration, beginning most memorably with Undersecretary of State Dean G. Acheson* characterizing Japan as the "workshop of Asia" in May 1947. Earlier that year, Edwin Martin, head of the Division of Japanese and Korean Affairs, advanced a more concrete agenda when he drafted a proposal for a $500 million package of U.S. aid to Japan intended to reduce economic constraints on Japanese industry and revive the prewar Triangular Trade*. Influential State Department officials endorsed Martin's plan, most notably George F. Kennan* and Paul Nitze, both of whom saw Japan as the key focal point for regional economic recovery and whose arguments led to the adoption of the Reverse Course* in the U.S. Occupation of Japan*. The diplomatic arguments for regional economic integration were buttressed by the views of U.S. military planners, who recognized that regional economic recovery would strengthen U.S. security in Asia.

Ultimately, the Truman administration's regional integration plans foundered on bureaucratic disagreements over where to direct scarce U.S. economic resources, how to coordinate the overlapping interests of Europe, Southeast Asia, and Japan, and how best to counter the challenge of Communism* in the People's Republic of China*. Whereas the U.S. military often viewed regional strategy through the distorting prism of support for the Republic of China* on Taiwan*, the State Department argued either for a policy of supporting moderate nationalists in the region or for an extensive Japan-centered regional economic program. These military-civilian tensions were partially alleviated with the introduction of the Mutual Assistance Program in 1949, providing support for a broad range of military programs. Various State and Defense Department missions in early 1950 continued to explore the possibilities for a regional economic strategy based around Japan's economic recovery, which received a strong endorsement from the Japanese themselves. Japanese prime ministers throughout the 1940s and 1950s, most notably Yoshida Shigeru*, Hatoyama Ichirō*, and Kishi Nobusuke*, all lobbied Washington to aid Japan in developing a close trading relationship with the markets of the region. But for much of the 1950s, Japan was itself financially vulnerable, with an unstable balance of payments, and was therefore economically, as well as politically, too weak to support a major regional assistance program. Furthermore, the Korean War* shifted U.S. containment policy in Asia to reliance on military means.

Support for the creation of the Great Crescent evaporated in the 1950s because the United States itself was not prepared to provide the needed capital outlay and was also very conscious of the potential backlash from other regional powers disinclined to assume the "role of hewers of wood and carriers of water for Japan." Moreover, by 1959, pursuing Japan-centered regional development would contradict the U.S. policy of encouraging greater European participation in East Asia, relying on international organiza-

tions, such as the International Bank for Reconstruction and Development, to administer development programs, and relying on bilateral projects in the region. It was not until much later, in 1977, under Prime Minister Fukuda Takeo* that Japan was in a position to begin to develop anything resembling a coherent regional economic strategy toward Southeast Asia. But this initiative was seen as self-serving and only beginning in the late 1980s, through Japan's involvement in the Asia-Pacific Economic Cooperation* (APEC) forum and cooperation with the Association of Southeast Asian Nations*, did the region move closer to realization of a redefined Great Crescent.

M. Schaller, *The American Occupation of Japan: The Origins of the Cold War in Asia* (New York, 1985); M. Schaller, "Securing the Great Crescent: Occupied Japan and the Origins of Containment in Southeast Asia," *Journal of American History* (September 1982); H. B. Schonberger, *Aftermath of War: Americans and the Remaking of Japan, 1945–1952* (Kent, OH, 1989).

John Swenson-Wright

GREAT MARIANAS TURKEY SHOOT

The Great Marianas Turkey Shoot was the air-to-air portion of the Battle of the Philippine Sea*, the largest carrier battle in history that marked the effective end of Japan's carrier aviation in World War II. It was fought by the combined Japanese First Mobile Fleet and Southern Force under Vice Admiral Ozawa Jisaburō against Task Force Fifty-eight under Vice Admiral Marc Mitschner of the Fifth Fleet under Vice Admiral Raymond Spruance. Ozawa's nine carriers with 473 aircraft were attempting to defeat a numerically superior (fifteen carriers and 956 aircraft), more experienced force and to prevent the Americans from seizing the Marianas Islands (Saipan, Guam*, and Tinian). Ozawa's plan was to use submarines and reconnaissance aircraft to give him advance warning of the American advance and then exploit the longer range of his aircraft (300-mile attack for the Japanese versus about 200 for U.S. bombers) to hit the U.S. fleet before it could attack him. By this time, however, the average American carrier pilot had two years of flying time; the average Japanese pilot only six months. Mitschner's Task Force Fifty-eight evaded Japanese surveillance and on 11 June 1944, attacked the Marianas by surprise, destroying more than fifty aircraft in the first strike. By 15 July, American air attacks had neutralized much of the Japanese land-based air forces, on which Ozawa also had counted.

Ozawa was able to remain undetected until his force launched the first strike on 19 June. American signals intelligence, the winning card at the Battle of Midway*, was now supplemented by extensive long-range radar coverage and a well-developed system to use both resources to direct their air battles. Once the first groups of aircraft headed toward Task Force fifty-eight, the radio chatter of the inexperienced Japanese air crews alerted the Americans. Massed U.S. fighters were vectored to advantageous intercept positions and attacked the Japanese bombers and their fighter escorts. The more experienced American pilots quickly broke up the attack and completely dominated the resulting dogfights. Only 56 of the 197 Japanese aircraft in the first two waves survived the American defenses. The third wave of 47 aircraft missed Task Force Fifty-eight completely, and as a result, only twelve were intercepted and seven of them shot down. The fourth wave also missed most of Task Force Fifty-eight and then attempted to land on Guam. It was mauled so badly by U.S. fighters that only 9 of the 82 returned to their carriers. In addition to Ozawa's losses, an estimated 50 land-based aircraft were shot down over the Marianas. American losses to all causes that day have been variously reported from 18 to 30. Japanese losses totaled between 290 and 350, including the land-based aircraft. Eighty more Japanese aircraft were lost the next day when Task Force Fifty-eight finally found and attacked Ozawa's carriers. Never again in the war would Japanese carrier-based aircraft be a threat to the U.S. Navy.

H. A. Gailey, *The War in the Pacific: From Pearl Harbor to Tokyo Bay* (Novato, CA, 1995); J. Prados, *Combined Fleet Decoded: Secret History of American Intelligence and the Japanese Navy in World War II* (New York, 1995); S. E. Morison, *The Two-Ocean War: A Short History of the United States Navy in the Second World War* (Boston, 1963); R. L. Spector, *Eagle Against the Sun: The American War with Japan* (New York, 1985); E. T. Wooldridge, *Carrier Warfare in the Pacific: An Oral History Collection* (Washington, DC, 1993).

Roger H. Hill

GREAT WHITE FLEET

President Theodore Roosevelt* was a great believer in the significance of naval power and had doubled the size of the U.S. Navy during his administration. As a means of showing the flag, in July 1907, he directed the U.S. Navy to embark upon what eventually became a worldwide cruise that was perhaps the most significant peacetime naval demonstration ever. On 16 December, sixteen battleships and other vessels of various sizes steamed out of Hampton Roads, Virginia. Not until the following March was it publicly announced that the fleet would continue around the world. After successful calls on ports throughout Latin America, the fleet traveled to New Zealand and Australia, where it was greeted by cheering crowds and government ministers, the latter most ecstatic about the demonstration of U.S. power as a counter to Japanese advances in the Pacific. A cholera epidemic in Manila made that stop in the Philippines* low-key in comparison with the others. While the voyage was under way, the Japanese government requested a visit by the fleet, a measure that was accepted with some trepidation by the Roosevelt administration out of fear of having the entire fleet inside Japanese waters. Nevertheless, on 18 October, the ships landed at Yokohama, Japan. There, the ships received the warmest and most enthusiastic welcome of the cruise. Thousands of schoolchildren sang rehearsed American songs, and many more people lined the streets with American flags. The Japanese government lavishly hosted the 14,000 men of the fleet for more than a week.

After the stay in Japan, part of the fleet returned to Manila while the rest visited China, where the regent appropriated 400,000 taels for the entertainment of American sailors. On 1 December, the fleet reunited in Manila and departed for home. A small crisis arose over the expensiveness of the voyage while it was in progress, but Roosevelt threatened to leave the flotilla at sea if Congress failed to provide sufficient funding. The rest of the journey was comparatively uneventful, and the fleet reached Hampton Roads on 22 February 1909, mere weeks before Roosevelt left office. A feat of historic proportions for U.S.–East Asian relations, the fleet had made its 46,000-mile voyage during a time of heightened discord between the United States and Japan. Its presence likely contributed to the easing of these tensions, but, despite the press at the time, the voyage in fact had not preempted any outbreak of war. The voyage had dispelled the growing clouds of ill feeling between Washington and Tōkyō. Also, the Great White Fleet compelled the Japanese government to enforce the provisions of the Gentlemen's Agreement* and facilitated the signing of several important bilateral conventions, such as the Taft-Katsura Agreement* and the Root-Takahira Agreement*. The cruise of the Great White Fleet marked the coming to prominence of the United States as a major power, not only in the Pacific, but in the world as a whole.

T. A. Bailey, *Theodore Roosevelt and the Japanese-American Crisis* (Stanford, CA, 1934); F. W. Marks III, *Velvet on Iron: The Diplomacy of Theodore Roosevelt* (Lincoln, NE, 1979); W. L. Neumann, *America Encounters Japan: From Perry to MacArthur* (Baltimore, MD 1963).

Kent G. Sieg

GREATER EAST ASIA CO-PROSPERITY SPHERE

During World War II, Japan announced as its objective the creation of a Greater East Asia Co-Prosperity Sphere in which the peoples of Asia would win their freedom from Western colonialism under the benevolent and enlightened leadership of Japan. Japanese interests in a Greater East Asia had been limited in the 1930s to Manchukuo* and north China. Not until 1936 did Japanese strategists contemplate a "southward advance." From 1937 to 1939, however, the strategic focus shifted to the army's traditional "northward advance" because of the outbreak of the Sino-Japanese War after the Marco Polo Bridge Incident* and the Soviet challenge at the Battle of Nomonhan* in Mongolia. German military successes in Western Europe in 1940 caused the Japanese to look southward again to the raw material–rich colonies of France, the Netherlands, and Britain, which were now defenseless. Finally, in 1941, with the Soviet Union combating German invasion and thus no further threat to Japan, the "strike south" faction prevailed in Japanese military and diplomatic circles. After the Pearl Harbor Attack*, Japan conquered Southeast Asia in a dazzling series of military campaigns that outran strategic planning for the area. On 1 November 1942, a Greater East Asia Ministry was established by Imperial Ordinance. It not only undermined the authority of the Foreign Ministry, but remained a center of discord among competing groups.

Initially, Japanese occupation forces ignored or suppressed native nationalists. Soon it became clear that in areas where there was pro-Japanese sentiment, the local nationalists might prove valuable in achieving Japan's strategic goals. The Japanese implemented an active propaganda campaign aimed at destroying the old order of racism, colonialism, and materialism. Instead, Western ideas were denigrated and Allied civilians humiliated and interned under harsh conditions, while the Japanese language and worldview were promoted. All public occasions were begun with a collective bow in the direction of Tōkyō and Emperor Hirohito*. The shock of Japan's military prowess over the Western powers was an irresistible force in causing many nationalist leaders to make pragmatic accommodations with Tōkyō. More important, the Japanese released prewar political prisoners and welcomed dissidents in exile. Local people filled the administrative and entrepreneurial vacuum created by the collapse of empire. A cultural revolution occurred as the Japanese encouraged and promoted the use of native languages in the media. Youth and women found a voice in Japan's "New Order" and were encouraged to participate in mass organizations, parades, rallies, and paramilitary formulations. Student exchange programs in Japan were initiated, as well as periodic Greater East Asia cultural exchange associations and literary and scientific conferences. Finally, Christians, Buddhists, and Muslims were all invited to participate in the holy war for the soul of Greater East Asia.

The year 1943 was the fulcrum of both World War II and the Greater East Asia Co-Prosperity Sphere. The Allies had challenged not only Japan's military and naval supremacy, but also her ideals in both the 1941 Atlantic Charter and at the 1943 Cairo Conference*. In response, Tōkyō announced her decision to grant "independence" to Burma* and the Philippines* in January 1943. An Indian National Army had been created from among the prisoners captured at Singapore* and a Burma Independence Army came into being. In addition, volunteer armies were raised all over Southeast Asia. The climax of Japan's effort to transform Southeast Asia came with the Greater East Asia Conference held in Tōkyō during early November 1943. Fifty leading Asian nationalists/collaborators attended, including Puyi* of Manchukuo, Wang Jingwei* of the Nanjing government, Ba Maw* of Burma, Wan

Waithayakon of Thailand*, José Laurel of the Philippines, and Subhas Chandra Bose of the Free State of India. Premier Tōjō Hideki* addressed the delegates, celebrating the dawning of a new age of harmony and co-prosperity in an Asia cleansed of Western colonialism. In 1944 and 1945, however, the fortunes of the Greater East Asia Co-Prosperity ebbed with Japanese military fortunes. Japan inadvertently began the revolutionary transformation of Southeast Asia. Seeking to enlist the loyalties of local nationalist elites, as well as extract strategic raw materials for the inevitable struggle to come, Japan's economic exploitation and terror drove many into opposition, resulting in the emergence of the anti-Japanese Vietminh* in French Indochina*, Hukbalahap* in the Philippines, and Free Thai Movement*. See also Amō Doctrine; Ōkuma Doctrine.

P. Duus, et al. (eds.), *The Japanese Wartime Empire, 1931–1945* (Princeton, NJ, 1996); J. C. Lebra-Chapman, *Japanese-Trained Armies in Southeast Asia: Independence and Volunteer Forces in World War II* (New York, 1977); C. Thorne, *The Issue of War: States, Societies, and the Far Eastern Conflict of 1941–1945* (New York, 1985).

Errol M. Clauss

GREEN BERETS

The U.S. Army Special Forces, popularly known as the Green Berets for their distinctive headgear, formed the backbone of U.S. efforts to combat Communism* in East Asia through counterinsurgency in the 1950s and 1960s. Some historians of the Second Indochina War* argue that if the United States had fought a counterinsurgency war—the forte of the Green Berets—rather than a conventional one, the result of the conflict could have been more positive. An outgrowth of World War II paratrooper-and Ranger-trained soldiers, the modern U.S. Army Special Forces were organized officially in 1952. Their original mission was to wage guerrilla warfare and organize resistance behind enemy lines.

Green Berets received the most intensive training of any U.S. Army combat troops. All members of the Special Forces were airborne-or paratroop-qualified; trained to infiltrate enemy-controlled territory and contact and organize local resistance forces for guerilla operations; subject to rigorous physical conditioning; familiar with foreign weapons, hand-to-hand combat, and night fighting; and cross-trained with basic medical knowledge. The Green Berets also were known as "snake eaters" for their ability to live off the land, which they exhibited at public relations demonstrations by capturing, skinning, and cooking a live snake.

The U.S. Special Forces commitment to East Asia dates from 1954, when a team was dispatched to Thailand* to train the Royal Thai Rangers. After June 1957, its teams helped for the next three years to develop and expand counterpart special units in the armed forces of the Republic of Korea*, the Republic of Vietnam*, Taiwan*, and the Philippines*. In July 1959, the Central Intelligence Agency* (CIA) began efforts to help Lao Royalists and neutralists fight the Communist Pathet Lao*, and Special Forces troops were assigned to Vientiane to train regular units of the Laotian army. Eventually, the Green Berets were forced to leave Laos*, along with other foreign military forces, as a result of the Geneva Accords of 1962*, which neutralized the country. But the most visible deployment of the Green Berets in Asia was in Vietnam. Special Forces involvement there started in 1957 when teams began training members of the Army of the Republic of Vietnam*, their primary mission for the next four years. President John F. Kennedy* made the Special Forces the centerpiece of his counterinsurgency strategy for combating "wars of national liberation" in developing countries. He expanded the Special Forces from 2,500 to 10,000 men and emphasized counterguerrilla operations in their training through a combination of civic action, political subversion, and psychological operations. The Green Berets's motto, *De Oppresso Liber* (To Free from Oppression), symbolized Kennedy's idealistic aims.

Under Kennedy, Green Beret teams were assigned to provide training and assistance to various South Vietnamese minority groups, such as the Montagnards, Cambodians, and ethnic Vietnamese from the Cao Dai* and Hoa Hao sects. These programs evolved into Civilian Irregular Defense Groups (CIDGs), and by February 1965, forty-eight CIDG camps had been established by Special Forces teams throughout South Vietnam. As the war progressed, these numbers increased and the mission of the Green Berets expanded as well. Special Forces units conducted top-secret intelligence operations throughout Southeast Asia and also were involved in the CIA's Phoenix Program*. In his 1967 "Report on the War in Vietnam," U.S. Commander General William C. Westmoreland* praised the Special Forces for being highly successful "in penetrating isolated enemy bases, disrupting the enemy's lines of communication, attacking his hidden logistical support bases, and gathering intelligence." The Green Berets became the embodiment of the ultimate American soldier. During the Vietnam War, they were immortalized in Robin Moore's best-selling novel *The Green Berets* (1965), Special Forces Sergeant Barry Sadler's hit song "The Ballad of the Green Berets" (1966), and John Wayne's laudatory motion picture *The Green Berets* (1968). *See also* Nation-Building Strategy.

L. E. Cable, *Conflict of Myths: The Development of American Counterinsurgency Doctrine and the Vietnam War* (New York, 1986); F. J. Kelly, *U.S. Army Special Forces, 1961–1971* (Washington, DC, 1973); S. L. Stanton, *Green Berets at War: U.S. Special Forces in Southeast Asia, 1956–1975* (Novato, CA, 1985).

Andrew L. Johns

GREEN, MARSHALL (1916–1998)

Ambassador Marshall Green, a career Foreign Service officer, was influential in developing postwar U.S. policy toward Japan, China, Korea, Indonesia*, and Vietnam. He was known as a cautious diplomat whose low-key approach and quick wit were legendary. A native of Massachusetts, Green, after graduation from Yale University, became a private secretary to Ambassador Joseph C. Grew* in prewar Japan. During World War II, Green was a Japanese-language officer in the U.S. Navy. Entering the Foreign Service after the war, Green continued to work on Japanese affairs, notably accompanying George F. Kennan*, director of the State Department's Policy Planning Staff, on his 1948 mission to Japan, which resulted in a final report that contributed to the Reverse Course* in the U.S. Occupation of Japan*. Following successive tours of duty in New Zealand, Sweden, at the National War College, and as Japan desk officer in Washington, he was regional planning adviser for the Bureau of Far Eastern Affairs. In this capacity, Green played a key role in 1955 as action officer in defusing the first of the Taiwan Straits Crises* by devising direct Sino-American negotiations in the Warsaw Talks*.

In 1960, Green became deputy chief of mission at the U.S. embassy in the Republic of Korea*. He witnessed both the demise of the corrupt regime of dictator Syngman Rhee* and the overthrow of the brief civilian government of Jang Myŏn* that followed. He achieved notoriety during the latter episode when, during a period when the ambassador had departed and without instructions from Washington, he publicly opposed the military coup led by General Pak Chŏng-hŭi*. From 1961 to 1963, he was consul general in Hong Kong*, the prime place from which Westerners observed and reported on events in mainland China during the Cold War. In 1963, Green returned to Washington as deputy assistant secretary of state for Far Eastern affairs. President Lyndon B. Johnson* appointed Green as ambassador to Indonesia on 4 June 1965, a post he held for nearly four years. He arrived in Indonesia at a time when rela-

tions with the United States were at their lowest ebb. However, Green quietly reached out to pro-Western segments in the Indonesian military and among student groups. This strategy bore fruit after an abortive Communist takeover on 30 September 1965. When General Suharto* was able after the Indonesia Crisis of 1965* to finally ease President Sukarno* out of office the following spring, Green requested aid, which he previously had recommended withholding, and established a complex international investment scheme to buttress Suharto's New Order.

While ambassador to Indonesia, Green had received former Vice President Richard M. Nixon* warmly. When Nixon became president in 1969, he fondly remembered Green and, after a brief period when Green was at the Paris Peace Talks* on Vietnam, offered him the position of assistant secretary of state for East Asian and Pacific affairs, a post Green assumed on 1 May 1969 and held until 10 May 1973. One of his major impacts was adoption of the Nixon Doctrine*. Throughout these years, though, Nixon and National Security Adviser Henry A. Kissinger* grew increasingly suspicious of Green because of his close ties to top-level people in past Democratic administrations. He did make an important contribution, however, when he accompanied Nixon and Kissinger to the People's Republic of China* during 1972. Green stood against tremendous pressure from Kissinger and insisted on refinements to the hastily drafted Shanghai Communique*. His next assignment was as ambassador to Australia and Nauru. In 1975, Green returned to Washington as government-wide coordinator for population affairs, leading the U.S. delegations to the United Nations Population Commission and devising policy guidelines to deal with the Indochinese Boat People*. He retired in 1979 with the rank of career minister.

M. Green, *Indonesia: Crisis and Transformation, 1965–1968* (Washington, DC, 1990); M. Green,

Pacific Encounters (Bethesda, MD, 1997); M. Green, *Population Pressures: Threat to Democracy and Stability* (Washington, DC, 1989); M. Green, *War and Peace with China: Firsthand Experiences in the Foreign Service of the United States* (Bethesda, MD, 1994).

Kent G. Sieg

GREENE, GRAHAM (1904–1991)

British author of numerous well-known and best-selling novels, Graham Greene's importance for U.S. relations with East Asia comes from his one novel that presciently, though not necessarily consciously, forewarned of American involvement in the Second Indochina War*. Titled *The Quiet American*, Greene's fictional account of events in Vietnam in the early 1950s was drawn from his travels there on behalf of *Life* magazine. He had been commissioned by John Emmet Hughes, himself a young Catholic protégé of *Time*, *Life*, and *Fortune* publisher Henry R. Luce*. The nonfiction article Greene eventually produced was not what Hughes and Luce had in mind, so he published it elsewhere. He then used his experiences to write *The Quiet American*.

In the novel, a young American named Alden Pyle arrives in the Republic of Vietnam* just after having left "the Common in Boston, his arms full of books he had been reading in advance on the Far East and the problems of China." Although some claimed that Greene based the character on the real-life Central Intelligence Agency* (CIA) operative Edward G. Lansdale*, who assisted South Vietnamese leader Ngo Dinh Diem* in the mid-fifties, Greene insisted otherwise, pointing out that he never had met Lansdale. Rather, it was Leo Hochstetter, a member of the U.S. economic aid mission to Saigon, who served as the basis for the character. The fictitious American Pyle meets a British journalist named Thomas Fowler, who teases Pyle for what he initially sees as his naivete. But Fowler misjudges Pyle and eventually decides that the American is far

more dangerous in his earnest desire to do good and involve himself in the affairs of Southeast Asia.

In many respects, Greene's novel expertly anticipates American involvement, from Pyle's unshakeable belief in a "Third Force" to the covert military assistance he supplies to the fictitious South Vietnamese General Thé in his pursuit of creating that force, which he intends to be neither colonial nor Communist. Also well done is Greene's depiction of the relationship between the youthful and vigorous American Pyle and the aging European colonist Fowler, as a parallel to what was happening internationally as European countries lost their colonies and the United States assumed the role of the world's primary superpower. *See also* Wesley R. Fishel; Nation-Building Strategy.

G. Greene, *The Quiet American* (London, 1955); M. Shelden, *Graham Greene: The Man Within* (London, 1994).

T. Christopher Jespersen

GREW, JOSEPH C. (1880–1965)

Joseph Clark Grew was U.S. ambassador to Japan during the decade before the Pearl Harbor Attack*. His diplomatic career began in 1904 with a posting to Cairo. In 1905, Grew married a descendant of Commodore Oliver Perry, Alice de Vermandois Perry, whose experience in Japan in her younger years served her husband well later in his career in Tōkyō. After being assigned to many cities, including Mexico City, Moscow, Berlin, and Vienna, he was named secretary to the U.S. Commission to the Versailles Peace Conference. After serving as minister to Denmark and as a negotiator at the Lausanne Conference, he became undersecretary to Secretary of State Charles Evans Hughes* in 1924 and contributed to the setting up of the Foreign Service. Not being on good terms with Frank B. Kellogg*, Grew took the opportunity to become ambassador to Turkey in 1927. His mentor at the State Department

William R. Castle Jr.* then successfully secured his appointment in 1932 as ambassador to Japan.

In Japan, Grew worked to promote cordial U.S.-Japan relations, recommending that Washington encourage moderates in Tōkyō by taking a less aggressive attitude toward Japan. He disagreed with the firm attitude of Stanley K. Hornbeck*, arguing that it might lead to war between the United States and Japan. Although Grew tried to realize his goal of promoting good relations through his personal connections with Japan's imperial counts and elder statesmen, their influence was less than Grew had estimated. His belief that Japan's pursuit of a Greater East Asia Co-Prosperity Sphere* was not a threat to U.S. security did not receive much attention in Washington. Grew also warned that the embargo of petroleum to Japan might push the Japanese toward French Indochina*. During 1941, he laid his last hope on a proposed meeting between Prime Minister Konoe Fumimaro* and President Franklin D. Roosevelt*, but it was thought that such a meeting would constitute a form of appeasement, and the plan was rejected in Washington.

After he returned to the United States in 1942, Grew became special assistant to Secretary of State Cordell Hull* and exerted himself in explaining the Japanese to the Americans. In 1944, he was named director of the Far Eastern Affairs Division and in December again appointed undersecretary of state. During those years, Grew tried to preserve the position of Japanese emperor and prevent the unconditional surrender of Japan. Although his ideas were not directly reflected in the Potsdam Declaration*, his opinions influenced the decision to preserve Emperor Hirohito*. Grew retired from the State Department immediately after Japan surrendered in 1945. His papers are in the Houghton Library at Harvard University.

E. M. Bennett, "Joseph C. Grew: The Diplomacy of Pacification," in R. D. Burns and E. M. Bennett (eds.), *Diplomats in Crisis: United States–Chinese-Japanese Relations, 1919–1941* (Santa Barbara, CA, 1974). J. C. Grew, *Turbulent Era: A Diplomatic Record of Forty Years, 1904–1945*, 2 vols. (Boston, 1952); W. H. Heinrichs Jr., *American Ambassador: Joseph C. Grew and the Development of the United States Diplomatic Tradition* (Boston, 1966);

Hirobe Izumi

GU WEIJUN (1887–1985)

Known as V. K. Wellington Koo in the West, Gu played an important role in the establishment of the League of Nations and the United Nations, as well as serving as ambassador for the Republic of China* (ROC) to France, England, and the United States. Born into an affluent family, he studied at St. John's University, a prestigious missionary school in Shanghai, from 1901 to 1904. After graduation, Gu went to the United States and enrolled in Columbia University, where he actively participated in extracurricular activities. He earned a master of art's degree in political science in 1909 and a doctorate in 1912. Columbia University Press published his dissertation in 1912 under the title of "The Status of Aliens in China." In April 1912, Gu went back to China and served as secretary in the cabinet and then councillor in the Ministry of Foreign Affairs of the newly established ROC.

From 1915 to 1919, Gu was Chinese minister to Mexico, the United States, and Cuba. In 1919, he participated in the negotiations for the Versailles Peace Treaty* after World War I as a member of the Chinese delegation and was an instrumental figure in negotiating the Shandong Agreement*, dealing with the question of Japanese treaty rights in that province. Gu played an important role in helping China become a nonpermanent member of the League Council in the League of Nations in 1920, advancing the theory of geographical representation, eventually accepted by the international community. Appointed

ROC foreign minister in August 1922, Gu began to negotiate with the Soviet Union over the establishment of diplomatic relations, the settlement of the Chinese Eastern Railway dispute, and the question of the political status of Outer Mongolia. Before talks produced any results, the cabinet he was serving fell to a military clique, forcing him to resign. During the subsequent changes of cabinets during the Warlord Era*, he was recalled and served as foreign minister, acting premier, and finance minister without much accomplishment.

When the Northern Expedition unified China in 1928, the Guomindang* (Nationalists) issued an order for Gu's arrest for his collaboration with the former military regime, forcing him into exile abroad. He returned to Shenyang in 1929, where his friend Zhang Xueliang* protected him and eventually persuaded Jiang Jieshi* to rescind the order for Gu's arrest in 1930. In 1932, Gu was China's assessor on the Lytton Commission investigating the Mukden Incident*. In that capacity, he worked on China's behalf and submitted a detailed report on Japan's aggression to the commission. That same year, Gu was appointed minister to France and China's delegate to the League of Nations. During 1933 and 1934, he was China's delegate to the Conference on Reduction and Limitation of Armaments at Geneva, the World Monetary and Economic Conference at London, and the Permanent Court of Arbitration at The Hague. After the Marco Polo Bridge Incident* in July 1937, he served again as China's chief representative in the League of Nations, defending China's interests there without much success.

When France fell to Nazi Germany in 1940, Gu stayed in Vichy for a short time, then went to Britain as ambassador. His achievements during World War II included arrangements of the Sino-British exchange of parliamentary missions in 1942, British relinquishment of extraterritorial rights in China in 1943, and the Sino-British Lend Lease* agreement in 1944. In March 1945, Gu became a member of Chinese delegation at the San Francisco Conference to create the United Nations. While serving as chairman of China's UN delegation, he was appointed in May 1946 as ambassador to the United States. After Jiang's government fled to Taiwan* following the Chinese Civil War*, he exerted great effort to negotiate and sign the U.S.-China Mutual Defense Treaty of 1954*. In 1956, he resigned the ambassadorship. Gu became a judge on the International Court of Justice at The Hague in 1957, serving from 1964 to 1967 as vice president of the body. *See also* Insular Cases.

H. L. Boorman (ed.), *Biographical Dictionary of Republican China* (New York, 1967–1971); W. Tung, *V. K. Wellington Koo and China's Wartime Diplomacy* (New York, 1977).

Song Yuwu

GUAM

U.S. acquisition of this island after the Spanish-American War* reflected the climax of American expansion into the Pacific during the nineteenth century. Guam lies roughly 1,500 miles east of Manila in the Philippines*, and is the southernmost island in the Marianas chain. About thirty miles long and ranging from four to eight miles in width, it is divided geographically into two parts. The southern end is mountainous and of volcanic origin, whereas the northern end consists of a high limestone plateau. Guam is surrounded by a coral reef and is within a typhoon belt, being struck by a major storm on average once every ten to twelve years. After Ferdinand Magellan landed on Guam in March 1521, various European navigators visited the island during the sixteenth century, using it as a source of fresh food and water. In 1565, a Spanish expedition claimed the island, laid the basis for Spanish control of the Philippines, and discovered a reliable return route to North America. This led to the establishment of direct trade between Manila and Acapulco by yearly voyage of the Manila galleons. Guam as a source of supplies for the galleons gave the island a strategic significance that eventually led to its conquest by Spain.

Throughout the sixteenth and the first two-thirds of the seventeenth century, Spain made no attempt to establish direct control over Guam. This situation changed in 1662 when Father Sanvitores first arrived on the island, devoting the rest of his life to Christianizing the Marianas. Initially, the mission was successful, but in 1670, the native Chamorros revolted. Two years later, the killing of Sanvitores initiated the Spanish-Chamorro Wars. Disunity, Spain's superiority in weapons, and the inability of the Chamorros to conceive of warfare as something other than a game led to Spanish victory in 1695. The Spanish colonial era then consisted of three periods. First, from 1700 to 1769, the Jesuit order administered Guam. Second, from 1769 to 1825, the Spanish state expelled the Jesuits and confiscated their property. With the end of the mission, a secular government under the viceroy of New Spain was established. Last, from 1825 to 1898, the collapse of the Spanish Empire in the Western Hemisphere resulted in the shift of Guam's administration from Mexico to the Philippines. This change, along with Spain's decision to use the island as a penal colony for both Filipino and Spanish criminals, intensified the Hispanization of Guam and introduced Filipino traits into mainstream Chamorro culture and society.

Guam became a U.S. territory in 1899 under the Treaty of Paris ending the war with Spain. Shortly thereafter, the island was made an unincorporated territory with administrative authority delegated to the Department of the Navy. From 1898 to 1941, Guam was a coaling and cable station for the U.S. Navy, and what development occurred took place was mainly in the fields of health and education. There also was some progress in developing political awareness within the local population. During World War II, the Japanese occupied Guam, incorporating it into their Greater East Asian Co-Prosperity Sphere*.

Administrative control was exercised primarily by the Japanese Imperial Navy. U.S. military operations between 21 July and 10 August 1944 ended Japanese rule, with the U.S. Navy resuming sole control of Guam in June 1946. Lasting until 1950, this second period of naval administration had a greater effect on the island than the first. The destruction caused by the war, the establishment of large military bases on the island, and the influx of large numbers of U.S. citizens and Asian construction workers began to alter the nature of the island's society.

In July 1950, the U.S. Congress passed the Organic Act of Guam, which replaced the naval governor with an appointed civilian, established a twenty-one-seat legislature, set up a civilian court system, and granted U.S. citizenship to all Chamorros. Although the U.S. military no longer controlled Guam, it continued to play a large role in local affairs. In 1962, the security clearance required for entrance to the island was abolished. That same year, Typhoon Karen struck Guam. The abolition of the security clearance and the rehabilitation program undertaken after the storm radically changed the lifestyle of the island's residents. Commerce and transportation systems were improved and expanded, media resources were enlarged, the population and immigration continued to increase, and the standard of living rose significantly. Typhoon Karen also affected Chamorro culture, which came increasingly under attack by the force of changes that the storm unleashed. Added to Guam's native way of life after 1700 are layers of Hispanic, Filipino, Mexican, and American cultural traits, which have combined to form the modern Chamorro culture. The maintenance and continued development of this culture, along with the need to revise the island's political status in light of the growing political sophistication of Guam's population, are probably the two major issues facing the island in the twenty-first century. *See also* Compact of Free Association for Micronesia; Insular Cases.

P. Carano and P. Sanchez, *History of Guam* (Rutland, VT, 1964); E. G. and F. J. Nelson, *The Island of Guam: Description and History from a 1934 Perspective* (Washington, DC, 1992); R. F. Rogers, *Destiny's Landfall: A History of Guam* (Honolulu, HI, 1995).

Dirk A. Ballendorf

GULF OF TONKIN INCIDENTS

A substantial escalation in the Second Indochina War* was triggered by two incidents in August 1964 in the Gulf of Tonkin between North Vietnam and the Chinese island of Hainan. The first of these incidents was rather small—three North Vietnamese torpedo boats attacked a U.S. destroyer on 2 August, but inflicted no casualties and no significant damage. The second was wholly imaginary—two U.S. destroyers, in darkness and poor weather, mistakenly believed they were being attacked by torpedo boats on the night of 4 August, when no hostile vessels were present. Aside from helping President Lyndon B. Johnson* gain passage of the Gulf of Tonkin Resolution, these incidents increased his popularity at a very convenient time, during his presidential campaign. By 1968, it was becoming apparent, however, that Congress and the public had been misled about many of the details of the August incidents. Some people not only doubted that there had been any attack on the two destroyers on the night of 4 August, but suspected that the report of such an attack had been a deliberate lie, rather than the honest mistake it initially had been.

The USS *Maddox* was sent into the Gulf of Tonkin on 31 July 1964 on one of the Desoto Patrols*, eavesdropping on radio communications, pinpointing coastal radar locations, and collecting less exciting information such as the depth and temperature of the water. The United States decided that the *Maddox* would obtain more useful information about the North Vietnamese

coastal defenses if they were in an aroused state. The United States therefore scheduled an unusually intense series of covert operations against the North Vietnamese coast, under a program called OPLAN 34A*, between 30 July and 5 August. On the afternoon of 2 August, near the island of Hon Me, which had been shelled by an OPLAN 34A raid three nights before, three North Vietnamese torpedo boats came out and attacked the *Maddox*. The torpedo boats were driven off, all of them damaged and one almost sunk by gunfire from the *Maddox* and four U.S. jets launched by a nearby aircraft carrier. The Americans mistakenly thought that they had sunk one of the torpedo boats, and the North Vietnamese mistakenly believed they had shot down one of the planes. President Johnson was annoyed that the torpedo boats had not all been sunk, but decided not to order any further retaliation.

The *Maddox* and another destroyer, the USS *C. Turner Joy*, went into the Gulf of Tonkin on 3 August to resume the patrol. On the night of 4 August, another incident occurred that is still hotly disputed. At the time, almost everyone on both destroyers believed they were being attacked by North Vietnamese torpedo boats. Many of them still believe this; others later decided that what had appeared on their radar had been ghost images generated by weather, seabirds, and low-flying U.S. aircraft. The available evidence indicates that no genuine torpedo boats were anywhere near the two destroyers. When Johnson was told that the U.S. Navy had been attacked for a second time, he quickly ordered retaliatory air strikes, code-named PIERCE ARROW. The targets were North Vietnamese naval vessels at a number of locations along the coast, and a fuel storage facility at Vinh, important to the supply systems supporting Communist forces in Laos* and in South Vietnam. The fuel facility at Vinh was destroyed, and at least one Swatow boat, and perhaps three, were sunk. Two U.S. aircraft were shot down. Both sides exaggerated their accomplishments by similar margins; the United States claimed eight vessels destroyed, and the Democratic Republic of Vietnam* claimed eight planes shot down.

Top officials expected that the United States would need to escalate the Vietnam War after the 1964 election, but Johnson was running as the peace candidate, so they had to conceal these plans. They wanted Congress to pass a resolution authorizing escalation, but did not wish to explain why they wanted it. The Tonkin Gulf Incidents provided the necessary pretext. They told Congress it must approve a resolution authorizing the president to take "all necessary measures . . . to prevent further aggression" not because major escalation of the war was needed, but simply to make it clear to North Vietnam that attacks against U.S. ships on the high seas would not be tolerated. What became known as the Tonkin Gulf Resolution passed unanimously in the House, and with only two dissenting votes in the Senate, on 7 August. But in 1970, Congress repealed it after realizing that it had been misled about the Gulf of Tonkin Incidents and the uses to which the president would put the resolution.

E. J. Marolda and O. P. Fitzgerald, *The United States Navy and the Vietnam Conflict*, Vol. 2: *From Military Assistance to Combat, 1959–1965* (Washington, DC, 1986); E. E. Moise, *Tonkin Gulf and the Escalation of the Vietnam War* (Chapel Hill, NC, 1996); E. G. Windchy, *Tonkin Gulf* (Garden City, NY, 1971).

Edwin E. Moise

GULICK, SIDNEY L. (1860–1945)

Sidney Lewis Gulick was a Congregational missionary born to a family of missionaries; hence his accepting the call to go to Japan in 1888 was in keeping with the family tradition. After a successful missionary career, he returned to the United States to become the "Japan expert" for the Federal Council of Churches of Christ in America, as his health did not permit a return to the mission field. He worked with equal fervor to convince his countrymen that Japan was not a menace, but such an undertaking in the years during and after World War I was not propitious. By the early 1920s, Gulick was being followed by the Bureau of Investigation, precursor to the Federal Bureau of Investigation. Prejudice against the Japanese, the so-called yellow peril of the Western world, ran high, although Japan had been the ally of Britain in World War I. The Versailles Peace Treaty* precluded the acceptance of the rising power of Asia, and although Gulick wrote five books and countless articles and tracts, he was unable to convince the church community or the wider public of Japan's merits. Oddly enough, he did not join the fight against the National Origins Act* of 1924 in the years after its passage; he seemed to be content to let time pass before attempting to gain a quota for the Japanese. But by the 1930s, as war clouds loomed on the horizon, Gulick mounted an ever increasing challenge to persuade the United States to change its policies toward Tōkyō. He knew that the Japanese would fight rather than be backed into a corner, and from his retirement home in Honolulu, he saw the bombs drop during the Pearl Harbor Attack*, marking the start of World War II for the United States. He relocated to his daughter's home in Idaho, where he died.

R. Daniels, *The Politics of Prejudice: The Anti-Japanese Movement in California, and the Struggle for Japanese Exclusion* (Berkeley, CA, 1968); R. Takaki, *Strangers from a Distant Shore: A History of Asian Americans* (Boston, 1990); S. C. Taylor, *Advocate of Understanding: Sidney Gulick and the Search for Peace with Japan* (Kent, OH, 1984).

Sandra C. Taylor

GUOMINDANG

In 1912, the Guomindang (GMD), known in English as the Chinese Nationalist Party, was formed in the context of the abortive efforts to create a democratic electoral system for the newly created Republic of

China* (ROC) after the Chinese Revolution of 1911*. It grew out of the Tongmenghui, or Revolutionary Alliance, which had been the main umbrella group for revolutionary activities against the Qing Dynasty in the decade after 1900. When Puyi*, the last Qing emperor, abdicated in February 1912, the Tongmenghui, in preparation for national assembly elections, joined forces with four minor political groups to form the Nationalist Party, with Song Jiaoren as chairman. Sun Zhongshan*, the Tongmenghui leader who briefly had been president of the new republic from January 1 to February 15, remained the real leader of the GMD, but did not run for office under its banner. But the initial efforts at electoral politics in China failed, as the assembly elected in the fall of 1912 was subverted by Yuan Shikai*, who had become president in a deal with the revolutionaries. Refusing to give real power to the GMD, which had won the majority of assembly seats, he drove the party from effective participation in government. Thereafter, the GMD remained marginal to political developments, as China dissolved into the Warlord Era*. But in the early 1920s, Sun, under the influence of the successful Russian Revolution and with the help of Bolshevik advisers, oversaw a reorganization of the party into a new, democratic centralist framework that became its permanent basic structure. At this time, the GMD also formed a United Front* with the new Chinese Communist Party* (CCP).

After Sun's death in 1925, the GMD went through an internal political struggle, with a left-wing faction eventually being defeated by the party's military leader Jiang Jieshi*. Jiang led the Northern Expedition after 1926, reuniting much of China under a single government for the first time since the fall of the Qing Dynasty. In April 1927, he split with the Communists and triggered the massacre of thousands of workers and CCP members in Shanghai. From 1927 until 1949, the GMD functioned as the ruling political party in China. Under Jiang's leadership, and with the help of his wife, Song Meiling*, the ROC developed strong ties within the United States. Through close connections with American missionary groups and positive media exposure in the publications owned by Jiang's friend and political admirer Henry R. Luce*, the GMD secured a positive image in American popular consciousness. Ironically, during the early 1930s, it also was building a close relationship with Germany, as Nazi military and economic advisers came to China to aid Jiang in his efforts to construct a strong authoritarian regime. As conflict with Japan deepened, however, especially following the Marco Polo Bridge Incident* in July 1937 and the full-scale Japanese invasion of China, Jiang's government distanced itself from Nazi Germany and emphasized the alliance with the United States. Then, after the Pearl Harbor Attack* in December 1941, the Jiang's Nationalist goverment formally became one of the major Allies in World War II. The United States poured large amounts of aid into the ROC's military, but much of it did not actually go for use against Japan and was hoarded by Jiang for eventual use against the Communists after the Japanese surrendered.

In 1945, the GMD and the CCP resumed fighting and, despite the efforts of the United States to create a coalition with the Marshall Mission*, the underlying conflict was simply too deep to be resolved other than through war. By October 1949, the GMD had lost the Chinese Civil War* and was forced to flee to Taiwan*. The way had been cleared for the mainlanders to dominate the island after the February 28 Incident of 1947*, when local resistance had been brutally suppressed. From 1949 to 1987, the GMD maintained itself as the government of the exiled ROC under a state of martial law. The United States provided a defense umbrella for Jiang's regime in the Korean War* with its Neutralization of Taiwan*, which placed its naval forces in the Taiwan Strait and has continued to provide protection for China's rump regime ever since. In 1972, the United States began to reconcile itself with the People's Republic of China* (PRC), resulting in U.S.-PRC Normalization of Relations* in 1979. But passage of the Taiwan Relations Act* maintained U.S. links to the GMD regime, particularly through ongoing military co-operation and arms sales. In 1987, the state of martial law finally was lifted, and the GMD began a new period of substantive electoral politics. In May 2000, its control over the ROC's central government ended when Dangwei* activist Chen Shuibian became the first opposition politician to be elected as president. The Nationalists remain, however, the largest and best-funded party, and their future role in Taiwan will no doubt be a powerful one. *See also* Jiang Nan Incident.

M. Bergere, *Sun Yatsen* (Stanford, CA, 1998); J. K. Fairbank, *The United States and China* (Cambridge, MA, 1983); T. B. Gold, *State and Society in the Taiwan Miracle* (Armonk, NY, 1990); I. C. Y. Hsu, *The Rise of Modern China* (New York, 2000).

Kenneth J. Hammond

GUOMINDANG INTERVENTION IN BURMA

The Chinese Guomindang* (Nationalist) Intervention in Burma is a little-understood and frequently overlooked aspect of U.S. and Nationalist attempts to destabilize the new People's Republic of China* (PRC) during the 1950s. Such efforts against the PRC included confrontations not only over Taiwan* and Korea, but also over Burma*, where the Central Intelligence Agency* (CIA) and the government of Jiang Jieshi* on Taiwan supplied arms to remnants of the Guomindang's army based there. Fleeing from the victorious People's Liberation Army in China, defeated Nationalist troops and deserters began to reach Burma in the summer of 1949. By early 1950, approximately 1,500 Guomindang troops had arrived. By April 1951,

troop strength had reached 4,000 soldiers. Reinforcements and supplies from Taiwan through Thailand* continued to arrive, and by 1952 there were as many as 30,000 soldiers. During the early 1950s, Nationalist forces repeatedly failed in attempts to seize Yunnan from its Burmese base. Meanwhile, Burma's leaders tried to remove these forces by military and diplomatic means. The Burmese initially worked through the United States to pressure the Republic of China*, but they gradually came to realize that Washington was supporting Guomindang efforts in Burma. As a result, the Burmese stopped taking U.S. economic aid in 1953, and turned to the United Nations for redress.

Initially, U.S. support for the intervention came from two camps. General Douglas MacArthur* and members of the China Lobby* advocated total war with the PRC, and the troops in Burma would provide the basis for another front. Moderates, such as President Harry S. Truman*, saw the troops as a defensive force hampering further Chinese Communist expansion into Southeast Asia. With the election in 1952 of Dwight D. Eisenhower*, the U.S. position changed, as the new president determined that Guomindang forces in Burma served no military purpose. However, with the expansion of Soviet and Vietminh* activities in the region and the ongoing civil war in Burma, some U.S. officials advocated supporting the troops as a countermeasure. Guomindang forces eventually withdrew, but the policy succeeded in destabilizing the fragile and newly independent Burmese state by heightening ethnic tensions and straining relations with neighboring countries while failing to secure a base of operations for a genuine military threat against the PRC on its southwest border.

Ministry of Information of Union of Burma, *Kuomintang Aggression Against Burma* (Rangoon, 1953); R. H. Taylor, *Foreign and Domestic Consequences of the KMT Intervention in Burma* (Ithaca, NY, 1973).

Karl Gerth

H

HAMAGUCHI YŪKŌ (1870–1931)

Hamaguchi Yūkō served as Japanese prime minister from 1929 to 1930. His public service, characterized by personal integrity and commitment to British-style parliamentary government, began in 1895 with an initially undistinguished career in the bureaucracy. After years of lackluster assignments at Finance Ministry outposts, Hamaguchi was promoted to head the Customs Office in 1902, serving thereafter in various government capacities. In 1915, he was elected to the Diet, where he became a founding member of the Kenseikai party the following year. In the 1920s, he twice served as finance minister, in which capacity he promoted government retrenchment and a balanced budget. Hamaguchi emerged from the party realignment of 1927 as inaugural president of the Rikken Minseitō, opposite the Seiyūkai under Tanaka Giichi*. In July 1929, he replaced Tanaka as prime minister amid a scandal spawned by the bombing death the prior year of Zhang Zuolin*, a Manchurian warlord.

Hamaguchi's tenure, the apogee of prewar Japan's parliamentary politics, was most notable for the deflationary policy of Finance Minister Inoue Junnosuke and the pro-Western diplomacy of Foreign Minis-

ter Shidehara Kijūrō*. In January 1930, he returned Japan to the gold standard. The lifting of the ban on overseas gold transfer, fiscal austerity, and the buffeting effects of the Great Depression combined to cause widespread unemployment, massive bankruptcies among small businesses, and an agricultural price depression. Blighted rural villages provided a breeding ground for the right-wing fanaticism and militarism that took Hamaguchi's life and pushed the nation into overseas adventurism in the 1930s.

Hamaguchi's greatest diplomatic triumph came in 1930 with the signing and ratification of the London Naval Treaty on cruisers and other auxiliary ships that had been left unrestricted by the 1922 Five Power Pact*. At the London Naval Conference of 1930*, Japan initially demanded a 10–10–7 ratio against the United States and Great Britain, but settled for a 10–10–6 ratio in heavy cruisers, with the possibility of future Japanese increases and equality in submarines. The Japanese Navy claimed that these limitations severely hampered its ability to meet a U.S. challenge in the western Pacific. The military and its supporters created a constitutional furor, arguing that the cabinet's action violated the doctrine of "command prerogative," or the right of the divine emperor and the military to determine the nation's defense needs. Hamaguchi overruled the opposition in the interest of cooperation with the West and fiscal responsibility. On 30 November 1930, he was shot by an ultranationalist, resigning the following April four months before dying from his wound.

Asada Sadao, *Ryotaisenkan no nichibei kankei* [U.S.-Japanese Relations in the Interwar Period] (Tōkyō, 1993); M. A. Barnhart, *Japan Prepares for Total War: The Search for Economic Security, 1919–1941* (Ithaca, NY, 1987); Ikei Masaru, et al. (eds.), *Hamaguchi Osachi nikki zuikanroku* [Hamaguchi Osachi Diaries and Essays] (Tōkyō, 1991); Sekine Minoru, *Hamaguchi Osachi den* [A Biography of Hamaguchi] (Tōkyō, 1931).

Shimizu Sayuri

HANOI CONVENTION (22 September 1940)

The Hanoi Convention, also known as the Nishihara-Martin Agreement, was an accord that permitted the Japanese to base military forces in French Indochina* in September 1940. In the weeks after France's surrender to Nazi Germany in June 1940, the Japanese government pressed authorities in Indochina to block the transit of war materials to China and to permit the establishment of Japanese military bases in the colony. After General Georges Catroux, the French governor-general, as well as his successor Admiral Jean Decoux, agreed to stop the shipment of war materials to China, Tōkyō sent a military mission headed by General Nishihara Issaku to Hanoi to monitor this embargo and to negotiate arrangements for the basing of Japanese air and ground units in northern Indochina. The talks, however, became deadlocked over the issue of French sovereignty in Indochina. The issues they addressed were taken up in Tōkyō on 1 August in negotiations between Foreign Minister Matsuoka Yōsuke* and Ambassador Charles Arsene-Henry. Meanwhile, the Vichy government asked for American and British promises of military support in resisting the Japanese demands. Although U.S. and British diplomats in Tōkyō raised strong objections to the basing of Japanese forces in Indochina, neither Washington nor London promised military aid to the French.

Negotiations in Tōkyō ended on 30 August when Matsuoka and Arsene-Henry exchanged letters that agreed to an acceleration of trade between Indochina and Japan, Japanese recognition of French sovereignty in Indochina and the territorial integrity of the colony, and the resumption of talks between Nishihara and French military authorities about the basing and transit of Japanese forces in Indochina. Negotiations between Nishihara and the French began on 3 September, resulting in the signing of an agreement on 22 September with General Maurice-Pierre Martin, the commander of French forces in Indochina. In the Hanoi Convention, the Japanese and the French agreed to Japanese use of four airfields in northern Indochina, the deployment of 6,000 Japanese troops to Indochina to garrison these bases, and further talks concerning the transit of 25,000 Japanese troops through Indochina to China. But the signing of the agreement did not prevent the outbreak of fighting between Japanese and French troops on the Chinese border on 23 September. However, the Japanese garrison force landed without resistance in Haiphong on 26 September. In response, the Roosevelt administration announced that it was granting a loan to the Chinese government and imposing an embargo on the sale of scrap iron to Japan. This was one of the first of the economic sanctions that the Roosevelt administration applied steadily against Japan in the months before the Pearl Harbor Attack*.

R. J. C. Butow, *Tojo and the Coming of the War* (Princeton, NJ, 1961); I. Hata, "The Army's Move into Northern Indochina," in James W. Morley (ed.), *The Fateful Choice: Japan's Advance into Southeast Asia, 1939–1941* (New York, 1980); W. L. Langer and S. E. Gleason, *The Undeclared War, 1940–1941* (New York, 1953); J. G. Utley,

Going to War with Japan, 1937–1941 (Knoxville, TN, 1985).

Joseph G. Morgan

HARA KEI (1856–1921)

Hara Kei, also known as Hara Takashi or Hara Satoshi, was the most influential party politician in Japan's Taishō period. He played an important role in formulating Japanese foreign policy toward Asia and the United States during and immediately after World War I. Born into a samurai family that remained loyal to the Tokugawa shōgunate, Hara started his political career after the Meiji Restoration as an outsider in the new government. After working as a newspaper reporter for three years, he began working in the Ministry of Foreign Affairs in 1882, exploiting political connections to climb quickly from the position of consul general in Tianjin, to first secretary in the embassy in Paris, to vice minister of foreign affairs in 1895. Hara served as ambassador to Korea in 1896, but he resigned the following year to become president and editor-in-chief of the newspaper *Ōsaka Mainichi*.

In 1900, Hara joined the Seiyūkai, the political party of Itō Hirobumi*, with the ultimate goal of establishing it as a permanent institution within the constitutional order. Holding a seat in the lower house of the Diet from 1902 until his death, he increased his party's power by penetrating the government bureaucracy while serving as home minister (1906–1908, 1911–1912, 1913–1914) and thus controlling the entire network of local government. In 1914, Hara became the president of the Seiyūkai. After Terauchi Masatake's cabinet resigned in the wake of the rice riots of 1918, Hara formed the first party cabinet, in which the head of the majority party in the lower house of the Diet became premier. However, despite his nickname as the "commoner" premier, Hara preferred gradual changes and stayed with cautious conservative reforms, supporting neither universal manhood suffrage nor labor union movements.

Hara always subordinated his foreign policy aspirations to domestic political needs. Although he personally believed cooperation with the Anglo-Saxon powers, especially the United States, was essential to the survival of Japan, he was fully aware of the importance of Japan's interests on the Asian continent in the context of domestic politics. For political expediency, he generally supported assertive policies to expand Japan's interests in Korea and China, so long as they would not antagonize the United States to the extent of irreparably damaging bilateral relations. As a member of the Advisory Council on Foreign Relations during and immediately after World War I, Hara supported the Terauchi cabinet's diplomatic efforts to make the United States recognize Japan's special interests in China through the Lansing-Ishii Agreement* of 1917. He opposed Japan's large-scale Siberian Intervention* in 1918 because of U.S. opposition to it, but once he was premier and after the expedition had begun, he worried more about the domestic repercussions of a hasty withdrawal from Siberia in compliance with American wishes.

Japanese actions at the Versailles Peace Conference confirmed the Hara cabinet's willingness to cooperate with the Anglo-Saxon powers on the issues that would not impair Japan's national interests. However, Hara stood firmly behind Japanese claims to German rights and concessions in Shandong, and did not hesitate to challenge President Woodrow Wilson*, who favored China's self-determination. Ever sensitive to the changing international environment, Premier Hara realized after Versailles that in deference to U.S. wishes, some sort of naval limitation was unavoidable. He made a crucial decision to send Admiral Katō Tomosaburō to the Washington Conference* because he would most likely be able to persuade the navy to accept any concessions Japan might be forced to make there. Reflecting the rise of militant nationalism in postwar Japan, Hara did not live to see the outcome of the Washington Conference. He was assassinated by a young ultranationalist in Tōkyō Station on 4 November 1921, just six days before the opening of the conference. *See also* Versailles Peace Treaty.

R. V. Dingman, *Power in the Pacific: The Origins of Naval Arms Limitation, 1914–1922* (Chicago, 1976); P. Duus, *Party Rivalry and Political Change in Taisho Japan* (Cambridge, MA, 1968); T. Najita, *Hara Kei in the Politics of Compromise, 1905–1915* (Cambridge, MA, 1967).

Kawamura Noriko

HARRIMAN, E. H. (1848–1909)

Edward H. Harriman was a railroad magnate who controlled a large part of American shipping in the Pacific. By the start of the twentieth century, when the United States emerged as a global power, his business interests had expanded proportionately. In 1905, Harriman visited Japan when the country was at war with Russia for control of Manchuria. Taking advantage of the Japanese desire to involve the United States in the Russo-Japanese War*, he made an arrangement with them to buy a controlling share in the South Manchuria Railway. From there, he developed a grand plan that was to leave a powerful mark on American diplomacy toward East Asia. While in Japan, Harriman explained his plan to the American minister:

There's no doubt about it. If I can secure control of the South Manchuria Railroad from Japan, I'll buy the Chinese Eastern from Russia, acquire trackage over the Trans-Siberian to the Baltic, and establish a line of steamers to the United States. Then I can connect with the American transcontinental lines, and join up with the Pacific Mail and the Japanese transpacific steamers. It'll be the most marvelous transportation system in the world. We'll girdle the earth.

This plan met its first frustration in September 1905 when Japan concluded the Treaty of Portsmouth* with Russia that gave Japan a free hand in southern Manchuria. Japan, therefore, decided to back out of the arrangement with Harriman, which it never signed, and exploited the interest in the South Manchuria Railway itself. As a private merchant, Harriman could do nothing about it and reluctantly abandoned his dream.

But American officials committed to curtailing the Japanese expansion in that region kept Harriman's vision alive. Willard D. Straight*, the U.S. consul in Manchuria, devised a plan to build a new railroad in southern Manchuria to compete with Japan's South Manchuria Railway. He presented this plan to Harriman and stressed the profitability of the opportunity. But the financial panic of 1907 in the United States drained available capital, and Harriman did not act on Straight's plan. In July 1907, Japan and Russia signed an agreement recognizing each other's sphere of influence in that region. When the financial panic ended, Harriman again renewed his interest. In 1908, at Harriman's request, Straight was recalled to Washington, where he became chief of the Division of Far Eastern Affairs. Harriman now worked with the State Department under Straight's coordination, devising new plans to direct Wall Street resources to China. President Theodore Roosevelt* showed little interest, but in 1909, William Howard Taft* became president and Dollar Diplomacy* began to drive U.S. foreign policy in East Asia. Finally gaining official support, Harriman resumed his effort to gain a foot in the Manchuria railway business. He attempted to persuade the Russians to sell to him the Chinese Eastern Railway so that he could expand the line southward, threatening Japan with competition. His ultimate goal was to force Japan to give up the South Manchuria Railway. However, Harriman's ambitious plan failed one more time—this time for good—with his sudden death in September.

A. DeConde, *A History of American Foreign Policy* (New York, 1978); W. I. Cohen, *America's Re-*

sponse to China: An Interpretation of Sino-American Relations (New York, 1980).

Li Yi

HARRIMAN, W. AVERELL (1891–1986)

W. Averell Harriman, son of railroad tycoon E. H. Harriman*, was among the founders of what came to be termed the foreign policy "Establishment" and was a leading architect of the Cold War. Under Presidents Franklin D. Roosevelt* and Harry S. Truman*, he served as special envoy to British Prime Minister Winston Churchill and Soviet Premier Joseph Stalin from 1941 to 1943; U.S. ambassador to Moscow, 1943 to 1946; U.S. ambassador to Britain in 1946; secretary of commerce from 1946 to 1948; U.S. special representative in Europe for the Economic Cooperation Administration, 1948 to 1950; special assistant to the president from 1950 to 1951; and head of the Mutual Security Administration from 1951 to 1953. Harriman's greatest effect on East Asian policy came during the Kennedy and Johnson administrations, when he was successively ambassador-at-large (1960–1961); assistant secretary of state for Far Eastern Affairs (1962–1963); undersecretary of state for political affairs (1963–1964); and ambassador-at-large (1965–1969).

As early as January 1946, Harriman was disturbed by the weakness of Jiang Jieshi* and his Guomindang* (Nationalist) government. He concluded that the United States was mistaken in trying to mediate a settlement between the Nationalists and the Chinese Communist Party*. In early August 1950, shortly after the Korean War* began, Harriman was despatched to see General Douglas MacArthur*, commander of the UN troops. Briefed by MacArthur on the forthcoming Inch'ŏn Landing* operation, whose approval he successfully recommended, Harriman also warned the latter that he should not sanction or endorse any effort by Jiang to instigate a war with the new People's Republic of China*. Two weeks later, MacArthur tried to ig-

nore this advice in a speech he planned—but was forbidden—to deliver, and in April 1951, he publicly called for using Nationalist troops in the Korean War. This final incident contributed to MacArthur's Recall* by Truman, a move Harriman recommended and applauded.

Harriman attempted to broker a settlement between warring factions in the Laotian Crisis of 1961*, which would have effectively neutralized Laos* and prevented passage through it to the Republic of Vietnam* of Viet Cong* guerrillas and supplies. After protracted negotiations involving the Soviet Union, the United States, and the three warring Laotian factions, the Geneva Accords of 1962* were reached. In practice, this understanding rarely was honored by the Communist Pathet Lao* and their Viet Cong allies. The Geneva meeting also saw an unsuccessful attempt by Harriman to begin exploiting the Sino-Soviet dispute and explore the possibility of closer relations with China by meeting with the Chinese foreign minister, and including China in the inner group of four other major powers at these talks. Both then and later in the 1960s, the Department of State rejected Harriman's suggestions.

In later years, Harriman's claims that he always had opposed U.S. intervention in the Second Indochina War* were an exaggeration. In 1954, he recommended the commitment of U.S. troops to French Indochina* to forestall the fall of Dien Bien Phu* and the region's possible loss to Communism*. Later, though, he was to become the most senior leader of Vietnam doves, favoring reforms in Vietnam and a negotiated settlement with the Viet Cong. As the United States military commitment to Vietnam grew in the early 1960s, Harriman visited Vietnam and warned that the government of President Ngo Dinh Diem* was corrupt and unstable. In late August 1963, over a weekend when most government officials were not in Washington, the undersecretary, working with Roger Hilsman*, his successor as assistant secretary of state for Far Eastern Affairs, and National Security Council staffer Michael V. Forrestal, drafted and dispatched a cable to Henry Cabot Lodge Jr.*, the new U.S. ambassador in Saigon, which implicitly authorized American support for a coup that resulted in Diem's Assassination*. Although this cable provoked bitter recriminations within the State and Defense Departments and Central Intelligence Agency*, whose secretaries and director had not seen the cable before its dispatch, it never was revoked.

Under Lyndon B. Johnson*, Harriman vigorously defended the administration's Vietnam policy in public while privately continually urging a bombing halt and the opening of negotiations with the Democratic Republic of Vietnam*. He was excluded from operational meetings about Vietnam and the Tuesday White House discussion luncheons of top policy makers. Harriman was generally restrained in expressing his criticisms directly to Johnson, an omission that distressed many of those closest to him, who ascribed his reticence to the fear of losing office. Even so, at a meeting of the president's most senior advisers, or "Wise Men," in November 1967, he dissented from the consensus reinforcing the policy on bombing, and called for the opening of negotiations. After the Tet Offensive* and the consequent reassessment of U.S. policy goals in Vietnam, Johnson appointed Harriman as his representative at the Paris Peace Talks*. Several months of lengthy discussions, both open and secret, finally succeeded in establishing procedural guidelines for the negotiations, at which the Soviet Union, the United States, North Vietnam, the Viet Cong, and South Vietnam were to be represented. At this stage, Richard M. Nixon* became president and Harriman returned to Washington, having completed his last formal government assignment.

R. Abramson, *Spanning the Century: The Life of W. Averell Harriman 1891–1986* (New York, 1992); D. Halberstam, *The Best and the Brightest* (New York, 1972); W. Isaacson and E. Thomas, *The Wise Men: Six Friends and the World They Made* (New York, 1983).

Priscilla Roberts

HARRIS, TOWNSEND (1804–1878)

After the momentous opening of Japan by Commodore Matthew C. Perry* two years earlier, diplomat Townsend Harris arrived in Japan as consul at Shimoda on 21 August 1856. A native of New York, Harris was a businessman who had turned to the shipping trade. He had no previous diplomatic experience, having been rejected for selection as consul in China and left off the Perry Mission*, but managed to convince President Franklin Pierce to offer him an appointment in Japan. On the way, he stopped off in Siam (Thailand*) and there negotiated a significant trade agreement. Armed with this experience, his sole mission in Japan was to negotiate a commercial treaty that would allow extensive foreign trade inside the previously closed island nation. Lacking the naval power that had so awed the Japanese during Perry's arrivals at Edo Bay, Harris was virtually on his own and had to rely on his skill at persuasion and manipulation. Shimoda was one of the ports opened to the Americans under the Treaty of Kanagawa*; it was here that Harris first arrived to find no housing available for him. Harris and his translator, the Dutch-American Henry Heusken, were forced to reside in a ramshackle temple miles from the town. They languished at Shimoda for months, awaiting permission to proceed to Edo. In the meantime, Heusken procured mistresses for himself and Harris, two young women forced by the governor of Shimoda to make the arrangement on patriotic grounds.

Harris did manage to make headway in spite of his isolation. By June 1857, he had negotiated the opening of Nagasaki to American ships, received permission for the establishment of a vice consulate at Hakodate, and secured greater freedom of movement around Japan. Yet he still had not obtained a commercial treaty. Finally, Harris traveled to Edo with a huge caravan of 250 retainers and in November arrived at the shōgun's court. After extremely slow negotiations caused by internal divisions in Japan's government, Harris and the shōgun's ministers concluded a commercial treaty on 29 July 1858. He transmitted to President James Buchanan the Harris Treaty* and the first official letter from a shōgun to a foreign ruler since Japan became secluded. On 19 January 1859, Harris was appointed minister-resident in Japan and opened a U.S. legation in Edo, presenting his credentials to the Japanese government in November of that year. On 13 February 1860, a delegation of seventy-seven Japanese officials left for the United States aboard an American vessel. Poet Walt Whitman was present for the arrival of the group in New York City on 16 June and penned "The Errand Bearers" in tribute. The U.S. Senate ratified the treaty on 22 May 1860.

The presence of foreigners in the port cities and the apparent humiliation at opening to foreigners generated a reaction against the foreign incursion, including the assassination of Ii Naosuke*, the shōgun's chief minister, and any Westerner foolish enough to venture out after dark or unescorted. Seven foreigners were killed over the next eighteen months, including, in January 1861, Heusken, for which Harris accepted an indemnity of $10,000 on behalf of Heusken's mother. Later, an armed attack on the British legation caused most of the foreign representatives to flee to the comparative safety of Yokohama, except for Harris, who still retained hope that Japan could be the one place where encroachment of the West did not bring about pillage and bloodshed. He did manage to persuade Secretary of State William H. Seward* against organizing a naval demonstration in Japanese waters. Despite a request from Japan's government that he be allowed to remain, Harris departed the country after being recalled on 26 April 1862. Successive American ministers thereafter never held comparable influence or prominence. Harris died in New York City and his exploits were immortalized in the 1958 Hollywood film *The Barbarian and the Geisha*.

M. E. Cosenza (ed.), *The Complete Journal of Townsend Harris: First American Consul General and Minister to Japan* (New York, 1930); H. H. Gowen, *Five Foreigners in Japan* (New York, 1936); E. Hahn, "A Yankee Barbarian at the Shogun's Court," *American Heritage* (June 1964); W. LaFeber, *The Clash: A History of U.S.-Japan Relations* (New York, 1997); C. Neu, *The Troubled Encounter: The United States and Japan* (New York, 1975).

Kent G. Sieg

HARRIS TREATY (29 July 1858)

The Treaty of Amity and Commerce negotiated by Townsend Harris* went beyond the Treaty of Kanagawa* and established full diplomatic and trade relations between the United States and Japan. In 1854, Matthew C. Perry* pressured Japan into signing a "wood and water" arrangement that also allowed the stationing of a U.S. consul at Shimoda. Harris's arrival at Shimoda in August 1856 as the first American consul general to Japan led to the completion of Perry's dream of fully opening Japan to American commerce and influence. Without naval support, Harris achieved his historic breakthrough mainly through patient and skillful diplomacy. In instructions dated 13 September and 4 October 1855, Secretary of State William L. Marcy directed Harris to secure three major aims: diplomatic representation, the freedom to trade at some ports in Japan, and the unambiguous right of Americans to reside at Hakodate and Shimoda. Because of the hostility of the Japanese to Christianity, Marcy did not expect Harris to acquire any religious concessions. Harris was authorized to threaten use of force if he could not secure privileges greater than those in the 1854 treaty.

With the Japanese government deeply

divided over whether to open its country to foreign trade and residence, Harris adopted a successful strategy of first seeking agreement on lesser issues. The Convention of Shimoda, signed on 17 June 1857, did not grant any trade privileges, but it added Nagasaki as a place where U.S. vessels could obtain coal and other supplies, allowed the appointment of a vice consul there, granted Americans permanent residence at Hakodate and Shimoda, stipulated that the U.S. consul general would try Americans accused of committing crimes in Japan, and gave that official the right to travel freely throughout Japan. Accordingly, on 7 December 1857, Harris became the first foreigner to be received by the shōgun at Edo in a diplomatic capacity. After his reception by Tokugawa Iesada, Harris initiated negotiations for a comprehensive treaty of friendship and commerce. He overcame the reluctance of his interlocutors to abandon Japan's policy of exclusion by pointing to the First Opium War* and the ongoing Second Opium War* as lessons in statecraft. Harris explained that if Japan hoped to avoid China's fate, it should come to terms with a benign nation such as the United States. On 29 July 1858, aboard the USS *Powhatan*, Japan signed its first major international agreement with a Western power.

The Japanese-American Treaty of Amity and Commerce fully opened Japan to diplomatic and economic relations with the United States. Incorporating the Convention of Shimoda, it established formal diplomatic ties between the two countries, with the U.S. minister to reside in Edo. Six ports were made available to American trade and residence, and, after a delay of a few years, Americans would be allowed to reside and carry on business in Edo and Ōsaka. Americans could lease or purchase homes and warehouses in all of these places. At three harbors, Kanagawa, Hakodate, and Nagasaki, the U.S. Navy could establish depots, with all supplies to be landed and stored duty-free. Americans accused of committing offenses against the Japanese were to be tried in American consular courts and punished according to U.S. law, and Japanese committing offenses against Americans would be judged and punished according to Japanese law. In addition to prohibiting importation of opium into Japan, the treaty authorized the Japanese to seize and destroy any opium brought to their country in an American ship. Americans were granted complete freedom to practice their religion and the right to build churches in Japan, and the Japanese would not offer any insults to American religious practices. To produce a favorable impression, Harris inserted a stipulation that upon the request of Japan's government, the president of the United States would act as a mediator in disputes between the Japanese and European nations. At the request of the Japanese, he also agreed that the Japanese would be permitted to purchase ships and "munitions of war" in the United States. Finally, the treaty established a fixed schedule for tariffs and tonnage duties.

The Harris Treaty provided the model for subsequent treaties negotiated in 1858 with the Netherlands, Russia, Great Britain, and France. From an American perspective, it was a highly favorable agreement. It led to a rapidly growing trade between the two nations and to the arrival of American businessmen and missionaries in Japan. Moreover, it formed the basis of Japanese-American relations until it was superseded by the American-Japanese Treaty of 1894*. Harris himself was most proud of having attained freedom of religion for Americans and the right to build suitable places of worship in Japan. A devout Episcopalian, he refused during his years in Japan to engage in business, to travel, or even to receive a gift from the shōgun on the Sabbath. From a Japanese perspective, the outcomes were more complicated. Although the Japanese gained access to American culture and technology, the unequal and extraterritorial provisions of the Harris Treaty, along with the growing presence of foreign trade and traders, disrupted the society and economy of a country that had sealed itself from outside influences since 1638. It contributed to a strong antiforeign movement, and ultimately the disruptive Western presence the treaty triggered helped to precipitate the Meiji Restoration of 1868, which ended the Tokugawa shōgunate.

M. E. Cosenza (ed.), *The Complete Journals of Townsend Harris: First American Consul General and Minister to Japan* (New York, 1930); M. E. Cosenza (ed.), *Some Unpublished Letters of Townsend Harris: First American Consul General and Minister to Japan* (New York, 1930); W. LaFeber, *The Clash: A History of U.S.-Japan Relations* (New York, 1997); H. Miller (ed.), *Treaties and Other International Acts of the United States of America,* vol. 7 (Washington, DC, 1942); S. Shio (ed.), *Some Unpublished Letters of Townsend Harris* (New York, 1941).

Kenneth E. Shewmaker

HATOYAMA ICHIRŌ (1883–1959)

As Japan's prime minister from December 1954 to December 1956, Hatoyama Ichirō implemented a more independent foreign policy that was less dependent on and subservient to the United States. Achieving a symbolic and practical break from the approach of his predecessor Yoshida Shigeru*, he sought to distance Japan from Washington through undertaking diplomatic negotiations with the Soviet Union and efforts to foster closer economic relations with the People's Republic of China* (PRC). By contrast with Yoshida's preference for independent decision making and relative disdain for public opinion, Hatoyama's style was much more self-consciously populist and focused on consensual, collective decision making. A lawyer by training, he was first elected to the Japanese Diet in 1915. Hatoyama acquired his political experience as a professional and successful parliamentarian, serving as secretary general of the Seiyūkai Party and, from 1931 to 1934, as minister of education. In April 1946, he was elected

president of the Liberal Party (Jiyūtō), the main conservative political party in early postwar Japan. His prewar political career and associations ensured that he was purged by the Supreme Commander for the Allied Powers (SCAP)*, and he retreated from political life until depurged in June 1951. Hatoyama and Yoshida apparently had agreed that Yoshida should assume leadership of the Liberal Party temporarily, on the assumption that Hatoyama could reclaim the position when he returned to active political life. But Yoshida's refusal to honor this understanding prompted a split in the Liberal Party, ultimately leading to the creation, under Hatoyama's leadership, of the rival Democratic Party (Minshutō).

During the U.S. Occupation of Japan*, the bitter personal rivalry between Yoshida and Hatoyama often undermined U.S. efforts to promote conservative policy initiatives favorable to American interests, including active security cooperation with the United States and rearmament. As prime minister, however, Hatoyama's main achievement was to preside over a critical conservative political consolidation that created a foundation for the long-term dominance of Japanese politics by the Liberal Democratic Party* (LDP), which would control the government from 1955 to 1993. But formal unity following the merger of the Jiyūtō and Minshutō initially was undercut by differences over who should head the new party. With the Liberals lobbying for Ogata Taketora and former Democrats backing Hatoyama as leader, agreement was reached only through a compromise allowing Hatoyama to assume the leadership for a provisional six-month period. Ogata's unexpected death in January 1956 allowed for Hatoyama's confirmation as the first official head of the LDP in April, but this did not translate into decisive political authority for him personally. Much of the impetus for conservative unity had come from other leading Democratic politicians, most notably Kishi Nobusuke* and Miki Bukichi. Moreover, once party unity had been achieved, the leaders shifted their focus to the question of leadership succession. Hatoyama had suffered a stroke in 1951 that had left him paralyzed on one side of his body. As late as 1956, he reportedly was receiving electric shock therapy for his condition.

Hatoyama's principal goals as prime minister were revision of the Japanese Constitution of 1947*, the rehabilitation and expansion of Japan's defense forces, and the conclusion of a peace treaty with the Soviet Union. He quickly faced determined opposition from the Japan Socialist Party (JSP), which fiercely resisted his attempts to rewrite the constitution. To bolster conservative political forces, Hatoyama promoted Diet legislation in March 1956 to replace the existing medium-size, multi-member constituency system with a small, single-member electoral system. Such a reform, he anticipated, would undercut opposition party support and allow the LDP to capture more than two-thirds of the seats in both houses of Japan's legislature—a necessary precondition for constitutional revision. Failure to pass this legislation in the face of fierce JSP resistance ultimately scuttled Hatoyama's constitutional reform initiative. Thereafter, Hatoyama concentrated on promoting policy proposals more commonly associated with the JSP, including social security, the development of public housing, and a commitment to full employment. These progressive initiatives, coupled with his public commitment to parliamentary democracy, ensured that the prime minister remained personally popular in Japan, but largely ineffectual politically. In fact, it was Socialist support that allowed Hatoyama, despite factional discord within the LDP, to achieve his other major policy goal of signing a treaty normalizing relations with the Soviet Union in October 1956. In December, he stepped down voluntarily as leader and Ishibashi Tanzan* replaced him as prime minister.

K. E. Calder, *Crisis and Compensation: Public Policy and Political Stability in Japan, 1949–1986*

(Princeton, NJ, 1988); Watanabe Akio (ed.), *Sengo Nihon no saishō tachi* [Japan's Postwar Prime Ministers] (Tōkyō, 1995).

John Swenson-Wright

HATTA, MOHAMMED (1902–1980)

Mohammed Hatta, along with his rival and sometimes colleague Sukarno*, led the independence movement in Indonesia* against the Netherlands before and after World War II. His commitment to a decentralized Indonesian state and a democratic, participatory government provoked frequent clashes with Sukarno and led eventually to his resignation from the government that he had helped to create. Born in West Sumatra, Hatta internalized the progressive values of his Minangkabau ethnic group, which emphasized egalitarianism and village democracy. These values decisively shaped his later views on independence and the form of government that he thought Indonesia should have. A studious, serious young man, Hatta excelled academically and gained access to Dutch colonial schools, where he was trained as an economist. He was both a devout Muslim and a modern thinker fascinated by the economic ideas of Karl Marx and his concern for social justice. Unlike many conservative Sumatran Muslims, Hatta was convinced that Islam and socialism were entirely compatible.

Hatta traveled to the Netherlands in 1921 to attend school and immediately became involved in nationalist student organizations. Inspired by the example of India, he advocated noncooperation with the Dutch and the formation of alternative Indonesian-led institutions that could become a "state within a state." Lacking both charisma or oratorical skills, Hatta concentrated on writing fiery nationalist tracts that condemned Dutch Colonialism* and challenged young Indonesians to devote themselves totally to the cause of independence. Upon returning to Indonesia in 1927, Dutch colonial authorities rightly viewed Hatta as a dangerous radical. They arrested him and three other leaders of the Partai Indonesia (PI) for incitement to rebellion, but they soon were acquitted and released. Disillusioned with the political direction of the PI (which Sukarno had joined), he founded the New Indonesian National Party, which emerged as the PI's main rival for leadership of the nationalist movement. He was arrested again in 1934 and exiled, first to a penal settlement in malaria-infested West New Guinea, and later to the island of Banda, but continued to organize for the nationalist cause. Colonial officials finally released him in February 1942.

During the Pacific war, both Hatta and Sukarno accommodated Japanese occupation authorities. As prominent nationalist leaders, they were granted a degree of autonomy, which they used to continue agitating for independence. They became known as the Dwi Tunngal (two in one), a formulation that stressed the unique skills each brought to the nationalist struggle. During the months before Japan's surrender, they formed a planning committee that prepared a draft constitution and proposed a presidential system of government, rather than a parliamentary system, as Hatta had urged. On 17 August 1945, under mounting pressure from radical Javanese youth, Sukarno and Hatta declared Indonesian independence. Hatta was Indonesia's first vice president, playing an increasingly important administrative and leadership role during the struggle over the next four years against Dutch attempts at reconquest. In 1949, Hatta again was imprisoned with Sukarno. Released under world pressure, he then headed the Indonesian delegation at The Hague that negotiated the settlement in December granting sovereignty to the Republic of Indonesia.

Hatta continued to serve as vice president until 1956, as well as prime minister from 1948 to 1950, but his status was largely symbolic. He found himself increasingly marginalized, having sharply diverged from Sukarno in advocating a decentralized state and opposing inclusion of the Indonesian Communist Party in the cabinet. Unable to reconcile himself with Sukarno's emerging vision of "Guided Democracy," Hatta finally resigned in December 1956. Thereafter, simmering regional discontent with the concentration of wealth and power in Java ignited a U.S.-supported regional rebellion and civil war. Hatta attempted to maneuver himself back into power, but by early 1958, Sukarno and Army Chief of Staff Abdul Haris Nasution* decided on a military campaign to crush the rebels. Hatta largely withdrew from active politics in the wake of the PRRI-Permesta Rebellion*, concentrating his energies on expanding the cooperative movement in Indonesia. His vision of a democratic Indonesian polity evaporated in 1965 when General Suharto* established his authoritarian regime.

M. Hatta, *Portrait of a Patriot: Selected Writings* (Jakarta, 1973); A. Kahin, *Rebellion to Integration: West Sumatra and the Indonesian Polity* (Amsterdam, 1999); G. McT. Kahin, *Nationalism and Revolution in Indonesia* (Ithaca, NY, 1952); M. Rose, *Indonesia Free: A Political Biography of Mohammed Hatta* (Ithaca, NY, 1987).

Bradley R. Simpson

HAWAIIAN ANNEXATION

Annexation of Hawaii in July 1898 concluded a long process of attaching the island nation to the United States. Early in the nineteenth century, the Hawaiian Islands had become an object of interest to American expansionists who saw their nation's "Manifest Destiny" as one of building a nation that extended to the Pacific coast and beyond. Beginning in the 1790s, American merchant ships and whaling vessels from New England ports began making frequent stops in the islands to trade and take on supplies. In the 1820s, American Congregationalist missionaries arrived to spread the gospel and instruct the native population in democratic political principles; by midcentury, the children of these missionaries had acquired much of Hawaii's wealth and political power. In 1842, President John Tyler declared a special relationship with Hawaii, warning that the United States would tolerate no foreign threat to the kingdom's independence. In 1849, the United States formally recognized the Hawaiian Kingdom and established closer ties through a treaty of friendship. In 1853, the Hawaiian monarch Kamehameha III, fearful of internal and external threats, negotiated a treaty of annexation with the United States, but his successor disavowed this document the next year.

After the American Civil War ended in 1865, American business interests, particularly in sugar plantations, grew and a reciprocity treaty in 1875 closely tied the Hawaiian economy to that of the United States. In 1887, this treaty was renewed, with a provision granting the United States the exclusive right to build a naval base at Pearl Harbor. The McKinley Tariff of 1890 ended the advantages Hawaiian sugar growers had enjoyed in the American market and led to a depression, but this did not weaken Hawaii's close ties to the United States. In fact, by then, expansionist American political leaders viewed Hawaii as essential to national security and the advancement of American trade with the nations of East Asia. White planters on the islands, who held strong ties to the United States, agreed, and their desire for annexation led to the Hawaiian Revolution* in 1893. A new provisional government, under the leadership of Sanford B. Dole*, dispatched a delegation to Washington in pursuit of annexation. Secretary of State John W. Foster* negotiated with the Hawaiians a hastily drafted treaty, but his desperate last-minute effort failed to secure Senate ratification. Many Americans and their elected leaders still believed that the United States should not abandon its tradition of anticolonialism, and incoming President Grover Cleveland held serious concerns about U.S. involvement in the ousting of Queen Lili'uokalani*.

After his inauguration, Cleveland withdrew the annexation treaty from the Senate and sent former Congressman James H. Blount* as special commissioner with "paramount" power to investigate the political situation in Hawaii. In April, upon his arrival in Honolulu, Blount had the U.S. flag removed from Hawaii's public buildings. He also interviewed some members of Dole's group (but not Dole, who refused to see Blount), met with the queen's loyalists, and issued a report concluding that the revolutionaries had acted only after receiving assurances of U.S. support from U.S. Minister John L. Stevens*. Furthermore, Blount's report claimed that recognition of the provisional government was improper, arguing that most of the islands' people remained loyal to the queen. Accepting Blount's conclusions, Cleveland expressed his desire to see Lili'uokalani returned to her throne. He appointed Albert S. Willis, a former Kentucky congressman, as minister to Hawaii with instructions to persuade Dole to restore the queen and Lili'uokalani to grant amnesty to the revolutionists. When asked in December 1893 to relinquish his office, Dole refused, sensing correctly that the Cleveland administration would not use force to restore the disposed monarch. On 4 July 1894, the Republic of Hawaii was declared, with Dole as president.

Dole and his allies in Washington were frustrated by the failure of annexation efforts in 1893, but they did not give up. By 1897, influential proponents of Hawaiian annexation included the newly elected Republican President William McKinley* and young expansionist Republican leaders such as Senator Henry Cabot Lodge* and Undersecretary of the Navy Theodore Roosevelt*. Still, opposition to annexation remained strong. In 1898, despite a visit to Washington by Dole, the anti-annexationists among Democrats, Populists, anti-imperialist intellectuals, and religious leaders, and western and southern sugar producers appeared to have the votes necessary to defeat a treaty of annexation. Military concerns associated with the declaration of war on Spain and the U.S. naval victory on 1 May 1898 at the Battle of Manila Bay* in the Philippines* finally provided the necessary momentum to secure annexation through a joint resolution of Congress, which did not require the two-thirds majority needed to approve a treaty. The resolution won passage in the Senate on 6 July 1898 by a vote of 42–21, with twenty-six senators abstaining and only one Republican voting against annexation. Although both Japan and Germany issued mild objections to this disruption of the status quo in the Pacific, the British refused to join them in any concerted protest. On 13 June 1900, an act of Congress created the Territory of Hawaii, but statehood was not granted to Hawaii until 21 August 1959 because conservatives in Congress opposed admitting into the Union a territory with a largely nonwhite population.

C. W. Calhoun, "Morality and Spite: Walter Q. Gresham and U.S. Relations with Hawaii," *Pacific Historical Review* (August 1983); M. J. Devine, "John W. Foster and the Struggle for the Annexation of Hawaii," *Pacific Historical Review* (February 1977); T. S. McWilliams, "James H. Blount, the South, and Hawaiian Annexation," *Pacific Historical Review* (February 1988); T. J. Osborne, *"Empire Can Wait": American Opposition to Hawaiian Annexation, 1893–1898* (Kent, OH, 1981); M. Tate, *The United States and the Hawaiian Kingdom: A Political History* (New Haven, CT, 1965).

Michael J. Devine

HAWAIIAN REVOLUTION

An important event in the history of U.S. expansion into the Pacific during the nineteeth century, the revolt of 1893 overthrew the Hawaiian monarchy and set off a chain of events that culminated in the Hawaiian Annexation* to the United States. It came as the result of King David Kalakaua* and Walter Murray Gibson, his chief adviser who became prime minister in 1882, challenging the domination of political and economic life by the white businessmen and professional people in the Hawaiian Kingdom. Their efforts to restore native Hawaiian influence led to serious government mismanagement, a heavy burden of debt, and the complete domination of the Hawaiian legislature by Gibson's Hawaiian supporters. This so alarmed white leaders that they staged a revolt in June 1887 that ousted Gibson and installed a new constitution drastically curtailing Kalakaua's nearly absolute power.

Upon Kalakaua's death in 1891, his sister Lili'uokalani* succeeded to the throne. She worked to regain control of the legislature and to set aside the constitution of 1887. Lili'uokalani succeeded in the first endeavor by the end of the legislative session of 1892, putting through several revenue measures, such as an opium licensing act and a national lottery, which were looked upon with horror by the whites. But when the queen announced on 14 January 1893 her intention to promulgate a new constitution, she ignited the Hawaiian Revolution. Refusing to accept restoration of the monarch's absolute power and fearing that economic instability might cause a takeover by either Britain or Japan, prominent white (haole) residents, mostly Americans, preferred annexation to the United States to a continuation of the existing situation. Mostly the same people with the same arms that had overawed Kalakaua and Gibson in 1887 now rose in rebellion against Lili'uokalani. A self-proclaimed Committee for Public Safety, led by Sanford B. Dole* and comprising Hawaii's most powerful planters and merchants, staged a coup on 16 January 1893. Native Hawaiians had not come to the support of Kalakaua in 1887 and did not rise in defense of Lili'uokalani in 1893 either. On the morning of 17 January, the leaders read a proclamation from the steps of the legislative building across the street from the palace that declared the Hawaiian monarchy at an end and announced the formation of a provisional government.

Historians later pointed to one glaring

incident to explain the success of the revolution. In the afternoon of 16 January, U.S. Minister John L. Stevens* ordered the landing of sailors and marines from the USS *Boston* anchored in Honolulu harbor to "secure the safety of American citizens" and they remained until well after the revolt had succeeded. Stevens also boldly declared a U.S. protectorate over the islands and extended official recognition to Dole's provisional government. Although he would deny in sworn testimony before the U.S. Congress that he assured the Committee of Public Safety of U.S. support prior to the coup, some assurances were at least implied. Secretary of State John W. Foster* was forced to disavow the protectorate, but the self-righteous and stubborn Stevens continued to fly the U.S. flag over public buildings in Hawaii. The queen later used the presence of the American troops to argue that they prevented her government from taking action against the rebels. Nearly all the major historical accounts of the events of January 1893 attributed the success of the rebellion to the U.S. intervention. In 1993, this argument became the basis for a congressional resolution apologizing to the Hawaiian people for the overthrow of the monarchy. In fact, there is no basis for the charges of U.S. culpability because the native government took no action against the incipient revolt during the two days prior to the landing of U.S. troops, and Lili'uokalani made clear to her advisers that she wanted no bloodshed. Moreover, the lack of opposition to the rebellion from the native Hawaiians probably assured the success of the revolt regardless of the presence of U.S. troops.

E. Andrade, *Unconquerable Rebel: Robert W. Wilcox and Hawaiian Politics, 1880–1903* (Boulder, CO, 1996); R. Kuykendall, *The Hawaiian Kingdom*. Vol. 3: *The Kalakaua Dynasty* (Honolulu, HI, 1967); W. A. Russ, *The Hawaiian Republic (1894–1898) and Its Struggle to Win Annexation* (Selingsgrove, PA, 1961); W. A. Russ, *The Hawaiian Revolution, 1893–1894* (Susquehanna, PA, 1959).

Ernest Andrade Jr.

HAY, JOHN (1838–1905)

John Hay served as secretary of state from 1898 to 1907, issuing his Open Door notes in 1899 and circular in 1900, which redefined U.S. policy toward China. He first achieved notoriety as assistant private secretary to President Abraham Lincoln. Later, Hay had successful careers as a writer and businessman. In 1879, he became assistant secretary of state. In 1897, he gained an appointment as ambassador to Britain, where he remained until 1898, when President William McKinley* named him secretary of state. Hay's experiences as ambassador in London made him an Anglophile who desired a diplomatic alliance between the United States and Britain at a time when American public opinion was often anti-British and opposed to entangling alliances.

Although most famous for the Open Door Policy*, Hay was not its architect. Alfred E. Hippisley, an Englishman serving in China as the inspectorate of maritime customs, persuaded W. W. Rockhill*, an adviser of Hay and an American expert on East Asia, that the United States could not prevent foreign powers from establishing spheres of influence in China, but that it could work to prevent preferential tariffs within those spheres. In a memorandum to Hay, Rockhill summarized Hippisley's argument and persuaded Hay to make an official unilateral declaration in favor of an Open Door policy toward China. On 6 September 1899, Hay sent diplomatic notes outlining this Open Door policy to Germany, Russia, and Great Britain. In November 1899, he sent notes to France, Italy, and Japan. As the Boxer Uprising* reached its height in the summer of 1900, Hay issued the Open Door circular of 3 July 1900, which reaffirmed the principle of equal opportunity for trade in China, but more important, urged foreign governments to respect the integrity of China and its government. He issued the circular to ease the fears of anticolonial Democrats in the United States, unite the foreign governments engaged in China, and earn the co-operation of Chinese officials not engaged in the rebellion.

During the siege of the legations in Beijing, Hay arranged for communications with the U.S. minister to China, Edwin H. Conger*, through the Chinese minister to the United States. His communication with Conger reassured the world that Boxers had not massacred legation personnel, as many believed. One of Hay's biographers has argued that his negotiations with the Chinese minister prevented this massacre. After the China Relief Expedition* lifted the siege, Hay closely followed the negotiations that led to the Boxer Protocol*. He instructed Conger, as the lead U.S. negotiator, and Rockhill to restrain the other powers from overburdening China with indemnities. Despite their efforts, the indemnities equaled $333 million, including $25 million owed to the United States. In late 1900, Hay, at the request of the U.S. Navy, had Conger petition China for territory at Samsah Bay to construct a naval base. But he withdrew his request when the Japanese, in whose sphere of influence Samsah Bay fell, reminded him of his 3 July 1900 Open Door circular, which argued for respecting the territorial integrity of China. The Open Door, most historians agree, did little to ensure the territorial or political integrity of China. Instead, it provided the U.S. government with an opportunity to advance the interests of its citizens in China without committing itself to a politically unpopular policy of active involvement.

K. J. Clymer, *John Hay: The Gentleman as Diplomat* (Ann Arbor, MI, 1975); T. Dennett, *John Hay: From Poetry to Politics* (New York, 1933); W. R. Thayer, *The Life and Letters of John Hay* (Boston, 1916).

William E. Emerson

HENG SAMRIN (1934–)

Former Khmer Rouge* commander of the 126th Regiment of the Eastern Zone insur-gents, Heng Samrin helped lead the final assault on Phnom Penh in April 1975 that toppled the government of Lon Nol*. He later fled Cambodia* when Pol Pot* instructed military commanders to attack the Socialist Republic of Vietnam*. Samrin returned with the Vietnamese during Hanoi's invasion of Cambodia in 1978, which ended the Khmer Rouge reign of terror. He initially shared power with other former officers, notably Hun Sen*, as leaders of the People's Republic of Kampuchea. By the early 1990s, Samrin's influence had waned as Hun Sen assumed greater authority.

D. Chandler, *A History of Cambodia* (Boulder, CO, 2000); W. Shawcross, *Deliver Us from Evil: Peacekeepers, Warlords and a World of Endless Conflict* (New York, 2000).

T. Christopher Jespersen

HILSMAN, ROGER (1919–)

Under President John F. Kennedy*, Roger Hilsman, especially as assistant secretary of state for Far Eastern affairs after 1963, bore much responsibility for the development of policies in Southeast Asia at the outset of the Second Indochina War*. Born in Texas to a military family, the young Hilsman had a flamboyant career in World War II, serving as one of Merrill's Marauders* and with the Office of Strategic Services in the China-Burma-India Theater* (CBI). In 1945, he headed a parachute rescue mission into Manchuria that freed American prisoners, among them his father, from a Japanese camp. After the war, Hilsman earned a doctorate in international relations from Yale University and taught international politics at Princeton University before becoming deputy director of the legislative reference service of the Library of Congress. He also worked on the early military planning for the North Atlantic Treaty Organization.

Hilsman joined the Kennedy administration in 1961 as director of the State Department's Bureau of Intelligence and Research. In February 1962, Hilsman defined the fundamental problem in Vietnam as political, rather than military in nature, although three months later, he criticized the U.S. military for what he perceived as its reluctance to take decisive action in Laos* or Vietnam. During late 1962, Hilsman and Michael V. Forrestal, head of the National Security Council's Vietnam Coordinating Committee, visited the Republic of Vietnam* to review the situation. Although both men were initially committed to U.S. intervention, they produced a mixed report on the Second Indochina War*, which reinforced growing doubts as to the viability of the existing South Vietnamese government. They pointed to ominous increases in Viet Cong* strength, which might lead to a lengthier and more costly war than predicted. Although agreeing with it in principle, they expressed doubts as to the effectiveness of the Strategic Hamlets Program*. A secret annex to the report recommended that the United States exert additional pressure upon South Vietnam's President Ngo Dinh Diem* to institute reforms and liberalize the "authoritarian political structure."

Hilsman became assistant secretary for Far Eastern Affairs in May 1963. Both he and Forrestal were central figures in the hectic maneuverings of late August 1963 when they worked with Undersecretary of State for Political Affairs W. Averell Harriman* to obtain presidential approval for the dispatch of a cable recommending the overthrow of the Diem government. Despite subsequent misgivings within the Kennedy administration, this cable never was revoked, and a coup, which led to Diem's Assassination* and his brother Ngo Dinh Nhu*, took place in November. The coup did little to improve the war's fortunes as its instigators had hoped. Hilsman clashed with the new president Lyndon B. Johnson* because he opposed the growing escalation of the war, arguing later that Kennedy would have withdrawn in a second term. In 1964, he left the government to teach at Columbia University. In 1967, he published a memoir based on his foreign policy experiences in the Kennedy years.

W. C. Gibbons, *The U.S. Government and the Vietnam War: Executive and Legislatives Roles and Relationships*, 4 parts (Princeton, NJ, 1986–1989); R. Hilsman, *American Guerrilla: My War Behind Japanese Lines* (Washington, DC, 1991); R. Hilsman, *To Move a Nation: The Politics of Foreign Policy in the Administration of John F. Kennedy* (New York, 1967); M. A. Nelson, "Roger Hilsman and Southeast Asia: Precursor to Failure?," M.A. thesis, Bowling Green State University, 1995; S. Pelz, " 'When Do I Have Time to Think?': John F. Kennedy, Roger Hilsman, and the Laotian Crisis of 1962," *Diplomatic History* (Spring 1979).

Priscilla Roberts

HIROHITO (1901–1989)

As Japan's emperor from 1926 to 1989, Hirohito remains the subject of controversy among historians who debate his responsibility for Japanese imperialist expansion in East Asia contributing to the outbreak of World War II. Michi no Miya Hirohito was the first crown prince to leave his country, traveling to England in 1921, where he was deeply influenced by the British-style constitutional monarchy. Later that year, he became regent for his ailing father, the Taishō emperor. Ascending the throne in December 1926 as Shōwa emperor, Hirohito's reign witnessed the rise of ultranationalism and militarism that would lead to the Mukden Incident* in 1931 and the Marco Polo Bridge Incident* in 1937. He gave final approval for the Pearl Harbor Attack* on 7 December 1941, which made him the most hated man in the United States. After Japan's surrender in August 1945, however, he escaped the International Military Tribunal for the Far East. But in the new Japanese Constitution of 1947*, the United States redefined his position as "symbol of the state." Hirohito's failure to take responsibility for the war, despite his legal status as the head of state, made him one of the most controversial figures in East Asian history.

The U.S. decision to preserve the imperial house and to exclude the emperor from the Tōkyō War Crimes Trials* came from practical considerations on the part of General Douglas MacArthur*, the Supreme Commander for the Allied Powers (SCAP*). MacArthur, who was responsible for the U.S. Occupation of Japan*, correctly anticipated that preserving the emperor would provide legitimacy for American rule in Japan and facilitate implementation of ambitious democratic reforms. Bolstering this decision was the inherent ambiguity of the role and function of the emperor under the Meiji constitution of 1889. The constitution declared the "sacred and inviolable" emperor to be the sole source of executive, legislative, and judicial powers, who also "exercised supreme command over the Army and Navy." But at the same time, the constitution contained an article that virtually absolved the emperor from personal responsibility for the government's behavior by making various ministers of state accountable for actions under their respective jurisdictions. Hirohito's closest advisers, such as Saionji Kinmochi*, Makino Nobuaki*, and Kidō Kōichi*, mostly succeeded in restraining the emperor from voicing his opinions even in private to political and military leaders, thereby shielding him from any direct responsibility for government decisions.

However, historians still debate the nature and extent of Hirohito's personal efforts to influence certain political and military decisions made before and during the Pacific war. For example, in 1928, the emperor was cautioned by his advisers when he suggested the resignation of Premier Tanaka Giichi* for failing to punish those army officers responsible for the assassination of Manchurian warlord Zhang Zuolin*. In the 26 February incident in 1936, Hirohito stood against the young military officers who attempted to achieve military rule by assassinating government officials. But the best-known imperial decision the emperor personally made was to

end the war and to accept Allied surrender terms in August 1945 in the wake of the Atomic Attacks* on Hiroshima and Nagasaki and the Soviet declaration of war on Japan. He intervened because the civilian and military leaders were deadlocked and asked for his opinion. Hirohito's exercise of imperial authority on these occasions prompted historians to question the orthodox view that he had no choice but to sanction the decision for war against the United States already made by his advisers. In the 1990s, Japanese scholars using primary sources made available after Hirohito's death began writing reappraisals criticizing his role in the events leading to World War II.

H. Bix, "The Showa Emperor's 'Monologue' and the Problem of War Responsibility," *Journal of Japanese Studies* (Summer 1992); R. J. C. Butow, *Japan's Decision to Surrender* (Stanford, CA, 1954); R. J. C. Butow, *Tojo and the Coming of the War* (Princeton, NJ, 1961); P. Wetzler, *Hirohito and War: Imperial Tradition and Military Decision Making in Prewar Japan* (Honolulu, HI, 1998).

Kawamura Noriko

HIRŌTA KOKI (1878–1948)

A leading career diplomat and politician in the Taishō and Shōwa periods, Hirōta Koki was Japanese prime minister during World War II. His role in the rise of Japanese militarism caused Hirōta to be the only civilian tried and found guilty as a Class-A war criminal at the Tōkyō War Crimes Trials*, resulting in his execution by hanging. Ascending the well-tested educational path to membership in modern Japan's power elites, he graduated from Tōkyō Imperial University's School of Law in 1905. During his career as a junior diplomat, Hirōta served in a series of important overseas missions, including embassies in China, Britain, and the United States. In 1923, in his capacity as the chief of the Bureau of European and American Affairs, he engineered the establishment of formal diplomatic relations with the Soviet Union.

Hirōta negotiated Tōkyō's rocky relationship with Moscow as ambassador after the Mukden Incident* 1931, but he was discharged the next year. In 1933, he returned to influence when Prime Minister Saitō Makoto* named him foreign minister. Okada Keisuke retained him when he formed a new cabinet.

Hirōta made an indelible mark on Japan's China policy in the critical period after the Manchurian crisis of 1931. The Amō Doctrine* of April 1934, widely interpreted at the time as proclaiming Japan's exclusionist design for East Asia, in essence reflected Hirōta's views. During his tenure as foreign minister, the Japanese Army accelerated its movement into northern China through the Umezu-Ho and Doihara-Qing agreements. The Okada cabinet's three-point manifesto, the so-called Hirōta Principles of October 1935, demanded that China end anti-Japanese agitation, recognize Japan's puppet regime of Manchukuo*, and launch a common defense against Communist threats from Inner Mongolia. Hirōta, by showing himself to be open to the use of force to attain these objectives, contributed to the erosion of Japan's relationship with the Chinese Guomindang* and the major powers in the mid-1930s.

Hirōta's meek acceptance of the military's initiatives also conditioned Japan's long-term strategic planning. As foreign minister in December 1934, he presided over Japan's abrogation of the Five Power Pact*. During his premiership, Japan's government adopted a series of long-term foreign and defense policy guidelines that reflected the military's institutional interests and policy objectives that included preparedness against the United States and the Soviet Union as prime enemies and entrenchment of political control over north Chinese provinces. The Anti-Comintern Pact* with Nazi Germany of November 1936 paved the way for the World War II Axis alliance. As foreign minister in the cabinet of Konoe Fumimaro*, Hirōta failed to contain the military clash in north China in July 1937 triggered by the Marco Polo Bridge Incident*. He was not able to reach a negotiated settlement with the Guomindang in the escalating conflict in China.

M. A. Barnhart, *Japan Prepares for Total War: The Search for Economic Security, 1919–1941* (Ithaca, NY, 1987); K. Denki, *Hirōta Koki* (Tōkyō, 1966); Uno Shigeaki, "Hirōta Koki no taigai seisaku to Shokaiseki" [Hirota Koki's Foreign Policy and Jiang Jieshi], *Kokusai Seiji*, 56 (Fall 1976).

Shimuzu Sayuri

HMONG

The Hmong tribal minority of Laos* provided the backbone of a clandestine army, supported by the Central Intelligence Agency* (CIA), that fought the Pathet Lao* and North Vietnamese in Laos during the Second Indochina War*. The Hmong originally came from southwest China and settled in the mountains of northern Laos. Known to non-Hmong as the Meo (a pejorative corruption of the Chinese *Miao* for barbarian), they did not integrate into the dominant lowland Lao society. They subsistence-farmed their hills and grew poppies for opium, their principal cash crop. During the First Indochina War*, the French used the Hmong as guerrillas against the Vietminh*, but with only limited success. The Royal Lao Government, successor to the colonial administration in French Indochina*, employed the Hmong as irregular forces to defend their own villages. In 1960, CIA officers persuaded the ambassador in Laos and key officials in Washington to approve a program to recruit Hmong into a secret army. Although some Hmong cast their lot with the Pathet Lao and the North Vietnamese, a large core group of them joined the U.S.–Royal Lao Government ranks.

Under two clan leaders, Touby Lyfoung and Vang Pao*, the Hmong accepted direct economic aid from the U.S. Agency for International Development and military weapons, supplies, and payment from the CIA. The program started modestly, but after the resumption of the Laos civil war in 1963, it grew quickly. In 1965, the CIA reorganized 10,000 Hmong into Special Guerrilla Units, a cross between light infantry and guerrillas, which were highly mobile, motivated, and willing to fight where required. The rest of the 20,000 Hmong under arms remained as village defenders. By the late 1960s, the Hmong clustered in towns and satellite villages on the southern end of the Plain of Jars. Long Tieng, their main headquarters, became the second-largest town in Laos. The CIA had expanded the secret Hmong army to just under 40,000 and upgraded their weapons. Increasingly, the Hmong became the principal opponent of the North Vietnamese in Laos. Air America* airlifted supplies, ammunition, and weapons to the Hmong. CIA and Thai officers provided training, military advice, and "volunteer" Thai artillery forces and infantry to fight with them. When engaged in combat, the Hmong were supported by a diverse array of U.S. air power, and in the 1970s, occasional U.S. B-52 bomber strikes.

The Hmong became a people at war. Farming declined, and families depended solely on U.S. aid to survive. A teenage boy came of age when he took up arms, and promising Hmong soldiers trained as pilots and forward air controllers directing U.S. air support. With the Paris Peace Accords* in January 1973, the Hmong lost their massive U.S. air and logistical support. A cease-fire was declared in Laos that year but mostly ignored. In 1974, the Royal Lao Government and the Pathet Lao joined together to form an uneasy coalition government. Old Hmong animosities with the North Vietnamese and Pathet Lao persisted, and fighting continued. The total collapse of U.S. power in South Vietnam and Cambodia* in 1975 left the Hmong dangerously exposed. Surrounded by North Vietnamese and facing a hopeless battle, Vang Pao fled his redoubt at Long Tieng for Thailand*. Word spread through Hmong villages, and many thousands set off to cross the Mekong River. Those

Hmong who stayed in Laos retreated to the mountains south of the Plain of Jars and fortified their villages. After the Pathet Lao overthrew the coalition, the Lao People's Democratic Republic in 1977 called on the Vietnamese to destroy the remnants of Hmong resistance, causing one-third of the remaining Hmong to flee to Thailand. The Hmong paid a high price for cooperating with the United States. Losing perhaps 30,000 killed in the war (about 10 percent of their total population), their traditional society was destroyed and many were forced to resettle in the United States. *See also* Secret U.S. Air War in Laos.

T. N. Castle, *At War in the Shadow of Vietnam: U.S. Military Aid to the Royal Lao Government, 1955–1975* (New York, 1993); J. Hamilton-Merritt, *Tragic Mountains: The Hmong, the Americans, and the Wars for Laos, 1942–1992* (Bloomington, IN, 1993); M. Stuart-Fox, *A History of Laos* (Cambridge, UK, 1997); R. Warner, *Back Fire: Secret War in Laos and Its Link to the War in Vietnam* (New York, 1995).

Edward C. Keefer

HO CHI MINH (1890?–1969)

Ho Chi Minh was the founder of the Vietnamese Communist Party, led the Vietnamese in wars against the French and the Americans, and was president of the Democratic Republic of Vietnam* from 1945 to his death. He was born Nguyen Sinh Cung sometime between 1890 and 1894 in Nghe An Province to a poor scholar gentry family. While a student at the National Academy in Hue, he joined in anticolonial activities protesting French Colonialism*. Ho left Vietnam for Europe in 1911. After traveling in southern France and northern Africa, and visiting New York City and London, he eventually settled in Paris, where he worked with anticolonial activists in the Vietnamese expatriate community. Under the pseudonym of Nguyen Ai Quoc (Nguyen the Patriot), Ho was the author of a proposal for the gradual emancipation of Vietnam from French colonial rule intended for presentation to Woodrow Wilson* at the Paris Peace Conference in 1919. In the wake of the conference's refusal to consider the petition or take action on French Indochina*, Ho turned from more gradualist anticolonial ideas and strategies to Marxism. He became a founding member of the French Communist Party in 1920, a student at the University of the Toilers of the East in Moscow in 1923, and a leading spokesman for the anticolonial cause at the Fifth Congress of the Communist International in 1924.

Sent to China as a Comintern agent in 1925, Ho founded the Vietnamese Revolutionary Youth League (Viet Nam Thanh Nien Kach Menh Hoi). In 1927, he authored the *Road to Revolution*, a training manual for the Youth League's members that included a sustained discussion of the American Revolution as a model for the Vietnamese anticolonial movement. In 1930, he oversaw creation of the Indochinese Communist Party. Arrested in Hong Kong in 1931, Ho was back in Moscow by 1934, and remained there until 1938. Apparently, he fell out of favor with Joseph Stalin for his unorthodox views favoring national liberation over class struggle and revolution. Ho returned to China in late 1938 to work as an adviser to the Chinese Communist armed forces. In 1941, he went to Vietnam and oversaw creation of the Vietminh*, an organization committed to winning independence from France. During World War II, Ho worked closely with the Deer Mission*, composed of U.S. military officers and intelligence operatives who provided tactical and logistical support for the war against the Japanese. As the war ended in 1945, Ho oversaw the August Revolution that brought the Vietnamese Communists to power. On 2 September, Ho Chi Minh proclaimed Vietnam independent, opening his address with the beginning of the American Declaration of Independence. Historians still debate the significance and sincerity of these actions, but Ho continued to seek U.S. support for the Vietnamese republic both directly through official U.S. personnel in Vietnam and in letters to President Harry S. Truman*.

In 1946, France's efforts to restore colonial rule ignited the First Indochina War*. Thereafter, perceptions of Ho's integrity and commitment to independence were a key factor in the widespread support for the Vietnamese Communist struggle against the French. In the aftermath of the war, and the division of the country under the Geneva Accords of 1954*, Ho turned toward the construction of a socialist state in the north by developing industry and collectivizing agriculture. The land reform campaigns, which sought to redistribute land to poorer peasants, quickly turned toward bloodshed, with estimates of upward of 10,000 people killed. By 1956, the campaign was brought to an end and Ho was forced to apologize for the regime's mistakes. As the Second Indochina War* with the United States began to escalate in the early 1960s, Ho's poor health forced him to occupy something of a symbolic role; most of the key decisions in this period were made by the collective leadership of the party. After his death in 1969, the Vietnamese state sought to use the memory of "Uncle Ho" to legitimate efforts at national liberation and socialist revolution. His remains were put on view in a public mausoleum in the center of Hanoi, attracting thousands of visitors each year. In the 1990s, however, Ho's memory became a site of friction between the state and civil society, as the failures of socialism in the Socialist Republic of Vietnam* gave way to the introduction of market economic reforms.

M. P. Bradley, *Imagining Vietnam and America: The Making of Postcolonial Vietnam, 1919–1950* (Chapel Hill, NC, 2000); W. J. Duiker, *Ho Chi Minh: A Life* (New York, 2000); H. K. Khanh, *Vietnamese Communism, 1925–1945* (Ithaca, NY, 1982); J. Lacouture, *Ho Chi Minh: A Political Biography* (New York, 1968); D. G. Marr, *Vietnam 1945: The Quest for Power* (Berkeley, CA, 1995).

Mark P. Bradley

HO CHI MINH TRAIL

Throughout the Second Indochina War*, the Democratic Republic of Vietnam* used the Ho Chi Minh Trail to transport soldiers, weapons, and supplies into the Republic of Vietnam* for combat operations. Originating in the panhandle of North Vietnam, it stretched 600 miles southward through southern Laos* into northeastern Cambodia* and ended at several distribution sites in the Central Highlands of South Vietnam. In 1964, when the United States began to escalate its military commitment in Vietnam, the route was primitive, comprising assorted roads, paths, and trails winding through mountainous and thick jungle terrain. During the First Indochina War*, the Vietminh* used the infiltration route as a communications link in fighting the French, with thousands of young and mostly female Vietnamese peasants maintaining the network of trails with campsites every nine miles. In May 1959, Communist leaders in Hanoi formed Group 559 to formulate measures for expanding and improving the Ho Chi Minh Trail, resulting in a greater infiltration of both cadres and modest amounts of arms, ammunition, and supplies to the Viet Cong*. Traveling down the artery was a physically arduous and exhausting trip, taking roughly five weeks to travel its course.

Early in 1964, Hanoi decided to escalate its military operations in the south. "We had to move from the guerrilla phase into conventional war," Communist leader Bui Tin said later. "Otherwise, our future would have been bleak." Commitment of North Vietnamese Army (NVA) regulars would require providing the force with tons of weapons, ammunition, food, and other assorted supplies. North Vietnam therefore implemented a grandiose plan that transformed the Ho Chi Minh Trail into a modern logistical supply system. Using Soviet and Chinese machinery, the Communists built roads and bridges capable of handling heavy trucks and other vehicles. After the U.S. bombing campaign started, they installed anti-aircraft defenses, as well as digging underground barracks, workshops, sanitary hospitals, storage facilities, and fuel depots. The Ho Chi Minh Trail allowed North Vietnam to match every American escalation after U.S. combat forces took control of the war in 1965. NVA units moved heavy machine guns, mortars, and rocket launchers for military action with now well-equipped Viet Cong battalions. By 1967, in addition to 5,000 men per month, Hanoi was moving an estimated 400 tons of supplies southward each week, an amount more than four times greater than in 1965.

American leaders understood that the Ho Chi Minh Trail was central to Hanoi's plan for victory. Secretary of Defense Robert S. McNamara*, while having limited confidence in Operation ROLLING THUNDER*, directed the weight of the bombing effort at the Communist transportation system south of the twentieth parallel and interdiction of the Ho Chi Minh Trail. Using various aircraft, the United States staged thousands of sorties, as well as waging a Secret U.S. Air War in Laos* and conducting Operation MENU* in Cambodia, but could not slow the flow of men and supplies southward. Roughly 90,000 North Vietnamese, many of them women and children, worked to keep the trail open. U.S. Special Forces also operated camps near the trail outlets in the south while the Central Intelligence Agency* (CIA) recruited Hmong* tribesmen to cut the artery in the north. Vietnamization* after 1969 led to the Army of the Republic of Vietnam* staging offensive operations Cambodia in 1970 and Laos in 1971 to disrupt the Ho Chi Minh Trail, but without effect. The Paris Peace Accords* in January 1973 ended U.S. bombing of the trail, ultimately allowing Hanoi to send about 30,000 soldiers into the south in March 1975 "along a modern highway," Stanley Karnow writes, "dotted with truck rest and service areas, oil tanks, machine shops, and other installations, all protected by hilltop anti-aircraft emplacements."

G. H. Herring, *America's Longest War: The United States in Vietnam, 1950–1975* (New York, 1996); S. Karnow, *Vietnam: A History* (New York, 1983); R. D. Schulzinger, *A Time for War: The United States in Vietnam, 1941–1975* (New York, 1997).

James I. Matray

HOAR, GEORGE F. (1826–1904)

George Hoar served in the U.S. Senate for Massachusetts from 1877 until his death, achieving national renown as an anti-imperialist at the end of the nineteenth century when he took a pronounced stand in favor of Philippine independence. A member of the Republican Party, he was a stalwart supporter of Abraham Lincoln and the Civil War. Hoar entered Congress in 1869, serving four terms in the House before elevation to the Senate. He was an idealist and supported good causes, such as that of African-Americans, Native Americans, and Boston Irishmen. His first large acquaintance with foreign relations was indirect: he spoke in favor of Chinese immigration and was an avowed enemy of the American Protective Association. Hoar took his stands out of principle, and on immigration surely did so not because of Chinese-American constituents, since he would have had very few of them. He opposed the initial 1880 exclusion bill, denounced the twenty-year suspension law of 1882, voted against the Sino-American Treaty of 1888 that prohibited immigration of coolies, and in 1902 cast the only Senate vote against continuing "temporary" suspension of immigration. When burned in effigy in Nevada in 1882, Hoar said he was singularly honored.

In the 1890s, Hoar at first opposed Hawaii Annexation*. "I have never been able to see," he said, "that our security was increased by a fortress three thousand miles off." Yet he voted for the joint resolution of 1898 that brought annexation, offering a New England reason. There were two dreams of empire, he said, one being "held

out to us in the Far East and in the West Indies as the result of military conquest; the other is held out to us in Hawaii by the children of the Puritans." By this he meant the Republic of Hawaii had sponsorship in part from missionaries of the Congregational Church. That same year, Hoar voted for war. But when President William McKinley* instructed the U.S. peace commissioners in Paris to acquire the Philippines*, it was too much, and he went into opposition against the leader of his own political party. Hoar wanted to advance the liberties of the Filipinos, but was far more concerned about the effect of empire upon American institutions, specifically the grave threat to past traditions and current social and political arrangements.

For Hoar, the issue of the future of the Philippines was a problem of balancing justice and self-interest. He decided not to stress a solution for the islands with which he toyed, namely a kind of tutelage that would not be imperial. Hoar took refuge in sinfulness and unconstitutionality. His Senate speech of 9 January 1899 against passage of the Treaty of Paris was the single-most important address of his life, and brought national attention. Asking his countrymen to look to their noble past, Hoar stressed the need to uphold principle and support the designs of the U.S. Constitution. He was one of only two Senate Republicans to vote against the treaty, which passed by the thinnest of margins, 57–27, one vote more than the required two-thirds. In the aftermath of Philippine Annexation*, Hoar proved no more successful than during the treaty fight. He repeated his commentaries in the Senate speech against the treaty, but there was little he could do to counter the logic of his Massachusetts colleague Henry Cabot Lodge*, who announced that "a great nation must have great responsibilities." By then, Hoar was considered more of a senior in the Senate than a wielder of power. With McKinley's assassination in September 1901, the new president was Theodore Roosevelt*, who, although not the fire-eater of 1898, still epitomized the new activist thrust in U.S. Asia policy. Hoar could only remark, "I appeal from the Present, bloated with material prosperity, drunk with the lust of empire, to another and a better age." *See also* Angell Treaty; Coolie Trade; Exclusion Acts; Spanish-American War.

R. L. Beisner, *Twelve Against Empire: The Anti-Imperialists, 1898–1900* (New York, 1968); R. E. Welch Jr., *George Frisbie Hoar and the Half-Breed Republicans* (Cambridge, MA, 1971).

Robert H. Ferrell

HODGE, JOHN R. (1893–1963)

Lieutenant General John Reed Hodge was the commander of the U.S. Armed Forces in Korea during the U.S. Occupation of Korea* from September 1945 until the formal establishment of the Republic of Korea* on 15 August 1948. Born in Golconda, Illinois, he attended Southern Illinois Teachers' College from 1912 to 1913 before enrolling at the University of Illinois to study architectural engineering. After the United States declared war on Germany in April 1917, Hodge earned an Infantry Reserve commission in August and traveled to France. During the St. Mihiel and Meuse-Argonne offensives, he saw combat as a company commander. After World War I, he was a professor of military science and tactics at Mississippi A&M College. In 1925, Hodge rejoined the U.S. Army and gained additional training before spending five years on the War Department General Staff. After the Pearl Harbor Attack*, he was assistant commander of the Twenty-fifth "Tropic Lightning" Infantry Division and fought at Guadalcanal before assuming command of the American Division in April 1943. Wounded at Bougainville, he also saw heavy action in the Solomons. In April 1944, Hodge became commander of the Twenty-fourth Corps, a unit formed to conduct amphibious operations against the Japanese in the Marianas and the Carolines. His unit fought with distinction at the Battle of Okinawa*. During World War

II, Hodge earned a reputation as a "soldier's soldier," sharing hardships with his troops at the front.

During August 1945, the War Department instructed Hodge and his Twenty-fourth Corps to occupy Korea south of the thirty-eighth parallel for the purpose of accepting the surrender of half of an estimated 375,000 Japanese troops. He received no detailed guidelines from Washington for six months, making even more difficult his task of responding to the revolutionary climate existing in Korea upon his arrival. From the outset, Hodge's highest priority was preserving law and order. Because he lacked administrative training, political experience, or familiarity with Korean history and culture, he committed numerous errors. Acting on instructions, Hodge at first retained Japanese administrators, but removed them after angry Korean protests. More significant was his reliance on wealthy and conservative Korean landlords and businessmen, including some who had collaborated with the Japanese. Unable to make progress toward ending the Thirty-Eighth Parallel Division*, Hodge worried constantly about Soviet occupation of northern Korea and the threat that it posed to his command. Simple, blunt, and direct in approach, he advocated early U.S. military withdrawal from Korea and was a persistent opponent of trusteeship.

Hodge neither understood nor dealt effectively with the challenge of Korean political factionalism. Shortly after his arrival, he requested a meeting with two representatives from each party and was shocked when 1,200 Koreans responded to his invitation. Hoping to promote political stability, Hodge then assisted Syngman Rhee*, Kim Gu*, and other Korean conservative exile leaders in their return to Korea in late 1945. Instead, political turmoil and violence increased, and in desperation, Hodge suggested his own recall, offering to serve as a "sacrificial goat." Ignoring Rhee's demand to hold quick elections for a separate government in the south, he then tried to work with Kim Kyu-sik* in creating a moderate political coalition in 1946. In another major blunder, Hodge proceeded to undermine the moderates, but without placating the conservatives. Rhee never forgave Hodge, and this led to his relief and return to the United States. After his recall, he held various posts before he assumed command of Army Field Forces in 1952, a post he held until he retired the next year. *See also* Moscow Agreement on Korea.

B. Cumings, *The Origins of the Korean War*, Vol. 1: *Liberation and the Creation of Separate Regimes, 1945–1947* (Princeton, NJ, 1981); C. M. Dobbs, *The Unwanted Symbol: American Foreign Policy, the Cold War, and Korea, 1945–1950* (Kent, OH, 1981); J. I. Matray, *The Reluctant Crusade: American Foreign Policy in Korea, 1941–1950* (Honolulu, HI, 1985); *New York Times*, 13 November 1963.

James I. Matray

HOME BY CHRISTMAS OFFENSIVE (24 November 1950)

General Douglas MacArthur* planned and executed this massive campaign to end the Korean War*, restore peace and unity to the peninsula, and allow the United Nations to gradually withdraw its forces. After the victorious Inch'ŏn Landing*, UN troops crossed the thirty-eighth parallel early in October 1950. The Yalu River and Manchuria appeared within easy striking distance as the UN offensive into North Korea got under way. In late October and early November, Chinese soldiers were captured in several engagements, showing the reality of Chinese Intervention in the Korean War*. MacArthur, however, saw full Chinese participation as unlikely and disregarded the incidents. On 24 November, he launched the Home by Christmas Offensive (as it became known) to force the Democratic People's Republic of Korea* to capitulate and end the war. MacArthur may have picked this date to intimidate the People's Republic of China* (PRC), since

the PRC's representative arrived at the United Nations that same day to discuss China's intentions regarding Korea.

The principal UN forces, consisting of the Eighth U.S. Army in Korea (EUSAK) and Tenth Corps, were each to strike separately toward the Yalu River before linking to engulf the North Korean Army. The EUSAK attacked first, driving north from Sinanju to Kangji and Chasan, and northeast to Sinŭiju. Three days later, on 27 November the Tenth Corps launched an attack on the western front from Changjin, cutting off the main road to the Yalu and striking the North Koreans from the rear. Initially, little resistance was encountered. However, fighting intensified as the Chinese People's Volunteers struck the UN line, driving a deep wedge into the center and dividing the EUSAK and the Tenth Corps. The campaign to end the war turned into a UN rout. Although reconnaissance failed to convince MacArthur of the scope of Chinese involvement, the early warning signs clearly were ignored by the veteran general. This military debacle ultimately persuaded President Harry S. Truman* to abandon reunification as a war aim in favor of pursuing an armistice based on restoring the division at the thirty-eighth parallel.

R. E. Appleman, *East of Chosin: Entrapment and Breakout in Korea, 1950* (College Station, TX, 1987); R. E. Appleman, *South to the Naktong, North to the Yalu* (Washington, DC, 1961); J. F. Schnabel, *Policy and Direction: The First Year* (Washington, DC, 1972); J. W. Spanier, *The Truman-MacArthur Controversy and the Korean War* (New York, 1959).

James I. Matray

HONG KONG

Hong Kong became a British colony in 1841, with further accessions of territory in 1860 and 1898, all of which were returned to mainland Chinese rule in 1997. British control of Hong Kong brought advantages to the United States. On several occasions in the nineteenth century, U.S. naval forces used Hong Kong as an anchorage when engaged in efforts to win concessions from Japan and China, and as a staging post against the Spanish fleet during the Spanish-American War*. There was also a major American commercial presence in the territory. Even so, the United States took relatively little interest in British Hong Kong until World War II, when unfulfilled Anglo-American strategic plans envisaged building up Hong Kong as a major naval base. But in December 1941, these schemes were overtaken by the Pearl Harbor Attack* and the rapid Japanese conquest and occupation. Committed to anticolonial ideology, President Franklin D. Roosevelt* pressed the British to return Hong Kong to China's Guomindang* (Nationalist) government of Jiang Jieshi*, a proposal stymied by Britain's recapture of Hong Kong in August 1945 and the subsequent British refusal to relinquish the territory. Until the Chinese Communist Party* seized control of mainland China in 1949, U.S. officials viewed British control of Hong Kong as an embarrassing anomaly. In 1949, the United States policy turned down a British request for American military assistance should Hong Kong be attacked by another power.

During the 1950s, the Korean War* and American support for the Republic of China* on Taiwan* led relations between mainland China and the United States to deteriorate and precipitated the Taiwan Strait Crises* over the offshore islands of Jinmen and Mazu. Hong Kong now served as a useful intelligence-gathering center for American spies and diplomats, who were excluded from the Chinese mainland. Points of contention in the Anglo-American relationship now focused on the degree to which Hong Kong served trade with the People's Republic of China* (PRC), on which the United States imposed a commercial embargo in 1950. Wary of causing overmuch offense to the mainland government, the United States in 1955 excluded Hong Kong from the military scope of the new Southeast Asia Treaty Organi-

zation*. In the late 1950s, under pressure from the Joint Chiefs of Staff, this long-standing policy was reversed, and in 1960, Washington determined that the United States would offer military assistance to Hong Kong should it be invaded by the PRC.

The American economic interest in Hong Kong increased dramatically after 1960, particularly with the increasing normalization of Sino-American diplomatic relations from 1971 onward. U.S. businesses used Hong Kong as a base from which to explore the possibility of trade and investment on the Chinese mainland, and by the early 1990s, had invested $7 billion in the territory, an economic stake far greater than that of Britain. Although the United States was not an interested party in the Sino-British Joint Declaration of 1984, under whose terms the PRC was to resume sovereignty over all Hong Kong in 1997, U.S. officials and congressmen displayed great concern over the future of Hong Kong. Between 1984 and 1997, governmental spokesmen, senators, congressmen, and private individuals frequently expressed their hope that Hong Kong would enjoy the greatest possible degree of democratization, judicial independence, and freedom from Chinese interference. The year after the Tiananmen Square Massacre* of June 1989, fears of restrictive future Chinese rule over Hong Kong led the U.S. Congress to pass legislation that charged the executive branch with monitoring conditions in Hong Kong. A massive influx of American and other international journalists into Hong Kong to cover the generally smooth July 1997 handover was followed by a precipitous drop in media interest immediately after that event. Press coverage did not revive until October 1997, when Hong Kong's stock market declined dramatically with the start of the East Asian Financial Crisis*. Meanwhile, the Chinese military stationed in Hong Kong maintained a low profile and, despite some tensions over ultimate jurisdiction in politically sensitive legal rulings, mainland interference in the daily affairs of government seemed minimal. *See also* First Opium War; Treaty of Nanjing.

W. I. Cohen and Z. Li, (eds.), *Hong Kong Under Chinese Rule: The Economic and Political Implications of Reversion* (New York, 1997); G. A. Postiglione and J. T. H. Tang (eds.), *Hong Kong's Reunion with China: Global Dimensions* (Hong Kong, 1997); S. Tsang, *A Modern History of Hong Kong: 1841–1998* (London, 1998); N. B. Tucker, *Uncertain Friendships: Taiwan, Hong Kong, and the United States, 1945–1992* (New York, 1994); F. Welsh, *A History of Hong Kong* (London, 1997).

Priscilla Roberts

HOOVER, HERBERT (1874–1964)

President of the United States from 1929 to 1933, Herbert Clark Hoover was born in West Branch, Iowa, the son of Quaker farmers. He was orphaned at age nine and raised by relatives in Iowa and Oregon. Hardworking, aggressive, and determined, he worked his way through Stanford University, majoring in geology and graduating with its first class in 1895. Hoover quickly established a reputation as a "great engineer" who had a special talent for scouting out mining opportunities and reorganizing sick enterprises. His work brought him to China during 1898 as chief engineer for the Chinese Engineering Company. The Boxer Uprising* forced Chinese officials to acquiesce in the conversion of this large business undertaking into an English corporation. Hoover participated in the reorganization, and his reward was a sizable number of shares in the company. He then traveled widely, becoming known as a skilled administrator, financial expert, and successful business promoter.

In 1914, Hoover, now wealthy, retired from business and devoted the rest of his life to philanthropy and government service. He repeatedly demonstrated his administrative abilities and Progressive tendencies in the various positions he held during and immediately after World War I. In 1921, Hoover became secretary of

commerce, serving in that capacity until he resigned to run for the presidency in 1928. He recruited able young administrators, ran an efficient organization, and made his department an important force in the economy of the New Era. Often clashing with the State and Treasury Departments, Hoover also demanded a voice in foreign policy making as he increased the role of the Commerce Department in expanding foreign markets and investment. In East Asia, his Commerce Department was a major factor in drafting and securing passage of the China Trade Act to encourage expansion of U.S. trade and investment by allowing federal incorporation of firms operating in China and exempting them from most federal taxes.

More than the State Department, Hoover was supportive of China against foreign encroachments, and he sought to encourage China's general economic development. He was willing to consider cooperating with Sun Zhongshan* in Guangzhou, if he purged the Communists from his Guomindang* regime. Hoover recommended a $250 million bankers' loan to stimulate economic progress in China. After the State Department rejected that proposal and the Second Chinese Consortium proved abortive, the Commerce Department proposed an industrial consortium that would guide private trade and investment in China. Nothing came of these ideas. Worried about preserving the Open Door Policy*, Hoover strongly opposed a J. P. Morgan loan to fund Japanese exploitation of Manchuria, working out a compromise with Thomas W. Lamont* and the State Department permitting a "general" Morgan loan to Japanese banks, thereby freeing Japanese capital for investment in Manchuria.

As president after 1929, Hoover became increasingly disenchanted with China and reluctant to challenge Japanese expansion in Northeast Asia. That became clear after the Mukden Incident* in September 1931, which, aside from the global Great Depression, was probably the greatest foreign policy crisis of his presidency. As the prime sponsor of the Nine Power Pact* and the Kellogg-Briand Pact, the United States had a stake in protecting its rights in China and maintaining the sanctity of treaties. Secretary of State Henry L. Stimson* was initially indifferent and, along with his Asia experts, equivocated about U.S. intervention. After Japanese forces seized Jinzhou and seemed bent on military conquest, however, he decided that something had to be done to check Japan. But Hoover refused to approve using sanctions, and Washington responded rhetorically with the Stimson Doctrine* of nonrecognition. Many historians later insisted on referring to it as the Hoover-Stimson Doctrine, arguing that the president had proposed the idea and restrained his voluable secretary of state. When the Japanese military attacked Shanghai in 1932, Hoover did order the American fleet to Hawaii and the landing of U.S. troops to protect American citizens and their property in the foreign settlements.

After leaving the White House, Hoover remained committed to avoiding recourse to military force. His consistency and independent thinking probably stemmed from his anxiety about preserving American capitalism, as well as his early Quaker beliefs. Hoover therefore criticized Washington policy makers who edged the nation toward war with Nazi Germany and Japan in 1940 and 1941 and later as they confronted the Soviet Union after 1945. He urged President Harry S. Truman* to make a concerted effort to end the war with Japan by relaxing insistence on unconditional surrender and condemned the president's decision to order the Atomic Bomb Attacks* against Japan. Similarly, Hoover later opposed U.S. participation in the North Atlantic Treaty Organization and its intervention in the Korean War*, advocating instead the concentration of U.S. resources on building a "Gibraltar America."

M. L. Fausold, *The Presidency of Herbert C. Hoover* (Lawrence, KS, 1985); H. Hoover, *Memoirs,*

1920–1933 (London, 1952); C. Thorne, *The Limits of Foreign Policy: The West, the League and the Far Eastern Crisis of 1931–1933* (London, 1972); J. H. Wilson, *Herbert Hoover: Forgotten Progressive* (Boston, 1975).

Noel H. Pugach

HORNBECK, STANLEY K. (1883–1966)

Stanley Kuhl Hornbeck was chief of the State Department's Division of Far Eastern Affairs from 1928 to 1937 and adviser on political relations from 1936 to 1944. His highly educated, pedagogical personality made him a formidable advocate of his opinion. Hornbeck was a member of Phi Beta Kappa, Colorado's first Rhodes scholar, a teacher in several Chinese colleges, and recipient of a doctorate from the University of Wisconsin, where Paul S. Reinsch* was one of his professors. As author of several books, including *Contemporary Politics in the Far East* (1916), and lecturer at Harvard, he brought a high level of erudition combined with a largely self-taught knowledge of East Asia to his profession. Hornbeck's diplomatic experience was likewise extensive. He was part of almost every major discussion on U.S. Asia policy from 1918 to 1944. Prior to becoming chief, he had served under Woodrow Wilson* on his "Inquiry" at the Versailles Peace Conference. He also was an adviser at the Washington Conference* of 1921 and 1922 and present at both the Beijing Tariff Conference of 1925 and the Commission on the Extraterritoriality in 1926. A cool and calculating master of bureaucratic infighting, Hornbeck was once described by an aide as a man who "handled power as a draper handles bolts of cloth." None before and few since have matched his combination of intellect, experience, and forceful leadership.

For most of the 1930s the formulation of U.S. Asia policy took place in the Department of State, as both Presidents Herbert Hoover* and Franklin D. Roosevelt* concentrated on domestic issues. Hornbeck, in a key position of influence, worked well with, and usually supported, the general strategies of Secretaries of State Henry L. Stimson* and Cordell Hull*, but sometimes disagreed on tactics. Often identified in outlook and opinion with Willard D. Straight* and Reinsch, he uncompromisingly supported China, was antagonistic to Japan, and made wild and untimely predictions, some of which proved wrong. Hornbeck's actual views were far more complex and evolving. His basic approach, not too different from that of his 1920s colleague John V. A. MacMurray*, looks realistic in retrospect. Hornbeck argued that Japan's *and* China's actions were contrary to not only their own long-range interests, but those of the entire world community. Both countries had an obligation to carry out their treaty commitments; neither nationalism understood rational compromise nor could U.S. policies in the region satisfy either one.

After the Mukden Incident* of 1931, Hornbeck tried to follow an evenhanded policy toward China and Japan, but after the Marco Polo Bridge Incident* in 1937, he began to promote a stronger stand of economic sanctions to force the Japanese to recognize the potentially enormous consequences of their actions. He consistently argued that Japan would find China a quagmire and never would succeed in controlling it. His call for careful naval and economic pressures was calculated not only to cripple the Japanese effort in China, but also to diminish Japan's capacity to fight the United States if war indeed occurred. In addition, Hornbeck counseled that "on the one hand Japan must be restrained; on the other Japan must be given a sense of political and economic security." Hull disagreed on the viability of economic sanctions, as did Ambassador Joseph C. Grew* in Japan, but Roosevelt leaned toward Hornbeck's position when he took a keener interest in 1940. Hornbeck kept his beliefs, and a week before the Pearl Harbor Attack*, in his most infamous prophecy,

said the odds were strongly against a war with Japan.

R. D. Burns, "Stanley K. Hornbeck, the Diplomacy of the Open Door," in R. D. Burns and E. M. Bennett (eds.), *Diplomats in Crisis: United States-Chinese-Japanese Relations, 1919–1941* (Santa Barbara, CA, 1974); J. D. Doenecke, *The Diplomacy of Frustration: The Manchurian Crisis of 1931–1933 as Revealed in the Papers of Stanley K. Hornbeck* (Stanford, CA, 1981); S. Hu, *Stanley Hornbeck and the Open Door Policy: 1919–1937* (Westport, CT, 1995).

Thomas H. Buckley

HOSOKAWA MORIHIRO (1938–)

Hosokawa Morihiro became prime minister of Japan in August 1993, ending the control of the Liberal Democratic Party* over the government that began in 1955. Grandson of Konoe Fumimaro*, a former three-time prime minister, he graduated from Sophia University, Tōkyō, and then became a pressman for the *Asabi Shimhun*. Hosokawa was a member of the House of Councilors from 1971 to 1983 and governor of Kumamoto Prefecture from 1983 to 1991. In 1992, he formed the Japan New Party and became its leader, gaining election to the Diet's lower house in July the following year. After inauguration as prime minister, he sought to reform the economic and the political-administrative structure, as well as satisfy U.S. demands for comprehensive relaxation of trade regulations and liberalization of rice import policy. In his address before the UN General Assembly on 27 September 1993, he stressed Japan's readiness to contribute to UN Peace Keeping Operations (PKO) and support for reform of the body's administration and finances. Hosokawa also mentioned reorganization of the UN Security Council to provide a permanent seat for Japan. That same day, he met U.S. President Bill Clinton* and agreed to continue steps toward reducing Japan's trade surplus. In this context, the U.S. government announced in October 1993 the postponing of enforcement of economic sanctions against Japan until January 1994.

Hosokawa attended the meeting of the Asia-Pacific Economic Cooperation* forum held at Seattle in November 1993, meeting with fifteen other Pacific Rim leaders. There, Clinton advanced the idea of an Asia-Pacific Community, but Hosokawa opposed creation of an Asian version of the European Community because of the diversities of the region. Clinton asked Hosokawa for progress in opening the rice market in Japan and cooperation to limit nuclear development by the Democratic People's Republic of Korea*, but Hosokawa's response was equivocal. Thereafter, he met with President Kim Young-sam* of the Republic of Korea* at Gyŏng-ju, Korea, in November 1993 and at Tōkyō in March 1994. In their talks, Hosokawa apologized for past Japanese Colonialism* in Korea. They agreed to cooperate in the new Asia-Pacific era after the Cold War and respond jointly to the North Korean Nuclear Controversy* in coordination with the United States. During a meeting in Beijing with the leaders of the People's Republic of China* in March 1994, he asked them to provide greater respect for human rights in China, but the Chinese leaders resisted his pressure.

Under Hosokawa, U.S.-Japan Postwar Trade Relations* still was a major source of friction. In January 1994, the U.S. trade representative suggested reviving the Super 301 Article, which specified punishment for nations following unfair trade practices. At his third summit with Clinton the next month, Hosokawa rejected the setting of numerical goals for imports to Japan in the three areas of government procurement of telecommunications and medical machines, insurance, and automobiles and their parts. Despite this disagreement, both leaders agreed that the U.S.-Japanese alliance remained unchanged regarding politics and security. In April 1994, a money scandal forced Hosokawa to resign as prime minister. His government never had been strong because it was a coalition comprising eight opposition parties. During May 1998, he left the Diet. That summer, his article "Are U.S. Troops in Japan Needed?" in *Foreign Affairs* asserted the advisability of U.S. troop withdrawal from Japan.

W. LaFeber, *The Clash: A History of U.S.-Japan Relations* (New York, 1997); J. I. Matray, *Japan's Emergence as a Global Power* (Westport, CT, 2000); Ozawa Eiji, *Hosokawa seiken 250 nichi no shinjitsu* [The Truth of 250 Days of the Hosokawa Administration] (Tōkyō, 1994).

Nagata Akifumi

HU SHI (1891–1962)

Hu Shi was an important Chinese intellectual, educator, and political commentator. He symbolized for many Americans the possibility of building a liberal democratic China, in effect re-creating and legitimizing an idealized version of the U.S. political order. Son of a scholar and degree-holder educated in the Confucian classics, Hu also received traditional instruction in his youth. His ties to the United States began in 1910, when he earned a Boxer Indemnity scholarship, which enabled him to obtain a bachelor of arts degree from Cornell University, and then a doctorate from Columbia University. After his return to China, he became an instructor at Beijing University, a national center of cultural and political debate. His writings played an important role in the New Culture Movement, a questioning of traditional culture and the search for outside ideas that might bring about China's internal unity and international strength. Hu became a vocal proponent of importing the Western ideas of liberal democracy, individualism, and the scientific method. Influenced by the pragmatism and experimentalism of John Dewey, one of his instructors at Columbia, Hu stressed the need for the Chinese people to avoid what he believed were vague ideologies such as Communism*.

Although not a supporter of the Chinese Communist Party* (CCP), Hu became a persistent critic of the Guomindang* (Nationalist) government led by Jiang Jieshi*. Despite his dissent, he advanced the moderate image Jiang sought to promote to obtain American support. In this capacity, Hu returned to the United States with a government-sponsored goodwill tour in 1937, served as ambassador to the United States from 1938 to 1942, and was a member of the Chinese delegation to the United Nations in 1945. After returning to China for four years, he once again came to the United States after the CCP victory in the Chinese Civil War*. Jiang continued to court Hu, and enticed him to move to Taiwan* in 1958 by naming him head of the Academia Sinica, the premier academic institution in the Republic of China*. Hu struggled to maintain his ideals and independence, even as his presence suggested at least a tacit acceptance of Jiang's regime. His last major moment in the limelight came in 1960, when he was a hesitant supporter of *Free China* (*Ziyou Zhongguo*) magazine, a publication critical of the Nationalists, until it was forced to close.

Hu illustrated both the influence and the limitations of Western ideas upon China. To Americans, he seemed a tangible sign that a liberal, democratic China—neither the Communism of Mao Zedong* nor Jiang's authoritarianism—was possible. In reality, Hu's career epitomized the weakness of Westernized intellectuals in Republican China and the barriers Americans faced in seeking to export their political system and ideology. He struggled to reconcile his harsh critique of traditional China with the demands of national loyalty in the face of Western and Japanese imperialism. Hu's advocacy of individualism seemed selfish to many of his compatriots, when placed in the context of the perceived need for collective action to strengthen, unify, and change China. He was a moderate without an army in a highly militarized era, whose ideas had little to offer the vast majority of Chinese, who were peasants struggling to survive. His independent stance made it difficult for him and

people like him to forge a viable alternative to the CCP or the Nationalists.

H. Boorman (ed.), *Biographical Dictionary of Republican China* (New York, 1968); J. Grieder, *Hu Shih and the Chinese Renaissance* (Cambridge, MA, 1970); V. Schwarcz, *The Chinese Enlightenment: Intellectuals and the Legacy of the May Fourth Movement of 1919* (Berkeley, CA, 1986).

Steven E. Phillips

HU YAOBANG (1915–1989)

Conservative forces within the leadership of the Chinese Communist Party (CCP) blamed Hu Yaobang for expressions of public unrest in 1989 that, after his unexpected death, resulted in the Tiananmen Square Massacre*. Born in Liuyang, Hunan, he was just twelve years old when the Autumn Harvest Uprising took place in 1927, at which time he joined the so-called Children's Corps. By 1933, Hu was active in youth work in the Jiangxi Soviet, and rose to a leading role in the Communist Youth League by the end of 1935. He was a survivor of the Long March, which placed him among the most honored ranks within the Chinese Communist movement. In 1941, he headed the General Political Department of the Eighteenth Corps of the Red Army and in 1947 became director of the Organization Department of the Revolutionary Military Council. When the People's Republic of China* (PRC) was established in October 1949, Hu was elected to the National Committee of the National People's Political Consultative Conference, a position he held until 1964. During the 1950s and early 1960s, he was active in the Youth League and, from 1953 through 1957, served on the Executive Council of the Federation of Trade Unions. Hu also took part during these years in several international delegations and came to know the world outside China, at least in the socialist bloc, better than many other leaders in the CCP.

When the Chinese Cultural Revolution* began, Hu was denounced by Red Guards as a member of Liu Shaoqi's antiparty clique, and disappeared from public view from January 1967 through April 1972. His reappearance coincided with the first rehabilitation of Deng Xiaoping*, with whose career Hu's came to be closely linked. He was elected to the Central Committee of the CCP in August 1977, and was named to the Standing Committee of the National People's Congress in March 1978. He also resumed international activities, serving on a delegation to Cambodia* late in 1978. As Deng put his Four Modernizations* into place, Hu became general secretary of the Central Committee of the CCP in 1979, a member of the Standing Committee of the Political Bureau in 1980, and a member of the Presidium of the State Council in 1982. During these years, he was an outspoken advocate of economic reform and opening to the outside world. Hu also associated with efforts to broaden political participation in China, and students and young professionals in particular saw him as more open and sensitive to their concerns than most senior CCP leaders. Hu's long years of work with the Communist Youth League helped develop and sustain his contacts with students and other groups of younger party members and professionals.

Yet it was this same association with more liberal elements that led to Hu's downfall. In December 1986, student demonstrations took place on campuses in several parts of China. Linked to the anniversary of anti-Japanese demonstrations in the 1930s, they benefited from some patriotic legitimacy. But they also included calls for greater political reform and expansion of political participation by educated elements in society. Blamed for the burgeoning democracy movement, in January 1987, Hu was removed from his leading posts and publicly criticized. Deng Xioaping acquiesced in his removal because he accepted the link between Hu's outspoken views and the student demonstrations. Although he had been forced to step down as CCP general secretary, Hu remained in the Political Bureau, suggest-

ing that his political base was broader than Deng's support alone. In April 1989, while addressing a meeting of the Political Bureau, he collapsed with a heart attack and died. Rumors spread that he had been arguing for further reforms in a heated debate. His funeral provided the occasion in Beijing's Tiananmen Square for public expressions of support for economic and political reform on the part of students and others, which rapidly developed into large-scale student demonstrations. These protests finally were suppressed militarily on the night of 3–4 June, with the loss of hundreds of lives.

M. Goldman and R. MacFarquhar (eds.), *The Paradox of China's Post-Mao Reforms* (Cambridge, MA, 1999); R. MacFarquhar, *The Politics of China: The Eras of Mao and Deng* (Cambridge, MA, 1997); M. Meisner, *Mao's China and After: A History of the People's Republic* (New York, 1999).

Kenneth J. Hammond

HUA GUOFENG (1921–)

When Mao Zedong* died, Hua Guofeng became the new chairman of the Chinese Communist Party* (CCP), thereafter traveling extensively abroad as the People's Republic of China* opened to the outside world. Born in Jiaocheng County, Shaanxi Province, Hua came from a poor peasant family who fled to northern Shaanxi Province because of natural disasters when he was still a young child. Late in 1935, the CCP forces arrived in northern Shaanxi at the end of the Long March, and shortly thereafter, at the age of fifteen, Hua began to serve in the Red Army. By 1949, he had risen to become CCP secretary of the Xiangyin County Party Committee in Hunan, Mao's native province. This link with Mao was enhanced by Hua's performance in the 1950s during the agricultural cooperatives movement and the Great Leap Forward, when he was in charge of a major reservoir project in Shaoshan, Mao's home district. In 1958, Hua became vice governor of Hunan and then secretary of the Hunan Party Committee. In 1964, he was elected to the National People's Congress.

When the Chinese Cultural Revolution* broke out, Hua was active on the Maoist side. In July 1967, Zhou Enlai* recommended him to play a leading role in the preparation of the Hunan Province Revolutionary Committee, the functional ruling group during the chaos of inner party struggle. Elected to the Central Committee of the CCP for the important Ninth Party Congress in April 1969, Hua became chairman of the Provincial Revolutionary Committee in 1970. Thereafter, Hua's career moved beyond Hunan, when he was brought to Beijing to share in the leadership of the secret group investigating the fall of Lin Biao*. In 1973, he was elected to the CCP Political Bureau and in 1975, named a vice premier and minister of public security. Early in 1976, after Zhou died and as Mao became aware of his own imminent death, Hua was elevated to the position of premier and first vice chairman of the CCP. In a famous meeting with the ailing chairman, Mao reportedly said to Hua, "With you in charge, I'm at ease." After Mao's death in September 1976, Hua became CCP chairman.

Hua's grasp of the leadership of the Chinese state and the CCP was tenuous at best. His position was wholly a result of Mao's personal support. Yet Hua was forced immediately to distance himself from Mao's closest supporters, the so-called Gang of Four. He authorized their arrest less than a month after Mao's death. Hua came to be identified with what was called the Whatever Faction, because he said he supported whatever Mao had said or done, but had no real ideas or policies of his own. Without an independent power base in the party, army, or political structure, he became an empty figurehead, as Deng Xiaoping* and his alliance of pragmatic bureaucrats came to hold real power. Hua retained his leading positions into the early 1980s, leading diplomatic delegations to Eastern Europe in 1978, Western Europe

in 1979, and Japan in 1980. But by 1982, he had fallen to being a simple member of the Central Committee. Hua returned to Hunan, and has remained a largely forgotten figure there.

W. Bartke and P. Schier (eds.), *China's New Party Leadership* (Armonk, NY, 1985); R. MacFarquhar, *The Politics of China: The Eras of Mao and Deng* (Cambridge, MA, 1997); M. Meisner, *Mao's China and After: A History of the People's Republic* (New York, 1999).

Kenneth J. Hammond

HUANG HUA (1913–)

Huang Hua was a senior diplomat of the People's Republic of China* (PRC) who studied under the American missionary educator J. Leighton Stuart*, the founder of Yanjing University. The young Huang became one of the first students to study there, where he earned his degree and developed a student-teacher relationship with Stuart. In the 1930s, Huang gradually leaned toward the left and became involved in the Communist revolution. As one of the very few well-educated men in the Chinese Communist Party* (CCP), Huang steadily rose in importance. From January 1949 to June 1950, Huang Hua's mission for the CCP was to develop and maintain good relations with the United States. Although ideologically different from the United States and often denouncing the American support for the Guomindang* (Nationalist) regime, the CCP had established cordial relations with the Roosevelt administration during World War II. It realized that recognition and support from the United States would be valuable in pursuit of victory in the Chinese Civil War*. As a former student of Yanjing University, Huang was instructed to contact his former teacher, Stuart, who now was the U.S. ambassador to the Nationalist regime at Nanjing.

In 1948, the United States was hesitant to maintain support for the retreating Nationalist regime, but was also reluctant to deal with the forthcoming Communist government. In early 1949, when the People's Liberation Army approached Nanjing, the Nationalist regime retreated, urging all foreign embassies to join it in flight. Although the Soviet ambassador did so, Stuart chose to remain in Nanjing, indicating that his government might be interested in communicating with the new regime. Before Nanjing fell, Huang sneaked into town under disguise and paid a few secret visits to Stuart. Their conversations focused on how to reset the relationship between the United States and the CCP. He tried to convince the U.S. government that the PRC would be able to maintain stability, and that it would be in Washington's best interest to recognize the new regime. Sufficient evidence suggests that Huang and Stuart reached a number of understandings, creating hope of normalizing relations between the two governments. The rapid development of the warfare, however, pushed aside the pledge Huang and his teacher had made. As the Nationalist Army disintegrated, the Communists raised their expectations, and U.S. skepticism grew. After the Korean War* broke out, a hostile relationship between Washington and Beijing was confirmed. Throughout the next three decades, Huang remained a Communist diplomat, and rose to the post of minister of foreign affairs in 1983. See also Zhou-Stuart conversations.

Y. Shaw, An American Missionary in China: John Leighton Stuart and Chinese-American Relations (Cambridge, MA, 1992); Song Jiang, Bainian waijiao fengyun lu [A Record of 100 Years of Rapid Change in Foreign Relations] (Shenyang, 1995); J. L. Stuart, Fifty Years in China: The Memoirs of John Leighton Stuart, Missionary and Ambassador (New York, 1954); U.S. Department of State, Foreign Relations of the United States, 1949, Vol. 8: China (Washington, 1978).

Li Yi

HUGHES, CHARLES EVANS (1862–1948)

Charles Evans Hughes was secretary of state from 1921 to 1925 under Presidents Warren G. Harding and Calvin Coolidge. Prior to that appointment, he worked for two decades as a practicing lawyer and at times as an investigative prosecutor. After being elected to two terms as governor of New York (1907–1910), Hughes served for six years as associate justice on the U.S. Supreme Court before resigning to run as the unsuccessful Republican candidate for the presidency in 1916. He later concluded his distinguished career as a public servant as chief justice of the Supreme Court from 1930 to 1941. His appointment as secretary of state brought prestige and integrity to an increasingly beleaguered Harding administration. Neither Harding nor Coolidge chose to emulate the active role in foreign affairs Woodrow Wilson* had undertaken. Both were content to let Hughes conduct U.S. foreign policy, even though he had not shown much interest in foreign affairs in his previous career and came into office with no experience in the area. He did possess, however, a formidable intellect, as well as leadership skills of a high order. A workaholic, sometimes to the point of exhaustion, Hughes applied to the study of foreign problems the same analytical skills and thoroughness of preparation that had served him so well in the law. His belief that "foreign policies are not built on abstractions" led him to pursue limited, pragmatic solutions to specific problems. Hughes feared budget deficits, recognized political restraints, and tried to build public support for his policies.

Hughes's most significant contribution to East Asian policies came with the Washington Conference* in 1921 and 1922. Concluding that American interests in the Pacific were not great enough to fight for in a war, and doubting that the American people or Congress would want to spend many tax dollars to build battleships, fortify Pacific islands, or defend China, he decided that diplomacy, rather than war, would best serve American interests. He viewed the Japanese, reluctant participants at the conference, as negotiators with whom he could do business. His Five

Power Pact* they could not afford to refuse—naval security in the western Pacific in exchange for limitations on their further building of capital ships (battleships and battlecruisers) and fortifications. Hughes also worked to end the Anglo-Japanese Alliance*, which he believed, contrary to perceived wisdom then and now, had not restrained Japan in China or elsewhere in Asia. His Four Power Pact* replaced what he saw only as Britain's hope that it might keep the Japanese from moving into its spheres of influence. As for the Chinese, the secretary wanted them to stabilize their nation, keep their word in international treaties, and maintain an open door for trade, resulting in foreign treaty rights being slowly, but surely, ameliorated and then abolished. Hughes's faith in the ability of the Nine Power Pact* to fend off challenges to China's territory and sovereignty was misplaced. It was the weakest link in the Washington treaties, reflecting a lack of understanding of the growing force of Chinese nationalism by Hughes and others at the conference.

Two other policies of Hughes's in Asia deserve attention. The National Origins Act* of 1924 unwisely gave the Japanese no quota, causing Japanese Ambassador Hanihara Masanao to send a letter of protest warning that "grave consequences" might occur if the law passed in its original version. Congress viewed this as a threat and overwhelmingly approved the bill. Although there has been speculation that John V. A. MacMurray* may have helped Hanihara draft the letter, Hughes, despite his disapproval of the bill, did not act to stem the congressional tide. The other incident involved the Lansing-Ishii Agreement* of 1917, which had recognized, as a temporary wartime expedient, that the Japanese had "special interests" in China. Although Hughes argued that the Nine Power Pact effectively negated that recognition, the agreement was not abrogated formally until 1923. But with or without U.S. consent, Japan seized Manchuria after he left office. By no definition could one

call Hughes an isolationist. "Cautious internationalist" comes the closest to describing his approach. He sought his goals in small steps, not in gigantic leaps. Hughes understood the limitations of the use of power and believed military means alone could not bring a stable peace.

D. J. Danelski and J. S. Tulchin (eds.), *The Autobiographical Notes of Charles Evans Hughes* (Cambridge, MA, 1973); M. J. Pusey, *Charles Evans Hughes*, 2 vols. (New York, 1951); J. C. Vinson "Charles Evans Hughes" in Norman A. Graebner (ed.), *An Uncertain Tradition: American Secretaries of State in the Twentieth Century* (New York, 1961).

Thomas H. Buckley

HUKBALAHAP

This Philippine term is the acronym for Hukbong Bayan Laban sa Hapon (People's Anti-Japanese Army), an anti-Japanese guerrilla army formed on 29 March 1939 by the Partido Komunista ng Pilipinas (PKP, the first Philippine Communist Party, established in 1930). The Hukbalahap, popularly known as the Huk, was created to resist the Japanese in the Philippines* and implement the general call of the Soviet Union for Communist parties to establish "antifascist" coalitions. But the PKP originally had additional plans for the Huk, intending to make this "people's army" one of the foundations of its future "people's republic." Among many Huk units, this was interpreted as a signal for armed peasants to eliminate landlordism in the areas they controlled. The party leadership, however, opted to postpone its dream of a "people's republic" and de-emphasized class contradictions in the countryside in the interest of the "united front of all anti-Japanese elements." The PKP was concerned especially not to alienate "middle classes and moderate landlords" who could provide vital economic support. The party also pledged loyalty to the United States and the Philippine Commonwealth as part of what it conceived as a united struggle of all "patriotic anti-Japanese groups," thus implicitly accepting the return of the United States and refraining from calling for immediate independence after the war.

After World War II, the United States shifted its attention from Japan to the purported growing "Communist threat" in Asia, and any ties Americans had with Communist-led guerrilla forces immediately were supplanted by vigorous support for postcolonial anti-Communist governments. In the Philippines, Washington extended military and political assistance to a new republic that was pro-landlord and anti-Communist. Communist and Huk representatives were removed from the legislature on false charges of electoral fraud, and police and paramilitary forces began harassing Huk units and their mass bases in the provinces. Manuel Roxas, the new president, announced a "mailed fist" policy against the Huks. In January 1950, the PKP formally proclaimed its intention to use the Huks as the leading force in an all-out revolution to overthrow the government and "U.S. imperialism." The high point of Huk mobilization was in early 1950, when more than 10,000 Huk guerrillas launched attacks and steadily advanced toward Manila. Government corruption and incompetence reinforced popular belief in an eventual Huk triumph.

Huk fortunes had changed by the summer of 1950. Massive American aid and the appointment of a popular politician (and close American ally) Ramón Magsaysay* as secretary of defense turned the tide against the Huks. The Central Intelligence Agency* provided assistance in this effort, which was public knowledge because of the open involvement of top agency operative Edward G. Lansdale* in the planning and implementation of the counterinsurgency campaigns. The PKP leadership suffered a major blow when several politburo members were captured in Manila, and the remaining leaders split into factions. The surrender of the charismatic Huk leader Luis Taruc and his "expulsion" from the

PKP by his rivals effectively ended the rebellion, as peasant units loyal to Taruc followed their leader's call to abandon the revolution, and others degenerated into brigandage and gangsterism. When Magsaysay became president in 1953, his popularity helped revive public trust in constitutional politics and further undermined the Huk's legitimacy as a people's movement. By the 1960s, the Huks were a spent force, one of the more famous failed Communist uprisings in postwar Southeast Asia. The counterinsurgency program launched by the U.S. and Philippine governments against the Huks served as a model for similar anti-Communist schemes in Vietnam, where the United States tried to create a Vietnamese version of Magsaysay in the person of Ngo Dinh Diem*.

B. Kerklviet, *The Huk Rebellion: A Study of Peasant Revolt in the Philippines* (Berkeley, CA, 1977); E. Lansdale, *In the Midst of Wars: An American's Mission to Southeast Asia* (New York, 1972); F. Nemenzo, "Rectification Process and the Philippine Communist Movement," in L. Joo-Jock (ed.), *Armed Communist Movements in Southeast Asia* (Singapore, 1984).

Patricio N. Abinales

HULBERT, HOMER B. (1863–1949)

Homer Bezaleel Hulbert was a missionary and an educator who became a close adviser to King Kojong* in Korea early in the twentieth century. He graduated from Dartmouth College and studied at Union Theological Seminary. When Kojong asked the seminary to send able teachers, Hulbert traveled to Korea in July 1886. He was a teacher in the Royal English School (Yukyong Kong-wŏn) until December 1891, when he returned to the United States. Two years later, Hulbert was back in Korea, where he managed the Trilingual Press (Sam-mun Chulpan-sa) and preached as a Methodist missionary. He also revived the magazine *The Korean Repository* and started publishing and editing the magazine *The Korea Review* in 1901, contributing many articles to both. Kojong gave much credit to Hulbert for the modernization of Korea and by 1904, had made him his adviser. Hulbert had not been optimistic about Japanese policy toward East Asia and Korea since arriving at Seoul. But during the Russo-Japanese War*, he decided that Korea needed reform and therefore supported in *The Korean Review* the Japanese cause against Russia, believing this would advance peace in East Asia and the independence of Korea. After Japanese troops entered Korea, however, Hulbert realized that Japan was destroying Korea's independence. This defied a protocol between Japan and Korea signed on 23 February 1904 guaranteeing Korean sovereignty, a point Hulbert made thereafter in his articles criticizing Japan.

In July 1905, Japan secured approval for control in Korea from the United States in the Taft-Katsura Agreement* (kept secret until 1924). Britain gave its consent in the second Anglo-Japanese Alliance* in August and Russia in the Treaty of Portsmouth* in September. In these circumstances, Kojong sent Hulbert to the United States with his letter to ask for aid to preserve Korea's independence under the Shufeldt Treaty* of 1882. He left Korea in October and arrived at Washington on 17 November, the day the second Japanese-Korean convention was signed in Seoul, providing for Japanese control of Korean diplomacy and establishing the post of resident general in Korea. Hulbert tried to meet President Theodore Roosevelt* and his Secretary of State Elihu Root*, but Roosevelt refused. However, Root met with Hulbert on 25 November and explained the impossibility of American intervention because of the existence of the convention. Hulbert was critical of the Roosevelt administration's responses to the Korean problem in his 1906 book *The Passing of Korea* and in an article in the *New York Times* on 5 March 1916. In *The Korean Review* in July 1906, he also criticized journalist George Kennan*, who strongly supported Japanese policy toward Korea.

After 1906, Hulbert often collaborated with Korean patriots for the realization of Korea's independence. He also participated in delivering Korean petitions to the Second Hague Peace Conference in 1907 and, after the Japanese Annexation of Korea* in 1910, the Versailles Peace Conference in 1919, the Washington Conference* in 1921 and 1922, and the Allies during World War II. Hulbert lived in Springfield, Massachusetts, after 1908 and in his articles continued to support the independence of Korea and to criticize Japanese Colonialism*. After the liberation of Korea in 1945 and the founding of the Republic of Korea* in 1948, President Syngman Rhee* sent a letter of invitation to Hulbert to visit Korea. Hulbert accepted and arrived at Seoul on 29 July 1949, but at age eighty-six, he was exhausted after the long journey and died on 5 August. His body was buried in the Seoul Foreigner's Cemetery in accordance with the stated wish in his will that "I would rather be buried in Korea than in Westminster Abbey."

H. B. Hulbert, *The Passing of Korea* (Seoul, 1969); C. N. Weems (ed.), *Hulbert's History of Korea*, 2 vols. (London, 1962).

Nagata Akifumi

HULL, CORDELL (1871–1955)

Cordell Hull was, as secretary of state from 1933 to 1944, prominently involved in the determination of policy toward Japan prior to the Pearl Harbor Attack* and in formulating U.S. plans for the postwar world. From humble origins in Tennessee, he became a lawyer and moved quickly into politics. Hull was elected to the U.S. House of Representatives in 1906, a seat that he held (with one two-year interruption) until 1931, when he won a seat in the U.S. Senate. In Congress, he became a vigorous advocate of free trade as the key to worldwide economic growth and political stability. When Franklin D. Roosevelt* was elected president in 1932, Hull became his secretary of state. With the president's support, he worked with considerable success for the liberalized trade policy that he cherished.

Hull's effectiveness was limited by his strained relationship with Roosevelt. Besides Roosevelt's disposition to be a strong leader on foreign and domestic issues, Hull's deliberative style and caution irritated him. Roosevelt went around Hull, working directly with the undersecretary of state and appointing special emissaries who reported directly to him. One area in which Hull was able to exert considerable influence was in defining the U.S. response to Japan's aggression, beginning with the attack on China after the Marco Polo Bridge Incident* of 1937. Hull tried to chart a middle course between "hawks" and "doves" within the administration. Although clearly opposed to Japan's expansionist "New Order" in East Asia, Hull also sought to avoid confrontation and to promote Japan's acceptance of a liberal international economic system. As relations worsened, Hull engaged in extensive diplomatic conversations with Japanese emissaries Kurusu Saburō* and Nomura Kichisaburō* in Washington throughout much of 1941. Hull was frustrated by his inability to change Japan's objectives and took the attack on Pearl Harbor, which occurred as negotiations were scheduled in Washington, as a personal affront.

During the war, the State Department worked on issues of long-term U.S. interest in Asia, including the planning for decolonization, a liberal economic order, and a new international organization. Although Hull supported these measures and contributed significantly to planning for the United Nations, his influence generally waned, a consequence of his declining health and of Roosevelt's domination of the most important policy issues. Hull resigned in November 1944, having held the position of secretary of state longer than any other person in American history. A year later, he received the Nobel Peace Prize in recognition of his role in establish-ing the United Nations. *See also* Nomura-Hull Conversations.

R. A. Dallek, *Franklin D. Roosevelt and American Foreign Policy, 1932–1945* (New York, 1979); I. Gelman, *Secret Affairs: Franklin Roosevelt, Cordell Hull, and Sumner Welles* (Baltimore, 1995); C. Hull, *The Memoirs of Cordell Hull*, 2 vols. (Garden City, NY, 1948); J. Pratt, *Cordell Hull, 1933–1944*, vols. 12–13, *American Secretaries of State and Their Diplomacy*, S. F. Bemis (ed.), (New York, 1964); J. Utley, *Going to War with Japan, 1937–1941* (Knoxville, TN, 1985).

Gary R. Hess

HUN SEN (1952–)

Hun Sen was a former Khmer Rouge* army officer who refused to engage in suicidal attacks on the Socialist Republic of Vietnam* (SRV) in 1977. Cambodian leader Pol Pot* thus forced him to flee to Vietnam for his life. Sen was part of the invasion force when Vietnam invaded Cambodia* in December 1978 and later became a member of the ruling group for the People's Republic of Kampuchea. By the mid-1980s, he had become the dominant figure in the coalition, assuming the position of prime minister under Vietnam's occupation, which technically ended during 1989 with the withdrawal of Vietnamese troops. As a result of elections sponsored and supervised by the United Nations Transitional Authority in Cambodia in 1993 and the losses suffered by Hun Sen's People's Party, a coalition government with two prime ministers emerged. One of them was Hun Sen and the other was Prince Norodom Ranariddh, son of Norodom Sihanouk*, who led the royalist party. Hun Sen forced Ranariddh out of the government in 1997.

D. Chandler, *A History of Cambodia* (Boulder, CO, 2000); W. Shawcross, *Deliver Us From Evil: Peacekeepers, Warlords and a World of Endless Conflict* (New York, 2000).

T. Christopher Jespersen

HURLEY, PATRICK J. (1883–1963)

Ambassador to China from 1944 to 1945, Patrick Jay Hurley publicly accused U.S. Foreign Service officers, known as the China Hands*, of disloyalty in encouraging a Communist victory in the Chinese Civil War*. Born in Oklahoma, he was an Indian Territory volunteer cavalryman and then a coal miner before teaching U.S. history at Baptist Indian University. Hurley earned a law degree in 1908 and opened his practice in Tulsa, later representing the Choctaw Nation. In World War I, he fought in France as an officer in the Oklahoma National Guard. Hurley was a staunch Republican who became a millionaire through oil, banking, and other ventures in the 1920s. After his efforts won Oklahoma for Herbert Hoover* in the 1928 presidential election, the new president soon appointed him secretary of war. In this position, he strongly opposed early independence for the Philippines*, and drew criticism during July 1932 for ordering the expulsion of jobless Bonus Marchers from federal property. Hurley then represented Sinclair Oil Company, negotiating a claims agreement with the Mexican government in 1940 that helped end a dispute over American oil properties Mexico had expropriated in 1938. During World War II, Brigadier General Hurley, as minister to New Zealand in 1942, supervised actions to break the blockade of Bataan. Although Hurley was a harsh critic of President Franklin D. Roosevelt*, the president sent him on missions to the Soviet Union and Iran in 1943 to arrange transportation and economic aid.

A rugged individualist, Hurley was known for his terse talk and forceful action. In 1944, as Roosevelt's personal representative, he attempted to mediate a prolonged disputed between General Joseph W. Stilwell*, commander of the China-Burma-India Theater*, and China's Guomindang* (Nationalist) leader Jiang Jieshi*. The two were at odds over military strategy, a situation made worse by mutual personal antipathy. Jiang's insistence on reserving his troops to fight the Communists, coupled with a major Japanese military offensive, brought bilateral relations to a crisis in the spring. After the Ichigo Offensive*, Roosevelt agreed to Stilwell's proposal to assume control of all troops, including Jiang's and forces of the Chinese Communist Party* (CCP). Incensed, Jiang asked for time to make adjustments and a personal emissary from the president to oversee the transition to the new arrangement. Hurley worked to resolve not only the conflicts between Jiang and Stilwell, but also the feud between Jiang and CCP leader Mao Zedong*. In each venture, he failed and then sided with Jiang when the Chinese leader successfully requested Stilwell's recall. But Hurley's mission became more significant later. In November 1945, he resigned his position as ambassador (to which he had been promoted after the Stilwell incident) and publicly accused State Department personnel with whom he had worked of disloyalty and undermining his efforts. His charges caused a sensation and were resurrected later by Asia-first politicians to discredit the Truman administration after Mao gained power on the mainland and established the People's Republic of China* in 1949.

R. D. Buhite, *Patrick J. Hurley and American Foreign Policy* (Ithaca, NY, 1973); R. Y. Koen, *The China Lobby in American Politics* (New York, 1974); *New York Times*, 31 July 1963; M. Schaller, *The U.S. Crusade in China, 1938–1945* (New York, 1979); B. W. Tuchman, *Stilwell and the American Experience in China, 1931–45* (New York, 1970).

T. Christopher Jespersen

I

IA DRANG VALLEY, BATTLE OF THE

See BATTLE OF THE IA DRANG VALLEY

ICHIGO OFFENSIVE (April–December 1944)

This occurred from April to December 1944 and was Japan's most formidable military operation of World War II in China. It effectively knocked Guomindang* (Nationalist) government forces under Jiang Jieshi* out of the war, politically and militarily. Imperial headquarters planned the offensive to establish a continental corridor to Southeast Asia in the face of the growing U.S. naval threat to the sea lanes to the southern regions. Also, the strategic bomber bases of General Claire L. Chennault* and his U.S. Fourteenth Air Force in south-central China threatened the Japanese Expeditionary Force throughout the country, installations on Taiwan*, and the home islands themselves. Japan massed the largest concentration of troops for a single campaign since the Russo-Japanese War* and proceeded to slice through the Chinese defenses of six provinces, exposing the military and political hollowness of Jiang's regime, destroying Chennault's air bases, threatening Kunming and Chongqing, cre-

ating a tenuous Japanese link between north China and French Indochina*, and resulting in the recall of General Joseph W. Stilwell* in the wake of criticism from Jiang to President Franklin D. Roosevelt*. Ichigo was finally brought to a halt when Chinese armies were reinforced with two American-trained divisions from Burma* and the Japanese finally felt the impact of heavy casualties, disease, and logistical problems. Nevertheless, U.S. interest in China as a base of operations against Japan ended. See also China-Burma-India Theater.

H. Chi, *Nationalist China at War* (Ann Arbor, MI, 1982); L. Eastman, *Seeds of Destruction: Nationalist China in War and Revolution, 1937–1949* (Stanford, CA, 1984); R. L. Spector, *Eagle Against the Sun: The American War with Japan* (New York, 1985).

Errol M. Clauss

II NAOSUKE (1815–1860)

Ii Naosuke was a senior adviser in the Tokugawa shōgunate who advocated Japan's national opening in the mid-nineteenth century. At age thirty-one, he was adopted by his oldest brother and placed at the top of the Ii clan's primogenital line and assumed the domain's mastership in 1850. Ii became a senior councilor to Japan's decaying government and made an indelible mark on its attitude toward contact with the West. His desire to squelch the opposition to national opening fed into a sweeping crackdown by his critics known as *Ansei no Taigoku*. The backlash against his repressive rule resulted in Ii's assassination and ushered in the "Expel the Barbarian" Movement* aimed at restoring imperial rule. His vision of an open Japan, however, informed by a shrewd assessment of Western power and interests, was inherited by a generation of leaders who shaped modern Japan's foreign relations after his death.

In the debate triggered by the not entirely unanticipated arrival of U.S. Navy Commodore Matthew C. Perry* in Edo Bay in July 1853, Ii initially argued against accommodating the U.S. demand for coaling and resupplying privileges, protection of shipwrecked U.S. sailors, and the opening of ports to trade. But estimates of the risks of war with Western powers possessed of supreme military technology led Ii to change his position. He became a leading advocate of national opening within the shōgun's advisory circles and pushed for the Treaty of Kanagawa* with the United States, modern Japan's first international treaty, which was signed in March 1854. Japan agreed to open the ports of Shimoda and Hakodate to U.S. vessels, guarantee safe haven to shipwrecked American sailors reaching those ports, and accept a U.S. consul. Nevertheless, the United States was unhappy that the treaty contained no explicit provisions for American trading rights and extraterritoriality.

In August 1856, Townsend Harris*, the first U.S. consul general, arrived in Shimoda, from where he demanded negotiations toward a formal trade accord. Ii held that bans on foreign trade must inevitably be lifted, and he was instrumental in drafting the Harris Treaty* of commerce, friendship, and navigation that provided for a resident minister in Edo, the opening of five ports to foreign commerce, and foreign residency in Ōsaka and Edo. The shōgunate's request for imperial approval of the draft treaty, however, became entangled in the dispute over shōgunate succession after the death of childless Tokugawa Iyesada. The imperial court, which already feared foreign influences, became embroiled in the feud between the Hitotsubashi faction, which opposed the treaty, and Ii's Kishū faction. In June 1958, Ii, the dean of the Kishū group, assumed the position of regent (tairō), and pushed the shōgunate to sign the treaty in the absence of an imperial ratification. The treaty served as the model for similar arrangements with Russia, Britain, France, and Holland.

W. LaFeber, *The Clash: A History of U.S.-Japan Relations* (New York, 1997); Masuda Hiroshi, *Nichibei kankei gaisetsu* [A Survey of U.S.-Japanese Relations] (Tōkyō, 1978); Yoshida Tsunekichi, *Ii Naosuke* (Tōkyō, 1963).

Shimizu Sayuri

IKEDA HAYATO (1899–1965)

As a prophet and architect of Japan's astounding economic growth in the 1950s and 1960s, Ikeda Hayato, especially as prime minister between 1960 and late 1964, moved his nation closer to the United States after the anti-American riots in the Anpo Crisis* during May and June 1960 badly eroded the relationship. Ikeda had political skills, although he rose to power mostly through the bureaucracy, rather than the political system. Born in Hiroshima prefecture to a prosperous sake dealer, he studied law at Kyōto University and then became a tax specialist in the Finance Ministry. Ikeda proved so skillful that in 1947, he became vice minister of finance. After winning election to the Diet in 1949, he was appointed minister of finance in 1952 by pro-American Prime Minister Yoshida Shigeru*. Unlike Japanese colleagues, he was sharp-tongued. When his economic discipline led to business failures, Ikeda said, "It cannot be helped if five or ten medium and small entrepreneurs go into bankruptcies and hang themselves."

In 1960, violent, if ultimately unsuccessful, rioting against the renewal of the U.S.-Japan Security Treaty of 1951* toppled the Liberal Democratic Party* (LDP) government of Kishi Nobusuke*, but Ikeda led another LDP faction into power. He stunningly promised to double national income by 1970. His announcement pleased U.S. officials; it took Japanese eyes off the explosive security issues and focused them on economics and liberalizing U.S.-Japan Postwar Trade Relations*. Ikeda's approach, however, turned out to be largely a one-way street: U.S. imports from Japan soared, whereas the Japanese bureaucracy, which Ikeda knew intimately, maintained tight controls over foreign access to Japan's trade and financial markets. Moreover, to Washington's chagrin, he moved his business community closer to the Communist market in the People's Republic of China* (PRC). He thus weakened the Japanese left-of-center parties, but opened vast economic opportunities to Japan even as U.S. businesses were forbidden by Washington to deal with China. Ikeda meanwhile placated U.S. officials by cultivating and developing Southeast Asian markets.

Ikeda won reelection as prime minister in 1963. In late 1964, after helping Emperor Hirohito* celebrate Japan's rebirth by hosting the Olympic Games, ill health forced him to resign. He had come to the United States on several trips after 1951 to build U.S.-Japanese economic cooperation, and he realized his economic program's success rested on U.S. military protection. But his Buddhism, preference for wearing traditional Japanese clothes, love of nature, and belief that the politically insulated bureaucracy best protected the national interest all made him a representative, as well as a pivotal, figure in postwar U.S.-Japan relations. The success of his economic plans, driven and protected by the bureaucracy, and his desire to move closer to the PRC, anticipated the reasons for the souring of the Japanese-American relationship after 1964. *See also* Kennedy-Ikeda Conference.

G. C. Allen, *A Short Economic History of Modern Japan* (London, 1981); J. I. Matray, *Japan's Emer-*

gence as a Global Power (Westport, CT, 2000); W. R. Nester, *Japan and the Third World* (New York, 1992); G. W. Waldner, "Japanese Foreign Policy and Economic Growth: Ikeda Hayato's Approach to the Liberalization Issue," Ph.D. dissertation, Princeton University, 1975.

Walter LaFeber

INCH'ŎN LANDING (15 September 1950)

On 15 September 1950, this amphibious landing of UN troops on the west coast of South Korea led by General Douglas MacArthur* reversed the course of the Korean War*. It led to the recapture of Seoul from the North Korean forces and the offensive across the thirty-eighth parallel. After invading the Republic of Korea* in late June 1950, the Korean People's Army (KPA) was able to occupy three-quarters of South Korea in a month. Inch'ŏn, the Yellow Sea port halfway up Korea's west coast, occupied a strategic position just twenty-five miles west of Seoul, where Korea's main roads and rail lines converged. MacArthur, who surveyed the situation in Korea shortly after the KPA occupied Seoul, contemplated the launching of an amphibious assault at Inch'ŏn, Haeju, or Chinnamp'o in July 1950. He favored Inch'ŏn as the landing site. A force landing at Inch'ŏn would have to move inland only a short distance to cut North Korean supply routes, and recapturing the capital city would have a great psychological impact. Combined with a general northward advance by the U.S. Eighth Army besieged within the Pusan Perimeter*, landing at Inch'ŏn could have decisive results and end the war. Retreating enemy troops would be cut off by the amphibious force behind them or be forced to make a slow and difficult withdrawal through the mountains farther east.

MacArthur's superiors and the U.S. Navy judged the Inch'ŏn plan dangerous. Naval officers considered the extreme Yellow Sea tides, which range as much as thirty feet, as well as narrow channel approaches to Inch'ŏn, as big risks to shipping. Marine officers saw danger in landing in the middle of a fortified area and in having to scale high sea walls to get ashore. The Joint Chiefs of Staff anticipated serious consequences if Inch'ŏn was strongly defended, because MacArthur would be committing his last major reserves at a time when there were no more units in the United States available for shipment to East Asia. But on 15 September, when sufficient strength was in place and the Pusan Perimeter had stabilized, UN forces carried out the daring amphibious landing at Inch'ŏn, trapping North Korean troops in the south. This brilliant landing far north of the battlefront succeeded in cutting KPA supply lines, and the Communist forces were shattered by the convergence of UN troops from north and south. MacArthur's forces captured more than 125,000 North Korean prisoners.

R. E. Appleman, *South to the Naktong, North to the Yalu (June–November 1950)* (Washington, DC, 1961); C. Blair, *The Forgotten War: America in Korea, 1950–1953* (New York, 1987); R. D. Heinl Jr., *Victory at High Tide: The Inchon-Seoul Campaign* (Philadelphia, 1968); M. Langley, *Inchon: MacArthur's Last Triumph* (London, 1979).

Han Kyu-sun

INDONESIA

U.S.-Indonesia relations commenced on 17 August 1945, when the popular nationalist leaders Sukarno* and Mohammed Hatta* announced establishment of the independent Republic of Indonesia just days after Japan's surrender in World War II. Dutch authorities, however, fully intended to reestablish colonial sovereignty over the sprawling archipelago that they had ruled with an iron hand prior to the Japanese wartime occupation. Familiar with the wartime pledges of Franklin D. Roosevelt* favoring self-determination for all peoples, the fledgling Indonesian regime looked to the United States for support. But U.S. policy makers were almost totally unprepared

for the depth and intensity of the postwar nationalist rebellions that erupted not only in the Netherlands East Indies, but throughout Southeast Asia. Caught in the middle, President Harry S. Truman*, Roosevelt's successor, adopted a neutral stance toward the Dutch-Indonesian dispute, much as he did initially toward the struggle emerging in French Indochina*. His administration did not want to alienate expectant Third World nationalists whose support it sought to cultivate. At the same time, it valued even more its relationships with European partners such as the Netherlands, countries central to American efforts to block Soviet expansion in Europe. Groping for a middle ground, U.S. leaders made it clear that they would not contest the legal right of the Netherlands to resume its position as "territorial sovereign," but implored the Dutch and Indonesians to seek a peaceful resolution of their differences.

After 1945, the Truman administration repeatedly emphasized its preference for progressive steps leading to eventual Indonesian self-government, but its "neutrality" tilted markedly toward the Netherlands, as U.S. Marshall Plan aid actually facilitated indirectly Dutch efforts to restore imperial control. Only after two unsuccessful Dutch "police actions" aimed at suppressing the Indonesian independence movement and preserving Dutch Colonialism* did U.S. policy shift. The Truman administration's threat to withhold economic and military assistance to the Netherlands unless it clearly and irrevocably committed itself to granting Indonesian independence paved the way for the emergence of a fully independent Indonesian state in December 1949. Thereafter, the United States and Indonesia enjoyed only a short-lived honeymoon. Indonesian leaders were grateful for U.S. support for the independence movement, however belated, and sought U.S. aid in the massive reconstruction efforts that they faced. Yet the determination of President Sukarno and nearly all other influential Indonesian politicians to pursue a nonaligned foreign policy clashed with the desire of both Truman and his successor Dwight D. Eisenhower* to convert Indonesia formally to the anti-Communist cause. All U.S. efforts to enlist Indonesia in bilateral or multilateral security pacts with the United States crashed on the rock of Indonesian neutralism. Sukarno's rabid support for the incorporation of the disputed territory of West Irian (West New Guinea) into the Indonesian state also generated tensions between Jakarta and Washington.

By the mid-1950s, several forces had combined to strain Indonesian-American ties severely, among them Sukarno's continued agitation on the West Irian question, his periodic anti-Western outbursts, Indonesia's prominent role in the nonaligned movement (whose inaugural Bandung Conference* was held at Java's central city in 1955), Jakarta's warm relations with both Moscow and Beijing, and, above all, the growing power and influence of the Indonesian Communist Party (PKI). The failure by early 1958 of the Eisenhower administration's bold effort to undermine, if not actually topple, Sukarno by encouraging the PRRI-Permesta Rebellion* dealt a major blow to U.S.-Indonesian relations. Shifting course, Washington began giving generous assistance to the Indonesian armed forces as a potential counter against the mercurial Sukarno and his PKI allies. President John F. Kennedy* went a step further. Convinced that a combination of patience, understanding, and adroit diplomacy might regain lost ground for the United States, he courted Sukarno. The principal fruit of that effort was the successful U.S.-led mediation of the West Irian dispute. Firm U.S. pressure on the Netherlands brought about an August 1962 agreement that authorized the transfer of the disputed territory to Indonesia. But the agreement did little to ease some of the more fundamental problems plaguing Indonesian-American relations. As the power of the PKI increased, Sukarno became more vocal in his criticism of the United States.

A new era in U.S.-Indonesian relations began after a failed coup ignited the Indonesia Crisis of 1965* that resulted in General Suharto* replacing Sukarno as president. Over the next three decades, Suharto ruled Indonesia in authoritarian fashion. He encouraged a great surge in Western trade and investment, bringing much-needed political stability and genuine, if wildly uneven, economic growth to Indonesia. But democratic institutions did not follow suit; Suharto's remained a closed system that stifled voices of dissent. Washington, although it periodically urged democratization and criticized Indonesia's 1975 invasion of and subsequent bloody repression in the former Portuguese colony of East Timor, proved a major prop of the Suharto regime. During a state visit to Indonesia in 1986, President Ronald Reagan* lauded Suharto as "a long-time friend of the United States" and praised him for bringing progress and economic growth to his country. Only after the severe East Asian Financial Crisis* of 1997 hit Indonesia with especial force, sparking widespread political unrest, did the United States waver in its support for the Indonesian autocrat. The administration of Bill Clinton* reluctantly came to see the longstanding U.S. ally as a barrier to needed political and economic reforms within Indonesia. When Suharto chose to step aside in May 1998, handing over power to his vice president, B. J. Habibie, U.S. officials applauded his statesmanship. The Clinton administration then quietly urged the new leadership to engineer far-reaching political and economic reforms—evidently hoping that yet another positive turn might be dawning in U.S.-Indonesian relations. Yet stability proved elusive in the vacuum left by Suharto's departure. Ethnic and regional rebellions proliferated, and the struggle for political power in Jakarta continued. Indonesia's first elected president, Abdurraham Wahid, was forced out of power early in 2001 and replaced by Megawati Sukarnoputri, daughter of the nation's founder.

P. F. Gardner, *Shared Hopes, Separate Fears: Fifty Years of U.S.-Indonesian Relations* (New York, 1997); H. P. Jones, *Indonesia: The Possible Dream* (New York, 1971); G. McT. Kahin and A. R. Kahin, *Subversion as Foreign Policy: The Secret Eisenhower and Dulles Debacle in Indonesia* (New York, 1995); R. J. McMahon, *Colonialism and Cold War: The United States and the Struggle for Indonesian Independence, 1945–49* (Ithaca, NY, 1981); R. J. McMahon, *The Limits of Empire: The United States and Southeast Asia Since World War II* (New York, 1999).

Robert J. McMahon

INDONESIA CRISIS OF 1965

This crisis was one of the decisive events of the postwar history of East Asia, permanently altering the political landscape of Indonesia* and leading to more than thirty years of corrupt authoritarian rule under the U.S.-supported anti-Communist General Suharto*. It began on the night of 30 September 1965, when forces loyal to a little-known Indonesian lieutenant colonel named Untung staged an alleged coup in which six Indonesian generals were kidnapped and killed. The power grab by middle-ranking military officers appears to have been aimed at forestalling a rumored coup attempt against President Sukarno* by a "Council of Generals" who had support from the Central Intelligence Agency* (CIA). Suharto, commander of the Army's Strategic Reserve, launched a countercoup and routed the meager forces under Untung's command. Suharto blamed the Indonesian Communist Party (PKI) for the deaths of the generals, providing the pretext for one of the worst massacres of modern history. An army campaign of extermination directed at alleged members of the PKI and its affiliated organizations resulted in the killing of between 500,000 and 1 million people within a few months. Liquidation of the PKI eliminated the only mass-based alternative to military rule. It is unclear whether President Sukarno knew about the coup beforehand, but the army accused him of involvement indi-

rectly and moved against him. Sukarno was powerless to stop either the destruction of the PKI or the slow disintegration of his own political position. Thereafter, Suharto slowly whittled away at his power until Sukarno transferred authority to him in March 1966. Sukarno was placed under house arrest in 1967, where he remained until his death in 1970.

Although the United States was not directly implicated in the events of September 1965, it bore a degree of responsibility for the coup and its bloody aftermath. Both the United States and Britain conducted covert operations over the course of 1964 and 1965 aimed at provoking a violent clash between the army and the PKI. Even as the United States reduced its overt presence in Indonesia in 1965, U.S. officials sent many signals to army leaders that they would support a coup against Sukarno. After the coup, U.S. and British intelligence conducted propaganda operations to spread accusations of PKI responsibility for the murder of the generals. U.S. officials also gave enthusiastic support for the mass killing of alleged PKI supporters, sending covert funds, weapons, medicine, communications equipment, cotton, and rice to Indonesia's army. Scholars have debated fiercely the origins of the 1965 Indonesian crisis, but not the fact that the social and political legitimacy of Suharto's New Order rested upon public acceptance of the army's official story of the PKI's responsibility for the deaths of the six generals. But even though the PKI very likely played a minor role in the coup, it did not orchestrate events. Persuasive evidence exists that General Suharto knew of Untung's plans and took advantage of this knowledge to organize his own bid for power. Beyond dispute is the fact that the Suharto regime was much more supportive of U.S. interests than was Sukarno's. Suharto quickly became a loyal anti-Communist ally of the United States, participated in regional military and economic groupings, such as the Association of Southeast Asian Nations*, installed U.S.-trained technocrats in key posts, and passed a major foreign investment law that welcomed Western capital back to Indonesia.

H. W. Brands, "The Limits of Manipulation: How the United States Didn't Topple Sukarno," *Journal of American History* (Fall 1989); F. Bunnell, *American "Low Posture" Policy Toward Indonesia in the Months Leading Up to the 1965 "Coup"* (Indonesia, 1990); R. Cribb (ed.), *The Indonesian Killings of 1965–1966* (Victoria, BC, Canada, 1990); H. Crouch, *The Army and Politics in Indonesia* (Ithaca, NY, 1978); U.S. Department of State, *Foreign Relations of the United States, 1964–1968*, Vol. 26: *Indonesia; Malaysia-Singapore; Philippines* (Washington, DC, 2001).

Bradley R. Simpson

INSTITUTE OF PACIFIC RELATIONS

The Institute of Pacific Relations (IPR) was one of the focal points for non-governmental diplomacy between the United States and East Asia, and the major center of research on Asia in the United States in the years before 1945. Throughout its life span, the IPR was characterized by unclear leadership at the top, stemming from its structure of autonomous national councils, its unclear political position, and resultant leeway given to individual members in positions of power. The IPR was founded in 1925 as an association to "study the conditions of the Pacific peoples with a view to the improvement of their mutual relations." The initiative for creation of this important non-governmental organization (NGO) came from a number of prominent figures in Japan and the United States, including Stanford president Ray Lyman Wilbur and Merle Davis of the YMCA*. Privately sponsored and financed in theory, it was made up of economically self-supporting councils in each of the participant countries. The Pacific Council was a convention of one representative from each national council and met once every two to three years. Thirteen council meetings took place, from the first meeting in Honolulu in 1927 to the last held in La-

hore in 1957. Davis envisioned the IPR as a nonaligned, apolitical cultural organization. But Edward Carter thought that political and economic issues should be addressed and ousted Davis in 1929.

The original roster had Australia, Canada, China, Japan, New Zealand, and U.S. councils, and representatives from seven other areas, Britain, France, the Philippines*, India, the Soviet Union, the Netherlands and Dutch East Indies, and Korea, took part at various times. As part of being in an NGO for promoting U.S.-Asia relations, all directors resigned their positions once they accepted a government post. In addition to organizing conferences, the IPR published hundreds of books and pamphlets, the best known among them the IPR journal *Pacific Affairs*, and the American Council journal, the *Far Eastern Survey*. Although heralded as the bridge over the Pacific by some, however, the IPR often was marked by tensions and conflicts among the various councils and its members. For example, the Japan Council never quite trusted the IPR leaders such as Carter and Owen Lattimore* for anti-Japanese statements made during their lectures and speeches. Conversely, the American Council looked upon the speeches of Nitobe Inazō and his colleagues justifying Japanese expansion after the Mukden Incident* in 1931 with considerable skepticism. With Nitobe's death in 1933, the Japan Council lost much of its drive, and began encountering funding difficulties. It merged in 1935 with the Japan International League (the former League of Nations Association), and did not send representatives to Pacific Council meetings until after World War II.

Although the IPR provided many personnel for the U.S. Occupation of Japan*, it experienced a steady decline after World War II. Lattimore wrote several controversial books on Asia and the U.S. role in the immediate postwar period, making him a target of conservative witch-hunts for individuals suspected of harboring Communist sympathies. The McCarran Committee of 1951–1952 labeled it a Communist front organization, and several academics who had become alienated from the IPR stepped forward to testify against it during the hearings. Funding from the Rockefeller Foundation was not renewed in 1953, pushing the American Council to the brink of bankruptcy. The Rockefeller Foundation established the Asia Society, and declined to have it merge with the IPR on the grounds that the new society was devoted strictly to cultural activities. From its prewar preeminence in the field of Asian studies, the IPR by 1961 had fallen into obscurity and irrelevance. With foundations transferring their grants to university research centers and programs, and university presses better able and willing to publish books on Asia, the IPR's role became peripheral. The attacks directed against it in the 1950s crystallized the left-right split among specialists of Asia in the United States and Canada. This rift continued to be reflected in North American studies of Asia, as exemplified by the Committee of Concerned Asian Scholars split from the Association for Asian Studies in 1968. The American Council dissolved itself in 1961, at the same time as the Japanese Council. *See also* Sakatani Yoshirō; Shibusawa Eiichi.

J. B. Condliffe, *Reminiscences of the Institute of Pacific Relations* (Vancouver, 1984); J. N. Thomas, *The Institute of Pacific Relations* (Seattle, WA, 1974); Yamaoka Michio, *Taiheiyō mondai chōsakai' kenkyū* [A Study of the Institute of Pacific Relations] (Tōkyō, 1997).

Hyung Gu Lynn

INSULAR CASES

In these nine cases, the U.S. Supreme Court collectively reconciled the U.S. Constitution with colonial rule by the United States over territories it acquired through Hawaiian Annexation* and the Treaty of Paris ending the Spanish-American War*. Specifically, the nine cases were *DeLima v. Bidwell; Downes v. Bidwell; Dooley v. U.S. (I, II);*

Grossman v. U.S.; Fourteen Diamond Rings v. U.S.; Armstrong v. U.S.; Goetze v. U.S.; Huus v. New York and *Porto Rico Steamship Company.* Some legal scholars construe the "insular cases" more broadly to include related cases decided from 1903 to 1922 (*Hawaii v. Mankichi; Gonzalez v. Williams; Kepner v. U.S.; Grafton v. U.S.; Kent v. Porto Rico; Kopel v. Bingham; Dowdell v. U.S.; Ochoa v. Hernandez; Ocampo v. U.S.; Balzac v. Porto Rico*). The most important principle articulated in the nine 1901 cases and reaffirmed in the later instances was that "the Constitution does not follow the flag." That meant that the United States may exercise sovereignty over "unincorporated" territories without being bound to grant anything more than "fundamental" rights and due process. The insular cases have long been construed as a racist American effort to control peoples and territories without extending to them full political rights. The insular cases were reversed insofar as they applied to American citizens outside the United States in *Reid v. Covert* (1957). However, as recently as 1977, the U.S. Supreme Court seemed to endorse the precedent with regard to noncitizens in *Torres v. Puerto Rico* (1977). *See also* Anti-Imperialist League.

J. Kerr, *The Insular Cases* (Port Washington, NY, 1982); G. Neuman, *Strangers to the Constitution: Immigrants, Borders, and Fundamental Law* (Princeton, NJ, 1996); E. R. Ramos, "The Legal Construction of American Colonialism: The Insular Cases (1901–1922)," *Revista Juridica Universidad de Puerto Rico* (1965); W. L. Thompson, *The Introduction of American Law in the Philippines and Puerto Rico, 1898–1905* (Fayetteville, NC, 1989).

Eileen Scully

INTERNATIONAL WHEAT AGREEMENT (23 March 1949)

The International Wheat Agreement (IWA) was a comprehensive agreement signed by wheat exporters and importers on 23 March 1949. The original concept of the organization was discussed as early as 1931, but six more conferences were convened before the IWA was signed. Forty-one countries originally signed the agreement, but three failed to ratify it, including the Soviet Union and Argentina (two wheat-exporting countries). Many importing nations became signatories in spite of the voluntary withdrawal of two of the biggest wheat importers. The accord was popular among importing countries because it benefited them in several ways. First, maximum and minimum wheat prices were fixed to prevent fluxuating wheat prices from affecting importers. Second, the importing countries were guaranteed a certain quantity of wheat for the duration of the agreement. Third, importers were not bound to any particular suppliers, and thus, were able to purchase the agreed-upon quota of wheat through commercial or government transactions.

The first IWA was in place for four years, until 1953. Subsequent agreements were signed in 1956, 1959, and 1962. Although no country was barred from joining the agreement, Germany and Japan faced initial opposition from importing nations. Importers, such as Britain, took a protectionist stance because they feared German and Japanese entry would diminish their portion of the nondollar wheat supplies and force them to seek wheat imports from the dollar area. Therefore, Germany and Japan were asked to sign a written statement agreeing to limit their wheat imports to a designated amount. After Germany complied, it was invited to join in 1950. Japan refused to sign and was unable to join until 1951. From the mid-1950s, the IWA began to promote the expansion of international trade in wheat and wheat flour because of a wheat surplus in the world market. In 1967, it was replaced by the Wheat Trade Convention during the Kennedy Round of the General Agreement on Tariffs and Trade*. Despite numerous revisions to the agreement, the structure of the IWA remained unchanged throughout its existence. The International Wheat Council

(IWC) continued to administer the IWA and an executive committee worked under its direction. Moreover, there was an Advisory Committee on Price Equivalents, which advised the council and the executive committee on technical matters. The IWC and the permanent secretariat had its headquarters in London.

IWC *Annual Report* (1949–1967).

Yokoi Noriko

INUKAI TSUYOSHI (1855–1932)

A native of Okayama, Inukai Tsuyoshi was Japanese prime minister from 1931 to 1932. His political career ran on a track roughly parallel to that of parliamentary rule in Japan before World War II. Inukai's assassination during an abortive military coup in May 1932 marked the onset of the atrophy of parliamentary government in prewar Japanese politics. He was tutored in the intricacies of party politics and civil-military relations during his early career as a journalist. In 1885, Inukai entered public service as a Tōkyō prefectural assemblyman, and a successful run in Japan's first national parliamentary election in 1890 followed. Save for a few short interludes, he was a permanent fixture in the Diet and held a handful of cabinet posts, until he formed his own cabinet as the head of the Seiyūkai Party in December 1931. Through his tenure as a parliamentarian, Inukai was involved in several different parties, earning notoriety as the dean of Japanese constitutionalism, a master politician, and a faithless turncoat.

Faced with the economic dislocation of the Great Depression and the political turmoil after the Mukden Incident*, the Inukai cabinet's record was mixed and truncated. Takahashi Korekiyo, his finance minister, took Japan off the gold standard in an effort to maximize latitude in fiscal and monetary policies. His macroeconomic management contributed to a moderate recovery of the economy in the early 1930s, but it also brought on inflationary pressures and charges of dumping from overseas. Inukai's handling of the fallout from the Manchurian crisis was constrained both by the popular fervor for safeguarding Japan's semicolonial possessions and his own support for Japan's dominion over north China. But whereas the military sought direct political control, he envisaged only economic dominance. This vision of economic power, informed by his belief that nationalism was the force driving modern China, prompted Inukai to patronize Chinese revolutionary leader Sun Zhongshan* during the latter's exile in Japan, and to travel to China following the Chinese Revolution of 1911* to mediate between Sun and his domestic rivals. In 1915, he also opposed Japan's Twenty-One Demands*. As prime minister, his belief that a foreign attempt to partition China permanently would fail, his concern about Japan's finite resources, and his fear of provoking the United States led Inukai to put a moratorium on recognition of Manchukuo*, the puppet regime the Japanese army had installed in Manchuria, and to try to settle the dispute through informal, personal emissaries.

N. Bamba, *Japanese Diplomacy in a Dilemma: New Light on Japan's China Policy, 1924–1929* (Vancouver, BC, 1972); S. Ogata, *Defiance in Manchuria: The Making of Japanese Foreign Policy, 1931–1932* (Berkeley, CA, 1964); A. Rappaport, *Henry Stimson and Japan, 1931–1933* (Chicago, 1963); Tokito Hideto, *Inukai Tsuyoshi: Riberarizumu no nashanarizumu no sokoku* (Tōkyō, 1991); Washio Yoshinao (ed.), *Inukai bokudo shokanshū* [The Personal Letters of Inukai Tsuyoshi] (Tōkyō, 1940).

Shimizu Sayuri

ISHIBASHI TANZAN (1884–1973)

Ishibashi Tanzan achieved distinction in Japan as a liberal thinker, journalist, and political leader before serving as prime minister from 1956 to 1957. As an establishment liberal, he entered politics in 1946 and cooperated with SCAP* at the outset of the U.S. Occupation of Japan*. Son of a Nichiren priest, Ishibashi attended Waseda University in Tōkyō. He contributed to the emergence of Japanese journalism in its modern form, particularly in his work for the influential business journal *Tōyō Keizai Shimpo* (Oriental Economist), becoming its editor-in-chief in 1924. He supported the Japanese Constitution of 1947*, although it was more radical than he expected and he did not favor its antiwar clause. Aware of the liberal tradition that would enable such reforms to succeed, however, Ishibashi objected to breaking up the *Zaibatsu** and large land holdings while leaving the "arrogant bureaucracy" intact. As a champion of liberalism, his career reflected the intellectual vitality of Japan's urban middle class early in the century and how it anticipated the direction of Japanese society after 1945.

Ishibashi wanted Japan to evolve gradually toward a new participatory political culture and consistently advocated pragmatic political reforms, the most important being universal suffrage. He also defended parliamentary government against its critics. In foreign policy, he opposed the Siberian Intervention* and supported the internationalist policies of Shidehara Kijūrō*, regarding possession of empire as a potential strain on Japan. After the Mukden Incident* of 1931 and Japan's turn toward militaristic imperialism, Ishibashi remained true to his principles. Although often sharply critical of the Western powers in his writings, he warned of the dangers of Japanese militarism. In his view, a "little Japan" rather than a Greater East Asia Co-Prosperity Sphere* offered the nation the best guarantee of security and prosperity. Ishibashi did not jeopardize his career with open dissent during the war, however. He maintained his wide network of contacts with corporate supporters, party politicians, bureaucrats, and intellectuals.

Ishibashi essentially advocated a different construction of liberalism than that of the SCAP reformers. The clash came while

Ishibashi was finance minister in the government of Yoshida Shigeru*, with his insistence that the Japanese government honor its debts to Japanese business incurred during the war by resorting to deficit spending. When forced to abrogate the guarantee payments, Ishibashi turned to the Reconstruction Finance Bank and the Economic Stabilization Board to implement his "priority production" policy. Production rose as intended, but his intransigence and rampant inflation prompted SCAP to purge him temporarily from politics. Returning in 1954 as head of the Ministry of International Trade and Industry*, he encouraged production of consumer goods, development of small and medium enterprises, and expanded foreign trade. In foreign affairs, Ishibashi advocated Sino-Japanese détente, expanded trade with the Communist bloc, and modest rearmament, and criticized the Cold War and the U.S.-Japan Security Treaty of 1951*. This advocacy of greater Japanese autonomy provoked U.S. suspicion of him at the time, but it anticipated both U.S. recognition of the People's Republic of China* and subsequent American concern with the unequal character of the U.S.-Japanese partnership. Ishibashi became prime minister in December 1956, but resigned two months later because of ill health. He recovered and remained a National Diet member until 1963.

Ishibashi Tanzan, *Ishibashi Tanzan zenshū* [The Complete Works of Ishibashi Tanzan] (Tōkyō, 1970–72); C. A. Johnson, *MITI and the Japanese Miracle: The Growth of Industrial Policy* (Stanford, CA, 1982); Masuda Hiroshi, *Ishibashi Tanzan: Senryō seisaku eno teikō* [Ishibashi Tanzan: Resistance Against Occupation Policies] (Tōkyō, 1988); S. H. Nolte, *Liberalism in Modern Japan: Ishibashi Tanzan and his Teachers, 1905–1960* (Berkeley, CA, 1987); K. Tsutsui, *Ishibashi Tanzan: Ichi jiyū-shugi seijika no kiseki* [Ishibashi Tanzan: The Track Record of One Liberal Politician] (Tōkyō, 1986).

Aaron Forsberg

ISHII KIKUJIRŌ (1866–1945)

Ishii Kikujirō, one of prewar Japan's most distinguished diplomats, tried to maintain cordial relations with the United States during World War I and the interwar years. Born in Chiba Prefecture, he studied law at Tōkyō Imperial University and entered the Foreign Ministry in 1890. Ishii first served as attaché at the legation of Paris until 1896, and then as consul in Korea until 1900. Upon becoming ambassador to France in 1912, he became the first Japanese diplomat abroad to predict the coming of World War I. While in Paris, he played the key role in achieving Japan's adherence to the London Declaration, in which Japan, as a member of the Allied powers, pledged no separate peace. As foreign minister from 1915 to 1916 under Ōkuma Shigenobu*, Ishii continued to make efforts to maintain unity among the Allies. He concluded the Russo-Japanese entente in 1916, primarily for the purpose of preventing Russia from signing a separate peace with Germany.

Ishii's greatest contribution during World War I was his diplomatic efforts to alleviate the tensions developing between his country and the United States. Reacting to Japan's Twenty-One Demands* in 1915, President Woodrow Wilson* emerged as a champion of the Open Door Policy* in China against Japan's ambitious expansionist policy on the continent. During the controversy between Washington and Tōkyō over the question of who should guide China into the war against Germany in the summer of 1917, Ishii was appointed as ambassador extraordinary and plenipotentiary to lead a special war mission to the United States. His task was to gain an agreement with the Wilson administration in which the United States would acknowledge Japan's special position, both political and economic, in China. However, Ishii's negotiations with U.S. Secretary of State Robert Lansing* were plagued by irreconcilable differences between U.S. insistence on respect for Open Door principles and Japan's determination to establish hegemony in China. The outcome was an amalgamation of incompatible ideas in the Lansing-Ishii Agreement* of November 1917, which gave the appearance of conciliation between the two and allowed them to concentrate on the war effort.

Ishii returned to Washington as ambassador in February 1918 and undertook the difficult task of negotiating the conditions for the U.S.-Japanese joint Siberian Intervention*. However, Wilson's ill-advised proposal for a limited joint expedition, Ishii's overzealousness to reach an acccord, and Tokyo's determination to assert leadership in the military venture resulted in further U.S.-Japanese estrangement. In the spring of 1919, Ishii resigned from his post in Washington because of his disagreement with Lansing regarding the employment of a Japanese official by the Chinese government. From 1920 until 1927, he was ambassador to France and also Japan's chief delegate to the League of Nations. He was the president of the Council and Assembly of the League of Nations in 1923 and 1926. Ishii also represented Japan at the Geneva Naval Conference of 1927*. In 1929, he became a member of the Privy Council and was best remembered for his warning against the aggressive and predatory tendency of Nazi Germany in the council's deliberations on signing the Tripartite Pact* in September 1940. Ishii was never found after a U.S. air raid over Tōkyō on 26 May 1945.

B. Beers, *Vain Endeavor: Robert Lansing's Attempts to End the American-Japanese Rivalry* (Durham, NC, 1962); K. Ishii, *Diplomatic Commentaries*, F. C. Langdon (trans. and ed.) (Baltimore, MD, 1936); N. Kawamura, *Turbulence in the Pacific: Japanese-U.S. Relations During World War I* (Westport, CT, 2000); I. Nish, *Alliance in Decline: A Study in Anglo-Japanese Relations, 1908–23* (London, 1972).

Kawamura Noriko

ISLAND-HOPPING STRATEGY

American military planners adopted this strategy during the campaigns in the Pacific in World War II to deal effectively with the immense distances to be covered to recapture Japanese conquests, reach the Japanese home islands, and bring the war to a successful conclusion in the least possible time. By the spring of 1942, Japanese forces had seized a huge area of the southwest Pacific in their drive for vital supplies of raw materials and had extended themselves in other directions as well. They had moved into the fringes of northern New Guinea, had taken New Britain and its major harbor at Rabaul from the Australians, and were poised to strike into southern New Guinea and possibly into northern Australia. A bit farther east, they had taken key positions and were building bases in the Solomon Islands not far from the vital U.S.-Australia supply line. Farther to the northeast and north, they had captured the British Gilbert Islands and the U.S. possessions of Guam* and Wake Island. These conquests formed a long perimeter encircling a vast area extending as far as 3,500 miles from Tōkyō.

After the Battles of the Coral Sea*, Midway*, and Guadalcanal, which ended the period of Japanese expansion and stopped the threat to Australia and Hawaii, the Americans took the initiative and began to clear Japanese forces out of the Solomons and to advance along the New Guinea coast toward New Britain. As a result of these operations in 1943, the expansion of U.S. air power and its importance in facilitating the capture of Japanese-held areas determined the success of the ground operations, particularly in New Guinea. The early objective of General Douglas MacArthur* in his advance along the coast of New Guinea had been Rabaul, the main Japanese base on New Britain. With the increase in U.S. air power, the decision was made to bypass Rabaul and strike out along the New Guinea coast to seize base areas in northwest New Guinea to support a return to the Philippines*. The key was to take areas about 200–250 miles apart, which was the operating radius of fighter aircraft, and to develop them into air bases to cover the next hop along the coast. If Japanese troops were there, they were cleared out; if not, base construction could begin immediately. In the case of Wewak, a large Japanese troop concentration was bypassed and left to sit out the rest of the war. By the end of July 1944, Sansapor, in the extreme northwest of New Guinea, had been secured, not far from the southern Philippines.

A much more dramatic example of the island-hopping strategy was carried out in the central Pacific. There, Admiral Chester W. Nimitz and the U.S. Pacific fleet spearheaded a drive that started in November 1943 with the capture of Tarawa and Makin Islands in the Gilberts. These were more than 2,500 miles from Pearl Harbor. What made such a long leap possible was the huge U.S. naval buildup during 1943. Now the fleet had more than a dozen large and medium aircraft carriers to provide air cover for landings on the island chains stretching to the Philippines and Japan. The Gilberts landings were followed by landings in the Marshall Islands in February 1944. Kwajalein atoll was the main target, and from there the carrier task forces and troop transports moved on to Eniwetok, bypassing several other Japanese bases. Then there was a pause, as the planners debated whether to assault the main Japanese naval and support base at Truk in the Eastern Carolines, or to go for the southern Marianas. The decision was for the Marianas, bypassing Truk and other bases in the Carolines.

On 15 June, a major landing took place at Saipan, nearly 1,800 miles from Kwajalein. Then, within another month, Tinian Island was taken and Guam was recaptured. The capture of the southern Mariannas was a heavy blow to Japan. At one stroke, it severed Japanese communications to the Carolines-New Guinea-New Britain area, brought American forces within striking distance of the Philippines and, most critically, put long-range U.S. bombers within range of the Japanese home islands. The last act in the leapfrogging strategy

came in late 1944, when the ground forces of MacArthur and the naval armada of Nimitz teamed up to carry out landings in the Philippines, which led to the severing of Japan's communications with all its Southeast Asian conquests. Then the Battles of Iwo Jima* and Okinawa* put southern Japan in danger of invasion. This invasion probably would have taken place in November 1945, if not for the surrender of Japan on August 14 after the Atomic Attacks*.

E. B. Potter and C. Nimitz, *Triumph in the Pacific: The Navy's Struggle Against Japan* (Englewood Cliffs, NJ, 1963); C. Reynolds, *The Fast Carriers: The Forging of an Air War* (New York, 1968); S. R. Taaffe, *MacArthur's Jungle War: The 1944 New Guinea Campaign* (Lawrence, KS, 1998); R. L. Spector, *Eagle Against the Sun: The American War with Japan* (New York, 1985).

Ernest Andrade Jr.

ITŌ HIROBUMI (1841–1909)

In the 1880s, Itō Hirobumi was the most prominent politician in Japan, and in 1885, he became the first prime minister. He also built the constitutional structure of imperial Japan by drafting the constitution of 1889. A lower-class samurai from Chōshū, he was a young patriot who participated in the turbulent political situation in Japan during the decline of the Tokugawa shōgunate and Japan's opening to the West. He helped set fire to the British legation in Japan in 1862, but after he went to study in Britain, he abandoned the "Expel the Barbarian" Movement*. However, in 1863 and 1864, Chōshū continued to fire on ships of the United States, Britain, France, and Holland at the Shimonoseki Strait. As the four countries prepared to retaliate, Itō hurried back to Japan to attempt mediation, but he failed. The four countries dispatched seventeen battleships to Shimonoseki in September 1864 and fired on the batteries, destroying the town.

After the Meiji Restoration in 1868, Itō was selected for one of the key positions in the new government. Japan's new leaders thought the "unequal treaties" signed between the Tokugawa shōgunate and the Western countries in the 1850s and 1860s were among the most important signs of weakness that they had to eliminate. Therefore, Tōkyō sent Itō as special envoy for negotiations with Western nations in December 1871. In Washington, the United States rejected the Japanese demand for abrogation of the Treaty of Kanagawa* and the Harris Treaty*. Itō and other members of the Iwakura Mission* stayed in the United States for more than half a year and later relied on their experiences to guide the modernization of Japan. After the end of the Sino-Japanese War, Russia, France, and Germany in April 1895 demanded that Japan return to China the Liaodong Peninsula, which was to be ceded to Japan. Prime Minister Itō wanted to evade the Triple Intervention* by securing U.S. help, but Washington refused.

Meanwhile, Itō had completed the 1889 constitution and served the first of five terms as prime minister. As an elder statesman at the start of the twentieth century, he tried to resolve the growing dispute with Russia over Korea, in which Japan would dominate Korea and Russia would control Manchuria. On his way to Russia in 1901, Itō stopped in the United States, where Yale University awarded him the degree of special professor emeritus. After Russia showed no interest, the Anglo-Japanese Alliance* was signed on 30 January 1902. The Russo-Japanese War* followed in February 1904. Itō then sent his aide, Kaneko Kentarō, a graduate of Harvard University, to lobby for American public support of Japan. After its victory over Russia, Japan's relations with the United States deteriorated because Japan imposed military rule on Manchuria in defiance of American protests defending the Open Door Policy*. At a meeting on 22 May 1906 attended by almost every leading Japanese politician, Itō, then resident general of Korea, insisted that Japanese military rule in Manchuria had to end at

once to ensure good relations with the United States, Britain, and China. Three years later in October, Itō was assassinated at Harbin, China, by a Korean patriot, Ahn Jung-gun. Many Americans after his death praised the accomplishments of Itō's career.

Itō Hirobumi den [Biography of Itō Hirobumi], 3 vols. (Tōkyō, 1940).

Nagata Akifumi

IWAKURA MISSION

In December 1871, the Japanese government dispatched a delegation of more than 100 high-ranking officials and students, mostly of aristocratic and former samurai backgrounds, to the United States and Europe to survey Western cultures and social institutions. Although not officially charged with the renegotiation of the "unequal treaties," signed by the Tokugawa shōgunate in the 1850s and up for renewal in 1872, the delegation, headed by ambassador plenipotentiary Iwakura Tomomi (1825–1883), held preliminary discussions of the treaties. The Meiji government demonstrated the importance it attached to the mission by allowing key officials, including Kido Kōin, Itō Hirobumi*, and Ōkubo Toshimichi, lengthy leave from service at home.

The delegation arrived at its first and longest stop, the United States, in March 1872, and was granted an audience with President Ulysses S. Grant. Iwakura and his associates exceeded their official charge and asked Secretary of State Hamilton Fish* to open negotiations toward a revision of the U.S.-Japan commercial treaty. In specific terms, they sought Japanese tariff autonomy and an end to U.S. extraterritorial rights. The Grant administration rejected the first proposition and made consideration of the second incumbent on the modernization of Japan's internal judicial system. Lacking proper diplomatic credentials, the delegation had to suspend negotiations in August. Learning from this experience, the Japanese emissaries simply presented European powers with a list of proposals to be considered in future negotiations.

This firsthand look by government leaders at advanced Western technology and modern social institutions produced several tangible results. Many European nations made it clear that guarantees of freedom of internal travel and religion were prerequisites for renegotiating their commercial treaties with Japan. Responding in part to Iwakura's advocacy of religious tolerance, the Meiji government lifted the ban on Christianity in February 1873. The mission also contributed to the modernization of Japan's education system. Among the achievements in this area was the founding of Tsuda College, Japan's first institution of higher education for women, by Tsuda Umeko, the mission's youngest member. Perspectives gained on the mission also shaped the position of its leaders on Korea, a key foreign policy concern of the early Meiji period. On returning to Japan in the fall of 1873, Iwakura and Ōkubo opposed the hardline policy advocated by Saigō Takamori on the grounds that domestic reform and development must receive top priority.

Gaimushō, *Nippon gaikō monjo* [Diplomatic Papers of Japan], *Meiji*. Vols. 4, 5, 6: *Joyoku kaisei kankei* [Treaty Revisions and Related Matters] (Tōkyō, 1964); Ishii Takashi, *Meiji shoki no kokusai kankei* [A Study of Treaty Revisions in the Early Meiji Period] (Tōkyō, 1977); Shimomura Fujio, *Meiji shonen joyaku kaiseishi no kenkyū* [International Relations in the Early Meiji Period] (Tōkyō, 1962).

Shimizu Sayuri

IWO JIMA, BATTLE OF

See BATTLE OF IWO JIMA

J

JANG MYŎN (1899–1966)

Jang Myŏn (John M. Chang) was an important postwar politician in the Republic of Korea* (ROK) who served as ambassador to the United States before and during the Korean War* and later as vice president and prime minister. Born in Seoul, he was a devout Catholic. He graduated from Suwŏn High Agriculture School in 1917, the English department of Seoul YMCA School in 1919, and Manhattan College, where he majored in education and religion, in 1925. Returning home, he worked with the Catholic Church in P'yŏngyang and Seoul. From 1931 to 1945, when Korea was liberated from Japan, he was teacher and later principal at Catholic schools in Seoul. For the entire period after Japanese Annexation of Korea*, he never resisted Japanese Colonialism*. He left a picture of himself in Japanese-style clothes and haircut, later used by his political opponents as evidence that he was a collaborator.

During the three years of the U.S. Occupation of Korea* (1945–1948), Jang was favored by Americans because of his fluent English and his Catholic background. This helped him to be appointed a member of the Democratic Representative Council and the Interim Legislative Assembly during 1946. Jang was elected in May 1948 to the National Assembly. With the establishment of the ROK and Syngman Rhee* as its president on 15 August 1948, he was appointed chief representative to the United Nations, which recognized the ROK government in December 1948. In February 1949, Jang was appointed ambassador to the United States. When Secretary of State Dean G. Acheson* publicly excluded South Korea from the U.S. defensive perimeter in January 1950, Jang visited the State Department to request an explanation for the apparent U.S. abandonment of the ROK in Acheson's National Press Club Speech*. He then appealed to President Harry S. Truman* for military aid, pointing out South Korea's military weakness without effect.

Immediately after the outbreak of the Korean War* on 25 June 1950, Jang appealed for American full-scale military intervention. After Truman took decisive action to resist the Communist invaders, he insisted on "unconditional surrender of North Korea as the only terms to be imposed at the conclusion of hostilities." In February 1951, Rhee promoted Jang to prime minister, because he wanted to reduce his difficulties with opposition members in the second National Assembly, with whom Jang had cordial relations. In November, Jang led the South Korean delegation to the UN General Assembly in

Paris, where he had to be hospitalized because of hepatitis. Returning home in 1952, still in ill health, he resigned from the premiership. Around this time, Rhee suspected that Jang was attempting to replace him as president, with the help of the Americans and the opposition members of the National Assembly, which was supposed to hold presidential elections before 15 August 1952. Rhee, through the "political crisis" of summer 1952, revised the ROK constitution to allow popular election of the president. Jang soon joined the anti-Rhee forces, which organized the Democratic Party in 1955. Elected the next year as ROK vice president, he was the target of an assassination attempt by a police-instigated agent.

In the notorious rigged election of 15 March 1960, Jang was "defeated" in the vice presidential race. But the student uprising of 19 April 1960 brought the ouster of Syngman Rhee and the subsequent National Assembly election of 27 July 1960 gave birth to the Second Republic, with a parliamentary cabinet system. Yun Po-sŏn was elected president, and Jang was elected prime minister. His cabinet members were usually former officials of the Japanese colonial administration or the U.S. military government. On 16 May 1961, the military coup overthrew the Jang government. He immediately took refuge in a Catholic convent at Seoul. The Kennedy administration could not find Jang to secure a request for U.S. intervention and three days later was forced to recognize the military regime under Pak Chŏng-hŭi*. Later, the military regime imprisoned him, but he soon was released. His government, usually called "the Democratic Party regime," has been remembered as "the weakest and most ineffective government" in the ROK's history.

B. Cumings, *The Origins of the Korean War*, 2 vols. (Princeton, NJ, 1981, 1990); J. C. Goulden, *Korea: The Untold Story of the War* (New York, 1982); S. Han, *The Failure of Democracy in South Korea* (Berkeley, CA, 1974); Jang Myŏn, *Han Arŭi miri Chŭkchi Ankonŭn: Jang Myŏn Paksa hoe-gorok* [Except a Grain of Wheat Fall into the Ground and Die: Memoirs of Dr. Chang Myon] (Seoul, 1967).

Kim Hakjoon

JAPAN-KOREA NORMALIZATION

On 22 June 1965, the Republic of Korea* (ROK) and Japan established formal diplomatic relations by signing the Treaty on Basic Relations, thus ending years of acrimonious relations and opening a new era of mutual economic benefit. The treaty confirmed that past treaties for the Japanese Annexation of Korea* in 1910 were void, and that the ROK was the only legitimate government on the Korean peninsula. Also, by signing four related agreements, the two governments settled disputes about the boundary line for fishing, legal status of Korean residents in Japan, Korean cultural treasures in Japan, and Korea's property claims. Specifically regarding the last issue, Japan was to provide South Korea with $45 million. But Japan was also to provide another assistance package of $800 million in grants and loans as a "gesture of goodwill." Although the treaty was the result of fourteen years of negotiations between Seoul and Tōkyō, the United States played a significant behind-the-scenes mediation role. Washington officials believed that an alliance between South Korea and Japan was the important step to ensure East Asian regional security. Furthermore, with growing concerns for its own balance-of-payments problem since the late 1950s, Washington wanted Japan to share the burden of assisting South Korea.

During the 1950s, little progress was made toward normalization because of the staunch anti-Japanese stance of ROK President Syngman Rhee* and the lack of serious motivations on the part of the Japanese government to improve its relations with South Korea, which claimed larger reparations than Japan was willing to pay. During the early 1960s, however, several factors contributed to progress in the negotiations. The regime of Pak Chŏng-hŭi* that came to power in May 1961 was eager to obtain Japanese capital to finance its economic development projects. Satō Eisaku*, who became Japan's prime minister in 1964, was more enthusiastic than his predecessors in pursuing a regional anti-Communist alliance as envisaged by the U.S. government. Moreover, as U.S. military involvement in Vietnam escalated, American efforts to conclude a Korea-Japan settlement became more evident. For example, in 1964, when Korean domestic opposition against "humiliating diplomacy with Japan" seriously challenged the Pak government, the Johnson administration made public its support for normalization. Also, to ease the South Korean public's anti-Japanese sentiment, the U.S. government pressured the Japanese government to make a statement of apology for its "past regrettable history" in relations with Korea and its people.

As the U.S. policy makers originally had intended, the settlement resulted in the U.S.-Korea-Japan tripartite alliance system in East Asia. This system also provided the political framework within which future economic relations between the three countries were patterned. However, the normalization did not solve the fundamental problem in Korea-Japan relations, which centered on the issue of the "past history" of Japanese Colonialism* in Korea. The subsequent controversy over the content of Japanese history textbooks demonstrated that despite deepening political and economic ties after normalization, the cultural and psychological gap between the two countries remained wide.

K. B. Kim, *The Korea-Japan Treaty Crisis and the Instability of the Korean Political System* (New York, 1971); C. S. Lee, *Japan and Korea: The Political Dimension* (Stanford, CA, 1985); J. W. Lee, "Kannichi kokko seijoka no seiritsu to Amerika, 1960–65" [Korea-Japan Normalization, and the United States, 1960–1965], in *Kindai Nihon kenkyū 16: Sengo kaiko no keisei* [Modern Japan Study 16: The Formation of Post-War Diplomacy] (Tōkyō, 1994).

Ma Sang-yoon

JAPANESE ANNEXATION OF KOREA

After the Sino-Japanese War (1894–1895), tensions between Russia and Japan heightened because of mutual expansionist ambitions in Korea and Manchuria. In 1900, Russia sent troops to Manchuria in the Boxer Uprising* and broke her promise to withdraw them by 1903, encouraging Britain and Japan to form the Anglo-Japanese Alliance* in January 1902. Fear of Russian imperialism also grew in the United States. For example, Theodore Roosevelt* was especially concerned that Russia would damage the promising American commercial interests in China. In August 1900, when he was candidate for vice president, Roosevelt publicly declared that "I should like to see Japan have Korea. She will be a check upon Russia, and she deserves it for what she has done." After Roosevelt became president in September 1901, he rejected the argument of Horace N. Allen*, the minister to Korea, for the necessity of checking Japan.

After failed negotiations between Russia and Japan for a settlement regarding Korea, the Russo-Japanese War* broke out in February 1904. Japan immediately concluded with Korea a protocol, and then the first Japanese-Korean Convention in August 1904, each recognizing the free use of Korean territory by Japan and the appointment of diplomatic and financial advisers through recommendation by Japan. In this situation, Roosevelt reiterated the desirability of Japanese superiority in Korea to check Russia, but feared that Japan might damage American economic interests in China and soon threaten the Philippines*. At Tōkyō in July 1905, Secretary of War William Howard Taft* and Japanese Prime Minister Katsura Tarō* secretly talked and then signed a memorandum to respect each other's interests in East Asia known as the Taft-Katsura Agreement*. Previous talks between Senator Henry Cabot Lodge*, a close friend of Roosevelt, and the British top leaders at London in June 1905 confirmed Anglo-American support for

Japanese control in Korea. The Second Anglo-Japanese Alliance of August 1905, in which Britain recognized Japanese supremacy over Korea, completed setting the stage for Japan's annexation of Korea. To prevent this outcome, Korea's Emperor Kojong* appealed to Washington to halt the Japanese penetration of Korea in compliance with the terms of the Shufeldt Treaty* of 1882. But the Roosevelt administration continued to reject the appeals.

With international acquiescence, Japan could conclude with Korea the second Japanese-Korean Convention in November 1905, removing Korean diplomacy to Japan and creating the office of the resident general in Korea. The United States was first to announce the withdrawal of its legation in Korea, and Roosevelt refused to meet Kojong's private messengers, Homer B. Hulbert* and Min Yŏng-chan, in late 1905. Thereafter, Japan concluded with Korea the third Japanese-Korean Convention, giving it the right to control the domestic affairs of Korea in July 1907. A year later, a treaty between the United States and Japan provided for U.S. trademark protection. By this, the United States partially abandoned its extraterritorial jurisdiction. But the Dollar Diplomacy* of the Taft administration after March 1909, especially the Knox Neutralization Scheme*, made Japan suspicious of U.S. policy along Korea's border with Manchuria. Sooner than expected, Japan annexed Korea under a treaty signed on 22 August 1910. By the Declaration of Japanese Government of 29 August 1910, Japan announced its annexation of Korea and pledged to maintain the existing tariff rate of the foreign powers there. There was almost no reason for U.S. intervention to block the process of Japanese penetration of Korea based on the limited American interests in Korea, but it is also undeniable that American nonintervention made Japan's penetration of Korea easier. *See also* Japanese Colonialism; Root-Takahira Agreement.

T. Dennett, *Roosevelt and the Russo-Japanese War* (New York, 1925); R. A. Esthus, *Theodore Roose-velt and Japan* (Seattle, WA, 1966); Moriyama Shigenori, *Kindai nikkan kankeishi kenkyū* [A Study on the History of Modern Japanese-Korean Relations] (Tōkyō, 1987); Nagata Akifumi, *Seodoa Ruuzuberuto to Kankoku* [Theodore Roosevelt and Korea] (Tōkyō, 1992).

Nagata Akifumi

JAPANESE COLONIALISM

Although one of the most common images invoked by the term "colonialism" may be a picture of an Englishman in khakis sipping tea in the tropical jungles, both Japan and the United States were major colonial powers in the twentieth century in the Pacific. But there are problems in defining the boundaries of Japanese colonialism. For example, both the islands of Okinawa to the south and Hokkaidō to the north conceivably could be included as colonies, that were assimilated into Japan proper over several decades. The "indirectly" controlled areas in China and Manchuria, or the wartime occupation of several Southeast Asian nations, also might fit under the rubric of "colonialism." Micronesia*, taken from Germany in 1914, was a League mandate, rather than an officially annexed colony, but it has often been included in studies of Japanese colonialism. Japan's expansion into Korea prior to annexation was clearly an example of imperialism, but the de facto conditions during the protectorate years (1905–1910) also could be classified under colonialism. Brief treatments of Taiwan*, Korea, and Micronesia will describe the essentials.

Successive U.S. governments were not particularly interested in the details of Japanese colonial rule in Korea or Taiwan*. The two colonies were not major markets for American exports, nor did they possess raw materials or products essential for U.S. economic growth. In the case of Taiwan, formally colonized as Formosa after the Sino-Japanese War in 1895, there were some concerns at first about its possible use as a staging base for attacks on Hawaii and the Philippines*, but these fears decreased with the Japanese government welcoming U.S. acquisition of Guam* and Samoa, as well as Hawaiian Annexation* and Philippine Annexation* in 1898. Although the first U.S. consular agency was established in Taibei in 1898, the State Department was generally indifferent to reports from the consul. The Taft-Katsura Agreement* of 1905 and the Root-Takahira Agreement* of 1908 gave mutual assurances of the status quo in the Philippines and Korea, further cementing the spheres of influence in the Pacific.

By contrast, Micronesia subsequently attracted consistent attention from the U.S. government, for obvious naval strategic reasons. In particular, the islands of Yap and the Carolines were subjects of countering claims as relay points for trans-Pacific cables. American charges about Japanese fortification of the islands (a violation of the League mandate) at the Washington Conference* led to insertion in the Five Power Pact* of a nonfortification clause. There was, however, no American protest raised over the Japanese immigration flow into Micronesia, where in some cases, the native population became outnumbered two to one.

Under Theodore Roosevelt*, Washington did not object to Japan's indifference to even the pretense of upholding the Open Door Policy* in Korea. Furthermore, when the Japanese foreign minister said in 1909 that Japan's expansion in Korea and Manchuria was a solution for the growing diplomatic problem with the United States over immigration, this struck a chord with American officials. By 1911, there were more Japanese in Korea than in the United States, and Woodrow Wilson* was happy that U.S. policy could support Japanese immigration ambitions in at least one area. Because the United States had no sphere of interest in China, the key was letting Japan close the door in Korea, as long as it was kept open in Manchuria. Washington displayed sympathy, but no strong interest in supporting Korean independence, when

the U.S. consulate in Seoul sent reports criticizing Japanese massacres of unarmed Koreans during the March First Movement* of 1919. Some American missionaries participated actively in independence demonstrations, but despite their protests on humanitarian grounds, the State Department sent repeated instructions to Seoul, Tōkyō, and the delegates at the Versailles Peace Conference not to encourage any belief that the United States would assist Korean nationalists. Many influential Americans thereafter viewed Korean independence as unrealistic, urging such Korean leaders as Syngman Rhee*, Kim Gu*, and Kim Kyu-sik* to focus more on concrete socioeconomic issues.

The Cairo Declaration of 1 December 1943 promised the return of Taiwan to China and independence "in due course" for Korea, and the Yalta Agreement on the Far East* of February 1945 promised the Kurile Islands to Russia, although the U.S. government had not questioned the legitimacy of Japanese occupation of those areas until then. The U.S. State Department established a Territorial Studies Committee for decolonization, but saw Taiwan as another Chinese province. U.S. intelligence reports on Korea noted the hydroelectric power plants in northern Korea and the role of Korean heavy industry in the Japanese war against China, but for most American soldiers on ships redirected from Japan to Korea after 15 August 1945, "Korea" had no meaning. The vaunted Japanese fortresses on Truk island in Micronesia turned out to be more impregnable in American intelligence reports than in actuality. During the immediate postwar era, Taiwan was taken over by China and became the seat of the Guomindang* (Nationalist) government. Korea was occupied by U.S. and Soviet troops and the Thirty-Eighth Parallel Division* resulted in the creation of the Democratic People's Republic of Korea* in the north and the Republic of Korea* in the south. Meanwhile, Micronesia was taken over by the United States as trust territories under the United

Nations. *See also* Greater East Asia Co-Prosperity Sphere; Japanese Annexation of Korea; Russo-Japanese War; Samoa Partition; Shandong Agreement; Yap Controversy.

F. Baldwin, "The March First Movement: Korean Challenge and Japanese Response," Ph.D. dissertation, Columbia University, 1969; G. Kerr, *Formosa: Licensed Revolution and the Home Rule Movement, 1895–1945* (Honolulu, HI, 1974); D. Y. Ku, *Korea Under Colonialism: The March First Movement and Anglo-Japanese Relations* (Seoul, 1985); R. Myers and M. Peattie (eds.), *The Japanese Colonial Empire, 1895–1945* (Princeton, NJ, 1984); M. Peattie, *Nanyo: The Rise and Fall of the Japanese in Micronesia, 1885–1945* (Honolulu, HI, 1985).

Hyung Gu Lynn

JAPANESE CONSTITUTION OF 1947

Japan's postwar constitution, often called the MacArthur Constitution, entered into effect on 3 May 1947. Replacing the Meiji constitution of 1889, the new document was a mosaic of provisions reflecting Japanese legal tradition, universal principles expressed elsewhere, and simple compromise. After General Douglas MacArthur* indicated his desire for revision in October 1945, the cabinet of Prime Minister Shidehara Kijūrō* delegated the matter to a special committee whose chairman was former Tōkyō University Professor Matsumoto Jōji. MacArthur rightly suspected that the Matsumoto Committee, whose draft the *Mainichi Shimbun* unexpectedly published on 1 February 1946, sought to preserve the status quo. Two days later, he ordered the Government Section of SCAP* to prepare an American draft in absolute secrecy. Colonel Charles L. Kades, a graduate of Harvard Law School, was chairman of the Government Section committee. Nine working subcommittees prepared different parts of the draft in a white heat. Few of the participants were deeply familiar with Japan, but they had extensive training in law and other fields, enjoyed a wide vari-

ety of international experience, and understood the significance of their responsibility. MacArthur set down three guiding principles: preservation of the emperor, renunciation of war, and an end to Japan's feudal system.

On 13 February, Japanese leaders, including Matsumoto and Foreign Minister Yoshida Shigeru*, were stunned when told that the Matsumoto draft was "completely unacceptable" and that SCAP's document was its substitute. Despite their shock, Japan's conservative political leaders reluctantly embraced the American draft as their own. MacArthur emphasized how acceptance of the draft would exclude Emperor Hirohito* from the Tōkyō War Crimes Trials* and preempt outside intervention in Japanese politics. Also mindful of domestic pressure for more extensive revision, Shidehara, Yoshida, and other conservatives pressed ahead to enact the constitution as quickly as possible. In translating the document, the Japanese began the process of "Japanizing" it. Newspapers published the complete text—written in colloquial Japanese—on 17 April, one week after a general election. After the Privy Council's approval, a special committee in the Diet's lower house, with Ashida Hitoshi* as chairman, reviewed the draft. The House of Representatives approved a modified version in August, and the House of Peers completed its review in October. The constitution was promulgated on 3 November 1946 and entered into force six months later. Written in accessible language (unlike the Meiji constitution) and promoted by the Committee to Popularize the Constitution, chaired by Ashida, the new constitution enjoyed genuine popular appeal.

Divided into chapters like the Meiji constitution, the 1947 constitution was a detailed document containing 103 articles. The first declared the emperor a "symbol of the state." The prewar nobility and advisory positions of the genrō (or elder statesmen) were abolished. The constitution assigned supreme political power to the Diet or national legislature. Article 9 renounced war and pledged that "land, sea, and air forces, as well as other war potential, will never be maintained." The document detailed many rights in a separate chapter. Most notable at the time were provisions guaranteeing sexual equality in a wide range of areas, including suffrage, property rights, inheritance, divorce, and other matters pertaining to marriage and the family. Echoing the voices of Japanese feminists, several female staff members of SCAP pressed for female equality during the U.S. Occupation of Japan*. Most notable was Beate Sirota, a member of the Government Section born in Vienna and raised in Japan, who participated in drafting the provisions of the constitution related to human rights. Other chapters dealt with the organization of the Diet, the cabinet, the judiciary, national finances, and local self-government. Amendment required a two-thirds vote of the Diet and approval of a majority of voters in a special referendum.

Politics cast a long shadow over how the Japanese viewed the constitution. The escalating Cold War, symbolized by the Reverse Course* in U.S. policy and the U.S.-Japan Security Treaty of 1951*, polarized Japanese politics. Conservative nationalists (who eventually found a home in the Liberal Democratic Party*) called for revision of the constitution "imposed" on Japan. Socialists vigorously defended the "peace constitution" in order to block revision, and with it, rearmament. The U.S. government favored revision of Article 9, but refused to press the point. Initial interpretations of the constitution focused on the break with Japan's past, but later revisionists with access to more archival records pointed to the continuities between the prewar and postwar eras. More recently, scholars have studied how the postwar constitution was new in different ways. Koseki Shōichi has emphasized how the 1947 constitution rests on principles of internationalism, and linguist Inoue Kyoko has studied the significance of differences

in meaning between the English and Japanese versions. Ambiguity, she has concluded, made it possible for the two sides to agree on "a document without fully agreeing on its fundamental meaning."

K. Inoue, *MacArthur's Japanese Constitution: A Linguistic and Cultural Study of Its Making* (Chicago, 1991), T. Kataoka, *The Price of a Constitution: The Origin of Japan's Postwar Politics* (Stanford, CA, 1991); S. Koseki, *The Birth of Japan's Postwar Constitution* (Boulder, CO, 1997).

Aaron Forsberg

JAPANESE PEACE TREATY (8 September 1951)

This agreement restored Japanese sovereignty after World War II. It sought to achieve the economic and political stabilization of Japan, and the reconstruction of the Asian economy around Japan—the region's only industrial power. The Japanese Peace Treaty, together with other, equally important elements of U.S. Asia policy, finally stimulated a much-belated postwar recovery in both Japan and the rest of Asia while helping link Japan closely in a Cold War partnership with the United States. Late in 1946, Undersecretary of State Dean G. Acheson* became convinced that an early peace treaty was essential to Japan's economic recovery, and ordered development of a draft treaty. In early 1947, Secretary of State George C. Marshall* pressed the issue, and Acheson then invited the ambassadors of key nations to a 1 July meeting. Here, the United States proposed an eleven-nation San Francisco Peace Conference for August. Despite general interest, Soviet recalcitrance and Acheson's resignation on 31 August robbed the issue of its impetus. George F. Kennan*, director of the Policy Planning Staff at the State Department, argued that Japan would be vulnerable to "Communist penetration" if "left to its own devices," and the first official policy statement on Japan (National Security Council [NSC] 13/2, 7 October 1948) tabled the issue.

Soon after Acheson became secretary of state in early 1949, he began a new drive for a treaty—allying himself with General Douglas MacArthur*, commander of the U.S. Occupation of Japan*, against the Pentagon on the treaty issue, and with the Pentagon against MacArthur on the *Zaibatsu* issue. At Acheson's request, the Joint Chiefs of Staff (JCS) reviewed the treaty question three times, each time concluding that termination of the U.S. occupation would render Japan too vulnerable. After the British threw their weight behind Acheson and President Harry S. Truman* authorized Acheson to fashion an NSC policy statement on the issue in February 1950, the JCS offered to accept a treaty, if it left the occupation unchanged. A stormy meeting on 24 April produced no further movement, but the Korean War* brought Truman down behind Acheson and the JCS followed suit—provided that Acheson would maintain U.S. bases in Japan and accept Japanese rearmament. Truman then sent John Foster Dulles*, the newly appointed Republican point man for bipartisanship, out to line up world support. In February 1951, Dulles announced an understanding with Japanese Prime Minister Yoshida Shigeru*, and corollary understandings with other interested governments followed. On 20 July, Acheson sent out invitations for a fifty-one-nation peace conference, enclosing with them copies of the Anglo-American draft treaty. The Soviets angrily denounced this, but agreed to attend on the assumption that they still could overhaul the draft treaty at the conference.

The San Francisco Peace Conference opened on 4 September 1951, with Acheson as its presiding officer. The first item on the agenda was the rules of procedure. When the Soviets offered motions to amend the Anglo-American draft treaty, Acheson ruled them out of order until the rules of procedure had been adopted. Then, once the rules were in place, the Soviets discovered that amendments were still out of order because the U.S. team had pushed through a set of rules that confined all deliberations to the existing draft treaty. "It took the Russians about three days to discover what had happened to them," Dean Rusk*, then assistant secretary for Far Eastern Affairs, later recalled. On 8 September, Yoshida signed the peace treaty, followed by the United States and forty-seven other nations; the Soviet Union, Poland, and Czechoslovakia refused to sign. On the same day, Yoshida also signed a security treaty with the United States, which Rusk had negotiated in secret over the preceding months. This gave the United States permanent bases in Japan. Most of Japan's victims wanted specific reparations targets and permanent Japanese disarmament; they got neither. In the seven major sections of the treaty, Japan simply relinquished all claims to its former empire, agreed to negotiate compensation for occupied nations, and accepted a few other minor conditions on subjects such as war crimes, commercial relations, and fishing rights. *See also* ANZUS Treaty; Reverse Course; U.S.-Japan Security Treaty of 1951.

R. L. McGlothlen, *Controlling the Waves: Dean Acheson and U.S. Foreign Policy in Asia* (New York, 1993); M. Schaller, *The American Occupation of Japan: The Origins of the Cold War in Asia* (New York, 1985).

Ronald L. McGlothlen

JIANG JIESHI (1887–1975)

Jiang Jieshi was among the most important figures of twentieth-century China. He was the leading protégé of Sun Zhongshan*, founder of the Guomindang* (Nationalist) Party. Upon the death of Sun in 1925, he held the post of commander in chief of the Nationalist Revolutionary Army, leading the Northern Expedition of 1926 and 1927 and then establishing his leadership over the whole nation. After the Sino-Japanese War broke out on 7 July 1937, Jiang desired assistance from the United States. Although he received little American help at that time because of lingering isolationism in the United States, Jiang still was firmly convinced that the United States would one day be involved in the war because of the Japanese military advance in the Pacific. The Pearl Harbor Attack* forced U.S. entry into the Pacific war. Jiang's suggestion resulted in a Chinese-American-British joint military conference at Chongqing on 23 December 1941, where a joint military council was established to coordinate efforts under U.S. leadership. To defend the Burma Road*, he organized and sent to Burma* the Chinese Expeditionary Army. President Franklin D. Roosevelt* dispatched General Joseph W. Stilwell* to China to command U.S. Army forces in the China-Burma-India Theater*, arrange Lend Lease* aid to China, and act as Jiang's chief of staff. In early 1942, the United States provided a $500 million loan to China.

In early 1943, China negotiated with the United States and Britain to abrogate the unequal treaties, resulting in the United States and Britain renouncing their consular jurisdiction and concessions in China. Together with President Roosevelt and Prime Minister Winston Churchill, Jiang conferred at the Cairo Conference* in 1943. The three leaders issued the Cairo Declaration, promising return to China of all her territories in Japanese hands, including Manchuria, Taiwan*, and the Penghus Islands. This was a great victory for Jiang and China. But then a series of conflicts emerged between Jiang and Stilwell because of different ideas about how to conduct the war in China after the Ichigo Offensive.* Relations deteriorated seriously until Roosevelt had to recall Stilwell in December 1944 and send General Albert C. Wedemeyer* as his replacement, with whom Jiang got along well. Meanwhile, Song Meiling*, Jiang's wife, actively lobbied leading U.S. politicians and influential citizens to expand American support for the Guomindang government during the war.

During the postwar period, the United States tried hard to make peace between Jiang's Guomindang (Nationalist) government and the Chinese Communist Party*

(CCP). U.S. Ambassador Patrick J. Hurley* urged the two parties to participate in talks in Chongqing. They signed the Double Tenth Agreement on 10 October 1945, but it never could be put into effect. In late 1945, President Harry S. Truman* sent General George C. Marshall* to China on a special mission to press the two parties to continue negotiations. But the Marshall Mission* failed and, in the middle of 1946, the Chinese Civil War* resumed. Jiang's government had fallen into financial crisis early in World War II and had to depend in large part on American economic assistance. As corruption grew after the war ended in August 1945, Jiang refused reforms, especially to address the grievances of the peasantry. The Guomindang government's situation politically, economically, and militarily deteriorated rapidly, and Truman lost faith in the Republic of China* (ROC). Having lost all political and military control on China's mainland, Jiang withdrew to Taiwan* in December 1949.

As the People's Republic of China* (PRC) affiliated itself with the Soviet Union completely, the United States again placed importance on the ROC and reestablished full relations with Jiang's government during the Korean War*. In December 1954, the ROC signed the U.S.-China Mutual Defense Treaty* with Washington. In July 1955, the U.S. Congress passed the Formosa Resolution* after the first of the Taiwan Strait Crises*. In October 1958, Jiang and U.S. Secretary of State John Foster Dulles*, who then was visiting Taibei, signed a joint statement, saying that the United States had assumed responsibility for defending Taiwan. Opposition to Jiang's regime grew internationally in the 1960s, with even the United States eventually adopting a Two China Policy*. His eldest son, Jiang Jingguo*, replaced Jiang as the ROC's leader upon his death, his dream of returning to the Chinese mainland still unfulfilled.

B. Crozier, *The Man Who Lost China: The First Full Biography of Chiang Kai-shek* (New York,

1976); Wang Fumin, *Jiang Jieshi pingzhuan* [Critical Biography of Jiang Jieshi] (Beijing, 1993); Yang Shubiao, *Jiang Jieshi zhuan* [Biography of Jiang Jieshi] (Beijing, 1989).

Xiang E

JIANG JINGGUO (1908–1988)

The promotion of Jiang Jingguo to the premiership of the Republic of China* (ROC) on 24 May 1972 began a new era on Taiwan*. On the domestic front, he shook up the entire government by handpicking native Taiwanese and promoting young bureaucrats to key positions. Diplomatically, Jiang faced his greatest challenge as the international community was about to isolate the Guomindang* (Nationalist) regime. The eldest son of Jiang Jieshi* and his first wife, Jiang Jingguo was born in Fenghua, Zhejiang. In 1925, he left for Moscow to study at the Sun Yat-sen University and graduated two years later. In 1928, the Soviet government selected him for advanced studies at the Central Tolmatchev Military and Political Institute in Leningrad, where he graduated in 1930. Detained in the Soviet Union for the next seven years, Jiang was finally allowed to return to China with his Russian wife and two children in 1937. In preparation for his eventual succession, he served in a number of important posts in the Chinese Nationalist government during the Sino-Japanese War from 1937 to 1945 and the Chinese Civil War*. During the first years of the ROC on Taiwan, Jiang held some of the most important and powerful positions in the government, including head of the secret police, deputy secretary general of the National Defense Council, and top-ranking member of the Central Committee of the Guomindang.

Taiwan's diplomatic problems began shortly before Jiang's promotion to the premiership. In October 1971, the General Assembly of the United Nations ousted the ROC and voted for the People's Republic of China* (PRC) to represent China. The next crisis came in February 1972, when President Richard M. Nixon* visited Beijing and issued the Shanghai Communiqué*, which acknowledged that Taiwan was a part of China. More pragmatic and flexible than his father, Jiang handled the diplomatic crises with great dexterity. After the United States announced plans to recognize the PRC as China's legitimate government, Jiang informed Washington of his desire that future U.S.-ROC relations should continue as before, with the United States continuing to provide defensive weapons to the ROC and maintaining cultural, economic, trade, scientific, technological, and travel relations. Moreover, he insisted on representation between the two governments being maintained to administer all future relations.

To end Taiwan's diplomatic isolation, Jiang announced in February 1973 his strategy of "total diplomacy." Under this approach, Taibei was to use every available channel—political, economic, trade, scientific, technological, cultural, and sports—to increase substantive cooperation and interaction with nations that had terminated diplomatic relations with Taiwan. Not long thereafter, Jiang's next major diplomatic crisis came in the fall of 1978 with the announcement from President Jimmy Carter* of his intention to establish formal relations between the United States and the PRC on 1 January 1979. To ensure continued U.S.-Taiwan relations, the two sides held a series of negotiations in the first months of 1979, which concluded with the creation of the American Institute in Taiwan and the Coordination Council for North American Affairs as the two institutions to implement "unofficial" ties between the United States and Taiwan. Although President Jiang regarded these manifestations of the new relationship as "bitter pills" that had to be swallowed, he was determined to "handle the current changed situation with all the fortitude at his command." Until his death, Jiang Jingguo not only worked to end Taiwan's diplomatic isolation, but also laid the foundation for a genuine democratic government there.

J. Fu, *Taiwan and the Geopolitics of the Asian-American Dilemma* (New York, 1992); C. Hughes, *Taiwan and Chinese Nationalism* (London, 1997); J. Taylor, *The Generalissimo's Son: Chiang Ching-kuo and the Revolutions in China and Taiwan* (Cambridge, MA, 2000); N. B. Tucker, *Taiwan, Hong Kong, and the United States, 1945–1992* (New York, 1994); Y. S. Wang (ed.), *Foreign Policy of the Republic of China on Taiwan: An Unorthodox Approach* (New York, 1990).

Roger Y. M. Chan

JIANG NAN INCIDENT

Jiang Nan was the pen name of Henry Liu, a naturalized American citizen and author of a critical biography of Jiang Jingguo*, son of Jiang Jieshi* and president of the Republic of China* (ROC) after his father's death. Liu was assassinated in 1984 by a criminal gang in the United States at the behest of the ROC officials on Taiwan*. After the trip of President Richard M. Nixon* to mainland China in 1972 and U.S. withdrawal of recognition from the ROC in 1979, the Jiang Nan Incident was perhaps the low point for relations between the Guomindang* (Nationalist) government and the United States. The incident exposed one of the little-understood aspects of relations between the United States and the ROC government—the latter's attempt to monitor, intimidate, and even eliminate dissent in the United States. Liu's death created a martyr for groups critical of the Nationalists, and increased scrutiny of the ROC's activities in the United States. It led to congressional hearings, protests in academic circles, and unfavorable editorial comment in American newspapers.

Henry Liu (Liu Yiliang) was born in China in 1932, then moved to Taiwan during the retreat of Jiang Jieshi's regime in the late 1940s. He served in the military, but left to pursue a career in journalism. Liu became a naturalized U.S. citizen in 1973, and wrote articles and biographies

about the lives of important Guomindang officials. He also appeared to dabble in the world of espionage, and perhaps had contacts with intelligence organizations in the United States, the ROC, and the People's Republic of China*. The book that led to his death was written under the pseudonym of Jiang Nan (literally "south of the river"). It addressed topics taboo on Taiwan at that time, including Jiang Jingguo's study in the Soviet Union, involvement with the military/secret police, and willingness to encourage violence against the United States during the 1950s to further his and his father's political agenda.

Liu was assassinated on 15 October 1984, in Daly City, California, by two men connected to the Bamboo Union Gang (*Zhu lian bang*) at the behest of top leaders in the ROC's Intelligence Bureau of the Ministry of National Defense. Liu was ambushed in his garage and shot three times before his assailants fled the suburban neighborhood on bicycles. Only one of the assassins was captured and tried in the United States. The perfunctory investigation in Taiwan became as serious an irritant to relations between the ROC and the United States as the actual murder itself. Guomindang government leaders did not provide meaningful assistance in the investigation, but did place some of those most obviously involved into prison or under house arrest. One of the killers was released after serving six years in a Taiwanese prison. Admiral Wang Xiling, the highest-ranking official connected directly to the murder, was under house arrest until 1991, when he and other officials were released during a general amnesty to celebrate the eightieth anniversary of the ROC. Thereafter, no evidence was found to trace the conspiracy any higher than Wang.

Jiang Nan (Liu Yiliang), *Jiang Jingguo zhuan* [A Biography of Jiang Jingguo] (Taibei, 1988); D. Kaplan, *Fire of the Dragon: Politics, Murder, and the Kuomintang* (New York, 1992); U.S. House of Representatives, *The Murder of Henry Liu: Hearings and Markup Before the Committee on Foreign Affairs and Its Subcommittee on Asian and Pacific*

Affairs, 99th Cong., 1st sess., 7 February, 21 March, and 3 April 1985 (Washington, DC, 1985).

Steven E. Phillips

JIANG TINGFU (1895–1965)

Jiang Tingfu was a prominent diplomatic representative for the Republic of China* (ROC), especially after World War II. He started his formal education at the Yizhi Academy, run by an American missionary, at Xiangtan in Hunan Province. In 1912, he entered Park Academy in Missouri. Two years later, he enrolled at Oberlin College, majoring in history. Upon graduation in 1918, he was sent to France by the YMCA to work with Chinese laborers there. After returning from Europe, he entered the doctoral program at Columbia University in 1919. After earning his doctorate in history there, Jiang began to teach at Nankai University in Tianjin in 1923. He joined the history faculty at Qinggua University in Beijing and became chairman of the history department in 1929. After Japan staged the Mukden Incident* in 1931 and invaded Manchuria, Jiang, together with Hu Shi* and Din Wenjiang, started the *Independent Reviews* (*Duli Pinglun*), a popular weekly magazine serving as an open forum for intellectuals to discuss current issues in China. Aware of the crucial role of the Soviet Union in China's resistance to Japan, Jiang spent three months there in 1934, studying its conduct of foreign relations. His articles and activities attracted attention from many people, including Jiang Jieshi*, the leader of the Guomindang* (Nationalist) government.

Jiang's political and diplomatic career began when he accepted Jiang Jieshi's appointment as the director of the Department of Political Affairs in November 1935, helping Jiang reorganize and run the central government. About a year later, Jiang Tingfu was appointed ambassador to the Soviet Union, working thereafter for better relations with Moscow. Although the Soviet Union refused to use force to stop Japan in its full-scale war with China, it did provide more weapons and loans to the Chinese in the early years of fighting after the Marco Polo Bridge Incident* in July 1937. After serving as director of the National Relief Rehabilitation Administration from 1944 to 1946, Jiang became China's standing representative to the United Nations in 1947. After the ROC fled to Taiwan* late in 1949, he gained passage of a resolution in the United Nations in 1952 that denounced the Soviet Union for violation of Chinese sovereignty in preventing Jiang's government from reasserting control in Manchuria and assisting the Chinese Communist Party* in its fight against the Guomindang. His greatest success was probably his successful defense of Taiwan's seat in the United Nations, which was challenged after Mao Zedong* won the Chinese Civil War* and established the People's Republic of China* (PRC) in October 1949.

While still holding his position as standing representative to the United Nations, Jiang began to serve as ambassador to the United States in 1961. During his tenure, he continued to defend Taiwan's seat in the United Nations and tried to keep a stable relationship with the United States. Jiang helped arrange the visits of several Guomindang leaders, such as Jiang Jingguo* and Chen Cheng, to the United States. However, he failed to obtain Washington's support for a projected Taiwan military attack on the mainland to replace the PRC. His diplomatic career ended in May 1965, when he retired from his ambassadorship. He did not have the opportunity to carry out his plan to return to history research and writing because of his sudden death on 9 October. His autobiography, *The Reminiscences of Tsiang T'ing-fu* was the finished part of the oral history project conducted with him at Columbia University and published in 1974. *See also* Chinese Representation in the United Nations; Kennedy-Chen Conference.

Ch'en Chih'mai, *Jiang Tingfu de zhishi yu ping-sheng* [The Career and Life of Jiang Tingfu] (Taibei, 1967); *Jiang Tingfu xuanji* [The Selected Works of Jiang Tingfu] (Taibei, 1969).

Li Hongshan

JIANG ZEMIN (1927–   )

Jiang Zemin became a top leader in the People's Republic of China* (PRC) during the 1990s. He was born into a Communist revolutionary family in China. Soon after the Chinese Communist Party* (CCP) victory in the Chinese Civil War* in 1949, Jiang was selected as one of the few lucky young people Beijing sent to the Soviet Union to study. There, he, like others with his background, was carefully groomed to be a loyalist to the Communist regime. Upon earning his degree in engineering and returning home, Jiang first became a techno-bureaucrat. But it was clear that he was more interested in politics than technology, which changed the direction of his career. After several decades of effort, he emerged as Shanghai's party secretary in the 1980s. His political fortune took a dramatic turn after the 1989 Tiananmen Square Massacre*. After the fall from power of then CCP Secretary Zhao Ziyang because of his explicit sympathy with the student demonstrators, party patriarch Deng Xiaoping* named Jiang as Zhao's successer. In the first few years of his tenure, Jiang carefully watched his steps in the extremely risky political arena of Beijing, and tried to avoid making enemies. Meanwhile, he gradually developed his own ruling basis under Deng's protection. By 1993, Jiang appeared increasingly confident in his foundation for leadership. That year, his visit to the United States to participate in the Asia-Pacific Economic Cooperation* (APEC) forum was one of his first high-profile exposures as the PRC's new leader.

During his tenure, Jiang basically has followed the direction that Deng set, aimed at encouraging the Four Modernizations*, but curtailing political freedom. Since 1992,

China's economic growth has ranked as the fastest in the world and the nation has become one of the most attractive targets for foreign investment. On the other hand, Jiang remained slow in improving China's human rights. To build political support and further attract foreign investment, he was passive in propagandizing Communist ideology, but praised Confucianism and Chinese tradition. Regarding China's U.S. policy, Jiang strenuously resisted American pressure on China to improve its human rights record, but, at the same time, reached out to build economic ties with the U.S. business community. By 1997, China had become a major source of the U.S. trade deficit, second only to Japan. Meanwhile, Jiang responded positively to the Constructive Engagement* policy that President Bill Clinton* followed toward the PRC.

By the time Deng Xiaoping died in early 1997, Jiang had established himself as the indisputable leader of the PRC. On the other hand, relations between the United States and China became contentious because of increasing vigilance among Americans concerning China's allegedly aggressive behavior, especially toward the Republic of China* on Taiwan*. Jiang soon became quite skillful in managing relations with the United States, maintaining a delicate balance between economic liberalism and political authoritarianism. For example, in October 1997, during his state visit to the United States, he took pains to project the dual image of himself as a fun-loving and easygoing person, playing guitar and swimming on a Hawaii beach, and the well-cultured gentleman who often quoted Confucius in his public speeches. His handling of public relations in the United States at minimum avoided further irritating those Americans monitoring human rights abuses in the PRC. By early 1998, his status as president was reaffirmed at the fifteenth National People's Congress and Clinton's visit in July confirmed his world role as China's recognized leader. *See also* Li Peng.

J. K. Fairbank, *China: A New History* (Cambridge, MA, 1992); *New York Times*, June and July 1998.

Li Yi

JOHNSON, LYNDON B. (1908–1973)

No American president devoted more time and energy to U.S.–East Asian relations than Lyndon Baines Johnson, although few presidents had less preparation for that aspect of American diplomacy. Born in the west Texas hill country, Johnson grew up in the Democratic Party and then headed the New Deal's National Youth Administration in his state. Elected to the House of Representatives in 1936, he served there until his 1948 election to the Senate, where he became minority leader in 1953 and majority leader in 1955. Ironically, in light of later events, Johnson in 1954 advised President Dwight D. Eisenhower* not to send U.S. combat troops to lift the siege at Dien Bien Phu* in the First Indochina War*. But he worked closely with Eisenhower on domestic policy, and hoped to win the 1960 Democratic nomination for president. When that prize went to Massachusetts Senator John F. Kennedy*, the nominee asked Johnson to be his vice presidential candidate. To the surprise of Kennedy's advisers, Johnson accepted, and his presence on the ticket proved crucial in Kennedy's November victory over Richard M. Nixon*.

At his accession to office upon the assassination of Kennedy, Johnson inherited an American commitment to the defense of South Vietnam that dated back to the mid-1950s, and was based on an American belief in the necessity of containing the southward expansion of Chinese Communist power. He initially hoped that the commitment to Saigon could be limited, not least because he much preferred domestic politics to foreign policy. But as the situation in the Republic of Vietnam* worsened after the overthrow of Ngo Dinh Diem*, Johnson found himself pulled further and further into the Vietnam conflict. In August 1964, after the Gulf of Tonkin Incidents*, he orchestrated congressional approval of the Gulf of Tonkin Resolution, authorizing "all necessary measures" to defend U.S. forces in Vietnam and to prevent additional aggression. Although Johnson delayed using this new authority until after the 1964 presidential election, which he won in a landslide over the more overtly belligerent Barry Goldwater, in early 1965 he commenced a major expansion of the Second Indochina War*. Bombing of North Vietnam—labeled Operation ROLLING THUNDER*—began in February, and was followed in July by a decision to expand American ground forces from 75,000 to nearly 200,000.

Even as Johnson's domestic program was sailing through Congress, his Vietnam policies were running into trouble on the ground in Southeast Asia. Air and land operations failed to prevent advances by the Viet Cong* and North Vietnamese, and in early 1966, Johnson approved another major escalation, to more than 400,000 troops. The Americanization of the conflict, and in particular its lack of success, provoked protests in the United States by congressional critics, including Arkansas Senator J. William Fulbright*, and by student activists on campuses across the country. Johnson sought to appease the dissenters by ordering periodic bombing halts, and by refusing to countenance such additional measures as an invasion of the Democratic Republic of Vietnam* (which he opposed anyway on grounds that it might draw the People's Republic of China* into the war). Despite the setbacks, Johnson and his advisers put the best face on the situation in Vietnam. Citing casualty rates and other statistics, they claimed to be making steady progress toward victory.

Early in 1968, the *Pueblo* Incident* embarrassed Johnson, as North Korea seized a U.S. surveillance ship and its crew. Far worse, the Tet Offensive* cast serious doubt over the administration's public optimism about Vietnam, and compelled

Johnson to change course. When General William C. Westmoreland* requested another 200,000 troops, Johnson refused. Instead, he suspended most of the bombing, proposed to negotiate an end to the war, and withdrew from the race for reelection as president. In January 1969, he handed responsibility for the war to Richard Nixon, his successor, who continued the Paris Peace Talks* begun during Johnson's last months in office and proceeded to deescalate the war. At the time of Johnson's death, his reputation remained in tatters, another American casualty among the very many in Southeast Asia. See also Johnson-Pak Conferences.

H. W. Brands, *The Wages of Globalism: Lyndon Johnson and the Limits of American Power* (New York, 1995); R. A. Dallek, *Flawed Giant: Lyndon Johnson and His Times* (New York, 1998); H. R. McMaster, *Dereliction of Duty: Lyndon Johnson, Robert McNamara, the Joint Chiefs of Staff, and the Lies that Led to Vietnam* (New York, 1997); R. S. McNamara, *In Retrospect: The Tragedy and Lessons of Vietnam* (New York, 1995); B. Van DeMark, *Into the Quagmire: Lyndon Johnson and the Escalation of the Vietnam War* (New York, 1991).

H. W. Brands

JOHNSON, NELSON T. (1887–1954)

Nelson Johnson was one of the first true "China experts" in the U.S. Foreign Service. He entered the Foreign Service in 1907 and was sent to Beijing to learn Chinese, serving thereafter from 1909 to 1911 as deputy consul general and interpreter in Mukden, Harbin, Hankou, and Shanghai. Named mixed court assessor in 1913, Johnson was during the next five years consul at Chongqing, Changsha, and Shanghai. He was assigned to the State Department in 1918, and named expert assistant for the Conference on the Limitation of Armament in 1920. Named consul general at large for the Far East and Australia in 1923, he became chief of the Division of Far Eastern Affairs two years later. Johnson succeeded

John V. A. MacMurray* as minister to China in November 1929, becoming ambassador in 1935, when the legation was upgraded to embassy status. After serving as minister to Australia from 1941 to 1945, he finished his career as secretary general of the Far Eastern Commission from 1946 to 1952.

Johnson's knowledge of Chinese language and culture, obtained during his long service in China, made him particularly sympathetic to Chinese nationalism. As chief of the State Department Division of Far Eastern Affairs, he influenced Secretary of State Frank B. Kellogg* to move toward revision of the unequal treaties, over the objections of MacMurray. The result was the treaty granting China Tariff Autonomy* in 1928. He also favored relinquishment of U.S. extraterritoriality in China, although the chaotic situation in China in the 1930s caused him to vacillate on this issue.

After becoming minister to China, Johnson alternated between sympathy for Chinese nationalism and frustration at the shortcomings he perceived in China's leaders. When the Japanese staged the Mukden Incident* and invaded Manchuria in 1931, he advocated invoking both the Kellogg-Briand Pact and the Nine Power Pact*. Believing that there were no vital American interests at stake, Johnson was concerned less with Japanese dominance of Manchuria than with the possibility that dissolution of the 1920s treaty system could lead to another world war. Although he supported the nonrecognition policy of Secretary of State Henry L. Stimson*, Johnson warned as early as 1932 that, faced with continued Japanese aggression, the United States "must be either prepared to shoot or to yield the street." He was an early critic of U.S. silver policy, arguing that the Silver Purchase Act of 1934 was devastating China's economy. Johnson later reversed himself, however, in the belief that the policy ultimately helped China resist Japan through large-scale U.S. purchases of Chinese silver.

After the 1937 Marco Polo Bridge Incident*, Johnson became more adamantly against appeasement of Japanese aggression. He opposed invoking U.S. neutrality laws, and although stopping short of advocating direct American intervention, thought that the United States should condemn clearly Japan's actions in China. By 1939, he was calling for direct U.S. aid to the Guomindang*, both to help stave off Japanese aggression and to prevent China from turning toward the Soviet Union. In the mid-1930s, Johnson had voiced sympathy for the Chinese Communist Party* (CCP), believing it to be more nationalistic than Communist, but by 1940, he was warning of a final showdown between the CCP and the Guomindang, although he thought that the United States should not intervene in the brewing Chinese Civil War*. Burned out by his long tenure in an increasingly difficult and dangerous situation, Johnson, in 1940, asked Stanley K. Hornbeck*, chief of the State Department Division of Far Eastern Affairs, for a transfer. He left his post as U.S. ambassador to China on 20 May 1941.

R. D. Buhite, *Nelson T. Johnson and American Policy Toward China, 1925–1941* (East Lansing, MI, 1968); W. I. Cohen, *America's Response to China: An Interpretive History of Sino-American Relations* (New York, 1990); A. X. Jiang, *The United States and China* (Chicago, 1988); C. R. Kitts, *The United States Odyssey in China, 1784–1990* (Lanham, MD, 1991).

Timothy L. Savage

JOHNSON-PAK CONFERENCES

President Lyndon B. Johnson* had three major conferences with President Pak Chŏng-hŭi* of the Republic of Korea* (ROK) during his time in office. In the context of his escalation of the Second Indochina War* and U.S Recruitment of Foreign Troops to Fight in Vietnam*, discussions throughout three meetings centered on the issue of South Korea's troop contribution. On 19 May 1965, during Pak's state visit to Washington, Johnson asked the ROK to contribute one combat division for service in Vietnam. As compensation, he pledged U.S. security commitments, reversing his administration's earlier secret plans to reduce the size of the U.S. military presence in South Korea. He also made a commitment for a $150 million development loan to assure Seoul of continuing U.S. aid, despite the impending signing of the Japan-Korea Normalization* Treaty. As a result of the conference, Pak in November dispatched one South Korean combat division to Vietnam. By September 1966, after further negotiations, he added one marine brigade and one army division to the ROK military in Vietnam.

On 1 November 1966, as a part of Johnson's Asian trip to enlist support of Asian countries for the war effort in Vietnam, he met Pak again, this time in Seoul. The two presidents agreed on the necessity of increased allied efforts in Vietnam. Considering adverse Korean public opinion on sending more troops to Vietnam and the upcoming Korean presidential election in 1967, however, it was agreed that the matter should be discussed later. Also, Johnson publicly reassured Pak of the U.S. security commitment to South Korea, because Pak was apprehensive of possible increased military pressure from the Democratic People's Republic of Korea* (DPRK). Then, on 17 April 1968, another meeting was held at Honolulu at Johnson's urgent request. Again, the main purpose was to request more ROK troops for Vietnam. Under the heightened military tension in Korea after North Korea's commando raid on Seoul and the *Pueblo* Incident*, when the DPRK seized a U.S. intelligence ship, both in January 1968, Pak was reluctant to send more troops. Pak only suggested that he would consider an additional troop contribution later, when security threats were less intense. Thus, to ease Pak's concern, and thereby to secure more Korean troops for Vietnam, President Johnson reaffirmed the U.S. security commitment to South Korea along with increased funding to assist modernization of the ROK military forces.

The conferences between Johnson and Pak demonstrated a shift in the dynamics of the alliance relationship between the United States and the ROK in 1960s. By 1964, the Johnson administration planned to reduce its military burden in South Korea and to concentrate more on the Vietnam situation. Johnson's determination to command multinational support in Vietnam since 1964, however, provided Seoul with effective bargaining leverage in its negotiations with Washington. Making full advantage of its position as the largest allied contributor to the Vietnam War, the ROK government succeeded in blocking a reduction of U.S. forces in South Korea. Seoul also exacted massive U.S. military and economic assistance that became one of the most important sources of South Korea's subsequent economic development.

B. Cumings, *Korea's Place in the Sun: A Modern History* (New York, 1997); N. E. Sarantakes, "In the Service of Pharaoh?: The United States and the Deployment of Korean Troops in Vietnam, 1965–1968," *Pacific Historical Review* (August 1999); N. B. Tucker, "Threats, Opportunities, and Frustrations in East Asia," in W. I. Cohen and N. B. Tucker (eds.), *Lyndon Johnson Confronts the World: American Foreign Policy, 1963–1968* (New York, 1994).

Ma Sang-yoon

JOHNSON, U. ALEXIS (1908–1997)

A career Foreign Service officer, U. Alexis Johnson was a highly influential shaper of U.S. foreign policy toward Asia, especially following World War II. After attending Occidental College, he pursued a career as a diplomat because the Great Depression made it impossible for him to afford law school. In 1935, he entered the Foreign Service and went to Japan as a language officer. Johnson spent the next seven years in Japan, or its controlled territories, doing consular work. After returning to the United States in 1942, and a brief assignment in Brazil, he was sent to a U.S. Army Civil Affairs Training School to prepare officers for the U.S. Occupation of Japan*. Near the end of the war, Johnson was briefly in the Philippines*, and with Japan's surrender, he became the consul general in Yokohama. His career took a giant step forward when he returned to Washington in 1949 to become the deputy director of the Office of Northeast Asian Affairs. By 1951, Johnson was deputy assistant secretary of state for Far Eastern Affairs, in charge of daily administration of State Department policy. Dean Rusk*, assistant secretary of state for Far Eastern Affairs, assigned him the task of drafting a plan for a cease-fire in the Korean War*. Rusk's successor in the Eisenhower administration, Walter S. Robertson*, kept him at work on this task until the Korean Armistice Agreement* was signed, when he insisted that Johnson be made an ambassador as a reward. Although Johnson was a bit junior in status, he became the U.S. ambassador to Czechoslovakia, an assignment he did not particularly enjoy.

During the Eisenhower administration, Johnson played a role in U.S. policy on a number of issues in East Asia. At the Geneva Conference of 1954*, called to achieve a settlement in Korea and French Indochina*, Secretary of State John Foster Dulles* made Johnson the delegation coordinator, requiring him to supervise the preparation of position papers and manage the U.S. staff. He also witnessed the famous incident when China's Foreign Minister Zhou Enlai* approached Dulles with an extended hand in front of photographers and the American turned his back on his counterpart. Since the United States was not a party to the negotiations on French Indochina, Dulles departed after the talks on Korea deadlocked, making Johnson the lead American observer. In Geneva, Dulles also assigned Johnson the assignment of negotiating with the People's Republic of China* (PRC) about obtaining the release of Americans being held in China against their will. These early meetings produced nothing, but in July 1955, he became the lead American negotiator when negotiations resumed in Warsaw. These Warsaw Talks* deadlocked before the year ended, but continued until Johnson went to Thailand* as the new ambassador. He enjoyed his stay there, finding the Thais far more willing to enter into meaningful negotiations than the Czechs. The most important issue during his tenure in Thailand was the civil war in Laos*, where the advance of the Communist Pathet Lao* threatened Thai security. Johnson convinced Foreign Minister Thanat Khoman that the United States would honor its obligations under the Southeast Asia Treaty Organization* (SEATO), even if the other signatories failed to do so.

When John F. Kennedy* became president, Rusk, the new secretary of state, asked Johnson to be his deputy undersecretary in 1962, which was the highest-ranking position for a career official. On 22 June 1964, Rusk informed Johnson that President Lyndon B. Johnson* was naming General Maxwell D. Taylor* as the U.S. ambassador to the Republic of Vietnam* and wanted the diplomat to go to Saigon as Taylor's number two man. He agreed to accept this demotion, but asked that he be called the deputy ambassador—a title he created on the spur of the moment. This appointment started the practice of sending a senior Foreign Service officer to Saigon who had been an ambassador to serve as the second-ranking diplomat. Johnson at first opposed the introduction of U.S. ground troops, until the president made this decision. In 1966, the president fulfilled his promise to Johnson's wife that he would reward her for going to Vietnam, and named her husband ambassador to Japan when Edwin O. Reischauer* resigned. At that time, political pressure in Japan was building for return of Iwo Jima and Okinawa, and the ten-year time limit on the U.S.-Japan Mutual Cooperation and Security Treaty* of 1960 made it imperative that Johnson alleviate tension, which he did by, among other concessions, persuading the State Department to support return

of the Bonin Islands*. Then, after Richard M. Nixon* became president, he arranged for reversion of Okinawa to Japan while serving as undersecretary for political affairs, formulating a compromise whereby the United States removed all nuclear weapons from the island, and Japan agreed to accept emergency consultations. In 1973, Nixon made Johnson the chief negotiator at the Strategic Arms Limitation Talks (SALT), a position he held until his retirement in 1977. *See also* Okinawa Controversy.

U. A. Johnson, *The Right Hand of Power* (Englewood Cliffs, NJ, 1984); M. Schaller, *Altered States: The United States and Japan Since the Occupation* (New York, 1997).

Nicholas Evan Sarantakes

JOINT COMMISSION ON RURAL RECONSTRUCTION

In a last-ditch effort to create a land reform program to assist the Guomindang* (Nationalist) regime of Jiang Jieshi*, the Sino-American Joint Commission on Rural Reconstruction (JCRR) was created under the China Assistance Act of 1948* passed by the U.S. Congress. On 3 July 1948, the United States and the Republic of China* (ROC) signed an economic aid agreement, and an exchange of notes on 5 August formally authorized the establishment of the Sino-American JCRR in China. However, before its formal initiation, defeat in the Chinese Civil War* forced Jiang's government and the JCRR to flee to Taiwan*. By the spring of 1950, the Pentagon considered the ROC a crucial ally to its defensive perimeter strategy for containing Communist expansion in the Pacific, and the Korean War* confirmed this approach as U.S. policy. The containment strategy required a politically stable and economically viable Taiwan, and U.S. advisers there pressed for changes and used U.S. aid to realize these policy goals. This conviction was confirmed by Wolf Ladejinsky, a land reform adviser on China's mainland, who believed that "only a major U.S. effort in the land reform area would win over the Asian peasants." Fearing a repetition of the debacle in the Chinese Civil War, U.S. policy makers acknowledged that in addition to U.S. military aid, the ROC also had to build a contented countryside that would support the military regime. Land reform, therefore, was intended as a crucial political weapon to win rural support for the Nationalists and thus reinforce social and political stability throughout Taiwan.

In 1949, two-thirds of the peasantry on Taiwan either were farm laborers or tenants. Some tenant farmers paid up to 70 percent of their harvest for rent. Once in operation, the JCRR immediately implemented a program of forced rent reduction, lowering rent to 37.5 percent. In 1951, Jiang's government began selling public land to working farmers. The passage of the Land-to-Tiller Act in 1953 forced landlords to sell all but three hectares of their land to the government, which in turn sold the land to former tenants. By 1959, the number of owner-cultivators on Taiwan had risen to 85.6 percent, and tenancy decreased to less than 15 percent. Besides land reform, the JCRR was responsible for establishment of farmers' associations and cooperatives, improved agricultural education, land use and soil conservation, plant industry, livestock, forestry, and fisheries. After 1965, gradual transfer of routine projects to appropriate governmental agencies began when U.S. economic aid to Taiwan ended. More important, many of Taiwan's future political leaders, notably President Li Denghui*, first gained stature as technical experts working for the JCRR.

T. B. Gold, *State and Society in the Taiwan Miracle* (New York, 1986); M. H. H. Hsiao, *Government Agricultural Strategies in Taiwan and South Korea* (Taibei, 1981); T. H. Shen, *The Sino-American Joint Commission on Rural Reconstruction : Twenty Years of Cooperation for Agricultural Development* (Ithaca, NY, 1970); M. M. C. Yang, *Socio-Economic Results of Land Reform in Taiwan* (Honolulu, HI, 1970).

Roger Y. M. Chan

JUCH'E

Juch'e, also called Kim Il Sung-ism after its founder, has been the ruling ideology dominating all sectors of life ranging from foreign policy to routine lifestyle in the Democratic People's Republic of Korea* (DPRK). An absolute religious dogma in North Korea, *juch'e* consists of four main concepts: self-determination in ideology, independence in politics, self-reliance in economics, and self-defense in military affairs. Commonly referred to as the concept of self-reliance, the word *"juch'e"* first appeared when Kim Il Sung* purged his political opponents, notably Pak Hŏn-yŏng*, in the course of power struggles after the Korean War* ended in July 1953. Kim Il Sung severely criticized the Chinese and Soviet factions for following the teachings of Marxism-Leninism dogmatically. He insisted instead on developing and adopting a Korean version of Marxism-Leninism, which allegedly harmonized with the realities of the Korean situation.

Juch'e ideology later was redefined by Kim Il Sung's son, Kim Jong Il*, into a political philosophy. In *On Juch'e Ideology*, published in 1982, Kim Jong Il described it as comprising six propositions: (1) man is the master of all things and man decides everything; (2) self-reliance is the soul of human existence; (3) all behaviors of man in historical development are decided by his ideological consciousness, and only when the masses of the working class people are guided by ideological consciousness can they become the masters of their destinies and the mighty creators of history; (4) the masses of the working class are the prime movers of revolution and construction; (5) revolution in one's country should be central to the thinking and revolutionary action of all men; (6) the masses of the working class people should take a masterly attitude with regard to revolution and construction because they are the masters.

Both Kims used *juch'e* as a political tool to justify the North Korean political system, government structure, and the personality cult of father and son. *Juch'e* has played a key role in the process of consolidating the North Korean political power structure and prevented the collapse of the DPRK, despite severe economic hardships beginning in the 1990s. Moreover, *juch'e* ideology was used as a tool to prepare the theoretical foundation to support the junior Kim's heirship. Originally, the socialist state in North Korea had been founded on the orthodox socialist principle that placed the party above all else. However, the DPRK's ruling hierarchy, by concocting *juch'e*, converted North Korea into a unique Communist state form in which the leader reigns over the party. In implementing its father-to-son power succession plan, a remnant of feudalism, North Korea was to become the target of criticism among socialists.

B. Cumings, *Korea's Place in the Sun: A Modern History* (New York, 1997); D. Oberdorfer, *The Two Koreas: A Contemporary History* (Reading, PA, 1997); D. Suh, *Kim Il Sung: The North Korean Leader* (New York, 1988).

Han Kyu-sun

JUDD, WALTER H. (1898–1994)

From 1942 to 1963, Walter Henry Judd was a member of the U.S. House of Representatives from Minnesota. Born in a small Nebraska town, he served as a medical missionary to China from 1926 to 1931 and 1934 to 1938, which gave him broad experience with the problems that contributed to the Chinese Civil War*. As a private citizen and congressman, Judd had an enormous impact on U.S. foreign policy regarding East Asia. From 1938 to 1940, he traveled the country delivering lectures on the danger of Japanese expansionism to U.S. interests. In Congress, he won approval of a bill to allow Chinese immigrants into the United States. Later in 1952, he wrote and saw passage of legislation to end racial discrimination in immigration laws. Judd was considered a member of the

China Lobby* because he was a staunch advocate for Jiang Jieshi* and his Guomindang* (Nationalist) government. He managed to obtain $338 million in aid for the Republic of China* (ROC) as part of the Marshall Plan, with another $125 million available under the China Assistance Act of 1948* to spend on Jiang's regime. Judd was also chiefly responsible for continued aid to Taiwan* by his work on the Joint Commission on Rural Reconstruction*, which he had created.

In 1947, Judd proposed extending the containment policy against Soviet expansion to the Pacific through formation of an alliance system of the United States and Asian nations, which he dubbed the Pacific Pact. Eventually in the Eisenhower administration, Secretary of State John Foster Dulles* created such a arrangement—the Southeast Asia Treaty Organization* (SEATO) of 1954. After the Chinese Communist Party* forced Jiang's government into exile on Taiwan, Judd argued forcefully and effectively against U.S. recognition of the People's Republic of China* (PRC). He was the prime mover in the operations of the Committee of One Million, a group devoted to preventing the PRC from gaining admittance to the United Nations. He worked effectively to isolate the PRC, until President Richard M. Nixon* sought to normalize relations with Beijing. When the United Nations admitted the PRC and expelled the ROC in 1971, the committee dissolved. Meanwhile, Judd had endorsed the decision of President Harry S. Truman* to intervene in the Korean War, but criticized his recall of General Douglas MacArthur*.

During the presidency of Dwight D. Eisenhower*, Judd vigorously supported the administration's efforts to pass its foreign aid programs, particularly assistance to Taiwan. On this issue, because of his experience in China, he had enormous clout with his fellow congressmen. He strongly endorsed Eisenhower's proposal of the Formosa Resolution*, which called for U.S. defense of the ROC on Taiwan. Later, Judd advised President Lyndon B. Johnson* on the Second Indochina War*, telling him to negotiate, but to be careful and not allow the Communists to stall. He argued that if the North Vietnamese were obstructionist, the United States should warn that it would resort to more extreme measures against the Democratic Republic of Vietnam*. But Judd also argued before the House Foreign Affairs Committee that the United States should not overwhelm the Republic of Vietnam* with too many men and too much material because this would destroy its culture. Judd died of cancer.

L. Edwards, *Missionary for Freedom: The Life and Times of Walter Judd* (New York, 1990); *New York Times*, 15 February 1994; E. J. Rozek, *Walter H. Judd: Chronicles of a Statesman* (Denver, CO, 1980).

Tracy S. Uebelhor

K

KAIFU TOSHIKI (1931–   )

Kaifu became Japan's prime minister on 9 August 1989 after the successive resignations of Prime Ministers Takeshita Noboru* and Uno Sōsuke in the wake of the Recruit-Cosmos money scandal and the losses of the Liberal Democratic Party* (LDP) that followed in the July Upper House election. Despite being a member of a small Komoto (previously Miki Takeo*) faction of the LDP, senior LDP leaders appreciated Kaifu's relative youth and "clean image" over other, more influential candidates, such as Miyazawa Kiichi* and Abe Shintarō, who were tainted by the scandal. Born in Aichi Prefecture, after graduating from Waseda University, he successfully gained a lower house Diet seat in 1960. Soon Kaifu became Miki's protégé, and Miki named him deputy cabinet secretary in his first cabinet. He was education minister under both Fukuda Takeo* and Nakasone Yasuhiro*, as well as chairman of the LDP's Education Policy Committee, gaining a reputation as an education expert in the party.

During the Kaifu administration, political reform, especially electoral reform, and *kokusai kōken* (international contribution) were two of the most important issues. Kaifu ultimately introduced a major political reform bill in August 1991, consisting of strengthening regulations on campaign funding and, more important, introducing a new electoral system providing for single-member constituencies in combination with proportional representation. The bill was strongly opposed by opposition parties, who feared the single-district system would be disadvantageous to them. When Kaifu pressed for the bill's passage with an undisguised threat of dissolving the lower house, most major factions withdrew support and Kaifu had to give up his hope for reelection in the coming LDP presidential election in October.

On the international scene, Kaifu, who had little experience in international affairs and was a dove in security matters, had to deal with the Persian Gulf War in 1991, which posed one of the biggest challenges in postwar Japanese foreign policy. Japan's international role as an economic superpower became a significant domestic and international political issue during the debate on its contribution to solving the crisis, which began in August 1990. Ultimately, the Kaifu administration, under strong pressure from U.S. President George H. W. Bush* for a major contribution of money and manpower to liberate Kuwait, contributed $13 billion, but failed to enact a UN Peace Cooperation bill, which would make possible the deployment of Japanese Self-Defense Forces in the Mideast. With a cease-fire established, the Kaifu administration successfully deployed minesweepers to the Persian Gulf in April 1991. Yet the national debate on the broader problem of Japan's kokusai koken continued. Kaifu also had to contend with the deepening of disputes related to U.S.-Japan Postwar Trade Relations*, which culminated in the Bush administration's Structural Impediments Initiative aimed at ending barriers to imports in Japan.

Fujimoto Kazumi, *Kaifu seiken to "Seiji Kaikaku"* [The Kaifu Administration and "Political Reform"] (Tōkyō, 1992); K. Hayao, *The Japanese Prime Minister and Public Policy* (Pittsburgh, PA, 1993); Watanabe Akio (ed.), *Sengo Nihon no saishō tachi* [Postwar Japanese Prime Ministers] (Tōkyō, 1995).

Kamimura Naoki

KAL 007 INCIDENT

Igniting a brief diplomatic crisis and even a threat of war, the KAL 007 incident worsened Soviet-American relations at a critical time. It also left more questions than answers. Shortly before 3:30 A.M., 31 August 1983, Korean Air Lines (KAL) Flight 007 left Anchorage, Alaska, on the final leg of its New York–Seoul schedule. On board was a cabin crew of twenty, 240 passengers, and nine other KAL employees. Only a few minutes after takeoff, the flight deviated from its assigned course, taking the jet twice over Soviet airspace (the Kamchatka Peninsula and then Sakhalin Island). The latter was the site of a major Soviet military installation. Only five hours after it left Alaska, two missiles struck KAL 007 as it flew over Sakhalin fired by veteran Soviet Air Defense Force Colonel Gennadiy N. Osipovich in his SU-15 interceptor. Twelve minutes later, the jumbo jet crashed into the Gulf of Tartary west of Sakhalin. No one survived, and sixty-one American citizens were on board.

An outraged President Ronald Reagan* claimed that the incident proved, as he had said in 1981, that the Soviet Union was an "evil empire." Calling the Soviets "barbarians," he denounced the Soviet claim that KAL 007 was a spy plane. Reagan put the U.S. Eighth Army in South Korea on full alert, and its commander, General Winfield Scott IV, commented to the press that the northern and western Pacific should prepare for the possibility of another world war. Although his comments especially frightened the inhabitants of the Pacific region, few in the U.S. news media believed him. Indeed, this incident would not be a rerun of the Cuban Missile Crisis of 1962. Yet it symbolized the collapse of Soviet-American détente in the early 1980s, and the possibility of successful arms limitations talks vanished. Meanwhile, an adequate explanation for what really happened over Sakhalin remained a mystery. One theory stressed that because an American RC-135 spy plane, in fact, had been over Sakhalin shortly before the Soviet attack, the whole affair had been a matter of mistaken identity or pilot incompetence. For years after the incident, the Soviet government refused to express any guilt in reference to it, and waged a campaign to keep all U.S. investigators away from the crash site.

Others explain that guilt rests with Korean Air Lines. In 1983, KAL suffered the unfortunate reputation of having one of the worst flight delay records in the airline industry. It also maintained an unusual company policy that paid pilots a bonus to arrive on time and in "any way they can." A popular airline industry joke quipped that KAL stood for Krash At Landing. There are even incredible tales about the disaster. Michel Brun, writing in 1996 and after ten years of research, claimed that an American-Soviet air battle was taking place at the time KAL 007 "allegedly" appeared over Sakhalin. Brun alleges that the jet wandered into the wrong place at the wrong time, intentionally or unintentionally, and was destroyed, for still unknown reasons, near Honshū, Japan, and not Sakhalin. Whatever happened to KAL 007, the incident underlined the reality of a still-disturbed Soviet-American relationship, as Cold War tension continued into the 1980s, with Washington opting for global sword-rattling over détente and Moscow preferring fabrication and denial of verifiable facts.

M. Brun, *Incident at Sakhalin: The True Mission of KAL Flight 007* (New York, 1996); A. Dallin, *Black Box: KAL 007 and the Superpowers* (Berkeley, CA, 1985); S. M. Hersh, *"The Target Is Destroyed": What Really Happened to Flight 007 and What America Knew About It* (New York, 1986); R. W. Johnson, *Shootdown: Flight 007 and the American Connection* (New York, 1986); F. Woodson, *The Last Flight of 007* (Costa Mesa, CA, 1993).

Timothy P. Maga

KALAKAUA (1836–1891)

David Kalakaua ruled the Hawaiian Kingdom from 1874 to 1891. During his reign, American residents revolted against him, which drastically reduced his power and gave much greater political influence to the whites living in Hawaii. Elected king of the islands in 1874, he presided over the negotiation of a reciprocity treaty with the United States in 1876 that mutually eliminated tariffs on Hawaiian sugar and on many goods imported to Hawaii from the United States. The treaty's effect was immediate and profound. Trade between the two countries greatly increased, and the United States reinforced its position as Hawaii's main trading partner. For Hawaii, it brought great prosperity and domination of the entire economy by sugar production, which grew enormously. Hawaii became an economic satellite of the United States.

Despite the treaty, Kalakaua was fundamentally hostile to Americans and their growing influence in Hawaiian life and culture. After a few years, with his prime minister Walter Murray Gibson, he began to pursue policies dedicated to reducing white influence in Hawaiian culture and restoring the old Hawaiian ways. These brought him into greater conflict with the whites living in the islands, especially the Americans. One project he developed with Gibson was the Primacy of the Pacific Policy. Kalakaua sought to set up a confederation of the Polynesian kingdoms in the Pacific not already controlled by another nation, with himself as head. He started with Samoa, which was a mistake since that was the very place where Britain, the United States, and Germany were contesting for control by backing factions in a civil war at the time. In 1886, Kalakaua's emissary succeeded in negotiating a treaty of confederation with the main chief. By so doing, however, he antagonized all three powers, who collectively objected. The project collapsed before a change of government in Honolulu officially ended it and eventually led to the Samoa Partition*.

The change of government in Hawaii was the culmination of the contest developing since 1882 between Kalakaua and the white community in the islands. He and Gibson carried out projects, such as the Samoan initiative, that brought increasing criticism. The nation's debt grew considerably, charges of corruption became more frequent, and the legislative assembly was controlled completely by the king. When Kalakaua was caught in an attempt to profit from a newly passed law to license the sale of opium, the whites rose up against him. On 30 June 1887, the white militia organization forced Gibson out of power and then required the king to sign a new constitution, taking from him his formerly absolute power, transforming the government into a constitutional monarchy, and increasing white power in the legislature. Thereafter, Kalakaua was ineffectual in weakening white influence. A counterrevolt, organized by disgruntled Hawaiians and designed either to overthrow him or to reestablish the older authoritarian constitution, was put down by the white militia on 30 July 1889. In November 1890, Kalakaua decided to travel to the United States in the hope of improving his health, which was failing. The trip did not succeed in its goal, and on 20 January 1983, Kalakaua died. He was succeeded by his sister Lili'uokalani*. *See also* Hawaiian Annexation; Hawaiian Rebellion.

E. Andrade, *Unconquerable Rebel: Robert W. Wilcox and Hawaiian Politics, 1880–1903* (Boulder, CO, 1996); R. S. Kuykendall, *The Hawaiian Kingdom*, Vol. 3: *The Kalakaua Dynasty* (Honolulu, HI, 1967); M. Tate, *Hawaii: Reciprocity or Annexation* (East Lansing, MI, 1968).

Ernest Andrade Jr.

KATAYAMA SEN (1860–1933)

A prominent social reformer, trade union activist, and radical in late-nineteenth- and early-twentieth-century Japan, Katayama Sen became known as the father of Asian Communism*. He edited Japan's first labor newspaper, organized Japan's Social Democratic Party, and was active in establishing the Japan Communist Party. Born into humble surroundings in Okayama prefecture and initially known as Yabuki Sugatarō, he later was adopted by the Katayama family to avoid conscription into Japan's imperial army. His early life was influenced by the turmoil of the overthrow of the Tokugawa shōgunate and the Meiji Restoration of 1868. He studied at Keiō University and, under the influence of such distinguished scholars as Oka Shikamon, moved from an initial interest in the Chinese classics and neo-Confucian scholarship to more practical involvement with contemporary social issues.

In 1884, Katayama traveled to the United States and converted to Christianity. Hampered by financial and linguistic difficulties, his education proceeded erratically, including enrollment at a preparatory school in Tennessee, Grinnell College in Iowa, the Andover Theological Seminary in Massachusetts, and eventually in 1894, the Yale Divinity School. His studies, together with exposure to urban deprivation in the slums of London and Glasgow during a brief visit to Britain, encouraged him to return to Japan in 1895. Thereafter, Ka-

tayama pursued a literary and journalistic career, after a brief stint teaching at Waseda University. During these years, he was affiliated with social reform, but more in a theoretical, rather than an active context. His first direct association was with the Society for the Promotion of Trade Unions and subsequently as a founding member of the Society for the Study of Socialism. In 1901, he helped to found the Social Democratic Party, a small group that survived only three years.

Katayama in late 1903 attended both the convention of the American Socialist Party in Chicago and the Second International in Amsterdam in 1904. On returning to Japan, he sought to advance socialist objectives through parliamentary obstructionism and the general strike, but in 1906 he split with fellow socialists advocating anarchism. After the government of Katsura Tarō* cracked down on radical movements in 1908, Katayama eventually was imprisoned for five months. Upon release in 1914, he left for the United States, motivated in part by a desire to participate in the burgeoning world socialist movement. He settled in New York City, where he was exposed to a heady combination of Russian and American revolutionary radicalism. He soon developed a more ambitious, revolutionary agenda, and published his most influential book, *The Labor Movement in Japan*, in 1917 and a series of articles in *International Socialist Review*. Embracing an optimistic, some would argue naive, outlook, he assumed that socialist revolution was an inevitability in Japan. In the United States, Katayama became a focal point for young, radical Japanese émigrés. But the U.S. government's crackdown on radicals in 1920 drove him into hiding and then to Mexico in 1921.

In 1922, Katayama went to Moscow, where he became an active and prominent figure in the Comintern while remaining largely insulated from the factionalism that affected the Russian Communist Party from 1924 to 1927. His standing reflected his willingness to place the interests of international Communism ahead of radical forces in his own country. Despite playing a key role in establishing the Japan Communist Party in 1922, Katayama could not counter the Japanese government's suppression of domestic progressive forces in 1923. From Moscow, Katayama's interest in Asian Communism broadened beyond Japan to also take in China and Korea. By the late 1920s, his initial optimism had been eclipsed by a reluctant realization that revolution in Japan was unlikely in his lifetime. His funeral in November 1933 was marked by official ceremonies in Moscow, but in Japan he received no official recognition.

E. S. Colbert, *The Left Wing in Japanese Politics* (New York, 1952); S. Katayama, *The Labor Movement in Japan* (Chicago, 1918); H. Kublin, *Asian Revolutionary: The Life of Sen Katayama* (Princeton, NJ, 1964); R. Scalapino, *Democracy and the Party Movement in Prewar Japan: The Failure of the First Attempt* (Berkeley, CA, 1953).

John Swenson-Wright

KATAYAMA TETSU (1887–1978)

Katayama Tetsu was the moderate socialist political leader who served as prime minister of a coalition government in Japan from May 1947 until February 1948. The shortlived government proved ineffective, but its record included significant political reforms associated with the U.S. Occupation of Japan*. Upon graduation from Tōkyō Imperial University, Katayama founded a law office. A Christian and a pacifist, he believed in social reform. One of the founders of the Socialist Party in 1926, Katayama was elected to the House of Representatives in the Diet in 1932. In 1940, he broke with his party over its turn toward militarism. After the war, he thus enjoyed a reputation as a principled advocate of social democracy. In November 1945, he was elected secretary-general of the newly formed Japan Socialist Party (JSP). Real power, however, rested in the hands of various factions. The party's

adoption of Social Democratic Party of Japan as its official name in English shows the dominance of those committed to parliamentary government.

Katayama led the JSP when it was a real contender for power. Although its organization was still rudimentary, the purge of 1946 severely depleted the ranks of conservative politicians in the Diet. In the election of April 1947, the JSP obtained a plurality, with 143 members in the lower house. After lengthy negotiations, Japanese lawmakers chose Katayama as the prime minister on 23 May. He then formed a coalition government that included the Democratic and National Cooperative parties. General Douglas MacArthur* welcomed his selection immediately. But the JSP had the misfortune of coming into partial power when economic conditions and U.S. policy were shifting away from socialist interests. Spiraling prices, increased labor militancy, and the threat of food shortages compelled Katayama's government to impose austerity measures. Its inability to enforce controls or to carry out a plan to nationalize the country's coal mines undermined public confidence in the coalition. Policy debates naturally highlighted tension across partisan and factional lines, and Katayama was incapable of resolving these differences. Under fire and unable to control the left wing of his own party, Katayama resigned in February 1948. Ashida Hitoshi* of the Democratic Party succeeded him, but his coalition also collapsed the following October. The elections of January 1949 swept the rightist Liberal Party of Yoshida Shigeru* back into power and strengthened the left wing of the JSP.

In retrospect, the coalition's failure, coupled with the defeat of Katayama and other moderate socialists in the 1949 elections, reduced prospects of future center-left cooperation and thereby contributed to conservative dominance of postwar Japanese politics. Nevertheless as the first government under the Japanese Constitution of 1947*, the Socialist-led cabinet attempted to strengthen the foundations of democracy in Japan. Working closely with (and sometimes under pressure from) SCAP*, the government secured passage of laws concerning antitrust and labor reform. By dissolving institutions such as the Ministry of Home Affairs, Katayama's government showed its commitment to removing traces of militarism from national life. Fittingly, it established a Ministry of Labor. It reorganized local government and the police, and appointed the first group of Japanese Supreme Court justices. It also revised the civil and criminal code. As for Katayama, even after temporary electoral defeat, he remained active in politics in an advisory role until 1963. In 1957, for example, he led a nine-man delegation to Beijing, Moscow, and Warsaw seeking to promote economic development in China, Siberia, and less-developed economies in Asia.

A. B. Cole, G. O. Totten, C. H. Uehara, *Socialist Parties in Postwar Japan* (New Haven, CT, 1966); M. Kohno, *Japan's Postwar Party Politics* (Princeton, NJ, 1997); T. Kataoka (ed.), *Creating Single-Party Democracy* (Stanford, CA, 1992).

Aaron Forsberg

KĀTO KŌMEI (1860–1926)

Kāto Takaaki (Kōmei) was foreign minister and, later, prime minister in Japan. He strongly favored close ties with Britain over those with Russia from the late 1880s into the 1920s. After graduating from the law department of Tōkyō Imperial University in 1881, he joined Mitsubishi Company and was sent to England to study. This experience made him an advocate for pro-British diplomacy throughout his life. In 1886, Kāto married the daughter of Iwasaki Yatarō, the founder of Mitsubishi. He joined the Foreign Office in 1887 and served as a secretary to Foreign Minister Ōkuma Shigenobu*. After working briefly as the director of a bureau in the Finance Ministry, Kāto returned to the Foreign Office. In 1895, he was sent to England as minister and worked there for about four years until his appointment as foreign min-

ister under Itō Hitobumi* in 1900. Although many members of the government were trying to solve the Korea question by entering into an alliance with Russia, Kāto ardently advocated an alliance with Britain. He criticized the idea of exchanging Manchuria for Korea as a weak-kneed policy toward Russia. Kāto rejected Russia's demands for neutralization of Korea and concessions at China's expense in Manchuria. He then served as a representative in the Diet's lower house between 1902 and 1904, and was president of a major Tōkyō newspaper from 1904 to 1906.

Kāto was appointed foreign minister under Saionji Kinmochi* in 1906, but soon resigned, partly in opposition to nationalization of the railway, which was against Mitsubishi interests. Another factor was his opposition to the army's management in Manchuria, which ran counter to his belief that the military should not intervene in diplomatic affairs. In 1908, Kāto was appointed ambassador to Britain. Asserting that the Anglo-Japanese Alliance* was at the center of Japanese diplomacy, he contributed to the conclusion of the second renewal of the agreement. In 1916, Kāto was named as foreign minister for the third time under Katsura Tarō*, and then remained in the post in the Ōkuma cabinet in 1914. During his tenure, the infamous Twenty-One Demands* were submitted to China in 1915. He then angered elder statesmen when he declared himself against a Russo-French proposal to join the Anglo-Japanese Alliance and soon resigned. Meanwhile, Kāto had formed the Constitutional Party (Kenseikai) and was its chairman in 1913. In 1924, Kāto finally became the prime minister of a coalition government. After his party's victory in the 1925 election, he persuaded the Diet to enact universal male suffrage and antisubversive acts. Kāto died while in office.

Itō Masanori (ed.), *Kāto Takaaki*, 2 vols. (Tōkyō, 1929); Kāto Takaaki (ed.), *Kāto Takaaki den* (Tōkyō, 1928); Kondo Misao (ed.), *Kāto Takaaki* (Tōkyō, 1959).

Hirobe Izumi

KATSURA TARŌ (1847–1913)

Katsura Tarō was a powerful Japanese political leader whose foreign policy vision helped direct Japan's expansion to the Asian continent in the first decade of the twentieth century. A scion of a Chōshū samurai family and protégé of Japanese Army doyen Yamagata Aritomo, he served four cabinets as war minister and three unconsecutive terms as prime minister. As a young army officer, he closely studied the German military system and promoted the professionalization of his service on the Prussian model. Katsura distinguished himself in his regional command in the Sino-Japanese War. In 1898, after a brief stint as consul general in the newly acquired territory of Taiwan*, he embarked on a career as war minister in the Itō cabinet. Katsura's vision for Japanese overseas expansion focused on Korea and Manchuria, dovetailing with the imperialist agenda articulated by Komura Jutarō, whom Katsura recruited in 1901 to be foreign minister in his own cabinet. Their efforts to cultivate an alliance with Britain capable of countering the Russian inroad into Manchuria after the Boxer Uprising* led to the Anglo-Japanese Alliance* in January 1902. The historic treaty recognized, among other things, Japan's special interest in Korea.

Katsura also believed that Japan had to work out a modus vivendi with the United States, which had established an imperial foothold in Asia with the acquisition of the Philippines*. In a secret memorandum signed by Katsura and Secretary of War William Howard Taft* in July 1905, after the cease-fire in the Russo-Japanese War*, Japan and the United States each recognized the other's special interests in Korea and the Philippines respectively. After the war with Russia, depleted national resources and the continued Russian presence in north Manchuria led Katsura to agree to sell E. H. Harriman*, a U.S. railroad magnate, the South Manchurian Railway, which had been ceded by Russia under the terms of the Treaty of Portsmouth*. In the event of war with China or Russia, the railway was to be placed under Japanese command. After Komura opposed the prospective deal, Katsura reneged on a tentative accord that provided for joint U.S.-Japanese control of the strategic transportation line.

During his second term as prime minister starting in 1908, Katsura continued policies to safeguard Japan's concessions in Manchuria while maintaining U.S. and British acquiescence in Japan's push toward exclusive control of Korea. To this end, the Japanese government signed the Root-Takahira Agreement* in 1908. When Secretary of State Philander C. Knox* proposed his Neutralization Scheme* regarding the South Manchurian Railway, it so alarmed Katsura's government that it signed an entente with Russia in July 1910. Formal Japanese Annexation of Korea* came the next month. Meanwhile, Katsura signed treaties of commerce and navigation with the United States and major Europeans powers, completing the treaty revision process.

W. G. Beasley, *Japanese Imperialism, 1894–1945* (London, 1987); H. Conroy, *The Japanese Seizure of Korea, 1868–1910: A Study of Realism and Idealism in International Relations* (Philadelphia, 1960); Gaimushō, *Komura gaikōshi* [The History of Komura Diplomacy], vol. 2 (Tōkyō, 1953); S. Okamoto, *The Japanese Oligarchy and the Russo-Japanese War* (New York, 1970); Tokutomi Ichirō, *Koshaku Katsura Tarō den* [A Biography of Duke Katsura Tarō] (Tōkyō, 1917).

Shimizu Sayuri

KELLOGG, FRANK B. (1856–1937)

From 1925 to 1929, Frank B. Kellogg, as U.S. secretary of state, was a friend to China during the turbulent Warlord Era* and played a central role in negotiating an international agreement outlawing war. As a child, he helped work the family farm in Minnesota, and nearly lost his life in a snowstorm. Pursuing a career in law, he became president of the American Bar Association in 1912. Kellogg then served in the U.S. Senate from 1917 to 1923, received appointment as ambassador to Britain, and became secretary of state under President Calvin Coolidge. In Asia, Secretary Kellogg sought to protect China against the great powers in accordance with the Open Door Policy*. He dealt mainly with a succession of Chinese governments in Beijing, all clamoring for formal recognition and willing to curry support by assailing foreign treaty rights and interests. Kellogg might have collaborated with the other treaty powers, principally Britain and Japan, forcing the Chinese to good or at least better behavior, but invariably rejected these opportunities.

Two crises threatened Kellogg's efforts to promote prosperity and stability in China. The first began on 30 May 1925, when British troops fired upon a mob that threatened to overwhelm a police station, killing twelve of the assailants. Even though the cause of the riot had been exploitation of Chinese workers in Japanese-owned cotton mills, Chinese public opinion turned against Britain, igniting the May Thirtieth Movement*. Months later, the government in London relented, but Kellogg refused to join Britain's belated move, issuing his own statement that his government was "ready then [at the Washington Conference* of 1921 and 1922] and is ready now . . . to take up negotiations on behalf of the United States alone." Second, on 24 March 1927 in Nanjing, Guomindang* (Nationalist) troops turned on missionaries and foreign businesses, ransacked residences, hospitals, churches, and places of business, killed several foreigners, including one American, and surrounded refugees on Socony Hill, a property of the Standard Oil Company. U.S. destroyers in the nearby river threw a cordon of shells around the hill and evacuated the refugees. Other powers desired indemnities and an apology, but Kellogg stood away from demands, arguing that the era of gunboat diplomacy in China had passed.

Kellogg set in motion a proviso of the Washington Conference that the Chinese should renegotiate their tariff treaties and undertake an end to extraterritoriality. The United States sent a delegate to accomplish both purposes, and signed a treaty in 1928 for China Tariff Autonomy* that, through its signature, recognized the Nationalist government of Jiang Jieshi*. But the extraterritoriality issue required time, creation of courts, and other legal arrangements that would protect U.S. citizens, and negotiations lingered until 1943. Kellogg's single failure was not so much exaggerating prospects for maintaining an Open Door in China as failing to sense the increasing weakness of the civilian government in Japan. Beset by military extremists, the Tōkyō cabinet and Diet could not prevent the seizure of Manchuria in the Mukden Incident* in 1931. But no statesman in the late 1920s sensed the danger, and Japan continued, largely without notice, to move in the direction of the Pearl Harbor Attack* of 1941.

D. Borg, *American Policy and the Chinese Revolution, 1925–1928* (New York, 1947); B. D. Cole, *Gunboats and Marines: The United States Navy in China, 1925–1929* (Newark, DE, 1983); L. E. Ellis, *Frank B. Kellogg and American Foreign Relations, 1925–1929* (New Brunswick, NJ, 1961); R. H. Ferrell, *Frank B. Kellogg—Henry L. Stimson*, in S. F. Bemis (ed.), *American Secretaries of State and Their Diplomacy* (New York, 1963); W. R. Fishel, *The End of Extraterritoriality in China* (Berkeley, CA, 1952).

Robert H. Ferrell

KENDRICK, JOHN (1740–1794)

John Kendrick was an American adventurer in East Asia in the late eighteenth and early nineteenth centuries. He was the first American to communicate with the Japanese. A rich merchant from Boston who owned an ocean vessel, the *Columbia*, Kendrick built his career as a captain and visited many parts of the world. After reading Captain James Cook's journals and particularly the successful story of the *Empress of China**, he became interested in the Pacific trade. In 1787, he organized a commercial expedition to East Asia. He planned to take his *Columbia* on a long voyage along the Northwest coast to collect a cargo of furs and, once obtained, sail on a sloop, *Lady Washington*, to Guangzhou. Kendrick's plan did not work out well, however. The *Columbia* did not reach the Northwest coast until too late in 1788 to collect any furs, and had to winter at Nootka. The following summer, as provisions ran short, Kendrick moved to the *Lady Washington* and remained on the coast, sending the *Columbia* to China under the command of Captain Robert Grey.

While waiting for the return of the *Columbia* from China, Kendrick began to purchase land from the Indians at Nootka Sound, and became a large landowner. The *Columbia* proceeded to Guangzhou, unloaded its cargo, and returned to Boston by way of the Cape of Good Hope with a cargo of tea and silk. The voyage was not successful as a business venture because by the time the *Columbia* arrived at Boston, prices were depressed. This initial failure did not discourage Kendrick, however. Shortly after his stay at Nootka, he resumed his commercial expedition on the *Lady Washington* in 1790, and again, East Asia was his destination. He went to Guangzhou first, trying unsuccessfully to sell his cargo of furs. Then he wandered up and down along the Chinese coast looking for opportunities.

In the spring of 1791, the *Lady Washington* ran into a seasonal typhoon and was forced to seek refuge in Kii Channel at the eastern entrance to Japan's Inland Sea. Knowing the reputation of the Japanese for being inhospitable, Kendrick apparently thought it wise to explain to local authorities why he had violated the isolation policy of Japan. In a letter to Japanese officials, he explained that he was on his way from China back to the United States, but that wind and wave had taken his ship to this land. He then petitioned for permission to

stay as long as the wind remained adverse, and promised to leave as soon as it became favorable. But when he declared his cargo, he mentioned only copper, iron, and guns, reporting "of naught else." There were in fact several hundred skins on board. Kendrick concealed the fact probably because he wanted to sell the skins illegally, as he had tried to do in China. Unintentionally, the *Lady Washington* was the first American ship that went to Japan. Unfortunately, this first recorded contact between the two countries was conceived in deceit. After a short stay in Kii Channel, the *Lady Washington* returned to the United States in August 1791.

T. Dennett, *Americans in Eastern Asia: A Critical Study of the Policy of the United States with Reference to China, Japan and Korea in the 19th Century* (New York, 1963); A. Walworth, *Black Ships off Japan: The Story of Commodore Perry's Expedition* (Hamden, CT, 1966).

Li Yi

KENNAN, GEORGE (1845–1924)

George Kennan started his career as a specialist on Russia after he had investigated the situation in Siberia during his stay there from September 1865 to April 1868 as a member of a study group for telegraphic communication between the United States and Russia. He had a positive feeling toward Russia and Russian people, but he became hostile toward the Romanov Dynasty after he saw the way the czar's regime punished innocent Russians with exile to Siberia and imprisonment. After publishing his book *Siberia and the Exile System* in 1891, he became even more anti-czar following the pogrom of Jewish people in Bessarabia in 1903. Kennan saw the advancing rivalry between Russia and Japan concerning Manchuria and Korea as the rivalry between "Brute" and "Civilization" respectively and was a supporter of Japan, hoping for the end of the czarist regime.

After the Russo-Japanese War* began in

February 1904, Kennan went to East Asia as a correspondent for the magazine *The Outlook* and traveled around Japan, Korea, and Manchuria, gathering information for articles concerning the situation in the area. In 1904 and 1905, he met many leading Japanese, including Prime Minister Katsura Tarō* on 23 May 1904, and visited many places in Japan, including the Naval Military Academy at Hiroshima, and Port Arthur in Manchuria. Kennan praised the Japanese character, especially the qualities of patriotism, cleanliness, good order, industry, and general prosperity. In Korea, he visited the suburbs of Seoul and Inch'ŏn, criticizing the Korean character, which he thought suffered from cowardice, filthiness, demoralization, laziness, and general lack of order. Accordingly, he judged Korea as "a degenerate state" and its people as the product of a "decayed civilization." Kennan expected Japan to take suzerainty over Korea to check Russia's expansion southward and thereby reduce the threat to the peace of East Asia. He also pointed out the negative aspects of Japanese Colonialism* in Korea, but nevertheless tried to arouse public opinion in the United States to support Japan.

Kennan tried to act as a diplomatic mediator between the governments of the United States and Japan. As U.S. skepticism toward future Japanese policies in East Asia, especially those of President Theodore Roosevelt*, became stronger, he met Katsura on 30 March 1905 and told him of the president's concerns. Katsura informed Kennan that Japan had no intention of harming the interests of the United States in Asia, and the exchange might have led to the Taft-Katsura Agreement* in July 1905. After the Treaty of Portsmouth* the following month, Kennan criticized Roosevelt in *The Outlook* in October, charging that his intervention in the Portsmouth Conference* had damaged Japanese interests. Roosevelt disagreed, insisting that Japan's military advantage might have evaporated had he not intervened. After

this exchange, Kennan continued to support Japan's position regarding such problems as Japanese immigration to the West Coast, instability in China during the Chinese Revolution of 1911*, Japanese Annexation of Korea*, the Korean Conspiracy Case* in 1911 and 1912, and Japanese participation in World War I. He worked to promote American understanding of Japanese culture in his articles in *The Outlook*. After the Russian Revolution in November 1917, Kennan also criticized the Bolshevik government.

F. F. Travis, *George Kennan and the Russian-American Relationship, 1865–1924* (Athens, OH, 1990).

Nagata Akifumi

KENNAN, GEORGE F. (1904–)

Diplomat George F. Kennan's greatest claim to fame was his famous "Long Telegram" during February 1946 while counselor in Moscow to the State Department. The telegram enunciated the "containment" strategy, which became the basis of U.S. Cold War policy until the Soviet Union collapsed in 1991. Summoned back to Washington in 1947, he served as first director of the State Department's Policy Planning Staff (PPS), with a mandate to devise overall global strategies for the United States. This think tank devoted much attention to East Asia, developing the concept of a Great Crescent* of Asian powers, stretching from Pakistan to Japan, which would serve as a barrier against future Communist expansion. In late 1948, Kennan was instrumental in recommending that U.S. policies toward Japan adopt a Reverse Course* and switch their emphasis from demilitarization and social reform to economic recovery aimed at enabling Japan to become a strong, stable, and democratic U.S. partner against the Soviet Union. These recommendations were adopted, and in late 1949 their successful implementation led Kennan to advocate the conclusion of a Japanese Peace Treaty*, achieved in September 1951. The PPS also advocated that the United States build up the Philippines* and other Southeast Asian countries as non-Communist bulwarks in Asia, and aid France's efforts to maintain its position in French Indochina*. Kennan opposed, however, U.S. military aid to the faltering Guomindang* (Nationalist) regime in China, which collapsed and fled to Taiwan* late in 1949.

On Korea, Kennan's policies were somewhat inconsistent. He recommended in 1947 that the United States withdraw from the peninsula, but he continued to support economic aid to the Republic of Korea* (ROK). When North Korean forces invaded South Korea in June 1950, however, he recommended prompt and unilateral dispatch of U.S. forces. Kennan then was instrumental in recommending that the Seventh Fleet be dispatched to the Taiwan Strait to prevent a Communist invasion, resulting in the Neutralization of Taiwan*. He opposed the U.S. decision to carry the Korean War* north of the thirty-eighth parallel and thereby attempt to unify the peninsula, advising unsuccessfully that the United States should seek a negotiated settlement that involved the neutralization and demilitarization of Japan and Taiwan, as well as French withdrawal from Indochina. Kennan's advice was ignored and, after Chinese Intervention in the Korean War* in late 1950, he wavered between recommending American determination to continue fighting and unilateral U.S. withdrawal. He feared the war's potential escalation into a general, potentially nuclear, conflict between the United States and the Soviet Union, and insisted that it must therefore remain an operation with limited objectives. In 1951, Kennan, then on sabbatical at Princeton University, held unofficial and ultimately successful talks with the Soviet delegate at the United Nations about opening negotiations for a cease-fire, leading to the P'anmunjŏm Truce Talks*.

In 1953, new Republican Secretary of State John Foster Dulles* dispensed with Kennan's diplomatic services, and he began a lengthy career as a historian and highly influential political commentator whose prolific and iconoclastic writings were often greatly at odds with the conventional wisdom of the foreign policy elite. Despite his 1950 advocacy of U.S. attempts to develop a non-Communist and nationalist "third force" in Indochina, by 1955 he was pessimistic about the prospects for such endeavors. During his service as ambassador to Yugoslavia during the Kennedy administration, Kennan showed little interest in Vietnam, and despite some misgivings, endorsed the Tonkin Gulf Resolution in 1964. Subsequent escalation of the Second Indochina War* persuaded him that the United States was overly involved militarily in a country of relatively slight strategic significance to its fundamental interests, but he did not recommend withdrawal. During widely publicized congressional hearings in 1967, he argued that use of the level of force necessary to attain victory would probably trigger Chinese intervention and a full-scale and probably nuclear war. Finally in November 1969, Kennan publicly advocated unilateral U.S. military withdrawal, notwithstanding the likelihood that this would lead to a Communist takeover of the Republic of Vietnam*. Even though Kennan had little real influence on policy on Vietnam or other issues in East Asia after 1950, his views always attracted wide publicity and a respectful hearing.

J. L. Gaddis, *Strategies of Containment: A Critical Appraisal of Postwar American National Security Policy* (New York, 1982); W. L. Hixson, *George F. Kennan: Cold War Iconoclast* (New York, 1989); G. F. Kennan, *Memoirs, 1925–1950* (Boston, 1967); G. F. Kennan, *Memoirs, 1950–1963* (Boston, 1972); D. A. Mayers, *George Kennan and the Dilemmas of U.S. Foreign Policy* (New York, 1988); W. D. Miscamble, *George F. Kennan and the Making of American Foreign Policy, 1947–1950* (Princeton, NJ, 1992).

Priscilla Roberts

KENNEDY, JOHN F. (1917–1963)

John F. Kennedy, as president of the United States from January 1961 to November 1963, deepened U.S. involvement in the Second Indochina War*. He sought a negotiated settlement to the Laotian Crisis of 1961*, but the Geneva Accords of 1962* made Kennedy all the more determined to keep South Vietnam out of Communist hands. This was not surprising, given the anti-Communist views he expressed first as representative and then as senator from Massachusetts in the U.S. Congress after 1946 before he won the 1960 presidential election over Republican Richard M. Nixon.* Kennedy's failure to topple Fidel Castro's regime at the Bay of Pigs in April 1961 meant that there also were political reasons for him to show his toughness in Indochina. In November 1961, after a lengthy debate within the administration, however, he rejected pressure from the Pentagon to dispatch U.S. combat troops in large numbers to the Republic of Vietnam*, but approved sending U.S. advisers—eventually numbering 16,000—some of whom participated in combat. The administration also built up paramilitary and counterinsurgency programs in support of the government of President Ngo Dinh Diem*. But Viet Cong* strength continued to grow not only because of increasing North Vietnamese infiltration through Laos*, but because of alienation of the populace by Diem and his brother Ngo Dinh Nhu*.

In mid-1963, Saigon's response to the Buddhist crisis raised serious doubts in Washington about Diem's ability to hold popular support. Growing pressure by South Vietnamese military leaders for the overthrow of Diem led to lengthy debates among Kennedy's advisers, including Roger Hilsman* and W. Averell Harriman*, about whether to continue to support Diem or whether a coup offered the only hope of successful resistance to the Communists. Kennedy finally authorized Ambassador Henry Cabot Lodge Jr.* to promise the generals, among them Duong Van Minh*, that a new government would have U.S. support. He thus indirectly encouraged the coup that overthrew Diem in November 1963, although he did not approve Diem's Assassination*. In the wake of the coup, Kennedy was still groping for a solution to the Vietnam dilemma. Some of Kennedy's associates maintained in later years that he had grave doubts about the U.S. involvement in Vietnam. If he had lived to serve a second term, they claimed, he would have withdrawn from Vietnam; others have disputed this. Evidence exists to support both views: Kennedy rejected many Pentagon proposals for military action in Laos and Vietnam, but he also repeatedly declared his determination to prevent a Communist takeover of South Vietnam.

Similar questions have been raised about Kennedy's China policies. During the 1960 campaign debates, Kennedy questioned U.S. policy regarding Guomindang* (Nationalist) control over the islands of Jinmen and Mazu. He directly criticized the Eisenhower administration's handling of the Taiwan Strait Crises*, suggesting the possibility of modification of U.S. policies toward the People's Republic of China* (PRC). During Kennedy's first few months in office, there was a lively ferment of ideas within the administration regarding China policy, especially on the question of Chinese Representation in the United Nations*, on which the United States increasingly was isolated. Kennedy took no action. Some administration members maintained later that he would have been more flexible in his second term. Not only domestic politics argued against a change of policy, however. Beijing's leaders, then immersed in a bitter political debate with Moscow, declared their fierce hostility toward Washington in a steady stream of invective. Both the PRC and the Republic of China* also made clear their adamant refusal to accept any suggestion of a Two China Policy*. See also Green Berets; Strategic Hamlets Program; Kennedy-Chen

Conference; Kennedy-Ikeda Conference; Kennedy-Pak Conference.

D. E. Kaiser, *American Tragedy: Kennedy, Johnson, and the Origins of the Vietnam War* (Cambridge, MA, 2000); F. Logevall, *Choosing War: The Lost Chance for Peace and the Escalation of War in Vietnam* (Berkeley, CA, 1999); J. M. Newman, *JFK and Vietnam: Deception, Intrigue, and the Struggle for Power* (New York, 1992); T. G. Paterson (ed.), *Kennedy's Quest for Victory: American Foreign Policy, 1961–1963* (New York, 1989).

Harriet Dashiell Schwar

KENNEDY-CHEN CONFERENCE

This conference between U.S. President John F. Kennedy* and Chen Cheng, the vice president of the Republic of China* (ROC) on Taiwan*, during July and August 1961, was designed to formulate a plan to battle Communism* on the world stage. Specifically, the United States demonstrated its support for Nationalist China's bid to retain its seat in the United Nations. Since 1950, the U.S. delegate to the United Nations had introduced annually a resolution designed to postpone consideration of Communist China's admission to that body. The effort always had been successful, but each year, the vote became closer and closer. On the heels of the Bay of Pigs and the erection of the Berlin Wall, it was imperative to both parties that the People's Republic of China* (PRC) be kept out of the United Nations. Kennedy was concerned that the PRC's admission would be a blow to U.S. prestige and undercut the American position in the world. Therefore, a strategy needed to be devised to prevent that eventuality. Kennedy noted that Brazil, Nigeria, and Pakistan planned to switch their votes of 1960 and now would support Beijing's admission to the United Nations.

However, there was sharp disagreement between the two allies on whether to seat the Communist nation of Outer Mongolia. Kennedy thought that denying the Mongolians a seat would alienate potential allies on the Chinese Representation in the United Nations* issue, particularly the newly independent nations of Africa, since the Soviet Union, with its veto threat, had linked Outer Mongolia's membership vote to that of Mauritania. Secretary of State Dean Rusk* believed this linkage involved ten to fifteen votes on the China issue. The Nationalist Chinese, who, as a member of the UN Security Council, also held veto power, believed that since Outer Mongolia was a Soviet creation and its satellite and not really independent, it did not deserve to be included in the United Nations. The ROC believed that any U.S. or UN recognition of Outer Mongolia would be appeasement and strengthen "World Communism." After all, Vice President Chen argued, the United States, as the leader of the Free World, should avoid any actions that would add to the prestige of the Soviet Union and Communist China.

In a testy exchange, UN Ambassador Jiang Tingfu* of the ROC questioned Washington's will in combating Communism in Asia, contrasting it with U.S. policy toward Europe, where it had drawn the line against further Communist expansion, whereas in Asia it was prepared to retreat. Kennedy responded that since World War II, the United States had fought only in Asia, not Europe. A frustrated Kennedy then added that "you can't have everything." He said that the goal of U.S. recognition of Outer Mongolia would be to win the UN vote against seating the PRC, not some "backhanded way of recognizing Peiping. We can't let those who don't understand this situation direct our strategy or we will end up beaten. Let's win this one." Rusk then asked Chen if it would not be "better to have Outer Mongolia than Communist China in the United Nations." ROC Ambassador to the United States Ye Gong Chao* responded that Taiwan wanted neither. Vice President Chen said that any Nationalist Chinese suspicions regarding U.S. motives in recognizing Outer Mongolia were put to rest by this meeting. At a dinner in his honor held by Vice President Chen, Kennedy asked the emissary to convey his belief that despite their differences, the United States and the ROC were united on the fundamental questions. *See also* Two China Policy.

O. T. Barck Jr., *A History of the United States Since 1945* (New York, 1965); T. Wicker, *New York Times*, 1–2 August 1961; Records of the U.S. Department of State, Foreign Service Posts, Record Group 84, National Archives, College Park, MD; *U.S. Public Papers of the President, John F. Kennedy*, Vol. 1: *1961* (Washington, DC, 1962).

Gregory J. Murphy

KENNEDY-IKEDA CONFERENCE

Meeting in the White House in late June 1961, Japanese Prime Minister Ikeda Hayato* and President John F. Kennedy* reaffirmed U.S.-Japan defense arrangements, agreed on new import-export policies, and charted the direction of modern U.S.-Japan relations. Ikeda, a founder of Japan's ruling Liberal Democratic Party* (LDP), had gained election only six months before Kennedy. Promising the electorate that his government would take "the first steps" to create an aggressive foreign economic policy that would lead, by 1970, to the dominance of the Japanese yen over the U.S. dollar, he insisted that the 1960s symbolized the emergence of a New Japan. Indeed, the Japanese press nicknamed his administration the "New Japan" government, for it also was meant to represent the dreams and ambitions of a new era divorced from the postoccupation concerns of the prior decade. Given his idealistic rhetoric, innovative policy making, and flashy, American-like political style, some Japanese called Ikeda the Kennedy of Japan, although the prime minister often quipped that Kennedy was the Ikeda of the United States. Ikeda was the first foreign leader to meet the new U.S. president in January 1961. At that time, the two men planned to meet again soon for the less social and more specific purpose of reaffirming and revising the delicate U.S.-Japan relationship.

At that June 1961 conference, Kennedy stressed that the U.S.-Japan Mutual Cooperation and Security Treaty* the Eisenhower administration had negotiated would continue to guide joint U.S.-Japan defense interests, but that it should not be seen in Japan as a U.S.-dictated treaty. To illustrate the point that the United States no longer saw Japan as "a stationary aircraft carrier" for its postwar military bases, he vowed to lobby the U.S. Congress to eliminate all protectionist legislation barriers to Japanese automobile, electronic, and other imports. Promising a Trade Expansion Act (TEA), Kennedy hoped to demonstrate the importance of the economic connections between fellow anti-Communist allies. However, he worried, without warrant or intelligence information to confirm it, that Japan might turn to Communism* if its plans for consumer exports to the United States were not welcomed. Knowing about Kennedy's concern, Ikeda exaggerated the internal Communist threat his country faced to win the American president's support. Publicly, both leaders announced that the postwar era of U.S.-Japan relations was over, ending a pattern whereby the United States treated Japan as either a "defeated nation" not worthy of consultation or as a "junior partner" in action against Communism in the Pacific. Especially for Japan, the conference represented the opening of a new era of optimism and pride. For the Kennedy administration, it meant more worries that Japan might waver toward Communism if its economic interests were not met. *See also* U.S.-Japan Postwar Trade Relations.

I. M. Destler, *Managing an Alliance: The Politics of U.S.-Japanese Relations* (Washington, DC, 1976); H. Fukui, *Party in Power: The Japanese Liberal Democrats and Policy-Making* (Canberra, 1970); W. S. Hunsberger, *Japan and the United States in World Trade* (New York, 1964); T. P. Maga, *Hands Across the Sea?: U.S.-Japan Relations, 1961–1981* (Athens, OH, 1997); T. P. Maga, *John F. Kennedy and the New Pacific Community, 1961–1963* (New York, 1990).

Timothy P. Maga

KENNEDY-PAK CONFERENCE

On 14 November 1961, six months after the South Korean military seized power in May 1961, the coup leader General Pak Chŏng-hŭi*, the chairman of the Supreme Council for National Reconstruction, met President John F. Kennedy* in Washington. During the meeting, Pak requested U.S. support for the Republic of Korea* (ROK) to maintain military strength at its current level, as well as to achieve rapid economic development. Interestingly, Pak offered to send South Korean troops to Vietnam. Although considerations behind this offer were complex, one of his calculations was that he might obtain as much U.S. assistance as possible by highlighting South Korea's value as a trustful U.S. ally in Asia. Although President Kennedy did not accept Pak's troop offer, he reassured Pak of maximum U.S. support to South Korea. Pointing out the global burden of the United States that made it difficult to maintain the past level of aid to South Korea, however, the president stressed the importance of the ROK's own efforts to improve its economy. These included, in particular, implementing a long-term economic development plan and achieving Japan-Korea Normalization* of diplomatic relations. In the joint communiqué that was released at the conclusion of the meeting, the Kennedy administration reconfirmed the U.S. security commitment to the ROK, and Pak pledged that the current military government in South Korea would return to civilian control by the summer of 1963.

The Kennedy-Pak meeting contained significant political symbolism. Having come into power by a coup, Pak and his military regime sought to compensate for its lack of political legitimacy by demonstrating a will and capability to improve rapidly the nation's dire economic conditions. Because of the heavy reliance of South Korea's economy on U.S. assistance at the time, however, this task could not be achieved without U.S. support. Kennedy's assurance of such support, then, could help Pak consolidate his domestic political footing. In fact, by inviting Pak to Washington, the administration aimed to increase Pak's prestige both in South Korea and abroad. For Washington officials, despite their initial unease about Pak's ideological predilection that arose from his past involvement in Communist activities, the chairman was seen as the only South Korean leader then able to stabilize the ROK's political situation and achieve social and economic progress. Furthermore, the Kennedy administration thought the visit would be a good chance to impress Pak with the power and capacity of the United States and thereby induce maximum cooperation with U.S. policy.

U.S. Department of State, *Foreign Relations of the United States, 1961–1963*, Vol. 22: *Northeast Asia* (Washington, DC, 1996).

Ma Sang-yoon

KHE SANH

The battle of Khe Sanh was the largest set-piece engagement of the Second Indochina War*. Although it was a tactical victory for the United States, the wisdom of the decision to stand and fight there was controversial at the time and remains so in retrospect. In August 1962, a detachment of U.S. Army Special Forces arrived at Khe Sanh, a small village in the northwest corner of South Vietnam, six miles from the Laotian border. Located on a plateau surrounded by high hills, the base at Khe Sanh was used to monitor the flow of North Vietnamese troops and supplies down nearby branches of the Ho Chi Minh Trail*. As the war grew in scale and intensity, General William C. Westmoreland*, the commander of U.S. Military Assistance Command, Vietnam* (MACV), shifted his attention to the northern provinces of South Vietnam. In September 1966, he ordered a U.S. Marine battalion to Khe Sanh and the upgrading of the airstrip there. In the spring of 1967, U.S. Marines and North Vietnamese units engaged in bloody clashes on the hills dominating the base, and in August enemy forces cut Route 9, the only road to the coast. Khe Sanh now could be resupplied only by air. Late in 1967, Westmoreland, informed that between 32,000 and 40,000 North Vietnamese troops were converging on the base, increased troop strength to 6,000 U.S. Marines and laid plans for a massive bombing campaign (Operation NIAGARA) to punish besieging troops. He hoped to lure the enemy into a conventional battle, where U.S. firepower would prevail, and soon to use Khe Sanh to support a large-scale operation into Laos* aimed at cutting off the Ho Chi Minh Trail.

The motives of General Vo Nguyen Giap*, the commander of the People's Army of Vietnam, in laying siege to Khe Sanh remain difficult to determine. Giap may have viewed the siege, which began on 21 January 1968, as a feint, designed to draw American troops away from the populated areas of the Republic of Vietnam* in preparation for the Tet Offensive*, which began on 31 January. Or he may have hoped to overrun the base, winning a stunning victory that would lead to a negotiated settlement on North Vietnamese terms. Throughout February and early March, North Vietnamese artillery shelled Khe Sanh and some limited assaults were made on the perimeter, and fierce battles were fought on nearby hills. U.S. Marines, reinforced by a battalion of South Vietnamese Rangers, frantically hardened their positions, while air power, including B-52 bombers, saturated the surrounding countryside. As the Tet Offensive waned, the attention of the U.S. government and people focused on Khe Sanh, where the U.S. Marine garrison seemed imperiled. President Lyndon B. Johnson* was haunted by his memory of Dien Bien Phu*, although Westmoreland reassured him that the base could not be overrun. By early March, Giap began to pull back his forces. On 1 April, U.S. troops on the coast started their advance up Route 9 and reached Khe Sanh on 15 April, formally ending the siege.

Roughly 10,000 North Vietnamese soldiers died during the battle, and American deaths numbered 650.

C. B. Currey, *Victory at Any Cost: The Genius of Viet Nam's General Vo Nguyen Giap* (Washington, DC, 1997); P. B. Davidson, *Vietnam at War: The History, 1946–1975* (New York, 1988); R. Pisor, *The End of the Line: The Siege of Khe Sanh* (New York, 1982); J. Prados and R. Stubbe, *Valley of Decision: The Siege of Khe Sanh* (Boston, 1991).

Charles E. Neu

KHIEU SAMPHAN (1931–   )

Khieu Samphan was a Khmer Rouge* party member and leader. He, along with Pol Pot* and Ieng Sary, spent time in France in the early 1950s and later worked to bring Communism* to Cambodia* (Kampuchea) in the aftermath of the Khmer Rouge's ascension to power in April 1975. As a result of their policies, Cambodia suffered a human catastrophe of unprecedented proportions, with 1.7 million of the nation's 8 million citizens dying during the three-and-and-a-half-year reign. Samphan began serving as the prime minister of Kampuchea in 1977 and also supervised the party's Central Committee. He later became Khmer Rouge president and opposed the 1993 elections sponsored by the United Nations Transitional Authority in Cambodia. Notwithstanding his insistence that Cambodians would not take part in what he termed "this stinking farce," 90 percent of the population turned out to vote, despite Khmer Rouge efforts at intimidation. Still, in a 1998 meeting with Hun Sen*, Khieu Samphan apologized for his role in Khmer Rouge actions during the 1970s.

D. Chandler, *A History of Cambodia* (Boulder, CO, 2000); W. Shawcross, *Deliver Us from Evil: Peacekeepers, Warlords and a World of Endless Conflict* (New York, 2000).

T. Christopher Jespersen

KHMER ROUGE

Khmer Rouge ("Red Cambodians") is a pejorative term that Cambodia's leader Prince Norodom Sihanouk* first used in the 1960s to describe his left-wing opponents. It became synonymous with genocide, mass murder, and starvation, which from 1975 to 1978 characterized its rule of Cambodia* (Kampuchea). U.S. policy toward Cambodia from 1969 to 1975 may inadvertently have created the conditions for the Khmer Rouge coming to power. Once the Vietnamese drove them from power at the end of 1978, the United States uncomfortably provided diplomatic support and, indirectly, material support to the Khmer Rouge remnants, a group that President Jimmy Carter* once characterized as the worse violators of human rights in the world.

The roots of the Khmer Rouge reach back to 1930 when the first Cambodian Communists participated in the Indochinese Communist Party founded that year by Ho Chi Minh*. After World War II, several of the Khmer movements seeking independence from France and liberation from the monarchy had Communist leaders. French efforts to continue their colonial rule only strengthened Communist elements in the independence movement. Many of the newer Khmer Communists had been educated in France, including Saloth Sar (later Pol Pot*), who returned to Phnom Penh, Cambodia's capital, in 1953.

Sihanouk now grasped the mantle of nationalism. His successful efforts to free Cambodia from French Colonialism*, culminating with the dissolution of French Indochina* at the Geneva Conference of 1954*, undercut support for the Communists. Pol Pot and other Communists taught courses in schools and colleges in Phnom Penh; many future left-wing militants graduated from these schools. During the early 1960s, some Communists served as government officials, and Pol Pot's wife, Khieu Ponnary, was on the staff of *Kambuja*, Sihanouk's official magazine.

In 1964, Sihanouk launched a strong attack on Cambodian leftists, and many of the Communists fled. In 1967 and 1968, they helped spur domestic rebellions, though there was little prospect of overthrowing the prince. Ironically, U.S. military actions related to the Second Indochina War* destabilized Cambodia and helped create the conditions that led to Sihanouk's ouster in March 1970, though by rightists. Sihanouk, bitter at his overthrow, urged his fellow Cambodians to defect to the Khmer Rouge. Many did, and in April 1975 their forces captured Phnom Penh.

Pol Pot and Khieu Samphan* then turned Cambodia into one giant slave labor camp. They were particularly harsh on racial minorities, such as the Vietnamese, Chinese, and Chams. Pol Pot was perhaps most brutal toward those Khmers who he thought were tainted by their association with the Vietnamese and were therefore no longer true Khmers. Approximately 1.7 million Cambodians in a national population of less than 8 million perished during the three-and-a-half years of the Khmer Rouge's rule. An end to the carnage came in December 1978 when the army of the Socialist Republic of Vietnam* invaded and drove the Khmer Rouge to the Thai border. Here, with support from the People's Republic of China* and, indirectly, the United States, its forces revived. They fought against Vietnamese troops and the Vietnamese-installed government, the People's Republic of Kampuchea (PRK), under Heng Samrin* and Hun Sen*.

In 1991, the PRK and all opposition factions, including the Khmer Rouge, agreed to participate in elections that the United Nations had organized. When the elections were held in 1993, however, the Khmer Rouge boycotted them and threatened violence, suffering major political damage as a result. Khmer Rouge armed forces continued to harass government troops, but with China having cut off support, they began to break apart. In 1996, Pol Pot ordered the assassination of a rival Khmer Rouge leader and his family; other Khmer Rouge then turned on Pol Pot and he was arrested. In June 1998, he died while under house arrest. Subsequently, most remaining Khmer Rouge adherents rallied either to the government or to the political opposition. By the end of 1998, they were no longer a threat to the country, and international efforts had begun to bring to justice those Khmer Rouge leaders who were still alive.

N. Chanda, *Brother Enemy: The War After the War: A History of Indochina Since the Fall of Saigon* (New York, 1986); D. Chandler, *The Tragedy of Cambodian History: Politics, War and Revolution Since 1945* (New Haven, CT, 1991); C. Etcheson, *The Rise and Demise of Democratic Kampuchea* (Boulder, CO, 1984); B. Kiernan, *How Pol Pot Came to Power* (London, 1985); B. Kiernan, *The Pol Pot Regime: Race, Power, and Genocide in Cambodia Under the Khmer Rouge, 1975–79* (New Haven, CT, 1996).

Kenton J. Clymer

KHUN SA (1934–)

Born Chang Chifu to a Shan (one of the ethnic groups in Myanmar) mother and ethnic Chinese father in northern Burma*, Khun Sa rose to become one of the most powerful opium and heroin merchants in the world. He would serve also as a symbol of the complexities inherent in U.S. drug policy. In March 1990, Khun Sa was indicted in Brooklyn, New York, on the charge of having imported more than 3,500 pounds of heroin into the United States. His indictment came a few months after U.S. President George H. W. Bush* had ordered U.S. soldiers to invade Panama to capture Manuel Noriega, indicted on similar charges. No troops were sent to capture Khun Sa, who was geographically and politically further from Washington's interest.

Khun Sa initially rose to power in the Drug Trade* as the commander of a local militia designed to help the Rangoon government control perennially restive ethnic areas of Burma. These militia received no

funding or arms. In 1967, in an effort to acquire these, and to expand his personal power, he challenged the Guomindang* (Nationalist) troops that controlled the opium trade in the region. His effort was crushed by parallel Guomindang and Lao efforts, and his influence waned. In 1969, Khun Sa was arrested and charged with treason on the basis of brief contacts with Shan rebels. He remained in prison until 1974.

Despite his clashes with the Guomindang, Khun Sa had no sympathy with Communism*. During the 1970s and 1980s, he concentrated his efforts on expanding and strengthening his Shan United Army (renamed the Mong Tai Army in 1985) to support his claim to be a Shan nationalist, and simultaneously rebuilt his opium business, this time including heroin refineries. His army fought when necessary to protect these interests. Fighting was rare, however, since Khun Sa had come to enjoy the protection of important Thai officials; his headquarters were for several years in Thailand*, near the Thai-Burma border. Officials in Rangoon also seemed content to allow Khun Sa to fight his rivals in the Communist Party of Burma for control of territory and the opium trade.

In 1977, Khun Sa acquiesced in a proposal from several Shan armies that the opium crop be sold to the U.S. government. Congressman Lester Wolff and Joseph Nellis, chief counsel of the Select Committee on Narcotics Abuse and Control, traveled to Southeast Asia. Nellis was impressed with Khun Sa's ambition and resolution, but Congress rejected the plan. Instead, it increased funding for law enforcement and eradication programs. Khun Sa was an intended target of these programs. U.S. authorities had deemed him the "kingpin of the Golden Triangle* heroin trade." Despite this overt pressure, and accompanying financial assistance, Rangoon authorities apparently only pretended to repress Khun Sa. By 1986, he controlled an estimated 80 percent of drug trade in the Golden Triangle, and 60 percent of the world's illicit opium supply.

The 1990s were less kind to Khun Sa. The U.S. indictment did not pose an immediate threat, but the ostracized government in Myanmar saw antinarcotics activity as a way to reestablish relations with countries such as the United States. During a 1993 visit by several U.S. senators, the Myanmar army launched a serious attack on the territory surrounding Khun Sa's Burmese headquarters. Khun Sa fought back fiercely. The military confrontation lasted until Khun Sa surrendered in January 1996. His surrender seems to have involved a deal, however, since he was not extradited to the United States. Apparently, he merely changed his name, and ran his businesses, including heroin, from Rangoon. Despite continued U.S. protests and further indictments of Burmese narcotics merchants, Khun Sa remained in Rangoon, ostensibly a businessman with profitable real estate and other investments, and close ties to important government officials. *See also* Guomindang Intervention in Burma.

A. Boucard and L. Boucard, *Burma's Golden Triangle: On the Trail of the Opium Warlords* (Bangkok, 1992); B. Lintner, *Burma in Revolt: Opium and Insurgency Since 1948* (Boulder, CO, 1994); A. W. McCoy, *The Politics of Heroin: CIA Complicity in the Global Drug Trade* (Chicago, 1991).

Anne L. Foster

KIDŌ KŌICHI (1889–1977)

Kidō Kōichi, who served as the lord keeper of the privy seal from 1940 to 1945, was the closest adviser to Emperor Hirohito* concerning Japan's critical decisions for war and peace during World War II. He was born as the oldest son of the Kidō family, which traditionally offered loyal service to the imperial house. His grandfather was one of the most important protagonists of the Meiji Restoration of 1868, and his father was in charge of young Crown Prince Hirohito's training at home. After graduating from Kyōto University, Kidō worked as a government bureaucrat between 1915 and 1930. He also became a member of the House of Peers in 1917. From 1930 to 1936, Kidō worked as chief private secretary to Makino Nobuaki*, the lord keeper of the privy seal. Both men shared the conviction that the primary task of the privy seal was to protect the imperial house from responsibility for political and military decisions. Kidō was minister of education in the first Konoe Fumimaro* cabinet (1937–1938) and home minister in the Hiranuma Kiichirō cabinet (1939).

In June 1940, the critical point in Japan's foreign policy, Kidō was appointed lord keeper of the privy seal and retained the position until the office was abolished in November 1945 under the U.S. Occupation of Japan*. Kidō, the closest adviser to the emperor, began to undertake unofficial responsibility that formally belonged to Saionji Kinmochi*, the last genrō, who was ill and unwilling to select a new premier. In July 1940, Kidō played the key role in calling a meeting of the senior statesmen and recommending Konoe to succeed the Yonai Mitsumasa cabinet, which was unable to reach a decision on signing the Tripartite Pact*. One of his hardest decisions, Kidō himself recalled, was the selection of Tōjō Hideki* as successor to Premier Konoe on the eve of the Pearl Harbor Attack* in October 1941. Coming to a deadlock in diplomatic negotiations with the United States, concerning in particular the U.S. oil embargo on Japan, Kidō and Hirohito opted to ask General Tōjō to form a cabinet. Premier Tōjō's task was to reverse the 6 September decision for war in the event of diplomatic failure and make one final attempt at negotiation with the United States. Kidō counted on Tōjō's loyalty to the emperor and his ability to restrain the militant young officers in the army, although this effort for peace failed to produce the desired outcome.

Kidō also played a crucial role in the peace faction's efforts to end the Pacific war. After the Foreign Ministry failed to realize peace through the Soviet mediation in the early summer of 1945, Kidō used the emperor's personal desire for peace and his authority to bring about the imperial conferences in August 1945, which set the stage for the imperial decision to end the war in the wake of the Atomic Attacks* and the Soviet declaration of war. After Japan's surrender, Kidō was tried as a Class-A war criminal at the International Military Tribunal for the Far East and was sentenced to life imprisonment. But he was released in 1955 because of ill health. His diary from January 1930 to December 1945 was presented at the Tōkyō War Crimes Trials* as evidence, and generally supported the accuracy of Kidō's testimony. Kidō's diary from 1930 to 1955 is one of the most valuable historical sources for Japanese politics.

R. J. C. Butow, *Tōjō and the Coming of the War* (Princeton, NJ, 1961); D. A. Titus, *Palace and Politics in Prewar Japan: The Context of Imperial Involvement in Politics and Palace Leadership in the Showa Period, 1929–1941* (New York, 1974); P. Wetzler, *Hirohito and War: Imperial Tradition and Military Decision Making* (Honolulu, HI, 1998).

Kawamura Noriko

KIM DAE-JUNG (1925–   )

Inaugurated president of the Republic of Korea* (ROK) early in 1998, Kim Dae-jung* was perhaps South Korea's most famous political dissident. Born in South Chŏlla Province, he graduated from Mok-p'o Commercial School in 1943 and began a career with a navigation ship company. During the U.S. Occupation of Korea*, Kim briefly joined a party led by leftist returnees from China and anti-Japan nationalists, which his political rivals later used to discredit him. In 1948, he founded a newspaper and a marine transportation company at Mokp'o. Two years later, when the Korean War* began, Kim was jailed by the North Koreans, but after the Inch'ŏn Landing* in September, he escaped, avoiding execution. After serving in the coast guard, Kim was defeated in 1954 for a seat in the

National Assembly. He joined the Democratic Party in 1956 at the recommendation of his godfather Jang Myŏn*, then vice president of the ROK. After fraud blocked his election to the assembly and left him bankrupt, his wife died of a medicinal overdose. In April 1960, Syngman Rhee's Ouster* led to Jang's election as prime minister, but Kim was defeated for an assembly seat. Three days after Kim's election to the assembly in May 1961, Major General Pak Chŏng-hŭi* seized power and arrested many politicians, including Kim. After the military junta released him, he remained on the list of those prohibited from engaging in political activities.

In January 1963, the military junta allowed civilians to reenter politics, and Kim joined in the rebuilding of the Democratic Party, becoming its spokesman. In the presidential election in October, he declared publicly that Pak's candidacy was illegal, allegedly earning the dictator's hatred. Pak was elected president, but Kim also won an assembly seat. Thereafter, the two men battled over assorted issues. In April 1971, Kim lost to Pak in the presidential election, but his opposition party won many seats in the next assembly elections. The Korean Central Intelligence Agency (KCIA) then tried, but failed to assassinate him, leaving Kim with a permanent limp. Pak, as Kim had predicted, declared martial law in October 1973, dissolved the National Assembly, and adopted the Yushin ("revitalization") constitution, under which a rubber-stamp national council elected the president without a limit on terms. Kim, who had gone to Japan for the treatment on his injured leg six days earlier, decided to live in exile. On 8 August 1973, KCIA agents kidnaped him in Tokyo and attempted to assassinate him. U.S. diplomatic intervention forced Kim's release, allowing him to return home.

Kim continued his efforts to topple the Pak regime until his arrest in 1976, which resulted in a sentence of five years in prison. Paroled in December, he was under house arrest when Pak was elected to his second six-year term. Three years later, Pak Chŏng-hŭi's Assassination* led to Major General Chŏn Du-hwan*, his protégé, declaring martial law and seizing power. Kim, along with Kim Young-sam* and Kim Jong-p'il*, worked to mobilize mass support for democratization. But the efforts of the "three Kims" could not stop Chŏn from consolidating power and then arresting Kim Dae-jung and other leaders. Protests against his incarceration led to the Kwangju Incident* in May 1980, when ROK special forces killed hundreds of demonstrators. The ROK Supreme Court sentenced Kim to death for allegedly staging "the Kwangju insurrection," but in response to strong protests from the Reagan administration and leaders in Europe, his sentence was commuted to life imprisonment in 1981. He then was allowed to leave the ROK for exile in the United States in 1982.

In February 1985, Kim returned to Korea to continue his efforts to foster democratization. One year later, he and Kim Young-sam led a "One Million People Signing Campaign to Petition for the Constitutional Revision" to allow for direct presidential election. The struggle reached a climax in June 1987, forcing the Chŏn government to surrender, resulting in the issuance of South Korea's Democracy Declaration*. In December 1987, Kim lost the popular election for president to No Tae-u* from the ruling party, mainly because the other two Kims also insisted on running, splitting the opposition vote. Kim Young-sam then joined No in forming the Democratic Liberal Party, setting the stage for him to defeat Kim Dae-jung in the presidential election of December 1992. Announcing his retirement from politics, Kim went to Cambridge University, but returned in 1993 and four years later won the presidency with Kim Jong-p'il's help. His tough measures to deal with the impact of the East Asian Financial Crisis* brought recovery from this economic disaster. Kim proposed a three-stage unification formula and then pursued the "Sunshine Policy" to promote engagement and reconciliation with the Democratic People's Republic of Korea*. In June 2000, Kim Dae-jung's meeting in P'yŏngyang with North Korean leader Kim Jong Il* resulted in his winning the Nobel Peace Prize.

Kim Dae-jung, *Kim Dae-jung jasŏjon* [Kim Dae-jung's Autobiography] (Seoul, 1999); Kim Dae-jung, *Mass Participatory Economy: Korea's Road to World Economic Power* (Cambridge, MA, 1996); D. S. Macdonald, *The Koreans: Contemporary Politics and Society* (Boulder, CO, 1988); D. Oberdorfer, *The Two Koreas: A Contemporary History* (Reading, PA, 1997).

Kim Hakjoon

KIM GU (1876–1949)

Kim Gu was a prominent Korean independence fighter who, from 1945 to 1948, bitterly confronted American military authorities during the U.S. Occupation of Korea*. Because of his staunch opposition to the four-power trusteeship plan the United States favored, he lost American support for his struggle for power in postwar Korea. Kim Gu was born in Haeju. After failing the civil servant exam, he joined the Tonghak movement and became one of its minor leaders. When he heard about Queen Min's murder in 1896, he killed a Japanese military officer, leaving the body at an inn with his name scrawled in blood on the wall. In 1909, the Japanese arrested and tortured him on suspicion of involvement in the assassination of Itō Hirobumi*, the Japanese resident general in Korea, handing him a seventeen-year jail sentence. By 1919, he was out of jail and in Shanghai, where he joined the Korean Provisional Government and became its leader in 1926. Kim Gu then gained fame for his anti-Japanese attack on 29 April 1932 in Shanghai that killed the head of the Japanese Residents Association and maimed Shigemitsu Mamoru*, Japanese minister to China. Thereafter, Jiang Jieshi* began supporting Kim and looking to him as a leader for postwar Korea who would align closely with his Guomindang* (Nationalist) government.

Kim Gu returned to Korea in November 1945 and became a leader of the right in southern Korea. Soon he was at odds with Lieutenant General John R. Hodge*, commanding general of U.S. forces in Korea. He mobilized mass demonstrations against trusteeship when the Moscow Agreement on Korea* was published late in December 1945. He also attempted a coup. On New Year's Eve, Kim issued a series of proclamations constituting a direct attempt to seize the government. But it ended in failure. As the United States proceeded to establish a separate government in South Korea after the failure of the Joint U.S.-Soviet Commission for a unified Korea in the autumn of 1947, Kim strongly objected. Thus, when elections under supervision of the United Nations were held in May 1948, he refused to participate. Instead, he attended a North-South unity conference in P'yŏngyang in April. North Korean leader Kim Il Sung* invited him and Kim Kyusik*, a leader of the South Korean moderates, to the meeting. After the Republic of Korea* (ROK) was created in August 1948, Kim was murdered by an ROK military officer presumably by order of President Syngman Rhee*. Kim Gu is still respected by many Koreans for his independence activities.

B. Cuming, *Korea's Place in the Sun: A Modern History* (New York, 1997); J. I. Matray, *The Reluctant Crusade: American Foreign Policy in Korea, 1941–1950* (Honolulu, HI, 1985); C. Sonu, *Paekbom Kim Ku* [White Bear Kim Gu] (Seoul, 1972); C. To, *Han'guk Minjokjuŭi wa Nambuk Kwangye* [Korean Democracy and Inter-Korean Relations] (Seoul, 1998).

Kim Jinwung

KIM IL SUNG (1912–1994)

Kim Il Sung was the founder of the Democratic People's Republic of Korea* (DPRK) and initiator of the Korean War*. Born Kim Sŏng-ju to a peasant family near

P'yŏngyang, he later assumed the name of a legendary guerrilla fighter, and under it became a well-known anti-Japanese guerrilla commander. Kim returned to Korea in September 1945, and subsequently used both his guerrilla record and the support of Soviet occupation authorities to become *the* leader of North Korea. He had a burning ambition to reunite the Korean peninsula and, with Soviet and Chinese acquiescence, invaded the Republic of Korea* (ROK) on 25 June 1950. But the assault was countered and repulsed by the forces of the ROK and the United States and fifteen other nations under the flag of the United Nations. Massive Chinese Intervention in the Korean War* saved the North Koreans from defeat and the DPRK from destruction.

In the aftermath of the Korean War, Kim systematically purged his political opponents, among them Pak Hŏn-yŏng*, creating a highly centralized system that accorded him unlimited power and generated a formidable cult of personality. He was referred to by his subjects as *suryŏng* or the Great Leader. He used the *Juch'e** or self-reliance ideology for legitimacy of his regime. Under his rule, the DPRK became isolated from the world community and hard-pressed economically. In particular, after his death, North Korea became increasingly unable to stabilize its sinking economy and feed its people. Kim collapsed with a massive heart attack and died just before the South-North Korean summit with ROK president Kim Young-sam* set for July 1994. With his death, Kim Jong Il*, his son, made a dynastic succession. Kim was as omnipresent in death as in life, and the junior Kim ruled North Korea in accordance with the teachings of the departed Great Leader as the nation's Dear Leader.

Kim had made the United States his number one enemy, blaming Washington for the Thirty-Eighth Parallel Decision* dividing the peninsula in 1945, intervening in 1950 to prevent reunification on his terms, and turning South Korea into its colony. Thus, he had pursued a hard-line policy toward the United States, as shown in the USS *Pueblo* Incident* in 1968 and the ax murders in 1976 of two American officers in the demilitarized zone. On the other hand, Kim had long sought to make contact with the United States in hopes of persuading Americans to withdraw from the peninsula. He also hoped that the beginning of a relationship with Washington could substitute for a collapse of the DPRK alliance with Moscow and the weakening of its relations with Beijing. After March 1993, P'yŏngyang used its nuclear weapons program as a bargaining chip to trade for recognition, security assurances, and economic benefits from the United States. For a failing and isolated regime with few other cards to play, the brinkmanship strategy proved successful. When Kim died, the U.S. government expressed its condolences to P'yŏngyang, which shocked the ROK government and many South Koreans. See also North Korean Nuclear Controversy.

B. Cumings, *Korea's Place in the Sun: A Modern History* (New York, 1997); D. Oberdorfer, *The Two Koreas: A Contemporary History* (Reading, PA, 1997); D. Suh, *Kim Il Sung: The North Korean Leader* (New York, 1988).

Kim Jinwung

KIM JONG-IL (1942–   )

Kim Jong Il became the leader of the Democratic People's Republic of Korea* (DPRK) after the death of his father Kim Il Sung*. He was born in Khabarovsk in the former Soviet Union and was called Yura in Russian. However, the DPRK has officially contended that Kim was born in Yanggang Province, near Mt. Paektu. After finishing elementary and secondary education in 1960, he majored in politics and philosophy at Kim Il Sung University in P'yŏngyang and graduated in 1964. Thereafter, his rise to a position where he would replace the Great Leader as the Dear Leader occurred in phases under a well-organized program his father directed. The junior Kim joined the ruling Workers' Party in 1964 as a staff member in the organizational section of its Central Committee. For the next decade, he rose in the DPRK's power hierarchy, learning how to lead the party's organization and deepening his relationships with potential followers from the younger generation. At the Central Committee meeting in February 1974, Kim officially was named as his father's successor. Before his status as a Communist "crown prince" was made public, he became party secretary in charge of organizations in 1973, the second-ranking post in the Workers' Party. This virtually drove out his uncle and presumed archrival Kim Yŏng-ju. From 1974 to 1992, Kim accelerated his participation in policy making, but also developed a reputation in the outside world as a playboy who liked to party and collect American movies.

Noteworthy in North Korea's process of hereditary succession was the major role Kim Jong Il played in explaining Kim Il Sung's *Juch'e** ideology. He was credited with launching a successful drive to infuse the whole North Korean society with *juch'e*, publishing a number of works that elaborated on these ideas, including *On the Juch'e Idea, On Some Questions in Understanding the Juch'e Philosophy, Let Us Establish More Firmly the Monolithic Ideological System in the Whole Party and Society*, and *On the Theory of Juch'e-Oriented Literature*. In North Korea, Kim thus became the exclusive authority on interpreting *juch'e*. In 1991, Kim was appointed supreme commander of the Korean People's Army, showing that he had a firm control over the military. When his father died on 8 July 1994, there was great skepticism about his ability to assert power, but soon Kim was a member of the Presidium of the Political Bureau and secretary of the Central Committee of the Workers' Party, as well as chairman of the National Defense Commission (NDC). In 1998, Kim Jong Il was reelected as chief of the NDC, a post equal to head of state under the Stalinist regime's newly revised constitution. This completed the world's first Communist dynastic succession. Meanwhile, North Korea was experiencing great economic hardship as a result of the fall of the Soviet Union in 1991. Despite floods causing widespread starvation, Kim refused to open his country and used the North Korean Nuclear Controversy* to frighten his neighbors and the United States. He did allow some cooperative economic ventures with the Republic of Korea*, however, and reacted positively to South Korea's engagement policy, meeting President Kim Dae-jung* in P'yŏngyang in June 2000.

C. Chung, *Kim Jong-il* (Seoul, 2000); D. Oberdorfer, *The Two Koreas: A Contemporary History* (Reading, PA, 1997); D. Suh, *Kim Il Sung: The North Korean Leader* (New York, 1988); C. Yi, *Kim Jong-il* (Seoul, 2001).

Han Kyu-sun

KIM JONG-P'IL (1926–)

Kim Jong-p'il became prime minister of the Republic of Korea* (ROK) in March 1998 after a long career of political maneuvers as an intelligence officer and protégé of Pak Chŏng-hŭi*. Despite his rural birth and modest background, he was able to enter Seoul National University. After graduating from Officers Candidate School in June 1949, Kim belonged to the first class directly entering the Republic of Korea* Army. In 1952, Major Kim, trained as an expert in counterintelligence, became the head of the North Korean section of the ROK Army Intelligence Bureau. In the wake of a student uprising, the aged South Korean President Syngman Rhee* resigned on 19 April 1960, leaving in place a weakly ruled civilian regime. Kim made common cause with Major General Pak Chŏng-hŭi, the leader of dissident senior military officers, as well as his father-in-law, to stage a military takeover. On 19 May 1961, Pak's troops seized key points in Seoul and deposed Prime Minister Jang Myŏn*, despite criticism from the U.S. embassy and the U.S. commander of United Nations forces.

By July 1961, Pak had set up the new government along strict military lines. Kim was not an official member, but became the spokesman of the new ruling group known as the Supreme Council for National Reconstruction. He also directed the creation of the Korean Central Intelligence Agency (KCIA), officially established on 19 June 1961. The KCIA served as the guarantor of Pak's regime for the rest of its existence. Having Pak's complete confidence, Kim exercised police and intelligence powers with impunity. With the legalization of political activity on 1 January 1963, Kim organized the Democratic Republican Party (DRP). He then negotiated in 1965 the Japan-Korea Normalization* Treaty, enriching himself with kickbacks along the way. In 1969, Kim resigned as DRP chairman following moves to block his succession to Pak, but he later returned as prime minister from June 1971 to December 1975 at a time when President Pak imposed a new constitution that perpetuated his dictatorship and wiped out the last remaining vestiges of democracy.

After Pak Chŏng-hŭi's Assassination*, Kim soon was at loggerheads with the Martial Law Command that had assumed power late in 1979. In May 1980, he and other politicians were arrested. Accused of corruption and stripped of his assets, Kim was forced into exile by President Chŏn Du-hwan* and was able to return only after repayment to the government of funds he had illegally acquired while in power. Remaining a force in Korean politics, Kim, in October 1987, declared his candidacy for president in the December elections. His "man of experience" theme won 7.9 percent of the vote, whereas the two other perennial opposition candidates, Kim Young-sam* and Kim Dae-jung*, split the remainder of the large opposition vote, thereby allowing the former general No Tae-u* to become president. In the next election, Kim joined forces with Kim Young-sam, helping him win the presidency. By 1995, he had formed his own organization, but in a surprise move in

1997, he threw his support to Kim Dae-jung and contributed to his election as president. In March 1998, Kim again became prime minister on the promise that constitutional change would give this office substantive power. But his political prominence soon evaporated. *See also* Rhee's Ouster.

S. Kim, *The Politics of Military Revolution in Korea* (Chapel Hill, NC, 1971); D. S. Macdonald, *The Koreans: Contemporary Politics and Society* (Boulder, CO, 1988); D. S. Macdonald, *U.S.-Korean Relations from Liberation to Self-Reliance: The Twenty-Year Record* (Boulder, CO, 1992); K. W. Nam, *South Korean Politics: The Search for Political Consensus and Stability* (Lanham, MD, 1989).

Kent G. Sieg

KIM KYU-SIK (1881–1950?)

Kim Kyu-sik was among the most selfless and moderate leaders in twentieth-century Korea. He probably was the only Korean capable of developing the political unity after World War II needed to prevent the formation of two governments on the peninsula. Born at Dong-nae, he went to the United States in 1897 to study at Roanoke College, Virginia, and graduated in 1903. After returning to Seoul, Kim worked over the next decade as a teacher and a clergyman. He planned to attend the Portsmouth Conference* to end the Russo-Japanese War* for the cause of Korea in August 1905, but the signing of the Treaty of Portsmouth* occurred sooner than he expected, so he did not do so. The Japanese Annexation of Korea* in 1910 and the Korean Conspiracy Case* in 1911 and 1912 made him take refuge in Shanghai in 1913. In response to the Fourteen Points address of President Woodrow Wilson* in January 1918 and the end of World War I in November, Korean exiles in China sent Kim Kyu-sik to appeal for the self-determination of Korea at the Versailles Peace Conference. He left Shanghai in February and arrived at Paris just as the March First Movement* began in Korea.

Kim prepared and submitted two petitions protesting the injustice of Japanese Colonialism* in Korea and asking for help to achieve independence for Korea, but Wilson and the U.S. delegation ignored them because they feared offending Japan and saw no benefit for U.S. interests in action upon them. Kim then tried to meet Wilson's Secretary of State Robert Lansing* unofficially in June 1919, but was unsuccessful.

Kim became a cabinet member of the Korean Provisional Government (KPG) in Shanghai when Korean exiles organized it in April 1919, but resigned in 1921 as a result of differences in strategy for liberating Korea. In early 1922, he attended the First Congress of the Toilers of the Far East at Moscow with more than forty Korean leftist political leaders. Kim and his associates hoped to gain support for the cause of Korean independence because the congress denounced the Washington Conference* as a forum for cooperation between the imperialist nations. Thereafter, he continued to participate in the Korean liberation movement in various ways, until the defeat of Japan in the Pacific War ended Japanese rule in Korea in August 1945. Kim returned to Korea as a private individual in November 1945 after the American Military Government (AMG) refused to accept his request for recognition as the vice chairman of the KPG, a position he had accepted in 1944.

After August 1945, the Thirty-Eighth Parallel Division* and Soviet-American military occupation created a tumultuous political scene in southern Korea. Kim initially participated in the anti-trusteeship movement, but after realizing that only fulfillment of the Moscow Agreement on Korea* would bring reunification, he became a Korean representative on the Joint American-Soviet Commission in March 1946. When the situation deadlocked, Kim, a representative of moderates on the right, joined with leftist leader Yŏ Un-hyŏng to form the Coalition Committee with AMG encouragement in southern Korea in June

1946. But Lieutenant General John R. Hodge*, the commander of the U.S. Occupation of Korea*, undermined Kim's efforts and ultimately betrayed him because he feared Communist domination of a united Korea. Hodge's actions led to the disbanding of the Coalition Committee in December 1947, ending a process that might have led to the emergence of a moderate majority as a political alternative to lead a united Korea.

Kim favored implementation of a plan that the United Nations approved in November 1947 calling for a supervised general election throughout Korea in 1948, but the Soviet Union rejected enforcement in the north. Kim Kyu-sik then opposed the U.S. plan to hold the election only in the south because he feared the fixation of Korea's division. He and Kim Gu* instead attended the North-South Conference in P'yŏngyang in April 1948 to discuss steps toward unification with Kim Il Sung* and Pak Hŏn-yŏng*, but failed to persuade northern leaders to moderate their plans to impose a Communist government on all Korea. When the Korean War* broke out on 25 June 1950, the withdrawing North Korean forces took Kim Kyu-sik to North Korea. Kim reportedly died of disease that December at the North Korean-Chinese border.

B. Cumings, *The Origins of the Korean War*, 2 vols. (Princeton, NJ, 1981, 1990); Yi Jŏng-sik, *Kim Kyu-sik ŭi saeng-ae* [The Life of Kim Kyu-sik] (Seoul, 1974); J. I. Matray, "Hodge Podge: U.S. Occupation Policy in Korea, 1945–1948," *Korean Studies* (1995).

Nagata Akifumi

KIM YOUNG-SAM (1928–   )

Kim Young-sam became president of the Republic of Korea* (ROK) after many years as a political dissident opposed to military rule. His ties with the United States generally were strained because of his reluctance to reach out to the Democratic People's Republic of Korea* (DPRK) in the north. Kim also is blamed for the collapse during the East Asian Financial Crisis* of the once prospering Korean economy and the ROK's receipt of an International Monetary Fund bailout loan that a majority of the South Korean people viewed as a national humiliation. Kim was born to a wealthy family on Kŏje Island near Pusan. He was elected to the National Assembly on the government ticket at the age of twenty-five, the youngest national legislator on record. He soon rebelled against the increasingly dictatorial rule of Syngman Rhee* and helped found the opposition Democratic Party, beginning a lifelong advocacy of democracy. As an opposition leader, Kim had long been outspoken and undaunted by oppression. In 1979, he was expelled from the assembly for publicly calling Pak Chŏng-hŭi* a dictator and asking the United States to intervene. After Chŏn Du-hwan* took power in 1980, Kim was placed under house arrest for two years for demanding democratic reforms and went on a hunger strike. Kim's 1960 family tragedy, in which his mother was killed by North Korean agents, shielded him from the Red-baiting commonly used against opposition politicians. His establishment roots and moderate political views made him acceptable to middle and upper class members of Korean society.

During the 1987 presidential election, Kim Young-sam was unwilling to withdraw his candidacy in favor of Kim Dae-jung* or Kim Jong-p'il*. No Tae-u*, Chŏn's protégé, thus won against the divided opposition. Discouraged by his defeat, he joined No's ruling party in 1990. Kim won the presidential election in December 1992 as the government candidate and took office in February 1993. He was the first civilian president since the military coup that overthrew Jang Myŏn* in 1961. But Kim was not well equipped to deal with ROK-U.S. relations or the new opportunities for reconciliation with the DPRK. Like much of the South Korean public, whose feelings about North Korea in the 1990s were a complicated mixture of kinship, disdain, and fear, the president's views were replete with inconsistency. Kim alternated between taking a hard line against the DPRK, calculated to bring about its early collapse, and pursuing an accommodation to bring about a "soft landing" leading to a gradual unification. Because he usually pursued the former and, therefore, often collided with the United States, who favored the latter, ROK-U.S. relations were tense during his term of office. In particular, strains between Washington and Seoul reached a peak after the North Korean submarine incursion in September 1996. South Koreans were angry at a comment by Secretary of State Warren R. Christopher that "all parties" should avoid further provocative steps, a statement that seemed to put the United States between the Koreas. *See also* North Korean Nuclear Controversy; South Korea's Democracy Declaration.

Chungang Ilbo (1992–1997); Korea Herald (1992–1997); D. Oberdorfer, The Two Koreas: A Contemporary History (Reading, PA, 1997).

Kim Jinwung

KISHI NOBUSUKE (1896–1987)

Kishi Nobusuke was prime minister of Japan, but was forced to resign as a result of the Anpo Crisis*. He was born Satō Nobusuke in Yamaguchi Prefecture, Chōshū. His father, whose original family name was Kishi, had been adopted into the Satō household and kept the Satō name. Only later, when Satō Nobusuke was adopted by his father's brother, did he take the name Kishi. After attending the Tōkyō Imperial University, he entered the Ministry of Agriculture and Commerce. In 1926, Kishi traveled to the United States to supervise and manage the Japanese pavilion at Philadelphia's World's Fair. Returning to Japan, he became an influential bureaucrat and politician with close ties to prominent businessmen. In the 1930s, he headed Manchuria's industrialization efforts, and later became vice minister of munitions and minister of commerce and industry in the

wartime cabinet of Prime Minister Tōjō Hideki*. On the day after the Pearl Harbor Attack* in 1941, Kishi and his cabinet colleagues signed the declaration of war against the United States and Britain.

Kishi was arrested in 1945 during the U.S. Occupation of Japan* and soon classified as a war criminal. Never prosecuted, he spent more than three years in Sugamo prison. Kishi returned to public prominence as a consequence of a decision taken during the Korean War* to allow former wartime politicians and bureaucrats to reenter domestic politics. In 1952, a year before he was depurged, Kishi befriended members of the American Council for Japan, including Harry Kern, a foreign editor of *Newsweek* who had regular contacts with the Central Intelligence Agency*. Council members tutored Kishi on English and helped organize trips for him to the United States and Europe. During 1955, Kern wrote articles in *Newsweek* that described the rehabilitated Kishi as a pro-American democrat. By that year, Kishi was a powerful force within the newly formed Liberal Democratic Party* (LDP). In 1956, he became Japan's foreign minister under Prime Minister Ishibashi Tanzan*. American officials were disgruntled with Ishibashi's premiership, particularly his desire to expand trade with the People's Republic of China*, and they were relieved when, in early 1957, the Japanese Diet voted to replace the ailing Ishibashi with Kishi.

Prime Minister Kishi soon developed a close working relationship with the new American ambassador to Tōkyō, Douglas MacArthur II*, nephew of the famous general. Kishi's first trip to Washington in the summer of 1957 centered around revisions to the U.S.-Japan Security Treaty of 1951*. During discussions in June, Secretary of State John Foster Dulles* told Kishi that he assumed the Japanese were willing to work with the United States to contain the Sino-Soviet alliance. He then said that if the Japanese preferred to divorce themselves from their anti-Communist alliance with the United States, Washington was prepared to develop Australia as an industrial base for Asia. Taken aback, Kishi reassured Dulles that the LDP was committed to the alliance. The two leaders then agreed to develop a revised treaty and administrative agreement, which were completed by January 1960. Although the U.S.-Japan Mutual Cooperation and Security Treaty* was supported by big business and former Prime Minister Yoshida Shigeru*, strong opposition emerged from a broad coalition of labor, intellectuals, student groups, and Diet members on the left. In the midst of the treaty revision crisis, President Dwight D. Eisenhower* canceled a planned visit to Japan. In June, MacArthur recognized Kishi's declining political fortunes, and told members of the Japanese cabinet that the prime minister should consider announcing his retirement from office after the treaty was ratified by both governments. Kishi resigned after he exchanged signed copies of the treaty on 23 June with MacArthur. After 1960, Kishi remained a very influential figure in Japan, and he maintained significant political and business interests in Taiwan* and Indonesia*.

P. Katzenstein and T. Shirashi (eds.), *Network Power: Japan and Asia* (Ithaca, NY, 1997); D. Kurzman, *Kishi and Japan: The Search for the Sun* (New York, 1960); J. I. Matray, *Japan's Emergence as a Global Power* (Westport, CT, 2000); M. Schaller, *Altered States: The United States and Japan Since the Occupation* (New York, 1997).

Steven Hugh Lee

KISSINGER, HENRY A. (1923–)

Henry A. Kissinger's academic background and theoretical knowledge of international politics and diplomatic history informed every aspect of his service in government, especially as national security adviser and later as secretary of state under President Richard M. Nixon*. Initially a professor at Harvard University, he was a great admirer of the realist tradition of foreign policy formulation, believing that the pursuit of a favorable balance of power and the in-terests of national security, rather than ideology, should guide the making of U.S. foreign policy. He was a protégé of Governor Nelson A. Rockefeller of New York and served as a consultant on foreign affairs to the Eisenhower, Kennedy, and Johnson administrations. In 1967 and 1968, Kissinger was privy to secret peace negotiations with the Democratic Republic of Vietnam*, and it appears that he provided classified information on the Paris Peace Talks* to Nixon, the successful Republican presidential candidate, possibly to ease his way into the coveted position of national security adviser, a job he received in 1969.

With Nixon's strong backing, in his position as national security adviser, which he combined with his service as secretary of state for two years after September 1973, Kissinger dominated the making of U.S. foreign policy, remaking the international balance of power and exploiting the Sino-Soviet split through policies of détente with the Soviet Union and rapprochement with the People's Republic of China* (PRC). In 1971, Kissinger secretly visited Beijing to arrange Nixon's Visit to China* in February 1972, where he and Qiao Guanhua*, the PRC vice foreign minister, wrote the Shanghai Communiqué* that led to U.S.-PRC Normalization of Relations* during the presidency of Jimmy Carter*. From 1969 onward, Kissinger also orchestrated secret talks aimed at ending the Second Indochina War*, which came to fruition in the Paris Peace Accords* of January 1973, a face-saving settlement that at least temporarily left the Nguyen Van Thieu* government in power in the Republic of Vietnam*.

Kissinger's and Nixon's penchant for secrecy was also apparent in the covert American and South Vietnamese military operations in the Cambodia Incursion* in 1970 and in Laos* in 1971. The pattern continued with the continuation and expansion of intensive secret American bombing raids on Laos and Cambodia* begun during the Johnson administration, with the objective of eradicating North Vietnamese bases and Communist opposition forces in those countries. These operations took place as part of U.S. attempts to enable South Vietnam to defend itself without outside assistance, a policy known as Vietnamization*, in anticipation of U.S. military withdrawal from the war. When Operation MENU* and the Secret U.S. Air War in Laos* were revealed, they exposed Kissinger to intense public criticism, and over his objections in August 1973, the U.S. Congress ordered the cessation of all bombing and barred all further U.S. military operations in Southeast Asia. In early 1975, when Viet Cong* and Khmer Rouge* forces renewed their respective assaults in Vietnam and Cambodia, Kissinger and President Gerald R. Ford*, who retained his services when he succeeded Nixon in August 1974, were unsuccessful in persuading Congress to furnish emergency aid to those countries, and in April 1975 both fell to Communist forces, a humiliating end to U.S. involvement in what had been French Indochina*.

In East Asia, Kissinger's most lasting legacy was the renewal of U.S. diplomatic relations with mainland China, a relationship whose importance to the United States he stressed thereafter in his prolific writings and speeches. In his dual roles as head of Kissinger Associates, a lucrative international consulting firm whose clients include leading American and overseas corporations, and respected elder statesman, whom PRC leaders consider an "old friend of China," he attempted to promote Sino-American concord, for example, urging U.S. moderation toward Beijing and opposing imposition of economic sanctions on the PRC after the Tiananmen Square Massacre* in June 1989, and welcoming the decision to award the 2008 Summer Olympic Games to Beijing.

P. Dickson, *Kissinger and the Meaning of History* (New York, 1979); S. Hersh, *The Price of Power: Kissinger in the Nixon White House* (New York, 1983); C. Hitchens, *The Trial of Henry Kissinger* (New York, 2001); W. Isaacson, *Kissinger: A Biography* (New York, 1992); R. D. Schulzinger, *Henry Kissinger: Doctor of Diplomacy* (New York, 1989).

Priscilla Roberts

KNOWLAND, WILLIAM F. (1908–1974)

A senator from California from 1945 to 1959, William F. Knowland was a close ally of the China Lobby*, which worked on behalf of the Guomindang* (Nationalist) government under Jiang Jieshi*. He was a stern critic of Mao Zedong* and the Chinese Communist Party* during the Chinese Civil War*, often advocating drastic action to ensure a Nationalist victory. For example, when the Chinese Communists imprisoned the U.S. consul general, Angus Ward*, Knowland called for a blockade of China until the U.S. diplomat was freed. On a visit to China in 1949, he barely escaped the besieged Nationalist-held city of Chongqing and again advocated a blockade, as well as President Harry S. Truman* naming General Douglas MacArthur* as U.S. high commissioner for Asia. Knowland also pressed for more aid to the Nationalists and opposed the Department of State's proposal for Jiang to join a coalition government with Mao. After the Nationalists fled to Taiwan* late in 1949, he was one of the most outspoken critics of the State Department, claiming that Secretary of State Dean G. Acheson* had betrayed the Republic of China* (ROC).

Knowland violently opposed U.S. recognition of the People's Republic of China* (PRC), and his speeches attracted many other senators to his strident stand endorsing the ROC. He utterly opposed the PRC's admission to the United Nations. At one point, angered at British pressure to admit Beijing, Knowland suggested that the United States terminate aid to Britain if it continued its campaign. In July 1954, he said that if the United Nations admitted Communist China, he would resign as Senate majority leader and work for U.S. withdrawal from the body. Knowland was even more outraged at signals that Truman planned to abandon Taiwan. He urged the dispatch of a U.S. military mission to show support for Jiang's regime, but opposed deploying troops to defend the island. When Acheson's National Press Club Speech* placed Taiwan outside the defensive perimeter in the Pacific, Knowland called for the secretary of state to resign. He backed Truman's intervention in the Korean War*, welcomed the Neutralization of Taiwan*, and urged bombing of supply lines to North Korea in China.

During the first of the Taiwan Straits Crises*, when the PRC began shelling Jinmen and Mazu in 1954, Knowland called for U.S. protection of the ROC's control over these offshore islands, as well as a blockade of China. He helped gain passage of the Formosa Resolution*, which authorized action to defend Taiwan and other ill-defined areas. But whereas President Dwight D. Eisenhower* wanted to defend the offshore islands only if their capture was a prelude to invading Taiwan, he wanted to defend them regardless of Beijing's intentions. When the PRC sentenced eleven U.S. airmen captured during the Korean War, Knowland called for a blockade of China and then criticized Eisenhower for not insisting on ROC participation in the negotiations to gain their release. By then, Asia expert Owen Lattimore* had labeled Knowland the Senator from Formosa, a sobriquet he hated. But his actions made a truly bipartisan policy on China almost impossible. Although considered a member of the Asia-First bloc in the Senate, Knowland supported aid to Western Europe. He never argued that the United States should make Asia its highest priority, but rather that it was not receiving the attention it deserved. Leaving the Senate after losing a race for governor of California in 1958, Knowland died more than a decade later of a self-inflicted gunshot wound. See also Chinese Representation in the United Nations.

S. E. Ambrose, *Eisenhower: The President* (New York, 1984); G. B. Montgomery and J. W. John-son, *One Step from the White House: The Rise and Fall of Senator William F. Knowland* (Berkeley, CA, 1998); D. W. Reinhard, *The Republican Right Since 1945* (Lexington, KY, 1983).

Tracy S. Uebelhor

KNOX NEUTRALIZATION SCHEME

The Knox Neutralization Scheme was a daring but clumsy American initiative to safeguard the open commercial door and enhance American economic interests in Manchuria. In November 1909, Secretary of State Philander C. Knox* proposed that the United States and Great Britain organize an international loan to enable China to buy Russia's Chinese Eastern Railway (CER) and Japan's South Manchurian Railway (SMR) and then build rail lines in its vast, undeveloped, and unpopulated Manchurian provinces. For the life of the loan, the international banking group would supervise and control the Manchurian railroads. As a fallback, Knox proposed Anglo-American collaboration in the Jinzhou-Aigun rail project, then being negotiated with China's government, that would compete with Japan's SMR. In either case, international financial cooperation would serve to neutralize both Russian and Japanese efforts to strengthen their spheres of influence in Manchuria and exclude other foreign nationals from exploiting the potentially rich area.

The American offensive was a major expression of the bold reaffirmation of the Open Door Policy* during the administration of William Howard Taft*, which aimed at securing a larger share of the fabled China market for American businessmen and bankers, undermining the spheres of influence, and protecting China's integrity from foreign encroachments. Taft's instrument was Dollar Diplomacy*, the utilization of American capital to expand and strengthen U.S. influence in East Asia (and elsewhere). The scheme also reflected the grandiose plans of E. H. Harriman* to incorporate the CER and SMR into a global transportation network. This aggressive U.S. posture was pushed by a group of young, dynamic, recently appointed State Department officials, including the restless Willard D. Straight*, who had worked closely with Harriman. It also received enthusiastic support from Taft, who had become disenchanted with the lukewarm commitment of Theodore Roosevelt* to the Open Door and his willingness to compromise with Japan. The aggressive scheme was a combination of self-interest and sympathy for China, ambition, and romanticism.

The proponents of neutralization, however, ignored international realities in East Asia and the substance of the Anglo-Japanese Alliance* and the Franco-Russian Entente. They also misread Britain's approval in "principle" of the Jinzhou-Aigun alternative. They miscalculated the vulnerability of Russia and Japan to international pressure and their determination to defend their spheres of influence; indeed, the Knox Neutralization Scheme brought the two powers closer together. They also misjudged the lukewarm support coming from the divided and disintegrating Qing government, which worried about defending its Manchurian frontier. Consequently, the Knox Neutralization Scheme, a dismal failure in conception and execution, set back U.S. efforts to revitalize the Open Door policy in East Asia. *See also* Six Power Consortium.

P. H. Clyde, *International Rivalries in Manchuria, 1689–1922* (New York, 1966); M. Hunt, *The Making of a Special Relationship: The United States and China to 1914* (New York, 1983); C. Vevier, *The United States and China, 1906–1913: A Study of Finance and Diplomacy* (New Brunswick, NJ, 1955).

Noel H. Pugach

KNOX, PHILANDER C. (1853–1921)

Philander Chase Knox served as secretary of state under William Howard Taft* from 1909 to 1913, and his reputation in the annals of U.S.–East Asian relations remains closely linked with the single-minded and largely fruitless pursuit of U.S. commercial interests in China known as Dollar Diplomacy*. He was a native of Pennsylvania who first made his national reputation as the legal mastermind behind the creation of the U.S. Steel Corporation in the 1890s. He was attorney general in the cabinets of Presidents William McKinley* and Theodore Roosevelt* from 1901 to 1904, senator from Pennsylvania from 1904 to 1907, and unsuccessful candidate for the Republican presidential nomination in 1908.

With a penchant for coffee-driven work early in the morning—and hurrying to the golf course after lunch, weather permitting—Knox, though only one of a long list of lawyers who have served as secretary of state, brought a particularly legalistic and precedent-driven approach to the office. Believing strongly in the potential for more U.S. profits in the inviting China market, and keeping a copy of John Basset Moore's influential *Digest of International Law* close at hand, Knox viewed the advancement of American economic interests in China as a practical and moral application of the Open Door Policy* that Secretary of State John Hay* had initiated and as a force for the preservation of Chinese territorial integrity. He played a key role in the reorganization of the State Department, which produced the first Division of Far Eastern Affairs and prominent U.S. officials, such as Willard D. Straight*, the first chief of the division, and Huntington Wilson, Knox's assistant secretary of state, who brought to U.S. policy in these years a strong suspicion of Japan, and installed an equally strong desire to outfox U.S. competitors in China. From their perspective, the United States—if it had ambitions to become more than a vocal spectator in the Chinese market—needed to acquire a genuine stake in China's major railway enterprises.

In the end, the Taft-Knox stewardship of U.S.–East Asian interests produced decidedly mixed results. Knox's boldest gambit was a plan launched in late 1909 calling for the neutralization or internationalization of all Manchurian railroads. It was founded, however, on optimistic assumptions about the likely reactions of the foreign powers, particularly Japan and Russia, and the Knox Neutralization Scheme* fell apart with embarrassing speed—prompting a haughtily disapproving reference by the *London Times* to Knox's "precipitous diplomacy." If Knox saw himself as the nation's "first lawyer" acting on behalf of U.S. interests in China, the American people would have been within their rights to demand his immediate resignation. But Knox defended his actions vigorously to all his detractors, including one particularly caustic critic, former President Roosevelt. Knox, with Taft's direct intervention, had greater success in securing U.S admittance to the Six Power Consortium*, an agreement that a group of European bankers had negotiated to lend the Chinese government money for railroad systems in southern China. But enthusiasm among U.S. bankers for private investment in China tended to dissipate as the Qing Dynasty disintegrated and anti-Western sentiment mounted. Knox, once memorably described by Roosevelt as a "sawed-off cherub," returned without fanfare to the U.S. Senate and ended his public career as an implacable opponent of Woodrow Wilson* and his League of Nations.

W. H. Becker, "1899–1920: America Adjusts to World Power," in W. H. Becker and S. F. Wells Jr. (eds.), *Economics and World Power: An Assessment of American Diplomacy Since 1789* (New York, 1984); M. H. Hunt, *The Making of a Special Relationship: The United States and China to 1914* (New York, 1983); W. V. and M. V. Scholes, *The Foreign Policies of the Taft Administration* (Columbia, MO, 1970); W. V. Scholes, "Philander C. Knox (1909–1913)" in N. A. Graebner (ed.), *An Uncertain Tradition: American Secretaries of State in the Twentieth Century* (New York, 1961).

Roger K. Hodgkins

KOJONG (1852–1919)

The twenty-sixth king of the Chosŏn Dynasty sought U.S. help in vain to save his falling kingdom in the intensified international power rivalries during the late nineteenth and early twentieth century, especially the threat from Russian, Japanese, and Chinese imperialism. Kojong succeeded Ch'ŏlchŏng in 1863 at the age of twelve. His father, known as the Taewŏn'gun (regent), ruled Korea in his name with an iron fist to create a strong monarchy until 1873, when he was forced to retire. The Taewŏn'gun and his primary political rival, the king's queen, swayed Kojong and shaped Korean politics for the rest of the century. Under the rule of the Taewŏn'gun, Korea's doors were kept tightly closed. When an American merchant schooner sailed up the Taedong toward P'yŏngyang in 1866, the Koreans killed its crew members in battle and burned the ship. This *General Sherman* Incident* prompted the U.S. government to open Korea's ports by force, and war broke out between the United States and Korea in May 1871. The brief conflict lasted from 21 May to 3 July, and Korean enmity toward the United States reached its zenith when U.S. Marines annihilated the fort at Kanghwa Island.

When Kojong began to rule in his own right in late 1873, he initiated a more moderate policy toward the outside world. Korea was forced to open its doors by Japan with the signing of the Kanghwa Treaty in February 1876, after a textbook display of gunboat diplomacy during the autumn of 1875. Then, in May 1882, as a defensive measure against its neighbors, Korea signed the Shufeldt Treaty* with the United States, its first with a Western power, in which the United States promised to provide its good offices in the event of external threat to Korea. Compared with the English-language version of the treaty, the Korean version employed the much more emphatic phrase *p'ilsu sangjo*, meaning "shall surely render mutual aid." King Kojong thought that the United States would come to Korea's assistance if Korean sovereignty and independence was threatened. Reportedly, he danced with joy when the first U.S. minister, Lucius H. Foote*, arrived in Korea. But his hope was shattered because of the U.S. policy of noninvolvement in Northeast Asia initially and friendly acquiescence to Japan's aggressive expansionism later under President Theodore Roosevelt*. In 1905, Secretary of War William Howard Taft* approved Japan's domination of Korea in the secret Taft-Katsura Agreement* with the Japanese, in exchange for assurances that Japan would not challenge U.S. colonial rule in the Philippines*.

Under the impact of Japanese Colonialism*, the Chosŏn Dynasty faltered and finally collapsed. Japan established a "protectorate" in 1905, taking control of Korean diplomacy. The Japanese forced recalcitrant Kojong to abdicate, in favor of his son Sunjong in 1907. Finally, on 29 August 1910, Sunjong, helpless to prevent the Japanese Annexation of Korea*, yielded the throne. When Kojong died in January 1919, rumors spread that a Japanese physician had poisoned him. The March First Movement* took place two days before his funeral. *See also* Horace N. Allen; Homer B. Hulbert; George Kennan; Korean Conspiracy Case.

B. Cumings, *Korea's Place in the Sun: A Modern History* (New York, 1997); W. Han, *The History of Korea* (Seoul, 1970); K. Lee, *A New History of Korea* (Seoul, 1984).

Kim Jinwung

KONG LE (1934–)

As a twenty-six-year-old captain commanding the elite Second Parachute Battalion of the Royal Lao Army, Kong Le staged a bloodless coup on 9 August 1960 against the then pro-American government of Laos*. A diminutive paratrooper trained at the U.S. Army Ranger School in the Philippines*, he was a Phou Thai tribesman (one of Lao highland minorities) who was politically inexperienced, idealistic, honest, and modest in lifestyle. His message of an end to the Lao civil war, no more "Lao fighting Lao," his opposition to endemic government corruption, and his call for international neutrality struck responsive chords among the people of Vientiane. The Eisenhower administration, however, saw Kong Le and all Lao neutralists as pro-Communists and a danger to U.S. interests in Southeast Asia. President Dwight D. Eisenhower* supported the efforts of right-wing military strongman Phoumi Nosavan* to retake Vientiane by military force. With clandestine American logistical, air, and financial support, Phoumi's forces began a slow—sometimes-sputtering—advance on the capital from their base in the southern Laos panhandle. The 13–16 December 1960 battle for Vientiane between the forces of Kong Le and Phoumi was an uncharacteristically fierce fight, in which almost a thousand combatants and civilians were killed or wounded. Heavily outnumbered and outgunned, Kong Le and his battalion retreated to the Plain of Jars, the strategic gateway to the Lao lowlands. There they regrouped, accepted military aid from the Democratic Republic of Vietnam*, and joined forces with the Pathet Lao* to drive Phoumi's troops off the Plain of Jars by the end of 1960.

President Eisenhower warned John F. Kennedy*, incoming president, that Laos was a potential flash point, but Kennedy decided to break with Eisenhower's policy in Laos and support neutralism there. Over the next year and a half, the new administration supported a neutralist government under Souvanna Phouma*. In October 1962, cooperation between Kong Le (now a general) and the Pathet Lao broke down over distribution of supplies and the Pathet Lao's assassination of a Kong Le associate. The Kennedy administration stepped in to keep Kong Le's small army intact with U.S. supplies delivered by Air America*. As the neutralist solution in Laos agreed to under the Geneva Accords of 1962* became frayed, and fighting between the coalition fractions resumed, Kong Le was caught in the middle. In April 1963, Kong Le finally broke with the Pathet

Lao, who with North Vietnamese forces attacked and pushed him off the Plain of Jars. Kong Le then allied with Souvanna's Royalist troops, but kept his demoralized 8,000-man army separate from its new comrades in arms. By this time, Washington had shifted support to Vang Pao* and his Hmong* adherents, who were far more effective in fighting the Pathet Lao and Vietnamese than Kong Le's forces or the Royal Lao Army. In 1966, Souvanna integrated Kong Le's troops into the Royal Armed Forces. Kong Le lost his power struggle within the Royal Lao Army and left Laos for exile in France, where he maintained a small following among exiled Laotians. *See also* Laotian Crisis of 1961; Souphanouvong.

M. Brown and J. J. Zasloff, *Apprentice Revolutionaries: The Communist Movement in Laos, 1930–1985* (Stanford, CA, 1986); T. N. Castle, *At War in the Shadow of Vietnam: U.S. Military Aid to the Royal Lao Government, 1955–1975* (New York, 1993); A. J. Dommen, *Conflict in Laos: The Politics of Neutralization* (New York, 1971); C. A. Stevenson, *The End of Nowhere: American Policy Toward Laos Since 1954* (Boston, 1972); R. Warner, *Back Fire: Secret War in Laos and Its Link to the War in Vietnam* (New York, 1995).

Edward C. Keefer

KONOE FUMIMARO (1891–1945)

Konoe Fumimaro was an influential Japanese politician who, as prime minister from 1940 to 1941, tried to avert war with the United States. He was born into the ancient and highly prestigious Fujiwara line of Japanese aristocracy. His father was a leading political figure during the Meiji period with pan-Asian sentiments. Konoe first came to prominence with the 1918 publication of "Reject the Anglo-American-Centered Peace," a stinging attack on Japan's compliance with the Versailles Peace Treaty* and later the treaty system emerging from the Washington Conference*. These opinions, coupled with an early infatuation with Marxism, led reformist bureaucrats and army officers in the interwar era to see in him an ideal political partner to help implement their various programs. As a prince, Konoe was guaranteed a seat in the Diet's House of Peers and was elected acting president of that body in 1921. By the end of the 1920s, he had established contacts with right-wing reformers and traditional conservatives.

Konoe was an ardent defender of Japan's seizure of Manchuria after the Mukden Incident* in 1931 and its decision to leave the League of Nations two years later. Ironically, his close association with the rightists convinced many senior leaders that he was their best chance to restrain right-wing extremism in the wake of the assassinations and an attempted coup by young army officers in February 1936. Konoe declined to become prime minister then, but accepted the post a year later, convinced he could lead Japan into a new era in which it would be the acknowledged leader of Asia abroad and secure a more "modern" (meaning centralized or even fascist-style) form of government at home. Opposition from the traditional parties in the Diet quashed these plans, although they were in part realized in the National General Mobilization Law of 1938. Unfortunately for Konoe, the law was passed only in reaction to the war in China after the Marco Polo Bridge Incident* in July 1937.

Konoe had hoped that fighting would be brief, but by the end of 1938, it was clear that it would be prolonged and draining. Konoe, who was often accused of having weak nerves, elected to resign and bide his time until the China situation was closer to resolution. By the spring of 1940, with Nazi Germany's crushing victories in Europe, that moment seemed to have arrived, and Konoe resumed the premiership. This time, he moved to create an all-encompassing political party—the Imperial Rule Assistance Association—under his direction to achieve his reforms within Japan. He also successfully oversaw the negotiation of the Tripartite Pact* with Germany and Italy in

September. He hoped this would end prospects of American aid to China and thus compel the Chinese to sue for peace. He was disappointed, as the alliance only ensnared Japan more deeply into the prospect of possible war with the United States.

During 1941, Konoe groped for a path to peace. He successfully dismissed the confrontational Matsuoka Yōsuke* from his cabinet in July, but could not persuade either the Americans or the Imperial Army to approve a personal summit between President Franklin D. Roosevelt* and himself that summer. Rather than lead Japan into a war with the United States, Konoe resigned. He spent the war years worrying, quietly and then openly using his personal connections to Emperor Hirohito*, that Japan's impending defeat would open the way to Communist revolution and that, as a result, a conditional peace with the Americans was advisable. Konoe himself thought, in fact, that the Potsdam Declaration* was such a peace. Then, during the U.S. Occupation of Japan*, when Supreme Commander for the Allied Powers (SCAP*) authorities demanded that the Meiji constitution of 1889 be eliminated, he wrote a new constitution barely less conservative. Its rejection by the Americans and his subsequent arrest as a war criminal embittered Konoe deeply. He wrote a long letter defending his actions and career and then committed suicide in December 1945 before he had to face the Tōkyō War Crimes Trials*. By the end of the century, Konoe enjoyed a revival among Japanese thinkers as an original figure who stood for Japanese independence from the West, especially the United States. *See also* Nomura-Hull Conversations.

G. M. Berger, "Japan's Young Prince: Konoe Fumimaro's Early Political Career, 1916–1931," *Monumenta Nipponica* 29 (Winter 1974); G. M. Berger, *Parties Out of Power in Japan, 1931–1941* (Princeton, NJ, 1977); Y. Oka, *Konoe Fumimaro: A Political Biography* (Tōkyō, 1983).

Michael A. Barnhart

KOO, V. K. WELLINGTON

See GU WEIJUN

KOREA

See DEMOCRATIC PEOPLE'S REPUBLIC OF KOREA; REPUBLIC OF KOREA

KOREAGATE

This scandal was the result of South Korean lobbying activities to influence U.S. policy toward the Republic of Korea* (ROK). According to American press reports in October 1976, Pak Dong-sŏn, a Korean agent, had distributed between a half and one million dollars annually to bribe members of the U.S. Congress. It was also reported that the Central Intelligence Agency* (CIA) had eavesdropped on the bribery planning session at the Blue House, the presidential residence in South Korea. Coming in the immediate wake of the Watergate scandal that forced President Richard M. Nixon* to resign in August 1974, the scandal became known as Koreagate.

Systematic ROK lobbying activities in the United States had started in response to the Nixon administration's unilateral 1970 decision for gradual withdrawal of U.S. ground forces from South Korea in accordance with the Nixon Doctrine*. However, the ROK believed that its country would be an exception and was frustrated at the "betrayal" by its most trusted ally. Seoul began to seek countermeasures beyond conventional diplomatic channels to prevent further reductions of U.S. troops in South Korea. The lobbying efforts were also aimed at securing approval from Congress of the Nixon administration's proposal for a $1.5 billion compensatory military aid package to the ROK. The government of Pak Chŏng-hǔi* also wanted to mitigate increasing criticism over political repression and human rights violations in South Korea.

Although the State Department and the

U.S. embassy in Seoul had been aware of Korean lobbying and bribery operations, it was not until late 1975 that President Gerald R. Ford* instructed the U.S. Justice Department to launch an investigation. More serious probes, however, followed after the newspaper revelations the next year. By the end of 1977, four full-scale congressional investigations of South Korean activities were under way. Despite the publicity surrounding the scandal, only two people, including one U.S. congressman, were convicted of bribery. Nonetheless, Koreagate seriously strained U.S.-ROK relations. The ugly implications of the scandal further hurt American public and congressional support for military aid to the ROK. On the other hand, the South Korean leadership was bitter about the way in which both the U.S. executive and legislative branches had sensationalized the scandal. *See also* Unification Church.

R. Boettcher, *Gifts of Deceit: Sun Myung Moon, Tongsun Park, and the Korean Scandal* (New York, 1980); C. J. Lee and H. Sato, *U.S. Policy Toward Japan and Korea: A Changing Influence Relationship* (New York, 1982); C. I. Moon, "Complex Interdependence and Transnational Lobbying: South Korea in the United States," *International Studies Quarterly* (Winter 1988); Cháng-guk Moon, *Hanmi kaldŭng ŭi haebu* [Anatomy of Korea-U.S. Conflicts] (Seoul, 1994).

Ma Sang-yoon

KOREAN AID ACT (14 February 1950)

In early 1947, the U.S. Army requested $138 million in basic assistance for southern Korea for fiscal 1948, and John Carter Vincent*, the State Department's director of Far Eastern Affairs, recommended an additional $50 million development grant. Undersecretary of State Dean G. Acheson*, however, hoped to rebuild all of Asia around Japan, what he called "the workshop of Asia," but the Japanese were starving. Acheson therefore proposed to rehabilitate Korea, which had provided two-thirds of Japan's prewar rice imports,

as a first step to reviving Japan. The Departments of State, War, and Agriculture sent a joint mission to Korea and Japan, and a joint committee considered four options: continuing limited aid, recognizing an independent South Korea as a means of liquidating the U.S. commitment there, referring the Korean issue to the United Nations, and adopting an "aggressive positive program." Both the mission and the committee supported the last option.

Acheson quickly forged a $600 million three-year Korean recovery program to follow those for Greece and Turkey under the Truman Doctrine. He won approval from the Pentagon and, after pruning the cost to $540 million, from the Office of Management and Budget. Arthur H. Vandenburg, chairman of the Senate Committee on Foreign Relations, agreed to take up the issue in early 1948. But after Acheson left the State Department on 31 June 1947, his plan had few supporters. On 4 August 1947, the Departments of State, War, and Navy approved a new Korea policy that killed Acheson's rehabilitation plan and kept Korean aid at low, basic support levels. In the fall of 1948, the assistant secretary of state for occupied areas submitted to Secretary of State George C. Marshall* a new three-year recovery plan. The current Korean policy, NSC 8, called for the "liquidation of the U.S. commitment of men and money in Korea," with only enough aid to "forestall economic breakdown" until the United States pulled out. Nevertheless, Marshall approved the plan, provided that its full extent could be kept secret to avoid any appearance of a U.S. commitment. When Acheson replaced Marshall in early 1949, he endorsed the three-year recovery plan, modeled on his own, but he also made it public—committing U.S. prestige in Korea.

In June, Acheson presented Congress with a $350–$385 million three-year rehabilitation program focused on production of coal, electrical power, and fertilizer. The coal would supply new electrical generating plants, which would service new fertilizer plants; these would restore both rice production and rice exports to Japan. Japan's economy had yet to recover; the United States supplied 25 percent of its food at a cost of $400 million—up from $330 million in 1947 and still climbing. In hearings before the Senate Committee on Foreign Relations, witness after witness extolled the Korean Aid Act's importance for Japan, eventually leading Chairman Tom Connally to ask if this might tempt the Russians to move militarily in Korea and " 'gum up' the Japanese situation." On 19 January 1950, the House of Representatives defeated the bill by one vote, and Acheson immediately warned President Harry S. Truman* that if permanent, this could be "disastrous." Truman lobbied Congress, Acheson reduced the cost to $320 million, and the House reversed itself. Truman signed the act into law on 14 February. The Korean War* slowed implementation of the three-year aid program, but it was completed. *See also* Republic of Korea.

R. L. McGlothlen, *Controlling the Waves: Dean Acheson and U.S. Foreign Policy in Asia* (New York, 1993); J. I. Matray, *The Reluctant Crusade: American Foreign Policy in Korea, 1941–1950* (Honolulu, HI, 1985); W. W. Stueck, *The Road to Confrontation: American Policy Toward China and Korea, 1947–1950* (Chapel Hill, NC, 1981).

Ronald L. McGlothlen

KOREAN ARMISTICE AGREEMENT (27 July 1953)

With the conclusion of this armistice agreement between the United Nations Command (UNC), on the one hand, and the Korean People's Army and the Chinese People's Volunteer forces, on the other, the Korean War* came to an end. The accord was the product of compromise of the U.S. containment and rollback policies against Communist expansionism after World War II. The agreement comprised five articles and sixty-three sections: Preamble; Article 1—Military Demarcation Line and Demilitarized Zone; Article 2—Concrete Arrangements for Cease-Fire and Armistice;

Article 3—Arrangements Relating to Prisoners of War; Article 4—Recommendation to the Governments Concerned on Both Sides; and Article 5—Miscellaneous. This armistice confirmed three key points. First, there was neither a winner nor a loser, because it restored the prewar division with only small territorial changes. Second, for the first time in history, a commander of UN forces signed a military agreement. The army of the Republic of Korea* (ROK) was not a signatory, which provided the Democratic People's Republic of Korea* with an excuse for refusing to include South Korea in later negotiations for a permanent peace treaty. Third, the armistice contributed to halting Communist expansion in Northeast Asia. The United States determined UNC negotiating positions, and the People's Republic of China* (PRC) dominated the Communist side, despite consultations throughout with Soviet leader Joseph Stalin.

Chinese Intervention in the Korean War* in October 1950 and the failure of the Home by Christmas Offensive* the next month caused U.S. policy makers to abandon reunification of Korea as a purpose of the war. Instead, President Harry S. Truman* decided in January 1951 that it was enough of a victory for the United States to halt the aggression, limit hostilities to the peninsula, and avoid escalation of the fighting to a global scale. When the Chinese failed to push UN forces out of Korea in April and May 1951, Washington intensified its efforts to end what had become a military stalemate. After private talks with George F. Kennan*, the Soviet delegate to the United Nations proposed on 23 June 1951 discussion of a cease-fire and an armistice. On 10 July, negotiations began between the UNC and the Communist commanders at Kaesŏng. At the first session, the negotiators agreed that hostilities would continue until an armistice agreement was signed. On 26 July, the delegations adopted an agenda for the points to be settled to achieve an armistice that paralleled the articles of the final agreement.

Negotiations deadlocked on the location of a demarcation line and demilitarized zone when the Communists rejected the UNC demand to control the southern half of North Korea, insisting instead on the thirty-eighth parallel. Talks adjourned in late August amidst Communist falsified charges that the UNC had violated the Kaesŏng neutrality zone.

Negotiations resumed on 25 October at P'anmunjŏm, a tiny settlement seven miles southeast of Kaesŏng. Both sides wanted an early armistice, the PRC because of heavy losses sustained in intensified UNC military operations and the United States because of pressure from its West European allies. The two delegations agreed in November on a line of demarcation during an armistice coinciding with the existing line of contact, provided an armistice agreement was reached within thirty days, and in February 1952 on a political conference to discuss Korean issues after an armistice. They also reached nearly complete agreement on measures for supervision of the cease-fire. But then discord over exchange of prisoners of war (POW) created an impasse in the armistice agreement negotiations early in May 1952. The Korean War POW Controversy* began in January 1952 after UNC delegates proposed to give captives a choice in repatriation to their homelands, a position inconsistent with the Geneva Convention of 1949. On this dispute, the negotiations adjourned in deadlock in October 1952 and did not resume until after the death of Joseph Stalin in March 1953. Meanwhile, Dwight D. Eisenhower* was elected president and visited South Korea in early December 1952, hoping to find a solution to bring about an "honorable peace" in the war. But he found it difficult to persuade ROK President Syngman Rhee* to accept the U.S. cease-fire plan that accepted Korea's continued division.

The armistice negotiations resumed in April 1953. An exchange of sick and wounded prisoners was carried out that same month. On 8 June, the prisoner re-patriation problem was settled through agreement that each side would have an opportunity to persuade those captives resisting repatriation to change their minds. But on 18 June, Rhee, who from the start had refused to participate in the armistice talks, ordered the release of North Korean prisoners who had refused to return to North Korea. The Communists promptly halted negotiations on this issue. On 20 July, negotiations resumed. Rhee relented and agreed to support the armistice, even though he would not sign it. In return, the United States promised to extend economic aid, enlarge the ROK military, and conclude a mutual security pact to protect South Korea against any future aggression. At 10:00 A.M. on 27 July 1953, chief delegates on both sides signed the military armistice agreement at P'anmunjŏm. All fighting stopped twelve hours after the first signing, ending the war started by the North Korean invasion three years earlier. *See also* Geneva Conference of 1954; Germ Warfare; U.S.-South Korea Mutual Security Treaty.

R. Foot, *Substitute for Victory: The Politics of Peacemaking at the Korean Armistice Talks* (Ithaca, NY, 1990); C. T. Joy, *How Communists Negotiate* (New York, 1955); M. B. Ridgway, *The Korean War* (Garden City, NY, 1967); W. H. Vatcher, *Panmunjom: The Story of the Korean Military Armistice Negotiations* (New York, 1958).

Han Kyu-sun

KOREAN CONSPIRACY CASE

This incident in 1911 and 1912 dramatized Korean opposition to Japanese Colonialism* and increased tensions between Japan and the United States because of the alleged involvement of American missionaries. The key figure in the Korean Conspiracy Case was Terauchi Masatake, Japanese minister of the army, who was also the resident general of Korea after May 1910. He played the final and decisive role in the Japanese Annexation of Korea*, forcing Korea's cabinet in August 1910 to sign the treaty confirming Japan's control and making Terauchi the governor general of Korea in October. He assumed full-time responsibilities in 1911 by resigning as minister of the army, remaining in the position until 1916, when he became the prime minister of Japan. Terauchi's rule in Korea became known as Government by the Bayonet after he conducted a personal inspection in December 1910 of P'yŏngyang, Songchŏn, and Sinŭiju in northwestern Korea. It was rumored that during his tour, Koreans planned to assassinate him several times but failed. In retaliation, Governor-General Terauchi had arrested about 700 Korean suspects by September 1911, the trials for 122 of them (the others released for lack of evidence) beginning in 1912. The Japanese governor general and the press suspected the complicity of American Presbyterian missionaries in Korea in this "incident" because many of the suspects were Christians in American Presbyterian churches of Korea. The U.S. government and the American Presbyterian church not only denied complicity, but voiced suspicion that the governor general of Korea had tortured the Korean suspects.

As U.S.-Japan tensions grew, three American missionaries in Korea, Oliver R. Avison, Samuel A. Moffett, and Norman C. Whitemore, sent letters to Terauchi and then met with him in January 1912 to deny the complicity of the Presbyterian church and ask for humane treatment of those arrested. Arthur J. Brown, the secretary of the Board of Foreign Missions of the Presbyterian Church in New York, though favorably disposed to Japanese rule in Korea, met with Hanihara Masanao, the chargé in the Japanese embassy, and asked for fair treatment of the suspects on 14 February 1912, later publishing a pamphlet titled *Korean Conspiracy Case*. Three U.S. senators met with Chinda Sutemi, the Japanese ambassador, and asked for the release of Yun Chiho, the most famous of those arrested in May, but Chinda rejected possible U.S. political intervention because Japan had unfettered jurisdiction. Then the *Washing-*

ton Post on 23 July 1912 reported that William Sulzer, the chairman of the U.S. Foreign Affairs Committee, was to ask President William Howard Taft* and Secretary of State Philander C. Knox* to press Japan for protection of the American missionaries in Korea, causing Chinda to meet with Sulzer and explain to him the Japanese position. Finally, journalist George Kennan* supported the Japanese stand with his article "Is Japan Persecuting Christians in Korea?" in *The Outlook* on 14 December 1912.

Responding to the concerns and pressure of the U.S. government and American missionaries, the Seoul district court judged seventeen suspects innocent, but the other 105 suspects were found guilty on 28 September 1912. On appeal to the higher court of those convicted, 99 suspects were found innocent, but the appeals of the other suspects, including Yun Chiho, were rejected on 9 October 1913. These six convicted suspects were given amnesty, owing to the coronation of Emperor Taishō on 16 February 1915, and were released. This outcome was the result of the intervention of the U.S. government and American missionaries. Without it, Japan could have uprooted many anti-Japanese Koreans, although this incident now is generally viewed as a Japanese fabrication. Thereafter, Korean dissatisfaction with Japanese and U.S.-Japan mutual distrust concerning American missionary activities in Korea increased, contributing to the March First Movement* in 1919.

Yŭn Kyŏng-no, *105 In Sagŏn kwa Shinminhŏ Yŏnku* [A Study on the 105 Persons Incident and the New Peoples Society] (Seoul, 1990).

Nagata Akifumi

KOREAN WAR (25 June 1950–27 July 1953)

The Korean War was the product of international and internal developments, including the Thirty-Eighth Parallel Division* and partition of the country by Soviet and U.S. armies after the Pacific war, the global and ideological rivalry between the two superpowers and their Korean client states, and a civil conflict within Korea itself, the first signs of which emerged as early as 1945 when the U.S. military government dismantled leftist people's committees at local levels of government. After rebellions on the island of Cheju and the town of Yŏsu were put down in 1948, South Korean guerrilla fighters adopted the Chiri Mountains as their principal fighting base. The Republic of Korea* (ROK) sent an armed force of several thousand that overwhelmed the guerrillas by the spring of 1950. Meanwhile, border fighting between the north and south erupted on the Ongjin peninsula and at Kaesŏng in the spring of 1949. The clashes intensified that summer. Syngman Rhee* and Kim Il Sung*, the southern and northern leaders, hoped to persuade their sponsors to help them launch an offensive to unify the peninsula, but neither the Soviet Union nor the United States at this time wanted their clients to fight a war. After the Americans obtained a promise from Rhee that he would not pursue a military option toward the north, U.S. troops left the peninsula in June 1949. The United States sent a military advisory group, the largest in the world, to replace the soldiers. In February 1950, Congress passed the Korea Aid Act* after initially rejecting it.

In January 1950, Soviet leader Joseph Stalin agreed to consider supporting Kim Il Sung's demand for a northern offensive. He formally approved his plans in April. After Chinese leader Mao Zedong* gave his consent in May, North Korea began its assault on the morning of 25 June 1950. Previously, U.S. officials frequently wrote about the need to defend the ROK and American prestige in the event of attack. Secretary of State Dean G. Acheson* said in January 1950 that the United Nations should be relied upon to protect nations against external aggression. Soviet documents have shown that Acheson's National

Press Club Speech* had no impact on the Communist decision to stage an invasion, but Acheson's prewar recommendation was acted upon immediately after the North Korean offensive. Following the advice of his secretary of state, President Harry S. Truman* committed American air power in Korea, brought the war to the United Nations, and ordered the Neutralization of Taiwan*, sending the Seventh Fleet to block a possible Chinese Communist assault on the island. Although the fighting in Korea was termed a UN "police action," the conflict emerged as an intense international war fought within a restricted geographical space.

In the early stages of the war, the northern army moved quickly to the Pusan Perimeter*. But on 15 September, under General Douglas MacArthur*, commander of the United Nations Command (UNC), the Tenth (X) U.S. Corps executed the brilliant amphibious Inch'ŏn Landing*, recapturing Seoul, cutting Communist supply lines, and forcing the northerners into retreat. South Korean forces crossed the thirty-eighth parallel at the end of September, the Truman administration already having decided to send U.S. and other UN troops across the border to destroy the North Korean army. Acheson was not as concerned about the local dimensions of the war as its global repercussions: a remilitarized United States under National Security Council Paper 68; a revitalized North Atlantic Treaty Organization; a unified Korea, which would strengthen U.S. plans for Japan's regional economic integration; a warning to Stalin not to use "puppet" troops to expand the Soviet empire; and a rollback of the borders of international Communism*. This fateful decision also guaranteed Chinese Intervention in the Korean War*. At his meeting with President Truman on Wake Island on 15 October, MacArthur had predicted boldly that China would not intervene in the war and that his Home by Christmas Offensive* would end the conflict. After the entry of Chinese "volunteers" forced UNC troops into full retreat, however, the general recognized that he faced an entirely new war.

In December, Truman told reporters that the use of the atomic bomb was under consideration. This brought a visit from British Prime Minister Clement Attlee, who was concerned about an expansion of the war. Attlee received only oral assurances from the president that the bomb would not be used without consultation. In the United Nations, the United States introduced a resolution on 20 January 1951 that condemned the People's Republic of China* (PRC) as an aggressor and called upon the United Nations to agree on additional measures to punish Beijing's aggression. After extensive debate and some compromise, this resolution passed on 1 February 1951 by a vote of 47–7 with nine abstentions. But Chinese troops were unable to evict the UNC from the peninsula. After the spring of 1951, the conflict was characterized by trench warfare roughly along the thirty-eighth parallel. Meanwhile, on 11 April, Truman had ordered MacArthur's Recall* largely because of concerns that his administration would not be able to control the general's efforts to expand the war to China. The decision was made several days after the administration had approved contingency plans for the use of atomic weapons in Northeast Asia. Lieutenant General Matthew B. Ridgway* replaced MacArthur as UNC commander.

Armistice negotiations began in July 1951, but dragged on over the unresolved prisoners of war (POW) issue for more than two years. Had the Korean War POW Controversy* been settled quickly, much death and destruction could have been avoided. About 45 percent of total American casualties during the war were suffered during the "peace" negotiations. As well, the United States military laid siege to the north, destroying dams, flooding villages, and leveling towns and cities. Military strategy toward the PRC also hardened in 1951 and, despite MacArthur's removal, discussions about blockading the

Chinese coast and using atomic weapons in Manchuria became commonplace. In the spring of 1951, the Truman administration endorsed NSC 48/5, a major document outlining U.S. objectives toward Korea and Asia. It contained contingency planning for naval and air action against China, and operational support for Guomindang* (Nationalist) troops should the United Nations have to evacuate Korea in the event of another sustained Communist attack.

In the winter and spring of 1953, the Eisenhower administration drew up plans for an expansion of the conflict in case the P'anmunjŏm Truce Talks* failed. These involved the utilization of atomic bombs against China coordinated with an offensive in Korea. At the end of May, in the context of allied pressures and concern over an expanded war at a time the Communists seemed willing to end the conflict, the United States threatened atomic destruction on China and Korea if its armistice proposals were not accepted. Secretary of State John Foster Dulles* would later claim in *Life* magazine that atomic diplomacy had compelled the Chinese to accept the armistice, but most historians believe that Mao and Zhou Enlai* were more concerned with resolving internal political and economic issues. With peace at hand, the ROK condemned the armistice talks and threatened to attack the north. The United States promised a mutual security pact with Korea, and Rhee eventually agreed not to take the war to the north, but not before his government unilaterally released about 27,000 North Korean POWs. Formal fighting then came to an end with the signing of the Korean Armistice Agreement* on 27 July 1953. The ROK government never signed the document and remained technically at war with the Democratic People's Republic of Korea.*

B. Cumings, *The Origins of the Korean War*, Vol. 2: *The Roaring of the Cataract, 1947–1950* (Princeton, NJ, 1990); R. Foot, *The Wrong War: American Policy and the Dimensions of the Korean Conflict,*

1950–1953 (Ithaca, NY, 1985); S. N. Goncharov, J. Lewis and L. Xue, *Uncertain Partners: Stalin, Mao, and the Korean War* (Stanford, CA, 1993); B. I. Kaufman, *The Korean War: Challenges in Crises, Credibility, and Command* (Philadelphia, 1986); S. H. Lee, *Outposts of Empire: Korea, Vietnam and the Origins of the Cold War in Asia, 1949–1954* (Montreal, 1995).

Steven Hugh Lee

KOREAN WAR POW CONTROVERSY

The Korean War* armistice negotiations began on 10 July 1951 at Kaesŏng. U.S. Vice Admiral C. Turner Joy represented the United Nations Command (UNC). The prisoner of war (POW) issue was the fourth item on the agenda. The initial UNC policy toward the POW issue was to demand a prisoner-for-prisoner exchange until all the UN prisoners were returned. The remaining Communist POWs then would be repatriated. On 5 July 1951, Major General Robert A. McClure, the chief of psychological warfare of the U.S. Army, wondered if all the Communist POWs should be repatriated, given the humanitarian and propaganda issues at stake. President Harry S. Truman* agreed. In October, the president decided that a free exchange of POWs was not equitable and that at the very least the United States should receive some major concession for an all-for-all exchange. Prisoner lists were exchanged by both sides in late 1951. The UNC listed 132,000 POWs and 37,000 civilian internees, and the Communist list counted 11,559, which the UNC disputed as too low. Partly as a result of Truman's continuing concerns about POWs, the administration began to reshape its bargaining stance.

In December 1951, Washington instructed UNC Commander General Matthew B. Ridgway* to initiate discussions about nonforcible repatriation of POWs, despite the fact that Article 118 of the 1949 Geneva Convention, which the United States had signed, stipulated that prisoners would be released and repatriated immediately after the cessation of hostilities. The Communist side immediately objected. In early April 1952, UNC negotiators told their Communist counterparts they estimated that about 116,000 of the 132,000 prisoners in their camps would accept repatriation, but a later UNC study found this initial estimate to be too high. In fact, the UNC policy toward the POWs was chaotic and many prisoners were intimidated. In addition, some 44,000 men refused to be questioned. The Chinese and North Koreans were informed on 19 April that 70,000 prisoners would return to their side. The Communists adamantly rejected this, saying that the figures could not be a basis for further discussion. The possibilities for settlement of the war thus hinged on the critical POW issue, and it was now clear that the negotiating process would be dragged out.

Soon thereafter, a riot broke out at the Kŏje-do POW camp, and the Communist prisoners forced Brigadier General Charles Colson, the commandant, to say that the UNC had treated the prisoners inhumanely and failed to follow international law. By the summer of 1952, the POW issue was entwined intricately with U.S. strategies for escalating the war and weakening the power of the Communist alliance system. To achieve greater success at the bargaining table, the UNC increased military pressure against the Communists. In 1952 and 1953, it bombed power plants and dams in an effort to flood villages, terrorize civilians, and weaken morale. Meanwhile, after much acrimonious behind-the-scenes debate at the United Nations in the fall of 1952, Washington supported an Indian proposal endorsing the principle of voluntary repatriation and calling for creation of a neutral commission to deal with those prisoners who refused to be repatriated. The Soviets rejected the resolution and Zhou Enlai* said on 28 November that only the Soviet proposal requiring forcible repatriation was acceptable. Meanwhile, the P'anmunjŏm Truce Talks* had adjourned in October after reaching a deadlock on the POW issue.

President Dwight D. Eisenhower* and his Secretary of State John Foster Dulles* took a more aggressive attitude toward the armistice negotiations, and used the POW issue as a means of creating a rift in the Sino-Soviet alliance after Soviet leader Joseph Stalin died on 5 March 1953. At the National Security Council meeting on 31 March, Eisenhower said the use of atomic weapons would be justified if the armistice line moved north to the "waist" of Korea. On 20 May, a final decision was made to expand the conflict if the Communists rejected UNC proposals, but on 4 June the Communists agreed to the principle of nonforcible repatriation and to the formation of a Neutral Nations Repatriation Commission (NNRC), which would take custody of the POWs and ensure that their decisions were authentic. Although Syngman Rhee* released 27,000 North Korean POWs two weeks later, the Korean Armistice Agreement* was signed on 27 July 1953. In August and September, the UNC transferred more than 75,000 POWs to the Chinese and North Koreans at the demilitarized zone, and 12,000 UNC soldiers were returned in this way. In late September, the nonrepatriates of both sides were turned over to the NNRC, and they began to explain their decisions to its members on 15 October. These discussions lasted ninety days, until 23 December. Of the 22,000 nonrepatriates turned over to the NNRC by the UNC, some 600 changed their minds and returned home. Of the 359 who had been in Communist custody, two Americans and eight Koreans decided on repatriation, and 21 Americans chose not to go home and were returned to the Communists.

R. Foot, *Substitute for Victory: The Politics of Peacemaking at the Korean Armistice Talks* (Ithaca, NY, 1990); W. G. Hermes, *Truce Tent and Fighting Front* (Washington, DC, 1966); S. H. Lee, *The Korean War* (London, 2001); S. H. Lee, *Outposts of Empire: Korea, Vietnam and the Origins of the Cold War in Asia, 1949–1954* (Montreal, 1995); W. W. Stueck, *The Korean War: An International History* (Princeton, NJ, 1995).

Steven Hugh Lee

KOWTOW

Kowtow (*ketou*), the act of supplication (three kneelings and nine prostrations) demanded of foreign emissaries before China's emperor, was a source of continued foreign conflict with the Chinese from about 1793 to 1860. The larger issue that what became known as "the audience question" symbolized was the clash between the principle of state-to-state equality and the Chinese effort to continue dealing with Westerners in the same manner as with tributary states. The ritual, prescribed and overseen by the Board of Rites, required an inferior to prostrate himself and knock his head to the floor before a superior. Until the British envoy Lord Macartney objected to the kowtow during his visit in 1793, Western representatives seeking trade concessions typically performed it without dissent. Macartney insisted—successfully—that he would show the emperor only the same deference shown the English throne: a bow on bended knee. However, a subsequent mission by Lord Amherst in 1816 ended in failure after he refused to perform the kowtow. After Anglo-French forces defeated Qing troops in 1860 in the Second Opium War*, Westerners won the right of ministerial residence in Beijing, but had to fight on for the right of an imperial audience without the kowtow. U.S. representatives consistently refused to perform the ritual prostration, or even to bow on bended knee. In 1873, China allowed foreigners to show respect in imperial audiences according to their own national customs, finally settling the issue.

Cambridge History of China, vol. 10 (New York, 1978); J. L. Cranmer-Byng, *An Embassy to China* (Hamden, CT, 1963); J. D. Spence, *The Search for Modern China* (New York, 1990); F. W. Williams,

The Middle Kingdom, vols. 1–2 (New York, 1913–14).

Eileen Scully

KUNG, H. H.

See KUNG XIANGXI

KUNG, PRINCE

See YIXIN

KUNG XIANGXI (1880–1967)

Kung Xiangxi (H. H. Kung), as finance minister for the Republic of China* (ROC), worked hard to win U.S. financial and military support from before and during World War II to finance China's war effort against Japan. His strong economic measures helped China sustain and win its long war against Japan. A descendant of Confucius, Kung attended American missionary schools for ten years before coming to the United States for higher education in 1901. After receiving his bachelor of arts degree from Oberlin College and master of arts degree from Yale University, Kung returned to China in 1907. Upon his return to his hometown, he established with the help of friends at Oberlin College the Mingxian Academy (Oberlin Shansi Memorial School) in Shanxi Province. Started as an elementary school, Mingxian soon expanded to offer high school education. Kung taught many subjects and was principal until 1947. Meanwhile, he became deeply involved in the antidynastic revolution. Kung met with Sun Zhongshan*, China's most famous revolutionary leader, while studying in the United States. His marriage to Song Ailing, the eldest of the three Song sisters, made Sun Zhongshan and Jiang Jieshi*, who later married Ailing's two sisters, his brothers-in-law. With such a unique background, Kung became the first minister of industry in the Guom-

indang* (Nationalist) government established at Nanjing in 1928.

Kung's greatest achievements were made during his long tenure as the minister of finance between 1933 and 1944, the most difficult years in Chinese modern history. In the first years of his tenure, he improved the tax system, finished currency reform, and imposed central control over Chinese banks. At the same time, Kung increased industrial and agricultural loans, established state monopoly over many staple goods, issued large sums of government bonds, and gave power to collect land taxes to the central government. These measures contributed to significant growth in Chinese industry, agriculture, transportation, trade, and government revenues in the 1930s. As a result, the Guomindang government was able to consolidate its power and continue its effort to defeat the Chinese Communist army. His success was highly recognized by the Chinese as well as foreign governments. After Japan launched its invasion of China in July 1937, Kung served first as premier of the Executive Yuan from January 1938 to December 1939 and then as vice premier from December 1939 to May 1945, while holding the position as minister of finance. His successful centralization of Chinese finance not only gave more power to the central government, but also provided opportunity for Kung and his family members to increase their personal wealth. His embezzlement of government funds, including U.S. loans to the ROC, caused strong resentment from the Chinese people as well as the U.S. government. Kung was forced to quit all his major government offices by 1945. He soon joined his wife in New York City and lived there in the last two decades of his life, with only four years spent in Taiwan*.

Gu Zheng, *Kung Hsiang-hsi yu Zhongguo caizheng* [Kung Xiangxi and China's Finance] (Taipei, 1979); Yan Su and Dong Junfeng, *Kung Hsiang-hsi he Song Ailing* [Kung Xiangxi and Song Ailing] (Beijing, 1994); Yu Liang, *Kung Hsiang-*

hsi zhuan [The Biography of Kung Xiangxi] (Hong Kong, 1970].

Li Hongshan

KURUSU SABURŌ (1886–1954)

A career Japanese diplomat, Kurusu Saburō participated in the last negotiations between Japan and the United States to avoid the Pearl Harbor Attack*. Born in Yokohama, he passed the foreign service examinations in 1909. In the mid-1930s, as director of the Commerce Bureau of the Foreign Ministry, Kurusu was responsible for settling trade disputes with other countries, including the United States, whose government raised tariffs on Japanese cotton goods in May 1936 after negotiations in Washington. As ambassador to Germany, Kurusu, together with Germany's Joachim Von Ribbentrop and Italy's Count Ciano, affixed his signature to the Tripartite Pact* in September 1940. Kurusu, who disagreed with his government about concluding the pact but had to obey orders, resigned from the Foreign Ministry after signing it.

In November 1941, Foreign Minister Tōgō Shigenori asked him to become a special envoy with the personal rank of ambassador for the purpose of assisting the Japanese ambassador to the United States, Nomura Kichisaburō*, in his negotiations, then at their last stage, to avoid war with the United States. Kurusu was a friend of Nomura's, and the latter, an admiral, needed an experienced career diplomat such as Kurusu at this crucial stage of the negotiations. Nomura was also fatigued. Kurusu arrived in Washington on 15 November and only three weeks later, war broke out between the United States and Japan. Early on the morning of 7 December 1941, a Japanese naval task force attacked the U.S. military installation at Pearl Harbor in Hawaii. Nomura and Kurusu, however, were in no position to know this secret military plan. The two visited U.S. Secretary of State Cordell Hull* to hand him a note informing the United States of Japan's intention to terminate negotiations, of which Hull had learned through the *Magic** decoding of the Japanese diplomatic messages. By then, Japan's attack already had been going on for fifty minutes. Hull greeted them coldly, not even asking them to sit down. "In all my fifty years of public service," he said, "I have never seen a document that was so crowded with infamous falsehoods and distortions." See also Nomura-Hull Conversations.

R. J. C. Butow, *Tōjō and the Coming of War* (Princeton, NJ, 1961); H. Feis, *The Road to Pearl Harbor: The Coming of the War Between the United States and Japan* (Princeton, NJ, 1950); I. C. Y. Hsu, "Kurusu's Mission to the United States and Abortive Modus Vivendi," *Journal of Modern History* (September 1952); P. W. Schroeder, *The Axis Alliance and Japanese-American Relations, 1941* (Ithaca, NY, 1958).

Ishii Osamu

KWANGJU INCIDENT

The Kwangju Incident of May 1980 in the Republic of Korea* (ROK), later officially termed the Kwangju Democratization Movement, provided permanent fuel for fervent South Korean Anti-Americanism* among citizens of the Chŏlla provinces and many Korean students. On 17 May 1980, General Chŏn Du-Hwan*, who had seized control of the South Korean armed forces in a bloody nighttime coup on 12 December 1979, declared martial law throughout Korea, bringing an abrupt end to the short-lived movement for democracy that followed President Pak Chŏng-hŭi's Assassination* in October 1979. The following day, students and citizens in Kwangju, the capital city of South Chŏlla Province, protested martial law and especially the arrest of Kim Dae-jung*, their favorite opposition leader, in street demonstrations that escalated almost into an armed revolt. The Kwangju uprising, however, ended after severe repression and the slaughter of many people by the ruling military. At first, Chŏn's government sent aggressive special forces troops to quell the demonstrations. Despite their brutal tactics, the special forces failed to subdue the citizens' revolt.

On 26 May, Chŏn requested that U.S. General John A. Wickham, commander of the Korean-American Combined Forces Command (CFC), release the ROK Army's Twentieth Division to put down the rebellion. The request was granted, and the next day regular army troops put an end to the resistance. Compared with the early brutal and bloody encounters, this second military action was relatively swift and effective. By the time the city was retaken, 170 people had been killed, by the official government estimate. The final death toll was raised to 240 after a reinvestigation in 1995, but the Kwangju people claim real casualties were far higher than either official number.

The tragedy has become a hot issue in Korean political life during subsequent years. In particular, it was the focus of much bitterness against Chŏn. It also inspired much of the anti-American rhetoric and action accompanying bitter demonstrations across the ROK. Anti-government dissidents charged the United States either with acquiescence or complicity in the slaughter. Many Koreans believed that the United States was at least indirectly responsible for the Kwangju tragedy by approving the commitment of Korean troops under the CFC's authority. To critics of the military dictatorship, "Kwangju" was symbolic of U.S. support for the authoritarian regime. Reacting to anti-Americanism in the ROK, the U.S. government took the unusual step of issuing an official explanation in June 1989 for the American role in the incident. Washington insisted that it was

never responsible for the tragedy because "neither troops of the Korean Special Warfare Command nor elements of the 20th Division, employed by the Martial Warfare Command in Kwangju," were under the CFC's operational command. Also, it "had neither prior knowledge of the deployment of the [special] forces to Kwangju nor responsibility for the actions there."

Unfortunately for the United States, its long-overdue account had little effect in calming rising anti-Americanism in the ROK. Anger over the American role in the Kwangju Incident increased in early 1996 when previously classified U.S. government documents were released showing that the June 1989 white paper was not the entire truth. According to these documents, top officials in the administration of President Jimmy Carter* knew of the ROK's military preparations to use military units against the pro-democracy demonstrators in Kwangju and approved of its plans. On 22 May 1980, in the midst of the Kwangju uprising, the U.S. government approved further use of force to "retake" the city and agreed to provide short-term support if Chŏn agreed to long-term political change. The May 1980 incident at Kwangju would remain a controversial and painful subject complicating U.S. relations with South Korea.

Kim Jinwung, *Hangukin ŭi Panmi Kamjŏng* [The Anti-Americanism of the Korean People] (Seoul, 1992); J. Kim, "Recent Anti-Americanism in South Korea: The Causes," *Asian Survey* (August 1989); D. Oberdorfer, *The Two Koreas: A Contemporary History* (Reading, PA, 1997); T. Shorrock, " 'Debacle in Kwangju': Were Washington's Cables Read as a Green Light for the 1980 Korean Massacre?," *Nation*, 9 December 1996; T. Shorrock, "U.S. Knew of South Korean Crackdown," *The Journal of Commerce*, 27 February 1996.

Kim Jinwung

L

LAMONT, THOMAS W. (1870–1948)

Thomas Lamont was one of the most influential partners at J. P. Morgan and Company and key architect of Morgan policy toward foreign loans, personally negotiating several key agreements with China and Japan. He became interested in Chinese investment through his firm's participation in the Six Power Consortium*, which systematized foreign loan practices in China by coordinating the actions of American, British, French, German, Japanese, and Russian banks. When President Woodrow Wilson* called for American withdrawal from the banking consortium in 1913, Lamont raised objections, but complied. Wilson's goals were to prevent foreign manipulation of China's economy and to encourage competition in the Chinese loan market. But Morgan and other American investment institutions remained reluctant to compete against foreign investment banks in the Chinese market. Another complication frustrating achievement of Wilson's goals was the subsequent outbreak of World War I. As the war absorbed the investment capital of the European powers, Japanese businessmen seized the initiative and assumed a dominant role in the continued economic development of China.

By the summer of 1918, Wilson recognized the failure of his policy. He agreed to support Lamont's efforts to resurrect the American Bankers Group as a means of coordinating U.S. investment in China. During the Paris Peace Conference, Lamont negotiated with representatives of the Japanese, British, and French banks to establish a new consortium for supervising foreign investment in China. He insisted that the postwar banking consortium would not exist to strengthen Japanese hegemony in Mongolia and Manchuria, but he also recognized the substantial advantage geographic proximity gave to Japan. After long, tense negotiations, Lamont persuaded the State Department that the consortium would concern itself with China's future economic development, not Japanese projects already well under way. This concession to Japanese interests raised the prestige of Morgan Bank in Japan, a circumstance that fostered a strong working relationship between Lamont and the governor of the Bank of Japan, Inoue Junnosuke.

During China's chaotic Warlord Era* after World War I, Lamont used his position within the American Bankers Group to discourage any large-scale loans to the Chinese government until stability could be assured. As a result, the consortium was effective in curtailing risky loans for questionable projects, but it also blocked loans designed to accelerate China's drive to a modern economy. However, Lamont's trips to China and Japan made him sensitive to the crises of natural disaster that both suffered after the war. He was involved in raising money for Chinese famine relief and responded to the Tōkyō earthquake by helping raise money for relief. But after 1924, Lamont's ability to influence U.S. policy in Asia declined as he became more sympathetic to European and Latin American financial problems. In addition, political instability in China enabled him to justify his objections to loans for that nation's modernization. As for Japan, he found the militaristic aspects of its culture offensive and, as the army exerted greater control over policy, lost interest in economic cooperation. After the Mukden Incident* in 1931, Lamont decried Japanese aggression but did not rally behind efforts to punish Japan or defend China.

R. Chernow, *The House of Morgan: An American Banking Dynasty and the Rise of Modern Finance* (New York, 1990); W. I. Cohen, *The Chinese Connection: Roger S. Green, Thomas W. Lamont, G. E. Sokolsky and American–East Asian Relations* (New York, 1978); E. M. Lamont, *The Ambassador from Wall Street: The Story of Thomas W. Lamont, J. P. Morgan's Chief Executive* (Lanham, MD, 1994).

Karen A. J. Miller

LANSDALE, EDWARD G. (1908–1987)

Edward Geary Lansdale served as a U.S. intelligence operative and Air Force officer who aided and advised the anti-Communist governments of the Philippines* and the Republic of Vietnam* during the Cold War. In World War II, he worked as an intelligence officer and in training programs for the Office of Strategic Services that took him to the Philippines and Ryūkyū Islands in 1945. Lansdale returned to the United States at the end of 1948 and was assigned to the Office of Policy Coordination, a covert operations group that eventually was absorbed into the Central Intelligence Agency*. He was sent to the Philippines in September 1950 to work closely with U.S. diplomats, military officers, and intelligence operatives in aiding the Filipino government against the Communist-led Hukbalahap* rebellion. Lansdale devised civic action and psychological warfare programs that the Filippino armed forces used effectively against the Huks. He was also deeply involved in promoting the political fortunes of Defense Secretary Ramón Magsaysay*, a politician whose integrity, strong leadership, and receptiveness to American advice had attracted the favorable attention of the Truman and Eisenhower administrations. Lansdale worked closely with him in building the organizational and financial support that helped Magsaysay win the presidency of the Philippines in September 1953.

Lansdale left the Philippines in January 1954, but returned to Asia in June to head a covert operations team, the Saigon Military Mission, that was formed in the aftermath of France's defeat at Dien Bien Phu*. His team operated in both North and South Vietnam to weaken the Communists and to strengthen the newly formed government of Ngo Dinh Diem*. When the leadership of the Binh Xuyen*, Hoa Hao, and Cao Dai* sects tried to topple Diem in the spring of 1955, Lansdale's assistance to Diem and reports to Washington played a major role in sustaining the Eisenhower administration's support for Diem. He remained in Saigon after Diem defeated the sect forces in May and gave him political advice when Diem staged a referendum that deposed Bao Dai* as Vietnam's chief of state in October 1955. Lansdale's activities initiated Eisenhower's Nation-Building Strategy* in the Republic of Vietnam*.

Lansdale returned to the United States at the end of 1956 and was assigned to work in the Pentagon as the deputy director of the defense secretary's Office of Special

Operations. He visited several Southeast Asian countries in this position in early 1959 and at the same time may have been involved in a plot by General Dap Chhuon to overthrow Cambodia's Norodom Sihanouk*. He briefly returned to Vietnam in late 1960 and described the Diem regime's troubles in a report that attracted the notice of incoming President John F. Kennedy*, who considered appointing him as ambassador to Saigon. But opposition from diplomatic and military officials, who had been antagonized by Lansdale's freewheeling behavior, blocked appointment. He nevertheless remained deeply involved in Vietnamese affairs.

Lansdale retired from the U.S. Air Force in October 1963, but was recalled to Vietnam two years later when Ambassador Henry Cabot Lodge Jr.* asked him to serve as a senior liaison officer in the embassy in Saigon. Lansdale was supposed to coordinate pacification programs in South Vietnam, but had no effective authority to carry out his responsibilities. He instead dispensed advice to U.S. and Vietnamese officials until he resigned in June 1968. Lansdale's departure from Saigon marked his retirement from public life, but he continued giving the U.S. government informal advice about Third World trouble spots until his death. He wrote *In the Midst of Wars*, a memoir of his work in the Philippines and Vietnam, an interesting anecdotal account of his exploits masking the extent of his covert activities. Some claimed that the lead character in *The Quiet American* was based on Lansdale, but author Graham Greene* denied this. However, Landsdale was the model for the title character in the 1957 best-selling novel *The Ugly American*.

D. L. Anderson, *Trapped by Success: The Eisenhower Administration and Vietnam, 1953–1961* (New York, 1991); C. B. Currey, *Edward Lansdale: The Unquiet American* (Boston, 1988); E. G. Lansdale, *In the Midst of Wars: An American's Mission to Southeast Asia* (New York, 1972).

Joseph G. Morgan

LANSING, ROBERT (1864–1928)

Robert Lansing played a key role in U.S. policy toward China and Japan as secretary of state from 1915 to 1920. Born in Watertown, New York, he graduated from Amherst College in 1886. Admitted to the bar in 1889, young Lansing's legal career changed dramatically after his marriage in 1890 to Eleanor Foster, the daughter of John W. Foster*, a noted international lawyer who soon would serve as secretary of state. He entered the field of international law and served as Foster's associate counsel for the U.S. government in the fur seal arbitration case in 1893. His legal work with international tribunals included the Alaskan Boundary Tribunal (1903), the North Atlantic Coast Fisheries Arbitration (1909), and the British-American Claims Arbitration (1912–1914). In April 1914, Lansing was appointed counselor for the State Department and over the next fourteen months, served as acting secretary of state during the frequent absences of William Jennings Bryan*. Much of Bryan's diplomatic correspondence was clearly the work of Lansing. Named secretary of state *ad interim* after Bryan resigned in 1915, he supervised the purchase of the Danish West Indies (Virgin Islands) in 1917 and worked to maintain U.S. support in Latin America amid ongoing friction with Mexico. As for World War I, he drafted protests of British violations of U.S. neutrality, using such harsh language that he upset U.S. Ambassador to Britain Walter Hines Page. Lansing was so decidedly pro-British, however, that he undercut the final U.S. attempt in December 1916 to mediate a settlement in the war.

Once the United States entered World War I in April 1917, Lansing turned his attention to smoothing relations with Japan to keep that nation as an ally in the war against Germany, culminating in the signing of the Lansing-Ishii Agreement*. As the war drew to a close, his suggestions for a peace settlement largely were ignored by

President Woodrow Wilson*, who, with Colonel Edward M. House, drafted plans for a new international organization without consulting the secretary of state. Although Lansing held serious reservations about the Versailles Peace Treaty*, he nevertheless advocated its passage as a better alternative to no treaty at all. He especially disagreed vehemently with Wilson on the Shandong Agreement*. In an effort to appease the Japanese and secure their participation in the League of Nations, Wilson agreed to allow Japan to hold the Shandong concession that Japan had seized from Germany during the war. Lansing considered this "an iniquitous agreement," yet he was seen by some members of the Chinese delegation in Paris as "the chief betrayer of China." Lansing's reservations about the treaty and the League of Nations became apparent during hearings on the treaty in the U.S. Senate during September 1919. Bedridden after a severe stroke, Wilson demanded Lansing's resignation, ostensibly because Lansing had presided over cabinet meetings during the president's five-month convalescence.

Following his resignation, Lansing returned to the practice of international law. He resumed his role as counsel to the Chinese legation in Washington, and in 1921 he advised the Chinese delegation to the Washington Conference*. However, Lansing found it difficult to advise representatives from a government in Beijing that could not speak for the entire nation, as the rival government of Sun Zhongshan* in Guangzhou refused to form a joint delegation. Also, the delegation that arrived in Washington was badly divided between those Lansing considered "idealistic," for their refusal to negotiate with Japan directly, and the "practical," who were intent on winning some kind of settlement. In February 1922, the Japanese agreed to withdraw their troops in return for monetary compensation. Although the Chinese were unhappy with this compromise, Lansing saw it as a "signal victory" for China. Lansing, known for his courtesy and tact,

enjoyed drawing, and frequently delighted his cabinet colleagues by sketching their portraits during meetings.

S. G. Craft, "John B. Moore, Robert Lansing and the Shandong Question," *Pacific Historical Review* (May 1997); D. D. Lazo, "A Question of Loyalty: Robert Lansing and the Treaty of Versailles," *Diplomatic History* (Winter 1985); J. W. Pratt, "Robert Lansing, Secretary of State, June 23, 1915, to February 13, 1920," in S. F. Bemis (ed.), *American Secretaries of State and Their Diplomacy* (New York, 1929); D. M. Smith, *Robert Lansing and American Neutrality, 1914–1917* (Berkeley, CA, 1958).

Michael J. Devine

LANSING-ISHII AGREEMENT (2 November 1917)

The Lansing-Ishii Agreement was an understanding between the United States and Japan regarding China. After the United States entered World War I in April 1917, U.S. policy makers, in particular Secretary of State Robert Lansing* and Colonel Edward M. House, pondered the most efficient means to contain Japanese expansion in Asia while avoiding confrontation. Specifically, they were eager to maintain the territorial integrity of China and preserve the Open Door Policy* regarding Chinese markets. With the Europeans at war, Japan sought to fill Asian markets deserted by the Western powers. The Japanese also endeavored to develop their possessions in Korea, Manchuria, and Taiwan* with greater energy and resolution. Japan enhanced and extended its political and economic position in China through its imposition of the Twenty-One Demands* of 1915. After accepting all but six of these demands, China requested U.S. aid to restrain Japan from acquiring the German possessions in Shandong. In response, Lansing said that although the U.S. friendship with China was "sincere," becoming engaged with Japan in China "would be quixotic in the extreme."

The Japanese were desirous of securing

American recognition of their gains in China. In September 1917, Viscount Ishii Kikujirō* arrived in Washington as head of a special diplomatic mission to discuss the conflicting interests between Japan and the United States. During the negotiations, Ishii argued that Japan's interests in China were similar to those the United States claimed in Latin America under the Monroe Doctrine. Under instructions from Japanese Foreign Minister Motono Ichirō, Ishii asserted that Japan held "paramount interests" in China, just as the United States did in Mexico. Lansing thought the term "paramount" was much too strong, substituting "peculiar interests." On 2 November 1917, his letter to Ishii expressed agreement that "territorial propinquity creates special relations" and recognized Japan's interests in those territories "to which her possessions are contiguous," meaning Manchuria and the recently seized Shandong. To avoid a break in diplomatic relations, Lansing and Ishii arrived at an agreement that not only was necessarily vague and ambiguous, but incorporated contradictory principles. It affirmed the "open door" in China, as well as its independence and respect for her integrity, but it also conceded in contradiction that Japan had "special interests in China."

Lansing pointed out to Ishii that the agreement left "ample room for suitable interpretations on both sides." Indeed, the Japanese saw the document as granting them a free hand to act as they pleased in their Chinese possessions, whereas President Woodrow Wilson* viewed the agreement as fully committing Japan to the principles of the Open Door Policy. The agreement maintained the status quo in China for the remainder of World War I. However, even though it temporarily calmed U.S.-Japanese differences, the agreement did nothing to address the basic causes of the tensions, and neither side was left completely happy. Eventually, the Lansing-Ishii Agreement was abrogated after the signing of the Nine Power Pact* in 1922 and formally announced the follow-ing year. The details of a secret protocol in the Lansing-Ishii Agreement, which pledged both nations to avoid taking advantage of the war to gain special privileges in China, was not made known until the U.S. State Department released the document in 1938. *See also* Shandong Agreement; Edward T. Williams.

B. F. Beers, *Vain Endeavor: Robert Lansing's Attempt to End the American-Japanese Rivalry* (Durham, NC, 1962); R. W. Curry, *Woodrow Wilson and Far Eastern Policy, 1913–1921* (New York, 1957); W. LaFeber, *The Clash: A History of U.S.-Japan Relations* (New York, 1997); C. Neu, *The Troubled Encounter: The United States and Japan* (New York, 1975).

Michael J. Devine

LAOS

Along with Vietnam and Cambodia*, Laos was part of French Indochina* at the beginning of the twentieth century. French Colonialism* left the nation economically exploited and politically oppressed until Japanese occupation during World War II. France's failure to reassert postwar control climaxed with its defeat at Dien Bien Phu*. Following separation under the Geneva Accords of 1954*, American influence in Laos soon eclipsed that of France. For example, the United States then extended its Southeast Asia Treaty Organization* (SEATO) umbrella over Laos in the event of external attack. It also "established a disguised military mission" in December 1955 known as the Programs Evaluation Office. Washington, using threats to withhold aid, was able to keep the Communist Pathet Lao* out of a coalition government. In November 1957, however, Prime Minister Souvanna Phouma* entered a "settlement" with half-brother and nominal Pathet Lao leader Souphanouvong* whereby the Communists would join a coalition government called National Union in return for Royal Lao government administrative control of the two northern provinces held by the Pathet Lao. Two battalions of Pathet Lao troops also were to be integrated into the national army.

Acute American anxiety about Communist expansion in Laos eased in 1959, when the pro-American Phoui Sananikone government arrested the Lao Patriotic Front deputies, including Souphanouvong. Fighting then broke out on the border with the Democratic Republic of Vietnam* in July. The deputies escaped from jail in May 1960. Then, in August, Kong Le* led a bloodless coup and called for restoration of Souvanna as prime minister. Phoumi Nosavan*, the ousted leader, then enlisted Eisenhower administration assistance through the Central Intelligence Agency*, receiving aircraft and military aid to topple Kong Le, but his forces were routed. After the neutralist Souvanna's return to power, the United States continued to support the anti-Communist Phoumi with aid. Phoumi attacked Vientiane late in 1960 and Souvanna asked for Soviet assistance. North Vietnamese troops arrived to join Kong Le's forces in the Plain of Jars. Hmong* tribal fighters under Vang Pao* then requested, and received, U.S. arms to fight the incursion. President Dwight D. Eisenhower* remarked that if not for the effect on the rest of East Asia, "we ought to let Laos go down the drain." Laos was considered "the front line" in Southeast Asia in the fight against Communism*. Washington therefore pledged to assist the Laotian government if it requested SEATO action.

When John F. Kennedy* became president, his first challenge was the Laotian Crisis of 1961*. At the June 1961 Vienna summit, Kennedy and Soviet leader Nikita Khrushchev agreed that the issue should not create a confrontation between them. Therefore, a neutral Laos was sought through the Geneva Accords of 1962*. As a result, the United States shifted its allegiance from the rightists in Laos, headed by Phoumi Nosavan, to the neutralists, represented by Souvanna Phouma and Kong Le. Souvanna's new cabinet that year consisted of seven neutralists, four Pathet Lao, and four rightists. But North Vietnam

refused to withdraw its 10,000 troops as stipulated by Geneva and proceeded to expand the Ho Chi Minh Trail*. This pushed Souvanna into closer cooperation with Lao rightists and the United States, causing the Pathet Lao members to vacate the cabinet. The United States used its air supremacy in Laos to drop supplies through Air America* to Hmong tribesmen, and authorized its ambassador to Laos to order air strikes (Project 404) against Communist installations and supply routes, including the use of napalm.

The civil war largely seesawed back and forth between 1965 and 1973, with Communist forces getting the upper hand during the dry season and the government regaining territory in the rainy season. U.S. bombing of the Ho Chi Minh Trail within Laos intensified after the U.S. bombing halt of North Vietnam in 1968. The "Laotian Incursion" of February 1971 found South Vietnamese troops, backed by American air and logistical support, driven out of Laos by North Vietnamese troops. A peace treaty between the Lao government and the Pathet Lao was signed on 21 February 1973, but the termination of the Secret U.S. Air War in Laos* allowed the Pathet Lao and North Vietnamese to continue their hostilities at will. The 1975 collapse of the Republic of Vietnam* and the Lon Nol* regime in Cambodia hastened the decline of the Royal Lao government, as Souvanna resigned and King Savang abdicated. The Lao People's Democratic Republic was proclaimed on 2 December 1975, with Souphanouvong as its first president. The new regime was repressive and isolated. In 1995, following a two-decade hiatus, American relations with Laos started to improve, as the United States announced it was no longer prohibiting assistance to the exceedingly poor country.

A. J. Dommen, *Conflict in Laos: The Politics of Neutralization* (New York, 1971); A. M. Savada (ed.), *Laos: A Country Study*, Department of State Central Files, National Archives, Washington, DC; C. A. Stevenson, *American Policy Toward*

Laos Since 1954 (Boston, 1972); M. Stuart-Fox, *A History of Laos* (Cambridge, MA, 1997).

Gregory J. Murphy

LAOTIAN CRISIS OF 1961

Laos* was the first international crisis John F. Kennedy* faced as president. The civil war between right-wing Lao forces supported by the United States and Thailand* and North Vietnamese–supported leftist Pathet Lao* and their neutralist allies turned sour from Washington's perspective in the last days of the Eisenhower administration. Forces under Phoumi Nosavan*, which had recaptured Vientiane in December 1960, proved incompetent and ineffectual, suffering a succession of humiliating military defeats in which they hardly put up even token resistance. Kennedy and Dwight D. Eisenhower* met on 19 January 1961, the day before the new president's inauguration. Multiple accounts of this meeting differ in slant, but clearly Eisenhower was putting Kennedy on notice that Laos was the number one trouble spot requiring urgent attention, if not U.S. military intervention. Kennedy did not follow the outgoing president's advice. Instead, as president, he initiated a policy debate in his administration on how best to respond to the crisis. As a result of these deliberations, the president realized that U.S. military options in Laos were very limited. U.S. military airlift capability was inadequate, Laos lacked airfields and facilities, and the Joint Chiefs of Staff were unwilling to commit to another limited conflict in Asia that resembled the Korean War*. Neutralization seemed the only solution, but it had to be negotiated from strength.

As Kennedy's advisers were deliberating, the continued military success of the Pathet Lao, North Vietnamese, and their neutralist allies under Kong Le* endangered the capital of Vientiane. To demonstrate U.S. concern, Kennedy ordered preliminary military moves, including placing U.S. forces on alert in Okinawa and dispatching the U.S. Seventh Fleet aircraft carriers with 1,400 marines to the Gulf of Thailand. The U.S. State Department orchestrated a diplomatic campaign among key allies, neutrals, and the Soviet Union in support of neutralization of Laos. Kennedy held a televised press conference on 23 March and, armed with three maps showing the Pathet Lao's advance from December 1960 to March 1961, warned of the dangers in Laos, blamed the North Vietnamese and Soviets for encouraging Pathet Lao aggression, backed neutralization of Laos, and threatened unspecified U.S. and Southeast Asia Treaty Organization* action if the Pathet Lao attacks did not stop. Washington asked Moscow to use its influence to bring the Democratic Republic of Vietnam* and the Pathet Lao to the conference table. Neutralist leader Souvanna Phouma* and Souphanouvong,* the leader of the Pathet Lao, conferred in Moscow and Beijing about neutralization.

In late April 1961, the important town of Vang Vieng fell to the Pathet Lao, opening the way to seizure of Vientiane. The Kennedy administration held another round of policy meetings. The president, already shaken by what he considered bad military advice in the Bay of Pigs fiasco in Cuba earlier that month, received so many conflicting recommendations that he pinned his hopes solely on neutralization by an international conference. After a temporary and tenuous cease-fire was declared in Laos, the Geneva Conference began on 16 May 1961 and the Laos crisis subsided, but the Lao factions continued to fight. Phoumi made a disastrous decision in early 1962 to contest the Pathet Lao in Nam Tha. The Pathet Lao routed Phoumi's troops in May 1962, mostly on the strength of unconfirmed and ultimately incorrect rumors that North Vietnamese and Chinese troops had joined the fight. Meanwhile, the Kennedy administration agreed to send a token force of 4,000 U.S. troops to Thailand and move 1,000 U.S. troops already there next to the Laos border to send the North Vietnamese a signal of U.S. determination and to re-assure the Thais of support. Soon after this deployment, the Lao factions agreed to the Geneva Accords of 1962* on Laos.

A. J. Dommen, *Conflict in Laos: The Politics of Neutralization* (New York, 1971); F. I. Greenstein and R. H. Immerman, "What Did Eisenhower Tell Kennedy About Indochina? The Politics of Misperception," *Journal of American History* (September 1992); C. A. Stevenson, *American Policy Toward Laos Since 1954* (Boston, 1972); M. Stuart-Fox, *A History of Laos* (Cambridge, MA, 1997).

Edward C. Keefer

LATTIMORE, OWEN (1900–1989)

Senator Joseph R. McCarthy* targeted Asia expert Owen Lattimore as a Soviet spy to prove his case that Communists were subverting the U.S. government. Born in Washington, D.C., Lattimore moved with his family to Shanghai in 1901, where his father taught language in Chinese government schools. From 1913 to 1917, he was educated in Switzerland and England, but insufficient family finances prevented him from pursuing a college degree. Returning to China in 1919, Lattimore worked for a newspaper, but in 1922 he joined a trade firm that exported produce from the frontier. Traveling throughout China, he learned the Chinese, Russian, and Mongol languages. From August 1926 to September 1927, an extended trip took him to Mongolia, Soviet Central Asia, and Chinese Turkestan, leading to the publication of his first two books. Thereafter, Lattimore held a fellowship at Harvard University's Yenching Institute, was editor of *Pacific Affairs*, the journal of the Institute of Pacific Relations* (IPR), and won fellowships from the Guggenheim Foundation, Social Science Research Council, and Royal Geographical Society that supported his residence in Beijing and travel for research in Manchuria and Mongolia. His fascination with the Mongols led to several influential publications that judged their nomadic lifestyle as more flexible than the sedentary Chinese. Lattimore joined journalists who visited the headquarters of the Chinese Communist Party* at Yan'an in 1937, concluding that Mao Zedong* represented China's agricultural society. Forced to leave after the Marco Polo Bridge Incident* that July, he joined Johns Hopkins University as a lecturer in history and then became director of the Walter Hines Page School of International Relations.

Lattimore was a widely known, highly respected, and extensively published Asia specialist when, on the recommendation of President Franklin D. Roosevelt*, he became an adviser to Generalissimo Jiang Jieshi* of the Republic of China* in July 1941. During his six months in Chongqing, he developed decidedly negative views toward the Guomindang* (Nationalist) government. After spending time with the Office of War Information, he traveled to Siberia and China with Vice President Henry A. Wallace in 1944. Reportedly, his *Solution in Asia* (1945) was one of only two books on East Asia on the desk of President Harry S. Truman* when he announced the surrender of Japan in August 1945, in which Lattimore warned the Allies not to ignore the demands of Asian nations for postwar self-determination. That fall, conservative commentators began raising doubts about Lattimore's loyalty because of his uncritical attitude toward the Soviet Union, adamant rejection that Mao was Moscow's puppet, and hostility toward Jiang's regime. In October 1949, he attended a State Department meeting where he spoke in favor of noninvolvement in the Chinese Civil War* and suggested possible future recognition of the People's Republic of China*. Just four months later, Senator McCarthy accused the China Hands* in the State Department of acting to ensure the Communist triumph in China. When his critics demanded proof, McCarthy said that he would "stand or fall" on his charge that Lattimore, who held no position in the U.S. government, was "the top Soviet agent in the United States."

In April 1950, Lattimore appeared before the Senate committee investigating the loyalty of State Department employees. After charges against him were dismissed in July, he publicly denounced McCarthy. This only incited more accusations from the senator that Lattimore was a Communist and guilty of treasonous behavior. Pressure grew on Johns Hopkins to fire him, and income he earned from his newspaper and invited lectures plummeted. Lattimore appeared before the Senate Internal Security Subcommittee as part of a probe of the IPR beginning in July 1951, which concluded a year later with a finding that he had been "a conscious articulate instrument of Soviet policy" and was guilty of perjury. Efforts by the Justice Department to convict him of perjury failed twice because the charges infringed on his constitutional rights, but the State Department denied him a passport. In 1953, Lattimore resigned as director, but stayed on as a lecturer at Johns Hopkins. It was not until 1960 and 1961 that he was allowed to visit the Soviet Union and Mongolia. In 1963, he became director of the Department of Chinese Studies at the University of Leeds in England. In 1970, he retired and returned to the United States, his dream of starting a Mongolian studies program at a major university unfulfilled. Admired for his tact and self-effacement, Lattimore was certainly among the greatest victims of McCarthyism.

D. D. Buck, "Lattimore, Owen," in J. A. Garraty and M. C. Carnes (eds.), *American National Biography* (New York, 1999); J. Cotton, *Asian Frontier Nationalism: Owen Lattimore and the American Policy Debate* (Atlantic Heights, NJ, 1989); O. Lattimore, *Ordeal by Slander* (Boston, 1950); *New York Times*, 1 June 1989; R. P. Newman, *Owen Lattimore and the "Loss" of China* (Berkeley, CA, 1992).

James I. Matray

LE DUC THO (1910–1990)

Le Duc Tho was a member of the Lao Dong (Communist) Political Bureau from 1951 to 1986 and chief negotiator for the Democratic Republic of Vietnam* (DRV) at the Paris Peace Talks*. Born in the northern province of Nam Dinh into a middle-class mandarin family, Phan Dinh Khai (his real name) joined the revolutionary cause against French Colonialism* at an early age. Although both his father and uncle were bureaucrats in the French colonial administration, three brothers were active members of the Vietnamese Communist Party. Tho was a founding member of the Indochinese Communist Party. Like most revolutionaries, he spent time during the 1930s in the French island prison of Poulo Condore, where he endured underground cells, heat, humidity, and disease. As the top Vietminh commissar during the First Indochina War*, Tho was responsible for directing the insurgency in southern Vietnam. He was involved in the southern insurgency and played a key role in directing the southern war until 1968. Tho also gained a reputation as a skilled theoretician and was often relied upon to guide party policy. After the death of Ho Chi Minh* in 1969, Le Duc Tho and Le Duan were the architects of the party's shift toward the Soviet Union.

In 1970, Tho was sent to Paris to head the DRV delegation. From 1970 to 1973, he met with Henry A. Kissinger* in covert negotiations for a peace settlement. For him, long, protracted negotiations were a form of guerrilla warfare, and the talks initially produced few substantive results. In the wake of a renewed U.S. bombing campaign against the north, Kissinger and Tho both agreed to compromises by the early summer of 1972. Kissinger backed away from unqualified support of the Republic of Vietnam* and its President Nguyen Van Thieu*, agreeing to support a tripartite electoral commission in the south. He also suggested that North Vietnam's troops remain in the south after a cease-fire. Tho dropped his unconditional demand for Thieu's removal from power. These compromises sparked angry reactions from southern allies of both the DRV and the

United States. Nevertheless, by October 1972, both sides appeared to have settled the major issues, but then haggled for weeks over the subtleties. President Richard M. Nixon* ordered a second round of LINEBACKER Bombings* against the north to force the DRV's hand. Historians still debate the impact of these massive and devastating airstrikes on the negotiations.

Tho and Kissinger ultimately reached a final agreement in January 1973 that differed little from the October draft. The Paris Peace Accords* provided for American withdrawal from Vietnam, but left the political future of South Vietnam unresolved. For this dubious achievement, Tho and Kissinger were jointly awarded the Nobel Peace Prize, which Tho rejected because the war continued. In 1975, he would return to the south and personally supervise the final stages of the Ho Chi Minh campaign for final military conquest of the south. Until his retirement in 1986, Tho remained an active member of the Vietnamese Communist Party Central Committee and helped plan the Cambodia* incursion in late 1978. He also directed the Party Organization Department, which supervised the assignment of cadres in party and state organs. Tho's influence weakened in the mid-1980s, however, and he resigned his post in 1986 in response to the introduction of sweeping economic reforms at the Sixth Party Congress.

G. C. Herring, *America's Longest War: The United States and Vietnam 1950–1975* (New York, 1996); S. Karnow, *Vietnam: A History* (New York, 1983); Truong Nhu Tang, *A Vietcong Memoir* (New York, 1985); M. B. Young, *The Vietnam Wars 1945–1990* (New York, 1991).

Robert K. Brigham

LEA, HOMER (1876–1912)

Homer Lea was a military trainer, adviser, and leader during the Chinese Revolution of 1911* for Kang Youwei and Sun Zhongshan*. Maimed in his childhood, he was a hunchback with poor eyesight, who topped not more than five feet and weighed less than eighty pounds. He entered Stanford University in 1895, but left before graduation to join the U.S. Army. Rejected because of his height, Lea began self-study in military strategy. Soon, he became interested in the anti-Qing activities producing unrest in China at the end of the nineteenth century. When Kang Youwei, who had failed in the 1898 protest for constitutional reform and modernization, escaped to the United States, Lea called on him and had a long talk about the Chinese situation. He asserted that if Kang had an army, he would drive straight into Beijing to clear away the conservative diehards in the court and support the Guangxu emperor in his implementation of reform. Lea added that he was willing to work for China without salary. In 1900, the Chinese royalists organized branches of their military institution titled "sports clubs" in San Francisco, Los Angeles, and New York and appointed Lea the commanding general. Lea trained four contingents of troops, all the soldiers sons of overseas Chinese and all the officers Americans, with himself as military leader. At that time, wherever there hung a portrait of Kang Youwei, there was a portrait of Lea beside it. In 1902, the Guangxu emperor appointed Lea as his senior general.

In 1904, Lea began to change his mind after reading a book by Sun Zhongshan. After Rong Hong* arranged his secret contact with Sun, he began to collect funds, train revolutionaries, and devise strategies for the revolutionary party. With Rong Hong and others, he devised a plan in 1909 to collect money from financial circles in the United States. Lea met Sun in Los Angeles in 1910 and presented a strategic plan to launch small-scale actions in preparation for a major operation, which Sun accepted. On hearing the news of the Wuchang Uprising on 10 October 1911, Lea, in London, cabled Sun, asking to accompany him to China. Sun arrived in London on 20 November and with Lea persuaded a banking consortium of the United States, Britain,

France and Germany to stop lending money to the Qing government. Though in very poor health, Lea then went to China with Sun, seeing his life as synonymous with China's revolutionary cause. Sun was elected provisional president of China and appointed Lea his military adviser. After the Taft administration strictly forbade him to hold the post, Lea wrote publicly that since he was not an officer on the active list, his private action was of no concern to the government. On 12 February 1912, Lea attended the ceremony at which the Qing emperor Puyi* gave up his throne. Three days later, he suffered a cerebral hemorrhage, and he returned to the United States in May 1913. Dying that December, his last wish expressed in his testament was to be buried in China.

Guo Shi Guan (ed.), *Zhonghua minguo shishi jiyao* [Summary of the History of the Republic of China] (Taibei); Huang Jilu, *General Homer Lea's Contribution to Chinese Revolution* (Taibei, 1974).

Xiang Liling

LEE KUAN YEW (1923–   )

Lee Kuan Yew held the position of prime minister of Singapore* from 1959 to 1990, when he was elevated to the elder statesman rank of senior minister. He was the founder of the People's Action Party, which led the fight to win independence from British rule. From the time Singapore became independent, the Cambridge-educated Lee used his intellectual brilliance, determination, and tactical skills to dominate his country's politics. These abilities ultimately made him a world figure whose influence greatly surpassed his country's intrinsic importance. Conscious of the vulnerability of a small island, a largely Chinese enclave with a population of only 1–2 million surrounded by Malay neighbors, he always was driven by the need to seek protection from friendly, larger powers. This was particularly the case after the acrimonious termination in 1965 of Singapore's brief union with its larger neighbor, Malaysia*, a partnership of which Lee had been a major architect and enthusiastic supporter.

Lee, once he attained power, was fiercely anti-Communist, which endeared him both to Britain, Singapore's colonial ruler until 1963, and the United States. In 1971, the closing of Britain's military bases in Singapore led Lee to look toward the United States as a substitute patron. In the mid-1960s, he made a brief show of sympathy with the nonaligned movement and condemned U.S. involvement in the Second Indochina War* as both unjustified and unwise. Soon, he was ready to request American aid to promote Singapore's economic development, assistance more readily given because of U.S. eagerness to build pro-Western bulwarks elsewhere in Southeast Asia. During a visit to the United States in 1967, Lee also warned U.S. leaders that their premature disengagement from Vietnam would be disastrous. Although no U.S. installations ever replaced the British bases and Singapore never signed any treaty of alliance with the United States, the warmer relationship won Singapore sophisticated U.S. military equipment precisely geared to the island's specific requirements. Despite Lee's often biting criticisms over the years of what he perceived as American gaucheness and ineptness, from the administration of Lyndon B. Johnson* onward, successive U.S. leaders courted Lee and characterized him as Southeast Asia's most dynamic figure, whose country's dazzling economic growth, order, and stability were a model of what well-managed non-Communist developing countries could achieve.

Simultaneously, however, leading American journalists and, on occasion, the U.S. government criticized Lee for being authoritarian in his domestic practices, especially the censorship of publications critical of the government, including on occasion leading Western journals and newspapers, and using the legal system to harass opponents of the People's Action Party. Lee defended strongly the right of Asians to run their own affairs according to their own cultural mores and traditions, emphasizing the manner in which Asians place the good of the entire community above the rights of the individual. He clearly believed these values were superior to those of the West and gave them much of the credit for Asian economic successes prior to the East Asian Financial Crisis*. Even so, Lee issued repeated public admonitions as the twentieth century ended against any potential U.S. military withdrawal from Asia, arguing that in the past, U.S. defense of Vietnam prevented the further spread of Communism*. To Lee, continued U.S. presence in the western Pacific was necessary to maintain stability and to check potentially overbearing regional powers such as Japan and China.

A. Josey, *Lee Kuan Yew*, 2 vols. (Singapore, 1980); Lee Kuan Yew, *The Singapore Story*, 2 vols. (Singapore, 1998, 2000); J. Minchin, *No Man Is an Island: A Study of Singapore's Lee Kuan Yew* (London, 1986); G. K. Pang, *Lee Kuan Yew: The Man and His Ideas* (Singapore, 1997).

Priscilla Roberts

LEGENDRE, CHARLES (1830–1899)

Charles LeGendre, as the U.S. consul at Xiamen, participated in the unsuccessful U.S. naval expedition against Taiwan* in 1867, which was a reaction to the killing of the crew members during the *General Sherman* Incident* the year before. Born in France, he migrated to the United States and later served in the Union Army, rising to the rank of brigadier general and losing one eye in the Battle of the Wildness. After the Civil War, however, the United States became too tame for his adventurous spirit. In 1866, LeGendre obtained his diplomatic appointment to China, but since Washington was not prepared for any large-scale overseas military involvement there, he decided to organize his own punitive force. Having gathered under him a Chinese gunboat and a battalion of mercenaries, he returned to Taiwan after 1867, swearing

destruction. When Chinese authorities in Taiwan promised that shipwrecked Americans would be protected in the future, a disappointed LeGendre had to end the hostile action. Unsatisfied, he occupied himself with collecting information concerning Taiwan, hoping for the day when he could extract appropriate retribution.

LeGendre did not have to wait for long. In 1872, he was on his way to the United States when he met in Japan with Charles DeLong, then U.S. minister to Japan. Convinced that Japan should be an ally of the United States, DeLong had been supportive of Japanese plans to conquer Korea and Taiwan. After introduction to the Japanese Foreign Office, LeGendre subsequently was hired as a second-rank counselor in Japan's embassy to Beijing. He played an important role in negotiations between Japan and China surrounding the killing of the Ryūkyū fishermen by the Taiwanese aborigines, and earned much respect from his Japanese superiors. The Japanese promised that if a war ensued, he would be made a general, and after Taiwan was conquered, the first governor of that island.

The Chinese government, realizing that LeGendre was working for the Japanese, tried to tempt him by offering a post in the Chinese custom house at a $20,000 annual salary. Determined to fulfill his ambition, LeGendre turned it down. The Chinese then protested to Washington that its citizens were engaged in activities hostile to Chinese interests. Having no interest in Asia beyond commerce, the United States ordered its citizens to disengage from the Japanese expedition. LeGendre was arrested for violating this neutrality edict. After his release, he returned to Japan for a few years, and became the first foreigner awarded the Order of the Rising Sun. Later, he moved to Korea and became the adviser on the Korean trade relations. Then, in 1891, he returned to Japan as the Korean envoy, seeking to revise the Korean-Japanese trade agreement.

T. Dennett, *Americans in Eastern Asia: A Critical Study of the Policy of the United States with Reference to China, Japan and Korea in the 19th Century* (New York, 1963); R. O'Connor, *Pacific Destiny: An Informal History of the U.S. in the Far East* (Boston, 1999).

Li Yi

LEMAY, CURTIS E. (1906–1990)

Major General Curtis E. LeMay was the U.S. Army Air Force (USAAF) commander most noted for his strategic bomber offensive against Japan from the Mariana Islands in 1945. Having developed the technique of "pattern bombing" in the daylight air war against Germany, LeMay was assigned to the China-Burma-India Theater* in 1944, where he supervised the "Over the Hump" Flights* into China, as well as the B-29 offensive against Japan mounted from India and staged through Chinese airfields. In January 1945, he assumed command of the twentieth USAAF's twenty-first bomber command based in the Marianas. Determined to demonstrate the critical effectiveness of air power before the onset of an amphibious invasion of Japan, LeMay changed offensive strategy from high-level precision attacks with high explosive bombs to low-level incendiary raids in specially lightened B-29s. This morally controversial tactical innovation had devastating effect. On the night of 9–10 March 1945, 25 percent of Tōkyō was destroyed in a firestorm. Further incendiary attacks were launched in rapid succession against Nagoya, Ōsaka, Kōbe, and Nagoya again. LeMay depleted his supply of incendiary bombs and, soon after, was ordered to prepare air support for the Battle of Okinawa*.

As with other horrors of World War II, LeMay was not ordered to incinerate Japanese cities. His commander, General Henry "Hap" Arnold, "merely expected action out of me," he later explained. Although the Joint Chiefs of Staff sanctioned firebombing of both Chinese and Japanese

cities and President Franklin D. Roosevelt* was informed of the fire raids, no one ever inquired about the consequences of such tactics. When the atomic bomb became available in July 1945, Le May considered it merely an extension of incendiary bombing. He, and his superiors, ignored the fact that the Tōkyō firestorm was a kind of "planned accident," whereas the Atomic Attacks* were a "planned certainty." After the war, LeMay served on the Joint Chiefs of Staff. He briefly resurfaced in the 1968 presidential campaign, calling for massive bombing of the Democratic Republic of Vietnam* to reduce it to "a parking lot" as vice presidential running mate with third-party candidate George Wallace.

C. E. LeMay and M. Kantor, *Mission with LeMay* (New York, 1965); R. Schaffer, *Wings of Judgment: American Bombing in World War II* (New York, 1985); M. S. Sherry, *The Rise of American Air Power: The Creation of Armageddon* (New Haven, CT, 1987).

Errol M. Clauss

LEND LEASE

Lend Lease was the major program of the U.S. government to aid the countries fighting the Axis powers early in World War II while still maintaining an official American neutrality toward the European and Asian wars. Britain's Winston Churchill compelled President Franklin D. Roosevelt* to challenge congressional isolationists directly when, on 8 December 1940, he informed the president that Britain had depleted its financial reserves and could continue its war effort only if the United States provided the means to maintain the flow of war materiel to Britain. Following Japan's decision of 1940 to join the Axis alliance with Germany and Italy in the Tripartite Pact*, the Roosevelt administration was moved to aid China as well. To obtain the necessary congressional and public support for his assistance program, the president informed a 17 December news conference that aiding the British was like lending a hose to a neighbor fighting a fire. Then, on 29 December, in a "fireside chat," he warned the American people that the Axis powers endangered the survival of not only those fighting the aggressors, but also the United States itself.

In his State of the Union message of 6 January 1941, Roosevelt announced that he was submitting to Congress a measure to provide support for the nations resisting Axis aggression. The Lend Lease bill, assigned the number 1776, passed Congress on 11 March. It empowered the president to "sell, transfer title to, exchange, lease, lend, or otherwise dispose of" war materiel to those countries whose security he deemed vital to the United States. Under the act, the president would determine the mode of repayment. The initial appropriation was $7 billion. Presidential aide Harry Hopkins directed the Lend Lease program until October 1941. Then Edward R. Stettinius Jr. administered Lend Lease until he became undersecretary of state in 1943. After the United States entered the war following the Pearl Harbor Attack* in December 1941, Lend Lease became the principal means whereby the United States continued to ship war materiel to its allies. When Lend Lease was terminated at the war's end in August 1945, the total assistance exceeded $50 billion, with $31 billion going to Britain and most of the remainder to the Republic of China*, the Soviet Union, and France. The United States recovered some $10 billion. In 1946, Washington settled Britain's Lend Lease obligations for $650 million.

R. A. Dallek, *Franklin D. Roosevelt and American Foreign Policy, 1932–1945* (New York, 1979); W. F. Kimball, *"The Most Unsordid Act": Lend-Lease, 1939–1941* (Baltimore, MD, 1969); W. L. Langer and S. E. Gleason, *The Undeclared War, 1940–1941* (New York, 1953).

Norman A. Graebner

LEYTE GULF, BATTLE OF

See BATTLE OF LEYTE GULF

LI DENGHUI (1923–   )

Son of a native-born Taiwanese farmer, Li Dengui was the reformist president of the Republic of China* (ROC) on Taiwan* from 1988 to 2000. He entered Kyōtō Imperial University in 1943 to study agricultural economics. In 1945, Li returned to Taiwan and in 1949, graduated with a degree in agricultural economics from Taiwan University. He taught briefly there before continuing his education in the United States, where he earned a master's degree in agronomy at Iowa State University and in 1968 a doctorate in agricultural economics from Cornell University. Li began his public service career in 1957, working for the U.S.-ROC Joint Commission on Rural Reconstruction* (JCRR). His political career took off while he was mayor of Taibei from 1978 to 1981. After serving as governor of Taiwan for three years, he was vice president until President Jiang Jingguo* died in 1988, when Li replaced him.

Li adopted a pragmatic foreign policy strategy during his tenure. Since the United States not only was Taiwan's largest trading partner, but also its main security provider, he concentrated his efforts at improving this vital relationship. First, his administration adopted a series of measures designed to open Taiwan's markets to American products and services and reduce its rising trade surplus with the United States. Taibei also initiated several "buy-American" purchase missions and other pledges to place American firms first to bid on large Taiwan infrastructure projects. Second, Li focused on strengthening the security clause in the Taiwan Relations Act* (TRA), in which the United States pledged to provide Taiwan with sufficient military weapons to enable it to maintain its self-defense. Washington's commitment to the defense of Taiwan was severely tested when Li attended a reunion at Cornell University to receive an honorary degree in June 1995. In retaliation, the People's Liberation Army staged a series of missile tests and military maneuvers around the Taiwan Strait. The dispatch of a U.S. carrier task force to the area between December 1995 and March 1996 clearly signaled Washington's continued commitment to the security of the ROC.

For his first two years as president, Li served in the shadow of the mainlander-dominated Guomindang* (Nationalist) Congress. But after winning the presidential election in 1990, he began the political transformation of Taiwan. Devoting his initial efforts to domestic political reforms, Li forced the lifetime parliamentarians to resign by the end of 1991. He then proceeded to revoke all of the repressive emergency legislation passed under martial law, thus paving the way for direct elections for the National Assembly. Meanwhile, Li targeted his "pragmatic diplomacy" in 1989 at ending Taiwan's diplomatic isolation and enhancing its international status. In his meetings with world leaders, he sidestepped the isolation policy of the People's Republic of China* by not meeting in presidential residences, but on golf courses. Making effective use of his version of "dollar diplomacy," Taiwan emerged as one of the world's ten largest donors of foreign aid in the 1990s. In 1998, Taiwan established a Southeast Asia Investment Company that aimed to raise $1 billion and strengthen Taiwan's ties with the Association of Southeast Asian Nations* after the East Asian Financial Crisis*. Li ended his presidency through a smooth transition of power to Chen Shuibian after the 2000 presidential election.

R. N. Clough, *Cooperation or Conflict in the Taiwan Strait* (London, 1999); C. Hughes, *Taiwan and Chinese Nationalism: National Identity and Status in International Society* (London, 1997); M. A. Rubinstein (ed.), *Taiwan: A New History* (New York, 1999); D. Shambaugh (ed.), *Contemporary Taiwan* (Oxford, UK, 1998).

Roger Y. M. Chan

LI HONGZHANG (1823–1901)

Leading scholar-general, modernizer, and regional governor, Li Hongzhang was a dominant figure in the later Qing Dynasty in China who played a central role in relations with Japan and the Western powers. U.S. Commodore Robert W. Shufeldt*, whom Li recruited to negotiate the Shufeldt Treaty* with Korea, wrote that he was

fifty-nine years old, six feet two inches in height, has a clear, cold, cruel eye, and an imperious manner. He is a thorough Oriental, & an intense Chinaman. These imply contempt for Western nations, and hatred for all foreigners. Li Hung Chang is the Bismarck of the East.

Li was born in Anhui Province, the son of a member of the Chinese scholar-gentry. In 1844, he went to Beijing to prepare for his final government examination, and in 1847, passed it, entering the highest rank of the gentry, becoming a member of the Hanlin Academy. After coming under the tutelage of Zeng Guofan, his political career was interrupted by the Taiping Rebellion*. With his father, Li went to Anhwei to organize resistance to the Taipings from 1853 to 1856. More important, however, was his continuing relationship with Zeng Guofan, who trained him as a personal assistant (*mu fu*) in the theory and pattern of military organization. In 1861, Zeng recommended to the court that Li be appointed governor of Jiangsu Province with responsibilities for holding it and Zhejiang against the Taiping rebels. By early 1862, Li had organized his Haui army into five battalions.

From 1862 to 1864, Li used his powerful, well-trained army to push back the Taipings to Nanjing before sending money and artillery support to Zeng's forces, who crushed them. He wanted control of weapons production, and built three small arsenals, including one at Nanjing and another at Jiangnan arsenal at Shanghai, which had a school and translation bureau attached to it. By 1865, Li was one of the strongest governors in China and a regional power. Three years later, faced with the threat of a French invasion in response to the Tianjn Massacre, he brought his army north to Tianjin. After negotiating an end to the French problem, Li replaced his mentor Zeng as governor general of the metropolitan province of Zhili, the highest provincial post in the empire, which he was to occupy for twenty-four years. He was placed there for his skill in dealing with Western diplomats, having demonstrated at Shanghai that he would respect their treaty rights. Thereafter, Li consolidated his power, attempting to control foreign affairs, and clashing with the Zongli Yamen* and the customs offices over northern trade revenue as superintendent of trade for the northern ports, the production and storage of armaments and control of arsenals, and retention of control over the northern military forces and the defense of the northern forts. He also built up considerable naval forces in a northern squadron, buying vessels in England and Germany. Li established a naval academy at Tianjin in 1880, and persuaded the court to establish an Admiralty or Board of Naval Affairs in 1885.

Foreign diplomats regarded Li as China's leading diplomat, especially because he resided at Tianjin, which controlled the waterways into northern China. Li worked with foreign representatives and cut off many diplomatic contacts with the Zongli Yamen, under the control of Prince Gong (Yixin)*. He encouraged the use of the telegraph, and examinations based on Western learning, and sent cadets to learn in military colleges abroad. Li enjoyed the support of the Empress Dowager Cixi* until the 1895 defeat of his army and annihilation of his northern naval squadron by the Japanese. His policy of using foreign treaties with Korea to preserve China's control over the peninsula backfired, as the Korean court turned to the Western powers and Japan for help in resisting the pretensions of Li's resident commissioner, Yuan Shikai*. China's defeat in the Sino-Japanese War led to Li being stripped of his governor generalship and his various honors, although at Japanese insistence, the court retained him to negotiate peace with Japan

in the Treaty of Shimonoseki*. Afterward, as an elder statesman without power, Li traveled and met world leaders. He represented China at the coronation of Czar Nicholas II of Russia, during which he negotiated a secret alliance against Japan, and ceded to Russia the right to extend the Trans-Siberian Railroad across Manchuria. Later, after the Boxer Uprising*, he refused to obey an imperial edict to wage war on the Western powers, and instead pledged to protect foreigners. After the China Relief Expedition* ended the seige at the legations, Li was recalled to negotiate the Boxer Protocol*. Reappointed as governor of Zhili, he died shortly thereafter, frustrated and embittered at his failed efforts to save China from further humiliation.

J. O. P. Bland, Li Hung-chang (London, 1917); S. C. Chu and Kwang-Ching Liu (eds.), Li Hung-chang and China's Early Modernization (Armonk, NY, 1994); K. E. Folsom, Friends, Guests, and Colleagues: A Study of the Mu-fu System in the Late Ch'ing Period (Berkeley, CA, 1964); A. H. Little, Li Hung Chang: His Life and Times (London, 1903); S. Spector, Li Hung-chang and the Huai Army: A Study in Nineteenth Century Chinese Regionalism (Seattle, WA, 1964).

Frederick C. Drake

LI PENG (1928–)

Li Peng was a Chinese Communist Party* (CCP) leader who was premier of the People's Republic of China (PRC) from 1987 to 1997. He lost his father when he was seven, and Zhou Enlai*, then CCP vice chairman, took care of him in Chongqing in 1939 and later in Yan'an, where Li joined the CCP in 1945. He was sent to the Soviet Union to study in 1948, majoring in hydroelectric engineering. After his return in 1955, he was promoted to director and chief engineer at different power plants and power supply administrations in northeast China and Beijing. Li escaped harm in the Chinese Cultural Revolution* because from 1966 to 1976, he was in charge of Beijing's power supply. He was vice minister and minister of the Power Industry Ministry from 1979 to 1983, as well as deputy premier in charge of energy, communications, and natural resources. Li was elected to the Politburo and the Secretariat of the CCP Central Committee in 1985. Among the third generation of Communist leadership, he implemented the Four Modernizations* policy of Deng Xiaoping*. To accomplish economic growth and establish a market economy in the PRC, he pursued a working relationship with the United States and other major powers such as Russia and Japan.

When Li became premier in 1987, China's reforms ran into troubles. Unable to solve social and economic problems and unwilling to implement political changes, he instead emphasized central planning and slowed economic reforms. In the spring of 1989, student protests for political reforms and against official corruption developed into huge mass demonstrations in Beijing, and the movement soon expanded to other major cities. After protesting students called on Li to resign, he declared martial law on 20 May and ordered the People's Liberation Army (PLA) to return order to the city. On 4 June, PLA troops and tanks entered Beijing, and hundreds of demonstrators were killed in the Tiananmen Square Massacre*. Thereafter, the PRC entered a period of repression and economic retrenchment brought on by international sanctions.

To break the international isolation, Li pursued a "good-neighbor policy" with Northeast and Southeast Asia. Japan responded favorably, agreeing in 1990 to resume its package of government loans to the PRC. That year, Beijing normalized relations with Indonesia* and Singapore*, and the Socialist Republic of Vietnam* in 1991. Li visited the Democratic People's Republic of Korea* in May 1991. Thereafter, North Korea made a dramatic change in its "one Korea" policy when it announced its desire to join the Republic of Korea* in support for "separate UN membership," a con-

cession coinciding with Li's support for "an interim measure" toward Korea's unification. In 1992, he visited Hanoi and signed agreements with Vietnam guaranteeing investment and encouraging economic, scientific, and cultural cooperation. In 1994, Li traveled to Myanmar (Burma*) with the aim of enhancing the "brotherly relationship" between the two countries. He also improved relations with Russia through technology and military cooperation, space exploration, and nuclear energy development.

It was not easy for Li to improve Sino-American relations after Tiananmen, although he had a brief meeting with President George H. W. Bush* in New York in 1992. His domestic and foreign policies often were criticized in the American media, the public, and Congress as too hard-line against democracy and human rights, causing Li to pay $1.5 billion for European airplanes from Airbus instead of buying American from Boeing. He said that if Taiwan* announced its independence, the PRC inevitably would employ nonpeaceful methods to punish the island. In 1996, Beijing fired missiles into the Taiwan Strait that fell only eight miles off Taiwan's coastline. Ignoring Li's warnings, President Bill Clinton* dispatched U.S. naval units, including two aircraft carriers, to the area. After retiring as premier, Li was elected in 1998 as the second-highest-ranking member on the Politburo's Standing Committee. See also Jiang Zemin.

H. Harding, *China's Foreign Relations in the 1980s* (New Haven, CT, 1984); K. Lieberthal and M. Oksenberg, *Policy Making in China: Leaders, Structures, and Processes* (Princeton, NJ, 1988); R. MacFarquhar, *The Politics of China, 1949–89* (Cambridge, MA, 1993); T. Robinson and D. Shambaugh, *Chinese Foreign Policy: Theory and Practice* (New York, 1994); J. Wang, *Contemporary Chinese Politics* (New York, 1999).

Li Xiaobing

LIBERAL DEMOCRATIC PARTY

The Liberal Democratic Party (LDP) has been the dominant political party in Japan since its creation in November 1955. After the right and left wings of the Japan Socialist Party (JSP) reunited in October that year, the 185 Democrats and 115 Liberals in the National Diet joined to form one conservative party. In the so-called "1955 system" that endured for the next thirty-eight years, the LDP ruled, and the radical JSP remained in the opposition. As the dominant party in a parliamentary system, the LDP has played a central role in mediating both the competition for power in government and the efforts of extraparty groups to influence government policy. The LDP has been fundamentally a parliamentary group rather than a mass party. The party president, who enjoys only a two-year term in office, also serves as prime minister. The LDP's factions compete vigorously for leadership of the party, which has strong ties with extraparty groups. Big business has been a vital source of funds and rural constituencies a reliable source of votes. Diet members have formed close alliances with civil servants throughout Japan's bureaucracy, who have in turn used these ties to enhance their own influence.

Owing to the JSP's advocacy of neutrality in the Cold War, the United States encouraged a conservative merger and then supported the LDP. The Central Intelligence Agency* even extended covert financial assistance to the party during the 1950s and 1960s. Although sensational, the influence of covert American action on Japanese politics was insignificant when compared with the overt impact of the U.S. Occupation of Japan* and the Cold War diplomacy of the Reverse Course*. Japanese Socialists defended the war-renouncing Japanese Constitution of 1947* and rejected the American alliance implicit in the U.S.-Japan Security Treaty of 1951*. For this reason, conservatives united to keep the JSP out of power. But underneath this two-party system was a three-way division on foreign policy that often led to inaction. During the early 1950s, Yoshida Shigeru* supported the alliance with the United States, but then later sided with the JSP to oppose the efforts of Hatoyama Ichirō* and Kishi Nobusuke* to revise the 1947 constitution and rearm Japan. This debate over foreign policy culminated in the Anpo Crisis* of 1960.

The LDP's dominance of politics contributed to postwar Japanese political stability. Conservative rule provided electoral support for the pro-business policies underpinning high-speed economic growth and Japan's alliance with the United States. The many ties established over the years between the LDP, the business community, and the bureaucracy also fostered corruption, complacency, and simmering public dissatisfaction with "money politics." Finally, following the Recruit-Cosmos Scandal of 1989, the LDP began to decline in strength. It temporarily lost power in 1993 when some Diet members left the party. Both the LDP and the JSP lost seats to new parties during the long recession of the 1990s. Having taken shape in a Cold War environment, the "1955 system" disintegrated with its end. The LDP, however, remains a primary political force in Japanese politics.

G. L. Curtis, *The Japanese Way of Politics* (New York, 1988); H. Fukui, *Party in Power* (Berkeley, CA, 1970); C. Johnson, *Japan: Who Governs?* (New York, 1995); T. Kataoka (ed.), *Creating Single-Party Democracy* (Stanford, CA, 1992); M. Kohno, *Japan's Postwar Party Politics* (Princeton, NJ, 1997); J. I. Matray, *Japan's Emergence as a Global Power* (Westport, CT, 2000).

Aaron Forsberg

LILI'UOKALANI (1838–1917)

Lili'uokalani Lydia Kamaka'eha was the last sovereign of the Hawaiian Kingdom, and was deposed by the Hawaiian Revolution* in 1893. She was born into a family of Hawaiian high chiefs. When her brother David Kalakaua* became king in 1874, she entered royalty and was destined for involvement in governmental affairs. When Kalakaua took a trip around the world in

1881, he left Lili'uokalani in charge of the government as princess regent. During that time, she had to deal with a serious epidemic of smallpox brought into the kingdom by Chinese immigrants and showed resolve by refusing to submit to demands for dismissal of certain government leaders. In 1889, an abortive revolt against Kalakaua to change Hawaii's constitution seems also to have involved Lili'uokalani, who believed her brother had exhibited cowardice in 1887 by submitting to demands by white businessmen and professional people that the sovereign's power be weakened. A failed coup in 1889 was likely intended to put Lili'uokalani on the throne in place of Kalakaua.

Lili'uokalani assumed the throne after the death of Kalakaua early in 1891. Her short reign was characterized by animosity between her and her white subjects, who criticized her attempts to get more revenue by questionable means and feared that she might attempt to change the constitution. After the legislature passed acts the queen favored to license the sale of opium and establish a national lottery, Sanford B. Dole* led the whites in revolt on 14 January 1893, when the queen tried to promulgate a new constitution restoring the absolute power of the monarch. The landing of U.S troops from a warship in Honolulu harbor intimidated Lili'uokalani's supporters, and when the rebels declared the monarchy ended and established a provisional government, she appealed to President Grover Cleveland to restore the monarchy. His attempt to do so failed when the provisional government refused to surrender power.

Lili'uokalani spent the next several years vainly trying to change the course of events. In 1895, she was involved in an unsuccessful attempt by Hawaiian royalists to overthrow the republic established the prior year, and she was tried and sentenced to prison for her activities. After less than a year of confinement in a room in the former royal palace, she was released. With Hawaiian Annexation* by the United States in 1898, no hope remained for res-

toration, but Lili'uokalani continued to justify her rule as the last monarch of the Hawaiian Islands. Her memoirs, *Hawaii's Story by Hawaii's Queen*, indicated her continuing belief that the United States was responsible for her overthrow. Thereafter, she lived quietly in Honolulu, a continuing symbol to the native Hawaiians, by then a distinct minority of the population in their own islands, of their lost independence. *See also* James H. Blount; John L. Stevens.

E. Andrade, *Unconquerable Rebel: Robert W. Wilcox and Hawaiian Politics, 1880–1903* (Boulder, CO, 1996); R. Kuykendall, *The Hawaiian Kingdom*, Vol. 3: *The Kalakaua Dynasty* (Honolulu, HI, 1967); Liliuokalani, *Hawaii's Story by Hawaii's Queen* (Boston, 1898); W. A. Russ, *The Hawaiian Revolution, 1893–1894* (Susquehanna, PA, 1959).

Ernest Andrade Jr.

LIN BIAO (1907–1971)

Chinese military leader Lin Biao was a close political ally of Mao Zedong* who rose to be the number two figure in the Chinese Communist Party* (CCP) before breaking with Mao and dying in mysterious circumstances. An early member of the CCP, he was also one of the first graduates of the Whampoa Military Academy in Guangzhou, run by the Guomindang* (Nationalist) Party with support and guidance from the Soviet Union in the early 1920s. Lin became a leader of the Red Army and participated in the armed uprisings of the late 1920s. After these failed, he was one of the Red Army leaders who set up the Chinese Soviet base area in Jiangxi, and later completed the Long March from Jiangxi to Yan'an in the northwest, which became the principal base area for the CCP from 1936 to 1945.

After victory in the Chinese Civil War* in 1949, Lin served as a top commander in the Korean War*. Ill health kept him out of prominent activities through most of the 1950s, but in August 1959, he became minister of defense after the purge of Peng Dehuai* at the CCP's Lushan Plenum. In this role, he undertook a campaign of political education within the People's Liberation Army (PLA), which included the compilation of *Quotations from Chairman Mao*, the famous "little red book" that played so prominent a role in the Chinese Cultural Revolution* in the late 1960s. During the Cultural Revolution, Lin became noted for another publication, his slim volume titled *Long Live the Victory of People's War*, in which he summarized the experience of guerrilla war in China and generalized from that a theory of global struggle, in which China would lead underdeveloped countries in a broad revolutionary alliance against U.S. imperialism. As Mao's "close comrade in arms and successor," a status that was formally written into the CCP constitution at the Ninth Party Congress in 1969, Lin was one of the major political beneficiaries of the inner party struggles after 1966.

At the beginning of the 1970s, however, Mao's strategic thinking underwent a profound change. He came to view the Soviet Union as the primary threat to the People's Republic of China*, and saw the United States as a declining power that had exhausted itself in the Second Indochina War*. By playing the American card and opening a new relationship with the United States, Mao hoped to undermine the rising power of the Soviets. Lin opposed this view, both because of his vested role as an opponent of U.S. imperialism and fear of a new political orientation threatening his leading role in the CCP. An outgrowth of this rift, the end of Lin's career and life remains shrouded in obscurity. Some kind of irrevocable breach developed between him and Mao, possibly involving the attempted assassination of Mao by Lin's agents. In September 1971, Lin and his family fled China on a PLA aircraft that crashed in Mongolia. It is unclear whether the plane was shot down or ran out of fuel after an overhasty departure. News of Lin's death was kept secret for a year, and was finally announced

through China's embassy in Algiers, after President Richard M. Nixon* had visited China and the new era of Chinese international relations had begun.

R. MacFarquhar (ed.), *The Politics of China: The Eras of Mao and Deng* (Cambridge, MA, 1997); L. Maitan, *Party, Army, and Masses in China* (London, 1976); F. Tiewes and W. Sun, *The Tragedy of Lin Biao: Riding the Tiger during the Cultural Revolution, 1966–71* (Hong Kong, 1996); J. Van Ginneken, *The Rise and Fall of Lin Biao* (New York, 1972).

Kenneth J. Hammond

LINEBACKER BOMBINGS

The LINEBACKER bombings were the final U.S. bombing operations against the Democratic Republic of Vietnam* during the Second Indochina War*. In response to North Vietnam's Easter Offensive* in March 1972, President Richard M. Nixon* had authorized the resumption of the bombing of North Vietnam, thus ending restrictions in place since November 1968. Operation LINEBACKER I began on 2 April 1972 and had several objectives, among them to disrupt the movement of men and supplies into the Republic of Vietnam*, to bolster the morale of South Vietnam's government, and to force negotiating concessions from North Vietnam. When the first month of bombings failed to alter Hanoi's negotiating position, Nixon, on 9 May, authorized the mining of Haiphong and other North Vietnamese harbors, and announced that the bombing would continue until an agreement ending the war was reached. The intensity of LINEBACKER I exceeded previous air operations, as round-the-clock missions bombed supply lines, depots, factories, power facilities, and virtually all targets of any military value. As negotiators at the Paris Peace Talks* approached a settlement, Nixon, on 22 October, ended LINEBACKER I.

When the tentative agreement reached in Paris unraveled, principally because of

South Vietnam's opposition to several provisions and North Vietnam's refusal in turn to make concessions to appease Saigon, Nixon resumed the all-out bombing of North Vietnam. LINEBACKER II, also known as the Christmas Bombings, was launched on 18 December. Its principal purpose was to weaken and intimidate North Vietnam, but it was intended also to reassure South Vietnam and thus gain the assent of President Nguyen Van Thieu* to the agreement. The eleven-day assault saw B-52 bombers and other aircraft dropping more than 40,000 tons of bombs principally in the Hanoi-Haiphong corridor. LINEBACKER II triggered considerable criticism internationally, as well as within the United States. Critics charged the United States with terrorizing civilians, but in fact LINEBACKER II, because of the use "smart bombs," was carried out with remarkable precision, thus largely missing nonmilitary targets. Although LINEBACKER operations devastated much of North Vietnam's warmaking capacity, their diplomatic effect remains controversial. To Nixon and his defenders, the bombing, especially LINEBACKER II, forced concessions that led to the January 1973 Paris Peace Accords*. Critics, however, charge that Hanoi made no significant concessions and that the final agreement differed only marginally from the preliminary settlement of October 1972.

M. Clodfelter, *The Limits of Air Power: The American Bombing of North Vietnam* (New York, 1989); M. Herz, *The Prestige Press and the Christmas Bombing, 1972: Images and Reality in Vietnam* (Washington, DC, 1980); A. Isaacs, *Without Honor: Defeat in Vietnam and Cambodia* (Baltimore, MD, 1983).

Gary R. Hess

LOCKHEED SCANDAL

This bribery case damaged relations between the United States and Japan, as well as having an important impact on domestic politics in both nations. In February 1976, during testimony before the U.S. Senate Subcommittee on Multinational Corporations, representatives from the Lockheed Aircraft Corporation admitted that they had used financial inducements to persuade senior members of the Japanese government to ensure that Japanese airline companies would purchase Lockheed's Tristar aircraft. Subsequent testimony exposed a clear case of political bribery starting in August 1972, when Lockheed Vice President A. Carl Kotchian had attempted to buy favorable access to the administration of Prime Minister Tanaka Kakuei*. A total of some $22 million was used to influence the government, and fifteen top political figures in the Liberal Democratic Party* (LDP), including the prime minister, ultimately were indicted by the Japanese courts for accepting bribes. By then, Tanaka already had been forced to resign in 1974, after publication of two lengthy investigative articles in a Japanese monthly periodical implicating him in questionable financial activities relating to real estate deals and contracts with construction firms.

The Lockheed scandal prompted a huge outcry from the Japanese citizenry and demands from some quarters that Tanaka, who was still a sitting member of the Diet, resign his parliamentary seat. Tanaka refused to stand down, not only proclaiming his innocence, but also arguing that the accusations were politically motivated by his rivals. His conservative supporters claimed that he was unfairly targeted for censure in a system in which the use of money to cement political and business deals was part of the political culture. Although Tanaka finally was sentenced in 1983 to four years in prison and ordered to pay a 500-million-yen fine, he avoided imprisonment thanks to a succession of appeals and died just before Japan's Supreme Court was to hear his case. Meanwhile, he remained a hugely powerful figure in the LDP, playing the role of kingmaker in selecting prime ministers until a stroke incapacitated him in 1985.

For U.S.-Japan relations, the Lockheed scandal risked creating additional bilateral instability just five years after the Nixon Shocks*. Initially, Secretary of State Henry A. Kissinger* refused to authorize the release of documentation related to the bribery case, despite a request from the Japanese government. It took a unanimous resolution from both houses of Japan's Diet and a personal request by Prime Minister Miki Takeo*, Tanaka's successor, for the material to be provided. Kissinger's behavior invited criticism from an American press and public still upset over the Watergate scandal that had forced President Richard M. Nixon* to resign. The Lockheed scandal, in combination with Koreagate*, may have contributed to President Gerald R. Ford* losing to Jimmy Carter* in the presidential election of 1976. As for Miki, his advocacy of reform and efforts to prosecute Tanaka alienated senior party members, who forced "Mr. Clean" to resign after the LDP's dismal showing in the December 1976 elections. But the Lockheed scandal fostered passage of two reform laws in Japan governing elections and helping shift political funds away from politicians and their factions toward a more party-centered campaign finance system.

J. Masumi, *Contemporary Politics in Japan* (Berkeley, CA, 1995); J. I. Matray, *Japan's Emergence as a Global Power* (Westport, CT, 2000); R. H. Mitchell, *Political Bribery in Japan* (Honolulu, HI, 1996); S. J. Pharr and E. S. Krauss, *Media and Politics in Japan* (Honolulu, HI, 1996).

John Swenson-Wright

LODGE, HENRY CABOT (1850–1924)

Henry Cabot Lodge served as one of the founders of a Republican foreign policy at the beginning of the twentieth century that assumed American culture was superior to all others, and that superior civilizations were obliged to impose a climate of order over international relations. He was well supported (both intellectually and politically) by other leading American nationalists, who also endorsed a "Large Policy" for the United States, including Theodore Roosevelt*, Albert J. Beveridge*, and Alfred Thayer Mahan*. Lodge's contribution to U.S. policy in East Asia was grounded in his support for a powerful navy capable of defending U.S. interests across the globe. His influence was exercised by means of his career representing Massachusetts in Congress. He began his tenure in 1886, first serving in the House of Representatives, where he was a member of the House Naval Affairs Committee. His influence over foreign policy rose substantially in 1892, when he was elected to the Senate, serving on the Senate Foreign Relations Committee. Lodge called for increased appropriations for construction of a navy that was technologically advanced.

Lodge did not believe in the seizure of colonies for the sake of empire building. When revolutionaries provided the United States with the opportunity for Hawaiian Annexation*, however, he thought it dishonorable to allow the primitive islanders to remain independent. Similarly, the Philippines* were not sought as a territory for conquest, but when they fell under U.S. control in the Spanish-American War*, he favored Philippine Annexation*. To refuse this responsibility would impede modernization of the Filipino, contradicting the notion of democratic stewardship that lay at the foundation of Lodge's foreign policy goals in the Pacific. His vision of the U.S. role in East Asia also assumed a rivalry with other hegemonic powers. His Anglophilia tempered his outlook toward British Colonialism* in Asia, but he sought to counterbalance the rising economic and military influence of Japan and Germany, particularly until World War I forced a realignment of colonial possessions. Japan posed the greatest threat to Lodge's objective of U.S. hegemony in East Asia. Cultural difference was compounded by Japan's growing economic and political influence over Korea, then Manchuria, then China and Siberia. The Lodge Corollary to the Monroe Doctrine, holding that no external power could use its nation's private enterprise to assert hegemonic control over territory in the Western Hemisphere, was a specific response to Japanese business involvement in Mexico. Furthermore, Lodge was a major proponent of limiting immigration to only those people who could assimilate smoothly into American culture, and thus he supported the efforts of Western politicians to curtail the entry of Japanese into the United States.

Lodge was one of the key figures responsible for blocking ratification of the Versailles Peace Treaty*. His motives derived from diplomatic goals in Europe, not East Asia. However, the U.S. failure to ratify the Versailles settlement had important implications for the balance of power in the Pacific. Former German island holdings were mandated to Japan instead of the United States. Combined with the Japanese wartime seizure of the Shandong Peninsula in China and military occupation of eastern Siberia, this provided an extraordinary boost to Japan's geopolitical power in East Asia. After thwarting President Woodrow Wilson* and his peace settlement, Lodge participated in postwar efforts to control the massive wartime naval-building programs of the United States, Britain, and Japan. When Secretary of State Charles Evans Hughes* prepared for the Washington Conference*, he insisted that Lodge be named a member of the U.S. delegation. His appointment served as a recognition of his stature as a senior Republican senator, but it also provided a pragmatic means of securing Lodge's support in shepherding any resulting treaties through the Senate Foreign Relations Committee. As a delegate, Lodge was a major force in negotiating the Four Power Pact*, which sought to secure the status quo in Asia. He was willing to support the Five Power Pact*, which was designed to protect the status of the U.S. Navy as a power "second to none." Lodge played the key role in securing Senate ratification of these two treaties and the Nine Power Pact*.

J. A. Garraty, *Henry Cabot Lodge: A Biography* (New York, 1953); W. C. Widenor, *Henry Cabot Lodge and the Search for American Foreign Policy* (Berkeley, CA, 1980).

Karen A. J. Miller

LODGE, HENRY CABOT JR. (1902–1985)

Henry Cabot Lodge Jr. was twice ambassador to the Republic of Vietnam during the height of the Second Indochina War*. The grandson of powerful U.S. Senator Henry Cabot Lodge*, he himself became a senator from Massachusetts in 1936. Resigning office to enter active duty during World War II, Lodge was reelected to his seat in 1946. John F. Kennedy* defeated Lodge in the 1952 campaign, during which Lodge headed the campaign of Dwight D. Eisenhower* for the presidency. Eisenhower named Lodge as U.S. representative to the United Nations, with the rank of ambassador, a post in which Lodge served from January 1953 to September 1960. At New York, he became involved in such issues as the P'anmunjŏm Truce Talks* to end the Korean War* and the Taiwan Strait Crises*. During the 1960 presidential campaign, Lodge was the vice presidential nominee on the Republican ticket headed by then Vice President Richard M. Nixon*.

In Vietnam, a Communist insurgency and internal instability appeared likely to topple the regime of President Ngo Dinh Diem* and thus to jeopardize the Cold War balance of power in Southeast Asia. As president, Kennedy designated Lodge as ambassador to the Republic of Vietnam, a post Lodge assumed on 1 August 1963. He had only minimal experience with former French Indochina* (consisting of his 1926 honeymoon cruise through the area and of briefings received while on reserve duty at the Pentagon), but the Kennedy administration needed a bipartisan public figure with the stature that Lodge had to oversee its effort in Vietnam. Soon after arrival, Lodge received a cable from the State Department authorizing him to support alternative leadership to the weakening Diem government, motivating him to make contact with coup leaders in the military. Although the coup did not occur and Washington soon retracted the authorization, Lodge continued in his efforts to reform the Diem regime and then to replace it as this effort seemingly failed. When the long-expected coup began on 1 November, Lodge made only lukewarm efforts to save Diem. Thereafter, he attempted to stabilize the successive military regimes that followed. Lodge left Vietnam in June 1964, the official reason being his wife's failing health, although it was more likely because of his desire to block Barry Goldwater from being the nominee for president of the Republican Party.

Lodge's involvement in the Second Indochina War continued under the next president. Lyndon B. Johnson* appointed him to another term as ambassador to South Vietnam on 31 July 1965. Lodge successfully stewarded South Vietnam's government through a major civil disturbance organized by militant Buddhists during 1966 and toward the formation of a civilian government the next year. He consistently placed a high priority on the pacification effort. Lodge also was involved in wider matters of a diplomatic nature. In the fall of 1966, he played a central role in the peace initiative known as MARIGOLD, helping to negotiate the opening of peace talks between the Democratic Republic of Vietnam* and the United States, only to be dashed literally on the eve of success by long-delayed U.S. bombings around Hanoi that December. After his return home in April 1967, Lodge served as Johnson's ambassador at large for the next year. He was an important participant in the reassessment of Vietnam policy as one of the "Wise Men" that occurred as a result of the Tet Offensive* in early 1968 and helped persuade Johnson to de-escalate the war. After Lodge's brief stint as ambassador to West Germany, Richard Nixon, now president, appointed him personal representative of

the president at the Paris Peace Talks* on Vietnam, where he stayed for ten frustrating months until resigning in December 1969. Thereafter, Lodge was U.S. representative to the Vatican until 6 July 1977. *See also* Diem's Assassination; Duong Van Minh.

A. Blair, *Lodge in Vietnam: A Patriot Abroad* (New Haven, CT, 1995); A. Hatch, *The Lodges of Massachusetts* (New York, 1973); H. C. Lodge, *As It Was* (New York, 1976); H. C. Lodge, *The Storm Has Many Eyes: A Personal Narrative* (New York, 1973).

Kent G. Sieg

LON NOL (1913–1985)

Lon Nol was prime minister of Cambodia* when the Communist Khmer Rouge* seized control of the nation in April 1975. He had risen through the ranks of the Cambodian civil service and was active in conservative political circles as one of the leaders of the Khmer Renovation Party, where he came to the favorable attention of King Norodom Sihanouk* in the late 1940s. He was defeated in the 1951 assembly elections, an event that soured him somewhat on democratic processes. After Cambodia's independence from France after the Geneva Conference of 1954*, Lon Nol entered the military and fought alongside the French against Communist insurgents. Thereafter, the United States began training the Cambodian military forces, and close ties developed between American advisers and the army under Lon Nol's control as minister of defense in various Sihanouk cabinets. In fact, Lon Nol expressed his regret at the deterioration in U.S.-Cambodian relations from 1963 to 1965, indicating that the armed forces would not allow Sihanouk to drift too far to the Communist side. All the while, however, he served Sihanouk well, foiling plots and arresting, torturing, and assassinating Communists.

Lon Nol was appointed prime minister in 1966, but resigned under pressure in

1967 amid accusations that he was a tool for Western intelligence agencies. He was again named prime minister in 1969 with a mandate to deal with Cambodia's pressing economic problems through policies of privatization and currency devaluation. Lon Nol and his deputy prime minister, Sirik Matak (later deprived of influence by Lon Nol's ambitious and corrupt brother Lon Non), formed a right-wing, pro-Western cabinet that acted without deference to Sihanouk. In March 1970, following a week of violent demonstrations in Phnom Penh against the Communists and the North Vietnamese in Cambodia, Lon Nol and Sirik hastily convened the National Assembly, which officially deposed the absent Sihanouk and gave the prime minister emergency powers. He immediately closed the port of Sihanoukville, which effectively denied the Democratic Republic of Vietnam* and Viet Cong* a vital logistic route for transporting military supplies. This caught Communist forces by surprise because Lon Nol had taken bribes (along with Sihanouk and other high Cambodian officials) over the years for allowing war material to pass through the port unmolested. In response, the Communists attacked government troops in the east in April, forcing Lon to withdraw his forces from the northeast. In retaliation, the Cambodian Army massacred thousands of Vietnamese civilians living in Phnom Penh.

Despite accusations to the contrary, Washington had no role in the Cambodian coup, but viewed it as a fortuitous opportunity. When Cambodia formally requested U.S. military aid, Washington eagerly complied. President Richard M. Nixon* called Lon Nol's regime "the only government in Cambodia in the last twenty-five years that had the guts to take a pro-Western and pro-American stand." He then launched the Cambodian Incursion*, with or without Lon Nol's permission (historians disagree), to disrupt Viet Cong supply lines. This had the effect of driving the Communists even deeper into central Cambodia. Following two disastrous military offensives directed by Lon Nol, the military situation stabilized in early 1972 because of U.S. bombing. Lon Nol held presidential elections that year, despite controlling only about 40 percent of Cambodian territory, and relied on widespread vote fraud to defeat National Assembly leader In Tam. The United States, its fingers burned in approving the 1963 coup against South Vietnam's Ngo Dinh Diem*, refused to intercede. After Congress halted U.S. bombing in August 1973, the Khmer Rouge prepared for a final offensive that began early in 1975. Lon Nol's inept and corrupt government and army, despite $1.18 billion in U.S. aid, was no match for the single-minded Communists. Although Washington vainly tried to arrange a peace agreement involving Sihanouk, Lon Nol fled to exile in Hawaii. After Khmer Rouge forces occupied Phnom Penh late in April 1975, Pol Pot* inflicted even more misery on the Cambodian people.

D. P. Chandler, *The Tragedy of Cambodian History: Politics, War and Revolution Since 1945* (New Haven, CT, 1991); R. Nixon, *RN: The Memoirs of Richard Nixon* (New York, 1990); Oral Histories of Andrew E. Antippas, Michael Rives, Marshall Green, Ambassador Emory C. Swank, William Harben, and Robert V. Keeley, Foreign Affairs Oral History Collection, Georgetown University.

Gregory J. Murphy

LONDON NAVAL CONFERENCE OF 1930

This conference was "the high water-mark of inter-war naval limitation." It was designed to extend the system that had been approved at the Washington Conference* by bringing within its ambit auxiliary vessels, especially cruisers. An earlier attempt to do so at the Geneva Naval Conference of 1927* had failed amid bitter Anglo-American recriminations. However, talks between President Herbert Hoover* and British Prime Minister Ramsay MacDonald in 1929 paved the way for a further limitation conference, which opened in London on 21 January 1930. In contrast to Geneva, where Italy and France had stood aside, all five Washington powers were present. The main outcome, which concluded with the signing of the London Naval Treaty on 22 April 1930, was limitation of the strength of the principal navies in auxiliary vessels, earlier obstacles having been overcome by Britain's concession to the U.S. position. A total British Commonwealth strength of fifty, in contrast to the seventy deemed necessary at Geneva, was accepted in an arrangement whereby the United States would have a numerical preponderance in heavy cruisers. Because Italy and France could not resolve their differences and did not sign this part of the treaty, an escalator clause was included to allow the three signatories—Britain, the United States, and Japan—to match any increases in their auxiliary strengths.

The main significance of the London Naval Conference lay in its impact on Anglo-American relations. A cruiser-building race between Britain and the United States, which would have further adversely affected their relations, was averted. In effect, Britain conceded naval primacy to the United States, relying on friendly Anglo-American relations to preserve its long-term position. Although Japan's strategic position in the western Pacific was strengthened by the treaty, its inferior status had been reaffirmed in the application of the Washington ratio to auxiliary vessels. But the escalator clause, and the fact that the auxiliary ratios were not to be in full effect until 31 December 1936, ensured that there would be little actual reduction of cruiser forces under the agreement. All five powers had agreed to the faster implementation of Washington provisions on capital ships (battleships and battlecruisers), in effect bringing the strict numerical ratio into operation earlier than expected. Domestic political controversy over ratification of the treaty contributed to the establishment of a militarist government in Japan in 1932. Japan thereafter

sought to evade the treaty's provisions. The London Naval Treaty merely had reinforced the major change in the balance of power in East Asia that the Five Power Pact* had reflected. Japan could pursue a sphere of influence in China with impunity after 1931. *See also* London Naval Conference of 1935–1936; War Plan Orange.

C. Hall, *Britain, America and Arms Control, 1921–37* (London, 1987); R. G. O'Connor, *Perilous Equilibrium: The United States and the London Naval Conference of 1930* (Lawrence, KS, 1962); S. Roskill, *Naval Policy Between the Wars*, Vol. 2: *The Period of Reluctant Rearmament, 1930–1939* (London, 1976).

Ian McGibbon

LONDON NAVAL CONFERENCE OF 1935–1936

The last arms limitation conference of the period before the outbreak of World War II, this meeting was a largely unsuccessful endeavor. By 1934, a need to negotiate new naval arms limitation agreements was clearly imperative. First, the Five Power Pact* and the London Naval Treaty of 1930 would both terminate at the end of 1936, leaving no limitations in naval armaments after that time. Second, the international situation was becoming more tense and uncertain as the rise of Nazi Germany and Italian and Japanese ambitions threatened the continuation of world peace. During 1934, the Americans and the British held talks to prepare the way for another naval conference, striving to present a common front to the Japanese, who were demanding a treaty to bring an end to the naval tonnage ratios for warship categories under the existing treaties. Unfortunately, the Americans found themselves unable to agree to the British desire to reduce the size of several categories of warship, especially battleships, to well below existing limits.

Led by British persistence, the naval powers decided to go along with the London Treaty's call for a conference before the expiration of the naval treaties. For their own reasons relating to their rivalry in the Mediterranean, France and Italy desired a conference to try to set up a new environment of naval limitations more favorable to the naval tonnage ratios. Convening in London on 7 December 1935, the conference quickly experienced difficulties. Attempts to extend or to establish new quantitative limits involving ratios along the lines of the existing treaties had to be abandoned, since neither France, Italy, nor Japan would support them any longer. The negotiators thereafter sought to establish qualitative limits on size and gunpower of warship types. This proved more successful. But Japan's insistence on what they called "a common upper limit" of tonnage for all warships, which admitted Japan's right to parity in naval power, was refused by the British and Americans. This caused the Japanese to leave the conference on 16 January.

The other four powers continued their discussions, and after several weeks of effort, they were able to agree on a treaty embodying qualitative limitations in the warship categories. Signed on 25 March 1936, the treaty would become effective on 1 January 1937 on expiration of the Five Power Pact and earlier London Naval Treaty. Of course, Japan's refusal to sign the treaty made it practically a dead letter, and the negotiators realized that fact when they included in it a number of escape clauses to allow any signatory the right to exceed the treaty limitations if it believed its security was threatened by a nonsignatory power's construction of warships exceeding those limits. The treaty was made even more futile by the actions of the Italians. Although they participated in the discussions and agreed with its provisions, they insisted on the removal of sanctions imposed upon them by Britain and France after invasion of Ethiopia. Failing to obtain this, the Italians refused to sign the treaty. The London Naval Treaty of 1936 collapsed quickly. When Japan began a large warship construction program in the spring of 1937, the other powers one after another invoked the treaty's escape clauses. Before the end of 1937, naval limitations of any kind were no longer in effect for any practical purposes, as the world prepared for the war clearly seen to be coming. *See also* London Naval Conference of 1930; War Plan Rainbow.

R. G. Kaufman, *Arms Control During the Prenuclear Era: The United States and Naval Limitation Between the Two World Wars* (New York, 1990); S. E. Pelz, *Race to Pearl Harbor: The Failure of the Second London Naval Conference and the Onset of World War II* (Cambridge, MA, 1974); U.S. State Department, *London Naval Conference of 1935* (Washington, DC, 1936).

Ernest Andrade Jr.

LOW, FREDERICK F. (1828–1894)

Frederick Ferdinand Low, as U.S. minister to China, led a mission to Korea in 1871 that provoked a military clash embittering U.S.-Korean relations. Born in Maine on a small farm, he was apprenticed to the Boston China trading firm of Russell and Company*. Low sailed to California in 1849, arriving at San Francisco harbor in June. After panning for gold, he then worked as a merchant in the city. In March 1854, Low brokered a shipping agreement between the inland steamship lines in San Francisco Bay and the Sacramento River area and set up a banking business. In 1861, he entered politics when nominated as a Union Republican representative-at-large for Congress, becoming California's third member in June 1862. Low became something of a journeyman Republican supporter, interested in safeguarding California land titles and banking regulations. When he retired, he worked as collector for the port of San Francisco and then won election as governor of California, serving from 1863 to 1867. His governorship was marked by strong vetoes, pocket vetoes, and calls for justice for Chinese immigrants under the Burlingame-Seward Treaty* of 1868.

In December 1869, Low was appointed minister to China, and he spent four years in Tianjin and Beijing. He participated with foreign representatives in the audience question, which forced the Chinese authorities to receive foreign representatives. In 1871, he notified Secretary of State Hamilton Fish* that the commerce of China, Japan, and Russian Manchuria required that vessels pass close to the coast of Korea, warning of the danger of shipwrecked American mariners and their property. Low informed Fish that Korea was an independent nation, which in 1870 ignored the strong claims of Chinese suzerainty. Fish instructed Low to join Admiral John Rodgers, in command of the U.S. Asiatic Squadron, in an attempt "to secure a treaty for the protection of shipwrecked mariners and a commercial treaty," but cautioned him "to avoid a conflict by force unless it cannot be avoided without dishonor." Low then persuaded Rodgers to take five ships and 1,200 seamen and marines to Korea to open trade, using the unsolved *General Sherman* Incident* as an excuse. In May 1871, the expedition proceeded to the mouth of the Han River, which was a vital point for the defense of the capital at Seoul. The Korean forces were extremely sensitive to the importance of their forts, for it was here that the French had made a prior invasion in 1866. Despite several Korean warnings not to approach, Rodgers landed marines on shore and the Korean forts eventually opened on the expedition.

Low seized on Fish's phrase about force "unless it cannot be avoided without dishonor" and promptly authorized an attack. Troops were landed, the war vessels returned fire, and more than 250 Koreans were slaughtered. The expedition, however, was a diplomatic failure. It did not open Korea, produced troubles for China and Korea with Japan, and led the Korean government to condemn the American action as aggression and assume that a state of war existed between the United States and Korea, a view that persisted until the first visit of Commodore Robert W. Shufeldt* to Korea in 1880. Homer B. Hulbert*

later described the expedition in unflattering terms:

A stranger comes into my yard and acts in a queer way. I order him off the place, but he proceeds to climb in at the window, I forcibly resist his entrance. This is an insult to him, which he resents.

Easterners saw the Low-Rodgers expedition as a military defeat, along the lines of the French withdrawal. The incident probably helped to undermine the power of the Taewŏn'gun, Korea's regent, hastened his retirement from office in 1873, and propelled progressive forces to consider opening the country to foreign trade, the first beneficiary of which was Japan at the Treaty of Kanghwa in 1876. Low meanwhile returned to San Francisco, where he worked as joint manager of the Anglo-California bank from 1874 to 1891. *See also* Lucius H. Foote; Kojong; Kowtow; Shufeldt Treaty.

D. L. Anderson, "Between Two Cultures: Frederick F. Low in China," *California History* (3, 1980); J. K. Bauer, "The Korean Expedition of 1871," *United States Naval Institute Proceedings* (1948); P. H. Clyde, "Frederick F. Low and the Tientsin Massacre," *Pacific Historical Review* (1933); H. A Gosnell, "The Navy in Korea, 1871," *American Neptune* (1947).

Frederick C. Drake

LUCE, CLARE BOOTHE (1903–1987)

As a writer, political figure, and diplomat, Clare Boothe Luce was tied to East Asia through her husband, Henry R. Luce*, publisher of *Time* and *Life* magazines. She gained her Asian perspective from Henry, but as a playwright, correspondent, editor, socialite, political spokeswoman, and congresswoman, Luce made these interests visible to a larger American audience. Her voice, added to that of her husband and the China Lobby*, was a powerful influence in the making of American public opinion in the Cold War era. Henry Luce met his future wife on the New York social scene, when she was editor of *Vanity Fair* and a beginning playwright. Following their 1935 marriage, Clare Boothe Luce continued writing for a while, but her life was characterized by shifting interests, movement from one career to another, and the kind of powerful personality that invited both fans and detractors. After the outbreak of war in Europe in 1939, Luce traveled there to report on the scene for *Life* magazine. Five of her articles appeared in *Life* from May to July 1940 and were published later that year with others as the book *Europe in the Spring* to bring the deepening crisis to the attention of a seemingly unconcerned American public. By this time, Clare Boothe Luce was well known.

In early 1941, the Luces visited China to observe the war conditions there. They met Generalissimo Jiang Jieshi* and other leaders of China's Guomindang* government, and visited the front line against Japan at the Yellow River. Clare accepted her husband's "uncritical enthusiasm" for Jiang's government—a perspective she retained throughout the Cold War. *Life* published her article "Wings Over China" in September 1941, recounting her observations and this soon-to-become-standard interpretation of the internal workings of China. Clare and Henry Luce became vocal proponents of the Republic of China* as well as advocates for strong American action in Asia before, during, and long after the war. Following a trip to the Philippines* in the fall of 1941, Luce's article "MacArthur of the Far East" ran as the cover story coincidentally in the 8 December 1941 issue of *Life*. This was another example of her bringing attention to U.S. interests abroad. After the United States entered World War II, Luce headed to India, Burma*, and China as a war correspondent for *Life*. Her series of articles on Claire L. Chennault* and his Flying Tigers, General Joseph W. Stilwell*, the China-Burma-India Theater*, and Madame Jiang Jieshi, (Song Meiling*) from April to September of 1942 brought the Pacific war into the homes of Americans in the days before "televised war," thus stimulating American sentiment for the Asian cause in a war that was focused largely on Europe at the time. The view of China "in distress" that Luce depicted later became a basic foundation of the China Lobby's worldview.

Luce's campaigning on behalf of Republican presidential candidate Wendell L. Willkie in 1940 gave her a taste of politics, so when she was approached in 1942 to run for Congress, she agreed. The Luces' country home in Fairfield County, Connecticut, made her eligible to run from that state, but in the largely Democratic district, her success took hard work. Once elected, her interests centered mostly on foreign affairs. Her first congressional speech in 1943 addressed a proposed "freedom-of-the-air" policy to allow unlimited access of airspace above all nations, an idea Luce condemned as "globaloney." During her two terms in Congress, Luce spoke out on such topics as Indian independence, postwar Sino-American relations, revocation of the Chinese Exclusion Acts*, immigration quotas from India, Java, and Korea, and U.S. policy toward the East Indies. In addition, she had more than two dozen articles, editorials, or speeches introduced into the *Congressional Record* on East Asian topics. She introduced bills on Indian immigration and Asian war relief and worked to focus the national attention on issues related to U.S.-Asian affairs. When Dwight D. Eisenhower* became president in 1953, he appointed Luce ambassador to Italy.

A. Hatch, *Ambassador Extraordinary: Clare Boothe Luce* (New York, 1956); S. Shadegg, *Clare Boothe Luce* (New York, 1970); W. Sheed, *Clare Boothe Luce* (New York, 1982); M. Thompson, "Biography: Clare Boothe Luce—Hell on Heels," Arts and Entertainment Network, 2 November 1998.

Catherine M. Forslund

LUCE, HENRY R. (1898–1967)

Henry R. Luce was the founder and publisher of the influential news magazines

Time, Life, and *Fortune.* Born in Dengzhou, China, to American missionary parents, he spent his first fourteen years in that country. Throughout his life, Luce retained an intense interest in the fortunes of China as it underwent vast and turbulent changes. His upbringing meant that, unlike most American internationalists, he showed more interest in Asia than in Europe. In the 1930s, Luce magazines gave unstinting support to the Guomindang* (Nationalist) government of Jiang Jieshi*, portraying him as a Westernized, Christian, democratic leader. The generalissimo and Song Meiling*, his American-educated wife, repeatedly adorned the cover of *Time* and were featured in scores of largely favorable stories. During and after World War II, Luce was the most prominent American supporter of the charitable organization United China Relief-United Service to China*, speaking often and raising several million dollars on its behalf. He ran some articles critical of the Guomindang regime's pervasive corruption and inefficiency but, considering Jiang's government, however flawed, far preferable to the increasingly strong Chinese Communist Party*, he ultimately fired Theodore H. White*, his correspondent in China, for being insufficiently pro-Nationalist.

Luce firmly believed that the twentieth century would be what he termed in his most famous article, a *Life* editorial of February 1941, the "American Century." In it, he argued that it was his country's destiny to dominate and, he believed, improve the world through providing technical and economic assistance and the dissemination of American ideals, a prediction that revealed his missionary heritage, and that he was determined to use his media position to facilitate. In 1940, *Time*'s support for the interventionist Wendell L. Willkie was instrumental in winning him the Republican nomination for the presidency. In 1940 and 1941, Luce assailed the policies of Franklin D. Roosevelt* as insufficiently bold in helping Britain, France, and China. He clearly hoped the United States would intervene in both the Pacific and the Atlantic. Despite his long-standing dislike for Roosevelt, Luce broadly endorsed the president's plans to enhance the American political and economic stake in the postwar world.

After World War II, Luce espoused firmly anti-Communist Cold War policies and advocated a strongly anti-Soviet line. Although the pro-Republican Luce media disdained what Luce saw as the unscrupulous extremism of Wisconsin Senator Joseph R. McCarthy*, it took up many of his charges, assailing the Truman administration for the 1949 Communist victory in the Chinese Civil War* and general softness on Communism*. Luce approved of U.S. intervention in the Korean War*, but attacked President Harry S. Truman* for firing General Douglas MacArthur*, when the latter provocatively suggested that Guomindang forces from Taiwan* should be used in combat against Communist forces. After MacArthur's Recall*, *Life* serialized his memoirs, for which it paid the general $600,000. Until the end of his life, Luce, a warm friend of the Republic of China* and a mainstay of the China Lobby*, opposed U.S. recognition of the People's Republic of China*. From the mid-1950s, he also gave strong support to the Republic of Vietnam* under Ngo Dinh Diem*. *Time* almost unquestioningly endorsed gradual escalation of the U.S. commitment in the Second Indochina War*, a posture that changed dramatically shortly after Luce's death. *See also* Clare Boothe Luce; Theodore H. White.

J. L. Baughman, *Henry R. Luce and the Rise of the American News Media* (Boston, 1987); R. E. Herzstein, *Henry R. Luce: A Political Portrait of the Man Who Created the American Century* (New York, 1994); T. C. Jespersen, *American Images of China, 1931–1949* (Stanford, CA, 1996); J. K. Jessup (ed.), *The Ideas of Henry Luce* (New York, 1979); P. Neils, *China Images in the Life and Times of Henry Luce* (Savage, MD, 1990).

Priscilla Roberts

LUCKY DRAGON INCIDENT

On 1 March 1954, the *Daigo Fukuryū Maru* (*Lucky Dragon* number five), a Japanese fishing vessel, while sailing some eighty-two miles east of Bikini atoll in the Marshall Islands, was inadvertently exposed to radioactive fallout from a U.S. hydrogen bomb test. The twenty-three crewmen soon exhibited traditional symptoms of radiation exposure, prompting a medical examination on their return to port in Japan. Although the initial examination was conducted privately and reassured the men concerned, and enabled them to distribute their fishing catch to the local market, a national Japanese journalist soon reported the incident, prompting a major public and official outcry and threatening serious harm to bilateral relations between Washington and Tōkyō. In light of understandable Japanese sensitivities regarding the use of nuclear weapons after the U.S. Atomic Attacks* of August 1945, public reaction quickly turned to panic and near-hysteria, as fish markets in Tōkyō and Ōsaka closed because of fear of the risk of contamination. Japanese media coverage was severely critical of the United States, citing both negligence and an inadequate official response, as well as suggesting that the incident had been engineered deliberately to examine the effects of new weaponry designed to yield high levels of lethal radiation. After the hospitalization and death of one of the crewmen, Japanese public and media criticism became more pronounced.

Bureaucratic confusion in both Japan and the United States, inaccurate media reporting, and larger strategic priorities all contributed to the bilateral tensions that arose from the *Lucky Dragon* incident. The argument that American officials had been insensitive and motivated by malicious intent is difficult to substantiate. Publicity announcing an official exclusion zone to prevent ships from being exposed to fallout had preceded the test. The *Lucky Dragon* was well outside this zone, but had been affected essentially because the de-signers of the bomb had miscalculated the size of the explosion, anticipating a roughly five-megaton detonation, but in fact eventually facing a far larger fifteen-megaton explosion. The internal response in the Eisenhower administration had been relatively swift, reflecting an awareness that the issue threatened to spin out of control. Moreover, American offers of technical and medical assistance either were turned down or misrepresented, with both the media and Japan's Ministry of Health and Welfare refusing to acknowledge that U.S. assistance had in fact been offered. The government of Prime Minister Yoshida Shigeru*, in private, acknowledged to the Americans that Japanese reporting had been confused, at times incorrect, and the result of bureaucratic and interest group pressures.

Yet, in other regards, Japanese grievances were well founded. Washington had been slow in issuing a formal apology, a point U.S. Ambassador to Japan John M. Allison* later freely acknowledged. Certain U.S. officials, notably Lewis Strauss, head of the Atomic Energy Commission, apparently had been intentionally misleading, claiming that the *Lucky Dragon* had been inside the testing zone. Furthermore, the United States would not cooperate when Japanese medical professionals requested specifics on the composition of the radioactive ash resulting from the Bikini test. Washington, fearing that a leak would reveal valuable details to the Soviet Union on the lithium core that accounted for the intensity of the Bikini test explosion, refused to divulge this information. Ultimately, the disagreement was resolved in January 1955, when the United States agreed to a $2 million compensation settlement for the affected fishermen. But Washington originally had offered only $1 million, only to face pressure for additional support from Japanese ministries that apparently were acting independently of Yoshida and his foreign minister, both of whom previously had acknowledged in private discussions with the Americans that the larger demand was unreasonable. Resolution of the incident fostered an easing of bilateral tensions. A second case of inadvertent exposure occurred in 1958, when two Japanese Maritime Safety Board vessels were subject to high levels of radiation after American nuclear tests near Eniwetok in the Marshall Islands. But this time the press in Japan uncharacteristically was subdued and the event passed largely unnoticed.

R. Buckley, *U.S.-Japan Alliance Diplomacy, 1945–1990* (Cambridge, MA, 1992); R. Dingman, "Alliances in Crisis: The Lucky Dragon Incident and Japanese-American Relations," in W. Cohen and A. Iriye (eds.), *The Great Powers in East Asia, 1953–1960* (New York, 1990); R. Hewlett and J. M. Holl, *Atoms for Peace and War, 1953–1961: Eisenhower and the Atomic Energy Commission* (Berkeley, CA, 1989); J. Swenson-Wright, *Unequal Allies?: United States Security and Alliance Policy Towards Japan, 1945–1960* (Stanford, CA, 2001).

John Swenson-Wright

LYTTON REPORT

This was the report of the Commission of Enquiry appointed by the League of Nations on the Mukden Incident*. After the Kwantung Army deliberately blew up a small portion of track on the South Manchuria Railway on 18 September 1931, Japan blamed the Chinese for the outrage, and then proceeded to overrun the city and the rest of Manchuria. China protested the aggressive actions taken by a fellow League member and finally, in January 1932, it was agreed that the Commission of Enquiry would be formed and sent to East Asia to investigate and recommend remedial steps. The commission's chairman was a distinguished Briton, the Earl of Lytton, who had gained considerable experience as a senior official working in India. France was represented by General Henri Claudel, a combat veteran well acquainted with colonial affairs, especially Asian. The Italian member was Count Luigi Aldrovandi-Marescotti,

who had served his country's delegation at the Versailles Peace Conference and had been ambassador to Argentina and Germany. Albert Schnee, the German member, was an expert on colonial matters at home and in East Africa. Although the United States was not a member of the League of Nations, President Herbert Hoover* and Secretary of State Henry L. Stimson* regarded the Manchurian crisis as vital to American interests, and they endorsed Major General Frank R. McCoy*, a respected soldier-diplomat, as the U.S. representative on the commission.

After arriving at Yokohama on 29 February by ship from San Francisco, commission members spent about a week in Japan interviewing civilian and military officials. Whatever hope existed for a softening in Japanese attitudes was shattered by the assassination of moderate leaders, which occurred in Tōkyō in early March 1932. The obduracy of the Japanese official position should have been immediately apparent when the Japanese authorities brazenly announced the creation of the puppet state of Manchukuo*. Nevertheless, the commission continued on to Shanghai, Nanjing, and Beijing and then to Manchuria itself, reaching Shenyang (Mukden) seven months after the original incident had erupted. Incessant Japanese obstruction in the guise of protection marked the six-week stay in Manchuria, but the commission managed to derive a good sense of conditions on the spot. The members spent the summer of 1932 in Beijing thrashing out a final report, completed on 4 September. It recognized the great importance of Manchuria to Japan's economic development and the advisability of a stable regime there to maintain order, as Japan demanded. Still, the members were obliged to conclude, as gently as possible, that the Kwantung Army's actions of 18 September could not be regarded as measures of legitimate self-defense, though it was possible that the local Japanese officers may have thought so. Restoring the original situation was out of the question, for Sino-

Japanese relations now amounted to "war in disguise." The future was dangerous, but the economic interests of both Japan and China in Manchuria were not irreconcilable.

These mild remarks did not mollify the Japanese, who thought the Lytton Commission was ignoring Communism* and banditry in Manchuria, and minimizing Japan's special interests there. On 24 February 1933, when the League Assembly in special session adopted the Lytton Report by a vote of 42–1, (with Thailand* abstaining and twelve countries absenting themselves), the Japanese were resentful and frustrated. They were irked by the League's insistence that Manchuria should be made autonomous under Chinese sovereignty, that the Kwantung Army should retreat to the old railway zone, and that Japan and China should negotiate directly. Particularly vexing was the stipulation that members of the League should withhold diplomatic recognition of Manchukuo after Japan already had done so. Thereupon, Matsuoka Yōsuke led the Japanese delegation in walking out of the League. On 27 March the final act occurred when the Japanese government gave formal notice of its intention to resign from the League, which it had helped found. The mission of the Lytton Commission had been doomed from the outset. Japan's actions undid the basic concept of collective security and marked a major first step in its defiance of the West leading to World War II.

A. J. Bacevich, *Diplomat in Khaki: Major General Frank Ross McCoy and American Foreign Policy, 1898–1949* (Lawrence, KS, 1989); A. Rappaport, *Henry L. Stimson and Japan, 1931–1933* (Chicago, 1963); C. Thorne, *The Limits of Foreign Policy: The West, The League, and the Far Eastern Crisis of 1931–1933* (New York, 1973).

Alvin D. Coox

M

MACARTHUR, ARTHUR (1845–1912)

Although perhaps best known as the father of General Douglas MacArthur*, Arthur MacArthur was in his own right an important figure during the Philippine-American War* of 1899–1902. Born in Massachusetts, he joined the Twenty-Fourth Wisconsin Infantry in 1862, eventually becoming its lieutenant colonel. In 1890, MacArthur was awarded the Medal of Honor for his actions at the Battle of Missionary Ridge in 1863. In 1866, he was commissioned into the Regular U.S. Army and served throughout the Indian War period in various infantry regiments until his transfer to the adjutant general's department in 1889. During the rapid expansion of the U.S. Army during the Spanish-American War* and the Philippine conflict, MacArthur received several temporary general officer commissions. Following brief service in stateside training camps, he was chosen to command a brigade and later a division in the Eighth Army Corps, the maneuver element that defeated the Philippine Republic's conventional field army in 1899 during the first phase of the Philippine war.

In 1900, MacArthur became military governor of the Philippines* as the war shifted from a conventional to a guerrilla struggle. He supervised the transition of the U.S. military effort there from a maneuver organization of divisions and brigades to a garrison force to carry out what could be described as a strategy of population control. MacArthur was acutely aware that the success of the U.S. pacification effort depended on severing the bond between the Filipino elite sponsoring resistance and the rural peasants actually serving as guerrilla fighters. He integrated several approaches to counterinsurgency: military efforts to capture or kill guerrillas in the field; "attractive" public health, sanitation, and education projects; grants of local political autonomy to secure districts; and coercive martial law measures to isolate guerrilla bands from their civilian supporters. His grasp on what was essentially a "hearts and minds" approach to defeating a guerrilla insurgency is best demonstrated in his fiscal year-end report for 1900. In the spring of 1901, MacArthur was replaced as military governor of the Philippines by General Adna R. Chaffee*. In spite of his accomplishments in the islands, he was frustrated in his efforts to become chief of staff of the U.S. Army. After promotion to major general in 1901 and lieutenant general in 1906, he retired from the service in 1909 as the U.S. Army's highest-ranking officer.

J. M. Gates, *Schoolbooks and Krags: The United States Army in the Philippines, 1898–1902* (Westport, CT, 1973); D. C. James, *The Years of Mac-Arthur*, Vol. 1: *1880–1941* (New York, 1970); B. R. Linn, *The Philippine War, 1899–1902* (Lawrence, KS, 2000); K. R. Young, *The General's General: The Life and Times of Arthur MacArthur* (Boulder, CO, 1994).

John S. Reed

MACARTHUR, DOUGLAS (1880–1964)

Few Americans are more identified with East Asia than General of the Army Douglas MacArthur, who was commander of the U.S. Occupation of Japan* and United Nations forces in the Korean War* from July 1950 to April 1951. Born in Little Rock, Arkansas, he was the son of General Arthur MacArthur*, the U.S. Army's highest-ranking officer from 1906 to 1909. Following his father's example, the younger MacArthur chose a military career, graduating from West Point with highest honors in 1903. Before World War I, he served as an engineering officer in the United States, the Philippines*, and Panama, eventually joining the War Department General Staff in 1913. MacArthur sailed to France after the United States declared war on Germany in April 1917, fighting with the Forty-second Division in the Champagne-Marne, St. Mihiel, and Meuse-Argonne operations. He earned many decorations for heroism and promotion to the rank of brigadier general. In 1919, MacArthur began a three-year stint as West Point's superintendent, later serving two command assignments in the Philippines and earning promotion to major general in 1925 and to general five years later. After becoming U.S. Army chief of staff in 1930, he commanded the U.S. troops sent to oust American veterans in July 1932 from the banks of the Anacostia River in Washington, D.C., following the Bonus March.

In the fall of 1935, MacArthur accepted a position as military adviser with the government of the Philippines, devoting six years to organizing Filipino defense forces.

But in July 1941, the U.S. government recalled him to active duty and named him commander of U.S. Army Forces in East Asia. After the Pearl Harbor Attack*, MacArthur commanded a stubborn defense of the Philippines at Corregidor*, but fled to Australia in March 1942. Over the next three years, he supervised Allied military operations in the Southwest Pacific Theater, until he was able in 1945 to liberate the Philippines and thus fulfill his pledge: "I shall return." Promoted to General of the Army in December 1944, he was appointed commanding general of U.S. Army Forces in the Pacific in April 1945. When the Japanese capitulated, MacArthur received the additional appointment of Supreme Commander for the Allied Powers (SCAP*) to accept formal surrender of the Japanese and then command the ensuing occupation. Though at times autocratic, from 1945 until 1951, MacArthur efficiently implemented a series of political, economic, and social reforms in Japan that eliminated militarist, ultranationalist, and feudal vestiges prior to approval of the Japanese Peace Treaty*.

After World War II, MacArthur, as head of the Far East Command, presided nominally over the U.S. Occupation of Korea* and Lieutenant General John R. Hodge*, who was in command of U.S. forces in southern Korea. He rarely played a direct role in policy formulation regarding Korea, but was a consistent advocate of early U.S. military withdrawal. Never enthusiastic about the Truman administration's efforts to provide military and economic assistance to the Republic of Korea*, a year before Secretary of State Dean Acheson* gave Acheson's National Press Club Speech*, MacArthur outlined a similar strategy excluding South Korea from guarantees of U.S. protection. In 1949 and 1950, the general lobbied intensively within government circles for a defense commitment to the Republic of China*. Following the North Korea invasion of South Korea, it was MacArthur's recommendation that caused President Harry S. Truman* to commit

ground troops in the Korean War. Theraf-
ter, as head of the United Nations Command, MacArthur consistently advocated a
full commitment of U.S. military power.
After his Inch'ŏn Landing* succeeded on
15 September 1950, he backed vigorously
the administration's decision to destroy the
North Korean regime. But already, Mac-
Arthur's relations with Truman were
strained because of the general's pressure
for an increase in U.S. support for Jiang Jieshi* against the People's Republic of
China* (PRC).

During October, as UN forces pushed
northward, MacArthur downplayed the
danger of Chinese Intervention in the Korean War*. At the Wake Island Conference,
he assured Truman that the PRC's threat to
intervene was a "bluff" and even if carried
out, would not impede achievement of U.S.
war aims. After China joined the fighting
in late October, compelling UN forces to
retreat south of the thirty-eighth parallel
after the Home by Christmas Offensive*,
MacArthur clashed more frequently with
both his civilian and military superiors. He
blamed his battlefield problems on restrictions against attacking China, and rejected
the wisdom or feasibility of seeking an armistice and restoring the prewar boundary.
Despite MacArthur's "gloom and doom"
predictions, during March 1951, battle lines
stabilized. When the Joint Chiefs of Staff
(JCS) informed him of Truman's impending cease-fire initiative, MacArthur sabotaged the effort with a public demand that
Chinese forces surrender or risk attacks
upon their homeland. Then came his public
letter to Congressman Joseph W. Martin
condemning administration policy in Korea as appeasement. These open and highly
partisan challenges led to MacArthur's Recall* by President Truman on 11 April
1951.

Among the most politically ambitious
generals in U.S. history, MacArthur sought
the Republican presidential nomination in
1944 and 1948. After Truman fired him
from his duties in Korea and Japan, the
general looked toward vindication as he

took his case directly to the American public. But despite broad popular affection for
MacArthur as a war hero, coupled with
frustration over the Korean stalemate, neither average citizens nor most civilian and
military officials favored a wider war. During the U.S. Senate's MacArthur hearings,
the JCS registered opposition to MacArthur's plan to escalate the war, and in Korea, Lieutenant General Matthew B.
Ridgway*, MacArthur's replacement, succeeded in stopping the Chinese spring offensive of 1951 and thereby opened the
way to P'anmunjŏm Truce Talks*. In 1952,
when the American people elected a general as president, it was not be MacArthur,
but Dwight D. Eisenhower*. MacArthur
then dropped out of public life, making occasional public appearances.

D. C. James, *The Years of MacArthur*, 3 vols. (Bos-
ton, 1970–1985); D. MacArthur, *Reminiscences*
(New York, 1964); G. Perrett, *Old Soldiers Never
Die: The Life of Douglas MacArthur* (New York,
1996); M. Schaller, *Douglas MacArthur: The Far
Eastern General* (New York, 1989); S. Weintraub,
*MacArthur's War: Korea and the Undoing of an
American Hero* (New York, 2000).

James I. Matray

MACARTHUR, DOUGLAS II (1909–1997)

The nephew of U.S. war hero General
Douglas MacArthur* was a career Foreign
Service officer who served as ambassador
to Japan in the late 1950s. After graduating
from Yale University in 1932, he followed
family tradition and joined the U.S. Army.
After two years, Douglas MacArthur II
joined the U.S. Foreign Service and spent
most of his early career in Europe. He was
interned in 1942 by France's Vichy government and held for two years. After returning to the United States, MacArthur was
assistant political adviser to General
Dwight D. Eisenhower*. In 1951, Eisenhower became the commander of North
Atlantic Treaty Organization forces and
took MacArthur along as political adviser.

In 1953, Secretary of State John Foster Dulles* made MacArthur the counselor of the State Department, in charge of the organization and planning for international conferences. Three years later, he went to Tōkyō, his first assignment as an ambassador. Although MacArthur spoke no Japanese and knew nothing about the nation's history, politics, or culture, his strengths outweighed these weaknesses. He found himself often referred to as the shōgun's nephew, and his name carried weight with the Japanese. Second, and more important, diplomats and politicians in Tōkyō knew he had a close relationship with both the secretary of state and the president.

MacArthur established a strong working relationship with Japanese Prime Minister Kishi Nobusuke*, adopting Kishi's belief that the relationship between the United States and Japan needed to enter a new period of equality. His first crisis came in January 1957, when a U.S. soldier shot a Japanese woman as she was collecting expended brass casings near a U.S. Army shooting range. Since the soldier was on a break at the time, Japan claimed jurisdiction under the Status of Forces Agreement. Republican leaders in Congress objected, but MacArthur warned Washington that if the United States failed to hand over the soldier, the case could eventually cost it bases not only in Japan, but throughout Asia. Eisenhower took steps to ensure that the soldier was turned over to the Japanese. MacArthur then used his influence to convince the administration that the U.S.-Japan Security Treaty of 1951* needed revision, warning that the one-sided agreement alienated the Japanese and only encouraged support for neutrality. In September 1957, after Dulles authorized him to negotiate a new treaty, MacArthur and Foreign Minister Fujiyama Aiichirō quickly agreed on a draft for the new U.S.-Japan Mutual Cooperation and Security Treaty*. Despite U.S. concessions, many Japanese raised objections about prior consultations over troop deployments and the introduction of nuclear weapons. MacAr-

thur successfully advised Dulles and Eisenhower to accept the Japanese position on these issues. Kishi's efforts to secure ratification, however, touched off the Anpo Crisis* during May and June 1960.

MacArthur believed Kishi was the only Japanese leader capable of sustaining the U.S.-Japan alliance. When Kishi traveled to Washington to sign the revised treaty in January 1960, a reciprocal visit was planned for Eisenhower in June. The turbulent protest demonstrations against the treaty caused MacArthur to fear for the future of the alliance and Japanese democracy. He met with top leaders of the ruling Liberal Democratic Party* and urged them to back Kishi. When Washington asked if the president's visit should be canceled, MacArthur said no, arguing that this would strengthen the opposition. Then, on 10 June, a U.S. Marine helicopter had to land and save the White House press secretary when a mob surrounded his car after he arrived in Japan to prepare for the presidential visit. When another crowd of a quarter-million people gathered near the U.S. embassy, the State Department instructed MacArthur to encourage Kishi to cancel the trip. MacArthur again refused. On 14 June, after police and protestors battled all night inside the Diet compound, Kishi canceled the trip. As a result, MacArthur and Fujiyama exchanged instruments of ratification at the foreign minister's home. Fujiyama had arranged to have MacArthur escape by climbing over the back fence into his neighbor's yard if mobs broke into his residence. MacArthur left Japan under less duress in 1961, serving later as ambassador to Belgium, Austria, and Iran. He was also assistant secretary for congressional relations for two years in the mid-1960s. He retired in 1972, living out his retirement in Washington, D.C.

G. Packard III, *Protest in Tokyo: The Security Treaty Crisis of 1960* (Princeton, NJ, 1966); M. Schaller, *Altered States: The United States and Japan Since the Occupation* (New York, 1997).

Nicholas Evan Sarantakes

MACARTHUR'S RECALL

President Harry S. Truman* relieved General Douglas MacArthur* as head of the United Nations Command (UNC) in the Korean War* and U.S. Occupation of Japan* on 11 April 1951. The president never had liked the general, remarking in July 1950 that MacArthur was a "supreme egoist," a failed commander in the Philippines*, and a "dictator" in Japan. When a controversial message from the general to the Veterans of Foreign Wars appeared in August 1950, Truman contemplated bringing him home. After Chinese Intervention in the Korean War* and the retreat of UNC forces late in 1950, MacArthur publicly criticized the administration for denying him the authority to strike back directly against the People's Republic of China* (PRC). Truman later wrote that he "should have relieved General MacArthur then and there," but chose to avoid giving the impression that he was being fired because the Home by Christmas Offensive* had failed. Instead, he ordered military officers not to comment publicly on sensitive issues.

As the administration turned down successive pleas from MacArthur to adopt his plan for victory and expand the war through attacking China, the general grew frustrated with the policy of settling for a truce near the thirty-eighth parallel. In March 1951, his demand for immediate Communist surrender sabotaged a planned cease-fire initiative. Conferring in Washington, U.S. military officials agreed that if any other general had acted as MacArthur had, "he would be relieved of his command at once." But for various reasons, many of them political, Truman and his advisers reprimanded, but did not recall, the general. By early April 1951, a combination of factors forced Truman to act. The Joint Chiefs of Staff worried about a Chinese and Soviet military buildup in East Asia, fearing that it might be unleashed against Japan as well as the UNC in Korea. They believed the UNC commander should have standing authority to retaliate against a Communist escalation, even recommending deploying atomic weapons to forward Pacific bases. They mistrusted MacArthur and guessed he might provoke an incident to widen the war.

On 5 April, MacArthur's letter to House Republican Minority Leader Joseph W. Martin once again criticizing the administration's efforts to contain the war showed Truman and his advisers that MacArthur would play partisan politics and manipulate the facts to get his way. Secretary of State Dean G. Acheson* argued that his push for a wider war threatened to destroy Western European and UN support for U.S. policy. Truman considered the Martin letter as "rank insubordination" and the "last straw." He believed that MacArthur provoked his own recall to escape a war without glory and to gain martyrdom. Acting on near-unanimous advice from his advisers, Truman signed the recall order on 10 April 1951. Although the White House tried to contact the general privately, fear of a news leak resulted in the recall announcement early in the morning of 11 April, infuriating MacArthur and his supporters, who then accused Truman of intentionally humiliating a national hero. Upon his return to the United States, MacArthur gave an emotional speech to Congress and then defended himself before a Senate committee investigating the recall. These hearings revealed the wisdom of Truman's decision. Meanwhile, Lieutenant General Matthew B. Ridgway* was implementing Truman's strategy in Korea successfully.

D. C. James, *The Years of MacArthur*, Vol. 3: *Triumph and Disaster, 1945–1964* (Boston, 1985); M. Schaller, *Douglas MacArthur: The Far Eastern General* (New York, 1989).

James I. Matray

MACMURRAY, JOHN V. A. (1881–1960)

John Van Antwerp MacMurray, as chief of the State Department's Far Eastern Affairs

Division (1919–1924), assistant secretary of state (1925), and minister to China (1925–1929), found himself at the center of the making and execution of U.S. policies in East Asia in the 1920s. He joined the U.S. Foreign Service in 1907 and his ideas proved congenial to Secretary of State Charles Evans Hughes*, but not to Hughes's successors, Frank B. Kellogg* and Henry L. Stimson*, with whom he had open disagreements. MacMurray had courage and intellectual ability. Both the polish of his dispatches and the tenor of his recommendations were not greatly dissimilar from those of George F. Kennan*, his contemporary as a Foreign Service officer. But he faltered from a lack of perspective; while in Washington he had lost sight of the new forces of nationalism building in Beijing during the Warlord Era*, and in Beijing he lost touch with the shifting political barometer in Washington. But even then, his realistic attitude dominated his approach. MacMurray supported nonintervention in China's domestic affairs, cooperative actions, including the use of force if necessary with other powers, and holding the Chinese government to its international treaty obligations. He saw no reason to choose sides in the Chinese Revolution of 1911* and described Zhang Zuolin* as a pirate and Sun Zhongshan* as a Chinese William Jennings Bryan*.

The Washington Conference* of 1921 and 1922 epitomized MacMurray's ideal of the powers working together both to protect their interests and to help China take responsible steps toward a stable future. His argument that the United States should not voluntarily give up its claims to extraterritorial rights, as American missionaries suggested, won Secretary Hughes' support. When he returned to China as minister in 1925, he advised Kellogg against concessions to China. He saw Chinese emotions against Western and Japanese positions in China as largely the result of racial and nationalist considerations, not Bolshevist ideologies or actions. Kellogg, however, told President Calvin Coolidge that it was time

to help China achieve her goals. Since the United States would lose its rights in China eventually, he reasoned, why not accommodate it and hope to win Chinese friendship? Not subject to domestic pressures, MacMurray, a strong believer in acting on the knowledge and advice of the ambassador on the spot, was bound to disagree. An incident at Dagu in March 1926, in which Chinese troops fired on foreign ships and Kellogg did not respond strongly, led MacMurray to complain to Undersecretary Joseph C. Grew*. A further incident at Nanjing in March 1927, in which Chinese troops entered the city and an American and five Europeans were killed, saw MacMurray calling for strong and immediate action, including the blockade of Chinese ports; none was forthcoming from Washington.

Despite rumors of MacMurray's probable firing, he held on until late 1929. He became restless in retirement and returned to the Foreign Service in 1933 as minister to Estonia, Latvia, and Lithuania, but he retained an interest in East Asia. Stanley K. Hornbeck* asked for his advice in 1935, and the result was the seminal memorandum titled "Developments Affecting American Policy in the Far East." In it, MacMurray wrote that U.S. alternatives were three: (1) actively oppose Japan, (2) acquiesce or even participate with the Japanese, or (3) take a passive attitude. The first would mean war and "nobody except Russia would gain from our victory in such a war." Avoidance of war must be a "major objective" of U.S. policy. Any large opposition to Japan might "lead them to make even a desperate attack," which would "force us into a war we do not want." The United States had no obligation to undertake any duties or responsibilities on behalf of China. Now was the time to husband U.S. strength, to write down U.S. interests in China to their present "depreciated value," to deal with Japan fairly and sympathetically, to be guided by national interests, and not to wander onto false trails, whether for or against China, or for or against Japan. There is no reason to believe that Franklin D. Roosevelt* ever saw or read the memorandum.

T. H. Buckley, "John Van Antwerp MacMurray: The Diplomacy of an American Mandarin," in R. D. Burns and E. M. Bennett (eds.), *Diplomats in Crisis: United States-Chinese-Japanese Relations, 1919–1941* (Santa Barbara, CA, 1974); A. Waldron, *How the Peace Was Lost: The 1935 Memorandum* (Stanford, CA, 1992).

Thomas H. Buckley

MCCARTHY, JOSEPH R. (1908–1957)

A senator from Wisconsin from 1947 to 1957, Joseph R. McCarthy's anti-Communist crusade occurred in an atmosphere in which Republicans blamed President Harry S. Truman* and Secretary of State Dean G. Acheson* for the "loss" of China, that is, the victory of the Chinese Communist Party* over the Guomindang* (Nationalists) in 1949. McCarthy believed that State Department experts on China, known as the China Hands*, had helped Mao Zedong* win the Chinese Civil War* over Jiang Jieshi*. The case of John S. Service* was very important to his charges. Service had called for the United States to be less supportive of the Nationalists in its policy toward China, believing that Jiang probably would lose his contest with Mao. He was one of four officials McCarthy named in his famed speech in Wheeling, West Virginia, in February 1950, in which he claimed that Acheson was protecting 205 Communists in the State Department. Service in fact had leaked classified information on China to the magazine *Amerasia*, but eventually was cleared of any charges of espionage. McCarthy pursued the case, however, making untrue statements damaging to Service. He decided later that Service was not a Communist, but definitely a security risk.

McCarthy's biggest case against an American Asian expert was that of Owen Lattimore*, who he named as a high-level Soviet spy. Although never a State Depart-ment employee, Lattimore had worked closely with other Asia experts during the 1940s at John Hopkins University as director of the Walter Hines Page School of International Relations. He certainly was antipathetic to the Chinese Nationalists, held pro-Soviet views, and, as later discovered, had a strange ability to attract Communist agents, but there was no proof that he was a Soviet spy. Democrats on the Senate committee that investigated McCarthy's charges, led by Millard Tydings, ridiculed McCarthy, saying that his attacks on Lattimore were distorted, and they found Service guilty only of an indiscretion. McCarthy angrily charged that the committee's report was a whitewash. Shortly thereafter, a hearing before maverick Democrat and stridently anti-Communist Pat McCarran's Senate Internal Security Committee charged Lattimore and John Carter Vincent* with shifting U.S. policy so that it favored Mao. Here, McCarthy's charges, however ill-founded, bore more fruit. Acheson dismissed Service from the State Department late in 1950. Vincent and other China Hands, including John Paton Davies*, O. Edmund Clubb*, and John F. Melby*, were forced into early retirement.

McCarthy damaged U.S.–East Asian relations in other ways. For example, he was a conduit for boosters of Jiang, such as Alfred Kohlberg, who owned a firm that imported Chinese embroideries. Kohlberg provided the senator with information on the alleged State Department "betrayal" of the Nationalists, which McCarthy repeated to the world. McCarthy also privately arranged a deal with Greek shipping magnates not to trade with the People's Republic of China* (PRC). In 1953, an investigation by McCarthy's aide Robert F. Kennedy determined that British and Greek ships flying the British flag were shipping strategic materials to the PRC. McCarthy contacted the Greek shipowners and obtained an agreement from them to stop trading with Communist China. His fall came in 1954 after Americans witnessed his obnoxious behavior in televised hearings probing his charges that U.S. officials were protecting known Communists in the U.S. Army. Later that year, the Senate condemned his conduct and stripped him of his powers. McCarthy died almost certainly of alcohol-related disease, but the detrimental impact of "McCarthyism" persisted. By freezing U.S. policy toward Asia, McCarthyism had made it impossible for the administration of John F. Kennedy* to deal realistically with China. And his purge of specialists on Asia from the State Department contributed to the disastrous U.S. involvement in the Second Indochina War*.

R. M. Fried, *Men Against McCarthy* (New York, 1976); D. Halberstam, *The Best and the Brightest* (New York, 1972); A. Herman, *Joseph McCarthy: Reexamining the Life and Legacy of America's Most Hated Senator* (New York, 2000); D. M. Oshinsky, *A Conspiracy So Immense: The World of Joe McCarthy* (New York, 1983); T. C. Reeves, *The Life and Times of Joe McCarthy: A Biography* (New York, 1982).

Tracy S. Uebelhor

MCCOY, FRANK R. (1874–1954)

Frank Ross McCoy was a career soldier and a protégé of President Theodore Roosevelt*, General Leonard Wood*, and Secretary of War Henry L. Stimson*. He belonged to a group of young diplomats, soldiers, and government officials who all believed the United States should play a greater world role. As aide to Wood in the Philippines* from 1903 to 1906, McCoy assisted in the brutal pacification of the native Moros. On leave in Asia in December 1905, McCoy helped other U.S. officers draw up a plan—never implemented—for an American military intervention and occupation in Guangzhou in response to a local boycott of American-made goods to protest his country's Exclusion Acts* and the mistreatment of Chinese living in the United States. In 1921, McCoy returned to the Philippines for four years as a member

of Governor Wood's unofficial "khaki cabinet," a post he held until his enforced resignation in 1925. The somewhat racist McCoy supported his superior's attempts to defer Philippine independence as long as possible. In 1931, he drafted an abortive bill that would have granted the Philippines dominion status, thereby, he hoped, defusing calls for complete independence. In 1923, McCoy, then on leave, witnessed the Yokohama and Tōkyō earthquakes and coordinated the American relief effort to Japan.

McCoy's most prominent public position was as the American member of the Lytton Commission, established by the League of Nations in 1931 to investigate the Mukden Incident*. The U.S. government nominated McCoy to this body and, though theoretically independent, he discussed his duties in great detail with Stimson, then secretary of state. The commission spent several months visiting Japan, Manchuria, and China, before writing the Lytton Report*, which recognized that Japan had a special position in Manchuria, but still strongly condemned Japanese aggression and demanded withdrawal. After retiring from the army, McCoy's final assignment was as head of the Far Eastern Commission (FEC), which was supposed to supervise policies during the U.S. Occupation of Japan*. His repeated efforts to make the FEC's authority effective were circumvented both by General Douglas MacArthur*, the occupation commander, who deeply resented and generally ignored its existence, and the Department of State, which refused to allow any other power, particularly the Soviet Union, any say in rehabilitating Japanese. A disillusioned McCoy left the FEC in late 1949 and enjoyed an active retirement in Washington, D.C.

A. J. Bacevich, *Diplomat in Khaki: Major General Frank Ross McCoy and American Foreign Policy, 1898–1949* (Lawrence, KS, 1989); W. S. Biddle, *Major General Frank Ross McCoy: Soldier-Statesman-American* (Lewistown, PA, 1956); S. Bradshaw, "The United States and East Asia: Frank Ross McCoy and the Lytton Commission,

1931–1933," Ph.D. dissertation, Georgetown University, 1974; N. B. Norton, "Frank R. McCoy and American Diplomacy, 1928–1932," Ph.D. dissertation, Columbia University, 1968.

Priscilla Roberts

MCKINLEY, WILLIAM (1843–1901)

William McKinley, as president of the United States from 1897 to 1901, played an essential role in the expansion of U.S.–East Asian relations through acquiring the Philippines* and establishing, with his secretary of state, John Hay*, the Open Door Policy* for the China trade. A former representative and senator from Ohio, he had defeated William Jennings Bryan* for the presidency in 1896. McKinley was an expansionist, and one of his first acts as president was to seek Hawaiian Annexation*, but the U.S. Senate refused to ratify his treaty. His success in achieving his goals in East Asia then came largely by inadvertence as a result of the Spanish-American War*. Commodore George Dewey's victory over the Spanish fleet in the Battle of Manila Bay* on 1 May 1898 presaged no annexationist movement. The Philippines, as Spanish territory, had been excluded from U.S. territorial ambitions. But McKinley's decision of 4 May to dispatch General Wesley Merritt to Manila, for the purpose of completing the destruction of Spanish power there, confronted Washington with the unanticipated dilemma of disposing of the islands, no longer under Spanish control. Following the path of least resistance, McKinley sought Philippine Annexation*. Late in November, his peace commission in Paris presented its final demands to the Spanish government: the cession of Puerto Rico, Guam*, and the Philippine Archipelago to the United States for $20 million. Spain accepted the terms on 10 December 1898.

What remained was the long, bitter debate in Congress and the press over the wisdom of extending U.S. imperial responsibilities across the Pacific. Senator George F. Hoar*, among other anti-expansionists, including members of the Anti-Imperialist League*, spoke against annexation. But in February 1899, the Senate approved the treaty, 57 to 27, just one more vote than the necessary two-thirds. McKinley's speaking tour the prior fall to promote support for ratification contributed to the outcome. Viewing the Philippines as a stepping-stone for American merchants to penetrate the China market, he then supported Secretary of State Hay's Open Door notes in September 1899, which sought to prevent transformation of the new leaseholds that the European powers had gained in the great ports of China into exclusive economic enclaves. In the second Open Door note of July 1900, the United States assumed responsibility for the administrative and territorial integrity of China against the ambitions of Russia and Japan, two countries that possessed far greater power and interests in China than did the United States. The McKinley administration thus transformed the United States into a major East Asian power, with commitments extending to the Asian mainland, with little concern for the warnings that the new obligations ultimately would carry great costs. Following reelection, McKinley began a second term in March 1901, but before the year was over, an assassin's bullet would put Theodore Roosevelt* in McKinley's place as president.

C. S. Campbell, *The Transformation of American Relations, 1865–1900* (New York, 1970); T. Dennett, *John Hay: From Poetry to Politics* (New York, 1934); E. R. May, *Imperial Democracy: The Emergence of America as a Great Power* (New York, 1961).

Norman A. Graebner

MCNAMARA, ROBERT S. (1916–)

Robert McNamara was the secretary of defense from 1961 to 1968, and strongly influenced U.S. policy in the Second Indochina War*. From a middle-class California background, he graduated from the University of California at Berkeley in 1937. Two years later, McNamara earned a master's degree in business administration from Harvard University, where he was trained in the new field of systems management and quantitative analysis. The U.S. Army Air Corps commissioned him in World War II to help apply statistical controls to the global air war. After the war, he joined Ford Motor Company and rose rapidly through the ranks, ultimately becoming its president in 1960, shortly before new President John F. Kennedy* named him to his cabinet. His relative youth, brilliance, and accomplishment cast him among "the best and the brightest" in the Kennedy inner circle. From the beginning of Kennedy's administration and continuing under his successor, Lyndon B. Johnson*, McNamara was the most visible official proponent of the escalating U.S. military involvement in the former French Indochina*. He had faith that the proper deployment of U.S. power, based on its advanced technology, could bring statistically verifiable political change to the Republic of Vietnam*. He was a vigorous advocate of the counterinsurgency efforts and the drastic increase in U.S. military advisers under Kennedy. Quickly gaining Johnson's confidence, McNamara urged the new president to increase the pressures on the Democratic Republic of Vietnam* through retaliatory air strikes after the Gulf of Tonkin Incidents* in 1964 and in 1965 through the launching of Operation ROLLING THUNDER*. He also advocated the introduction of combat troops and the open-ended troop commitment that Johnson approved in July 1965.

Behind the scenes, McNamara soon became a skeptic. He recognized that the bombing was failing to intimidate North Vietnam and to reduce significantly its war-making capacity. He was also increasingly troubled by the corruption and narrow base of the South Vietnamese government and the ineffectiveness of the Army of the Republic of Vietnam*. Accordingly, McNamara consistently pressed Johnson to seek a diplomatic solution, such

as the San Antonio Formula*, to stabilize troop levels, and to limit the bombing. As the war dragged on, McNamara's relations with the Joint Chiefs of Staff, never strong to begin with, steadily worsened. His refusal to approve expanded operations alienated the military leadership and their hawkish supporters. At the same time, McNamara was criticized by antiwar protesters for his prominent public role in taking the country to war. In late 1967, Johnson engineered McNamara's appointment to become president of the World Bank. Characteristically, he immersed himself in that position and became a strong advocate of programs to improve the living standards of Third World peoples. He retired in 1983. But then in 1995, McNamara published *In Retrospect*, in which he admitted that the war had been "terribly wrong" and faulted himself and other officials for failing to recognize the strength of Vietnamese nationalism. Although such self-criticism is rare in a memoir, McNamara's touched off more criticism than praise. Vietnam veterans were incensed over revelations of his doubts as he was orchestrating escalation. Other readers were troubled by McNamara's excuses, especially an evident misplaced loyalty to Johnson. *See also* Green Berets; Strategic Hamlets Program.

L. Gelb and R. Betts, *The Irony of Vietnam: The System Worked* (Washington, DC, 1978; R. McNamara, *In Retrospect: The Tragedy and Lessons of Vietnam* (New York, 1995); D. Shapley, *Promise and Power: The Life and Times of Robert McNamara* (Boston, 1993).

Gary R. Hess

MAGIC

This was the American code word to identify deciphered Japanese diplomatic communications before and during World War II. The word was often used to designate deciphered Japanese military communications and, to further complicate definitions, all these messages were classified Top Secret Ultra. The origins of the decrypts were quite distinct: *Magic* dealt with diplomatic codes, whereas Ultra was military and naval (and not to be confused with the British Ultra, which penetrated only German Enigma codes). *Magic* included all decrypted diplomatic codes and ciphers, but most notably those encrypted by the cypher machine known to the Americans as Purple. The Americans first broke Purple with *Magic* on 25 September 1940, two days before the Tripartite Pact*, and continued to do so for the duration of the war. Ultimately, the BRUSA (Britain and United States of America) agreement of 17 May 1943 formalized the sharing of intelligence information on an equal basis.

General George C. Marshall* regarded it as a "priceless asset" and ordered extraordinary measures to keep it secure. Consequently, these precautions became so onerous that they hampered effective use of this intelligence source in the days before the Pearl Harbor Attack*. Both the U.S. Navy and U.S. Army commanders in Hawaii and, for a time, President Franklin D. Roosevelt* were denied access to *Magic*. In addition, *Magic* was treated with such secrecy that it was almost impossible to integrate it with other forms of intelligence, since the United States possessed no central intelligence agency until the creation of the Office of Strategic Services in June 1942. *Magic* also served as an invaluable source of information on German resources and intentions. Japanese diplomats, especially General Ōshima Hiroshi in Berlin, kept Tōkyō closely informed on developments in Europe, from the possibility of an invasion of the Soviet Union in 1941, to German morale on the Eastern front, the Atlantic Wall defenses, and specifics of the new guided missiles and snorkel submarines. Finally, *Magic* revealed the desperate efforts of Tōkyō in the summer of 1945 to secure neutral Soviet mediation of the Pacific war.

E. J. Drea, *MacArthur's ULTRA: Codebreaking and the War Against Japan, 1942–1945* (Lawrence, KS, 1992); R. Lewin, *The American Magic: Codes, Ciphers, and the Defeat of Japan* (New York, 1982); E. Van Der Rhoer, *Deadly Magic: A Personal Account of Communication Intelligence in World War II in the Pacific* (New York, 1978).

Errol M. Clauss

MAGSAYSAY, RAMÓN (1907–1957)

Ramón Magsaysay was president of the Philippines* from 1953 to 1957. First and foremost, he fancied himself a man of the people, often opening up his palace to the people—so much so that U.S. officials thought that he sometimes neglected his governing duties. But the United States had great faith in his ability, reliability, and integrity, relying on him to prevent the triumph of Communism* in the Philippines. He fought in the Filipino guerrilla movement against the Japanese during the Pacific war, becoming a successful commander in Zambeles Province. With U.S. liberation, he was named military governor of the province, as the Americans were impressed with his determination and pro-American attitude. After independence in 1946, Magsaysay was twice elected to Congress as a Liberal Party member. President Elpidio Quirino appointed him as secretary of defense in September 1950 and, with much aid and advice from the United States, he directed the successful repulsion of the Communist-led Hukbalahap* insurgency. In fact, Magsaysay's chief adviser was U.S. Colonel Edward G. Lansdale*, a Central Intelligence Agency* icon, who, from 1950 through 1953, was Washington's greatest intelligence asset in the Philippines.

Magsaysay's campaign revolved around two central facets: having the previously ineffective army employ a "win-the-hearts-and-minds-of-the-people" strategy by ending harsh pacification tactics and forced evacuations of villages, and offering land to rebels who surrendered. The use of Huk informers was also a factor. He went so far as to favor the use of napalm attacks against the Huks. By 1953, the Huks were finished as a fighting force. Simultaneously, Magsaysay used the army to patrol polling places and ensure clean legislative elections in 1951. The victorious leaders of the Nacionalista Party praised his performance. His national reputation thereby was enhanced as the one honest man in the Quirino administration, although critics complained about his dependence on the United States. Lansdale groomed Magsaysay, the most prominent Filipino to support the continuance of American bases in the Philippines, to succeed the corrupt Quirino as president of the Philippines. Thus, the American provided propaganda on Magsaysay's behalf through American newspapers, American-owned Filipino newspapers, and supportive Filipino-owned papers. Lansdale even arranged for Magsaysay to journey to Washington to meet with President Harry S. Truman*, Secretary of State Dean G. Acheson*, and Secretary of Defense George C. Marshall*. Magsaysay impressed his American hosts by asking for a modest $500,000 to finance his counterinsurgency efforts.

In 1953, Magsaysay resigned from the Quirino government, charging the government with corruption. He joined the Nacionalista Party and ran for president, easily winning a four-year term on December 1953 over Quirino. Magsaysay's success in battling the Huks culminated as president in May 1954 with the surrender of their leader, Luis Taruc. Relations between Manila and Washington were at an all-time high under Magsaysay. Significantly, Manila was the site of the conference in 1954 that resulted in creation of the anti-Communist Southeast Asia Treaty Organization*. The revised U.S.-Philippine Trade Agreement was signed in 1955, which gradually increased Philippine tariffs on U.S. products while enabling the Philippines to increase exports to the United States. On the domestic front, Magsaysay pushed for reforms in land distribution and the political process. His efforts won him enormous popularity from the masses, but only the bitter enmity of the landowning and political elite. Magsaysay began building a coalition of younger, reform-minded politicians, implementing a program of building bridges, roads, and irrigation canals. Special courts were established in the countryside to settle landlord-tenant disputes. In 1955, Magsaysay pushed land reform legislation through the legislature, which enabled the newly established Land Tenure Administration to acquire private lands by purchase or expropriation and then sell plots at reasonable rates to farmers. Magsaysay died in an airplane crash in March 1957, an event U.S. Vice President Richard M. Nixon* called "a tragedy for the Philippines and for all of free Asia."

C. B. Currey, *Edward Lansdale: The Unquiet American* (Boston, 1988); M. M. Gray, *Island Hero: The Story of Ramon Magsaysay* (New York, 1965).

Gregory J. Murphy

MAHAN, ALFRED THAYER (1840–1914)

Admiral Alfred Thayer Mahan developed the concept of sea power in his works on the history of the British Navy, which shaped the growth of naval policies of Great Britain, Germany, Japan, and the United States both before and after World War I. He was born at West Point, and his father, Captain Dennis Hart Mahan, was a famous instructor at the U.S. Army Academy. Alfred chose to enter the naval service, to his father's mild annoyance, entered the Naval Academy at Annapolis, and graduated in 1859 second in his class of twenty. Quiet and studious, his service on various ships was undistinguished, reinforcing Mahan's interest in study and writing, rather than command. In the period before 1885, he published a few well-received articles on naval affairs. In 1884, the major turning point came when he was offered and accepted a position as lecturer at the newly established Naval War College in Newport, Rhode Island. Two years later, he became president of the college. Now in a position where he could devote adequate time to research and writing, Mahan developed his ideas on sea power in lectures, which were collated and published in 1890 under the title *The Influence of Sea Power upon History, 1660–1783*.

Within a short time, Mahan and his sea power concepts received attention and acceptance in naval circles abroad. Later in his career, he published several works, the most important being *The Influence of Sea Power upon the French Revolution and Empire* (1892), the sequel to his first work on sea power. His other major works, *The Life of Nelson: The Embodiment of the Sea Power in Great Britain* (1897), and *Sea Power in Its Relations to the War of 1812* (1905), were based on earlier research and published after his retirement from the navy in 1895. Mahan's sea power doctrines were based upon his study particularly of the history of the British Navy in the later seventeenth and the eighteenth centuries. Simply put, he saw the victorious career of the Royal Navy as largely the result of the principle of blockade and the deliberate seeking out of the enemy fleets at sea. Mahan said that decisive results in naval warfare could be achieved only by the destruction of the enemy's main battle fleets, for only this would gain the command of the sea. This presupposed a strong naval policy focused on the building and operation of a major navy, along with secure bases from which to operate. As important was a favorable geography, and a seafaring population versed in commerce and overseas trade. According to Mahan, the possession of these factors enabled the British to dominate the world's oceans for more than two centuries.

Ironically, Mahan's ideas were not easily accepted in the United States. American naval policy had long been based upon the defensive concept of coast defense forts, supplemented by a small fleet to protect American shores. Mahan pointed out that the policy had been found wanting during the War of 1812, and also in the experience of other nations. Theodore Roosevelt* was a disciple of Mahan and, during his presidency, he built up a strong navy based on battleships. But it was not until the promotion of the idea of "a navy second to none" beginning in 1916 that the sea power doctrine took hold in the United States. His sea power doctrine was accepted most completely in Great Britain, Germany, and Japan. In Germany, it was a factor in the fateful decision to challenge British naval supremacy by building a strong battleship fleet, and in Japan the idea so influenced naval thinking that most of Japanese naval strategy between World Wars I and II was dominated by the idea of a decisive naval battle with the U.S. Navy to gain control of the western Pacific at one blow. Mahan, who was promoted to admiral in 1906, was naturally much sought after for lectures and articles. He commented particularly upon the international situation in the momentous years from 1900 to 1914. Events confirmed many of his conclusions and predictions, especially the coming of world war.

W. E. Livezey, *Mahan on Sea Power* (Norman, OK, 1981); W. D. Puleston, *Mahan: The Life and Work of Captain Alfred Thayer Mahan* (New Haven, CT, 1939); R. Seager II, *Alfred Thayer Mahan: The Man and His Letters* (Annapolis, MD, 1977).

Ernest Andrade Jr.

MAHATHIR, MOHAMAD (1925–   )

Mohamad bin Mahathir was born in Kedah, British Malaya. He trained as a doctor before entering politics in the 1960s, and became prime minister of Malaysia* in 1981. He has been an uninhibited promoter of "Asian values" and has led Malaysia during the years when per capita gross national product had risen to approximately US$3,000 by the late 1980s, higher than Portugal or Hungary at that time. Mahathir has not hesitated to take credit for his development program, which has emphasized both ready acceptance of technology and a redistribution of some economic power from ethnic Chinese to ethnic Malays.

Despite Mahathir's well-known "Look East" policy, and during the late 1990s his inflammatory rhetoric blaming international currency traders (especially from the United States) for his country's economic woes after the East Asian Financial Crisis*, Mahathir also has been a foreign policy realist. Malaysia was a founding member of the Association of Southeast Asian Nations*, and Mahathir has been a consistent, if sometimes uneasy, supporter. During the Gulf War with Iraq, Mahathir attempted to find a middle road. Malaysia objected to Iraq's invasion of Kuwait, but did not freeze Iraqi assets. By late November 1990, Mahathir, having abandoned his initial position that force was not necessary, voted for the "use of force" resolution in the United Nations. After the United States closed its naval bases in the Philippines*, Mahathir entertained the idea of allowing U.S. ships to have docking privileges in Malaysian ports; Singapore* ultimately granted this privilege.

Most of the 1990s witnessed rocky U.S.-Malaysian relations. Mahathir relied on a populist and stridently sovereign tone unusual for the pro-growth leader of a small country. In 1990, when the U.S. Congress cut off some aid to Malaysia because it had sent refugees from the Socialist Republic of Vietnam* back to sea, Mahathir declared that Malaysia "is our country. We have the right to decide who can come in and who cannot. The U.S. cannot force us." The next year, Mahathir accused the United States of maintaining a double standard after Washington supported Asian-Pacific Economic Cooperation* (APEC) over the East Asian Economic Caucus Mahathir had proposed in 1990: "Can it be that what is right and proper for the rich and powerful is not right and proper for the poor?" The Asian economic crisis beginning in 1997 hurt Malaysia less than many countries, but Mahathir's invective against currency speculators, as he called them, did not help his relations with Washington. Mahathir

remained a strong supporter of APEC, however, although at times primarily for the purpose of turning it toward Asia and away from the United States. In the late 1990s, economic challenges stemming from international problems had emboldened some of his political rivals.

A. R. A. Baginda (ed.), *Malaysia's Defence and Foreign Policies* (Petaling Jaya, Selangor, Darul Ehsam, 1995); R. Stubbs, "The Foreign Policy of Malaysia," in D. Wurfel (ed.), *The Political Economy of Foreign Policy in Southeast Asia* (New York, 1990); Khoo B. Teik, *Paradoxes of Mathirism: An Intellectual Biography of Mahathir Mohamad* (Kuala Lumpur, 1995).

Anne L. Foster

MAKINO NOBUAKI (1861–1949)

Makino Nobuaki was one of the leading political figures in Japan during the interwar period and the closest adviser to Emperor Hirohito* from 1925 to 1935. Having studied in the United States and served as diplomat in Europe, he was seen by his contemporaries as a pro-Western, liberal diplomat and politician. Throughout his political career, Makino exerted some influence for moderation in Japan's foreign policy toward the Western powers, including the United States. The son of Ōkubo Toshimichi (the leading advocate of Westernization in the Meiji government), Makino accompanied his father on the Iwakura Mission* in 1871 and remained in the United States to attend school until 1874. He joined the Ministry of Foreign Affairs in 1880 and spent the next three years at the Japanese legation in London. He was ambassador to Italy and Austria-Hungary before he served from 1906 to 1908 as minister of education.

When Makino became foreign minister in 1913, the state of California passed alien land legislation banning Japanese immigrants from owning land and straining relations between the two nations. He had to undertake the difficult task of standing firm against the racially motivated discriminatory legislation in the United States while preventing the event from becoming a diplomatic crisis. However, Makino's attempt to press President Woodrow Wilson* to intervene on behalf of Japan was unsuccessful. Upon the resignation of the Yamamoto cabinet, Makino was appointed to the House of Peers as well as the Privy Council.

During World War I, Makino joined the Advisory Council on Foreign Relations, which the government of Terauchi Masatake established in an effort to make bipartisan wartime foreign policy. Makino played an important role in the council's debate over the Siberian Intervention*. He insisted on the primacy of cooperation with the United States, but, along with Hara Kei*, firmly opposed the sending of an independent Japanese expeditionary force that did not have the support of the Wilson administration. At the Paris Peace Conference of 1919, Makino acted as the chief delegate from Japan under the nominal head, Saionji Kinmochi*. Although he personally favored Japan's participation in the League of Nations and detested the military's aggressive expansionist policy in China, Makino followed Tōkyō's instructions and firmly maintained in negotiating the terms of the Versailles Peace Treaty* Japanese claims above all to German rights and concessions in Shandong and the declaration of racial equality in the League of Nations.

Makino became one of the key advisers to Crown Prince Hirohito when he was appointed imperial household minister in February 1921. Having assumed the post of lord keeper of the privy seal in 1925, he continued to guide young Emperor Hirohito until he resigned from the position in 1935. Makino's main task was to preserve the image and reputation of the imperial house and the nation. As a true believer in constitutional monarchy, he tried to prevent the emperor from directly participating in the political and military decision-making process. Because of his strong opposition to the army's aggressive

actions, such as the assassination of Zhang Zuolin* in 1928 and the Mukden Incident* in 1931, Makino, under heavy criticism from the military and the right-wing politicians, resigned from the privy seal in 1935. Unlike some of his unfortunate colleagues, Makino narrowly escaped ultranationalist young officers' attempt to assassinate him in the 26 February Incident in 1936.

N. Kawamura, *Turbulence in the Pacific: Japanese-U.S. Relations During World War I* (Westport, CT, 2000); P. Wetzler, *Hirohito and War: Imperial Tradition and Military Decision Making in Prewar Japan* (Honolulu, HI, 1998).

Kawamura Noriko

MALAYSIA/MALAYA

Located south of Thailand*, Malaya occupies roughly three-fourths of the Malay Peninsula. Its population is predominantly Moslem, but there are many Indian and Chinese inhabitants. Britain established Malaya as a colony in 1826, ruling there until Japan occupied the country in 1942 after the Pearl Harbor Attack*. During World War II, the Allies relegated East Asia, and along with it Malaya, to a position of secondary significance, in spite of the widespread U.S. temptation throughout the war to make the defeat of Japan its first priority. At the Arcadia Conference held in Washington from December 1941 to January 1942, U.S. President Franklin D. Roosevelt* and British Prime Minister Winston Churchill agreed that until Nazi Germany was defeated, the Allies would remain on the defensive against Japan. Although the British viewed this agreement as a major diplomatic victory, it came at a price: a considerable portion of the British Empire, including Malaya, had fallen to Japanese conquest by early 1942.

On its return to Malaya in early 1946, Britain confronted almost immediately its old antagonist the Malay Communist Party, which drew nearly all of its membership from the sizable Chinese community in Malaya. In response, the British offered a new constitution that proposed the transferral of authority from Malay rulers to the British crown, the unification of all Malay states except Singapore* into a Malayan Union, and the granting of citizenship and equal rights to all Chinese and Indian immigrants. Formally introduced in April 1946, the union met with such resistance from the Malay community's new political grouping—the United Malays National Organization (UMNO)—that its provisions never were fully realized. Talks between Britain, the UMNO, and the Malay rulers produced in its stead the Federation of Malaya (inaugurated in February 1948), which formalized the policy of unification, left sovereign control with the sultans, and introduced restricted citizenship provisions for the Chinese and Indian minorities.

To have political power offered and then suddenly taken away aggrieved the Chinese community. Drawing inspiration from the increasing political and military success of the Chinese Communist Party* in the Chinese Civil War*, the Malay Communist Party turned to military means. On 16 June 1948, after a series of murders, the British colonial authorities declared a state of emergency. By the end of the year, more than 900 people had died. Three years later, with a unified command under General Sir Gerald Templer, the British shelved the union and reendorsed Malay status. This demonstrated Britain's willingness to cede independence to Malaya, and support for the Communists declined. By 1954, the insurgency had been reduced significantly, and in 1960, the "Malay Emergency" was lifted. Washington viewed the crisis in Malay with alarm, recognizing it as part of a wider trend in Asia. American policy makers by now perceived Communist insurgency as virtually endemic to a region in which Japanese conquest had weakened the fabric of European colonialism and instead given impetus to nationalistic movements. The Malay Emergency seemed to exemplify the danger that in Southeast Asia, as in China, the victory of nationalism could be accompanied by subversion to Communism*.

President Roosevelt's policy of accelerating the liberation of colonial peoples was overturned after his death in April 1945 by his successor Harry S. Truman*, whose primary concern became containment first of Soviet and then Sino-Soviet imperialism in East Asia. Despite Communist victories in the People's Republic of China*, the Democratic Republic of Vietnam*, and the Democratic People's Republic of Korea*, Britain gave independence to Malaya in 1957, as well as India, Pakistan, Ceylon, Singapore, Burma*, and other minor colonies. Except for Burma, all these states elected to remain in the British Commonwealth. In 1963, Singapore, North Borneo, and Sarawak were federated with Malaya to form Malaysia, but Singapore resumed its independence two years later. Indonesia*, with U.S. belated encouragement, had won its independence from the Netherlands. There, in Malaya and other former British colonies, and in the Philippines*, U.S. leaders saw some realization of their hopes in 1945. Indeed, Malaya was among those nations that formed the Association of Southeast Asian Nations* in 1967, which worked thereafter to promote mutual economic development, as well as social progress and political democracy in the region. *See also* British Colonialism.

R. Clutterbuck, *The Long, Long War: The Emergency in Malaya, 1948–1960* (London, 1967); A. Short, *The Communist Insurrection in Malaya, 1948–1960* (London, 1975).

Peter Mauch

MANCHUKUO

"Manchukuo" was the name of the regime, created under the auspices of Japanese military (mainly the Kwantung Army) and commercial interests (primarily the Southern Manchuria Railway Company) in Manchuria, that existed between 1932 and the defeat of Japan in World War II. When

China's Qing Dynasty ended in 1912, some members of the ruling house, as well as their supporters, almost immediately became acquainted with Japanese military officers working to advance Japanese interests in China. These operatives exploited the resentments and ambitions of the displaced remnants of the Qing court, especially the young Puyi*, who had abdicated as China's "last emperor" at the age of six. His advisers, tutors, and entourage were consistently encouraged by Japanese agents to attempt a restoration of the dynasty. Loyalist movements and uprisings in Mongolia, as well as Manchuria, were abetted and in some cases aided by the Japanese, and regionalist or separatist leaders were undermined or even murdered—such as Zhang Zuolin* in Manchuria. These covert Japanese attempts to dominate Manchuria were part of a larger strategy for control of Northeast Asia, Mongolia, and eastern China that had contributed to the start of the Russo-Japanese War* in 1904. After the Japanese Annexation of Korea* in 1910, Japanese commercial interests had established themselves rapidly in Manchuria, where there were not only rich agricultural lands, but abundant supplies of coal and iron.

China's fragmented government during the Warlord Era* could not resist Japanese encroachments. Most local leaders came to understand that resistance was very dangerous, whereas cooperation could be profitable. During this period of Chinese weakness, Japanese strategists used the theme of "independence" to pry Manchuria and northern China from the control of the Republic of China* under Jiang Jieshi*. Formal establishment of this "independent" state in Manchuria finally came after the Mukden Incident* on 18 September 1931. After staging an explosion of railroad track, Japanese troops occupied Manchuria, reassigning the ancient Manchu name of Mukden to the provincial capital of Shenyang. Puyi, who then was residing under the protection of Japanese diplomats in Tianjin, was invited to assume the presidency of the new state of Manchukuo in 1932. China's protests and international alarm at Japan's blatant expansionism led to creation of the Lytton Commission by the League of Nations to examine the situation in Manchuria and assess the legitimacy of the Manchukuo state. The Lytton Report* condemned Manchukuo as a "puppet state" of Japan, which caused a diplomatic break between Japan and the League of Nations, but otherwise did not alter the situation. The United States, with the Stimson Doctrine*, refused to recognize Japanese seizure of Manchuria. China's actions against the Japanese usurpation were limited to military assaults on Japanese compounds and property in Shanghai in 1932.

In 1934, Japan elevated Puyi from "president" of Manchukuo to its "emperor" (formally a "younger brother" of the Japanese emperor). Though the institutions and terminology of a state bureaucracy were established in Manchukuo, policies remained in the control of the Kwantung Army and South Manchuria Railway Company. Prior to establishment of Manchukuo, the region had been outstanding for its production of staple crops, particularly soybeans. The worldwide depression from 1930 constricted markets for export, and under Manchukuo, the economy of the region was redirected toward heavy industries that would aid in the development of Japan's domestic and colonial enterprises. Railway systems linking Korea and Manchuria were developed, and many Koreans were forcibly removed to Manchukuo as slave laborers in mining, smelting, refining, and building enterprises. Manchukuo ultimately became the most industrially advanced region of continental East Asia. Perhaps equally striking was the assiduous use of new media, particularly film, to promote Manchukuo and Puyi. The public relations effort included a number of glowing accounts by European and American authors of the economy and society of Manchukuo, published in Tōkyō or the Japanese enclave in Shanghai. Outside of

Japan the propaganda had little effect, although as a historical record of an early attempt to use film and photography for political purposes, the Manchukuo materials remain of great interest. With the defeat of Japan in 1945, the Manchukuo regime ended. Puyi and others members of the elite were arrested as prisoners of war by the Soviet Union, and in 1950 transferred to the custody of the People's Republic of China.*

P. Duus, R. H. Myers, and M. R. Peattie (eds.), *The Japanese Informal Empire in China, 1895–1937* (Princeton, NJ, 1989); *The League and "Manchukuo": The Sixth Phase of the Chinese-Japanese Conflict, January 1, 1933–August 1, 1934* (Geneva, 1934).

Pamela K. Crossley

MANDATE SYSTEM

In the aftermath of World War I, the mandate system was a provision of the Versailles Peace Treaty*. It was a compromise between the victorious powers, who wanted to annex parts of the defunct German and Ottoman empires, and President Woodrow Wilson* of the United States, who favored a form of international control. Wilson threw his support to the mandate idea, while Japan, whereas along with others had favored the annexation option, acquiesced. The League of Nations supervised the mandates through a Permanent Mandates Commission, the actual administration and control of the mandated territories being carried out by specific powers that had been awarded the territories. Based on its wartime occupation of the Marianas, the Carolines, and the Marshalls, all formerly ruled by Germany, and the agreements with Britain, France, Russia, and Italy supporting its claims to them, Japan received the mandate for these islands from the Supreme Council of the Allied Powers in May 1919, a decision confirmed by the Council of the League of Nations in December 1920. Also, the council confirmed the mandates of Great Britain

for Nauru, Australia for New Guinea, and New Zealand for Western Samoa.

The United States, however, had expressed reservations about assigning the island of Yap in the Carolines as part of Japan's mandate. Japan had cut and relanded a cable during the war to provide direct communications between Yap and Japan. But this cable previously had provided communications between U.S.-held Guam* and Shanghai in China via Yap. Consequently, after extensive diplomatic wranglings, Japan and the United States signed a treaty in February 1922 that resolved the Yap Controversy*. By contrast, the mandates for South-West Africa, New Guinea, Western Samoa, Nauru, and the north Pacific islands were "C" category mandates. This meant the mandatory powers could rule them as integral parts of their territories. Unlike "A" and "B" mandates, the "C" mandates did not enjoin on the mandatory powers the facilitation of rapid transition to independence, because the people of these territories were thought to be less ready to exercise sovereignty. Instead, the mandatory powers such as Japan were to adopt a paternalistic or protective approach to the native peoples, prohibiting for instance the sale of alcoholic beverages to them and prohibiting the slave trade. The powers also were not to establish military or naval bases and fortifications in these territories. But what angered Japan was that it had to accept a situation that would allow other mandatory powers to apply their discriminatory immigration and economic legislation to the detriment of Japanese in the mandated territories because it failed to gain a clause in the League Covenant dedicated to racial equality,

Japan appears to have abided by these terms as well as, if not better, than the other mandatories. Indeed, there was a marked reduction in racial prejudice toward the native populations, in contrast to the prior German colonial administration. By March 1922, the Japanese government had established the South Seas Bureau to govern its north Pacific islands mandate. Natives participated in government as local officials and village policemen. Expenditures increased for social welfare, but much more was spent on economic development. Most notably, a sugar industry developed during the Japanese mandate period to complement the already existing copra and phosphate industries. Trade between Japan and the islands expanded, but it still was negligible. Most of the skilled industrial labor was provided by Japanese who immigrated to the islands, their numbers growing to about 55,000 by the end of the 1930s. Many also became tenant farmers. The traditional society of the islanders began to atrophy under the effect of this modernization, excepting the Marianas, where it already had vanished by the time of the German occupation. Japan's withdrawal from the League of Nations in late March 1933 as a result of the Mukden Incident* did not affect its status as mandatory. It pledged to abide by the terms of the mandate and issue annual reports to the Permanent Mandates Commission. Japan's mandate ended in 1945 with its defeat in World War II, and the United States assumed control over the islands of Micronesia* as strategic trust territories under supervision of the United Nations.

P. H. Clyde, *Japan's Pacific Mandate* (New York, 1935); L. H. Evans, "The Mandates System and the Administration of Territories under C Mandates," Ph.D. dissertation, Stanford University, 1927; D. C. Purcell, "Japanese Expansion in the South Pacific 1890–1935," Ph.D. dissertation, University of Pennsylvania, 1967; Q. Wright, *Mandates Under the League of Nations* (Chicago, 1930); Y. Tadao, *Pacific Islands Under Japanese Mandate* (New York, 1940).

Harold H. Tollefson

MANILA BAY, BATTLE OF

See BATTLE OF MANILA BAY

MANSFIELD, MIKE (1903–2001)

Mike Mansfield was active in U.S.–East Asian relations as a congressional representative, senator, and diplomat. He claimed that his interest in Asian affairs had been sparked by his service as a U.S. Marine in the Philippines* and Tianjin in 1921 and 1922. After returning to the United States, Mansfield studied and later taught history at the University of Montana. He was elected as a Democratic member to the House of Representatives in 1942 and then served on the House Foreign Affairs Committee. Mansfield established his credentials as a congressional expert on Asian affairs when he traveled to China in 1944 and wrote a report criticizing the failings of the Guomindang* (Nationalist) regime and claimed that the Chinese Communist Party* seemed to be principally interested in "agrarian reform." He made another trip to Asia in 1946 and served on the U.S. delegation in 1951 at the UN General Assembly. Mansfield was elected as a senator from Montana in 1952 after a close election campaign in which the Republicans bitterly attacked his wartime analysis of Chinese politics.

In the Senate, Mansfield was assigned a seat on the Senate Foreign Relations Committee after he supported Lyndon B. Johnson* as minority leader. He developed an interest in French Indochina* after listening to testimony given by French Defense Minister René Pleven and meeting Ngo Dinh Diem* in May 1953. Mansfield was a U.S. delegate at the Manila Conference in September 1954 and supported ratification of the Southeast Asia Treaty Organization*. After Diem became Vietnamese premier in June 1954, he was his most vocal congressional supporter. When General J. Lawton Collins* expressed repeated doubts about Diem's leadership abilities in the spring of 1955, Mansfield voiced strong opposition to any plans to replace Diem and at first supported the Nation-Building* strategy. Soon, however, he became increasingly critical of U.S. aid programs to the Republic of Vietnam* and other Southeast Asian governments, arguing that they were costly, overemphasized military aid, and created a dependency relationship with recipient countries. In 1959 and 1960, he was chairman of a Senate subcommittee that investigated charges of waste in the South Vietnamese aid program and recommended changes to make it more effective.

Mansfield was elected Senate majority leader in January 1961, holding the post until he retired from the Senate in 1977. During the Laotian Crisis of 1961*, he urged President John F. Kennedy* to refrain from a military intervention. Mansfield also advised against taking control of the war effort in South Vietnam, but recommended that the United States press the Diem regime into making significant reforms. By the time Lyndon Johnson took office in November 1963, his pessimism about the prospect of U.S. success in the Second Indochina War* caused him to urge Johnson privately to seek a negotiated settlement. He nevertheless publicly supported the Gulf of Tonkin Resolution in 1964 and Johnson's decision to use combat forces in 1965. He was more outspoken in criticizing the war after Richard M. Nixon* took office in 1969, especially after the Cambodian Incursion* in April 1970. Thereafter, Mansfield backed measures to end U.S. ground operations in Cambodia*, set a deadline for withdrawal of U.S. combat forces from Indochina, and halt U.S. bombing operations in Cambodia. In the spring of 1975, he opposed emergency military aid to the governments of Lon Nol* and Nguyen Van Thieu*. Mansfield did support Nixon's actions to improve relations with the People's Republic of China* and visited China himself in 1972 and 1974.

After retiring from the Senate, Mansfield served with Ambassador Leonard Woodcock* on the delegation to the Socialist Republic of Vietnam* in 1977. He then became U.S. ambassador to Japan in April 1977, serving in this post under both Presidents Jimmy Carter* and Ronald Reagan*. During his tenure of office, he dealt with such issues as rising friction in U.S.-Japan Postwar Trade Relations*, the sale of Japanese technology to the Soviet Union, and Japanese spending for defense and foreign aid. The Japanese applauded Mansfield for his tact and honesty, but some American critics claimed that Mansfield lacked firmness in dealing with Japan. His resignation from the ambassadorship in 1989 brought his public career to an end.

R. K. Baker, "Mike Mansfield and the Birth of the Modern Senate," in R. A. Baker and R. H. Davidson (eds.), *First Among Equals: Outstanding Senate Leaders of the Twentieth Century* (Washington, DC, 1991); S. Chira, "Mansfield San Bids Sayonara as an Envoy," *New York Times*, 15 November 1988; *Current Biography*, 1978; G. A. Olson, *Mansfield and Vietnam: A Study in Rhetorical Adaptation* (East Lansing, MI, 1995).

Joseph G. Morgan

MAO ZEDONG (1893–1976)

Mao Zedong was chairman of the Chinese Communist Party* (CCP) when he established the People's Republic of China* (PRC) after defeating Jiang Jieshi* in the Chinese Civil War*. As a Marxist-Leninist disciple in the early 1920s, he attended the first CCP national meeting in 1921 as one of the party's twelve founders. Believing that the peasantry, rather than the working class, was the major societal force leading the Communist revolution, Mao organized rural-centered, armed revolts in his home province of Hunan in 1927. After the first CCP coalition with Jiang's Guomindang* (Nationalist) Party collapsed and the Communists left cities for the countryside, he created the first revolutionary base in 1928 in Jinggangshan, a remote mountainous region in South China, where he was elected chairman of the Executive Committee of the Chinese Soviet Republic in 1931. He led the Long March during 1934 and 1935 to save the Red Army and to find a new base to escape Guomindang campaigns to eliminate the CCP armed forces, emerging as the unquestioned leader. In World War II, his successful strategy of working with Jiang in a United Front* and mobilizing guerrilla warfare behind Japanese lines increased CCP members from 40,000 in 1937 to 1.2 million and won the admiration of U.S. diplomats known as the China Hands*. He became chairman of both the Politburo and Secretariat in 1943, and chairman of the Central Committee in 1945. Unable to cooperate with Jiang after the war, Mao resumed the civil war.

General George C. Marshall* attempted after December 1945 to form a coalition government in China. At first, Mao cooperated with the Marshall Mission*, although he resented that the United States continued to provide Jiang with military equipment and financial assistance. After the CCP defeated his forces, Jiang moved the Republic of China* to Taiwan* late in 1949. By then, Mao had announced that the PRC would "lean to one side" in the Cold War, meaning that China would align with the Soviet Union. As president of China's new government, he traveled to Moscow in December 1949 and signed the Sino-Soviet Treaty of Friendship and Alliance* early in 1950. The United States refused to recognize the PRC, but President Harry S. Truman* evidently was prepared for contacts with Mao's regime after its anticipated conquest of Taiwan before the Korean War* began in June. Following the Neutralization of Taiwan*, Mao's decision to order Chinese Intervention in the Korean War* led the PRC and the United States into a long period of hostility. Although Soviet leader Joseph Stalin had asked Mao following the Inch'ŏn Landing* to rescue Kim Il Sung* and the Democratic People's Republic of Korea*, he sent the Chinese People's Volunteers (CPV) to demonstrate that China was the leader of the revolutionary movement in Asia. Although Chinese forces compelled UN troops to retreat after the Home by Christmas Offensive*, they could not unify Korea. U.S. air and naval superiority inflicted heavy casualties on the Chinese, including Mao's son, who was killed as a Russian translator at the CPV headquarters in an air raid.

Mao considered it a great victory when the United States signed the Korean Armistice Agreement* in July 1953 because China had saved the Communist regime in North Korea, prevented a U.S. invasion of China, acquired more Russian military and economic aid, and established itself as a world power. But Chinese intervention had provoked a deep antagonism to Communism* in the United States and throughout much of Asia. Nevertheless, Mao saw the Cold War as a competition for control of an "intermediate zone" in the developing world. His commitments to French Indochina* and other revolutionary movements in Asia reflected his ideological commitment to achieve World Communism. With Moscow pursuing "peaceful coexistence" with the United States after 1953, Mao had concluded by 1957 that Beijing should assume global leadership of the Communist movement. He sent more than half a million Chinese troops to Vietnam in the early 1960s, provided weapons and aid to Communist guerrillas in Southeast Asia, and supported Third World nations struggling against the imperialist policies of the United States and its Western allies. His attacks on Guomindang-held offshore islands ignited the Taiwan Strait Crises* in the 1950s, resulting in the United States strengthening its protection of Jiang's regime. Presidents John F. Kennedy* and Lyndon B. Johnson* continued the trade embargo against the PRC under the China Committee (CHINCOM*) and denied it admission to the United Nations and most international organizations.

In defiance, Mao mobilized the Chinese masses to continue the revolution and staged first the Great Leap Forward from 1958 to 1960 and then the Chinese Cultural Revolution* from 1966 to 1976. These radical political campaigns led to deaths in the tens of millions, fostered great disasters and disorder among the Chinese people, and portrayed Mao to the world as a ruthless dictator obsessed with creating a personality cult. His extremism derived from his ideological idealism, and also from his concerns for national security and his party's survival. After the Sino-Soviet split in the early 1960s and Chinese-Russian military border conflicts later in the decade, Mao criticized the Soviet Union as "imperialist" and "hegemonic" and more threatening to the PRC than the United States. In a dramatic policy shift, he worked to create a world alliance against Moscow through improving China's relations with the major Western powers and Japan. The PRC replaced Taiwan in the United Nations in 1971 and took its seat in the UN Security Council, resolving the Chinese Representation in the United Nations*. President Richard M. Nixon* also reacted positively, ending the trade embargo that year. Playing the "American card" against the Soviet Union, Mao restored relations with the United States during Nixon's Visit to China* in 1972, issuing the Shanghai Communiqué* to undercut the U.S. Two China Policy*. After reciprocal liaison offices opened during 1973, Mao met many U.S. officials, such as Secretary of State Henry A. Kissinger* eight times and President Gerald R. Ford* in 1975, working for better U.S.-PRC relations. His policies in the 1970s eased Cold War tensions in Asia, contributing to the Paris Peace Accords* ending the Vietnam War and normalization of Sino-Japan relations. After 1974, Mao suffered from Parkinson's disease, but still met former President Nixon in February 1976, seven months before his death. *See also* Hua Guofeng; Huang Hua; Lin Biao; Peng Dehuai; Zhou Enlai.

S. Breslin, *Mao* (New York, 1998); J. Chen, *Mao and China's Foreign Policy* (Chapel Hill, NC, 1997); Z. Li, *The Private Life of Chairman Mao: The Memoirs of Mao's Personal Physician* (New York, 1994); M. J. Meisner, *Mao's China and After: A History of the People's Republic* (New York, 1977); S. R. Schram, *The Thought of Mao Tse-Tung* (Cambridge, MA, 1989).

Li Xiaobing

MARCH FIRST MOVEMENT

This historic Korean nationalist movement was encouraged to a great extent by the principle of national self-determination put forward by U.S. President Woodrow Wilson*. The doctrine naturally appealed to the Korean people, who were suffering under harsh Japanese Colonialism*, and provided the impetus to transform the Korean nationalist movement—a movement that hitherto had trusted in the activities of exiles and clandestine organizations—into a full-scale national effort to regain Korea's lost independence. This massive independence movement began with the promulgation of a declaration of independence framed by the thirty-three "representatives of the Korean people" on 1 March 1919, two days before the funeral of King Kojong*. When he died in January, rumors spread that a Japanese physician had poisoned him, which provoked Korean's hostility against Japan. The proclamation of independence gave the main impetus to a struggle for freedom among the entire Korean people. The independence movement quickly spread to the countryside, and an estimated 1.1 million people actively joined the mass parades, marching and shouting, *"Taehan toknip manse"* (Long live Korean independence). Stunned by the enormousness of the movement, Japan violently suppressed the peaceful demonstrations in March and April, killing more than 7,500, wounding more than 16,000, and arresting more than 46,000 Koreans.

Although the March First Movement failed to win the support of the Western powers, it awakened an independence-oriented Korean nationalism. Syngman Rhee*, Kim Gu*, Kim Kyu-sik*, and other Korean leaders became members of the Korean Provisional Government (KPG) established in Shanghai during April 1919. The KPG included both those already active overseas and others who had gone into exile after the independence movement. It failed, however, to enlist support from the United States, one of its primary goals. Despite the well-known antipathy of the Korean people to their Japanese overlords, Washington rebuffed efforts by the KPG for recognition during World War II. But the Korean nationalist movement attracted U.S. attention. Many American journalists reported the independence movement and denounced Japanese brutality in subduing the demonstrations. In addition, some members of Congress criticized the U.S. government's pro-Japanese attitudes and expressed support for Korean independence. See also Japanese Annexation of Korea; Homer B. Hulbert; Korean Conspiracy Case.

W. Han, The History of Korea (Seoul, 1970); K. Lee, A New History of Korea (Seoul, 1984); U. Pak, Han'guk T'ongsa [History of Korea] (Seoul, 1915).

Kim Jinwung

MARCO POLO BRIDGE INCIDENT

The Marco Polo Bridge Incident of July 1937, also known as the China Incident, ignited World War II in East Asia between Japan and China. During the 1930s, few Chinese had any illusions about Japanese imperialist designs on their nation. Hungry for raw materials and pressed by the problem of overpopulation, Japanese militarists initiated the seizure of China's Manchuria after the Mukden Incident* in September 1931. Japan then established Puyi*, ex-emperor of the Qing Dynasty, as head of the puppet regime of Manchukuo* in 1932. The loss of Manchuria, the industrial base of China, worsened the existing depression in China's economy. The League of Nations reacted to the occupation of Manchuria with an investigation resulting in the Lytton Report*. In defiance, the Japanese withdrew from the League and began to push from Manchuria into northern China. Chinese resistance to Japanese encroachments finally stiffened on 7 July 1937, when a skirmish between Chinese and Japanese troops took place outside Beijing near the Marco Polo Bridge. This clash not only marked the beginning of open, but undeclared, war between China and Japan, but also hastened formal announcement of the second United Front* between the Guomindang* (Nationalists) and the Chinese Communist Party* against Japan.

On the night of 7 July 1937, Chinese troops fired on Japanese troops conducting field exercises again at the Marco Polo Bridge. After an exchange of fire, the Japanese commander found that one of his soldiers was missing. The Japanese approached the nearby city Wanbing and asked the Chinese authorities for permission to enter the city to search for the missing man. Upon refusal, the Japanese attacked and occupied the city of Wanbing on 8 July. Konoe Fumimaro*, the new Japanese prime minister, then allowed the Japanese army to punish China. Ten days after the Marco Polo Bridge incident, Jiang Jieshi*, leader of the Republic of China*, sent troops to the north into the demilitarized areas in accordance with the Ho-Umezu Truce Agreement of 1935. Jiang then called on Chinese people to resist Japan, receiving encouragement from his German adviser General Alexander von Falkenhausen, who predicted that Chinese forces would drive the Japanese "over the Great Wall." Although his optimism was unjustified, Jiang had no other choice but to fight while hoping for assistance from the United States and other Western powers. On 28 July, Japanese bombers attacked three cities. On 13 August, Japan began terror bombing of Shanghai. By 1938, Japan controlled most of northern China and most of its coast, forcing Jiang to retreat from Nanjing to the western city of Chongqing. Japan now fought a protracted war. See also Tao Xingzhi.

F. F. Liu, A Military History of Modern China, 1924–1949 (Princeton, NJ, 1956); D. J. Lu, From Marco Polo Bridge to Pearl Harbor: Japan's Entry into World War II (Washington, D.C, 1961); J. W. Morley, The China Quagmire: Japan's Expansion on the Asian Continent, 1933–1941 (New York, 1983).

Song Yuwu

MARCOS, FERDINAND E. (1917–1989)

From 1963 to 1986, Ferdinand Edralin Marcos was president of the Philippines* and received strong support from the United States despite his authoritarian rule. He was born in northern Luzon, and like many children of Filipino oligarchic families, enrolled at the University of the Philippines in Manila. While studying law, he was convicted of assassinating his father's political rival, but the Supreme Court of the Philippines, after his superb self-defense, freed him on grounds of insufficient and contradictory evidence. Marcos claimed he had a courageous military record in World War II, but later it was revealed that he had forged the records of his exploits and medals. Elected in 1949 to the legislature, he served three terms, becoming a powerful congressman through adept use of patronage politics and long-term alliances, including marriage to Imelda Romualdez, the niece of powerful Speaker Eduardo Romualdez. Marcos was elected to the Senate in 1959 and in 1963 won the presidency. He was reelected in 1969 amid charges of massive fraud and violence. By 1972, Marco faced opposition, as exposés of corruption by a hostile media were reinforced by the growing radicalism among Filipino youth. The Philippine economy also was in a crisis after devaluation of the currency, government overspending, and the flight of foreign capital. In the south, the Muslim minority was promoting separatism, and radical demonstrations and random bombings in the cities created a sense of imminent political collapse.

Marcos responded to the crisis by declaring martial law on 21 September 1972. He imprisoned more than 30,000 people, including his principal political opponents, student radicals, labor leaders, and journalists. He closed Congress, declaring he would rule by decree. During the next fourteen years under "constitutional authoritarianism," Marcos expanded Philippine connections abroad, establishing diplomatic ties with the People's Republic of China* and a host of eastern European states. The normalization strengthened Marcos at home, as Beijing immediately terminated its support to the Communist Party of the Philippines. He also gave greater prominence to Philippine involvement in the Association of Southeast Asian Nations*. Marcos sought to establish himself as a leader of the Third World by expanding diplomatic links with activist states such as Nigeria, Egypt, and Libya. The dictatorship at first benefited from a boom in world sugar prices, but then falling prices left the Marcos government with a surplus of sugar that it withheld in hopes that prices would rise again. Frenetic borrowing abroad and an unprecedented increase in U.S. military and economic aid mitigated the devastating impact of the economic crisis. Earnings from Filipino migrant labor and remittances from Filipino families in the United States brought in the capital that kept the economy afloat as the dictatorship tottered into near-bankruptcy.

By 1975, the Muslim separatist movement had erupted into a major war and the Communist Party had emerged as a powerful and popular force opposing the Marcos dictatorship. The Catholic Church had sent out human rights monitors in the country, and the economic elite resented "crony capitalism" or the practice of giving Marcos relatives and close friends monopolies and privileging these corporations with cheap loans, subsidies, and other preferences. All along, U.S. aid remained steady, despite tensions with President Jimmy Carter* over human rights. Marcos was no "puppet" and exploited the Subic Naval Base Controversy* for his private gain. The Americans, especially Ronald Reagan*, obliged because Marcos was a steady ally. Also, early in 1981, he "lifted" martial law. He then easily "won" a presidential election in June boycotted by all opposition groups. As the Philippine economy deteriorated, the extravagances of Imelda and the excesses of crony capitalism became untenable. The most serious shock came in August 1983, when Marcos opponent Benigno Aquino Jr. was assassinated by his military escorts at Manila's airport. This set in motion events that led to Marcos's Ouster* in February 1986. He left the country with a $27 billion debt, a shattered industrial sector, and more than 50 percent of Filipinos living in poverty. His successors largely distanced themselves from his legacy, but Marcos's foreign policy initiatives ensured that the Philippines retained a broad network of diplomatic relations, especially after U.S.-Philippine ties waned in the late 1990s.

B. Aquino, *Politics of Plunder: The Philippines Under Marcos* (Manila, 1987); R. Bonner, *Waltzing with a Dictator: The Marcoses and the Making of American Policy* (New York, 1987); J. Boyce, *The Philippines: The Political Economy of Growth and Impoverishment* (Honolulu, HI, 1993); D. Rosenberg (ed.), *Marcos and Martial Law in the Philippines* (Ithaca, NY, 1979); M. Thompson, *The Anti-Marcos Struggle: Personalistic Rule and Democratic Transition in the Philippines* (New Haven, CT, 1995).

Patricio N. Abinales

MARCOS'S OUSTER

After twenty years of despotic rule in the Republic of the Philippines*, the government of Ferdinand E. Marcos* was deposed in 1986 by the "people power" movement of Corazon Aquino*, defecting members of Marcos's own regime, and a White House request to resign. Ruling under a personally defined martial law since 1971, Marcos once had been a powerful representative of U.S.-led Cold War interests in the western Pacific and Southeast Asia. As host to Clark Air Base, the largest U.S. Air Force installation in its overseas basing system, Subic Bay, a major U.S. Navy Seventh Fleet base, supply/refitting facility, rest and rehabilitation center, and home to other military installations, the Marcos government remained the region's strongest U.S. ally during the Second Indochina War*. Enriching himself and his

family on U.S. aid and complicated American military base land lease arrangements, Marcos was praised by both Democratic and Republican presidents for his unswerving anti-Communist support during the Cold War. With the collapse of the U.S. effort in Vietnam during 1975 and the waning of Soviet-American tensions by the mid-1980s, Marcos's value as an American ally faded in Washington. Meanwhile, the corruption and tyranny of his government stimulated a powerful movement for democratic justice.

Although leadership of the democratic movement was claimed by a variety of anti-Marcos activists, the Marcos regime viewed the charismatic Benigno Aquino Jr. as its most formidable opponent. Aquino and his supporters saw themselves as the democratic alternative to the Maoist-like New People's Army (NPA). Headquartered largely in Mindanao, the NPA, drawing support especially from the rural poor of the Philippines, used Viet Cong*-style terrorist tactics to harass, and, it was hoped, destroy the Marcos government. Albeit slowly, its support grew throughout the early 1980s, and Marcos's military was hard-pressed to stop it. Implicated in the 1983 assassination of Benigno Aquino, Marcos reportedly feared Aquino's reasoned and eloquent appeals for democratic reform. Corazon Aquino assumed her dead husband's role, adding both a sense of drama and her own high moral tone to the anti-Marcos movement.

Preferring nonviolence and mass demonstrations against the Marcos regime, Aquino's "people power" effort still needed U.S. acknowledgment to succeed. In early 1986, at the height of street demonstrations, President Ronald Reagan* still considered himself a friend to Marcos. He urged respect for a long time, trusted U.S. ally, worrying that the Communist NPA might emerge to the post-Marcos leadership. Hence, the U.S. abandonment of the Marcos regime took many days of patient negotiations with Reagan by former Marcos supporters in the U.S. Congress, such as fellow Republicans Richard Luger and Orin Hatch on the U.S. Senate Foreign Relations Committee. The defection of key Marcos supporters, especially highly respected General Fidel Ramos, to the Aquino cause, helped Reagan conclude that the "people power" movement had order, cohesion, and the potential to form a working government. Although it was a tearful request, Reagan personally asked the ailing Marcos to resign with a guarantee of safe passage out of the country (if possible). Marcos fled to Hawaii, and Corazon Aquino, inheriting a struggling economy, the NPA battle, and a bitter Subic Naval Base Controversy* among her followers, became the new Philippine president.

E. Hamilton, *America's Global Interests: A New Agenda* (New York, 1989); S. Karnow, *In Our Image: America's Empire in the Philippines* (New York, 1989); B. D. Romulo, *Inside the Palace: The Rise and Fall of Ferdinand and Imelda Marcos* (New York, 1987); G. Slack, *Ferdinand Marcos* (New York, 1988).

Timothy P. Maga

MARSHALL, GEORGE C. (1880–1959)

General George C. Marshall was U.S. Army chief of staff during World War II and later served as both secretary of state and defense in the administration of President Harry S. Truman*. His most important impact on East Asia was leading the Marshall Mission* to China in 1945 and 1946. Born in Pennsylvania, Marshall graduated from Virginia Military Institute and pursued a military career. After obtaining his regular commission in 1902, he rose steadily through the ranks, serving in World War I and in various postwar assignments. During World War II, Marshall became a war hero, earning widespread respect among the American people. His bipartisan support was responsible for Truman's selection of Marshall to attempt to mediate an end to the Chinese Civil War*. But his mission failed, as did another

in 1947 under Lieutenant General Albert C. Wedemeyer*. As secretary of state from 1947 to 1949, he was not involved in the U.S. Occupation of Japan*, but he did help to negotiate an agreement with the Soviets to resume talks to end the Thirty-Eighth Parallel Division* in Korea. Marshall then spoke to the United Nations in September 1947, asking it to supervise elections there. The general (as he was known to his contemporaries) focused his attention mainly on Europe, where his Marshall Plan brought economic recovery.

When Marshall returned from China and became secretary of state early in 1947, he thoroughly acquainted Truman with what he came to see as the impossibility that any outsider could bring the Guomindang* (Nationalists) and the Chinese Communist Party* to an agreement. Since both were determined to fight through to a military decision, he urged that the United States remain uninvolved in the conflict. Marshall talked privately about the gross incompetence of Guomindang generals, whom Jiang Jieshi* would not dismiss because they were old military classmates. "I have tortured my brain," he related, "and I can't now see the answer." The same commentary appeared when he spoke at hearings on his nomination to be secretary of defense in September 1950. By that time, the Korean War* had begun and Truman again looked to Marshall to build bipartisan support in Congress. After the failure of the Home by Christmas Offensive* and Chinese Intervention in the Korean War*, Marshall opposed the plans General Douglas MacArthur* advanced to escalate the conflict. He did not lobby for MacArthur's Recall* in April 1951, but strongly supported Truman's decision. At the MacArthur Hearings in June, Marshall repeated his views on China and endorsed fighting a limited war in Korea. He retired from public service later that year.

D. Acheson, *Present at the Creation: My Years in the State Department* (New York, 1969); R. H. Ferrell, *George C. Marshall* (New York, 1966);

F. C. Pogue, *George C. Marshall: Statesman* (New York, 1987).

Robert H. Ferrell

MARSHALL MISSION

With Japan's surrender in August 1945, the Chinese Civil War* between the Guomindang* (Nationalists) and the Chinese Communist Party* resumed. Japan's defeat prompted a race between the forces of Jiang Jieshi* and Mao Zedong* for territorial control in China. During World War II, the U.S. government had anticipated that a unified and pro-American China would be a stabilizing force in postwar East Asia. By the fall of 1945, however, Washington was more concerned about the spread of Soviet influence in the region and was apprehensive about a Communist victory in China. Fearful that a chaotic and divided China would allow for the Soviet expansion into Manchuria, President Harry S. Truman* sent the highly respected U.S. Army Chief of Staff General George C Marshall* as his special representative to China in late 1945. His task was to mediate a settlement between Jiang's Guomindang and Mao's Communists.

Marshall's efforts, supposedly impartial, were compromised from the outset because the United States recognized Jiang's Republic of China* as the sole legitimate government. Accordingly, Marshall strove to integrate the Communist armed forces into the Guomindang army, and continued programs of aid and support to the Nationalists exclusively. Continued American support of Guomindang forces, however, bolstered Jiang's confidence that he could crush his longtime rival through military means, and further deepened the Communist suspicion of U.S. intentions. Nevertheless, Marshall did achieve some initial success, as the Nationalists and the Communists agreed to a cease-fire on 10 January 1946.

Meanwhile, Marshall also created an executive headquarters in Beijing to direct truce terms for field investigation, and help supervise the agreement between the two Chinese parties. It consisted of three commissioners, one American as chairman, one representative from the Chinese Nationalist government, and one from the Chinese Communist Party. The truce, however, turned out to be short-lived. Very soon the Nationalists and the Communists started accusing each other of violating the ceasefire. After June 1946, the situation in north China, and especially Manchuria, progressively worsened as Jiang's and Mao's forces intensified their fighting. When Soviet troops withdrew from Manchuria, a full-scale war between the two contending parties commenced. The Marshall Mission failed to end China's civil war. In January 1947, a disappointed Marshall returned to the United States to become secretary of state. *See also* China Assistance Act of 1948; China Hands; Patrick J. Hurley; Wedemeyer Mission.

S. Levine, *Anvil of Victory: The Communist Revolution in Manchuria, 1945–1948* (New York, 1987); L. P. Van Slyke (ed.), *Marshall's Mission to China, December 1945–January 1947: The Report and Appended Documents* (Arlington, VA, 1976).

Zhang Hong

MATSUOKA YŌSUKE (1880–1946)

Little was conventional about Matsuoka Yōsuke. After going to school in the United States at age thirteen and graduating from the University of Oregon nine years later, he was one of the first to undergo and pass in 1904 the rigorous entrance examinations into the Foreign Ministry. Although on track to rise high in the ministry, Matsuoka left it in 1921 to become a director of the South Manchuria Railway Company, which was the backbone of the Japanese Empire's presence there. For the next nine years, he cultivated connections with leading military figures, especially in Japan's Kwantung Army (stationed in Manchuria), and political leaders, especially those most hostile to Foreign Minister Shidehara Ki-jūrō* and his policy of accommodation to the West and the rising Nationalist Chinese. In 1930, Matsuoka returned to Japan to win election to the Diet. His success in negotiating an end to the Shanghai Incident of 1932 led to his appointment as delegate to the League of Nations a year later. At Geneva, Matsuoka illustrated his considerable skills as a debater, as well as his fluency in English, in criticizing the League's Lytton Report* that charged the Japanese military was guilty of creating a puppet state in Manchukuo* that did not represent a satisfactory solution to Sino-Japanese differences. Even his threat to pull Japan out of the League was not sufficient to block its adoption, so Matsuoka led Japan out in 1933.

These steps solidified Matsuoka's popularity with the military. Thereafter, he became a strong and vocal advocate of closer ties with Germany, loudly criticizing the Foreign Ministry's misgivings over the Anti-Comintern Pact* of 1936. This crusade led Konoe Fumimaro* to name him to the Cabinet Advisory Council upon formation of his first cabinet in 1937. Two years later, the stunning Nazi-Soviet Pact in August temporarily ended his campaign for an alliance with Germany, but in some respects it paved the way for the makeup of Konoe's second cabinet in July 1940 with Matsuoka as foreign minister. He came to office supremely confident in Germany's military supremacy, certain that firmness was the best way to deal with the United States, the only remaining democracy capable of threatening Japan. His bold leadership in his first weeks swiftly led to serious discussions with Germany and the Tripartite Pact* in September, a scarcely veiled attempt to confront the Americans with the prospect of a two-ocean war if they intervened against either Germany or Japan. Intoxicated by what he regarded as his personal success in creating a global coalition, Matsuoka toured Europe in the spring of 1941. His main goal was to obtain Soviet membership in the Axis, but he had

to settle for a neutrality pact in April. This annoyed the Germans, who had hinted broadly to Matsuoka that Nazi-Soviet difficulties were imminent.

Matsuoka returned to Tōkyō to discover high hopes for a possible resolution of differences with the United States as a consequence of the Nomura-Hull Conversations*. He moved swiftly to torpedo these and advocate an attack on Singapore*, only to find that Germany meant to attack the Soviet Union almost immediately. Wedded to his Germany-first outlook, Matsuoka now argued for war against the Russians. Every other Japanese leader thought his stance—hostility toward the Soviet Union, Britain, and the United States—exceedingly rash. When Matsuoka overstepped his bounds in attempting to insert unauthorized conditions into discussions with U.S. Secretary of State Cordell Hull*, he was removed as foreign minister in July. Matsuoka remained supremely confident, expecting to return to power as soon as Germany had crushed Soviet resistance, but was wrong. The Soviets survived; the Americans were neither deterred nor intimidated. Matsuoka fell ill and was compelled to retire from politics. The Allies arrested him as a war criminal, but he died before a verdict was passed.

C. Hosoya, "The Japanese-Soviet Neutrality Pact," in J. W. Morley (ed.), *The Fateful Choice: Japan's Advance into Southeast Asia, 1939–1941* (New York, 1980); J. Huizenga, "Yosuke Matsuoka and the Japanese-German Alliance," in G. A. Craig and F. Gilbert (eds.), *The Diplomats, 1919–1939*, Vol. 2: *The Thirties* (Princeton, NJ, 1953); K. Usui, "The Role of the Foreign Ministry," in D. Borg and Shumpei Okamoto (eds.), *Pearl Harbor as History: Japanese-American Relations, 1931–1941* (New York, 1973).

Michael A. Barnhart

MAY FOURTH MOVEMENT

This was a mass uprising of Chinese in May 1919 against continuing imperialist exploitation of China. When World War I ended, Japan still held German rights over the Shandong Province, though China was a victorious nation. President Woodrow Wilson* had enunciated his famous Fourteen Points, the fifth point of which stated, "When the question of colonies is being settled the interests of the colonial peoples themselves must be given equal right with those of the governments putting forward claims to title over them." In response, the Chinese were deeply grateful to Wilson. Chen Duxiu, the pioneer of the Chinese New Culture Movement, praised Wilson for his decision to "uphold justice" and be "anti-might," calling him "the first good man in the world of today." The Chinese government consequently placed on the United States its hope for restitution of its right to Shandong.

At the Paris Peace Conference in January 1919, the U.S. delegation supported China's claim of the restitution at first, but later compromised with Japan. Together with the leaders of Britain and France, Wilson decided to award the German rights in Shandong to Japan. This news enraged the Chinese people, and in Beijing on 4 May, thousands of students marched through streets, demonstrating against the Versailles Peace Treaty*, under the slogan "Return our Shandong" and "Externally resist the foreign powers; internally get rid of Chinese traitors." Students all over the country rallied to this cause. Merchants and workers everywhere closed shops and went on strike to show their support of the students. Shocked by the cry of rage that erupted in the country, China's representatives at the conference stiffened, and the government that had been prepared to submit adopted the policy of remaining undecided.

Among the U.S. delegates, Secretary of State Robert Lansing* consistently and firmly supported China's claim. At his meeting with Chinese representatives Gu Weijun* and Lu Zhengxiang on 20 May, he suggested that China withhold approval on the Shandong clause. But Wilson did not share this viewpoint. He indicated at his meeting with Lu and Gu that Japan might refuse to fulfill her promise of cooperation at the conference and support for the League of Nations under the pretext of China's reservation. Chinese President Xu Shichang now favored signing the treaty without reservation. This stimulated the mass movement to reach a climax, resulting in angry demands that the Chinese government punish the three officers who had participated in negotiations with Japan and had signed the Twenty-One Demands* in 1915.

The May Fourth Movement resulted in the Chinese government developing a compromise. It instructed the Chinese mission to withhold approval of the Shandong clause first and then, in case of failure and with no alternative, to sign. Yet China's representatives did not follow this instruction to the letter. After the Council of Four had rejected China's request for a reservation, they refused to sign the treaty. Paul S. Reinsch*, the U.S. representative to China, did not regard Wilson's position as right and therefore resigned on 7 June. The U.S. Congress debated the Versailles Treaty in July and the Shandong clause received criticism. On 6 August, Wilson said that the fact that he agreed to the Shandong clause did not mean he approved of the Twenty-One Demands. Unsatisfied, the Congress adopted a resolution during August identifying the Shandong clause as a U.S. reservation and reserving the right to act if this caused conflict between China and Japan. *See also* Mandate System; Shandong Agreement.

P. S. Reinsch, *An American Diplomat in China* (New York, 1922); Tianjing Museum of History (ed.), *Mi ji lu cun* [Records of Secret Papers] (Beijing, 1984).

Xiang Liling

MAY THIRTIETH MOVEMENT

The May Thirtieth Movement was triggered when the British and Japanese policemen of the concession in Shanghai fired at Chinese students participating in a demonstration on that date in 1925. Many students were injured and some were killed. The incident aroused popular indignation that developed into a mass strike of workers, students, and shopkeepers on 1 June. Facing the protest, local British administrators proposed to all the consular representatives in Shanghai to assemble a joint army to land at Shanghai for protecting foreign residents there. U.S. Consul General Edwin S. Cunningham in Shanghai agreed. The U.S. government's stand on the incident was, though regretting the death of the students, identical with the other powers that "on no account should the interests of powers be infringed upon." On 4 June, Secretary of State Frank B. Kellogg* approved the proposal to send U.S. troops. As a result, among the thirty-three warships anchored at Shanghai in early June, there were thirteen U.S. vessels carrying 1,450 American soldiers.

Yet the U.S. government maintained a conciliatory attitude. At the diplomatic corps meeting in Beijing on 4 June, U.S. Chargé Ferdinand L. Mayer suggested sending a fact-finding mission to Shanghai to investigate the incident. After approval of the proposal, a mission with members from six nations—the United States, Britain, Japan, France, Italy, and Belgium—was founded. However, many Chinese figures called for a joint mission consisting of both foreigners and Chinese. Cunningham indicated in his report on 9 June that a joint mission would cause serious damage to the concession administration, even though it would promote a reconciliation with the Chinese. The next day, Kellogg directed Cunningham that a joint mission with Chinese was not advisable. To maintain a good impression for the United States among the Chinese people, Cunningham proposed at the consular corps meeting to invite some Chinese representatives to observe the investigation. Some American newspapers objected, arguing that since the target of the May Thirtieth Movement was Britain and Japan, the United States should not be associated with action against the Chinese students. To counter this criticism, Kellogg directed Mayer on 12 June that the U.S. government did not seek to exploit the situation to obtain either advantages or disadvantages.

On 16 June, the talks between the investigators and the Chinese representatives began in Shanghai and then moved to Beijing. On 25 June, the Chinese government sent two notes to the foreign diplomats. The first note related directly to the 30 May incident, demanding the punishment of the murderers, indemnity for the killed and injured, and issuance of an apology for the incident. The second note called for the revision of the unequal treaties. To respond to the first note, a joint group consisting of judges from Britain, Japan, and the United States was formed. Whereas the British and Japanese judges regarded police authorities as innocent, the American judge held the British chief police responsible. The group made the ultimate decision to recommend that the chief police resign, the policeman who had given the order to fire be discharged, and the concession administration pay 150 thousand silver dollars to the Chinese. As for the second note, U.S. government agreed that it would propose a special conference on the Chinese tariff, acting on this promise in July. On 26 October, the conference convened in Beijing with delegations from the nine nations that had attended the Washington Conference*. The May Thirtieth Movement thus started the long and tortuous process toward granting China Tariff Autonomy*.

Cheng Daode, Zheng Yueming, and Rao Geping (eds.), *Zhonghua minguo waijiao ziliao xuanji, 1919–1931* [Selected Diplomatic Data of the Republic of China, 1919–1931] (Beijing, 1985); Fu Daohui, *Wusa yundong* [May Thirtieth Movement] (Fudan, 1985).

Xiang Liling

MAYAGUEZ INCIDENT

On 11 May 1975, an unarmed American merchant vessel, the *Mayaguez*, was boarded at gunpoint by Cambodian naval personnel many miles off the Cambodian coast and hauled into port with its thirty-nine American crewmen. President Gerald R. Ford* condemned the seizure as an act of piracy by the new Communist government of Cambodia*, which had assumed power when Khmer Rouge* forces under Pol Pot* captured Phnom Penh less than two weeks earlier. Ford instructed the State Department to demand the immediate release of the ship, adding that the "failure to do so would have the most serious consequences." While U.S. officials asked the People's Republic of China* through its liaison office in Washington for help in obtaining release of the ship, the U.S. commander in charge ordered the aircraft carrier USS *Coral Sea* and other ships from the Seventh Fleet to sail for the Gulf of Thailand. The Cambodians did not have long to wait. On 14 May, U.S. forces recaptured the *Mayaguez* and rescued the crew. This daring operation, in which forty-one U.S. soldiers died, won popular approval until it was revealed that the Cambodians had agreed to release the captured Americans. Secretary of State Henry A. Kissinger* said at the time that "there were limits beyond which the United States cannot be pushed." He was probably right.

G. R. Ford, *A Time to Heal: The Autobiography of Gerald R. Ford* (New York, 1979); H. A. Kissinger, *Years of Upheaval* (New York, 1982); R. Rown, *The Four Days of the* Mayaguez (New York, 1975); R. G. Head et al. (eds.), *Crisis Resolution: Presidential Decision Making in the Mayaguez and Korean Confrontations* (Boulder, CO, 1978).

Joseph M. Siracusa

MELBY, JOHN F. (1913–1992)

A career U.S. Foreign Service officer, John Fremont Melby served in the U.S. embassy in China from November 1945 to December 1948 during the climactic phase of the Chinese Civil War*. Subsequently assigned to the State Department, he played a major role in preparation of the China White Paper* and occupied several influential posts dealing with Philippine and Southeast Asian affairs. Born in Portland, Oregon, Melby graduated from Illinois Wesleyan University in 1934 and earned his doctorate in international relations at the University of Chicago two years after joining the U.S. Foreign Service in 1937. A Latin American specialist, he first served in Ciudad Juárez, Mexico, and Carcacas, Venezuela, before being assigned to the Peru-Ecuador desk in the State Department. In June 1943, Melby transferred to the embassy in Moscow, where, during a nearly two-year stay, he gained firsthand experience in Soviet affairs. After a brief stint in April–June 1945 at the founding conference of the United Nations in San Francisco, he was posted to the embassy in Chongqing as a press and political officer, with special instructions to keep a watch on Soviet activities. While in China, Melby assisted General George C. Marshall* (whom he greatly admired) during his mediation, as well as Lieutenant General Albert C. Wedemeyer* during a fact-finding trip in 1947. By the end of the Marshall Mission*, he had grown disillusioned with the Chinese Communist Party*, but was convinced that the United States could do little to salvage the decrepit Republic of China* under Guomindang* (Nationalist) leader Jiang Jieshi*.

After leaving China, Melby took charge of the Philippine desk at the State Department. Shortly thereafter, he coordinated preparation of the China White Paper, editing the document and writing some parts himself. After returning to his duties at the Philippine desk, Melby saw an ominous similarity between the existing domestic situation in the Philippines* and postwar China. If the former U.S. colony were to avoid the same fate, he said, he saw an urgent need to deal with the interrelated problems of the Hukbalahap* rebellion, the dubious leadership of President Elpidio Quirino, and the nation's political and economic failings. He was prominent in the planning of an economic survey mission to the Philippines in June 1950 that resulted in large-scale development aid tied to economic and fiscal reforms. After the Korean War* began that month, Melby became the State Department representative until October on a Joint Mutual Defense Assistance Program survey mission to Southeast Asia. He and his military counterpart, Major General Graves B. Erskine, with a team of assistants, visited French Indochina*, Malaya*, Thailand*, Indonesia*, and the Philippines to determine the potential effect of U.S. military aid and recommended increased assistance to block Communism* in Southeast Asia. Soon after, Melby was promoted to deputy director of the Office of Philippine and Southeast Asian Affairs and was involved in negotiation of the U.S.-Philippines Mutual Defense Pact* and in grooming Ramón Magsaysay* as a successor to Quirino. In June 1952, he moved to the post of assistant to the director of the Mutual Security Administration in the Pacific.

Meanwhile, Melby had come under investigation by the State Department's Loyalty Security Board in 1951. In November 1952, the board suspended him from duty on the grounds that he was a security risk, despite his reputation as a stalwart anti-Communist, his superb efficiency reports, and affidavits attesting to his loyalty from an impressive list of State Department officials. After two unsuccessful appeals, he was terminated in April 1953. Although no reason was given for his dismissal, the explanation almost certainly lay in his relationship with Lillian Hellman, the famous playwright and well-known advocate of left-wing causes. He and Hellman had once been lovers and had maintained a personal connection after their affair ended. After being fired from the State Department, Melby did educational work of various kinds. In 1966, he became chairman of the Department of Political Studies at the University of Guelph in Ontario, Canada, and remained a professor there until his retirement. Finally, in 1980, nearly three decades after his wrongful dismissal, the State De-

partment cleared his record and reinstated his security clearance.

N. Cullather, *Illusions of Influence: The Political Economy of United States–Philippine Relations, 1942–1960* (Stanford, CA, 1994); G. R. Hess, *The United States' Emergence as a Southeast Asian Power, 1940–1950* (New York, 1987); J. F. Melby, *The Mandate of Heaven: Record of a Civil War, China 1945–49* (Toronto, 1968); R. P. Newman, *The Cold War Romance of Lillian Hellman and John Melby* (Chapel Hill, NC, 1989).

Robert D. Accinelli

MENZIES, ROBERT G. (1894–1978)

Robert Gordon Menzies, Australia's longest-serving prime minister (1949–1966), was a strong proponent of U.S. involvement in the Second Indochina War*. Because of his policies, every known opinion poll of the Australian public persuasively indicated a firm commitment to fighting the Vietnam conflict and to overseas service for those conscripted. President Lyndon B. Johnson* first asked Menzies on 14 December 1964 for some minesweepers, tank landing craft, salvage and repair vessels, and hospital ships, as well as 200 advisers. Unable to fill this request, the Defense Department proposed as a compromise to offer another seventeen advisers, to bring the Vietnam team up to an even 100. Menzies decided, however, to inform Johnson that Australia could supply neither the ships nor the instructors at present, but asked for clarification as to exactly how far the United States was prepared to commit itself in Vietnam, meanwhile assuring Johnson that Australia would "do whatever lies within our physical capacity," which was evidently less than the Americans had imagined.

Nevertheless, Australian leaders wanted the United States to undertake strong and effective action. Minister for External Affairs Paul Hasluck did not see any reason for the delay into early 1965, informing his ambassador in Washington "to suggest that Australia would give full public and diplomatic support if the United States were to initiate air strikes against North Vietnam's infiltration system." When Washington asked Canberra about supplying another thirty combat instructors, Hasluck replied in January that seventeen more advisers would be sent, as well as a combat battalion and a crack Special Air Service squadron. He also gave full support in Parliament for air strikes delivered in February after the Pleiku Incident*, arguing that aggression had to stop. Thereafter, Canberra publicly supported the U.S. commitment of ground forces and sent an Australian delegation led by the chairman of the Chiefs of Staff Committee, Air Chief Marshall Frederick Scherger, to attend military staff talks in Honolulu from 30 March to 1 April. The Australians obtained vital information on U.S. military aims in Vietnam, but the United States reached no decision on an operational strategy.

On 2 April, Secretary of State Dean Rusk* hinted to Australia's ambassador that the United States was sending additional forces to Vietnam and that "Australia might consider giving some help." When a formal request was communicated to Canberra, he asked for 150 more Australian advisers. On 7 April, at the Foreign Affairs and Defence Committee meeting, Hasluck advocated deferring any decision because Washington's strategy was not yet clear. Prime Minister Menzies and other ministers overruled this position. Harold Holt, deputy leader of the Liberal Party, argued that whatever the final outcome of U.S. intervention in Vietnam, Australia had to provide the maximum contribution possible. Menzies said that Australia should commit a battalion if it was requested because it was in Australia's interests to assist the United States in Vietnam, and it was vital that the Republic of Vietnam* not fall to Communism*. Although he was rejecting the request for more advisers, the battalion would be offered to assist in a strategy that was yet to be finalized. After receiving approval from Saigon in April,

Menzies announced the commitment of a battalion, although it was inaccurately implied that this was the result of a formal request for military assistance from Saigon. Between 1962 and 1972, 50,000 Australians served in the Vietnam War, resulting in 400 killed, 2,500 wounded, and a cost of $162 million. The anti–Vietnam War movement soon became one of the largest pressure groups in Australia's history. *See also* U.S. Recruitment of Foreign Troops to Fight in Vietnam.

G. Barclay, *A Very Small Insurance Policy: The Politics of Australian Involvement in Vietnam, 1954–1967* (St. Lucia, BWI, 1988); J. Gray and J. Doyle (eds.), *Vietnam: War, Myth and Memory* (Sydney, 1992); R. G. Menzies, *Afternoon Light* (London, 1967); J. M. Siracusa and Y. Cheong, *America's Australia: Australia's America: Some Memories of Men and Events* (Claremont, CA, 1997).

Joseph M. Siracusa

MERRILL'S MARAUDERS

The War Department named the first American infantry regimental-sized unit to fight in the China-Burma-India Theater* (CBI) Galahad. It was activated as the 5307th Composite Unit (Provisional), but became known to the world as Merrill's Marauders after a reporter used the title, taking the name of the unit's commander, Brigadier General Frank Merrill. Galahad grew out of the Quebec Conference in August 1943, where President Franklin D. Roosevelt* and British Prime Minister Winston Churchill voiced the desire to take the offensive on the Asia mainland. Admiral Lord Louis Mountbatten was selected as commander of the Southeast Asia Command, with Lieutenant General Joseph W. Stilwell* as his U.S. deputy and liaison to the Guomindang* (Nationalist) government. U.S. combat presence was to be in the form of three long-range penetration groups modeled after the Chindits of Major General Orde Wingate, who had gained fame after a three-month expedition in northern Burma* behind Japanese lines in 1943. The units were to be resupplied entirely by air every four to five days. The War Department issued a call for jungle-trained volunteers: 960 from the Caribbean Defense Command, 970 from U.S. Army ground forces, 674 from the South Pacific, and 274 from General Douglas MacArthur*.

Merrill's Marauders arrived in Burma in November and began training for a dry-season offensive. From 24 February to 27 May, the unit engaged in three operations, fighting five major and seven minor engagements in conjunction with Guomindang forces. It drove the Japanese out of northern Burma, securing territory for the Ledo Road, which connected to the old Burma Road* to send supplies overland to China. After this grueling 600–700 mile offensive, the unit was physically and emotionally exhausted. Only 1,310 of the original 3,000 reached the final battle at Myitkyina, and those were being evacuated at a rate of 75 to 100 per day. At this point, Chinese units proved ineffective in capturing the city, so Stilwell sent engineer units into battle and pulled wounded survivors from hospitals back to the front lines. Merrill's Marauders now experienced what a War Department investigation called "an almost complete breakdown of morale." Colonel Charles Hunter, who had assumed command of the unit when General Merrill had a heart attack, was relieved. The unit was awarded the Distinguished Unit Citation and disbanded after the fall of Myitkyina on 2 August 1944. One of Merrill's Marauders was Roger Hilsman*, who would play an important role in policy making regarding the Second Indochina War*.

E. Hoyt, *Merrill's Marauders* (Baton Rouge, LA, 1980); C. Ogburn, *The Marauders* (New York, 1956); B. Tuchman, *Stilwell and the American Experience in China, 1911–1945* (New York, 1971).

Larry R. Beck

MICRONESIA

Japan conquered these Pacific islands during World War II. Following Allied liberation, the United Nations assigned Micronesia as a trust territory to the United States. Located in the northern Pacific Ocean, this collection of island groups includes the Marianas, Carolines, Marshalls, Kiribati (Gilbert Islands), and the island nation of Nauru. In all, there are some 2,106 islands covering 1,104 square miles. In 1997, the estimated population was 346,000, including some 2,000 expatriates from Australia, Britain, the United States, China, Taiwan*, and Japan. Culturally diverse, Micronesia incorporates characteristics of the same groups, although there is a heavy Polynesian influence at Kapinga-marangi Atol, which is near the equator south of Chuuk (Truk), and Pohnpei, and a Melanesian influence at Tobi Island in Palau. Some ethnographers have considered Tuvalu (Ellice Islands) to be culturally Micronesian. Politically, the definition is more complicated. Until the 1990s, Micronesia was usually considered synonymous with the U.S.-administered Trust Territory of the Pacific Islands (TTPI), which included all the Marshalls, Marianas, and Carolines, except for Guam*. The original TTPI, established in 1947, covered approximately 3 million square miles in geographic Micronesia. It was the only one of the trusteeships the United Nations established after World War II that was designated as a "strategic trusteeship." This provided ultimate UN authority to reside with its Security Council, rather than with the Trusteeship Council, although the latter handled regular administration processes and annual reporting from the the United States, the administering power.

In 1969, the people living under the TTPI entered into formal future political status negotiations with the United States. The Northern Mariana Islands broke away from the rest of the island groups in 1972 and entered into separate negotiations with the U.S. government, and subsequently the

Commonwealth of the Northern Mariana Islands was formed. Carlos Camacho took office as the first governor on 9 January 1978 at Saipan, having authority over all of the Mariana Islands except Guam. In 1975, the other islands in the TTPI held a constitutional convention and the people voted on adoption of this document on 12 July 1978. Yap, Pohnpei, Chuuk, and Kosrae ratified the new constitution, but Palau and the Marshall Islands did not. The four states that ratified formed the Federated States of Micronesia, and their government took power officially on 10 May 1979, under an elected president, Nakayama Tosiwo, and a vice president, Petrus Tun. Elected as governor in each state were Leo Falcam of Pohnpei, John Mangafel of Yap, Erhart Aten of Chuuk, and Jacob Nena of Kosrae. The Marshall Islands drafted a constitution, which was passed in a referendum in 1979. In April, an election was held for their new legislature, which had thirty-three members, and they elected one president from among its members. Amata Kabua was inaugurated on 1 May 1979 as the first president. In April 1979 the Palauans also held a constitutional convention, approving a document providing for general election of president and vice president. Palau ratified its Compact of Free Association for Micronesia* with the United States in 1994, and on 1 October the TTPI officially was terminated.

R. D. Craig and F. P. King, *Historical Dictionary of Oceania* (Westport, CT, 1980); D. Farrell, *History of the Northern Mariana Islands* (Saipan, 1991); W. L. Wuerch and D. A. Ballendorf, *Historical Dictionary of Guam and Micronesia* (Metuchen, NJ, 1994).

Dirk A. Ballendorf

MIDWAY, BATTLE OF

See BATTLE OF MIDWAY

MIKI TAKEO (1907–1988)

Miki Takeo became prime minister of Japan on 19 December 1974 after Tanaka Kakuei* resigned in the wake of a money scandal. Even though Miki was leader of one of the smallest factions in the Liberal Democratic Party* (LDP), he became party president and then prime minister as a compromise candidate because the LDP's leadership had misgivings about the party's image as a corrupt money machine after the Tanaka resignation. During his previous thirty-seven years in the Diet, Miki had cultivated the image of "Mr. Clean" with long advocacy of reforming the party's "money culture." The LDP's leaders hoped to exploit Miki's clean image, choosing him over other, more influential candidates, such as Ōhira Masayoshi* and Fukuda Takeo*. Because of this, however, the Miki administration critically depended on the support of other stronger factional leaders, and his political base remained weak. He ultimately was removed from power in 1976 by the coalition of major factional leaders led by Fukuda.

Miki was born in a farm town in Tokushima Prefecture. After graduating from Meiji University, he gained election in 1937 to the lower house of the Diet, keeping his seat continuously for more than fifty years until his death. His campaign slogans for his first election were "The purification of politics and political parties" and "Down with the undemocratic bureaucratic government," which summarized his lifelong political beliefs. During his early political career, Miki flirted with a "cooperative" movement, which was influenced by the ideas of Robert Owen and popular in devastated postwar Japan. This developed in him another lifelong belief in the necessity to seek social justice within the framework of capitalism, which he characterized as "progressive conservatism." Miki participated in the establishment of the LDP in 1955, but his reformist orientation kept him on the fringe of the party's mainstream conservatism. He developed highly pragmatic political skills, often compromising with stronger political forces behind the scenes.

As prime minister, Miki represented Ja-

MILITARY ASSISTANCE ADVISORY GROUP, TAIWAN

pan at the first economic summit of the advanced industrialized countries in 1975. He introduced the first National Defense Program Outline in 1976, placing limits on Japanese force levels in peacetime with the doctrine of "defensive defense" and the standard force concept. His administration also established the important policy guideline of limiting annual defense spending to less than 1 percent of Japan's gross national product. Domestically, Miki sought stronger regulations of campaign funds, strengthening the Anti-Monopoly Law, and introducing primary elections for the LDP president. But what damaged his standing in his party was the Lockheed Scandal* during 1976, in which Miki sought a thorough investigation of international bribery and allowed the arrest of Tanaka. His handling of this issue estranged most LDP leaders and led a majority of factions to unite behind the Miki Oroshi (Down-with-Miki Movement). Miki ultimately had to resign after the December 1976 elections, in which the LDP for the first time failed to gain a majority of Diet seats in the lower house. Always a maverick, Miki remained influential in party politics after resigning, traveling widely and consulting with world leaders.

K. Hayao, *The Japanese Prime Minister and Public Policy* (Pittsburgh, PA, 1993); J. I. Matray, *Japan's Emergence as a Global Power* (Westport, CT, 2000); Miki Takeo, *Gikai seiji to tomoni* [In Parliamentary Politics] (Tōkyō, 1984); Watanabe Akio (ed.), *Sengo Nihon no Saishō tachi* [Postwar Japanese Prime Ministers] (Tōkyō, 1995).

Kamimura Naoki

MILITARY ASSISTANCE ADVISORY GROUP, TAIWAN

In U.S. military shorthand, MAAG stood for Military Assistance Advisory Group. This was the designation of the unit of American military personnel stationed on Taiwan* to assist and counsel the Guomindang* (Nationalist) armed forces. The MAAG was established officially in May

1951, after a decision by the Truman administration to extend substantial military aid to the exiled Republic of China*. The assignment of a MAAG team to Taiwan publicly signaled that the United States had decided to resume long-term military support for the displaced regime of Jiang Jieshi*. Early in 1950, Washington had curtailed further military assistance to the Nationalists and appeared ready to allow Taiwan to fall to the People's Republic of China* (PRC). The Korean War* persuaded the Truman adminstration to support Jiang. During its first four years, the MAAG, Taiwan was headed by Major General William C. Chase, a career U.S. Army officer and self-described "MacArthur man," who had served in East Asia under General Douglas MacArthur* during and after World War II. The MAAG's mission was to train, equip, and advise the Nationalist armed forces, which were mostly ill-trained and ill-equipped when Chase first arrived at his post. The MAAG concentrated on preparing these forces to defend Taiwan and the Penghus (Pescadores), but it also lent assistance to harassing Guomindang raids against the mainland and sought to build a strategic reserve of troops with limited offensive capability for possible use in operations outside the Taiwan area.

From the start, the MAAG advisers encountered a fundamental problem in carrying out their basic mission because of the Nationalist government's insistence, in line with its oft-proclaimed goal to recapture the mainland, on maintaining an overly large and costly military establishment. Washington refused to subscribe to Jiang's militant liberationist goal and was loathe to finance his efforts in that direction. Despite this and other differences, the MAAG advisers established effective working relationships with their Guomindang counterparts and made significant progress in modernizing Taiwan's military services, as well as improving their skills and morale. Along with military equipment, Jiang's forces absorbed U.S. military organization, techniques, and tactics. The MAAG grew from about 250 just after its establishment to some 2,300 by the late 1950s, making it one of the largest U.S. advisory groups in the world. The MAAG, Taiwan was a target of the Taibei Anti-U.S. Riot of 1957*, when on 24 May, a mob of 25,000 wrecked the U.S. embassy and the U.S. Information Service headquarters, and threatened the MAAG offices. The proximate cause of this outburst was popular anger over the acquittal in a U.S. military court of a MAAG sergeant accused of murdering a Chinese man. But the more deep-seated cause was resentment against the large number of American civilian and military personnel on the island. These personnel lived separately from the local citizenry, enjoyed a higher standard of living, and were immune from Chinese law.

During the period of U.S. escalation of the Second Indochina War* in the 1960s, the U.S. military presence on Taiwan mushroomed. Until 1967, military aid remained at relatively high levels. The basic mission of the MAAG remained to train, supply, and advise the Nationalist armed forces, who acquired more sophisticated equipment and weaponry, but remained incapable of an independent large-scale landing on the mainland. As a result of the reconciliation between Washington and the Beijing under President Richard M. Nixon*, the tight military connection between the United States and Taiwan loosened considerably. The Shanghai Communiqué*, jointly issued in February 1972, pledged the United States to withdraw its military forces from Taiwan "as the tension in the area diminishes." In 1974, U.S. military grants aid to Nationalist China ceased, except for a small amount for training. By the middle of 1977, the size of the military advisory group had dropped to less than fifty. The withdrawal of U.S. recognition from the Republic of China on 1 January 1979 (the same day on which Washington normalized relations with the PRC), together with the termination of the U.S.-China Mutual Defense Treaty of 1954* a

year later, spelled the end of the MAAG, Taiwan.

R. D. Accinelli, *Crisis and Commitment: United States Policy Toward Taiwan, 1950–1955* (Chapel Hill, NC, 1996); W. C. Chase, *Front Line General* (Houston, TX, 1975); R. N. Clough, *Island China* (Cambridge, MA, 1978); N. B. Tucker, *Taiwan, Hong Kong, and the United States, 1945–1992: Uncertain Friendships* (New York, 1994).

Robert D. Accinelli

MILITARY ASSISTANCE COMMAND, VIETNAM

When President John F. Kennedy* began increasing military aid to the Republic of Vietnam* in late 1961, the Joint Chiefs of Staff (JCS) recommended establishment of a military command to direct military operational and logistic support to the South Vietnamese. This resulted in the formation of the Military Assistance Command, Vietnam (MACV) on 8 February 1962, under the command of U.S. Army General Paul D. Harkins. Its predecessor, the Military Assistance and Advisory Group, Vietnam (MAAG-V) continued to operate as an independent agency overseeing organization and training of the Army of the Republic of Vietnam* (ARVN) until May 1964, when the MACV absorbed its functions. The MACV served as a joint service headquarters directing the U.S. effort in South Vietnam during the Second Indochina War* until its deactivation in March 1973.

The MACV, in addition to having overlapping functions with MAAG-V, suffered from being a "subordinate unified command" under the Commander in Chief, Pacific (CINCPAC) in Honolulu. It did not report directly to the JCS and it did not control strategic planning, the Secret U.S. Air War in Laos*, air strikes against the Democratic Republic of Vietnam*, or offshore naval operations. As ground forces in South Vietnam grew, General William C. Westmoreland*, General Harkins's successor, refused to establish a field army headquarters, maintaining command of army forces himself, in addition to the advisory and political roles of the MACV. Thus, the role of the MACV was at the same time too limited and too broad. This command structure combined with detailed civilian involvement from President Lyndon B. Johnson* and the Department of Defense hampered the efficient prosecution of the war. General Westmoreland assumed command of the MACV in June 1964. He was replaced by General Creighton Abrams* in July 1968, who in turn was succeeded by General Frederick Weyland in June 1972. Both Westmoreland and Abrams left the MACV to become chief of staff of the U.S. Army. *See also* Green Berets.

M. Matloff (ed.), *American Military History* (Washington, DC, 1969); N. Sheehan, *A Bright Shining Lie: John Paul Vann and America in Vietnam* (New York, 1988); W. C. Westmoreland, *A Soldier Reports* (Garden City, NY, 1972).

Larry R. Beck

MINISTRY OF INTERNATIONAL TRADE AND INDUSTRY

Japan's Ministry of International Trade and Industry (MITI) was established in 1949, quickly establishing itself as a rival to the Ministry of Foreign Affairs in shaping government policy. MITI bureaucrats vigorously pushed industrial development and export growth in Japan. This state guidance of the economy caused friction in U.S.-Japan Postwar Trade Relations*, and provoked intense debate over the Japanese model of capitalist development. In its personnel, institutional structure, and guiding philosophy, Japan's postwar economic bureaucracy showed strong continuity with the prewar era. MITI was the postwar incarnation of the long-established Ministry of Commerce and Industry and the wartime Ministry of Munitions. Bureaucrats in these ministries advocated strategic economic planning, but they lacked the necessary power. Rising figures, such as Kishi Nobusuke*, who became minister of munitions, experimented with economic plan-

ning in occupied Manchuria beginning in the 1930s. Dependent upon the bureaucracy during the U.S. Occupation of Japan*, SCAP* purged fewer than fifty Ministry of Munitions officials.

Sympathetic observers have likened MITI to an "economic general staff" because of the wide scope of its authority. The ministry was organized into general policy-making bureaus and those corresponding with specific industries. Ministry leaders sought to accelerate Japan's economic development, and they acquired a large domestic policy-making role. MITI, rather than the market, decided the levels of production, the rationalization of enterprises, and the introduction of new technology. Rejecting rigid government planning, the bureaucrats instead perfected various forms of "administrative guidance" to secure the cooperation of Japanese enterprises. U.S. policies also unwittingly contributed to MITI's power. During the occupation, U.S. officials controlled vital economic transactions, such as purchases of imports. They expected that when SCAP divested itself of supervisory powers, Japan's government gradually would relax them, but the controls endured. Owing to legitimate concerns about Japan's precarious balance of payments position, in 1953, the U.S.-Japan Treaty of Friendship, Commerce, and Navigation granted Japan the right to put restrictions on foreign trade and investment. Even in the early years, industrial policy amounted to much more than simple trade protectionism. MITI bureaucrats promoted high value–added industries, such as chemicals, automobiles, and electronics. This effort also included protecting the domestic market from foreign competition until Japanese companies were themselves competitive abroad and confining domestic consumption to achieve the economies of scale required for international competitiveness.

Economic success led to great interest in MITI and Japan's distinctive brand of capitalism by the 1980s. Although the Japanese gradually relaxed these and other controls during subsequent decades, MITI policies became the source of friction in U.S.-Japanese economic relations. American criticism of Japanese industrial policy grew as Japan's trade surplus rose. This tension peaked during the 1980s and early 1990s. For Ambassadors Mike Mansfield* and Michael H. Armacost*, along with other officials, trade conflicts were a political issue of prime importance. As Americans in greater numbers considered MITI either a threat to the United States or a model for the future, scholars began to view it more critically. Analysts of high-technology policy rightly emphasized that MITI was not alone at the top, but part of a wider system. Changes in technology and market needs rendered the various MITI policies obsolete. Contrary to the popular perceptions abroad, Japanese high-tech consortia have been marked by conflict and have yielded less than expected. In short, Japanese bureaucrats found that policies associated with "catch-up capitalism" were inadequate to meet the challenges facing a market leader. The long recession of the 1990s further tarnished the luster of Japanese industrial policy. Ironically, some MITI officials emerged as prominent advocates of deregulation.

M. H. Armacost, *Friends or Rivals?: The Insider's Account of U.S.-Japan Relations* (New York, 1996); S. Callon, *Divided Sun: MITI and the Breakdown of Japanese High-Tech Industrial Policy, 1975–1993* (Stanford, CA, 1995); C. A. Johnson, *MITI and the Japanese Miracle: The Growth of Industrial Policy* (Stanford, CA, 1982); D. I. Okimoto, *Between MITI and the Market Japanese: Industrial Policy for High Technology* (Stanford, CA, 1989); F. K. Upham, *Law and Social Change in Postwar Japan* (Cambridge, MA, 1987).

Aaron Forsberg

MIYAZAWA KIICHI (1921–)

Serving as prime minister of Japan during the early 1990s, Miyazawa Kiichi became the first Liberal Democratic Party* (LDP) standard-bearer to face defeat in a genera-

tion. Once regarded as "the power behind the throne" of a number of prime ministers, he was especially responsible for the establishment and maintenance of Japan's "bubble economy" of the 1970s and 1980s. The economic collapse of 1992 and 1993 also triggered the collapse of Miyazawa's LDP Party rule. Miyazawa was elected to the upper house in the Diet in 1953. At age thirty-two, he was the youngest member of this body at the time and the focus of many press accounts because of it. A former official in the Finance Ministry, his expertise was in foreign trade policy and exports.

Thoroughly bilingual in American-accented English, Miyazawa also served as private secretary to Finance Minister Ikeda Hayato* from 1949 to 1952. He sometimes acted as Ikeda's interpreter and translator in U.S.-Japan trade discussions, including the Colombo Plan* Conference in 1958. By late 1959 and early 1960, this 1941 Tōkyō University graduate was the vice minister of education in the third cabinet of Prime Minister Kishi Nobusuke*, as well as the deputy chief of the LDP's Finance Division. Known for his gentlemanly manners and an early interest in an export policy that targeted the consumerism of the United States, Miyazawa also maintained an unusual commitment to ethics in government at a time when corruption was often tolerated in the LDP itself. Ikeda, who became prime minister in 1960, had not forgotten about his young, innovative assistant and appointed Miyazawa his chief adviser on all foreign economic policy matters. Much of Ikeda's agenda for a "New Japan," which embraced an aggressive trade policy, was scripted by Miyazawa. The term "bubble economy," which denotes Japan's rapid rise to economic power and its successful penetration of the American market, is sometimes attributed to Miyazawa's efforts alone.

Although Miyazawa often described himself as a struggling amateur who, like some of the American political heroes that he admired, emerged as a "dark horse" in an otherwise crowded political field, he came from a privileged, influential political family. His grandfather served as minister of justice in the 1920s and was elected ten times to the House of Representatives. His father served six terms there. It was Miyazawa Kiichi, however, who was most remembered from this family. By the mid-1970s, his blueprint for rapid industrial development linked to frenetic export policies to North America had led to the shedding of Japan's postwar image of defeat and junior partner status to the Americans. With characteristic reluctance, he finally entered the prime minister's office. Ironically, he took command of the country at a time when it faced growing unemployment and a youthful "populist" movement in his own party to keep Japan's "best products home." His time in office was marked by a certain national soul-searching over its 1990s future. His fall from power left Japan in the hands of successive coalition governments, the first under Hosokawa Morihiro*, until in 1998, Obuchi Keizō brought Miyazawa back into government as his finance minister to revive a tottering economy during the East Asian Financial Crisis*. *See also* U.S.-Japan Postwar Trade Relations.

Japan Times, "Interview with Kiichi Miyazawa: An Elder Statesman Reflects on Postwar and Future Japan," *Japan Times Weekly International Edition*, 28 August–3 September 1995; T. P. Maga, *Hands Across the Sea?: U.S.-Japan Relations, 1961–1981* (Athens, OH, 1997); K. Yamamura, *Japan's Economic Structure: Should It Change?* (Tōkyō, 1990).

Timothy P. Maga

MOON, SUN MYUNG

See UNIFICATION CHURCH

MOSCOW AGREEMENT ON KOREA (21 December 1945)

The Moscow Conference, held 16–26 December 1945, was the second meeting after World War II between the foreign minis-

ters of the United States, Britain, and the Soviet Union. It was organized on the initiative of U.S. Secretary of State James F. Byrnes and represented an effort to make progress on the details of postwar settlements, which had stalled at the London Council of Foreign Ministers Conference in September. The major issues discussed in Moscow were atomic energy, peace treaties, withdrawal of Soviet troops from Iran, occupation machinery for Japan, Soviet and U.S. troops in China, and policies regarding the joint occupation of Korea. The latter issue emerged out of the Thirty-Eighth Parallel Division* of Korea into Soviet and U.S. zones in August 1945. The conference amounted to a working out of spheres of influence, particularly those of the Soviet Union and the United States.

On Korea, Byrnes and Soviet Foreign Minister Vyacheslav Molotov agreed to create a Joint Soviet-American Commission composed of American and Soviet occupation officials. The Joint Commission was to consult with Korean democratic parties and social organizations and to make recommendations for the formation of a democratic provisional government for all of Korea. The recommendations of the commission would be submitted to the governments of the United States, the Soviet Union, China, and Britain for comment, but the United States and the Soviet Union would have the final say. The commission then would negotiate with the provisional Korean government and the four powers to work out a four-power trusteeship for Korea for a period of up to five years. Finally, there were to be discussions between the occupation commanders to increase contacts across the thirty-eighth parallel.

Many U.S. officials, particularly those in southern Korea, were not fully committed to trusteeship. They realized that continued adherence to an unpopular political program would weaken the U.S. position in southern Korea and strengthen the power of the left. After October 1945, the U.S. occupation commander, Lieutenant General John R. Hodge*, recommended that trusteeship be abandoned. In November 1945, Byrnes informed William R. Langdon, acting political adviser in Korea, that if adequate guarantees for Korea's independence could be found, it might be possible for the United States to end its commitment to trusteeship. After the Moscow Conference, Byrnes announced in a radio address that the Joint Commission might find it possible to dispense with trusteeship if a sovereign Korean government were established quickly. Prominent Koreans, including Kim Gu* and Syngman Rhee*, also openly criticized trusteeship. In the north, the left soon embraced trusteeship, as the Soviets claimed that only those Korean political parties who agreed with trusteeship should be consulted about forming a Korean provisional government.

The Moscow Conference was a short term success for tenuous postwar unity, but it failed to diminish the increasing suspicion between the former Allies. President Harry S. Truman* was angry that Byrnes had not taken a stronger position on Korea at the conference, and criticized his secretary of state for failing to demand a central government and immediate measures for the joint economic reconstruction of Korea. These comments were contained in a famous unsent letter to Byrnes dated 5 January 1946, in which Truman also said that he was now tired of "babying" the Soviets. The Joint Soviet-American Commission reached a deadlock by the summer of 1947 and the United States then unilaterally brought the Korean issue to the United Nations.

B. Cumings, *The Origins of the Korean War*, Vol. 1: *Liberation and the Emergence of Separate Regimes, 1945–1947* (Princeton, NJ, 1981); J. L. Gaddis, *The United States and the Origins of the Cold War, 1941–1947* (New York, 1972); J. I. Matray, *The Reluctant Crusade: American Foreign Policy and Korea, 1941–1950* (Honolulu, HI, 1985); U.S. Department of State, *Foreign Relations of the United States, 1945*, Vol. 2: *General: Political and Economic Matters* (Washington, DC, 1967); U.S. Department of State, *Foreign Relations of the United States, 1945*, Vol. 6: *The British Commonwealth, The Far East* (Washington, DC, 1969); D. Yergin, *Shattered Peace: The Origins of the Cold War* (New York, 1990).

Steven Hugh Lee

MU OUCHU (1876–1943)

Deeply influenced by the reformist ideological trend prevailing in China at the beginning of twentieth century, Mu Ouchu held the thought that "to save the nation demands prospering industry and to prosper industry demands real knowledge." Mu was on his way to study in the United States in the summer of 1909, when at his first stop in San Francisco, he made contact with modern technology and admired the Americans' excellent industrial techniques. He studied agriculture at the University of Wisconsin and then the University of Illinois and Texas Agricultural and Mechanical College. During his stay, he observed the country and studied the people in the United States and made comparisons with his homeland. He paid most attention to the American management system and wrote a book contrasting it with that in China.

Returning home with a master's degree in 1914, Mu built a fund with his elder brother to construct a cotton mill named Deda in Shanghai. Not long after Deda came into operation, it became the "cotton king" and its brand name Pagoda ranked first in the 1916 commodity-quality competition in Beijing. Mu attributed the reasons for his success to American industrial techniques and management. Imitating a U.S. trust, Mu built a new mill named Housheng, forming a limited joint-stock company. He equipped Housheng with American machinery, made purchases through Andersen, Meyer and Company Limited, and ran the mill in the way of American management. Housheng came into operation in 1918 and soon became the "achievement show and practicing place of American Spinning machinery." As reported at that time, "any Chinese who intend to initiate a cotton mill must, to begin with, visit Housheng and send people to practice there." He set up a third mill named Yu Feng in the same way in Zheng-zhou at the end of 1918. In addition, Mu established sixteen farms in provinces for planting long-fiber cotton, the seeds of which were imported from the United States.

Mu purchased American commodities, he explained, because he "knew best the quality of American goods" and because of "the friendship that I cultivated with the American people during my stay in the United States." In his memoirs, he wrote that "much of the increased importation of machinery and other manufactures from the United States that aided the develop-ment of Chinese industries could be as-cribed to American University men working in industrial enterprises in China." Holding the view that the failure of China's modern enterprises resulted from a lack of qualified entrepreneurs and poor education, Mu asked the famous ed-ucationalist Cai Yuanpei to select for him some young men and funded them to study in the United States, most of whom later became famous scholars. From 1914 to 1923, he translated a book about manage-ment science into Chinese and wrote many articles to introduce American manage-ment to the Chinese. In October 1922, Mu attended and delivered a speech at the Pa-cific Commercial Conference in Hawaii as China's chief representative.

Kong Lingren (ed.), *Zhongguo jindai qiye de kai-chuang zhe* [The Man Who Opened Up Chinese Modern Enterprise] (Jinan, 1991); Mu Ouchu, *Mu Ouchu wushi zizhuan* [Autobiography of Mu Ouchu at 50 Years of Age] (Shanghai, 1926).

Xiang Liling

MUCCIO, JOHN J. (1900–1989)

John J. Muccio was the first U.S. ambassa-dor to the Republic of Korea and remained in this position until two years after the start of the Korean War*. Born near Naples in Italy, his parents came to the United States when he was an infant and settled in Providence, Rhode Island. World War I interrupted his college education. After serving in the U.S. Army in 1918, Muccio graduated from Brown University in 1921. That same year, he became a U.S. citizen and entered the consular service, later earning a master of arts degree at George Washington University. In 1924, Muccio's first posting was as vice consul in Ham-burg, Germany, serving thereafter in China at Hong Kong (1926–1928), Fuzhao (1928–1930), and Shanghai (1930–1934). For the next nine years, he held postings in Latin America. In 1945, Muccio returned to Ger-many as an assistant to Robert D. Murphy*, U.S. political adviser on German affairs, and attended the Potsdam Conference. Af-ter a brief stay in the United States, he spent 1947 in China and Manchuria as a member of the Inspector Corps of the For-eign Service.

In August 1948, when the United States accorded conditional recognition to the Re-public of Korea* (ROK), President Harry S. Truman selected Muccio as his special rep-resentative to replace Lieutenant General John R. Hodge*, commander of the U.S. Occupation of Korea*, as head of the U.S. diplomatic mission in Seoul. Undoubtedly, Truman chose him because he had both ex-perience in Asia and familiarity with the problems of military occupation and divi-sion in Germany. In March 1949, Muccio became the first U.S. ambassador to the ROK, when Washington raised its mission in South Korea to embassy rank. His greatest challenge was maintaining good relations with President Syngman Rhee*. Previously, he had criticized the Rhee re-gime for its political repression, but now he faced the difficult task of overcoming ROK opposition to U.S. plans for an early mili-tary withdrawal. After negotiating an agreement for U.S. economic assistance to South Korea, Muccio displayed considera-ble diplomatic skill in pacifying Rhee. He then persuaded Rhee to enact strong mea-sures to control inflation and hold the May

1950 assembly elections on schedule. During the six months before the start of the Korean War, he vigorously advocated with modest success an expansion of U.S. economic and military aid for the ROK, both in private cables and in congressional testimony.

It was Muccio who notified Washington of the North Korean invasion of South Korea on 25 June 1950. As the North Korean forces moved southward, he supervised the evacuation of U.S. personnel. Muccio seriously considered staying in Seoul, but left after Secretary of State Dean G. Acheson* persuaded him that his capture would not serve U.S. interests. During the retreat to the Pusan Perimeter*, Muccio argued that the war was not lost and victory was indeed possible, thus reinforcing the morale of Rhee and other South Korean officials. His pressure led the U.S. Army to fill out its understrength battalions with Korean soldiers. After the Inch'ŏn Landing* in September, Muccio returned his embassy to the capital. He attended the Wake Island Conference with General Douglas MacArthur* and spoke in favor of permitting the Rhee government to play an active role in occupation of North Korea. After Chinese Intervention in the Korean War*, he moved his embassy directly to Pusan, where it remained for the balance of his tenure as ambassador. With the start of armistice talks in July 1951, Muccio struggled unsuccessfully to persuade Rhee that the United States never would permit the Communists to conquer South Korea and that a negotiated settlement was therefore in the interests of the ROK. Similarly, his efforts to promote democracy failed, as Rhee crushed his enemies and strengthened his dictatorial rule in June 1952. Two months later, Muccio was replaced and he soon was named to the UN Trusteeship Council. His career ended with appointments as envoy extraordinary to Iceland (1954–1956) and ambassador to Guatemala (1959–1961).

Current Biography, 1951; H. J. Noble, *Embassy at War* (Seattle, WA, 1975); J. I. Matray, *The Reluc-*

tant Crusade: American Foreign Policy in Korea, 1941–1950 (Honolulu, HI, 1985); U.S. Department of State, *Foreign Relations of the United States, 1950*, Vol. 7: *Korea* (Washington, DC, 1976); U.S. Department of State, *Foreign Relations of the United States, 1951*, Vol. 7: *Korea and China* (Washington, DC, 1983); U.S. Department of State, *Foreign Relations of the United States, 1952–1954*, Vol. 15: *Korea* (Washington, DC, 1984).

James I. Matray

MUKDEN INCIDENT

World War II began at Mukden (Shenyang) in September 1931, when Japan flouted the moral authority of the League of Nations and got away with it. By 1931, the officers at Japan's Kwantung Army Headquarters in Manchuria, then at Port Arthur, like many of their comrades in Japan, had become entirely exasperated by the social, political, and economic reverses afflicting Japan both domestically and internationally. The threat of expanding Communist influence from China and from the Soviet Union by means of the latter's rights in the Chinese Eastern Railway was very real. Development of Japanese interests in Manchuria was regarded as a matter of national security, for northeast China constituted a buffer against Russia or China, or a springboard for operations against those nations or Mongolia. Kwantung Army Headquarters, in particular, clamored for Tōkyō to adopt a policy to compel China to abandon its efforts to recapture national rights. Chinese unification posed potentially a fatal threat to the Japanese hold on Manchuria, although Jiang Jieshi* had not yet eliminated powerful Guomindang* (Nationalist) rivals or the Chinese Communist Party*.

The plot prepared at Kwantung Army Headquarters during 1931 to conquer Manchuria reflected a much larger military movement designed to renovate Japan itself by bringing down the civilian government, which allegedly was characterized by corrupt politicians addicted to the spoils system. The arrival at Port Arthur in 1928 and 1929 of Lieutenant Colonel Ishiwara Kanji and Colonel Itagaki Seishirō, two new activist staff officers, both with important associates in Tōkyō and who ruled out any early peaceful resolution of pending Sino-Japanese problems, signaled crystallization of the well-planned plot. New commanders of both the Kwantung Army and Korea Army, Generals Shigeru Honjō and Senjūrō Hayashi respectively, took over in 1931. Both were thought to be sympathetic with the aims of the plotters, but were not directly implicated. The Mukden area, a railway hub and military base for the Chinese, was seen as crucial. The Kwantung Army, though vastly outnumbered, was elite and mobile, with emphasis on careful operational planning and rigorous training. Tipped off that Tōkyō's government and High Command might seek to restrain intemperate action in Manchuria, the conspirators moved up the date for the proposed coup at Mukden to 18 September, even before a homeland terrorist plot could be unleashed.

A phony explosion on the tracks of the South Manchuria Railway was fomented on the night of 18 September and blamed on the Chinese, followed by the swift concentration of Japanese troops and the overrunning of the unsuspecting main Chinese military encampment. By afternoon on 23 September, the whole Mukden sector had been seized, and Kwantung Army Headquarters was relocated from Port Arthur. Invaluable but unlawful assistance was provided by Hayashi's Korean Army. Soon afterward, the Kwantung Army fanned out and occupied all of Manchuria, thus bringing it to the borders of Soviet Siberia. Japan's civilian government could do nothing to thwart the fait accompli, which soon would be followed by the creation of the puppet state of Manchukuo* and the withdrawal of Japan from the League of Nations, whose protests were feckless. The United States responded with the Stimson Doctrine* of nonrecognition in January 1932. Without concomitant force, threats of imposing sanctions or conducting an eco-

nomic blockade were empty words. Japanese forces proceeded to carve up north China, leading in due course to full-scale Sino-Japanese hostilities after the Marco Polo Bridge Incident* in July 1937.

A. D. Coox, *Nomonhan: Japan Against Russia, 1939*, 2 vols. (Stanford, CA, 1985); S. Ogata, *Defiance in Manchuria: The Making of Japanese Foreign Policy, 1931–1932* (Berkeley, CA, 1964); J. Penlington, *The Mukden Mandate: Acts and Aims in Manchuria* (Tokyo, 1932); Y. Takehiko, *Conspiracy at Mukden: The Rise of the Japanese Military* (New Haven, CT, 1963).

Alvin D. Coox

MURPHY, ROBERT D. (1894–1978)

From May 1952 to April 1953, Robert D. Murphy was the first U.S. ambassador in Tōkyō after the U.S. Occupation of Japan*. With considerable and varied exposure in the field of foreign policy, his long involvement in European affairs overshadowed his contribution to East Asian affairs. Murphy was born in Milwaukee and attended Marquette University. After joining the Foreign Service in 1917 and then graduating from George Washington University Law School in 1920, he had held postings by 1930 in Zurich, Munich, Seville, and Washington. Thereafter, Murphy served in Paris as consul, first secretary, counselor, and chargé until 1940, when he became the personal representative of President Franklin D. Roosevelt* in secretly preparing the way for the Allied invasion of French North Africa. He then was chief civil affairs officer on the staff of General Dwight D. Eisenhower*, the supreme commander, Allied Forces Headquarters. In the postwar period, Murphy served as political adviser to the U.S. Occupation of Germany until 1949, when he became ambassador to Belgium, and worked to implement the Marshall Plan.

In 1952, President Harry S. Truman* named Murphy U.S. ambassador to Japan. During his tenure, he was associated closely with three principal issues. First was the highly contentious question of postwar Japanese rearmament, which the United States favored despite prohibitions against it in the Japanese Constitution of 1947*. Second was Murphy's role in the drafting and eventual signing of the U.S.-Japan Treaty of Friendship, Commerce, and Navigation in April 1953. Third was the debate over the status of Okinawa and the Ryūkyū and Ogasawara Islands. In this last case, Murphy, together with Admiral Arthur W. Radford*, the commander in chief in the Pacific, advised, after an inspection visit to the Ogasawara Islands to the southeast of Japan in October 1952, against satisfying the request of Japan's government under Prime Minister Yoshida Shigeru* for the return of the territories to Japanese administrative control. The islands, they concluded, were strategically important to the United States, and political pressures for return of the territories were not considered sufficiently strong to warrant compliance with the Japanese request.

A staunch Cold Warrior, Murphy gained a reputation as a skilled diplomatic troubleshooter. In 1953, after his brief tenure in Japan, he became assistant secretary of state for United Nations Affairs and was replaced as ambassador in Tōkyō by John M. Allison*. Murphy also served as political adviser to the United Nations Command in the Korean War* and helped persuade President Syngman Rhee* of the Republic of Korea* to accept the Korean Armistice Agreement* in the summer of 1953. A close friend and professional associate of President Eisenhower, he then occupied from 1953 to 1959 an influential position as deputy undersecretary of state under Secretary of State John Foster Dulles*. He concerned himself primarily with Soviet affairs, but also helped in the negotiations over Trieste and was special representative in Lebanon during the intervention in 1958. Murphy was promoted to undersecretary of state for political affairs in 1959, before retiring that year. A decade later, he advised President Rich-ard M. Nixon* on his initial diplomatic appointments.

W. H. McNeill, *America, Britain, and Russia: Their Co-operation and Conflict, 1941–1946* (New York, 1970); R. D. Murphy, *Diplomat Among Warriors* (Garden City, NY, 1964); *New York Times*, 10 January 1978.

John Swenson-Wright

MY LAI MASSACRE

During the Second Indochina War*, in the village of Son My, mainly in the hamlet or subunit known as My Lai Four, in Quang Ngai province of the Republic of Vietnam*, U.S. Army Infantry Company C, Task Force Barker, Eleventh Infantry Brigade, Americal Division, and especially the platoon within that company commanded by Lieutenant William Calley, killed several hundred peasants on 16 March 1968. The company was sent to the village that morning expecting to find an enemy military unit, the Viet Cong* Forty-eighth Local Force Battalion. The information they had been given was incorrect; no enemy unit was present. Three guerrillas who were in the village fled when they heard the helicopters approaching, and were killed outside the village by gunfire from helicopters. But by the time C Company entered the village, no armed enemies were there. The killing began while the U.S. troops were searching the village for guerrillas, but it continued after they realized that no guerrillas seemed to be present. Many peasants were gathered together, held under guard for several minutes, and then gunned down. There is no way to be sure how many were killed; a later investigation by the Criminal Investigation Division of the U.S. Army estimated 347 peasants killed in My Lai Four, but some of the killing was in the adjoining hamlet of Binh Tay and would not have been included. Some of the U.S. troops also burned down homes, killed livestock, and raped women.

The massacre was covered up; what was reported officially was that the Viet Cong local force battalion had been found in the village as expected, and that there had been a battle in which C Company had killed ninety guerrillas and another company had killed thirty-eight more. This story was generally accepted for more than a year, despite the protests of Warrant Officer Hugh Thompson, a helicopter pilot who had twice landed to try to stop the killing while it was in progress. He once ordered his door gunner to cover the troops on the ground with a machine gun to stop them from interfering while Thompson rescued some peasants and got them on the helicopter to carry them to safety. The U.S. Army finally launched a serious investigation in 1969, after Ronald Ridenour, an Eleventh Brigade helicopter door gunner who had not been present at the massacre, sent a letter describing the atrocity to a large number of high government officials and senators. Charges of murder were filed against Calley on 5 September, and the story hit the national media on 13 November 1969. My Lai became a major public scandal partly because a soldier decided to protest and bring it to public notice but also because it was proved beyond doubt that Calley, in what was not actually a combat situation, had ordered men in his platoon to kill women and children who both Calley and the men knew were unarmed. Moreover, Calley and others reported that Captain Ernest Medina, the company commander, had said a few hours before the operation that everyone in the village was to be killed.

Calley was tried and convicted on twenty-two counts of murder, but public reaction sympathized with him. Officers who answered calls at the Pentagon discovered that most callers knew civilians had been killed at My Lai, but believed that this had occurred during genuine combat against the Viet Cong. On 31 March, Calley was sentenced to life at hard labor. But three days later, by order of President Richard M. Nixon*, he was transferred from the stockade to his apartment to reside there under house arrest. Released on $1,000 bail in February 1974, he returned to the stockade at Fort Benning for six days on 20 June. Then Calley was transferred to Fort Leavenworth, where he did prison labor as a clerk-typist until his final release in November. The U.S. Army's investigators also recommended charges against many other officers and men, both for the massacre and for its cover-up, but Calley was the only one convicted. Although Captain Medina was tried and acquitted, most of the other soldiers involved never came to trial.

M. Bilton and K. Sim, *Four Hours in My Lai: A War Crime and Its Aftermath* (New York, 1992); J. Goldstein, B. Marshall, and J. Schwartz (eds.), *The My Lai Massacre and Its Cover-up: Beyond the Reach of Law?: The Peers Commission Report* (New York, 1976); W. R. Peers, *The My Lai Inquiry* (New York, 1979); K. Willenson, *The Bad War: An Oral History of the Vietnam War* (New York, 1987); N. L. Zaroulis and G. I. Sullivan, *Who Spoke Up?: American Protest Against the War in Vietnam, 1963–1975* (Garden City, NY, 1984).

Edwin E. Moise

MYANMAR

See BURMA